The Synthesizer

The Synthesizer

A COMPREHENSIVE GUIDE TO UNDERSTANDING, PROGRAMMING, PLAYING, AND RECORDING THE ULTIMATE ELECTRONIC MUSIC INSTRUMENT

Mark Vail

OXFORD
UNIVERSITY PRESS

OXFORD
UNIVERSITY PRESS

Oxford University Press is a department of the University of Oxford. It furthers the University's objective of excellence in research, scholarship, and education by publishing worldwide.

Oxford   New York
Auckland   Cape Town   Dar es Salaam   Hong Kong   Karachi
Kuala Lumpur   Madrid   Melbourne   Mexico City   Nairobi
New Delhi   Shanghai   Taipei   Toronto

With offices in
Argentina   Austria   Brazil   Chile   Czech Republic   France   Greece
Guatemala   Hungary   Italy   Japan   Poland   Portugal   Singapore
South Korea   Switzerland   Thailand   Turkey   Ukraine   Vietnam

Oxford is a registered trade mark of Oxford University Press in the UK and certain other countries.

Published in the United States of America by
Oxford University Press
198 Madison Avenue, New York, NY 10016

© Mark Vail 2014

All rights reserved. No part of this publication may be reproduced, stored in a retrieval system, or transmitted, in any form or by any means, without the prior permission in writing of Oxford University Press, or as expressly permitted by law, by license, or under terms agreed with the appropriate reproduction rights organization. Inquiries concerning reproduction outside the scope of the above should be sent to the Rights Department, Oxford University Press, at the address above.

You must not circulate this work in any other form
and you must impose this same condition on any acquirer.

Library of Congress Cataloging-in-Publication Data
Vail, Mark.
The synthesizer : a comprehensive guide to understanding, programming, playing, and recording the ultimate electronic music instrument / Mark Vail.
pages cm
Includes bibliographical references and index.
ISBN 978-0-19-539481-8 (alk. paper) — ISBN 978-0-19-539489-4 (alk. paper)   1. Synthesizer (Musical instrument)—Instruction and study.   2. Electronic music—Instruction and study.   I. Title.
MT723.V35 2013
786.7'419—dc23   2013008727

1 3 5 7 9 8 6 4 2

Printed in the United States of America on acid-free paper

CONTENTS

Foreword by Michelle Moog-Koussa • ix

Preface • xi

About the Companion Website • xv

1. Trendsetting All-Stars • 3

Control • 4
    No Touch Required • 4
    For *The Birds* • 8
    Waggling Keyboard • 10
    Timbral Flowage • 11
    Tape-to-Electronics Transition • 13
    Voltage and Digital (Fingertip) Control • 17
    Synth Italia • 24
    Armand Pascetta's Pratt-Reed Polyphony • 26
    Heavyweight Polyphony and Control • 28
    Multitimbral Polyphony • 29
    Physical Modeling • 29
    Finger-Controlled Speech • 31

Sound • 33
    Quantized Note Selection • 34
    Polyphonic Progenitor • 36
    Polyphony from an Expander • 38
    Switched-On Additive Synthesis • 41
    Groundbreaking German Digital Synthesizers • 45
    Realizing John Chowning's Linear FM Synthesis • 47
    Phase Distortion • 50
    Linear Arithmetic • 53
    Vector Synthesis • 55
    MultiSynthesis and –Processing Environment • 58
    Open Architecture • 61
    Virtual Analog • 63
    Neural Modeling • 64

Performance • 67
    Keyboard-Controlled Tape Player • 68
    Optical Sonics, Part 1 • 69
    Optical Sonics, Part 2 • 71
    Digital-Sampling Trailblazer from Down Under • 72
    More Affordable Digital Sampling • 73
    The Volksampler • 75
    Multitimbral Sample Playback, Sampling Optional • 76
    Direct-from-Disk Sample Playback • 79
    First Programmable Polysynth • 80
    Classic Beat Boxes • 82

First Programmable Sample-Playback Drum Machine • 85
Small-Scale Improvisation Instrument • 86
Interface • 88
Patchboard-Matrix British Synths • 88
Educational Instruments that Went Well Beyond • 91
Unique Improvisation Machine • 94
Multitasking Pre-MIDI Wonder Workstation • 95
Original Resynthesizer • 99
Hybrid Modular • 100
Early Electronic Music Applications from Max Mathews • 102
Barry Vercoe's Long-Lived Synthesis and Processing Software • 102
Personal Computer with a Built-In Synth Chip • 103
Graphically Programmable Computer Music Language • 104
"Obsolete" and Ever-Evolving Sonic Software • 104
Premier Softsynths for Discriminating Enthusiasts • 107
DIY Softsynth Apps and Their Potent Offspring • 109
Reliable Softsynth Platform for the Road • 112
Composition • 113
The First Synthesizer • 114
Room-Filling Automated Composition Machine • 114
Photo-Optic Instrument from Russia • 117
Instantaneous Composing/Performance Machine • 118
Hybrid Music Workstation that Arrived Too Late • 119
Gigabuck Digital Audio System • 121
Economical Multitimbral Sequencing Synth • 123
Musical Playstation for the Masses • 124
Instrument that Launched Hip-Hop • 126
Multipurpose Environment for Composition and Performance • 127
Beyond • 129

2 Acoustics and Synthesis Basics • 130

Real-World Acoustics • 131
Types of Synthesis • 132
Audio Sources: Oscillators, Noise, and More • 137
VCAs, Envelopes, and LFOs • 150
Envelope Followers and Pitch-to-Voltage Converters • 156
Filters • 157
EQs and Filter Banks • 166
Analog Sequencers • 172
Arpeggiators • 180
Reverb • 182
Analog Delay • 187
Digital Delay • 193
Loopers • 197
Other Effects • 200

3 Choosing Your Synthesizer(s) • 210

Options • 213
What's Your Budget? • 213

Musical Tastes and Goals • 213
Hardware vs. Software • 216
Portability and Power • 221
Programmability: Pros and Cons • 223
Expandability • 223
As Others Have Done • 224
Perspective • 244
Modular Synthesizers in the Twenty-first Century • 245
An Overview • 245
Modular Synth Shopping • 254
More on Eurorack Modular • 262
More on FracRak Modular • 265
More on Serge Modular • 265
Connectivity • 266
Convincing Analog and MIDI Synths to Coexist • 266
MIDI-to-CV Conversion • 267
CV-to-MIDI Conversion • 273
Controllers • 276
Synths and Controllers with Keyboards • 276
Alternative Controllers • 283
Wind Controllers • 284
Touch Controllers • 286
Hand-Held Controllers • 301
Struck Controllers • 302
Controllers for Microtonal Tunings • 305
Noise Toys • 306

4 Composition, Programming, and Performance Techniques • 310

Composition • 310
Scoring to Picture • 310
Composing for Living Art • 316
Following Through on a Thought • 317
Sage Advice from a Master • 318
Scoring with Intent, Even When Intimidated • 319
Patching, aka Programming • 321
Encouraging Synthesists' Creativity • 321
When and How to Experiment with Sounds • 322
The Good and Bad of Non-Programmability • 327
Programming for Progress • 329
Fun with Modular Synths • 331
Layering Synth Sounds • 334
Programming for Expression • 338
Performance • 339
Tools of the Trade • 339
Dependence on the Tried and True, but Moving Forward • 342
Modular Apparitions • 345
Defying the Dependence on Visuals • 349

5 Recording the Synthesizer • 352

As It Was and How It's Become for the *Switched-On* Innovator • 352
Serial vs. Random-Access Media • 353
Strategies for Recording Film and TV Scores • 354
Harnessing the Power of Modular Synths with Ableton Live • 359
Automated Mixing • 360
Outboard Processing: Preparing Audio for Recording • 361
Recording Direct and Expanding for Surround-Sound • 364

APPENDICES • 367

Appendix A. Selected Bibliography, Films, and Museums • 369

Appendix B. Manufacturers, Forums, Blogs, Dealers, and Stores • 375

Index • 385

FOREWORD

When Bob Moog introduced the Moog modular synthesizer in the 1960s, it was the first new popularized instrument invented since Adolphe Sax created the saxophone in 1846. While almost a century separated these developments in musical technology, the efforts that led to the modern-day synthesizer were many. Pioneers such as Thaddeus Cahill, Leon Theremin, Friedrich Trautwein, Raymond Scott, Vladimir Ussachevsky, Paul Ketoff, Harald Bode, and many more each made important steps toward exploring the possibilities of sound sculpting by electronic means. Bob Moog's work, and the work of every other synth manufacturer, is built on the shoulders of those giants.

Even prior to formal education in the fields of engineering and physics, Bob devoted his time in his father's basement workshop educating himself about the history and technology of electronic music. This early passion led to his double undergraduate degrees and to his PhD from Cornell University in Engineering Physics. He remained a student of both the technical rigors of engineering and the rich and varied history of electronic music throughout his career. His intertwined understanding informed his professional path; his path informed an industry.

At the Bob Moog Foundation we embrace the ultimate importance of music, science, and history education as a force to inspire children to blaze new paths. With Bob's life and career—and those of so many other synthesizer pioneers—as our inspiration, we created *Dr. Bob's SoundSchool* to teach kids the science of sound. Waveforms, vibrations, pitch, amplitude, and the components of sound creation and transmission inform the students' knowledge of basic physics. The concepts are also used to ignite their sense of curiosity, exploration, and creativity.

Through this book, Mark Vail is echoing Bob's very own sentiments of the importance of both technical and historical information as forces to true understanding of the vast and glorious world of sound synthesis. The thorough and methodical exploration laid forth in the following pages provides for an inspired path of learning, understanding, and creating. In particular, the section on controllers is something Bob would have felt to be of utmost importance. From the magical elegance of the Theremin to the then-unprecedented touch sensitivity of the little-known Eaton-Moog MTS keyboard to the touchpad on the Moog Voyager synthesizer, he was impassioned about the creation of new control interfaces for musicians; he saw them as the most viable means to provide musicians with increased means of access and creativity in synthesis. On one of his last days at work he said to a colleague, "The keyboard is an antiquated interface. It's time to move on."

Moving on, or looking toward the future, we will see a continuation of the ever expanding offerings in synthesis. It's an exciting time for unprecedented creativity, should people be bold enough to explore it to that end. With Mark Vail as our guide, we have the tools to do so.

Michelle Moog-Koussa
Bob Moog Foundation
Asheville, NC
moogfoundation.org
May 1, 2013

PREFACE

Shop via the Internet or enter a good music instrument store and you can find a huge assortment of synthesizers for sale. They come in many forms: analog, digital, hybrid, hardware, software, modular, patchable, fixed-architecture, programmable, brand new, quite old, and handmade from scratch or a kit. Lucky me, I've had the opportunity to play with almost every kind.

How did I get here? Wendy Carlos's astute "On Synthesizers" article for the May 1973 printing of *The Last Whole Earth Catalog: Access to Tools* instilled in me a great interest in these instruments. I bought my first synth—a Minimoog—in 1976, soon after I'd discovered *Keyboard* magazine. After moving to the San Francisco Bay Area in 1977, I earned an MFA in electronic music at Mills College in Oakland in 1983 and got married the same year. Toward the end of 1987 my wife, Christy, found an alluring ad in the *San Francisco Chronicle*: *Keyboard* was in search of an editor. I was very fortunate to land the position—thanks, Dominic—and worked on *Keyboard*'s editorial staff from January 1988 until April 2001.

My goal with this book is to inspire existing and potential synthesists to get the most out of and make the kinds of music they most enjoy with synthesizers of as many types as possible. I wanted to create a book that I haven't seen elsewhere. I dedicate it to the dreamers, designers, developers, programmers, performers, users, artists, technicians, fixers, modifiers, and owners of synthesizers of all sorts.

I extend my utmost thanks to my parents, Chuck and Jean (aka Kemosabe and Bubbles), who nurtured my interest in music and afforded me lessons and instruments; David Brodie for helping me find and purchase a Minimoog; Ellie Latz, who introduced me to her daughter Christy; Gordon Mumma, Lou Harrison, David Rosenboom, Maggi Payne, and Ed Tywoniak for their tutelage at Mills College; everyone at *Keyboard*, GPI, Miller Freeman Publications, and Backbeat Books, including Dominic Milano, Jim Aikin, Bob Doerschuk, Jim Crockett, Tom Darter, Ted Greenwald, Brent Hurtig, Andy Ellis, Michael Marans, Kyle Kevorkian, Debbie Greenberg, David Battino, Ken Hughes, Mitch Gallagher, Tom Wheeler, Art Thompson, Joe Gore, Jas Obrecht, Tom "Ferd" Mulhern, Richard Johnston, Bill Leigh, Matt Kelsey, Marty Cutler, Phil Hood, Sanford Forte, Jay Kahn, Mark Hanson, Andy Doerschuk, Jeff Burger, Kent Carmical, Jim Hatlo, Jim Roberts, Scott Malandrone, Ernie Rideout, Greg Rule, Karl Coryat, Pat Cameron, Charlie Bach, Michael Gallant, Marvin Sanders, Stephen Fortner, David Leytze, Amy Miller, Randy Alberts, Ned Torney, Rich Leeds, Linda Jacobsen, David Williamson, Ed Sengstack, Paul Haggard, Valerie Pippin, Gabe Echeverria and Chandra Lynn, Xandria Duncan, Perry Fotos, Jon Sievert, Robbie Gennet, Chris and Liz Ledgerwood, Sam Miranda, Cynthia Smith, Chris Eaton, Ricc Sandoval, Joanne McGowan, Matt Gallagher, Anthony Comisso, Rick Eberly and Margaret Anderson, Vicki Hartung, Dave "Feeney" Arnold, Pete Sembler, Diane Gurshuny, and Dan Brown, plus the many editors, authors, and publishers with whom I've had the pleasure of working, including Craig Anderton, Marvin Jones, Steve Oppenheimer, Gino Robair, Julian Colbeck, Tim Tully, Peter Forrest,

Preface

Peter Gorges, Matthias Becker, Ralf Kleinermanns, Gerald Dellmann, Ian Gilby, Paul White, Gordon Reid, and Jörg Sunderkötter; Dave Stewart, for sharing his keen British wit and expert contractual consultations; Dave Amels and Tom Rhea, who assisted me with the historical chapter content; and all of my very good friends in the music industry, namely Jerry Kovarsky, Jack Hotop, Amin Bhatia, Drew Neumann, Starr Parodi and Jeff Fair, Dave Smith, Bob Moog, Barbara Gaskin, Avery Burdette, Chris Martirano, Phil Clendeninn, Dale Ockerman, David Rosenthal, Laurie Spiegel, Don and Julie Lewis, Ikutaro Kakehashi, Roger Linn, Wendy Carlos, Don Muro, Mike Kovins, Charlie Bright, John "Skippy" Lehmkuhl, Suzanne Ciani, George Mattson, Hans Nordelius, Christoph Kemper, Dan Phillips, Chris Meyer, Andrew Lubman, Mike Groh, Roger Powell, James Grunke, J.L. Leimseider, Keith Emerson, Brian Kehew, Ben Dowling, Keiichi Goto, John L. Rice, Jordan Rudess, Jan Hammer, Malcolm Doak, John Bowen, Frédéric Brun, Colin McDowell, Herb Deutsch, Ernst Nathorst-Böös, Timothy Self, Morton Subotnick, Tom Coster, Kevin Lightner, David Zicarelli, Darwin Grosse, Alan R. Pearlman, Philip Dodds, Tina "Bean" Blaine, Ray Kurzweil, Candice Pacheco, Tage Widsell, Jennifer Hruska, Tim Ryan, Patti Clemens, Paul Wiffen, Marc Doty, Christopher Franke, Serge Tcherepnin, Rex Probe, Larry Fast, Kevin Braheny Fortune, Scott Kinsey, Dieter Doepfer, Tim Caswell, Eric Persing, Don Buchla, John Loffink, Mary, Greg and Marc St. Regis, Rick Smith, John Medeski, Bryan Bell, David Mash, Matt Traum, Geoff Farr, Gary Chang, Greg Kurstin, Pamelia Kurstin, Peter "Ski" Schwartz, Paul Lehrman, Andrew Schlesinger, Axel Hartmann, Moe Denham, Robert Bond, Tom Oberheim, Denis Labrecque, Tom White, Bill Mauchly, Milton Babbitt, Max Mathews, Lance Abair, Dave Rossum, John Chowning, Doug Curtis, Marcus Ryle, Kristoffer Wallman, Curtis Roads, Robert Rich, Dan Del Fiorentino, Robbie Clyne, Bob Yannes, Dave Bristow, Jeff Rona, Roy Elkins, Paul de Benedictis, Gerry Basserman, Scott and Kellie Wilkie, Dennis Houlihan, Jean-Jacques Perrey, Kevin Monahan and Denise Gallant, David Kean, TJ Martin, Tony Karavidas, Andrew McGowan, Paul Schreiber, Marsha Vdovin, James Bernard, David Van Koevering, Bryan Lanser, Philippe Chatiliez, Don Leslie, Alan Young, Mike McRoberts, James and Elisabeth Lewin, Paul Sommer, Kevin Jarvis, David Vogel, Barry Gould, Francis Preve, Keith McMillen, Virgil Franklin, John Eaton, Terry Riley, Lee Sebel, Gene Radzik, Gary Nester, Erik Norlander, Emile Tobenfeld, Bruno Spoerri, Geary Yelton, Bob Williams, Chester Smith, Alain Seghir, Dan Armandy, Felix Visser, Howard Massey, Pea Hicks, Timothy Smith, Jon Appleton, Jonathan Sa'adah, David Abernethy, and David Gross for their friendship and contributions to my synth knowledge and to the synth industry.

My sincere gratitude also goes to Stephen Masucci for sharing his knowledge and experience of restoring vintage modular synthesizers, preparing state-of-the-art synth-based systems for recording and performance, and introducing me to the graphic artist extraordinaire and synthesizer aficionado John Blackford; and to John Blackford for creating the astounding and beautiful cover of this book.

Thank you, Michelle Moog-Koussa, for filling the enormous gap left after your father and my friend Bob passed, for determinedly directing the Bob Moog Foundation under extremely adverse and distressing conditions, and for contributing the foreword to this book.

Thank you as well, Norm Hirschy, editor of Music Books at Oxford University Press, for the opportunity to complete this book and for caring guidance, enthusiastic encouragement, and utmost patience throughout the process.

Finally, thank you especially, Christy, for decades of love, support, devotion, forgiveness, singing with me, immense knowledge of grammar, acute editing-with-a-hatchet approach when needed, and letting me buy so many wonderful music-making toys.

Mark Vail

ABOUT THE COMPANION WEBSITE

www.oup.com/us/thesynthesizer

Oxford University Press has created a password-protected companion website for *The Synthesizer,* and I urge readers to take full advantage of it. The site features contributions from synthesists Drew Neumann and Niklas Winde to supplement material in the book. While Drew provided screenshots and audio using Digidesign Turbosynth and U&I MetaSynth to create specific sounds described in the book, Niklas produced three video examples of the Buchla 296e Spectral Processor in action, demonstrating possibilities afforded by a special module from synthesizer pioneer Don Buchla. Oxford's 🔊 and 🌐 symbols respectively indicate these audio and video examples in chapters 1 and 2.

In addition, the companion website includes lists of synthesizer books, films, museums, manufacturers, forums, blogs, dealers, and stores combined with links to immediately transport you to most of those sites. Finally, you'll find an extensive discography of synthesizer music from past to present.

You may access the site using the username **Music2** and the password **Book4416.**

The Synthesizer

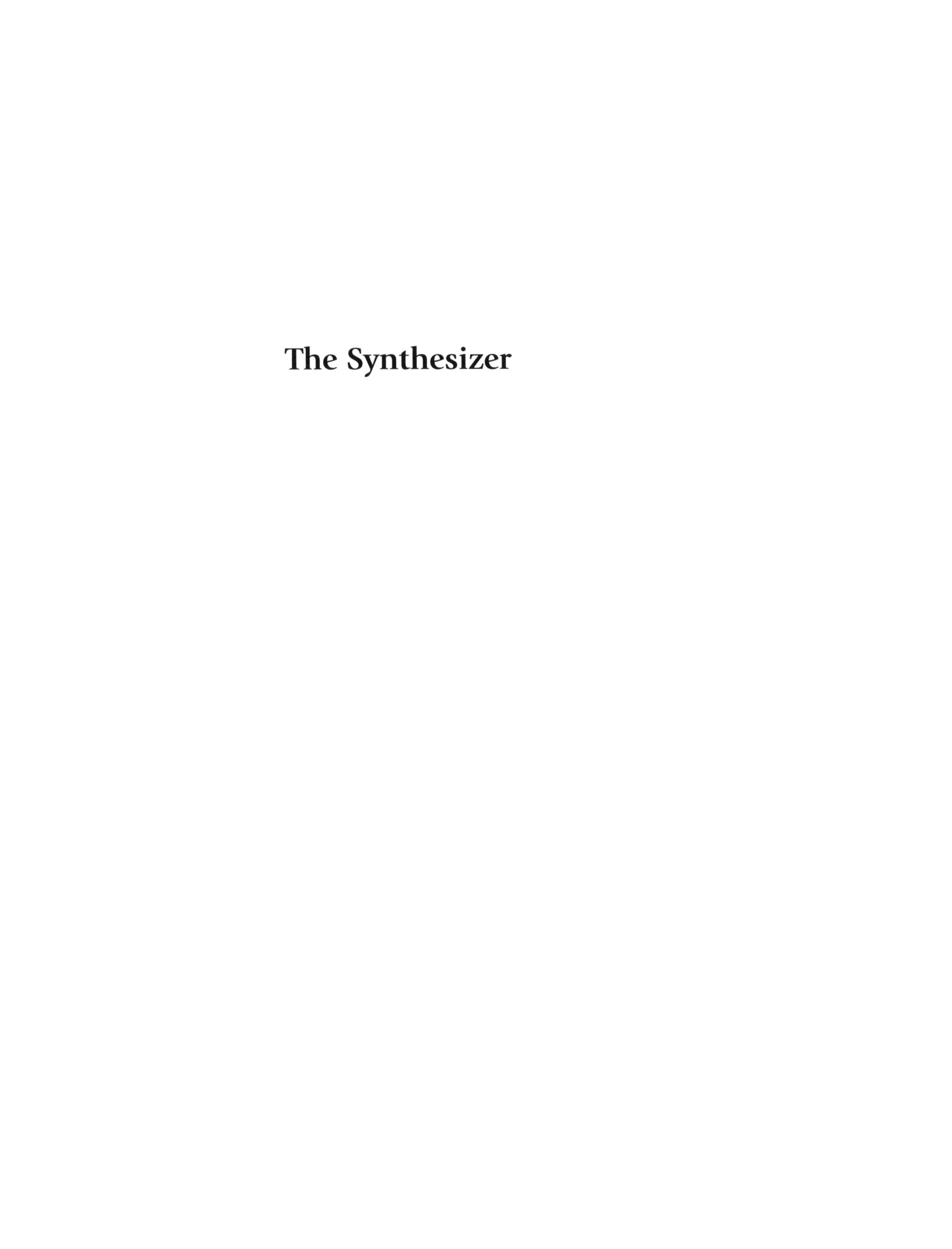

1

Trendsetting All-Stars

The lineage of purely electronic musical instruments dates back to 1919. It's fascinating to consider important developments and innovative ideas that have occurred since then, and a good way to lay a foundation for understanding the wide variety of synths currently available and where they came from.

The use of electricity for musical purposes actually dates back to 1759, when Parisian Jean-Baptiste de La Borde made the *Clavecin Electrique*, or Electric Harpsichord. Its static electricity–charged clappers under keyboard control struck bells, much like a carillon, except that carillons are purely mechanical. By the turn of the twentieth century, Thaddeus Cahill had developed the Telharmonium, comprised of spinning electric generators called alternators or dynamos to produce musical tones, along with organ-style keyboard consoles from which to play the enormous device that was so big it required several railroad cars to be transported. Cahill intended the Telharmonium to transmit music through phone lines to paying subscribers, but the venture failed. Cahill's designs eventually influenced Laurens Hammond in the development of tonewheel organs beginning in the early 1930s and subsequently led to such instruments as the popular Hammond B-3.

To limit the focus of this synthesizer history so that it's a manageable universe, we'll avoid electro-mechanical instruments and instead concentrate on those that generate(d) sound electronically, whether it be via analog and/or digital circuitry, magnetic tape, optical disc, software, or some other means. Among the following instruments are many that you're familiar with and others of which you've never heard. In no way is this intended to be a complete catalog of every electronic instrument or synthesizer. Instead, I've chosen those that are important because they introduced novel capabilities or implemented existing concepts in significant new ways.

The instruments are organized by what their makers intended them to do, or what they turned out to be best at doing. I've arranged them in five categories: Control, Sound, Performance, Interface, and Composition. *Control* features instruments that offered new and/or advanced methods of controlling sound. *Sound* highlights instruments that advanced the art of electronic sound generation. You'll find instruments optimal for use in live situations under *Performance*. The *Interface* section touts instruments with highly developed and conceptualized methods of interaction between the user and the synthesizer. And synthesizers that delivered extensively improved or extraordinary methods of creating music appear in the *Composition* area.

This is not to imply an instrument that winds up in the Interface section couldn't, for instance, produce exceptional timbres or provide outstanding features for composing new music. In such cases where any synth excels at other functions, I'll share this information.

Control

One of the major limitations suffered by many electronic instruments has been a lack of the musician's expressive control. An instrument's tone may be astounding, but if the timbre remains static and unchanging throughout a note's duration—and if every note exhibits the same **attack**, **release**, and **amplitude** characteristics—the listeners' emotional involvement and interest will quickly fade. A performance that lacks expression can quickly become tedious, but the performer can also become bored and the performance itself dull.

> *attack:* the audible onset of a sound, which may occur quickly as with a note or chord played on a piano, or more slowly like a softly blown flute
> *release:* how a sound ends, whether it disappears abruptly or fades slowly until it's inaudible
> *amplitude:* the loudness of a sound, normally quantified in terms of the logarithmic decibel (dB) scale, where 0dB is the threshold of hearing, a quiet whisper at three feet is 30dB, a normal conversation 60dB, loud singing at three feet 75dB, inside a subway 94dB, and amplified rock 'n' roll at six feet 120dB

Since the introductions of the earliest electronic instruments, musicians have challenged makers to address control issues so they can add expression to their performances. Thankfully, many inventors rose to the challenge.

No Touch Required

In late 1919, the Russian inventor Lev Sergeyevich Termen (1896–1993) began concertizing with the Etherphone. Also known as the Termenvox, it generates tones within a frequency range of about four octaves—similar to that of a cello—by combining signals from two high-frequency **heterodyning oscillators** to output a pitch based on the difference of the oscillators' frequencies. You might know its inventor by his Gallicized name: Leon Theremin. Performers play his instrument, which eventually became known simply as the Theremin, without touching it.

> *heterodyning:* frequencies generated by two sources are combined to create a third frequency, which equals the difference of the source frequencies
> *oscillator:* a circuit that generates periodic fluctuations in voltage to produce an analog signal of frequency measured in Hertz (Hz), or cycles-per-second

The Theremin is monophonic, capable of producing only one pitch at a time. The proximity of one hand in relation to a vertical antenna determines pitch. Rather than offering a note scale with fixed frequencies such as a piano or organ, the Theremin's pitch

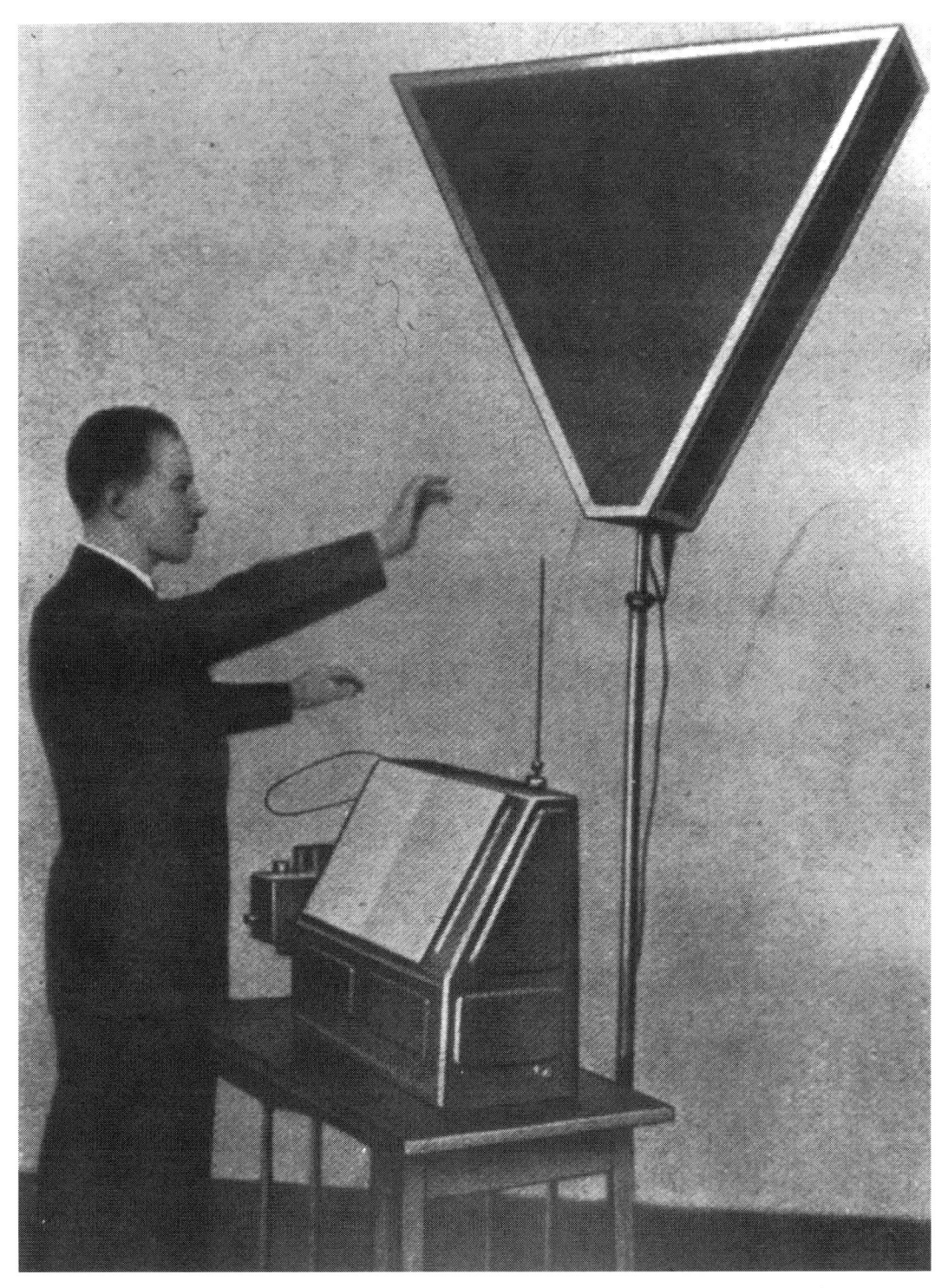

Leon Theremin ca. 1927 in performance with a Theremin amplified by one of his speaker systems of that era. (Courtesy of Tom Rhea)

varies continuously. A performer controls the instrument's volume with his second hand, moving it nearer to a second antenna to quiet the Theremin's output and pulling it away to make the sound louder. While it may sound simple and easy to play, it's extremely difficult to master, but it is also one of the most expressive electronic instruments. On one hand, it's easy to mimic sirens and old science-fiction sound effects; on the other, it

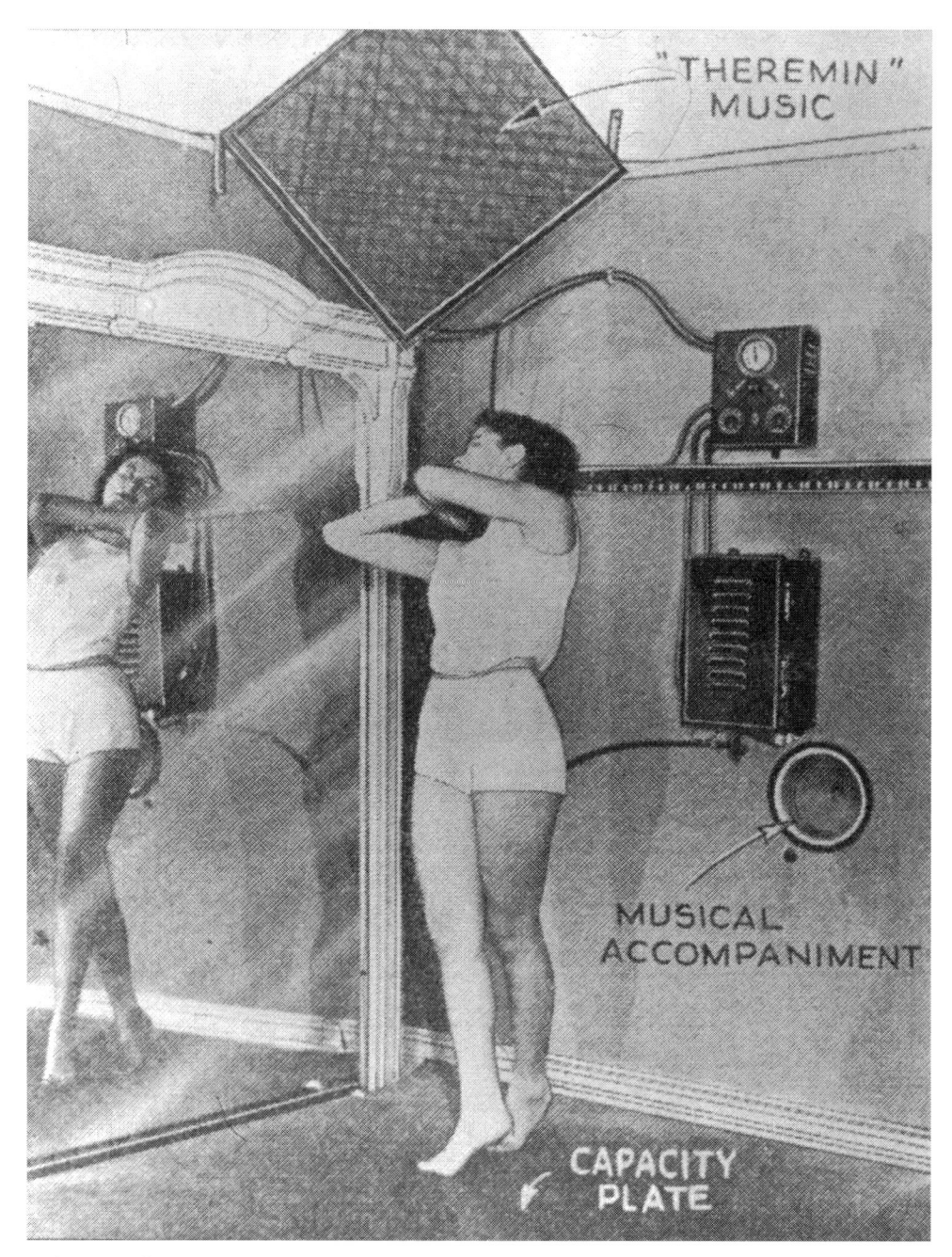

A dancer performs on Leon Theremin's Terpsitone during the early 1930s. (Courtesy of Tom Rhea)

may take years of concentrated study and practice before someone can confidently play melodies.

Leon Theremin dabbled with many different instrument designs. One was the Terpsitone, also known as the Etherwave Dance Stage, a platform on which the performer controlled pitch with vertical movements of her body and volume by moving toward or away from the rear of the platform. Another series of Theremin's devices resembled the cello, except that no strings were involved. On one of these, the performer moved fingers up and down a touchplate surface—a fingerboard—to play one note at a time. The other hand rested on a lever that jutted out of the "fingerboard Theremin" to control note articulation and volume.

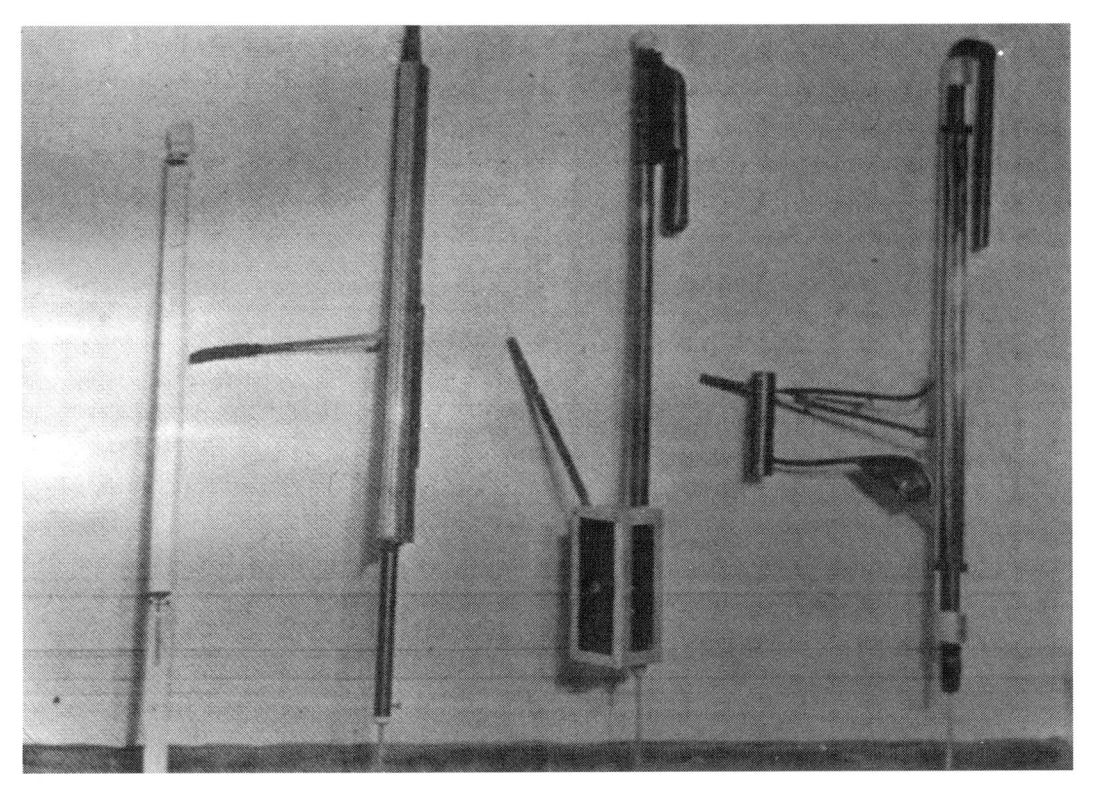

Three examples—to the right—of the fingerboard instruments Leon Theremin developed during the 1930s. On the left is an incomplete instrument. (Courtesy of Tom Rhea)

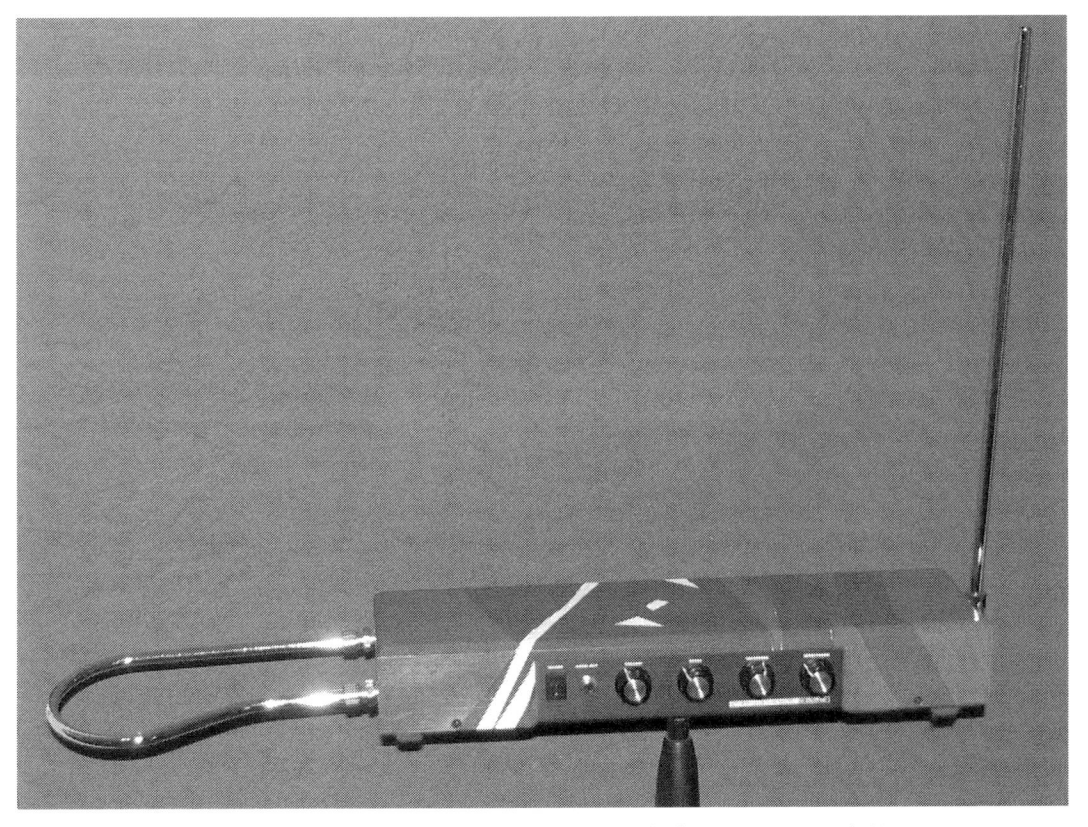

In early 2001, I painted and assembled this Etherwave Theremin, a kit from Big Briar—Bob Moog's company name before he recovered the legal rights to his name in 2002. Moog Music still offers the Etherwave in assembled and kit forms. (Mark Vail)

For *The Birds*

The German acoustician Friedrich Trautwein (1888–1956) introduced another innovative and expressive monophonic electronic instrument in 1928, the Trautonium. For pitch control, it incorporated a metal bar onto which the performer depressed a wire that closed a circuit and generated a tone. Protrusions extending above the bar indicated specific notes, but the pitch varied continuously. While earlier versions of his instrument produced every note with the same abrupt attack, Trautwein later equipped the instrument with a mechanism that allowed the performer to vary note attack by changing how hard or soft he depressed the wire onto the bar. Given enough practice, a performer could play the Trautonium very expressively.

Unlike the Theremin, the Trautonium incorporated a neon-tube oscillator to produce a rich-sounding **sawtooth waveform** replete with high **harmonics**, which could be filtered for timbral variation. Trautwein understood the nature of **formants** in acoustic instruments and equipped the Trautonium with a series of formant filters, or resonators, which the performer could tune over extended frequency ranges in real time, thus allowing a wide variety of tonal variations. This illustrates an important contrast between electronic and acoustic instruments: the physical attributes of an acoustic instrument—

A young Oskar Sala performs in concert on a Telefunken Trautonium. (Courtesy of Tom Rhea)

including the shape of its body and resonance properties—force its formant to be fixed to a specific frequency range.

> *sawtooth:* a **waveform** with a voltage that begins at a low value, climbs steadily to a high value, then drops immediately to the beginning value before repeating the shape; a *reverse sawtooth* does the opposite, jumping immediately from low to high, falling steadily to the low point, and so on
> *waveform:* a signal generated by an oscillator with certain harmonic content
> *harmonics:* overtones, or higher frequencies, in a tone that are integer multiples of the **fundamental**
> *fundamental:* the root or lowest frequency of a note, typically perceived as its pitch
> *formant:* one or more frequencies that are emphasized by the resonant qualities of an acoustic instrument's body or by filters in an electronic instrument

In the early 1930s, Trautwein's colleague Paul Hindemith (1895–1963) composed music such as Trio Pieces for Three Trautonia and Concerto for Solo Trautonium and Orchestra. Telefunken produced a limited run of Trautoniums beginning in 1932. Alfred Hitchcock's *The Birds* featured sounds produced by the instrument's descendant, the Mixtur Trautonium, to which the virtuoso Oskar Sala (1910–2002) made extensive enhancements.

Oskar Sala plays the Mixtur Trautonium in 1932. Sala made many contributions to this instrument beyond Friedrich Trautwein's original Trautonium. (Courtesy of Tom Rhea)

Waggling Keyboard

It's a bit of a stretch to fathom, but a monophonic keyboard, developed to enhance pianos and organs in the mid-twentieth-century home, offers more expressive control than many contemporary synthesizers. The thirty-seven-note keyboard for Georges Jenny's Ondioline—which he began developing in 1938, patented in 1941, and produced until 1974—mounts underneath a piano or organ keybed. Its keys are similar to those on an accordion, but the keyboard is spring-loaded to allow finger-generated **vibrato** with horizontal motions. The Ondioline's keyboard also responds to pressure: After you've played a note, you can vary its volume and timbre by changing how hard you depress the key. You can transpose the Ondioline to cover an eight-octave range. Its separate speaker

Dana Countryman bought this blond Ondioline in 2000 and used it on several albums, including two with Jean-Jacques Perrey: *Destination Space* and *The Happy Electropop Music Machine!*. (Dana Countryman, © 2007 Dana Countryman)

cabinet contains most of the electronics—all vacuum tubes originally, but solid-state transistor circuits appear in later models. Using switches at the top of the speaker cabinet, you can vary timbre by routing the audio signal through a variety of filter paths.

> *vibrato:* a (hopefully) pleasant and periodic wavering or modulation of pitch produced manually or using automation, typically modulated in a synthesizer with a **sine** or **triangle waveform** oscillating at around 7Hz
>
> *sine waveform:* a periodic, single-frequency, sinusoidal waveform; at audible frequencies, it consists only the fundamental frequency and no harmonics and is also known as a *pure tone*
>
> *triangle waveform:* named for its triangular shape, a periodic signal that rises and falls in a linear fashion with sharp corners at the waveform's apex and lowest point; useful as an LFO (low-frequency oscillator) waveform for pitch modulation as a vibrato effect; at audible frequencies, a triangle wave contains the fundamental frequency and all of the odd-numbered harmonics whose ascending amplitudes decrease in ratios of 1:9, 1:25, 1:49, 1:64, 1:81, etc., sounding similar to a sine wave except with weak harmonics, whereas a sine wave has no harmonics, only the fundamental

Jean-Jacques Perrey is the best known Ondioline player. He left medical school to work with Jenny (d. 1976) in 1951 as a demonstrator and salesman, and continues to perform and record with the instrument well into the twenty-first century. Perrey proved that the Ondioline can produce unique and diverse timbres, and that the expression it affords can equal that of a violin.

Timbral Flowage

Borrowing the medieval moniker for what became the trombone—the "sackbut"—the Canadian Hugh Le Caine (1914–77) created an extremely expressive instrument with components and capabilities found on voltage-controlled synthesizers that it preceded by decades. Le Caine's monophonic Electronic Sackbut, which he developed between 1945 and 1948 and continued to redesign and improve until 1973, had a familiar-looking musical keyboard for note selection, but one that was quite unusual. For one thing, it was horizontally spring-loaded. Lateral movements to a key altered the pitch, allowing a gradual bend up or down to a different note—even one "between the cracks" of a scale. Wobbling a key back and forth imparted vibrato to the pitch. Not only was the bend range adjustable up to a whole octave, but pitch could also be controlled via a touch-sensitive ribbon.

The Electronic Sackbut's four-octave keyboard also provided **velocity response** for variations in note attack: playing softly resulted in a note with a slow entrance, and hitting a key harder made the response more immediate. Continuous pressure sensing allowed real-time variation in note volume for producing crescendos and diminuendos after a note began playing.

Hugh Le Caine with a prototype of his Electronic Sackbut in 1954. (Courtesy of Gustav Ciamaga, the Institute of Radio Engineers, and the Electronic Music Foundation)

To address timbre, Le Caine equipped the Electronic Sackbut with a lefthand control section for precise parameter manipulation using fingertip pressure. The performer's left index finger varied among basic waveforms, some of which were evocative replications of clarinet, flute, oboe, trumpet, and organ. Other waveforms stressed the fundamental or certain harmonic intervals. As a note sounded, the player could morph through different timbres. In addition, the left thumb and remaining fingers shaped the Electronic Sackbut's tone: while the performer used his or her thumb to control **filter resonance** and the formant, or peak in the frequency spectrum, he or she could modulate amplitude and frequency and add noise or periodic voltages using other fingers.

> *velocity response:* a touch sensitivity that detects the force or speed with which the instrument has been struck
> *filter resonance:* an emphasized peak of a narrow band of frequencies

Le Caine was striving for an electronic instrument that would play as expressively as an acoustic instrument such as the violin, but with the extended timbral opportunities afforded by electronics. Continuous variation of the harmonic content of the Electronic Sackbut's tone made the instrument much more expressive than it otherwise would have been. Unfortunately, it never went into production due to Le Caine's inability to finalize its design.

Tape-to-Electronics Transition

During the late 1950s and early '60s, *musique concrète* was the most familiar method of creating electro-acoustic music by recording acoustic sounds—sometimes electronically processed—and timbres output by electronic test equipment onto 1/4″ magnetic reel-to-reel tape, which the composer then cut into snippets and meticulously spliced together to create astounding and often rhythmic sequences of unrelated sounds. Creating a few minutes of taped music could take weeks or even months.

Some of the earliest efforts to replace *musique concrète* techniques with musical **voltage-controlled** instruments took place at the San Francisco Tape Music Center, co-founded by Morton Subotnick and Ramon Sender in the early 1960s. They engaged Don Buchla to begin designing electronic music devices in early 1963, drawing on his knowledge of physics and electronics, as well as his experience in building acoustic and electro-acoustic instruments of welded steel and other materials. Buchla's approach to designing instruments has always been scientific, organic, and user-oriented.

> *voltage-controlled:* analog circuitry whose status can be regulated or changed using electromotive force or a flow of electricity

Control over what those elements do over time was critical to Buchla. One characteristic that distinguishes most of his instruments from competitors' is the absence of an organ-style keyboard. Instead, he prefers capacitance- or resistance-sensitive touchplates organized in various arrangements. The touchplates are area-sensitive, with each plate transmitting three control voltages depending on finger position and the amount of force exerted, which increases or decreases the amount of skin coming into contact with the touchplate.

Alternative Controllers

In case an organ-style keyboard, or any of its equivalents, isn't your first choice to play a synthesizer, you have many other options. While Don Buchla has contributed his fair share of *alternative controllers*, he isn't alone in their development. There are, for instance, wind controllers from sources including Nyle Steiner, Softwind Instruments, Eigenlabs, and Akai; percussion pads and instruments such as those from Alternate Mode Kat, Korg, and Alesis; complete electronic drum systems from Roland, Yamaha, and others; ribbons from Doepfer, Kurzweil, and Eowave; and a huge variety of unique controllers and electronic instruments. In addition, for those who'd rather do it themselves, manufacturers such as Electrotap, I-Cube, and Eowave offer sensors for tracking changes in acceleration, temperature, distance, light, pressure, and other physical actions, as well as interfaces for connecting these sensors to synths and computers to control specific aspects and parameters. See ch. 3 for more information about what's available and how you might use these instruments and devices to make music.

This is the first modular synthesizer Don Buchla built for and delivered to the San Francisco Tape Music Center in 1964. Included in this original member of the Buchla 100 Series were a Model 146 16-Stage Sequential Voltage Source, a Model 123 Eight-Stage Sequential Voltage Source, two Model 110 Dual Voltage-Controlled Gates, three Model 106 Six-Channel Mixers, a Model 111 Dual Ring Modulator, and two Model 112 Touch-Controlled Voltage Sources. This instrument has resided in the Center for Contemporary Music at Mills College since the late 1960s. (Bill Reitzel)

Buchla also developed some of the earliest **analog sequencers**. His first synth had three of them, two with eight stages or steps apiece, the third with sixteen. Each stage generated three voltage-control outputs. You could synchronize two sequencers to get six voltages per stage, and you could create complex rhythm patterns by setting the sequencers to different numbers of stages—for example, five stages against thirteen.

Over the years Don Buchla has created numerous series of **modular synthesizers** and custom instruments, including the original 200 Series Electric Music Box and (ca. 2005) its modernized and current 200e descendants, as well as the 300, 400, 500, and 700 Series. Control has always played an important role in Don's instruments.

Rick Smith completely refurbished this Buchla 200 Series Electric Music Box system, for which he began collecting modules in February 2000 and finished in 2004. He succeeded in his goal of making it classic, 200 Series era-correct with components from 1970 to 1972. (Rick Smith, Buchla Restorations, www.electricmusicbox.com)

Don Buchla revived his favorite synthesizer line, the 200 Series, in 2005 as the 200e Series. Among those touring and giving live concerts with a 200e modular is Morton Subotnick, who played a key part in getting Buchla to design synthesizer modules in the first place. (Paul Haggard)

> *analog sequencer:* an analog module with multiple stages or steps, each of which outputs a set of one or more user-defined voltages; the sequencer may repeat all or some of the stages in the same order over and over, only once through, or one stage at a time according to input from the user or another module
>
> *modular synthesizer:* an instrument comprising independent modules that you can buy and/or assemble separately, freely arrange and mount in a case, cabinet, or rack during the assembly process according to your wishes, and subsequently rearrange and replace modules later on; in order for the instrument to generate audible sounds, you need to interconnect specific modules using patch cords, a pin matrix, or some other signal-routing arrangement, depending on the modular system
>
> *MIDI:* acronym for Musical Instrument Digital Interface, the protocol introduced in 1983 that allows performance data created on one electronic instrument to be transmitted to other instruments—even those from different manufacturers—for voice layering, recording, sequencing, editing, and much more

In the early 1980s, Buchla co-developed WIMP (Wideband Interface for Music Performance) and included its connectors alongside those for **MIDI** on some of his instruments. Most synth manufacturers adopted MIDI and nobody else incorporated WIMP, so you don't hear much about it any more. During the late 1980s and early '90s, Buchla shifted his focus almost exclusively to alternative controllers, developing the Thunder pad and Lightning wireless controllers. They were followed in 2002 by the Buchla-designed Piano Bar, a retrofit that converts any acoustic piano into a complex MIDI controller and synthesizer. Ironically, the Piano Bar was for a time distributed by Moog Music—the company founded by Buchla's cross-country contemporary in New York, Bob Moog.

Voltage and Digital (Fingertip) Control

Before his death at age seventy-one on August 21, 2005, Dr. Robert A. Moog (rhymes with "rogue") made many groundbreaking contributions to the electronic-music industry, especially in terms of control and sound quality. He began building and selling Theremins in 1954. Inspired by the electronic music pioneer Harald Bode's 1961 article "Sound Synthesizer Creates New Musical Effects: New Frontiers in Electronic Music," Bob collaborated with the composer Herbert A. Deutsch in 1963 to design and construct a modular synthesizer, which he demonstrated at the Audio Engineering Society (AES) convention in October 1964. He introduced the first Moog Modular synthesizers in 1965.

At the age of seventeen, Bob Moog demonstrates his Theremin at Bronx High School of Science. (With the permission of Ileana Grams-Moog)

The Synthesizer

Wendy Carlos recorded her transcendental *Switched-On Bach* with a custom Moog Modular. Released by Columbia Records in November 1968, *Switched-On Bach* became the first album of classical music to go platinum—eventually selling millions of copies—and put Moog's name and instruments on the map.

Carlos and Deutsch were among numerous composers who influenced Bob in designing new synth modules. Besides assisting Bob on technical issues, modifications, and improvements, Wendy helped Moog add touch-sensitivity to the synthesizer's keyboard, which had previously responded like an organ or harpsichord: all notes played the same no matter how hard keys were struck. Bob also modified two **fixed-filter banks** as encoder and decoder filters for her custom **vocoder**.

> *fixed-filter bank, aka a formant filter:* a series of bandpass filters with specific audible-range frequency centers and level controls for boosting or cutting the frequency content and harmonics of an incoming audio signal
>
> *vocoder:* a circuit or device that imparts the spectral characteristics of one incoming audio signal—the program—onto another input signal—the carrier—resulting in an output that has the pitch of the carrier signal with some or most of the timbral character and articulation of the program signal; for example, if the program is a spoken voice and the carrier is a synthesized violin, the vocoder will make the violin voice seem to talk—provided both signals are present simultaneously

Synth pioneer Bob Moog poses during the mid-1970s with, from *left to right*, a Sonic Six, a Moog Modular, and a Minimoog. Out in *front* is a Moog Percussion Controller. (With the permission of Ileana Grams-Moog)

Bob Moog and Keith Emerson stand before Keith's big Modular Moog and Hammond C-3 organ in the mid-'70s. (Mark Hockman, with the permission of Ileana Grams-Moog)

In this 1974 photo taken at Radio City Music Hall, Roger Powell (synthesist for Todd Rundgren's Utopia) plays his custom dual-manual keyboard controller while Bob Moog surveys Roger's Moog Modular system, the equivalent of two Synthesizer 55s. (Alan Blumenthal, courtesy of Roger Powell)

The Synthesizer

A complete Moog Modular Series 900 system from the late 1960s. (With the permission of Ileana Grams-Moog)

Another contributor was Vladmir Ussachevsky, who provided specifications for an **envelope follower** and **envelope generator**, and it was Gustav Ciamaga of the University of Toronto whose module description led to Bob's first voltage-controlled **lowpass filter**. Moog's lineup of voltage-controlled oscillators, **noise generators**, lowpass and **highpass filters**, **sample-and-hold**, and analog sequencers—as well as **ribbon**, **joystick**, and drum controllers—set standards that defined the synth industry and continues to do so in a modular/**patchable synthesizer** market, which rebounded to a remarkable extent during the late 1990s.

---

envelope: a two-dimensional shape or contour of acoustic elements of a sound, such as its amplitude; envelopes are typically illustrated with level or intensity mapped on the vertical (y) axis and time on the horizontal (x) axis

envelope follower: a device that monitors incoming audio signals and generates a control-voltage envelope proportional to the changes in amplitude of those signals

envelope generator (EG): a device or circuit that generates a control signal that simulates the sequence of an acoustic sound, which has a beginning, middle, and end; the parameters for one of the most common EGs in analog synthesizers are attack, decay, sustain, and release (ADSR), where the attack, decay, and release parameters signify time or rate values and sustain is a signal level

filter: a circuit that can be used to attenuate or emphasize specific frequencies in an electronic audio signal

lowpass filter: a circuit that attenuates higher frequencies while allowing lower frequencies to pass unattenuated

noise generator: a circuit that produces a random collection of multiple frequencies that can be perceived as hiss, wind, static, and other non-pitched sounds, depending on the noise "color," filtering, and envelope control; also described as a source of random frequencies that may sound like radio static or a sizzle; the most common types for synthesis are: white noise, a hissing-like sound weighted such that there is equal energy per unit bandwidth throughout the frequency spectrum; and pink noise, sounding lower pitched than white noise and weighted such that there is equal energy in every octave of the pitch range

highpass filter: a circuit that attenuates lower frequencies while allowing higher frequencies to pass unattenuated

sample-and-hold: a circuit that continually scans a voltage or numerical-generating source, measures its level when triggered, then locks on and outputs this voltage or value until the next measurement; the resulting output seems to be a random voltage or value

ribbon controller: an elongated touch-sensing strip of material that tracks the movement of a performer's finger across its surface and outputs a corresponding voltage or value to control oscillator pitch or some other parameter

joystick: a two-dimensional controller in the form of a vertical shaft that can be smoothly moved forward, backward, and from side to side to output control signals according to current x and y axis positions

patchable synthesizer: an instrument consisting of modules that are configured and arranged according to a manufacturer's control-panel design; unless they're **normalled**, modules must be interconnected for the instrument to generate audible sounds

normalled: all of the synthesizer circuitry has been wired together behind the control panel, negating the need for patch cords with which to connect modules—although some normalled synths have front-panel patch points for custom signal routing

During the late 1960s Bob decided there was a need for a performance-oriented synthesizer, so he teamed with Bill Hemsath, Jim Scott, and Chad Hunt to design the Minimoog. Its signal-routing structure—oscillator, noise, and external input signals go into a mixer, which passes the aggregate signal through the envelope-controlled lowpass filter and amplifier before reaching the main outputs—became a standard in the synth industry. The Minimoog proved so popular, thanks in good part to Keith Emerson, Jan Hammer, Chick Corea, Rick Wakeman, and many others who played it onstage and in studios, that Moog Music made more than 12,000 of them from 1970 to 1981, making it the most popular American-made monophonic analog synthesizer of the twentieth century.

The Synthesizer

A shot of the Moog studio in Trumansburg, New York, where Moog instruments were manufactured between 1963 and 1971. Note the conveniently placed patch cord tree directly to the *left* of the big Moog Modular. (With the permission of Ileana Grams-Moog)

After reluctantly leaving Moog Music in 1977 and subsequently losing the legal right to put his own name on musical instruments, Bob Moog founded Big Briar in 1977 and continued to develop new Theremins and other products. He finally reclaimed the legal right to his name in 2002. Bob spent several years developing a Minimoog for the twenty-first century, what became the Minimoog Voyager—complete with modern circuitry to not only duplicate as closely as possible the original's tone and functionality, but also to deliver extras such as a three-dimensional touch surface, secondary **VCF**, MIDI I/O, programmability and patch memory, and dedicated LFO. It began shipping in 2002. A variety of models are available, including the Old School—which like the original Minimoog lacks MIDI and patch memory for synthesists who want to work the old-fashioned way—and Minimoog Voyager XL, featuring a sixty-one-note keyboard that responds to velocity and **aftertouch** and a front-panel **patchbay** for extended signal-routing flexibility. Moog Music has also released the Little Phatty analog performance synth series, the unique Moog Guitar, a contemporary re-creation of the Taurus synth-bass pedals, and even iOS applications for Apple's iPhone, iPod Touch, and iPad. Throughout the years, Bob Moog's companies have produced Theremins.

Bob Moog poses with five Moogerfooger processors and an Etherwave Theremin at the Smithsonian Institution in April 2000. The occasion was a two-day conference called "The Keyboard Meets Modern Technology," a series of programs specifically honoring synthesizers during the Smithsonian's "Piano 300: Celebrating Three Centuries of People and Pianos." (Mark Vail)

Posing in the Moog Music office in July 2004 behind the guts of an Etherwave Pro Theremin are Steve Dunnington holding a Moogerfooger MF-105 MuRF stompbox, Bob Moog behind a Minimoog Voyager, and Mike Adams holding the control box from a Buchla Piano Bar. (Mark Vail)

> *aftertouch:* the varying amount of downward force or pressure applied to a key after it has been struck and reaches the bottom of its travel
> *patchbay:* a panel or **rackmount** unit containing multiple jacks that are interconnected to allow flexible patching and rerouting of signals
> *rackmount:* a device with permanent or removable "ears"—vertical, perpendicular extensions on either side of its front panel—perforated with two or more holes and measuring 19 inches across, allowing the device to be mounted in industrial-standard 19" racks; the letter "U" identifies the device's height, 1U indicating a single-space rackmount unit, with 1U being equal to 1.75"

Perhaps a little-known keyboard controller best epitomizes Bob's dedication to the craft of control: the Multiple-Touch-Sensitive Keyboard, on which Bob began working with the composer John Eaton in 1968. They finally completed it as a MIDI controller in 1991. Each of its forty-nine keys can sense finger position, how much skin is touching the key surface, how far down the key is pressed, and how hard the key is depressed at the bottom of its travel, so the instrument can transmit **polyphonic aftertouch**. When he began working with the finished Eaton-Moog keyboard, Eaton discovered it generated more MIDI controller data than he could find interesting parameters to control on synthesizers of the early 1990s. However, he returned to working with it in late 2006 and discovered the situation had much improved with contemporary software instruments.

> *polyphonic aftertouch:* each key of a keyboard senses pressure exerted on that key independently of other keys; allows the performer, for example, to impart LFO-driven vibrato on individual notes within a chord or play melodies inside a sustained chord by increasing the amplitude of single notes; also referred to as "poly pressure" and "poly aftertouch"

Synth Italia

What mostly inspired John Eaton to work with Bob Moog on the Multiple-Touch-Sensitive Keyboard? An electronic instrument called the Syn-Ket from the early 1960s, when electronic music and various arts thrived at the American Academy in Rome, Italy. Eaton was one of several American composers who worked there, alongside Otto Luening, William O. Smith, and George Balch Wilson. A talented sound engineer named Paul Ketoff had constructed a large, studio-confined instrument called the Phonosynth with the composer Gino Marinuzzi. After Ketoff demonstrated it for the Americans, they persuaded him to make a smaller, less elaborate version. Thus was born in 1963 the Syn-Ket, the Synthesizer Ketoff.

Paul Ketoff and John Eaton pose with a Syn-Ket in 1965. From the *top down* are modulation generators; a nine-band fixed filter bank; a patchbay matrix; three voice channels; a module containing a white-noise generator, spring reverb, and VU meter; and three twenty-four-note keyboards. (Courtesy of John Eaton)

Following completion of the original, Eaton recommended numerous musical features that Ketoff added to subsequent models. In essence, the Syn-Ket contained three synthesizers. It had three cascading twenty-four-note keyboards like the manuals of an organ console. The keys were small, like those on a toy piano, but you could wiggle them back and forth to bend notes and produce vibrato. On the second Syn-Ket, made specifically for Eaton, the keys also responded to velocity for control of amplitude and the filters. Each keyboard controlled its own voice, or "sound-combiner" as Ketoff referred to them, consisting of a square-wave oscillator; a series of button-controlled frequency dividers capable of dividing the incoming frequency by factors of 2, 3, 4, 5, and 8 to produce different harmonics; three complex filters; an amplifier; and three independent modulators. Vacuum-tube and solid-state circuitry made up the sound-combiners, which you could interconnect for a wider range of timbral possibilities. Eaton felt the Syn-Ket offered a human nuance missing from other early electronic instruments, and he enjoyed the ability to perform counterpoint parts with it alone.

Ketoff hand-made about a dozen Syn-Kets between 1963 and 1977, and there were considerable differences among them. Designed for live performance, the Syn-Ket proved challenging and difficult to learn—much like an acoustic instrument—but very rewarding given enough effort. Eaton, a renowned opera composer who frequently combined synths with orchestra and voice, wrote many pieces for Syn-Ket and toured extensively with one or two of these instruments between 1964 and 1977. Over time the aging instruments began to malfunction and eventually failed entirely.

Armand Pascetta's Pratt-Reed Polyphony

As synthesizers became more prevalent during the early 1970s, many players lamented their monophonic nature. The musician/technician Armand Pascetta was among the first to tackle synthesizer polyphony. Doing business as Electro Group, Pascetta wired Pratt-Reed keyboards to a unique processor (before microprocessors were commonly available) he had hand-assembled from transistors, resistors, diodes, and military-grade surplus integrated circuits to develop keyboards that responded to note velocity, **release velocity**, and aftertouch, and also allowed advance functionality including **keyboard splits** and **polyphonic portamento**. By the mid-1970s he'd created pre-MIDI keyboard controllers capable of transmitting more than twelve separate channels of gate and voltage-control data and handling multiple synth modules, even across multiple networked keyboards.

> *release velocity:* how quickly a finger is pulled from a key
> *keyboard splits:* dividing a keyboard into two or more sections, each capable of triggering different sounds either from different synthesizers or samplers, or from a synthesizer or sampler capable of **multitimbral** operation
> *multitimbral:* capable of generating more than one timbre simultaneously, with independent control of the individual timbres
> *polyphonic portamento:* when multiple notes are played, pitches glide at an adjustable rate from those previously sounding to the newly played notes rather than the pitches of the individual notes sounding immediately; other names for portamento include glissando and glide
> *CPU:* central processing unit, the circuitry in a computer that executes instructions from programs

Pascetta's polyphonic keyboard operated particularly effectively because it electronically sensed activity without continuously scanning the entire keyboard. If no keys were played, no processing time was spent. If you hit a single key, the system took one **CPU** clock tick to acquire the information from the keyboard. Playing two keys took only two clock ticks. Microprocessors in typical polyphonic keyboards scan all of the keys all of the time, which eats up processing power.

Among those whom Pascetta credits for making his keyboards happen is the organ builder and repairman Vince Treanor III. Malcolm Cecil, one of the first synthesists to discover Pascetta's work, incorporated a polyphonic keyboard into his massive TONTO (The Original New Timbral Orchestra) system, which Stevie Wonder played on *Music of My Mind*, *Talking Book*, *Innervisions*, and *Fulfillingness' First Finale*. The multitalented jazz/pop/gospel organist/synthesist/singer Don Lewis was another client, working with Pascetta to improve the keyboard's capabilities and user interface. In 1974, Lewis added a four-channel Pascetta keyboard that drove four Oberheim SEMs and two ARP 2600s in LEO (Live Electronic Orchestra), Don's fabulous electronic performance system. Other notable musicians who used Pascetta keyboards were Sergio Mendes, Quincy Jones, and Henry Mancini.

A 1975-era polyphonic, multitimbral synthesizer system consisting of an Armand Pascetta keyboard connected to, at the *upper left*, a pair of Pascetta's networked, four-channel processors stacked above four modified Oberheim SEMs. (Courtesy of Armand Pascetta, Electro Group)

Relatively few people are aware of Pascetta's work; his controller system never made it into full production, and he tells me he sold only twenty of these systems. However, his ideas were revolutionary and many have yet to be duplicated or surpassed. He reported in 2011 that he's once again working at perfecting and producing his keyboard controllers because, he said, "it would be fun to push the envelope again" and "I found MIDI to be obsolete from the day it was invented."

Three Armand Pascetta polyphonic keyboards along with a pair of his four-channel processors, photographed in 1975. (Courtesy of Armand Pascetta, Electro Group)

Heavyweight Polyphony and Control

Prior to 1976, Yamaha's only synthesizers were the little-known SY-1 and SY-2 keyboards. What they released that year, however, was special indeed. The CS-80 polyphonic synth was hefty in terms of both weight and suggested retail price: 220 pounds and $6,900. Even though it didn't crush its competition—the Polymoog, ARP Omni, Oberheim Four Voice, and Sequential Circuits Prophet-5, all built in the United States—it introduced fresh timbres and ushered into the synth industry some novel controller features, and remains one of the most coveted instruments today.

The CS-80 produces a distinctive, fat synth sound and is simple to use and play—once you get it to its destination and situated on a stand or tabletop ready to go. Not only was the CS-80 one of the first synths with a velocity-sensitive keyboard, but it also introduced polyphonic aftertouch. Instead of **pitchbend** and **modulation** wheels, the CS-80 has a unique ribbon controller; wherever you touch it becomes the center point, and moving away from there bends the pitch, allowing more extensive bends than possible on other ribbons. (Back then, synths didn't offer programmable bend ranges like a majority do today.) One of its earliest proponents was Stevie Wonder, who played the CS-80 so often that he wore out its ribbon.

---

pitchbend: a manual or automated upward and/or downward movement of pitch as a note is playing

modulation: fluctuations induced into a parameter, such as filter cutoff or oscillator frequency, using manual or automated techniques

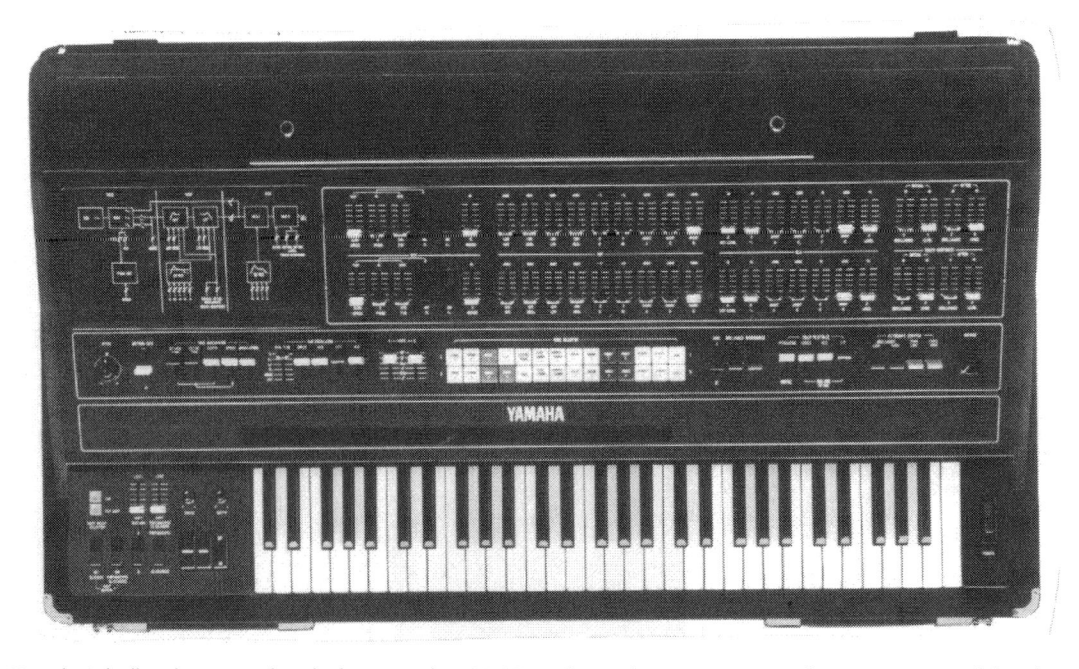

Yamaha's brilliantly executed, polyphonic analog CS-80 synth is as heavy—220 pounds!—as it is powerful and sonically stunning. Electronically temperamental, fragile, and challenging, as well. (Courtesy of Yamaha Corporation of America)

The Chroma rose like a phoenix from ARP's ashes in 1981 and survived through several years of development and production. It remains a highly prized vintage synthesizer, but its mylar membrane front panels are prone to failure and extremely rare today. (Courtesy of Alan R. Pearlman)

Multitimbral Polyphony

Until the mid-1970s, there were two giants in the synth-making universe: Moog Music and ARP Instruments. The electrical engineer Alan R. Pearlman founded ARP in 1969, then directed the release of a succession of synthesizers and keyboards over an eleven-year period. Some ARPs were popular and successful—the 2600, Odyssey, Pro-Soloist, and Omni—but others languished due to failures in quality control and/or design flaws—the Electronic Piano, Centaur, and Avatar guitar synth.

When ARP went bankrupt in 1981, two-year-old plans for a synth called the Chroma were seemingly squandered. Philip Dodds (1951–2007), the vice president of engineering, remained alone at ARP, but he managed to sell the Chroma design to CBS and get hired by the Rhodes division as the director of its production.

The Chroma, which Rhodes manufactured in 1982 and '83, is a programmable, sixteen-channel multitimbral, polyphonic synthesizer with an exquisite-feeling sixty-four-note weighted-action keyboard that offers accurate and sensitive velocity response. One concept the Chroma helped usher in, however, annoyed many synthesists: deep menu-driven voice programming with one data slider, two minimal LED displays, and fifty dual-function membrane switches. Previously, single-function buttons, switches, knobs, and sliders—one control per parameter—abounded on synthesizers, and affirmed knob-twisters and switch-throwers typically find the Chroma programming model foreign, cumbersome, and downright unfriendly. At least its pre-MIDI computer interface allowed connection to a personal computer for digital recording and reproduction of performance data. Tony Williams, a key engineer in designing the Chroma, developed voicing and sequencing software for it that ran on Apple IIe and IBM-PC computers. In fact, the PC had yet to ship when the Chroma first hit the market.

Physical Modeling

Some synthesists are content to load a complex patch, play a note, and luxuriate in multi-timbral bliss. Perhaps they'll tweak a knob or two to appear as if they're actually working hard to produce such a marvelous auditory experience.

Many players thankfully strive for more control and real-time expressivity, and synth developers and manufacturers from time to time address these enthusiasts. One synth that

Introduced in 1993, Yamaha's VL1 delivered powerful new synthesis and control capabilities, but it requires considerable patience and practice to be played expressively. (Courtesy of Yamaha Corporation of America)

truly requires active participation is Yamaha's VL1, the first commercially available **physical-modeling** synthesizer. Not only did it introduce a radically new type of synthesis, but it also requires considerable practice for a performer to make it sound good. Its Virtual Lead (VL) synthesis engine is based on the waveguide equation developed by Dr. Julius O. Smith of **CCRMA** at Stanford University. Toshifumi Kunimoto, acknowledged as the father of VL technology, led an engineering team to convert Smith's waveguide equation into the system that became a real-time musical instrument.

> *physical modeling:* the use of mathematical equations to represent physical laws and actions
> *CCRMA:* the Center for Computer Research in Music and Acoustics
> *duophonic:* capable of sounding two different notes simultaneously, each controlled independently
> *breath controller:* a device that fits between the performer's lips and senses pressure created by blowing
> *wind controller:* an electronic instrument with sensors to measure a performer's breath force, finger movements, lip and jaw activity, and other expressions; it may or may not have a built-in sound generator and may or may not appear similar to an acoustic wind instrument; and it transmits performance activity and expressions via MIDI or analog control voltages, gates, and triggers to built-in or external synthesizers and electronic musical instruments
> *sample playback:* capable of triggering sounds from memory, but not actually able to record sounds in the first place

When it appeared in 1993, the VL1 faced a challenging synthesis market. Pricey at $4,995 and merely **duophonic**, the VL1—as with an acoustic instrument—requires lots of dedicated practice to sound good and for the synthesist to develop expressive performance techniques. Playing it with a **breath controller** can add to its expressive capabilities. Experienced woodwind and brass players might even forgo the VL1's forty-nine-note velocity- and pressure-sensing keyboard, and play the VL1 with a **wind controller** such as a Steiner MIDI EVI, Softwind Instruments Synthophone, Yamaha WX5, or Akai EWI400s.

The VL1 can reward its player with dynamic musical articulation, which can't be achieved using most other types of synthesis—especially **sample playback**. Not only is the VL1 tricky to play, but programming patches is extremely difficult because timbre and pitch are interrelated. You might start with a beautiful tone only to ruin the timbre by trying to tune it. Likewise, modifying the timbre of a sound that's in tune can make it untunable, perhaps even unplayable.

Finger-Controlled Speech

Among the many innovative electronic devices that came from the creative minds at Bell Laboratories decades before they appeared in consumer products was a speech synthesizer called the Voder (Voice Operation DEmonstratoR). Speech engineer Homer W. Dudley developed it in time for demonstrations at the 1939 New York World's Fair. The Voder used finger-controlled levers and foot pedals with continuous—as opposed to switched—responses to control parameters that allowed the simulation of human speech.

It's doubtful any working Bell Voders remain today, but thanks to programming wizard Bill Mauchly and Waveboy Industries there's Voder software, which transforms Ensoniq's EPS-16 Plus and ASR-10 **samplers** into instruments as close as anything to embodying the original Voder's spirit. At the core of the Waveboy Voder, which is as of August 2013 still available from Chicken Systems, is an effect algorithm that creates a bank of filter frames. Provided on the Voder 3.5″ floppy disk are sixteen frames based on common phonemes from the English language: nine vowels and seven sustained consonants such as V, L, and M. When you load the Voder software, the frames are assigned to the bottom sixteen notes of the sampler's sixty-one-note keyboard, from C2 to E♭3. Playing any of these keys recalls a filter frame, but the keys themselves don't trigger sounds. The speed at which the new filter configuration evolves from the previous one depends on how hard you hit the key. In essence, you can make the sampler talk—although it will take lots of practice to make the results intelligible.

A total of sixty-four filter frames are available at one time, and you can use sources besides a keyboard to sequence through frames—including pressure, the mod wheel, an **LFO**, and sample-and-hold for random frame selection. **Chorusing** and **delay** effects are also part of the Voder algorithm.

---

samplers: instruments that can digitally capture acoustically and electronically generated sounds, store and trigger them from memory, and perhaps allow those sounds to be edited in memory in ways such as truncating silence from the beginning and/or end of the sample, normalizing the sample's audio content to increase the

The Synthesizer

An operator works the Bell Lab Voder's levers and pedals to synthesize speech. View a filmed Voder presentation at www.youtube.com/watch?v=mSdFu1xdoZk. (Courtesy of Tom Rhea)

> amplitude of quieter parts so that they're nearly as loud as those with higher amplitude, and looping some or all of the sample so that it repeats in various ways
> *LFO:* low-frequency oscillator, one that typically cycles at a rate slower than audible frequencies, or below 20Hz, although possibly capable of oscillating at an audible rate, which is generally accepted as 20Hz to 20kHz
> *chorusing:* an effect created by using a delayed or detuned version of an audio signal mixed with the original to emphasize and reduce harmonic content, resulting in a fatter and more animated sound
> *delay:* an analog or digital circuit that creates echoes from incoming audio signals
> *equalizer:* a circuit or device that allows the amplitudes of selected bands of incoming frequency content to be boosted or reduced

The Ensoniqs' sampling inputs can be activated so that you can route sounds from an external source through the Voder effect for real-time processing. The Voder will not, however, function as a vocoder—another Homer W. Dudley invention—because the Ensoniq samplers' microprocessor isn't capable of processing an input at the same time that it synthesizes sound. Given its capacity to process external signals in real time, however, the Voder-equipped Ensoniq sampler can function as a unique MIDI-controlled **equalizer**.

Sound

Man's quest to create new musical timbres stretches far back in history, maybe even farther than you'd imagined. Consider these prophetic words:

> We have also sound-houses, where we practise and demonstrate all sounds and their generation. We have harmonies which you have not, of quarter-sounds and lesser slides of sounds. Divers instruments of music likewise to you unknown, some sweeter than any you have; together with bells and rings that are dainty and sweet. We represent small sounds as great and deep; likewise great sounds, extenuate and sharp; we make divers tremblings and warblings of sounds, which in their original are entire. We represent and imitate all articulate sounds and letters, and the voices and notes of beasts and birds. We have certain helps which, set to the ear, do further the hearing greatly. We have also divers strange and artificial echoes, reflecting the voice many times, and, as it were, tossing it; and some that give back the voice louder than it came, some shriller and some deeper; yea, some rendering the voice, differing in the letters or articulate sound from that they receive. We have also means to convey sounds in trunks and pipes, in strange lines and distances. (from *The New Atlantis* by Francis Bacon, 1626)

Could Francis Bacon have been any more prescient? He might have been referring to synthesizers and other gear for making electronic music today. Bacon might even have foreseen the Internet.

The Synthesizer

A seventy-four-key Ondes Martenot with its three diffusers—*clockwise* from *lower left:* the Haut-parleur, Palme, and Métallique. (David Kean, courtesy of the Audities Foundation and the National Music Centre)

Quantized Note Selection

The development of all the different types of synthesis available to us now has taken many years, almost a century. At times progress has been slow, and at other times there have been leaps and bounds in technology. Nearly three centuries after Bacon penned *The New Atlantis*, the earliest electronic instruments began to appear. Developed about a decade after the Theremin, the Ondes Martenot came from France. Like the Theremin it uses a heterodyning-oscillator sound-generation technique, but it isn't as well known—even though it's more user-friendly for pitch accuracy.

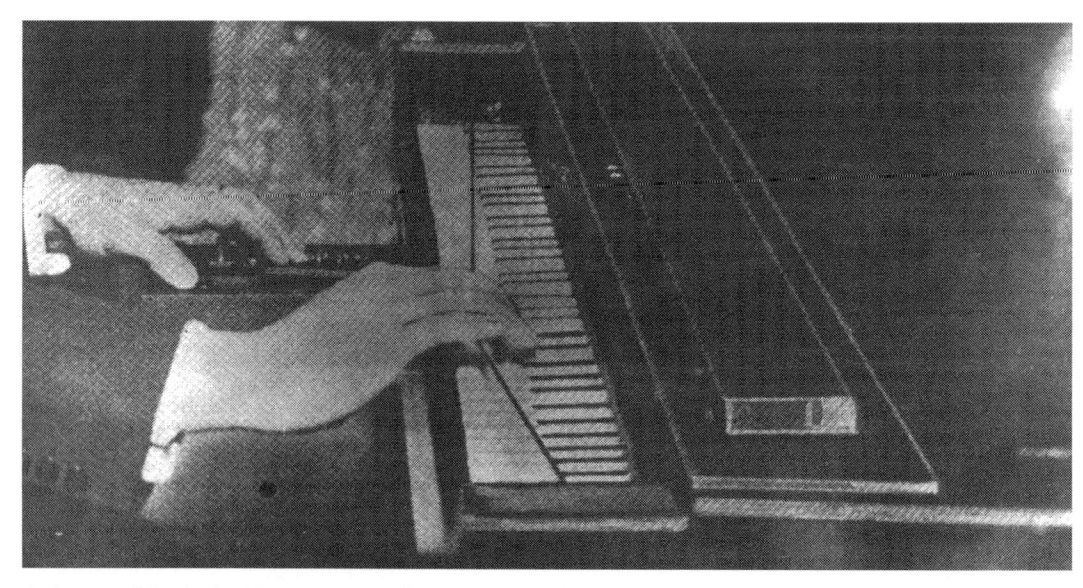

A closeup of the Ondes Martenot's controllers, comprising this early model's etched fingerboard and ring-connected band for pitch selection via the right hand, and articulation and timbre selectors for the left. (Courtesy of Tom Rhea)

Maurice Martenot (1898-1980) invented the Ondes Martenot—also known as the Ondes Musicales—in 1918, introduced it in Paris in 1928, and handmade them until his death in October 1980. Only around three hundred ever existed. It's easier to play specific notes than with the Theremin thanks to an etched chromatic fingerboard and a celluloid ring worn on a finger and attached to a continuous wire ribbon. The performer simply moves the ring to the desired note in order to hear it. Later models feature a mini-key mechanical keyboard along with the wire ribbon. The keyboard is spring-loaded and can be wobbled back and forth to add vibrato. Depressing a bar with the left hand triggers and articulates notes.

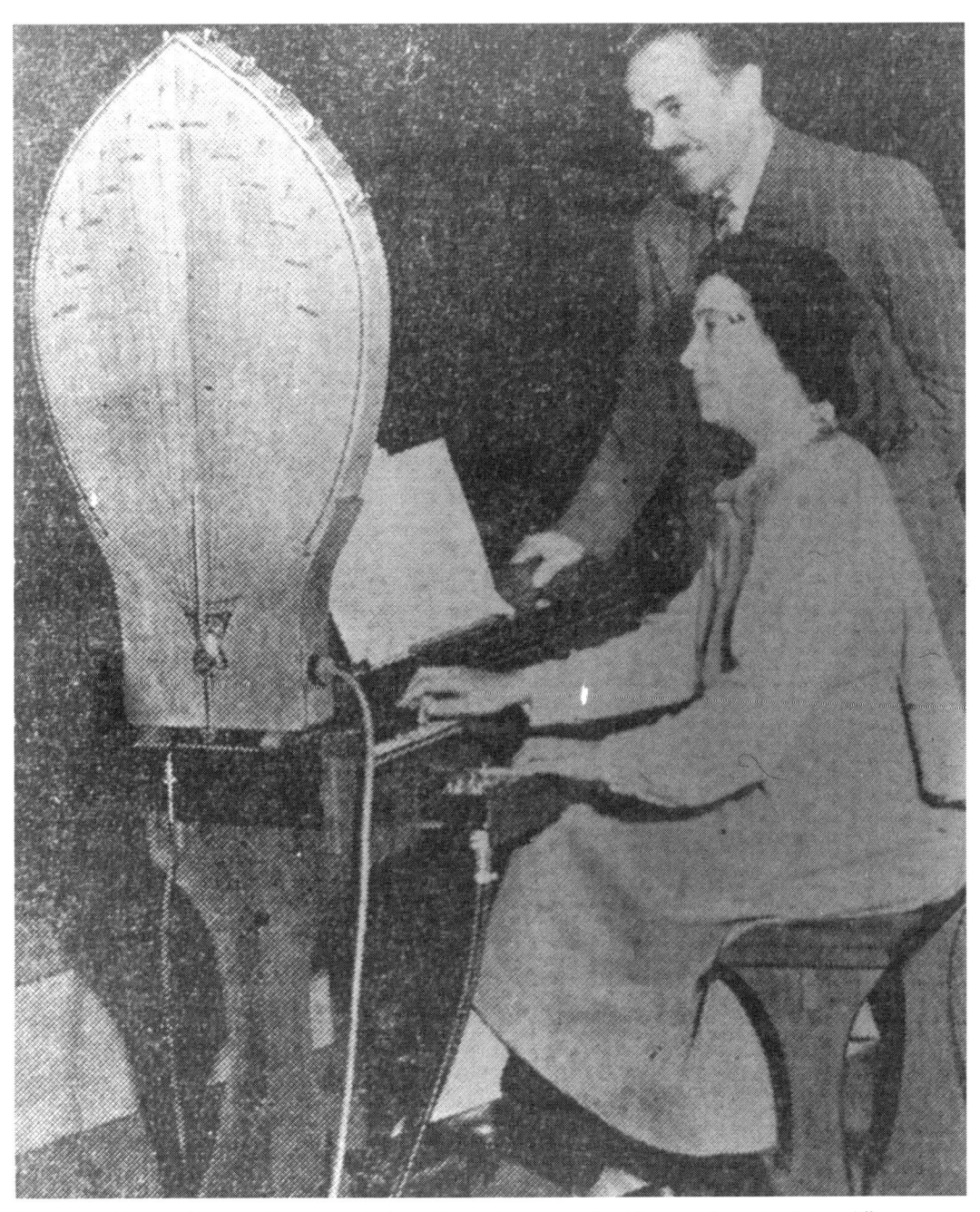

As inventor Maurice Martenot looks on, his sister Ginett plays an Ondes Martenot through a Palme diffuser. (Courtesy of Tom Rhea)

Maurice and Ginett Martenot pose with a Palme diffuser. (Courtesy of Tom Rhea)

Incorporating fixed filters for timbral selection, the Martenot generates sounds named in terms familiar to organists of the time, such as "Hollow," "Tutti," "Wave," "Gambe," "Nasillard," and "Octaviant." A knee lever mounted on the instrument's underside allows continuous control of the chosen timbre. Martenot also designed sound projectors called "diffusers." While the *Haut-parleur* resembles a contemporary speaker cabinet with a forward-facing loudspeaker, the other two diffusers are unique. The exquisite *Palme* combines a resonant body and a sound hole like an acoustic guitar with a dozen taut brass wires stretched and tuned over the front and rear surfaces, meeting at a transducer that oscillates according to the note played and creating sympathetic vibrations acoustically amplified by the resonant body. The innovative *Métallique* houses a gong suspended in a polygon-shaped box. A transducer vibrates the gong to resonate in sympathy with the Martenot-generated note. From the instrument's control panel, the Martenot player can select among the individual diffusers or pipe audio to all of them at once.

Polyphonic Progenitor

Among the various relatives of the famous Hammond B-3 organ is a little-known but distinguished electronic instrument called the Novachord. It's often regarded as a forerunner of modern polyphonic synthesizers thanks to the programmability of its individual parameters.

Hammond engineers virtually stumbled onto a new method of generating tones electronically by connecting a **triode** as an amplifier, then routing a sawtooth wave into

Hammond's Novachord shown in an early 1940s publicity shot. The late Alan Young (1926-2004), who worked for thirty years as a research and development engineer for Hammond, once said the Novachord "was the forerunner of today's polyphonic synthesizers. In ways it was far ahead of its time. Even today, with all the modern electronic instruments we hear, the Novachord is still distinctive." (Courtesy of Hammond Suzuki USA Inc.)

this circuit. The output was an octave lower than its original pitch, and this 2:1 **frequency divider**—supplemented with a type of **distorter** called a "control tube," which adds multiple harmonics to the tone—became the basis of the Novachord.

Produced from 1939 to 1942, the five-hundred-pound instrument features twelve oscillators with five frequency dividers each; lowpass, **bandpass**, and highpass filters; and a seventy-two-note keyboard. Its distinctive timbres range from mellow to brilliant and have been described as hauntingly beautiful and slightly eerie, as if there's a strong fundamental layered with string-like overtones. Onboard envelopes allow note attacks to vary from instantaneous to very slow.

> *triode:* typically a vacuum tube, one of the earliest electronic components for amplifying signals
>
> *frequency divider:* a circuit that lowers the frequency of an electronic signal; dividing a frequency by two results in a drop of one octave

> *distorter:* a circuit for purposely altering and modulating a waveform, introducing harmonics and other artifacts to the signal, or feeding audio back onto itself to overload the signal path and alter the sound quality
>
> *bandpass filtering:* circuitry that attenuates frequencies below and above specified cutoff points and allows frequencies between the cutoff points to pass unattenuated

Although the Novachord is capable or producing gorgeous sounds, it failed in the instrumental marketplace mainly due to its unreliability. Its voicing circuits consist of scores of primitive capacitors, essentially metal cans filled with wax, and their likelihood of failure proved overwhelming. The Hammond Organ Company manufactured more than 1,700 Novachords during its three-year production, but few remain in functional condition.

Polyphony from an Expander

More significant advancements took place beyond the electronic production of musical sounds between the 1940s and 1970s, but during the late '70s many synthesists craved polyphonic keyboards that generated distinctive analog timbres capable of competing with electric guitars, bass, drums, and other instruments in a loud rock band. Tom Oberheim provided some outstanding solutions.

From 1975 through the 1980s, synthesizers bearing the Oberheim name were among the most desirable money could buy. But Tom's story goes back farther. Beginning in the 1960s, he created popular **stompbox** effects for Norlin under the Maestro label. In 1970 Oberheim decided to make a digital sequencer to drive his ARP 2600 and Minimoog synthesizers. By 1971 he'd developed the monophonic DS-2 digital sequencer, which could record and repeat monophonic lines played on a keyboard. However, once you sequence a **monosynth**, no voices remain to play along with the sequence on the same synth. Coincidentally, many synthesists searched for ways to add voices and/or fatten the sound of their instruments by layering voices on top of each other.

> *stompbox:* an effects processor often used by guitar players who typically position them on the floor at their feet where they can be switched on and off with an easily accessible pushbutton, commonly referred to as a footswitch
>
> *monosynth:* a synthesizer with a single voice channel, typically comprising one, two, or three oscillators, a filter, an amplifier, and one or more envelope generators; while capable of producing only one note at a time, the note could conceivably consist of two or more frequencies, depending on the number of oscillators in the voice channel
>
> *VCO:* voltage-controlled oscillator, an analog circuit that generates a variety of waveforms, usually at audible frequencies (20Hz to 20kHz), although also commonly

> capable of frequencies below and above that range, depending on the incoming DC voltage
>
> *two-pole multimode VCF:* a voltage-controlled filter that provides different filtering modes—such as lowpass, bandpass, and highpass characteristics—with a 12dB-per-octave cutoff slope; a single pole exhibits a cutoff slope of 6dB per octave
>
> *ASR envelope generator:* a contour or transient generator with attack, sustain, and release time or rate parameters

Tom Oberheim eventually undertook his true calling: the development of superb-sounding analog synthesizers. First he created the Synthesizer Expander Module (SEM), featuring two **VCOs**, a **two-pole multimode VCF**, an LFO, and two **ASR envelope generators**. Not only did it meet Oberheim's personal needs, but it also saved him financially after the Norlin company unexpectedly cancelled all of their Maestro stompbox orders at the beginning of 1975. Tom subsequently licensed the polyphonic scanning keyboard developed by E-mu's Dave Rossum and paired it with multiple SEMs. By June 1975 he'd completed his Two Voice and Four Voice synths, the first polyphonic synthesizers to use individual voltage-controlled circuits for each voice. By 1977 there was the Oberheim Eight Voice, available in single- and dual-manual configurations.

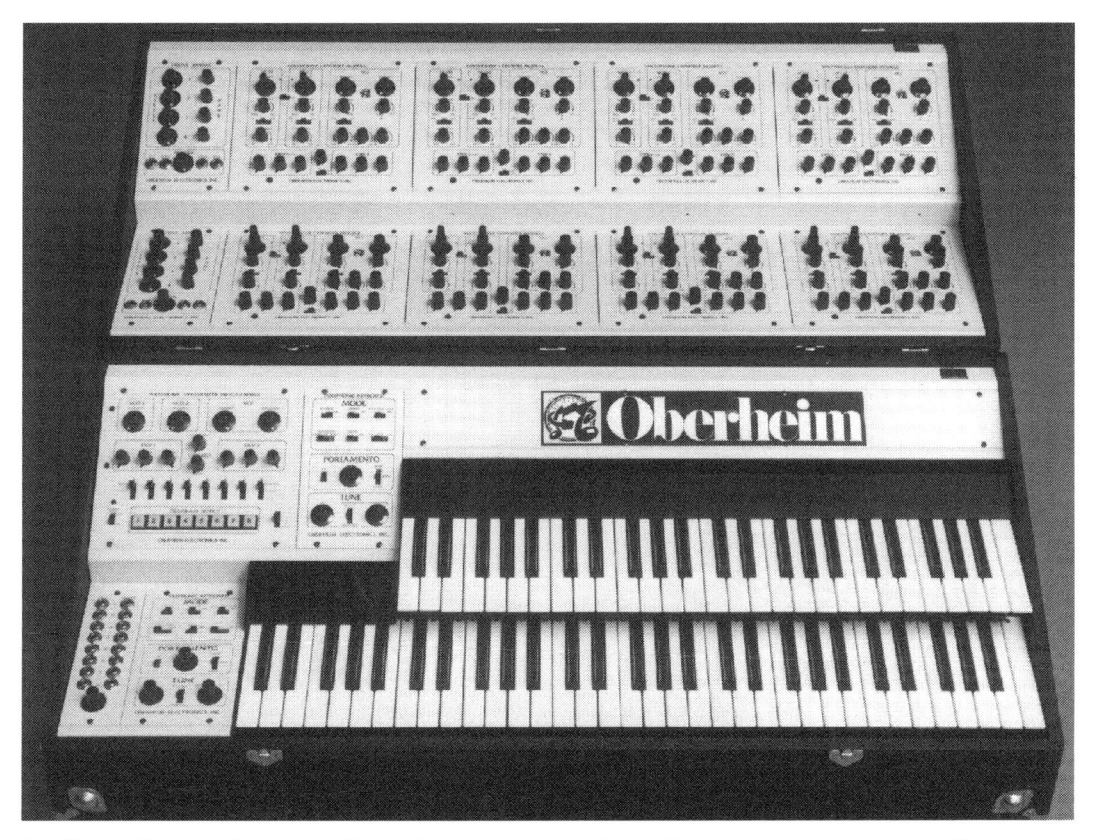

A full-blown Oberheim Dual-Manual Eight Voice synthesizer, packed with two output modules, four- and five-octave keyboards (each with its own controller module), eight SEMs, and a Polyphonic Synthesizer Programmer for loading patches into the SEMs. This version appeared during the late '70s. (Photo courtesy of Gibson Guitar Corp.)

The Synthesizer

Tom Oberheim unveiled the Two Voice Pro analog synth in 2012. Along with a pair of modern versions of his SEM, Tom equipped it with a three-octave keyboard that senses both velocity and aftertouch, fifty 3.5mm patch jacks for ultraflexible signal-routing, and a sixteen-step sequencer that can play two different sequences simultaneously, syncs to MIDI clock, allows sequence-chaining into songs, and provides memory for ninety-nine sequences. (Courtesy of Tom Oberheim)

Another Oberheim development proved equally groundbreaking: the programmability, storage, and recall of most of the SEM's parameters, delivered by the Polyphonic Synthesizer Programmer module. Introduced in 1976, the Programmer allowed a nearly immediate change in the sound generated by multiple SEMs at once, although it didn't store values for a few SEM parameters.

Before losing his company in 1985, Tom Oberheim oversaw the development of powerful and popular synths including the OB-X, OB-1, Xpander, and Matrix-12, as well as the pre-MIDI Oberheim Parallel Buss for synchronizing the OB-X with his multitrack DSX digital sequencer and the DMX drum machine. He founded Marion Systems in 1989 and introduced a sixteen-bit upgrade for the twelve-bit Akai S900 sampler and a **SCSI** interface for the Akai MPC60 music workstation. Toward the end of 1993 Tom introduced the 1U rackmount MSR2 synth module that could house one or two proprietary analog synth circuit boards. From 1998 to 2002 he served as the president of SeaSound, manufacturer of computer audio interfaces. Oberheim also helped design and assemble Radio Baton controllers for Max Mathews, found time to work on computer programming, and experimented with analog synthesizer and audio circuits.

> *SCSI:* Small Computer System Interface, intended for file transfers between computers, hard drives, and other gear; originally developed in 1978 and first marketed in 1981; the acronym is pronounced "scuzzy"
> *cross-platform:* capable of running on both Macintosh and Windows operating systems

To the greater synthesis community, Tom Oberheim's most significant contribution during the twenty-first century was his reintroduction on June 3, 2009, of the SEM. He makes three versions: one with a patchbay panel of thirty-three 3.5mm jacks that allows you to override normalled circuit connections for audio routing and voltage-control of components; the second with a built-in MIDI-to-CV (control voltage) converter; and the third with MIDI-to-CV conversion and twenty-one 3.5mm patch points. True to the original, there's no patch memory and—beyond a few component upgrades and improved audio quality—the old and new versions are essentially identical. In 2012 Tom delivered the Son of 4-Voice as well as the Two Voice Pro, analog Oberheims for the twenty-first century. Coincidentally, Arturia released a virtual, **cross-platform** version of Tom's original synth module in the form of Oberheim SEM V.

Switched-On Additive Synthesis

While many synthesists crave state-of-the-art technology, others latch onto specific instruments and stick with them for years, squeezing all of the musicality out of them as possible. Case in point, Wendy Carlos with the MTI General Development System (GDS) and Digital Keyboards Synergy, which are capable of advanced sound-generation techniques including **additive synthesis** and **phase**, **frequency**, and **amplitude modulation**.

> *additive synthesis:* the use of multiple waveforms—traditionally sine waves—with independent control of each wave's frequency, amplitude, and phase to create complex timbres
> *phase modulation:* manual or automated adjustments by degrees to the cycle stages of one or more oscillators' output signals; the complete cycle of a periodic waveform measures 360 degrees
> *frequency modulation (FM):* controlling the output frequency of one oscillator (the carrier) with another oscillator (the modulator); at slow FM rates around 7Hz using a sine or triangle waveform as the modulator, the results can sound like vibrato; at audible and higher frequencies with a variety of periodic modulation waveforms, you can produce elaborate timbral changes and extra harmonics; John Chowning's linear FM synthesis technology, licensed by Yamaha, uses multiple carriers and modulators with complex signal routings to generate timbres
> *amplitude modulation (AM):* changes in an audio signal's loudness under manual or automated control; modulation by a sine or triangular wave at around 7Hz results

> in **tremolo**, or a periodic wavering in amplitude; modulating amplitude at audible frequencies can result in timbres similar to those you get from FM
>
> *tremolo:* a periodic modulation of amplitude; often mistakenly referred to as *vibrato*, which is instead a modulation of pitch

During the late 1970s, while working at Bell Labs on an echo-cancellation solution for telephone lines, Dr. Hal Alles designed the synthesis engine that eventually powered the GDS and Synergy. After reading Alles's article "An Inexpensive Digital Sound Synthesizer" (*Computer Music Journal* 3, no. 3, Sept. 1979), Ernie Briefel and his son Dennis co-founded MTI (Music Technology, Inc.), a New York–based division of the Italian company Crumar. They enlisted Dr. Alles as an advisor; hired a development staff that included Mercer "Stoney" Stockell, Kevin Doren, Wing Moi, and Jerry Kaplan; and fi-

The General Development System (GDS), which Music Technology, Inc., manufactured under the Crumar name, descended from work done by Dr. Hal Alles at Bell Labs. Its keyboard unit featured multiple sliders, knobs, and buttons, but they served no functions early on because the GDS designers weren't sure what they were supposed to do. (Courtesy of Ernie & Dennis Briefel, Music Technology, Inc.)

A third-generation Digital Keyboards Synergy II+. It interfaced with a Kaypro computer like the one shown here so that users could edit and enter their own patches. Previously, alternative patches could be created only on a Crumar/MTI GDS, burned onto a ROM chip, and transferred into a Synergy via a cartridge like the one shown to the *right* of the Kaypro keyboard. (Dominic Milano)

nanced the development and production of the GDS. MTI manufactured only five or six of them because the GDS was intended primarily for internal use, but they sold a few for $27,500 each. For their investment, GDS buyers received an instrument with thirty-two programmable digital oscillators and a complex internal patching network. Its sixty-one-note velocity-sensitive keyboard was accompanied by an impressive array of controllers: thirty-two sliders, twelve rotary knobs, sixteen lighted pushbuttons, a joystick, a spring-loaded pitchbend knob, and an expression-pedal input.

With the development system up and running, the MTI team—by then known as Digital Keyboards—focused on making the less expensive Synergy ($5,295), a pushbutton synth with a seventy-four-note velocity-sensing keyboard, **cross-switching** between voices, four-**voice layering** with innovative voice-assignment modes (with rotating mode engaged, each note triggered the next available voice round-robin style), a four-track polyphonic sequencer, and a joystick for pitchbends and modulation control. Two keyboard-split options were available: a fixed-point mode and a **floating-point keyboard split mode** that fairly accurately followed the player's hands across up to six keyboard zones.

> *cross-switching:* velocity-controlled triggering of different waveforms or sound samples assigned to independent ranges of velocity values
>
> *voice layering:* stacking multiple sounds to be played simultaneously by incoming note commands
>
> *floating-point keyboard split:* a keyboard-assignment mode that allows you to define a point between two notes on the keyboard on either side of which triggers a different sound, then tracks the notes you play with either hand and attempts to assign the proper sound to play for one hand or the other, even if the notes played extend below or above the defined split point

Wendy Carlos particularly enjoyed working with the GDS and Synergy because they were voiced in two dimensions—from low to high pitches with a full range of dynamics. She could assign the dimensions to alternative axes and manage the results using note velocity, knobs, and other controllers. Voices responded in a graduated manner through custom curves in look-up tables to evenly tie dynamic changes together. "It created a continuity of timbral variation that was smooth over all of the keys and levels," Wendy explains, "very much like most acoustic instruments."

Prior to the development of a computer interface and software for a Kaypro computer running CP/M (Control Program for Microcomputers) to allow programming on the Synergy itself, Carlos created all of her Synergy timbres on the GDS. Stoney Stockell helped her achieve a long-desired goal of exploring microtonal tunings by retrofitting her Synergys to load pitches from a desktop computer in real time. This allowed Wendy to design and explore different scales and instrumental tunings, including—very important to her—"the crucial tie between timbres and tunings, and even timings, durations, and tempi."

> **Microtonal Tunings**
> Synthesists interested in exploring the art of just intonation and microtonal-tuning temperaments are fortunate on two fronts. First, you'll find a number of electronic instruments equipped to support alternative tunings. While the number of hardware synths that allow microtonal scales has decreased since 2000, many software instruments can do so. Second, there are plenty of resources for such exploration. As a starting point, I recommend John Loffink's Microtonal Synthesis website (www.microtonal-synthesis.com), where you'll find links to pages that reveal microtonal synthesizer charts, terms, and definitions; a help page that includes tips, information, and further links; sources of microtonal scales and software; a discography of microtonal synthesis recordings; and information about just-intonation pioneer Harry Partch (1901–74). An excellent and comprehensive book on the subject is Scott R. Wilkinson's *Tuning In: Microtonality in Electronic Music*. Working with microtonal tunings isn't a simple task, nor is it for everyone, but the rewards can be enlightening and fulfilling for those willing and committed to seriously delve into the art.

Carlos exploited this work to the utmost for *Beauty in the Beast*. Among the **non-equal-tempered tunings** she explored were **Balinese pelog and slendro scales**, custom scales called **alpha** and **beta**, and her own "perfect" **just-intonation tuning** with 144 notes per octave. Her specially expanded just tunings are actually a family of two—"Harmonic" and "Super-Just"—that to her are the most useful, especially in extended forms for 144 pitches per octave.

> *non-equal-tempered tunings:* whereas twelve-tone equal temperament, in which octaves are divided into twelve equal steps of 100 cents per step, became an accepted musical scale in Western music at the beginning of the nineteenth century and is

the most prevalent scale in use today, it's an unnatural compromise; although French monk, mathematician, and music theorist Marin Mersenne originally developed equal temperament in 1635 to allow key changes while maintaining frequency ratios within the scale, some tuning ratios between keys are noticeably sharp or flat in comparison with an integer-proportioned—or just intonation—scale, in which no tuning beats occur between notes, but transpositions are limited without the ability to quickly retune note frequencies; twelve-tone equal-temperament tuning is so ingrained in most listeners' ears that music in just intonation or other microtonal temperaments sounds strange and out of tune

Balinese pelog and slendro scales: **gamelan** musicians on Bali and Java developed pelog, a scale of seven notes, although players are typically limited to only five of these notes by their instruments; slendro, an older gamelan scale, comes from a different region in Indonesia and bears resemblance to five-note-per-octave equal temperament

gamelan: a musical orchestra or ensemble, traditionally from Indonesia, or a collection of instruments they play, which can include bowed string instruments, xylophones, drums, gongs, bamboo flutes, and others, many handmade

alpha scale: an exotic 15.3 note-per-octave scale with steps of 78 cents between individual notes; Wendy Carlos developed it by dividing a minor third into equal halves, and then equally halving that into the alpha scale

beta scale: another Wendy Carlos scale, which she developed by splitting a fourth in half, resulting in a scale of approximately 18.8 notes per octave with steps of 63.8 cents between the notes

just-intonation tuning: a microtonal scale in which octaves are unequally divided into frequency ratios according to integer proportions; for example, in traditional just intonation, the ratio of a perfect fifth is 3:2, or 701.955 cents higher than the octave's beginning note frequency, making it slightly sharp in comparison with twelve-note-per-octave equal temperament's 700 cents above the starting pitch, or an imperfect ratio of 1.498307:1; Carlos's "perfect" just-intonation scale works out to 144 pitches per octave because she developed tuning tables for each key to allow transpositions into different keys

Groundbreaking German Digital Synthesizers

The German engineer Wolfgang Palm proved one of the most influential and prescient pioneers of digital synthesis. His efforts, beginning in 1975, resulted in a collection of digital instruments that found their way into the hands of artists including Christopher Franke and Edgar Froese of Tangerine Dream and Thomas Dolby when analog was all anybody knew anything about.

Palm's lineup of PPG Wave instruments are known for their piercing eight-bit digital sound, which brazenly includes **aliasing** in higher registers—musical grunge that gives the PPG a special sonic squawk. Its ability to sweep through digital **wavetables** using

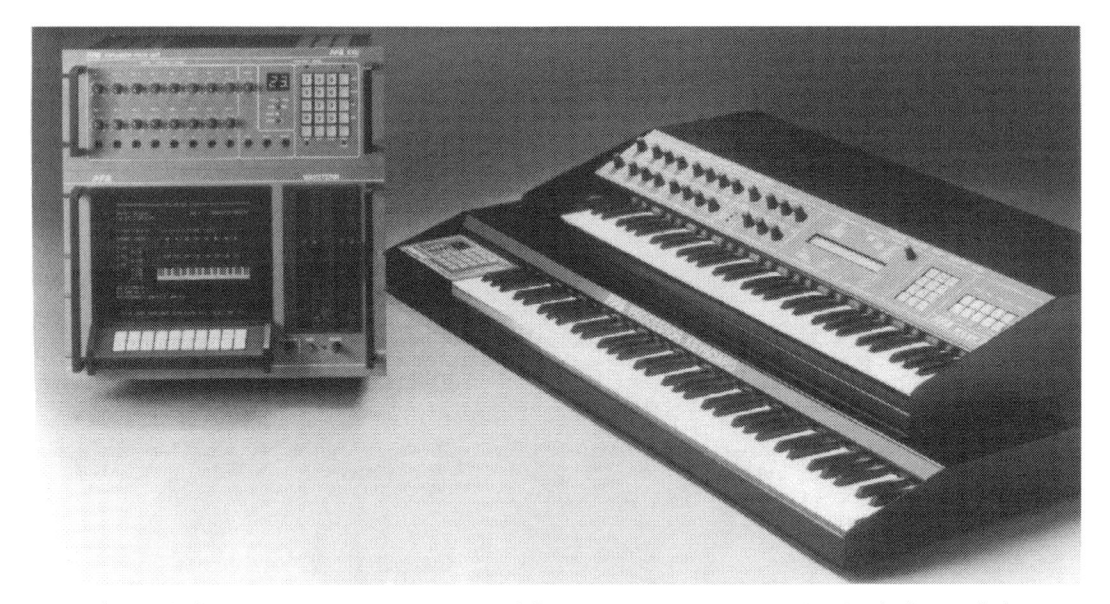

A complete PPG Wave system, ca. 1982. On *top at left* is an Expansion Voice Unit (EVU), which provided sixteen additional voices for the Wave 2.2 (*top right*). MIDI didn't yet exist, so the EVU and Wave 2.2 communicated via PPG's twelve-pin parallel communication bus. Beneath the EVU is an original Waveterm, with which you could create eight-bit waveshapes by specifying points on a graph or by sampling externally generated sounds and then display the results on the CRT screen and perform a Fourier analysis, which represents a waveform as a collection of sine waves at various frequencies and amplitudes. Data storage went onto 10.5" floppy disks. Under the Wave 2.2 to the *right* is a PRK Processor keyboard, which sported a seventy-two-note (F to E) velocity-sensitive, weighted-action keyboard. The PRK could be loaded with up to eight PPG voice cards, each with four wavetables. (Dominic Milano)

envelope generators created perhaps the most popular PPG Wave sound. Although PPG no longer exists, Palm's ideas and developments live on in the synthesis circuitry of the Waldorf Microwave (1990), full-blown Wave (1993), and 2007-vintage Blofeld.

aliasing: nonharmonic overtones induced into a digital audio signal at frequencies exceeding half the sampling rate, also known as the *Nyquist* frequency and based on the **Nyquist theorem**

Nyquist theorem: published by Harry Nyquist (1889–1976) in 1929, the highest frequency that can accurately be reproduced when a signal is digitally encoded at a certain sample rate; theoretically, the Nyquist frequency is one-half of the sampling rate, and digital audio containing frequencies above the Nyquist limit can suffer from aliasing

wavetables: collections of single-cycle digital waveforms

analog modeling: using digital components and math to virtually produce analog-like timbres

wavetable synthesis: the creation of timbres using digital oscillators to scan through collections of digitized single-cycle waveforms, sometimes in a linear fashion from the beginning of one wavetable to its end, or across a variety of wavetables under user control

sampling: digitally recording or encoding audio

Over the years there have been elite synths that possess an extremely high drool factor—synths that look so cool they make you slobber from wanting a chance to play them. One of the all-time beauties in anyone's book would be the Waldorf Wave, manufactured from 1993 to 1998. Its control panel was so big and heavy that the designers incorporated two shock absorbers in its tilt assembly. (Courtesy of Waldorf Music GmbH)

As the synth industry exploded in the mid-'80s, Palm saw many of his customers opt for American and Japanese instruments. To maintain his business, he decided to develop different products. One was a multipurpose, all-digital music machine called the Realizer, which combined digital sound production, processing, recording, sequencing, and mixing in one system. Although PPG didn't stay in business long enough to manufacture the Realizer, Palm got it to emulate four basic kinds of sound generation: **analog modeling**, frequency modulation, **wavetable synthesis**, and **sampling**. In 2011 Palm released a free Windows application called the Plex 2 Restructuring Synthesizer. He introduced the PPG WaveGenerator and PPG WaveMapper—both for the iPad—in 2012 and 2013, respectively, as well as the PPG MiniMapper for the iPhone and iPod Touch in 2013.

Realizing John Chowning's Linear FM Synthesis

Two introductions in 1983 rocked the music industry. One was MIDI, the Musical Instrument Digital Interface—the communications protocol that transformed and invigorated

Thanks to MIDI's development and introduction in 1983, you can connect multiple MIDI synths together and play them all from one controller. Provided seven of them have MIDI thru connectors, you could connect them in series. However, many current MIDI devices don't have a MIDI thru. MIDI Solutions' T8 MIDI thru box—shown here from *behind*, where its single MIDI in and eight MIDI thrus are located—is a 1U rackmount unit that allows you to drive up to eight slave devices from one MIDI controller. (© MIDI Solutions Inc.)

The Synthesizer

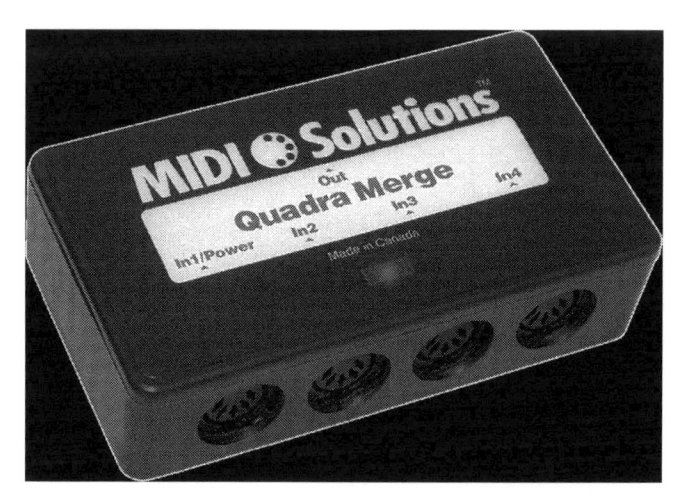

MIDI Solutions makes a wide range of rackmount and tabletop devices for routing and processing MIDI data. This is their Quadra Merge, which combines MIDI data from four sources—one of which provides power—for output through its single MIDI out. (© MIDI Solutions Inc.)

the electronic-music universe. Also introduced that year was one of the best-selling synthesizers of all time: the Yamaha DX7.

Polyphonic analog synths such as the Sequential Circuits Prophet-5 ruled the roost at the time, but the DX7 shattered all previous synth-sales records and offered a powerful new form of digital synthesis—linear frequency modulation (FM)—at a price many players could afford. Together with digital samplers, the digital synths including the DX7 practically buried interest in analog synthesis for nearly a decade.

Yamaha licensed linear FM synthesis from John Chowning, who had begun working on FM during the 1960s, and Stanford University in 1973. The company released

So popular was the Yamaha DX7 that it was the first synthesizer to earn six-digit sales numbers. (Courtesy of Yamaha Corporation of America)

its first FM synths—the non-user-programmable GS1 and GS2, respectively priced at $16,000 and $6,900—in 1981. Yamaha flew Dave Bristow and Gary Leuenberger—British and American experts on Yamaha's analog CS-80 synth—to Japan to voice the GS synths, whose programming interface made the notoriously difficult-to-program DX7 look easy.

Bristow and Leuenberger found Yamaha's programming interface much improved in late '82 when they again traveled to Japan to voice the DX7, a sixteen-voice FM synth with thirty-two patch memories, a five-octave keyboard, and MIDI—all for a list price of $1,995. They had less than four days to produce 128 patches. It was a huge challenge to create so many different sounds in such a short time, but they also had to come up with names for the sounds. The DX7 was the first synth that had an LCD and allowed users to name patches.

Yamaha hadn't previously had a major-selling synthesizer. According to Bristow, the company hoped the DX7 would be a no. 1 seller, which meant moving more than 20,000 units. Within a year orders totaled 150,000 to 160,000. Until then, no one realized the synth market was so big. Not only were FM and digital synthesis big selling points, but so was the DX7's velocity- and aftertouch-sensitive keyboard, of which the factory patches took full advantage.

Yamaha hoped to repeat its success in 1987 with the follow-up DX7II, which has stereo outputs and a cleaner sound. However, competitors had upped the ante with attractive alternatives to the FM sound, so the DX7II didn't match its predecessor's success. Yamaha remains at the forefront of synthesizer development, adding multitimbral operation, internal sequencing, and effects processing in their workstation synths, often combining linear FM with other forms of synthesis such as sample-playback. The company found great success with their Motif series, introduced in 2001. By 2012, Yamaha's flagship Motif XF8 packed 741MB of waveforms in **ROM**, user sampling into 128MB of internal **RAM**, automapping of sounds, a customizable user interface, direct computer connectivity (USB, Ethernet, and optional Firewire), wireless control and file transfers with devices like the iPad, multiple types of expandability for items such as up to 2GB **Flash WAV memory**, and much more. The MO and MOX models are more affordable versions of the Motif line. If you'd prefer a dedicated synth without all of the workstation features, Yamaha offers the MM music synthesizer and S stage-piano series, both complete with many Motif sounds and attributes geared toward slightly different players.

ROM: read-only memory, which retains its contents regardless of whether it remains powered; the contents are permanent and users can't store their own data into ROM

RAM: random access memory, which loses its contents when power is disconnected; RAM patch cartridges include built-in batteries to maintain stored data, and users can store their own patches on RAM cartridges supported by many synthesizers

Flash WAV memory: nonvolatile, user-programmable storage of digital audio data that can instantly be accessed for playback

In spite of its small size, tiny keys, plastic case, and availability in department stores, Casio's CZ-101 was capable of generating some really cool digital timbres, even as many as four at the same time. (Courtesy of Casio America, Inc.)

Phase Distortion

What's the most unlikely store in which you'd shop for a synthesizer? In 1985 you might have stopped by Macy's, one of many outlets for the little Casio CZ-101. Its original retail price was $499.

The CZ-101 is a digital synth with four- or eight-note polyphony, depending on whether you want one or two oscillators per note. It also provides **ring modulation**, polyphonic portamento, sixteen factory and sixteen user patches, a cartridge memory slot, multitimbral operation via MIDI, guitar-strap buttons, and a forty-nine-note mini-keyboard. The bigger CZ-1000 (originally listing for $699) offers a full-size forty-nine-note keyboard, but is otherwise electronically identical to the CZ-101. You can power either with six D batteries, which are necessary for the instrument to retain user patches.

> *ring modulation:* a processing circuit that combines two incoming signals and outputs only the sum and differences of their frequencies; while ring-modulating simple audio waveforms often produces clangorous, bell-like timbres, using percussion loops and voice can lead to interesting and effective results as well; some ring modulators have built-in oscillators to serve as the modulator for the incoming carrier signal

Not only is the CZ-101 relatively tiny—measuring a mere 26″ w × 8.25″ d × 2.5″ h—but it also introduced a previously unheard-of method of synthesis: phase distortion. Casio engineer Mark Fukuda championed this technique, which evolved from the Cosmo Synth System developed for the legendary synthesist Isao Tomita. Phase distortion has been described as "planned error" in reading waveform data from tables. Whereas FM essentially works with pure mathematics, phase distortion incorporates custom-crafted tables that actually distort the acquisition of data.

Each CZ-101 voice channel features three eight-stage envelope generators, and users can define any stage as the **sustain segment**—a remarkably flexible innovation that was

Casio's RZ-1, introduced in 1986, is an eight-bit sampling drum machine with twelve preset sampled drum sounds, ten sliders for controlling individual voice volume levels, memory for one hundred patterns and twenty songs, and real-time or step-entry pattern programming via the front panel or MIDI. The sample rate is only 20kHz, so there isn't much high end, but the lo-fi, eight-bit audio quality grew in popularity for certain music styles at a later date. (Courtesy of Casio America, Inc.)

extremely rare at the time. This allows the programmer to, for example, create triple attacks before the sustain segment or delay echoes afterward.

sustain segment: the steady portion of an envelope that determines the output signal level

For a time during the 1980s and early '90s Casio offered an array of professionally oriented gear, including the VZ-1 synthesizer with an expanded phase-distortion implementation, the FZ-1 sampling keyboard, the RZ-1 sampling drum machine, and the

One of the first aspects you might notice about the Casio VZ-1 is that it has three performance wheels. Two are for modulating parameters independently of each other—a rarely found convenience—and the third does pitchbends. Other VZ niceties include sixteen-bit sound, eight-oscillator voices, a generously sized LCD that will display envelopes, and a cool pitchbend mode that bends only physically held notes, not those sustained with a footswitch, which is great for simulating steel-guitar-style playing. (Courtesy of Casio America, Inc.)

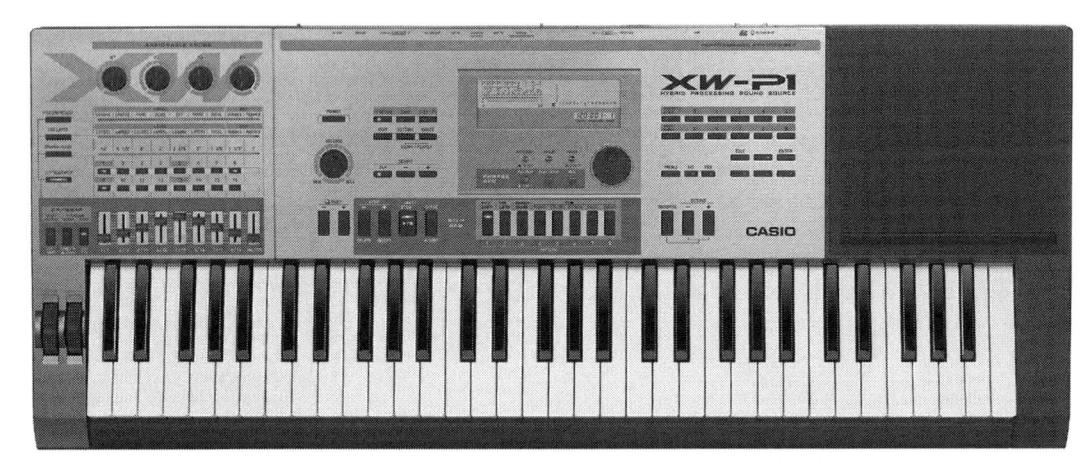

Special to Casio's XW-P1 performance synthesizer are Hammond organ sounds and HexLayer mode, which allows you to stack six synthesizer components complete with voice layering and keyboard split zones. (Courtesy of Casio America, Inc.)

AZ-1 strap-on MIDI keyboard controller. While the company stayed in the portable keyboard and digital piano businesses all along, they dropped their pro line during the early 1990s.

To the delight of many fans of affordable, well-endowed synthesizers, Casio reentered the pro market in 2012 with the XW-P1 performance synthesizer and XW-G1 groove synthesizer. Both have sixty-one-note keyboards and house a six-oscillator monosynth, a polyphonic sample player with sounds of popular instruments (pianos, **EPs**, strings, guitars, etc.), a thirteen-track step sequencer, a programmable sixteen-step **arpeggiator**, a phrase sequencer that can record and play back riffs, a multitimbral performance mode with four assignable keyboard zones, four multipurpose real-time controller knobs and nine sliders, MIDI and USB connectors, and the ability to run on six D batteries—although each XW conveniently comes with an AC power supply. With the XW-P1 you get a Drawbar Organ mode and with the XW-G1 you get a sample looper with up to nineteen seconds of sampling time.

Casio's XW-G1 groove synthesizer includes user sampling and a sample looper, with DJ-style rhythm and pattern creation and playback, and nonvolatile Flash memory storage. (Courtesy of Casio America, Inc.)

> *EPs:* electric pianos, epitomized by the Rhodes Suitcase and Wurlitzer 200A
>
> *arpeggiator:* a performance aid that automatically steps one note at a time through a group of held or latched notes at a manually adjustable rate or synchronized to an external clock, often at speeds that would be extremely difficult if not impossible for a human to play; arpeggiators commonly provide modes for playing note patterns through multiple octaves and in order of ascending, descending, up and down, as-played, and random; some arpeggiators are capable of playing chords and allow programmable rhythm patterns

Linear Arithmetic

After sales of Yamaha's DX7 rocketed so high during the early '80s, Roland decided to develop a DX7 killer. The result was the D-50, which arrived in March 1987, garnered around 100,000 units in sales, and played a big part in keeping Yamaha's DX7II from duplicating its predecessor's success.

Roland created a new type of synthesis for the D-50 called linear arithmetic. The LA recipe combines sample-playback, **subtractive synthesis**, and built-in reverb, delay, chorus, and EQ effects—making the D-50 the first mass-produced synth to have built-in digital effects. Tucked into its smaller-than-1MB of ROM were one hundred brief samples, many of them **attack transients**. Roland's intent was to combine the initial attack of a sampled acoustic sound with a sustained, synthesized sound, fooling one's ears into believing it's a single, complete sample. The D-50 also provides sixteen-voice polyphony and a sixty-one-note keyboard with velocity and pressure response. Optionally available was the PG-1000 programmer, which sports fifty-six sliders for synthesists wanting thorough real-time parameter control and fewer menu treks.

Impressing listeners in the late '80s with the Roland D-50 was as simple as calling up one particular patch and hitting a low note. Thanks in great part to potent built-in effects and magnificently executed factory patches, the D-50 sold really well. (Courtesy of Roland Corporation)

> *subtractive synthesis:* electronically generating sound using oscillators capable of generating complex waveforms with lots of harmonic content and routing their signals through voltage-controlled filters to attenuate specific harmonics and contour the resulting timbre
> *attack transient:* the initial part of a sound; in the music world, a snare has an immediate attack and a flute a much smoother entrance
> *softsynth:* a synthesizer rendered virtually in software
> *PCM:* pulse-code modulation, the conversion of an analog audio signal to digital by periodically capturing its amplitude and quantizing the result to the nearest available digital step; PCM sampling delivers high audio quality, but consumes much more digital storage space and sounds better than a compressed audio format such as MP3

Eric Persing and Adrian Scott designed sounds for the entire Roland D-series, among many other synths. Both were present for the D-50's birth. After sitting through an eight-hour dissertation on the theory of its technology, they finally got to hear the prototype and quickly realized it made possibly the thinnest tones either had ever heard. They then discovered what they thought was purely a hardware instrument was actually based entirely in code that could be changed—a new and foreign concept at the time, and a harbinger of the world of **softsynth**s to come. Not coincidentally, since 1994 Eric has created and distributed some of the most popular softsynths available via his company, Spectrasonics.

Multiple teams at Roland worked on different parts of the D-50, and soon all of the pieces fell into place. Along the way Persing and Scott dubbed the heads of divisions with suitable names, such as Mr. Chorus and Mr. Reverb. They worked exclusively with the engineer they'd dubbed Mr. **PCM**, who encoded all of the samples they'd provided and developed a sequencer that would cycle through the synth's waveforms. As a joke, Mr. PCM included some sequenced loops in a late ROM set. Persing and Scott loved these loops so much that they convinced him to keep them in the factory soundbank. Thus were born the astounding DigitalNativeDance and other patches based on sequenced waveform loops. DigitalNativeDance alone likely sold thousands of D-50s. All a demonstrator had to do was load the patch, hit a low C, and peoples' jaws would hit the floor.

What the D-50 lacked was a stellar signal-to-noise ratio, which many of its superb factory patches masked. The culprit? An extra digital-to-analog-to-digital conversion between the oscillators and effects processors.

Since the introductions of its System 100M and System 700 modular synthesizer lines in the mid-1970s, as well as awesome instruments such as the Jupiter-8 polyphonic analog synth in 1981 through and beyond the twenty-first century V-Synth series, Fantom workstations, Gaia SH-01, and Jupiter-80, Roland has maintained a stellar track record in the synth industry.

Roland resurrected the age-old name "Jupiter"—the moniker of their most powerful polyphonic analog synth of the early '80s, the Jupiter-8—in early 2011 with the Jupiter-80. The new digital Jupiter offers many capabilities that weren't available in the analog model, thanks to twenty-first-century technology. (Courtesy of Roland Corporation)

Vector Synthesis

An especially potent form of digital synthesis first appeared in the Sequential Circuits Prophet-VS, which had the distinction of becoming popular well after it and its manufacturer were history. What made the Prophet-VS special was **vector synthesis**, which incorporates four oscillators per voice along with dynamic waveform **cross-fading** via a dedicated envelope and joystick. The resulting tones and timbral animation can be stunning.

Chris Meyer first conceived of vector synthesis in 1985 while pondering the sound of scanning four waveforms in two dimensions. By patching together his Oberheim Two Voice, numerous Korg and Paia modules, a custom-made Gentle Electric **VCA** cabinet, Dennis Electronics voltage-control processors, and a Sequential Model 700 programmer, he was able to generate a single voice with four coordinated oscillators that he could mix among. After recording some sounds—"struck attacks that faded into shimmering flutes," Meyer recalls, and "clarinets that opened up into raw sawtooths"—he played the tape for

VS stands for vector synthesis. What's that? Whereas many synthesizers sport a mere two oscillators per voice, the Prophet-VS incorporates four, each capable of generating any of 127 waveforms—thirty-two of which are user-programmable—along with dynamic waveform cross-fading via a dedicated envelope and joystick. (Courtesy of Dave Smith)

others at Sequential, whose founder Dave Smith was anxious to make a digital synth. The VS fit the bill and went into production in 1986.

> *vector synthesis:* dynamically cross-fading between two or among more than two timbres using automated or manual techniques
>
> *cross-fading:* a smooth transition between at least two timbres manually or using automation
>
> *VCA:* voltage-controlled amplifier, which attenuates the level of an audio signal passing through its circuitry according to incoming control voltages

Its audio quality, however, suffered from noise issues, mostly due to aliasing artifacts at high frequencies. Digital synthesis was still in its infancy, and oscillators capable of generating really high pitches cost too much to include in reasonably affordable instruments. Sequential's Prophet-2000 sampler used much of the same audio technology and couldn't sound high frequencies without tuning problems. Meyer and other Sequential engineers decided this was unacceptable on the VS, so they designed its oscillators to average the correct pitch, resulting in considerable noise artifacts in the upper range—although many musicians found those attributes desirable and useful in their music.

In spite of its distinctive, mostly brilliant timbres and vector-synthesis capabilities, the VS didn't sell well. Sequential Circuits folded in 1987, and Yamaha bought its assets in 1988. Vector synthesis later reappeared in Yamaha's SY22 and TG33 and Korg's Wavestation—all developed under Dave Smith's direction. Korg later included vector synthesis in the Wavestation Legacy softsynth and the OAYSys and Kronos workstations. In addition, Arturia included it in Prophet V, a softsynth combo of Sequential's Prophet-5 and Prophet-VS.

Following his consultation days with Yamaha and Korg, Dave Smith served as the president and head engineer for Seer Systems, which developed and in 1997 released Reality, one of the first software synths. Since 2002 he's run Dave Smith Instruments, designing and making the analog/digital Evolver series and the analog eight-voice Prophet '08, the analog Mopho monophonic desktop module and Mopho x4 four-voice keyboard synths, the polyphonic Tetra tabletop synth module, and the twelve-voice hybrid Prophet 12 keyboard synth. Dave also collaborated with drum-machine innovator Roger Linn to produce the Tempest **analog/digital hybrid** drum machine/synthesizer and the Linndrum II digital/analog drum machine/MIDI sequencer. Dave Smith was hugely responsible for the development of MIDI and, with Roland founder Ikutaro Kakehashi, received a Technical Grammy Award on February 10, 2013, in acknowledgement of MIDI's introduction thirty years earlier.

> *analog/digital hybrid:* a musical instrument that generates sound using both analog and digital circuitry

Vector synthesis appears in Arturia's Prophet-V2, a softsynth hybrid of both Sequential's Prophet-5 and Prophet VS. (Image courtesy of Arturia)

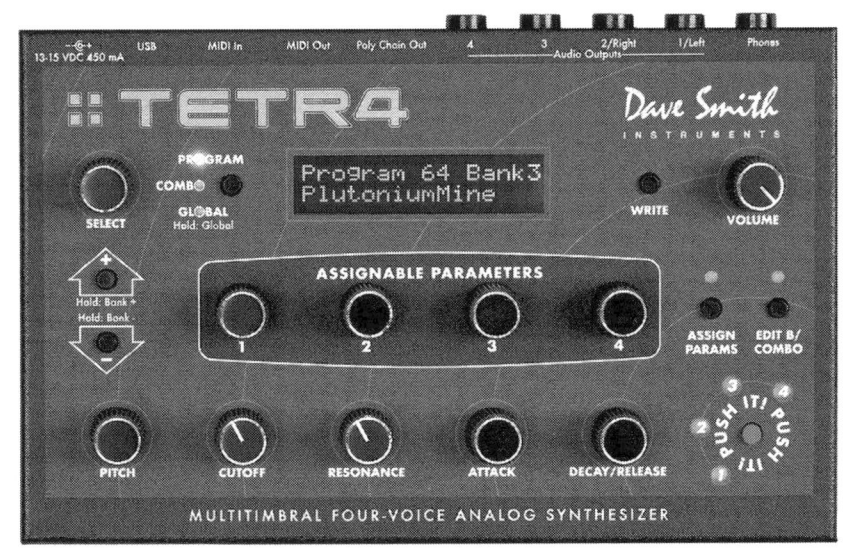

Among the synthesizers introduced by Dave Smith Instruments since its formation in 2002 is the Tetra module, which delivers four-voice analog multitimbral polyphony in a tabletop unit measuring only 7.9" × 5" × 2.7" and weighing less than two pounds. (Courtesy of Dave Smith Instruments)

Dave Smith poses at the January 2005 NAMM convention with the then-new DSI PEK, the Dave Smith Instruments Poly Evolver Keyboard. It's a four-voice polyphonic synth with four oscillators per voice—two that are analog and two digital. (Mark Vail)

MultiSynthesis and –Processing Environment

Combine the patchability of modular synthesizers with state-of-the-art synthesis, sound-design, **DSP**, and composition software running on a dedicated, multiprocessor computer platform, and you might have the astounding Kyma system that Carla Scaletti and Kurt Hebel developed at Symbolic Sound Corporation.

> *DSP:* digital signal processing

First in 1984 came the Platypus digital signal processor, on which Hebel worked with Lippold Haken. Meanwhile, Scaletti had earned a doctorate in music composition at the University of Illinois at Urbana-Champaign (UIUC), taught computer music classes, decided she'd rather create software, and returned to UIUC to earn a master's degree in computer science. She began working on Kyma in 1985. Running on an Apple Mac Plus, it took five minutes to generate a one-second sine waveform. By 1987 she had Kyma doing real-time synthesis on the Platypus. Kurt finished his doctorate in electrical engineering—specializing in digital signal processing—in 1989, then began designing the Capybara, the next hardware core for the Kyma system. In early 1990 Scaletti and Hebel founded Symbolic Sound Corporation, and by fall they were shipping systems.

A view from the front of Symbolic Sound's Pacarana, the flagship hardware component that generates and processes sound for Kyma. (Courtesy of Symbolic Sound Corporation)

FireWire 800, Ethernet, USB, and expansion jacks on the back of Symbolic Sound's Pacarana. (Courtesy of Symbolic Sound Corporation)

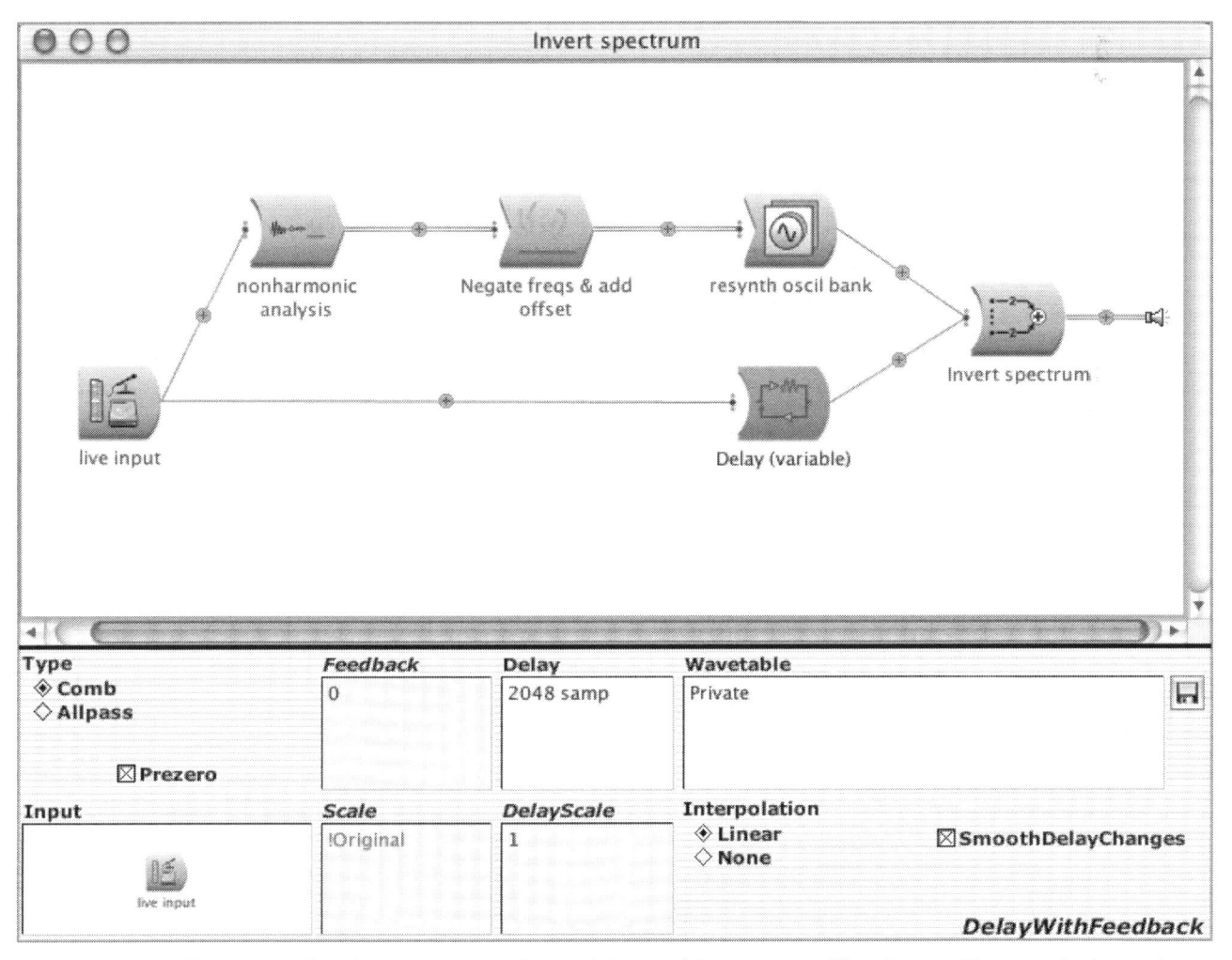

To create new sound-processing algorithms in Kyma, you drag and drop modules into a signal-flow diagram. This example shows a live spectral analysis, spectral inversion, and resynthesis. The *rightmost* module mixes the inverted spectrum with the live input delayed. (Image courtesy of Symbolic Sound Corporation)

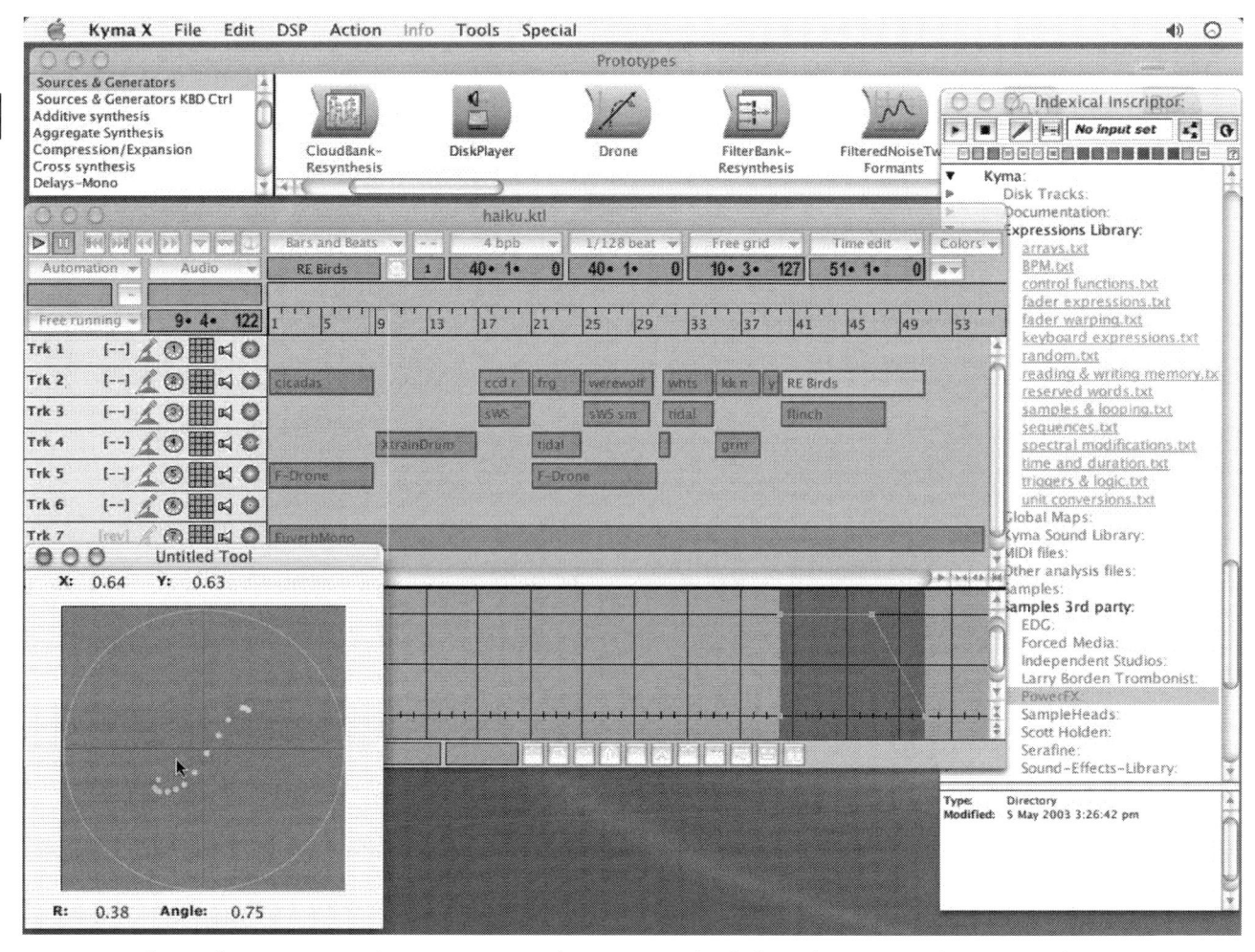

The Synthesizer

Once you've designed your Kyma sounds, you can arrange them in time and multichannel space using the Kyma Timeline to create a live-performance environment. (Image courtesy of Symbolic Sound Corporation)

Kyma is an environment in which you graphically patch together virtual synthesis and processing modules to create sounds and compose music. As of mid-2013, two sound-computation engines were available: the entry-level Paca with two processors and 1GB of sample RAM, and the pro-oriented Pacarana with four processors and 2GB of RAM. Both have two FireWire 800 ports, two USB ports, two multipin expansion ports so you can connect multiple sound-computation engines and use them as a sonic supercomputer, and an Ethernet jack for connecting to **OSC** and to a wireless router for Apple iPad control. The cross-platform Kyma X software is included, as are more than 1,000 presets and 360 or so modules for sound synthesis, processing, and sampling. Among Kyma's capabilities are subtractive, additive, AM, FM, granular, and aggregate synthesis; physical modeling; audio morphing; sampling; effects and spectral processing; spectral analysis-FFT; live looping; stereo, surround, and multichannel output; vocoding; and much more.

OSC: an acronym for Open Sound Control, an open-ended protocol originally developed at the University of California, Berkeley, Center for New Music and Audio

> Technology (CNMAT) and optimized for networking computers, synthesizers, and multimedia gear for real-time data processing, the creation of sensor and gesture-based musical instruments, mapping nonmusical data to sound, and much more

Open Architecture

Hidden in a Hilton suite at the January 1995 **NAMM** convention in Anaheim, California, Korg had a prototype keyboard called the OASys set up for private viewing. Sporting the company's custom DSP chips, the OASys (Open Architecture Synthesis System) could do additive synthesis, analog and physical modeling, sample playback, FM, **wave sequencing**, vector synthesis, and signal processing. DSP assignments were dynamically allocated, so the OASys could perform different types of synthesis simultaneously. As demonstrated by Korg's Benjamin Dowling, the superb-sounding OASys could quickly convert from emulating a Hammond B-3 to a Minimoog or DX7. It was scheduled for release later that year, and synthesists worldwide hungrily awaited.

> *NAMM:* the acronym for National Association of Music Merchants, which briefly changed its name in 2000 to the International Music Products Association; "NAMM" is often used in reference to semiannual tradeshows held in January in Anaheim, California, and in July in Nashville, Tennessee
> *wave sequencing:* oscillator playback of two or more waveforms individually while switching or cross-fading from one waveform to another
> *PCI:* Peripheral Component Interconnect, a computer expansion slot

More than four years later, during the summer of 1999, Korg partially sated synthesists' appetites with the $2,300 OASys **PCI** computer card, complete with twenty synth algorithms and room for more loaded as plug-ins. There were also more than one hundred effects algorithms for simultaneously processing onboard synth sounds, tracks from digital audio applications, and inputs from external audio sources. There were, however, two major drawbacks: (1) the OASys card wasn't compatible with PCI slots in newer computers, and (2) support for computer operating systems ended at Windows 98 and Mac OS 9.

Korg implemented physical-modeling in their expressive Prophecy lead monosynth in 1995 and the twelve-note polyphonic, six-part multitimbral Z1 synth in 1996. But still synthesists awaited the OASys, and in 2005 they finally got their wish. Billed as an Open Architecture Synthesis Studio, the OASYS sports multitrack MIDI sequencing, hard-disk recording, sampling, and effects galore, along with sample playback, an advanced tonewheel-organ emulation, tons of onboard controllers, and a 10.4" touchscreen LCD that tilts up from the front panel. Korg offered two versions of the OASYS, one with seventy-six synth-action keys, the other with eighty-eight keys and a weighted, grand piano–style hammer action.

The Synthesizer

Korg's premier sound programmer Jack Hotop puts the OASys synthesizer workstation through its paces at the January 2008 NAMM show in Anaheim, California. Jack has worked for Korg since the early 1980s and has played a pivotal role in the voicing and development of many of the company's synthesizers, including the trendsetting M1. (Mark Vail)

In January 2011, Korg introduced the Kronos synthesizer workstation, which borrows from and improves on much of the technology found in the discontinued OASYS. Available with a sixty-one-note semi-weighted keyboard or a seventy-three- or eighty-eight-note hammer-action keyboard, the Kronos delivers nine types of synthesis, including three different analog models, physical modeling, waveshaping, and sample-playback. The year 2012 saw Korg's introduction of the Krome, a slightly downscaled version of the flagship Kronos workstation.

Virtual Analog

When I first saw a February '95 ad depicting a new red synth from Sweden, I thought it looked cheesy and cheap. Within days said red synth found its way into my possession, and enthusiasm quickly replaced my cynicism.

Thus I met the Clavia Nord Lead (NL) virtual analog synthesizer, a four-voice (expandable to twelve), dual-oscillator, modeled-analog synth with **hard oscillator sync**, FM, **pulse-width modulation** of its **pulse wave**, four-voice layering, four-channel multitimbral operation, a multimode **resonant digital filter**, two LFOs—one capable of sample-and-hold, the other offering an arpeggiator mode—polyphonic portamento, and a forty-nine-note velocity-sensing keyboard.

What mostly changed my mind about the NL were its reintroduction of multiple, dedicated knobs for real-time parameter control and its convincing analog-like timbres. The red synth appeared amid the crystalline-sounding, pushbutton-synth universe conceived by the Chroma and DX7. Here at last was an electronic instrument whose timbre I could once again control in real time.

---

hard oscillator sync: a control connection between two oscillators in which the master oscillator forces the slave oscillator to restart its cycle simultaneously with that of the master oscillator; if the slave's frequency differs from the master's, modulations of the slave's frequency can result in timbral variations

pulse-width modulation: a manual or automated variation in the width of a pulse wave's duty cycle; in the case of an audio wave, pulse-width modulation has the effect of changing timbre and, in extreme cases, the perceived pitch

pulse wave: an oscillator-generated signal with alternating positive and negative voltages of equal and steady-state values; there is no gradual transition between the positive and negative states, only an immediate change between; the pulse wave's *duty cycle* determines the length of the positive-state duration in relation to the negative—specified in ratios such as 1:3 and 1:2—as well as the harmonic content generated by the wave

resonant digital filter: a virtual, digital rendition in software of a **resonant VCF**

resonant VCF: a voltage-controlled analog filter that allows a manual or automated boost to a specific range of frequencies—the resonance peak—near the filter's cutoff frequency; some synth manufacturers refer to resonance as "emphasis" or "Q"

Not only is the NL's control panel adorned with twenty-six fixed-function knobs and forty-eight LEDs, but it introduced some fresh concepts and capabilities. First, there's only a single wheel, albeit one that feels gritty like pumice rock. It's assignable for modulation functions that include sound "morphing," which allows you to assign multiple parameters to be varied between two values using the mod wheel and key velocity. Thus you can morph, or cross-fade, between two similar or very different timbres.

Clavia's first modeled-analog synth, the original Nord Lead. Although you can't tell from this black-and-white photo, all Nord instruments brandish a distinctively red sheen. (Mark Vail)

Next to the mod wheel is the innovative "pitch stick," which promptly became my favorite note-bender. Clavia's cofounder Hans Nordelius invented and patented the pitch stick, so you won't find it on non-Nord instruments. It offers stiff resistance and a tactile response, and there's no dead zone or center detent to cause unwanted jerkiness in note bends.

Another NL function that I enjoy using during performance makes use of its four voice-channel slots. In Program mode with one of the slot buttons activated, you can step on your sustain pedal while the slot is sounding—arpeggiated patches work well—and select a different slot before releasing the pedal. The previous patch continues to sound, and you can accompany it with the patches assigned to the other three slots. You can also return to a slot that's sounding and tweak patch parameters or step on and release the sustain pedal to stifle the sound. With four slots, you can get a lot happening under your immediate control.

Clavia started a virtual-analog craze with the Nord Lead. Soon to follow were analog-sounding digital synths with real-time knobs and sliders from Access, Korg, Novation, Roland, Waldorf, Yamaha, and other companies.

Neural Modeling

Consider these neologisms in a synthesis context: neural modeling, neuronal **resynthesis**, and neural network-controlled adaptive sound analysis. They describe the Hartmann Neuron, introduced at the January 2002 NAMM show.

Clavia cofounder Hans Nordelius poses in front of many of his creations in March 2007. Now you know where the Nord name comes from. (Mark Vail)

It sports quite a long name for a relatively small synthesizer: the Access Virus TI Polar WhiteOut Special Edition. Packed inside its metal cabinet is a fabulous virtual-analog synthesis system—fabulous in terms of both sound and synthesis capabilities. While Christoph Kemper of Access Music was the brains behind the synthesis parts, Axel Hartmann designed the synth's front-panel layout and overall look. (Courtesy of Access Music)

The Synthesizer

Axel Hartmann's Neuron introduced some fantastic new synthesis techniques in 2002. Sadly, the hardware and software weren't quite up to the challenge. (Courtesy of Hartmann Music)

Futuristic in appearance and sound generation, the Neuron delivers a voice that begins with two Resynators, or resynthesis oscillators, each loaded with either a sound model selected from the two hundred provided by the manufacturer or any created using Hartmann's ModelMaker software and the user's **AIFFs**. You can adjust twelve parameters per sound model in real time using a generous collection of front-panel joysticks, or control them via envelopes, LFOs, **key tracking**, and key velocity.

---

resynthesis: an electronic approximation of a timbre created after analyzing its frequency and amplitude characteristics; the results aren't a mere snapshot of a sound like a sample is, and therefore are far more malleable as the timbre is generated fresh by the resynthesis process

AIFFs: Audio Interchange File Format digital sound files, which are commonly supported by Macintosh computers

key tracking: a synthesizer's recognition of which notes are played in order to adjust parameters such as oscillator pitch and filter cutoff frequency

---

Internally connecting the Resynators is the wheel-controlled Blender that determines what kind of interaction occurs between the Resynators with modes called Dynamic Transsphere, Cromophonic, and Intermorph. Another module, the Slicer, induces tremolo or **panning** to the audio signal before it arrives at the Silver module, where it's processed with a multimode filter and effects such as reverb, delay, EQ, compression, ring modulation, a **bit-reducing decimator**, distortion, and a variety of more exotic signal processors. Eventually sounds exit from the Neuron's six audio outputs, which can be configured for 5.1 surround-sound.

> *panning:* adjusting the position of a sound in a stereo field between far left and far right; "pan" is short for panorama
>
> *bit-reducing decimator:* a digital-processing effect that distorts an audio signal by decreasing the length of its data bits, (i.e., from sixteen bits to eight or fewer bits)

Axel Hartmann was mainly responsible for the Neuron's development. Assisting Axel in the Neuron venture was the DSP guru Stephan Bernsee. What types of sounds can it produce? Complex swirls of tonal beauty or sonic madness, multispectrum layers with shifting harmonics, huge sci-fi landscapes, Mellotron choir simulations, and more. Regrettably the expensive ($4,995) and polyphonically challenged (five voices at best) Neuron failed to attract enough buyers to remain in production. In 2005 Hartmann released Neuron VS, an $899 Mac/Windows application that featured the Neuron's synthesis engine and came with the Nuke, a tabletop controller with four knobs, a joystick, and a pushbutton, but it too was discontinued. Axel Hartmann and Stephan Bernsee deserve lots of cheers for their attempts to raise the synthesis bar for the twenty-first century.

Axel remains optimistic about the Neuron's eventual return and success. In the meantime, while he continues to design products and equipment for more lucrative industries including medical and automotive, Axel most enjoys designing synthesizers. His track record is totally impressive, having created control panels and user interfaces or otherwise contributed to the appearance of synths including the Waldorf Wave, Q, MicroWave, and Blofeld; Access Virus synths up to and including the Polar; Alesis Andromeda; Moog Music's Minimoog Voyager, Voyager Old School, Voyager XL, Little Phatty, Slim Phatty, and Taurus III; and Arturia's Origin, Origin Keyboard, Minibrute, and Spark drum machine.

Performance

Certain synthesizers offer great control facilities and produce outstanding timbres, but not all of them excel in live performance. To understand how far electronic instruments have come, we need to look back to the 1960s and the earliest implementations of one of the most successful forms of synthesis: sample playback. Along with performance-oriented synthesizers and instruments that reproduce recorded sounds are those that can also record and reproduce sounds—samplers—and another subset of electronic performance instruments, **drum machines**.

> *drum machines:* instruments capable of reproducing user-programmed sequences of samples or analog or digitally synthesized events that typically sound like drum and percussion instruments, although other timbres are perfectly acceptable

Keyboard-Controlled Tape Player

Beneath each of the Mellotron Model 400's thirty-five keys is a six-foot long, 3/8″ wide strip of magnetic tape. That isn't a standard tape width, so Britian Leslie Bradley (1917–97) with his brothers Frank (d. 1979) and Norman built a special cutting machine to trim ½″ tape down to size. Playing a Mellotron key results in a rotating spindle catching the front end of the tape and pulling it over a playback head for about eight seconds before coming to the tape's end, when a spring-based mechanism quickly pulls the tape back in preparation for the note to play again.

During that eight-second span, you might hear flutes, brass, tenor sax, string sections, Hammond organ, boys' choirs, marimba, glockenspiel, or timpani rolls. Also available were tapes of canned laughter, cuckoo clocks, frogs and toads, ship horns, and a thunderstorm. The sounds were quite impressive in the mid-'60s. Since the Mellotron plays analog recordings of acoustic instruments, it qualifies as one of the first sample players. Every Mellotron tape has three tracks, each with a different sound. Multitrack tape heads were prohibitively expensive at the time, so the Bradleys incorporated a

This Mellotron Model 400 encased in a clear Plexiglas cabinet was custom-made for the London Music Expo in 1972. (Mark Vail, courtesy of the Audities Foundation)

Harry Chamberlin's Riviera—a gorgeous instrument suitable for nearly anyone's family room—was a forerunner to the Mellotron. (Mark Vail, courtesy of the Audities Foundation)

single-track head per key and mounted a rotary switch on the front panel to shift tape-head positions.

In order for notes to have attack transients instead of playing steady tones like an electronic organ, the Bradley brothers used strips of tape as opposed to looped tapes that would play continuously. This differed from the Mellotron's predecessor, the Chamberlin Rhythmate. Californian Harry Chamberlin (d. 1986) designed and built numerous keyboard-controlled tape instruments before enlisting the Bradleys to refine his designs to make the Mellotron.

Optical Sonics, Part 1

Many a '60s-era hand puppet and doll contained a little mechanical talkbox with a ring on a string that you pulled and released to make the toy speak. Mattel made most of these toys and developed the talkbox, which surprisingly led to a quirky home organ of sorts.

At the end of the '60s, company executives decided to make a musical toy keyboard. Their engineers first assembled a prototype incorporating the equivalent of an **Edison cylinder** with grooves of recorded loops and key-activated styli that fit into the grooves. The contraption didn't work well, so they began experimenting with magnetic tapes as used in the Chamberlin and Mellotron. Mattel even purchased Harry Chamberlin's patents before learning that Packard Bell had patented but never produced a photo-electric organ in the early '60s. The company purchased those patents and produced the Optigan, a three-octave "organ" that plays notes, melodies, chords, and rhythms from flexible, 12" diameter celluloid discs. The company manufactured several models of the instrument from 1971 to 1975.

The Synthesizer

Lots of people might confuse an Optigan for an ordinary home organ, but they'd be wrong. Mattel manufactured them during the early 1970s, and the Optigan plays sounds and loops from floppy optical discs. Optigan expert Pea Hicks produces new discs and offers support for the instrument from his website, and is working on an Optigan iOS application. (Courtesy of Pea Hicks, optigan.com)

> *Edison cylinder:* Tomas Edison's original audio-recording device, which he invented in 1877; early versions consisted of a cylinder of aluminum foil before Edison incorporated wax

Fifty-seven rings of analog waveforms appear on each Optigan disc, providing thirty-seven scale tones and twenty accompaniment patterns. To create experimental music, you could load two discs together to create layered sounds and loops, or flip a disc upside-down to play loops in reverse.

Mattel produced forty Optigan discs and two for diagnostics. Optigan expert Pea Hicks began producing new discs for the instrument in 2008, provides technical documents and support, and produces CDs that feature the instrument. Should you find an Optigan for sale, don't expect much because they tend to be unreliable and noisy. Although it didn't score big in sales, major artists including Tom Waits, Fiona Apple, Elvis Costello, Devo, Aimee Mann, and the Clash were inspired to make music with the Optigan.

Optical Sonics, Part 2

Another important analog sample player that often gets overlooked is the Vako Orchestron, a brainchild of David Van Koevering. While touring and performing live on a Moog Modular system during the early '70s, Van Koevering yearned to play chords in a more orchestral vein. He tried the Mellotron, but quickly discovered its deficiencies. After helping develop Mattel's Optigan, Van Koevering licensed its technology to be implemented in instruments for professional musicians.

A Model C dual-manual Vako Orchestron complete with pedalboard and an ATA-approved flight case. Like the Optigan, the Vako Orchestron played sounds stored on optical discs. One major difference between them was that David Van Koevering designed the Orchestron line of instruments for touring synthesists such as Patrick Moraz. (Courtesy of David Van Koevering)

From 1975 to 1979 Vako Synthesizers Inc. produced the Orchestron, a series of polyphonic analog sample-playback keyboards. The Orchestron disc reader used a 40-watt aquarium bulb to shine light through a slit about one-tenth the width of a human hair onto a disc of thirty-seven tracks, each about 1/8″ wide and containing waveform data of an instrument sampled at a specific pitch. Each note had an attack followed by a sustain phase. To mask the attack transient during lengthy notes, a counter kept track of the reader head's position in reference to the attack section and the Orchestron phased the audio signal.

Electronic music pioneer Paul Beaver recorded instruments for the Orchestron, including violins, brass, vocals, and Hammond organs. Before adopting a laser-encoding process, Vako wrote samples on Orchestron discs incorporating galvanometers like those used to write film soundtracks prior to the employment of magnetic audio tracks. They compressed unexposed film emulsion on 3″ optical glass to squeeze out distortion-inducing microscopic bubbles, then exposed the film to the accompanying master disc with a flashing arc light.

Digital-Sampling Trailblazer from Down Under

By today's standards, the first keyboard-based, polyphonic digital sampler's eight-bit resolution and sub-10kHz top-end frequency response seem pitiful. However, the original Fairlight Computer Musical Instrument (CMI), which included additive synthesis capabilities and first appeared in 1979, certainly proved adequate for Stevie Wonder, Kate Bush, Jan Hammer, Peter Gabriel, Mike Oldfield, Thomas Dolby, Jean-Michel Jarre, Keith Emerson, and many others who made it a centerpiece in their studios.

It came from Kim Ryrie and Peter Vogel of Sydney, Australia. After founding Fairlight in 1975, they licensed engineer Tony Furse's dual-processor computer and converted it into a device that allowed the digital recording of any sound, its storage on disk, editing of its harmonic content using a light-pen on a video monitor, and playback along with seven other independent sounds simultaneously from the CMI's eighty-eight-note keyboard. Digital synthesis was new and rare at the time, and very expensive. Early CMI systems, later referred to as the Series I, cost from $25,000 to $36,000. One reason it was so expensive is that each note required an entire circuit board.

Improvements to the channel cards, which increased the sampling rate and boosted the high-end frequency up to 16kHz, showed up in the Series II in 1982. In 1984 Fairlight released the Series IIx, in which they'd upgraded the processing chips and implemented MIDI. By 1985 Ryrie and Vogel had ditched their earlier designs in favor of a new architecture, with specs that included sixteen-bit sample resolution, sixteen-voice polyphony, and two thirty-two-bit 68000 processors, one for master control and waveform generation, the other for **SMPTE** and MIDI functions—along with a 6809 for each sound channel and two 6809s for sequencing and graphics.

SMPTE: the acronym for Society of Motion Picture and Television Engineers, typically used to identify a standard time code for synchronizing sequencers to audio and video tape

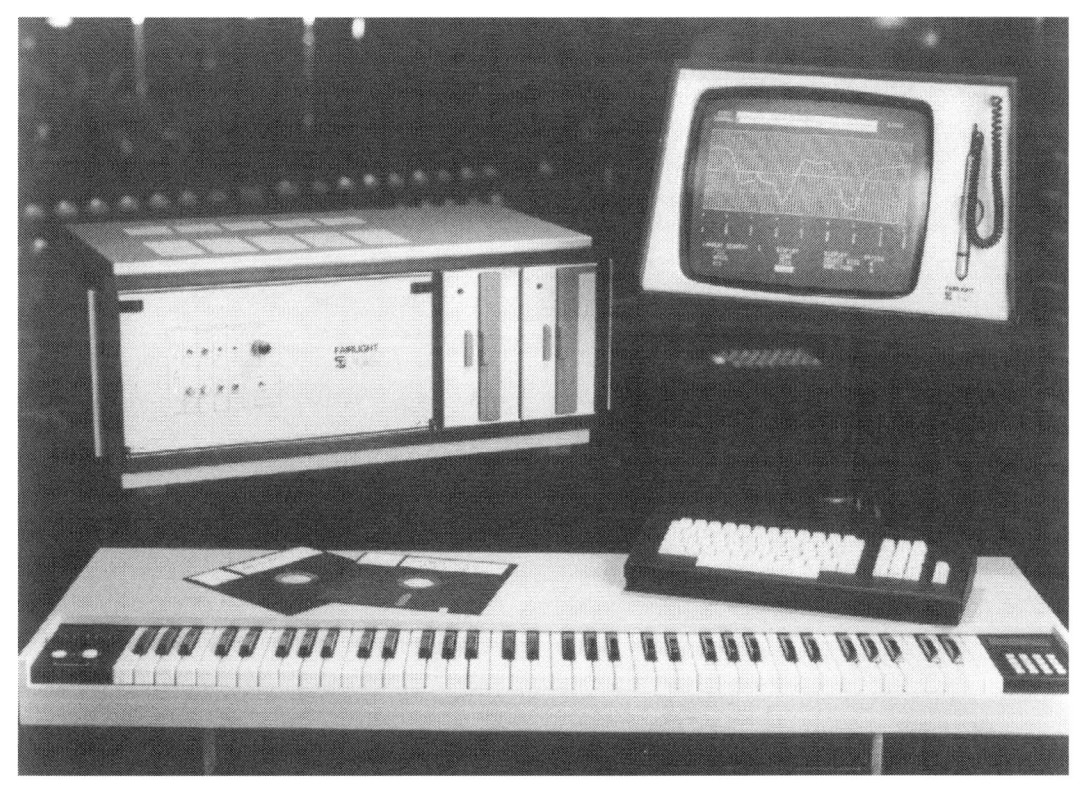

A Fairlight CMI system, ca. 1980. A new version called the CMI-30A, which looks exactly like this, showed up with Fairlight co-founder Peter Vogel at the January 2011 NAMM show. (Courtesy of Fairlight Instruments)

As the Fairlight design team refined the CMI, they developed its software sequencer. Initially the program could only record notes and their velocities, and it allowed overdubbing, but editing was difficult. Inspired by the pattern programming features of Roger Linn's LM-1 Drum Computer, Ryrie and Vogel assigned programmer Michael Carlos to create Page R, an interactive sequencing environment that evolved throughout the CMI's lifetime and had a great deal to do with the instrument's popularity.

Speaking of lifetimes, attendees of the 2011 Winter NAMM Show may have spotted the Fairlight CMI-30A, the thirtieth anniversary edition. If its price of nearly $21,000 is beyond your means, you could opt for an iOS simulation for significantly less. Fairlight co-founder Peter Vogel now runs the company as Peter Vogel Instruments.

More Affordable Digital Sampling

The earliest American-made digital sampler came from the Northern California surfer-and-boardwalk town of Santa Cruz, where Scott Wedge and Dave Rossum began making modular synthesizers in 1970 and incorporated their business as E-mu Systems in 1972. After witnessing Fairlight's original CMI at the May 1980 AES convention, Rossum realized he could design a less expensive sampling instrument. Thus was born the Emulator. When Stevie Wonder discovered the Emulator prototype at the February '81 NAMM convention, he was fascinated by its ability to sample and reproduce his voice across the keyboard, even though transposed up a couple of octaves it sounded **Munchkinized**.

The Synthesizer

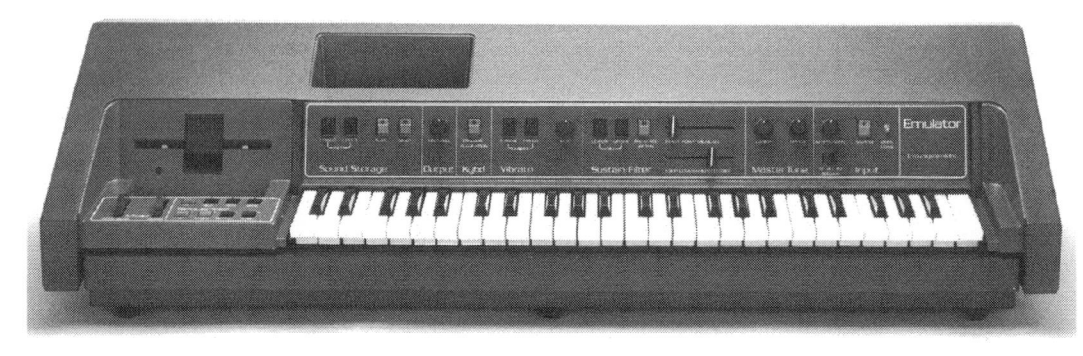

An original E-mu Emulator, introduced in 1981. While perfecting the Emulator's looping capabilities, engineer Dave Rossum and his cohorts created the Big Bladder Simulator by sampling the sound of someone peeing in a toilet and looping it for two to three minutes. (Courtesy of Dave Rossum/E-mu Systems)

Sales were slow in the beginning. While cheaper than a Fairlight, an eight-voice Emulator with memory for seventeen seconds of samples was still a high-ticket item, retailing for $9,995. The original Emulator also suffered from numerous impediments. Its four-octave keyboard was always split in two; to play the same sample across the entire keyboard, you had to load it into both the upper and lower memory banks. Every sample was a fixed two seconds in length, and editing functions were limited to **sample start point** and **sample duration**. Since DSP was so expensive at the time, the Emulator transposed samples by changing the playback rate. It also lacked a VCA; when you played and released a key, a lengthy sample would continue until its decay. You could loop short sounds to play as long as you held the key, and they quickly decayed when you let go, but triggering a longer sample could be annoying. Rossum soon designed an "ugly 50-wire kludge" VCA to fix the problem and toured worldwide to retrofit Emulators in the field with both the VCA and E-mu's just-completed sequencer. The revised Emulator appeared at the January '82 NAMM at a reduced price of just under $8,000. E-mu also began promoting its sample library of twenty-five to thirty disks, a strategy that paid off and kept the company solvent.

> *Munchkinized:* a term applied to the results of pitch-shifting a sample too high above its original frequency, which can make sampled speech sound like the voices of the Munchkins in *The Wizard of Oz*
> *sample start point:* an adjustable location from which an existing sample begins playing
> *sample duration:* the length of time a sample will play

E-mu produced both hardware and software Emulators throughout its existence, along with the more affordable Emax and rackmount ESI samplers, the Drumulator sample-playback and SP-12/1200 sampling drum machines, and the Proteus line of sample players. In March 1993 Creative Technology Ltd. purchased E-mu Systems, which later produced sampling plug-ins and sound libraries and, in hardware form, USB keyboard controllers and audio and MIDI interfaces.

The Volksampler

Among the first truly affordable digital samplers was the Mirage, Ensoniq's first product. Prior to that Pennsylvania company's formation, four employees of Commodore Business Machines—Charlie Winterble, Al Charpentier, Bruce Crockett, and Bob Yannes, designer of the Sound Interface Device (SID) chip for the Commodore 64—left the company in 1982 to start Peripheral Visions with the goal of creating the next great home computer. However, so popular was the C64 that no one else could match its success. Yannes therefore recommended they apply their newly designed sound generator—the Digital Oscillator Chip (DOC)—to musical instruments. Since that direction didn't appeal to Winterble he went elsewhere, leaving Charpentier, Yannes, and Crockett to start doing business as Ensoniq.

Yannes initially wanted to make a polyphonic synthesizer, but the synth market was saturated at the time, so they decided instead to make a low-cost sampler based on the DOC. Bill Mauchly, Alex Limberis, Mats Myrberg, and John Senior assisted Yannes in developing the Mirage, which Ensoniq introduced in 1984. An eight-voice multitimbral sampler with a five-octave, velocity-sensitive keyboard, the Mirage's less-than-stellar audio quality is due more to the DOC than its eight-bit sample resolution. Instead of using variable sample-rate technology to transpose like the Fairlight CMI and E-mu Emulator, the DOC incorporates a fixed-rate sample-skipping—aka drop/add—architecture without interpolation. When transpositions require finer factors than doubling or halving the sample's original frequency, which respectively shifts a sample up or down an octave, the DOC drops or adds samples to change pitch and, since there's no interpolation, it imparts a grungy quality to the sound.

Polyphonic variable-rate sample playback costs more than drop/add because, for one thing, you need a **DAC** for each voice so it can vary its playback rate independently of the others. The Ensoniq team had designed the DOC—which also appears in Ensoniq's ESQ-1, SQ-80, and SDP-1 digital piano—for a low-cost home computer, so it's audio quality isn't stellar.

The Ensoniq Mirage came to market at a price far below earlier samplers such as the Fairlight CMI and E-mu's Emulator. This is an original version, complete with a mushy Pratt-Reed keyboard and black cabinet with silk-screened labeling and aluminum endcaps. (Courtesy of Perfect Circuit Audio)

> *DAC:* digital-to-analog converter

The Mirage—complete with a built-in MIDI sequencer; 144K of internal sample RAM; 3.5″ floppy-disk drive for sample, sequence, and operating-system storage; and an original retail price of $1,695—proved very popular, selling nearly 8,000 units within its first year. That was more than all of the other samplers that preceded it combined. Various versions of the sampler stayed in production until 1988 and reached about 25,000 units in total sales. After supposedly becoming obsolete, the Mirage rebounded in popularity during the '90s when grungy audio became a fad.

Ensoniq engineers later developed the thirteen-bit, sample-interpolating, digital-filtering DOC II chip for their EPS sampler (late '87), then quickly replaced it with OTIS, a sixteen-bit chip with digital audio busses for direct communication with the Ensoniq Signal Processor, their ESP I DSP effects chip; OTIS appeared in the VFX synth and EPS-16 Plus sampler ('89 and '90). After OTIS came OTTO for the ASR-series products (late '92 to '97) and the DSP-processing OTTO-FX for the Fizmo (1999), Ensoniq's final synth before Creative Labs purchased the company in 1998.

Multitimbral Sample Playback, Sampling Optional

In an appearance on NBC TV's *The Today Show* in January 1976, the inventor/futurist Raymond Kurzweil demonstrated the Kurzweil Reading Machine, a product that could vocalize printed words for the blind. Stevie Wonder heard the broadcast, soon visited Kurzweil's office, and walked away with the first production unit, beginning a long and productive friendship between the two.

The friendship, funds from financiers, and the sale of the Reading Machine business to Xerox eventually led to the development of an important series of synthesizers bearing the Kurzweil name. Ray Kurzweil went to Stevie's Wonderland studio in 1982 and saw the various acoustic and electronic instruments that Wonder had collected. Wonder explained that he lamented the lack of a bridge between these two worlds. While electronic instruments gave musicians access to powerful control techniques, their timbres tended to be thin and uninspiring. As for the acoustic world, thanks to a long history of development, instruments could produce complex and rich timbres, but the sounds were inaccessible to those who failed to master the techniques necessary to make the instruments sound their best. Wonder and Kurzweil devoted themselves to finding and developing ways to apply modern control methods to play stimulating, electronically generated, acoustic-like sounds.

Setting up shop in Waltham, Massachusetts, Kurzweil assembled a team of specialists with whom to work on the creation of what would become the legendary K250 sample-playback synthesizer. Among the team members was John Shykun, who'd previously worked at ARP and became Kurzweil Music Systems' director of marketing. According to Shykun, Kurzweil's engineers had plenty of funding to work with and they had many great ideas, but they didn't understand how to design something that could be

Spotted at the January 1984 NAMM show are a waving director of marketing John Shykun, on the *left*, and a relieved Ray Kurzweil with the nearly-ready-to-ship Kurzweil 250. (Dominic Milano)

The Kurzweil K250 is a big synthesizer, measuring 54" across × 27" deep × 9" high. Bob Moog, who served as Kurzweil Music Systems' vice president of New Product Research from 1989 to 1992, once explained the company's approach to building instruments: "Kurzweil starts out with a no-compromises instrument using completely new technology and then tries to develop that technology to where it can be produced more cheaply." (Courtesy of Ray Kurzweil, Kurzweil Technologies)

mass-produced. They soon needed to define what the instrument was actually going to be so that it would exist within a year.

Actual K250 development began in 1983. Every week, its designers had to delete more features. The instrument was supposed to contain 250 sounds—thus its name—but **EPROM** was still exceedingly expensive, and filling the K250 with adequate memory for that many sounds using existing techniques could have cost $50,000 or more. The engineers therefore developed Contoured Sound Modeling, which allowed the compression of samples into a reasonable amount of memory. Even so, the team had to decrease the number of onboard sounds to one hundred.

> *EPROM:* erasable programmable read-only memory, which users can reprogram according to their needs

Eventually the K250 appeared as a ninety-five-pound behemoth with a then-impressive synth engine: ten-bit samples, twelve-voice multitimbral operation, six-voice layering, a remarkable 256-segment amplitude envelope generator, and twenty-four multi-waveform LFOs. It also has a built-in twelve-track MIDI sequencer. Sampling was optionally available. The first units shipped in June 1984. Besides Ray Kurzweil, the K250's main creators were software developer Chet Graham and signal-processing guru Bob Chidlaw.

The K250 remained in production until 1990, an impressive tour of duty for a synth in the hi-tech music industry. It was continuously revised throughout its lifetime. The final version actually represented the instrument that was originally intended, but by then its price had climbed to $20,000. Eventually the price dropped to $10,715 for a basic model, or $14,960 for a fully expanded unit with sampling.

In 1988 Kurzweil Music Systems introduced the K1000 Series of sample-playback instruments, which provided sixteen-bit versions of the best K250 sounds. In July 1990, the Korean piano manufacturer Young Chang purchased the company. The next year saw the release of the K2000, Kurzweil's initial VAST machine (**Variable Architecture Synthesis Technology**). A K2000 with an "s" in its name can sample. The upgraded K2500 series appeared in 1995, followed by the K2600 in 1999. The entire K2XXX lineup

Introduced in 1999, Kurzweil's K2600 continued VAST's development by delivering 12MB of sampled sounds (expandable to 44MB), built-in effects, master stereo and independent outputs, an interactive thirty-two-track sequencer, optional twenty-bit sampling, a four-and-a-half-octave-long ribbon controller, and configurations including seventy-six- and eighty-eight-note keyboards. There's also a 3U rackmount-module version. Shown here is a K2600XS, which includes Kurzweil's KB-3 Organ Mode, a Hammond tonewheel organ simulation with harmonics controllable from the nine faders. (Courtesy of Ray Kurzweil, Kurzweil Technologies)

Kurzweil's PC3K series extends the company's synthesis expertise well into the twenty-first century with such features as user-created DSP algorithms and comprehensive signal-routing capabilities while maintaining compatibility with K2XXX synthesizers. In addition, Kurzweil resurrected its VA-1 Virtual Analog Synthesizer technology for the PC3K, which is available in sixty-one-, seventy-six-, and eighty-eight-key versions (models PC3K6, PC3K7, and PC3K8, respectively). (Courtesy of Ray Kurzweil, Kurzweil Technologies)

has enjoyed great popularity thanks to its dedicated user base. In 2006 Hyundai bought Young Chang and invited Ray Kurzweil to return as their chief strategy officer, which he became in February 2007.

> *Variable Architecture Synthesis Technology (VAST):* a virtual means of nonstandard signal routing through digital synthesizer modules using Kurzweil-defined algorithms or signal-routing configurations

Direct-from-Disk Sample Playback

Since the advent of digital sampling, there's been one expensive requirement: lots of RAM to contain multiple high-resolution samples. While the price of RAM has steadily dropped over the years, you still can't consider it a cheap commodity—especially given the gigabytes needed to contain all of the great samples you want to play live. Wouldn't it be much more cost effective to play samples directly from a hard drive?

NemeSys introduced a near-perfect solution in late 1998: GigaSampler. They'd licensed Rockwell Semiconductor's EndlessWave technology, which could stream audio directly from hard drives. With GigaSampler you could play 2GB stereo piano samples that had no loops, and it included synthesis and sample-editing functions. The downside as far as Macintosh users were concerned was that GigaSampler ran only on Windows PCs.

The Synthesizer

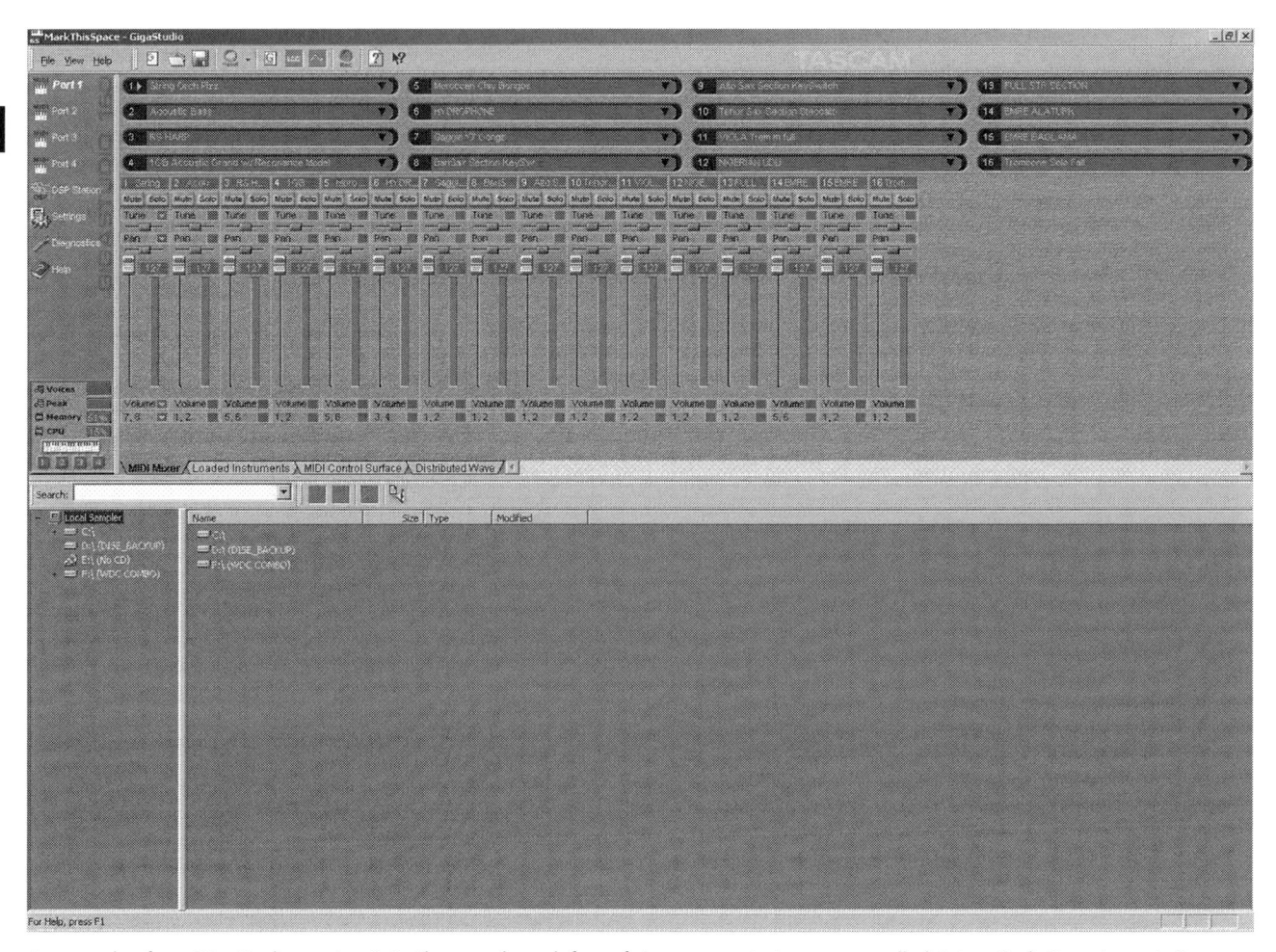

A screenshot from GigaStudio version 2.5. Slots one through four of sixteen contain instruments called String Orch Pizz, Acoustic Bass, RS Harp, and 1GB Acoustic Grand w/Resonance Model. Using the onscreen mixer, you can mute, solo, pan, and tune instruments, adjust their volumes, and assign them to different outputs. You browse for sounds and instruments in the lower part of the screen. Although GigaSampler/GigaStudio progressed to versions 3 and 4, Drew Neumann stuck with version 2.5 because it worked well for him, sounded good, and he didn't want to troubleshoot the upgrade process. He reports that since Gigastudio's unexpected early demise, many studios have migrated to plug-ins such as Soundlib G-Player, Native Instruments Kontakt, and Apple EXS24. (Drew Neumann, Droomusic)

During GigaSampler's lifetime, its name changed to GigaStudio, and it passed from NemeSys to Tascam and then to Garritan in 2009 before being discontinued.

First Programmable Polysynth

I don't mean to imply that only samplers and sample players are geared toward live performance. Prior to the mid-1970s, true polyphonic synthesizers—as opposed to a few that were merely organs with a few synth-style features—were new to the market and total programmability was virtually unheard of. Then came the January 1978 NAMM show at the Disneyland Hotel in Anaheim, California. While Moog Music and ARP Instruments were reveling in their heyday as king-of-the-hill synth-industry giants, Roland and Yamaha were still trying to figure out how to make a synthesizer that would sell in the United States. Tom Oberheim's modular Four Voice and Eight Voice synths, the Polymoog, and ARP's two-voice 2600 were the only polyphonic synths in production so far. The Oberheims, complete with the Programmer module, were the only polyphonic

A rev 3—the final version—of the Sequential Circuits Prophet-5, which can be identified by the tape cassette control buttons to the *upper right*. While rev 1 and 2 models features SSM chips, Curtis Music chips appeared in all of the rev 3 synths, which explains why earlier versions sound different from rev 3s. (Courtesy of Dave Smith)

synths with user patch memory, but the Programmer couldn't store all of the SEMs' parameter settings.

Tucked in a tiny booth, Dave Smith, former Moog clinician John Bowen, and businesswoman Barb Fairhurst—the staff of Sequential Circuits—were showing a barely working prototype of a synthesizer called the Prophet-5. The company, a self-funded outfit begun in the confines of Smith's San Jose garage, sold a digital sequencer and a generic synth programmer.

Sequential was hardly the company you'd expect to send industry leaders running for cover, but while Moog and ARP were battling over the relative merits of pitchbend wheels vs. ribbons vs. spongy little rectangles called Proportional Pressure Controllers (PPCs), Sequential was cranking out exactly the kind of instrument—with exactly the kind of sound and features—that musicians needed. By today's standards, those features look pathetic: forty user patches, five **monotimbral voices,** and a non-touch-sensitive keyboard. But the Prophet was the first fully programmable polyphonic synth. You could store settings for every one of its parameters in memory.

> *monotimbral voices:* all notes play the same sound
> *filter cutoff frequency:* the point in the audible spectrum at which a filter begins attenuating frequencies

If there was a single feature that defined the Prophet sound, it was the poly-mod section, which enabled you to use the filter envelope and osc 2 to modulate osc 1's frequency and pulse-width and/or the **filter cutoff frequency.** These modulation routings, combined with osc 1's sync function, produced the trademark—and at one time hopelessly overused—oscillator sweeping-sync sound.

Many exciting performance-oriented instruments came from Sequential Circuits before Yamaha purchased its assets in 1988. Although essentially an eight-voice spinoff of

A big, beautiful, hefty, and expensive Prophet-T8 from Sequential Circuits. Each of its seventy-six keys has a spring-loaded wooden hammer assembly and two sets of optical sensors for velocity detection. Calibration of these sensors can be tricky because of slight warping in all of the T8's wooden parts. Some T8 keyboards are better than others, and humidity and transportation mileage can be factors in the keyboard's response accuracy. (Courtesy of Dave Smith)

the Prophet-5, the Prophet-T8 (1983–84) delivered a comprehensive MIDI implementation; a seventy-six-note weighted-action keyboard that sensed velocity, release velocity, and polyphonic aftertouch; keyboard splitting and voice layering; and knobs galore—all at a hefty list price of $5,895. At the other end of the price scale was the Pro-One ($745, 1981–84), a popular, dual-oscillator monosynth with an arpeggiator and a forty-note step-entry sequencer. The company even dabbled in samplers, first the twelve-bit Prophet-2000 keyboard and later the potent, but extremely rare, sixteen-bit Prophet-3000 rackmount module.

Classic Beat Boxes

Two entities that electronic musicians take for granted today didn't yet exist during the 1960s: computerized, programmable drum machines and Roland. The development of both came about thanks to Ikutaro Kakehashi. At the time Mr. K—as he's affectionately known—ran Ace Electronics, a manufacturer of organs, amplifiers, and rhythm machines. Two of his early designs were hints of what was to come: the Rhythm Ace R-1, a hand-operated machine that attached to an organ, and the Rhythm Ace FR-1, his first electronic rhythm machine, each respectively introduced in 1964 and 1967.

Mr. K founded Roland in 1972, and preset-pattern rhythm machines were among the new company's first products. By the late '70s when microprocessors started appearing in musical instruments, Mr. K incorporated one in Roland's seventh rhythm instrument, the CR-78. Although Paia's Programmable Drum Set, which came out in 1975, was the first programmable drum machine, the CR-78 was the first rhythm machine that had a microprocessor.

Roland's second programmable drum machine caused a big splash on the music scene only after its production had ended. The TR-808 became the rhythm machine of choice for making hip-hop and techno music. Five analog percussion sounds characterize its sonic prowess: hum kick, ticky snare, tishy hi-hats, and spacy cowbell. An event-accent

Roland founder Ikutaro Kakehashi poses with me at the January 2006 NAMM show in Anaheim, California. (Roland Corporation U.S.)

function, which is integral in making an automatic rhythm machine musically useful, survived the transition from the earlier CR-78. The 808 also incorporated volume knobs for each voice, multiple audio outputs, and the immediate precursor to MIDI—Roland's proprietary communications protocol called the DCB Bus. In fact, the DCB connector is identical to that used for MIDI I/O. Mr. K played major roles in developing and getting the MIDI protocol accepted industry-wide in 1983, for which he and Dave Smith received Technical Grammy awards on February 10, 2013. Since Mr. K was unable to

Roland's programmable CompuRhythm CR-78 came to market in 1978 and was the first programmable drum machine to incorporate a microprocessor. (Courtesy of Roland Corporation)

The Synthesizer

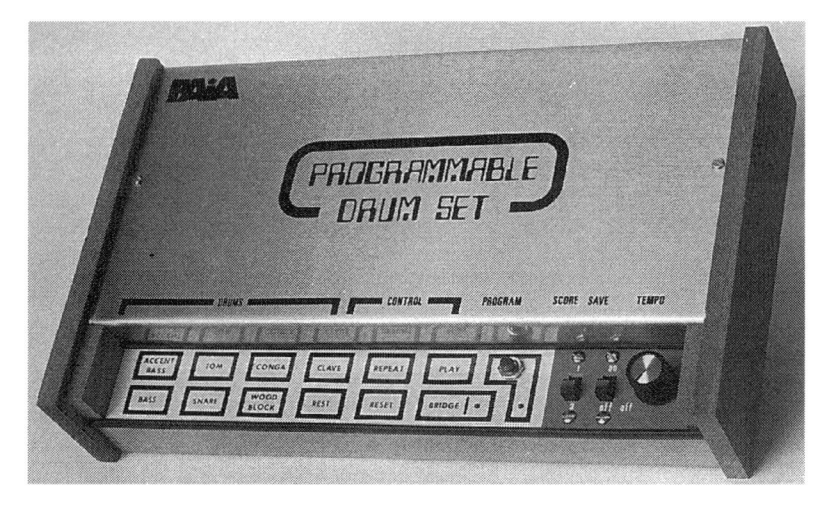

John Simonton's Programmable Drum Set, Paia Model 3750, was the first programmable drum machine. Unlike Roland's CR-78, the 3750 used TTL (transistor-transistor-logic) circuitry instead of a microprocessor. Both generated sounds using analog components. Simonton passed away in 2005 at the young age of sixty-two. (Courtesy of Paia Electronics, Inc.)

travel from Japan for the Grammy ceremony, his second son—Ikuo Kakehashi, a professional percussionist who has recorded and performed with trail-blazing synthesists Isao Tomita and Don Lewis, among many other musicians—accepted the award on behalf of his father. Ikuo explained that their family name means "bridge" and that Mr. K has always strived to make products that serve as a bridge to new generations of musicians.

At about the same time Mr. K foresaw the value of implanting a microprocessor in a rhythm machine, Roger Linn began developing the Linn LM-1, which upon its release in 1980 qualified as the first programmable drum machine that featured sampled sounds. But Mr. K wasn't prepared to abandon analog sound generation in his rhythm instruments, even by the time the TR-909 was introduced in 1984. Only one of the 909's eleven percussion sounds—the crash cymbal—was sampled. It was Roland's first rhythm

Roland's TR-808 became the fave percussion source for hip-hop and techno musicians after it went out of production in 1983. (Courtesy of Roland Corporation)

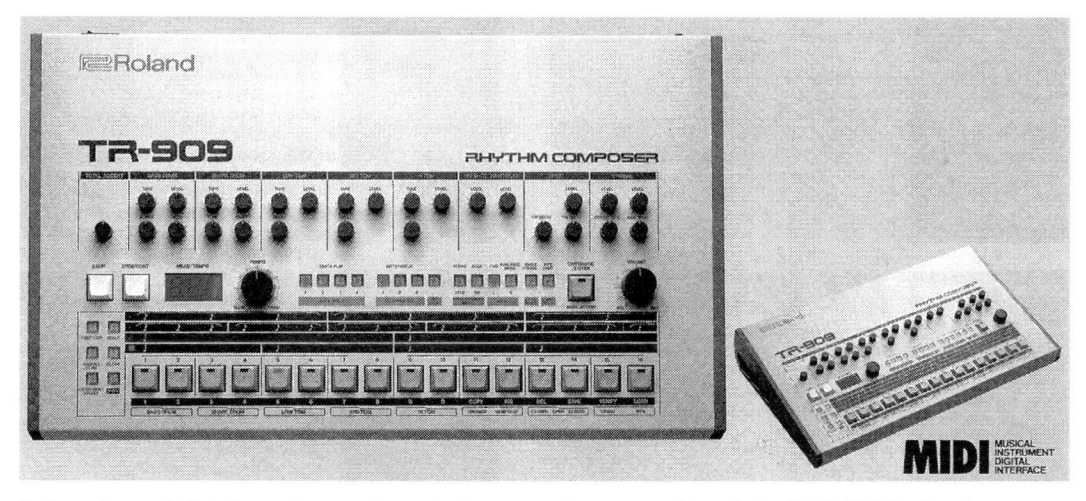

Both analog and digital sound-generation techniques were incorporated into Roland's TR-909 Rhythm Composer, the company's first drum machine with MIDI. By the time the 909 was unleashed in 1984, the Linn LM-1—whose drum sounds were sampled—had attracted most buyers in the drum machine market. Like the TR-808, however, the 909 gained popularity after its production ended. (Courtesy of Roland Corporation)

machine with MIDI, but it only stayed in production for one year. Since the LM-1 drew many more buyers, Roland quickly replaced the 909 with the TR-707, which played only sampled sounds. But like the 808, the 909 became a favorite of dance music producers following the termination of its production.

The pre-MIDI TB-303 Bass Line tabletop module was another Roland product that enjoyed remarkable postmortem popularity. Introduced in late 1981 at a list price of $395 and discontinued in 1984, the 303 could be had on the used market for spare change before it caught fire and drew exorbitant prices during the 1990s because it became *the* bass synth of choice in techno, house, and acid music.

First Programmable Sample-Playback Drum Machine

In this day of sixteen- to sixty-four-bit arrogance, mention the word "great" in reference to an eight-bit device and you're bound to raise a few cynical eyebrows. But if it weren't for an eight-bit marvel known as the Linn LM-1, it might have taken us a lot longer to reach this enlightened age of the digital drum machine, be it hardware or software.

Before the LM-1, 99 percent of all drum machines were essentially organ add-ons that exclusively featured preset rhythm patterns. The final 1 percent comprised John Simonton's Paia Programmable Drum Set, the Roland CR-78, and a 6′ × 2′ beast that Bob Moog built in the late '60s but never put into production. Not only that, but they made sounds using analog circuits. Roger Linn changed all that with the LM-1. It wasn't cheap—going for $4,995—but unlike typical $500 drum machines that played preset samba patterns and sounded like crickets, the LM-1 triggered samples of real drums.

Sampling was a little-known term back in 1978 when Roger began his quest. Besides developing his own drum-machine programming ideas such as **quantizing** and **shuffle-play**, Linn had to pave his own way into the sampling world. He took the advice of an engineering friend and incorporated a compounding digital-to-analog converter (ComDAC), which provided a better dynamic range than eight-bit linear sampling would have. He also disregarded the Nyquist theorem and used unfiltered

The Synthesizer

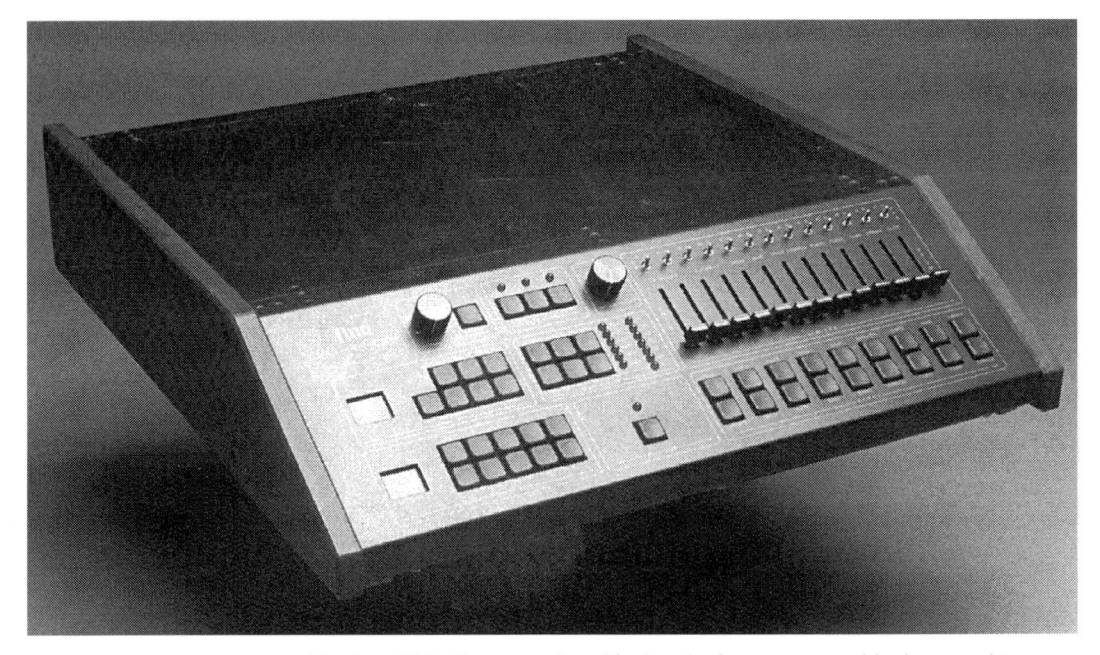

A second-generation version of the Linn LM-1. The original qualified as the first programmable drum machine to feature sampled sounds. After Roger Linn assembled the first 35 LM-1s at home, he made some improvements and Bob Easton of 360 Systems assumed production, upgrading the quality control of the later units. (Paul Haggard)

samples that contained harmonic content higher than half his 27kHz sampling rate, resulting in a sizzling, sometimes distorted sound that proved more lively and natural than those produced by competing machines.

> *quantizing:* adjustments to the timing of played notes or events to coincide with a particular rhythm
>
> *shuffle-play:* percentage adjustments to a sequence of notes or events to give a jazzy swing feel to a rhythm pattern

Linn's shuffle feature was unique in the drum machine world, and it's found on every device he's designed. Linn's method of creating a sixteenth-note swing or shuffle feel was to unevenly split the timing of an eighth note and delaying every second sixteenth note by a specific time factor. There's something about the LM-1 feel that drum machines from other manufacturers have rarely if ever quite matched. Little wonder, then, why the National Academy of Recording Arts and Sciences rewarded Roger Linn a Technical Grammy Award on February 12, 2011, for his groundbreaking work in creating programmable drum machines.

Small-Scale Improvisation Instrument

Portable, dedicated performance hardware rarely comes smaller, as flexible, and more affordable than Korg's Kaossilator, a battery-powered synthesizer with a two-dimensional

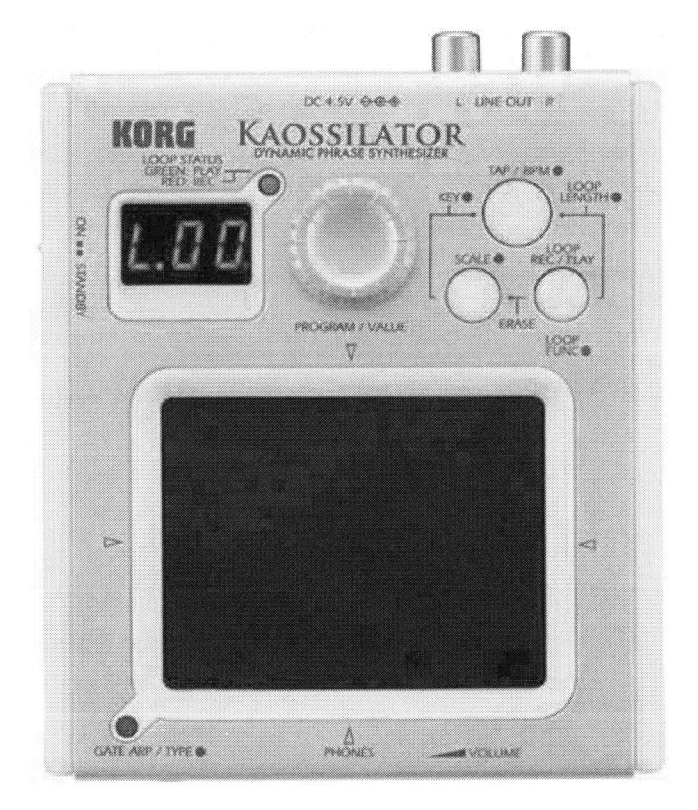

Measuring a mere 4-1/8" × 5" × 1", Korg's Kaossilator is about as portable as a synthesizer in hardware form can get. (Courtesy of Korg)

touchpad, built-in sampled and synthesized preset sounds complete with effects, a **gate arpeggiator**, and creative **looping functions**—all for a surprisingly reasonable list price of $199. Introduced in 2008, the Kaossilator is packed with one hundred presets in seven categories: lead, acoustic, bass, and percussion sounds; chords; patterns; and sound effects. With pitched sounds, while the touchpad's x-axis often controls frequency, the y-axis might vary filter cutoff frequency, timbre, LFO speed, volume, or distortion amount; add vibrato; or pan the sound across the stereo soundfield. Dial up a chord preset and the y-axis might switch between major and minor voicings.

Although melodies can be challenging to execute due to the lack of key indicators, there are scale choices ranging from chromatic and whole tone to modal (Ionian, Dorian, Phrygian, etc.) to thirds, fifths, and octaves—or the pitch can vary continuously like a Theremin's. Engage the gate arpeggiator and the Kaossilator will play the sound in a pattern ranging from simple to complex—depending on which of the fifty patterns you've selected—as long as you touch the pad. Record four- or eight-bar patterns with unlimited **overdubs**. One caveat, however, is that memory isn't battery-backed. Once you turn the Kaossilator off or manually clear memory, your marvelous loop will have disappeared. In spite of that, the Kaossilator is an addictive and productive performance synth that you can take almost anywhere—with earbuds, a headset, or amplified speakers as there isn't a built-in speaker system.

> *gate arpeggiator:* a performance accessory that converts a sustained sound into repeated bursts in a rhythm determined by the selected pattern
> *looping functions:* recording and repeated playback of performance activity, with the ability to remove some parts
> *overdubs:* recording new parts on top of those that you previously recorded

As an alternative, if you absolutely want to store your work for later recall, consider the Kaossilator Pro, introduced in January 2010. With a list price of $399, the Kaossilator Pro trades battery-powered convenience for four independent loop banks of up to four measures or sixteen beats in length, MIDI I/O, one hundred eighty-five preset sounds and fifteen effects—including ten for vocoder-style processing—with a mic input for processing your own voice, user sampling, and a whole lot more. The handheld Kaossilator 2 ($230 list) arrived in 2012 and is even smaller than the original and packs advanced capabilities including audio recording using its built-in mic or the audio input, as well as a microSD/SDHC card slot for storage of loops and recorded performances. Korg also developed an iOS version called iKaossilator, which runs on an Apple iPhone, iPod Touch, or iPad and costs only $9.99.

Interface

One of the most interesting aspects of synthesizer design is the user interface. How does the synthesist make music with an instrument, let alone just getting it to generate sounds? Are features and capabilities presented in intuitive, easy-to-use ways? In the case of a programmable synth, are its factory presets so fun and outstanding that you just want to spend the day auditioning and jamming with them one by one, or does the instrument invite you to tweak each sound as you play it, encouraging you with its front-panel controls to caress what you're hearing and store your personalized patch before continuing to the next one?

Over the years, some user interfaces have been extraordinary; others simply novel, if not particularly effective. Here we'll concentrate on those that have in any manner been particularly groundbreaking.

Patchboard-Matrix British Synths

Take, for example, the lineup of instruments from Electronic Music Studios (EMS). Out of an advanced—for 1969—computer-music studio near London came a series of synthesizers and related gear, including a patchable tabletop synthesizer known in America as the Putney. Its true name is the VCS3, which stands for the Voltage-Controlled Studio, attempt #3. The VCS3 is smaller than its behemoth American-made Moog Modular counterparts of the same generation mostly because, instead of having dozens of jacks arranged among gobs of knobs across several square feet of panel space, the VCS3 has a tiny patchboard matrix into which you insert pins to route audio and control signals through the device. David Cockerell, who designed many of EMS's products, admits they chose the patchboard because the company bought hundreds of them surplus.

The earliest synthesizers from Electronic Music Studios (EMS), ca. 1971. *Clockwise from the left* are the VCS3 Mark I with a DK2 keyboard; the prototype Synthi A, which was called the Portabella at the time; and the Synthi KB-1 prototype. (Courtesy of Robin Wood, Electronic Music Studios)

Beginning in 1965, Cockerell worked for Peter Zinovieff, who'd purchased a Digital Equipment Corporation (DEC) PDP-8—the first minicomputer—and assembled one of the earliest computer-music studios. According to Robin Wood, who joined EMS in 1970 and purchased the company in 1995, EMS in the early days was actually a complex studio in which Cockerell designed a sophisticated sixty-four-channel filter bank for analyzing sounds along with prototype analog circuits for generating audio—all under computer control.

Zinovieff and cofounder Tristram Cary (1925–2008) were into toneless avant-garde music and thought a keyboard was of secondary importance. In fact, the VCS3 didn't have a keyboard, but they developed one as an afterthought. The DK2 was a three-octave, duophonic mechanical unit installed with control electronics in a wooden cabinet that matched the VCS3.

Portability was obviously an afterthought as well because—given the VCS3's bulk—it's awkward to transport. Compared with EMS's Synthi 100, though, it's tiny. Originally based on three VCS3s, the Synthi 100 appeared in 1971 and grew to encompass twelve oscillators and associated filters, envelopes, and more. It also had a three-track monophonic digital sequencer and two 64-X-64 patch matrices. Production of the Synthi 100 was quite limited and it sold for around £10,000 (US$25,000 at the time). BBC's Radiophonic

Synthesizer pioneer David Cockerell sets up a Synthi AKS in his London lab in March 2007. If you've ever made music with an EMS synth, Akai sampler or MPC, or something from Electro-Harmonix, David was most likely involved in its development and production. (Mark Vail)

Not many synthesizers are bigger than the EMS Synthi 100, an oversized system complete with sequencing capabilities and built inside a large console. EMS introduced it in 1971. (Courtesy of Robin Wood, Electronic Music Studios)

Workshop invested in one for use in the electronic music and sound effects created for a myriad of TV programs such as *Doctor Who*.

To meet the demand for a small, portable synth, Cockerell squeezed the VCS3's electronics into an oversized briefcase by 1971 and dubbed it the Synthi A. He also designed the KS, a two-and-a-half-octave capacitive touchplate keyboard with a 256-event monophonic digital sequencer—all of which fit inside the Synthi A's briefcase lid to become the Synthi AKS. The Dutch composer Felix Visser scored many early '70s European films with an AKS, producing music and sounds none of his competitors could match. Numerous rock bands and artists made use of the EMS VCS3, Synthi A, and Synthi AKS synths onstage and in studios during the 1970s. Among them were Pink Floyd, The Who, Jean-Michel Jarre, King Crimson, Tangerine Dream, Klaus Schulze, Moody Blues, Curved Air, Gong, and Yes. The VCS3 has also served well in the teaching of acoustics, synthesis, and audio signal processing.

David Cockerell has designed and contributed to the production of many excellent musical products. During the '80s and '90s, he designed the twelve-bit S612, S700, and S900 samplers for Akai, making them flexible and easy to use. Cockerell teamed with another British synth designer, Chris Huggett—famed for the Electronic Dream Plant Wasp, Oxford OSCar, Novation Supernova, and many others—to design Akai's lineup of sixteen-bit samplers starting in 1988 with the popular S1000. David also worked with Roger Linn to develop the original Akai MPC60 MIDI production workstation. In addition, Cockerell has done extensive development for Mike Matthews and his company Electro-Harmonix over the years.

Educational Instruments that Went Well Beyond

One of America's most prominent synth manufacturers of the 1970s started doing business mainly for educational purposes. Boston-area electrical engineer Alan R. Pearlman wanted to make a modular synthesizer for music education. You may have seen a result of his early efforts in Steven Spielberg's *Close Encounters of the Third Kind*, when aliens exchange the familiar five-note motif with musician Jean Claude, who's standing behind a huge synthesizer console. It was a rare ARP 2500, a big modular from Pearlman's com-

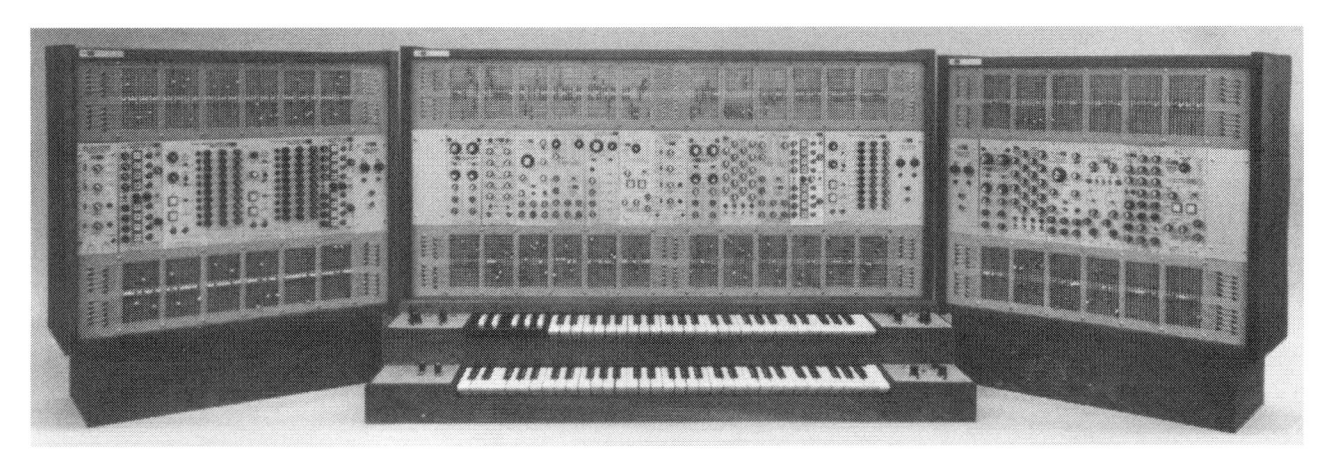

A very well-endowed ARP 2500, which was in production from 1969 to 1976. ARP founder Alan Pearlman credits David Friend for spreading the word about ARP Instruments, demonstrating the 2500 for New York filmmakers and recording artists, and taking one to Europe to visit Karlheinz Stockhausen in his studio in Germany. (Courtesy of Alan R. Pearlman)

The Synthesizer

ARP Instruments produced the potent 2600 in several different forms between 1970 and 1981. This is a third-generation model, shown with its 3620 keyboard. (Courtesy of Alan R. Pearlman)

Don Muro poses in 1971 with a rare "Blue Marvin" ARP 2600, one assembled in a garage before the ARP factory opened. ARP insiders called it the "Blue Marvin" as a tribute to then ARP president Marvin Cohen. Everyone else knew of it as the "Blue Meanie"—in reference to the evil creatures in the Beatles' *Yellow Submarine*—because all of its components were hidden inside an impenetrable aluminum cabinet, and the crucial modules were coated in epoxy to discourage outsiders from copying and reproducing them. (Courtesy of Don Muro)

pany ARP Instruments—originally called Tonus, Inc. The guy who played Jean Claude wasn't actually a movie actor; he was Philip Dodds (1951–2007), vice president of engineering for ARP.

During the late '60s, Pearlman learned that not only would his main competitors be Moog Music and Buchla and Associates, but the synthesizers from both manufacturers suffered from tuning instabilities. He therefore began to develop oscillators and filters that were more stable. Pearlman also consulted with Brown University music professor Gerald "Shep" Shapiro, who provided a list of features he would like to see in a synthesizer for studio use. One goal was to minimize the number of patch cords required. Pearlman incorporated many of Shapiro's ideas, including a patch matrix similar to what EMS used, which made for a cleaner front panel; however, the matrix patchbays were notoriously noisy due to crosstalk.

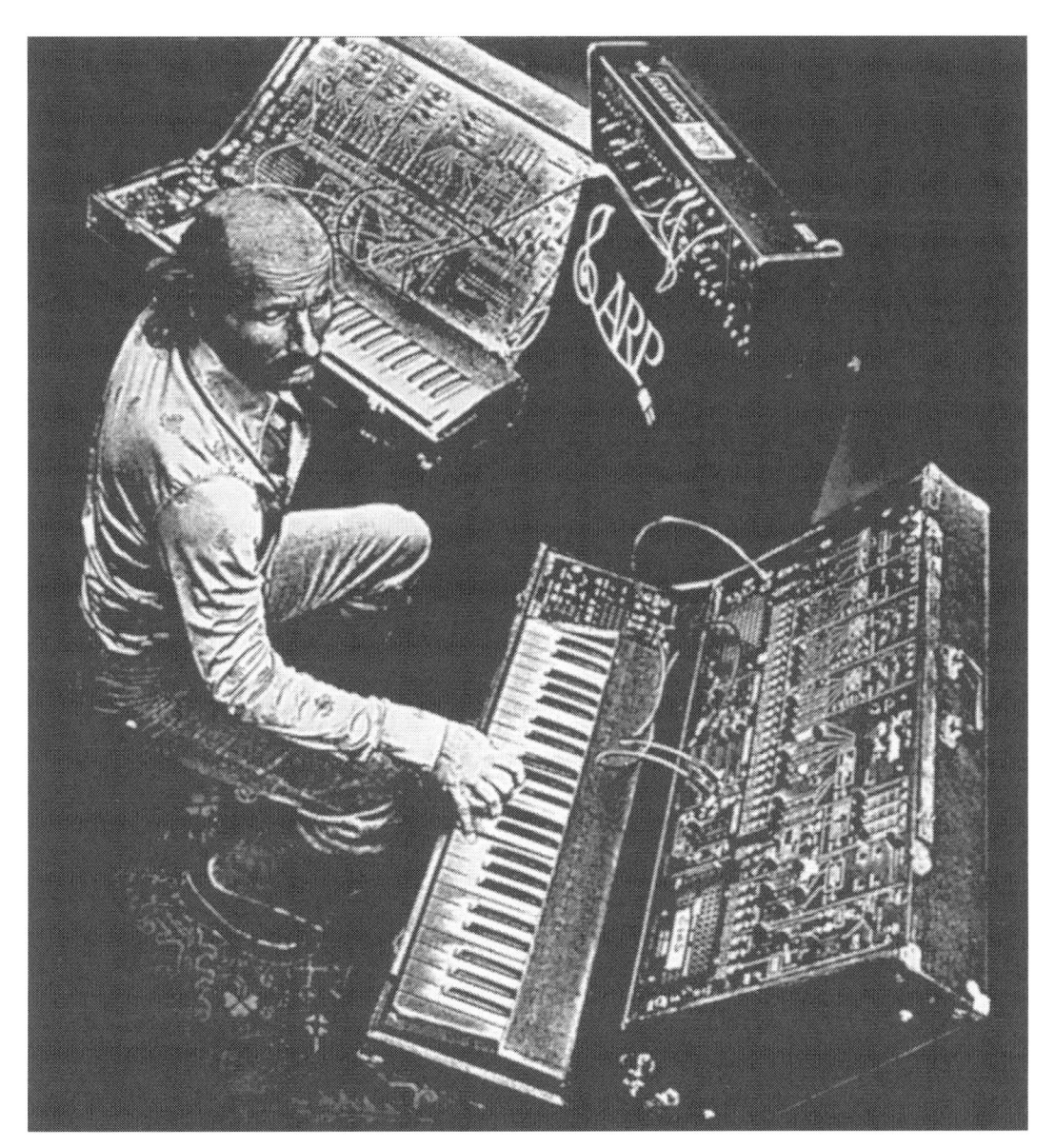

ARP Instruments used this photo of Joe Zawinul (1932–2007) playing two ARP 2600s in some of their ads. He challenged himself by inverting the voltage of one 2600 so that high notes triggered low frequencies and vice versa, and then by playing counterpoint parts on both synths together. Who wouldn't want to be a synthesist after hearing Zawinul play them with Weather Report? (Courtesy of Alan R. Pearlman)

ARP Instruments conducted business from 1969 to 1981. The synthesizer that initially put the company on the map in 1970 was the 2600, another that Pearlman designed from an educational standpoint with the intent of teaching synthesis techniques to musicians who were studying traditional instruments. Front-panel graphics illustrated the 2600's normalled (hard-wired) signal paths, which could be overridden using patch cords to reroute signals and create more bizarre and complex timbres than were possible on a totally normalled synth. In addition, Pearlman chose sliders and extended-throw switches to make parameter settings easier to see than they were on a knob-laden synth.

Unique Improvisation Machine

A user interface once described as "a conductivity matrix" appears on the four-hundred-pound SalMar Construction, as do patch cables strewn like spaghetti across one of its oversized panels. Their presence, however, pales due to the size and other attributes of Salvatore Martirano's entire machine itself.

Martirano (1927–95) created the SalMar Construction between 1968 and 1972 with the assistance of faculty, students, and others—James Divilbiss, Sergio Franco, Richard Borovec, Gregory Danner, Jay Barr, Josef Sekon, and Terry Mohn—at the University of Illinois at Champaign-Urbana. The massive musical instrument/industrial sculpture measures 4.5′ across, 2.5′ deep, and a hulking 8′ tall. Within its open, slotted L-channel framework are custom-made analog synth modules, digital control circuits, and a panel of 291 patching and control touch-switches. Steven Curtin, a composition student of Martirano's, has written that the SalMar Construction was among the first digital, interactive composition instruments. It sports an interface consisting of a touch-sensitive digital-logic programming system with which the performer selects among melodies and sequences generated by logic circuits.

At the heart of the SalMar's synthesis engine are sixteen oscillators that independently scan a pair of waveforms from two thirty-two-sample long by eight-bit sample memories. Their outputs continue to a differential multiplier where incoming control voltages determine the oscillator mix of the audio output, allowing the creation of an extensive variety of waveforms and time-varying spectra. In addition, you can load waveform memories in real time using the same logic circuits that generate notes. The SalMar can produce microtonal temperaments including sixteen, twenty, and a variable number of notes per octave. There are also panning circuits, basic **waveshapers**, and thirty-two percussion instruments generated by self-oscillating filters.

> *waveshaper:* a type of synthesis distortion that alters a simple waveform to generate complex overtones

The still-functioning SalMar Construction resides in the Sousa Archives and Center for American Music museum at the University of Illinois at Champaign-Urbana. On December 11, 2011, Sal's widow Dorothy Martirano performed on violin with an assortment of musicians playing a variety of acoustic and electronic instruments in a delightful

Salvatore Martirano's SalMar Construction set up for performance. (Courtesy of the Martirano Foundation and the Electronic Music Foundation)

two-hour improvisation centered around the SalMar, under the expert guidance of Ken Beck. See the performance in its entirety at www.library.illinois.edu/sousa/?p=collections.

Multitasking Pre-MIDI Wonder Workstation

Picture a do-it-all computer-music system capable of multiple types of synthesis, sequencing, and music printing, and geared toward both composition and—thanks to effective real-time control functions—live performance. Now consider the system was

Salvatore Martirano at the helm of his SalMar Construction. (Courtesy of the Martirano Foundation and the Electronic Music Foundation)

developed during the mid-1970s, which you'd assume would make it sluggish since microprocessors of the time were rather slow, memory was prohibitively expensive so there wouldn't be much of it to work with, and the technology involved was primitive and limited in comparison with what we have today. You might also assume its synthesis techniques and sound quality would be inferior, especially with a system that several college students conceived and developed. Check your assumptions and preconceptions at the door because we're talking about the Con Brio Advanced Digital Synthesizer (ADS).

The Con Brio ADS 100 prototype. Its makers—Tim Ryan, Don Lieberman, and Alan Danziger—took advantage of Caltech theoretical physics professor George Zweig's offer of lab space in which to assemble the instrument in exchange for his use of it to map the cerebral cortex of cats. Ryan, Lieberman, and Danziger later disassembled the ADS 100 for parts to make the first of two ADS 200 systems. (© Con Brio 1988, courtesy of Tim Ryan)

In 1975, Con Brio's founders Tim Ryan and Don Lieberman were physics majors and Alan Danziger was an applied physics major at the California Institute of Technology (Caltech) in Pasadena. After deciding to build a synthesizer composed of a dozen or so manually wire-wrapped circuit boards and completing the original, sixteen-oscillator, monophonic ADS 100 prototype in 1977, they disassembled it in 1980 for parts to make an ADS 200. Each of the two ADS 200 and single 200-R instruments they eventually made has sixty-four digital oscillators (expandable to 256 if you had enough handmade circuit-board oscillators), 128 sixteen-stage envelope generators, sixteen-bit DACs, multitimbral voice operation, sixteen-track sequencing, a CRT video display, and a patch-bay matrix with gate and CV I/O for connection to analog modular and patchable synths. In real time, you can create multichannel, multitimbral compositions and mixdowns complete with automated changes to track volumes, tempo, and sounds. Whereas all of the ADS 200's components reside in a single cabinet, Ryan, Lieberman, and Danziger fashioned the ADS 200-R as a two-piece "roadable" model in 1982. The 200 systems can produce sound via additive, frequency-modulation, and phase-modulation synthesis, and the adventurous programmer can create unique synthesis algorithms using any combination of them.

All user interaction with a Con Brio takes place via a control panel laden with knobs and buttons. There's purposely no QWERTY keyboard because the developers found it nonmusical. Before you assume the Con Brio's one-hundred-plus buttons would be daunting to deal with, consider that only active buttons are lit depending on the operating

The Synthesizer

A Con Brio ADS 200 (*left*) that Brian Kehew has owned since the 1990s sits next to the one and only Con Brio ADS 200-R, property of its co-maker, Don Lieberman. It still works! An ADS 200 contributed sound effects to *Star Trek: The Motion Picture* and *Star Trek II: The Wrath of Khan*. (Don Lieberman)

Don Lieberman (*left*) and Brian Kehew delivered their Con Brio ADS 200-R and ADS 200 synths to the Computer History Museum in Mountain View, California, in November 2007 for that year's Vintage Computer Festival. (Mark Vail)

mode. As you progress from one mode to another, sections of the front panel light up, and those that aren't functional remain dark. It's very intuitive to work with and fast, too—much faster than paging through the deep menus on many contemporary instruments.

Other Con Brio functions are likewise expeditious, including defining split points across either of the two sixty-one-note keyboards and assigning sounds to play within specific zones, layering sounds on top of each other, and transposing and changing the volume of individual sounds. Storing and recalling parameter and assignment settings to and from floppies works faster than some state-of-the-art computers can access data from a hard drive.

Con Brios also respond to performance activity almost immediately. Thanks to direct memory access (DMA) and the transistor-transistor logic (TTL) circuitry that make up their synthesis engine, they're capable of consistently producing sound within 0.003 of a second (3ms) of receiving note requests. Not to be overlooked is the quality of the Con Brio's marvelous sound, to which I can attest after hearing the fully functioning ADS 200-R Don Lieberman and producer/vintage-synth expert Brian Kehew demonstrated at the Computer History Museum in Mountain View, California, in November 2007.

Original Resynthesizer

A little-known but visually and sonically impressive and technologically advanced instrument called the Technos Acxel Resynthesizer came from Québec, Canada, in 1987. Serving as the user interface for this unique sampling, audio-editing and -analysis, and sample-playback instrument is the Grapher, which prominently features a 64-×-32 matrix

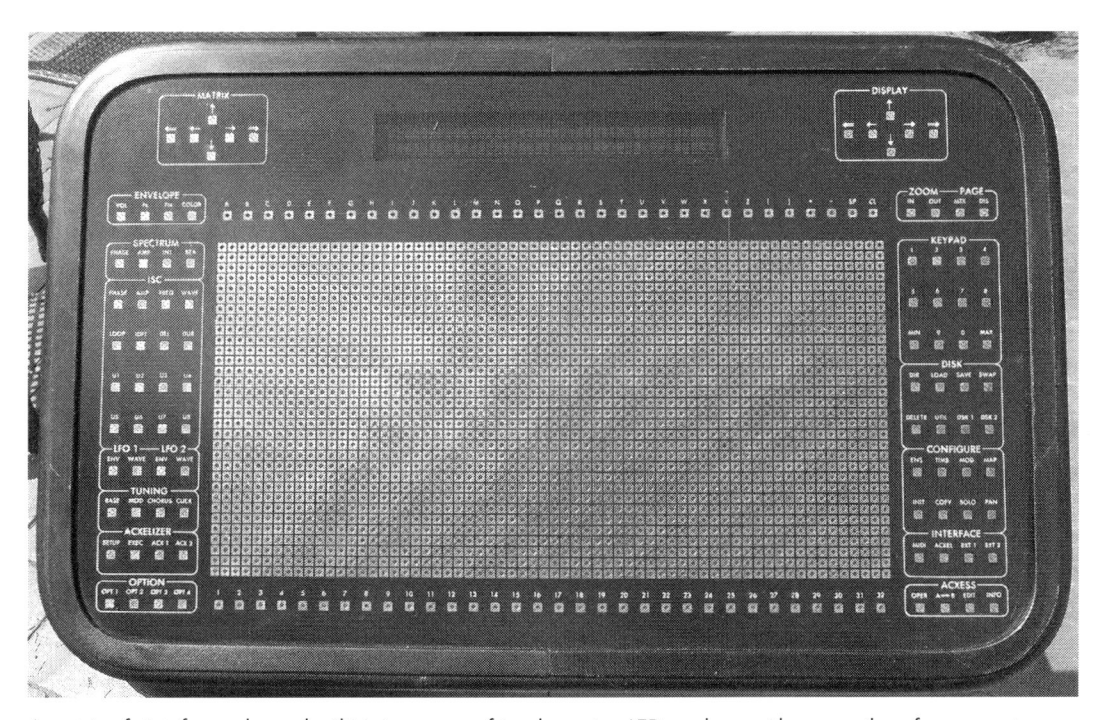

A matrix of sixty-four columns by thirty-two rows of touch-sensing LEDs—along with many others for parameter selection and programming functions and a two-line by forty-character numerical display—inhabits the Grapher, the Technos Acxel Resynthesizer's user interface. By tracing shapes with your finger across the matrix, you can enter waveforms and envelopes. The Acxel responds with timbral changes in real time. Not shown are the Acxel's default display message—"Forget Technology! Think Music"—and the separate rackmount card cage, called the Solitary. (Gary Nester)

of touch-sensing LEDs that display and allow the user to draw waveforms and envelopes and perform other functions with the touch of a finger.

A resynthesizer can sample a sound, analyze it, and divide the analyzed waveform into individual elements. Just as "pixel" stands for PIcture ELement in the video industry, "Acxel" stood for ACoustics and ELements in reference to how the Acxel divides a sample into elements and recombines them to re-create the original sound. Technos cofounders Nil Parent and Pierre Guilmette called the process "Acxelization," and it includes all of the parameters related to the harmonics and transients of the original sound. The system can autoprogram itself in order to reproduce the sound as accurately as possible using a form of additive synthesis. Once the rendition of the original sound is complete—or "Acxelized"—you can edit the results and individually adjust any of the parameters associated with its elements, including the duration, pitch, amplitude, and frequency of each harmonic. You can also add modulation, filtering, flanging, and phasing, and even delay selected harmonics.

Along with accurate reproductions of sampled sounds, the Acxel is capable of other various mind-blowing audio tricks. While a sample is essentially a photograph of a sound, Acxelized sounds are substantially variable in real time. Consider a sampled note with vibrato: transposing the sample up an octave will double the vibrato rate; with an Acxelized version of that sample, you can play multiple notes anywhere across the frequency spectrum and each note will feature vibrato at the same rate. You can also morph between sounds, smoothly transitioning, for example, from the sound of a barking dog to that of a talking child. It also allows you to apply formants taken from spoken words onto other sounds.

The Acxel, however, suffers from a few bugs and imperfections. Complex waveforms such as a snare hit often lead to problems with attack transients. In addition, the Acxel's audio is sometimes of low fidelity compared to equivalent samples.

Technos manufactured and sold thirty-nine Acxel Resynthesizers and had enough parts to build fifteen more when they went bankrupt in 1992. As you might expect, it was a high-ticket item. While a four-voice Starter-Stage playback-only system went for $11,995, an Acxel 32 Master system cost $57,995.

Hybrid Modular

Patching a traditional modular synthesizer can stimulate your creativity. However, retracing specific patch points when dozens of cables are involved can boggle the mind, and reproducing the patch after you've removed or repatched cables is close to impossible. Another challenge involves the patch cords: having enough of them and keeping them perfectly functional, on hand, untangled, of adequate length, and prepared for a patching session.

In 1997 Hans Nordelius and his Swedish team at Clavia introduced an exceptional synthesizer that uniquely addressed these issues. The Nord Modular combines hardware with a software editor to digitally transform the modular synthesizer concept. The hardware portion consists of either a two-octave velocity-sensing keyboard or a tabletop/rackmountable module, both of which provide eighteen user-assignable knobs and four independent voice channels or "slots." Four DSP sound engines power the Nord Modu-

Introduced in 1997, Clavia's Nord Modular combines a hardware synth, which can function stand-alone, along with cross-platform editor for creating patches from dozens of software modules. It was also available as a tabletop unit minus the keyboard, or as the small, single-channel Nord Micro Modular. (Image courtesy of Clavia DMI AB)

lar, but you could increase DSP power via an optional expansion board. A single-channel tabletop module, the Nord Micro Modular, came out in 1998, providing a single DSP and up to four notes of polyphony, depending on patch complexity.

The Nord Modular's editor software allows you to configure your own synthesizers on a Macintosh or Windows computer—complete with a bevy of module types and virtual cables for conducting audio, control, logic, and slave signals among modules—and then download them to the hardware unit via MIDI. As long as you don't need to add new modules or reconfigure cable routings, the synth doesn't require a computer and can function as a stand-alone instrument. Among the available modules are multiple types of oscillators, envelope generators, filters, EQs, LFOs, step sequencers, waveshapers, audio and logic processors, control modifiers, and mixers. You can design complex patches without hitting the DSP ceiling, the supply of patch cords is essentially endless, and available synthesis types include subtractive, additive, FM, AM, and ring modulation.

Possibilities for sonic experimentation abound with the Nord Modular, as do educational applications. One potential downside, however, is compatibility issues with advancing computer operating systems. Since Clavia replaced the original Nord Modular line with the Nord Modular G2 in 2003, they stopped developing the editor at Windows 95/98/NT and Mac OS 9—although you'll find an unsupported public beta version for Mac OS X on the Clavia website. As for the G2 version, Clavia added many new modules—including many for effects processing—and greatly improved the keyboard version's user interface with digital encoder knobs encircled by LEDs, a keyboard that senses aftertouch as well as velocity, and the same pitchstick and mod wheel found on Clavia's first synthesizer, the Nord Lead. Unfortunately, the G2 went out of production in 2009 and there's no indication Clavia will resurrect the Nord Modular line.

Early Electronic Music Applications from Max Mathews

The use of computers for creating electronic music goes back to the 1950s, when Max Mathews (1926–2011)—the father of computer music—first developed Music I, a program capable of producing only a triangle waveform and providing scant parameters for the frequency, amplitude, and duration of individual notes. Using Music I, Mathews programmed a seventeen-second composition in 1957 for an IBM 704 vacuum-tube computer at IBM's headquarters in New York City, recorded the results on digital magnetic tape that he took to Bell Labs in Marray Hill, New Jersey, to output the computer-generated audio through a twelve-bit vacuum-tube DAC before he could hear the music.

By 1958 Bell Labs had purchased a second-generation IBM 7094 computer, allowing Mathews to refine his software and create Music II, a considerably more powerful program capable of a variety of signal-processing functions. Throughout the 1960s, Mathews gradually improved the software through successive versions to Music V, which provided unit generators consisting of virtual oscillators, filters, envelope generators, and other building blocks of sound to generate various types of synthesis, including additive, subtractive, and FM. Users could develop and add new blocks, provided they had the programming chops.

While some programmers have used Music V to develop softsynths (and it has served as a model for other music applications), it requires users to input lines of code ranging from assembly-language subroutines to higher level programming of instrument definitions and complete compositions. Beginning in 1967, Mathews and F. Richard Moore first addressed real-time computer synthesis with GROOVE (Generating Realtime Operations On Voltage-controlled Equipment), a hybrid of computer and voltage-controlled analog modules intended for live performance. GROOVE could generate sounds immediately and allowed the composer to work with and shape them interactively, rather than waiting for a huge mainframe to process the source code, generate and route data through DACs, and record the results onto magnetic tape.

Barry Vercoe's Long-Lived Synthesis and Processing Software

About the same time that affordable PCs began appearing in the early '80s, Barry Vercoe was developing Csound at the MIT Media Lab. Finished in 1985, Csound is a virtual synthesizer and signal-processing application based on Max Mathews' Music V, but it originally ran only on PCs. By the mid-'90s, PC CPUs and soundcards got fast enough to generate digital audio in real time. If a particular computer ran too slow for real-time auditions, Csound could render the music as an audio file on hard disk. Csound has been ported to many platforms, including Macintosh and Windows machines. Not only can you download Csound for free, but graphical editors are available so users aren't forced to work in a source-code environment—although those familiar with the C programming language can get much more out of Csound. As of early 2012, you can get a version of Csound called csGrain for the Apple iPad, thanks to Boulanger Labs (www.boulangerlabs.com).

Personal Computer with a Built-In Synth Chip

During the early 1980s, microcomputer owners who could afford $1,000 or more typically invested in an IBM-PC or Apple II. Serious but less lofty users who were developing their machine-language programming chops often opted for something like a KIM-1 (Keyboard Input Monitor), a single-board 6502 micro with a user interface comprising a tiny multidigit LED display and a calculator keypad. In those days, programmers considered 2,000 bytes of memory huge.

Thanks to its affordability and built-in SID synthesis chip, the Commodore 64 allowed scads of musicians to enter the computer-music arena. In celebration of MIDI's thirtieth anniversary at the January 2013 NAMM show, the MIDI Manufacturers Association displayed this Commodore 64 with its CRT monitor communicating via MIDI with an Apple iPad running Moog Music's Animoog softsynth. (Mark Vail)

Then in 1982, Commodore Business Machines shook the PC industry by releasing the Commodore 64. For $600 retail, the C64 provided programmable color graphics and a whopping 64K of RAM. What grabbed musicians' interest was the C64's built-in 6581 Sound Interface Device (SID), which boasted three oscillators, three **ADSR** envelope generators, a resonant 12dB/octave multimode filter, ring modulation, oscillator sync, and four LFOs on a twenty-eight-pin chip. Designed for Commodore by Bob Yannes, who later cofounded Ensoniq, the SID was capable of generating some dazzling, albeit grungy, timbres suitable for wicked leads, punchy bass, and wild sound effects.

> *ADSR:* attack, decay, sustain, release, one of the most familiar types of envelope generators

Numerous companies—including Moog Music, Passport Designs, and Dr. T's Music Software—created MIDI software and interfaces for the C64. As late as 1999, the Swedish company Elektron ESI AB introduced the SidStation, a MIDI synth module with a lone SID inside. As of late 2013, you can still find SID chips for sale.

Graphically Programmable Computer Music Language

One of the most interesting and potent computer-music applications is Max, the graphic programming environment Miller Puckette originally developed from 1980 to 1990 under the name Patcher at IRCAM (Institut de Recherche et Coordination Acoustique/Musique) in Paris, France. Intended as an interactive MIDI application for live electronic music, it was in use at IRCAM for four years before its commercial release, received considerable enhancements by David Zicarelli, was renamed in honor of Max Mathews, and went on the market in 1990 from Opcode Systems.

In 1999, Zicarelli founded Cycling '74 and took over distribution of and support for Max. David also developed a new version of the program—Max/MSP—which includes digital audio processing and generation utilities. Likewise, while IRCAM's Joseph Francis, Paul Foley, and François Déchelle developed an audio-and-MIDI version of the original Max application called Jmax, Puckette relocated to the University of California at San Diego and implemented more of his own ideas into the program Pd, which stands for Pure Data. Programmers later developed interactive video and three-dimensional multimedia extensions for all three applications.

"Obsolete" and Ever-Evolving Sonic Software

Audio-editing applications for personal computers—Apple's Macintosh in particular—have immensely extended the sonic-generating capabilities of sound designers and synthesists. Two of the best merit mention here.

Several years before Digidesign introduced Pro Tools—the computer-based recording system that eventually became an industry standard—the Digi programmer Mark Jeffery developed Turbosynth in 1988. Functioning somewhat like a software-realm modular

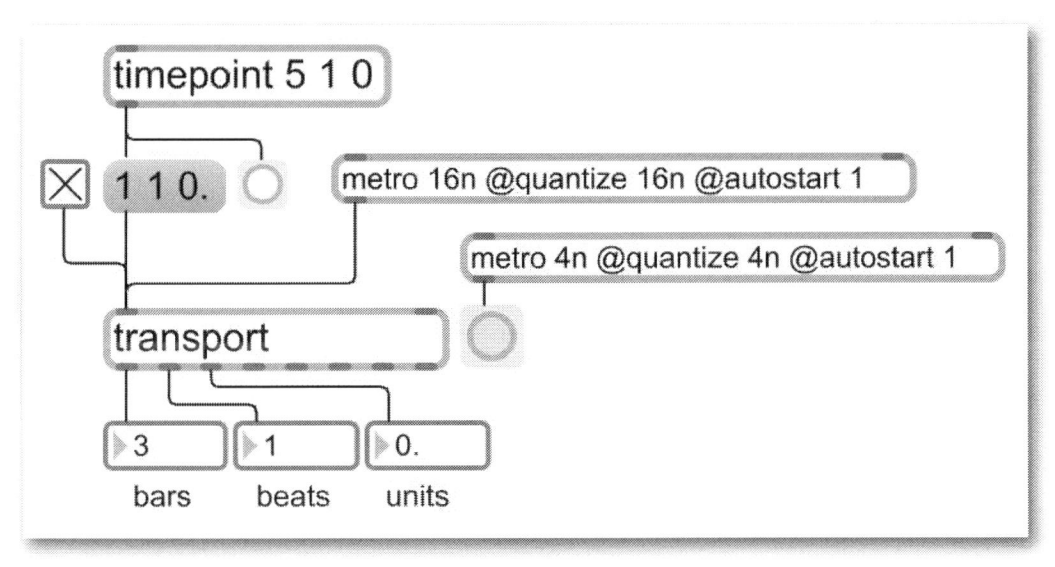

Cycling '74 programmer Darwin Grosse created this Max/MSP version 5 patch, which allows you to load an audio file and select a portion of it. "The selected area is broken up into rows by the 2d.wave~ object, creating a two-dimensional grid of samples," says Darwin. "Playback is accomplished using two triangle-wave scanners that move through the x and y axes of this grid, morphing between samples and rows and creating a complex waveform. The output is also modified by two short delay lines, providing a psychoacoustic panning effect. The result is an ever-changing, ever-moving drone influenced by the sample file, file selection area, and scanner settings." (Max 5 patch by Darwin Grosse, courtesy of Cycling '74)

synthesizer, Turbosynth delivered synthesis and processing tools for concocting special sounds to be downloaded into a sampler for playback. Graphic boxes that you dragged around in its patch window and connected like components in a modular synthesizer represented many of Turbosynth's functions. Among its tools were oscillators with preset waveforms that you could stretch and deform, or you could draw your own; a 6dB-per-octave, nonresonant lowpass filter; a modulator for frequency, amplitude, and pitch modulation; a spectral inverter that would analyze incoming audio and flip low frequencies to high and vice versa; digital delay for echo effects; a resonator module that functioned somewhat like a parametric EQ; a waveshaper for mangling and warping a sound's harmonic content; a stretching algorithm that represented an early form of **granular synthesis**; onboard **normalization** for keeping amplitude at a good level from one module to the next; and some rudimentary looping functions. The more RAM in your computer, the more modules you could use in a patch, which you could save for later editing and processing.

> *granular synthesis:* the generation of sounds from brief bits or particles of audio, typically ranging from 5ms to 100ms in length, strung together for playback to create timbres; reordering the bits or altering their amplitude, duration, or pitch characteristics can considerably alter the resulting timbre
>
> *normalization:* a digital-audio-editing process that can increase amplitude levels without inducing distortion from clipping or overdriving audio circuitry

The Synthesizer

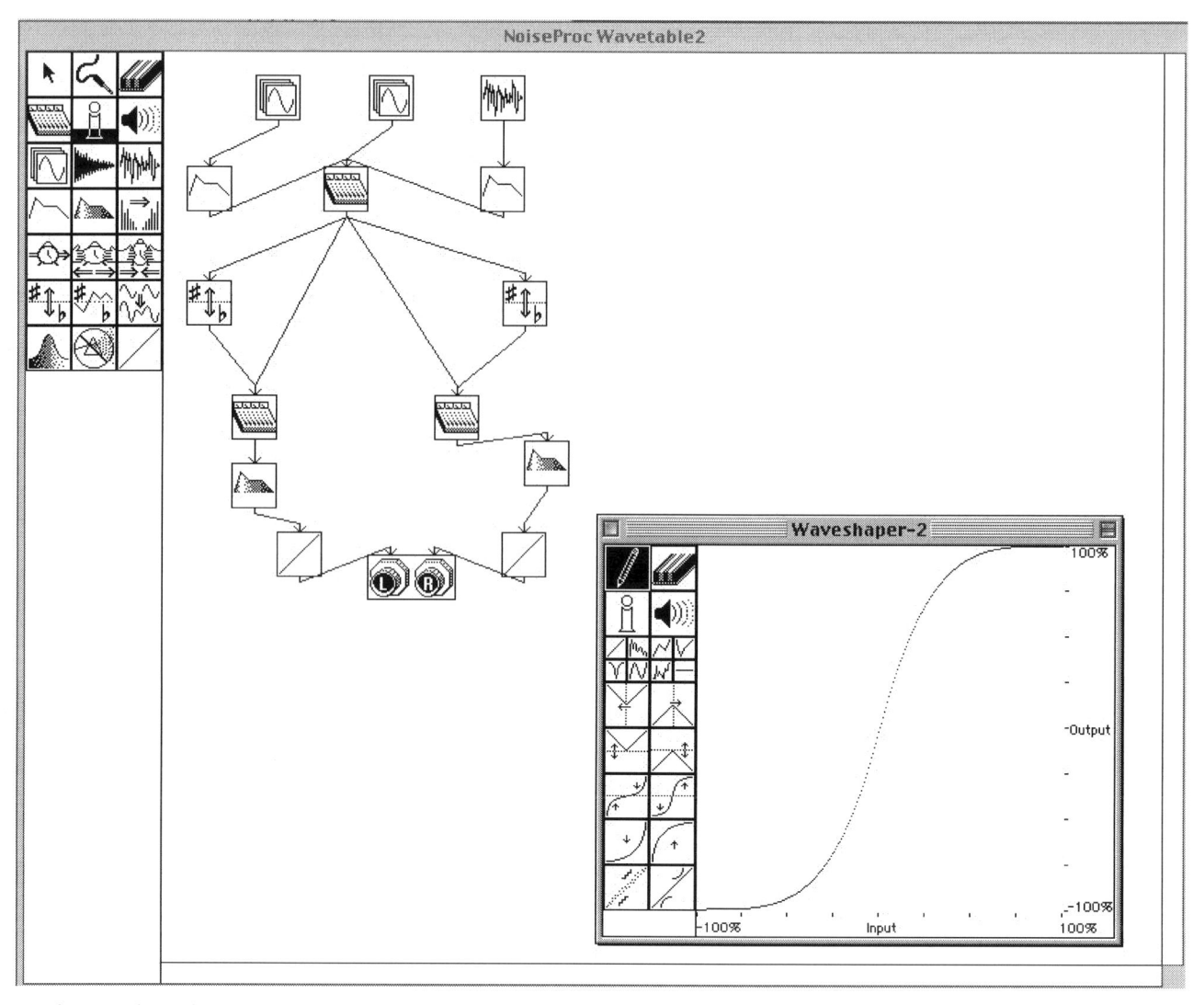

Digidesign Turbosynth provided a wealth of audio-editing and audio-processing tools, as divulged by the matrix of symbolic icons to the *uppermost left* in this screenshot. In this patch, which Drew Neumann programmed to "pluck off fractally generated chunks of white noise and sweep and smear between two different wavetables," he mixed two samples and white noise ("to provide some attack")—two with ADSR-controlled attenuation—and routed the mixed signal through pitch-shifters, filters, and a nonlinear wave transform, which Drew says "tends to boost the bass frequencies while increasing distortion in a pleasant way." Processing functions provided by the Waveshaper included compression, soft-clipping, frequency-dependent, and user-drawn curves. (Drew Neumann, Droomusic)

Composer/synthesist Drew Neumann is so fond of Turbosynth that he keeps an outdated Mac G4 running OS 9 to operate the discontinued application. He calls Turbosynth "an extraordinarily flexible modular environment that allows you to develop 16-bit sampled sounds in Sound Designer and AIFF formats." Drew is particularly fond of its Convert to Oscillator function, which allows you to start with a sampled sound, select a pitch, and the software will resynthesize the sample into an oscillator wavetable that you can squash, stretch, delete bits, and edit further. For MTV's animated *Aeon Flux* series, he altered wimpy recordings of 9mm semi-automatic gunshots using Turbosynth's waveshaper saturation process to create extremely percussive and massive blasts.

Neumann is also a big fan of another sound-creation and -editing environment that appeared ten years after Turbosynth. Beginning in 1998, the visionary Eric Wenger of U&I Software applied unique graphical concepts to create MetaSynth for the Macintosh.

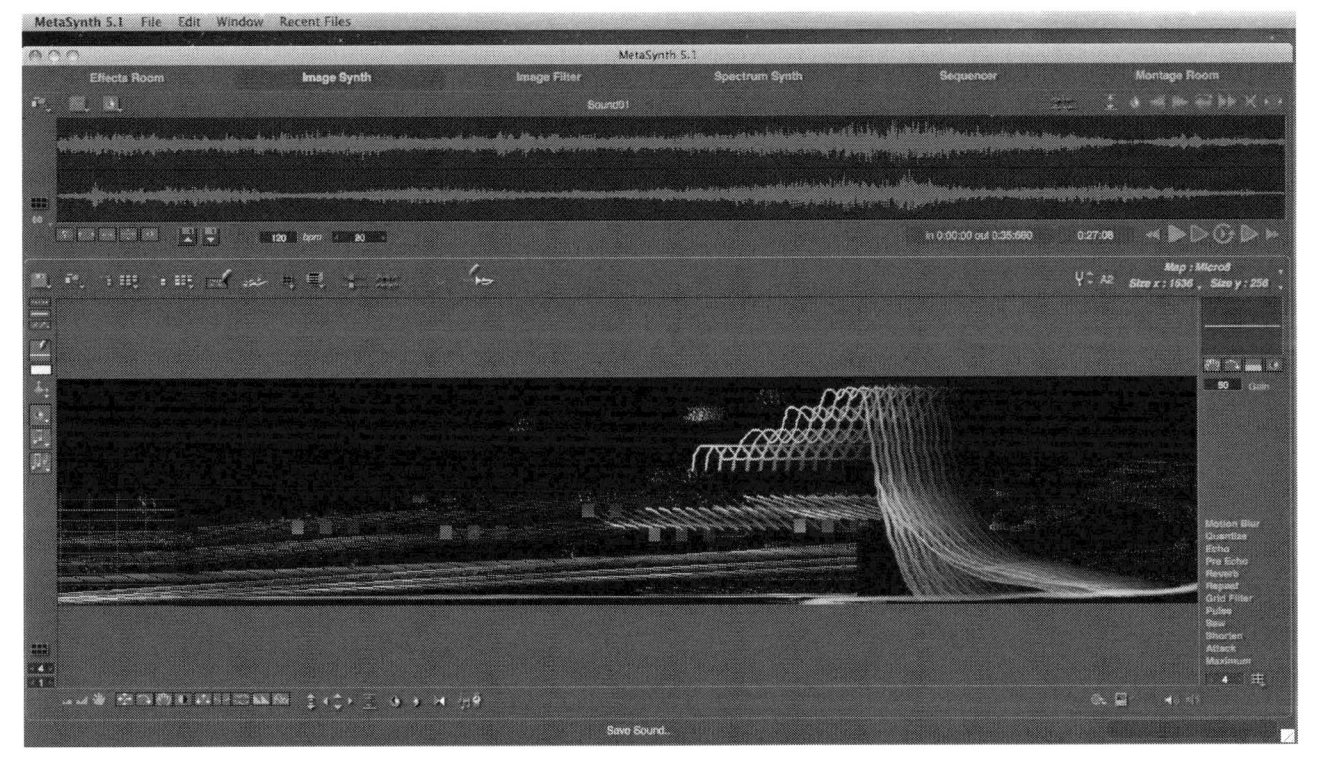

Within the Image Synth page of U&I Software's MetaSynth 5.1, Drew Neumann demonstrates an attempt to simulate sections of Louis and Bebe Barron's soundtrack for *Forbidden Planet*. He used tuning tables to create an eight-tone microtonal scale that doesn't allow notes to resolve into specific, recognizable pitches. Drew also created multiple layers including an underlying, writhing tone that build to an apex before cascading downward and added pre- and post-echo events to enhance the spooky aural sequence. (Drew Neumann, Droomusic)

It provides a variety of windows—called "rooms"—in which you can render and edit exotic, frightening, astonishing, outlandish, rhythmic, and abstract timbres; work in a wide range of temperaments; define spatial location by color choices and determine volume with pixel brightness; impose dynamic filters of all sorts onto existing timbres; work with spectral granular sequencing; process sounds with envelope-controlled DSP effects; compose melodies, phrases, and loops; and mix up to twenty-four separate audio tracks.

Sound design with MetaSynth is practically addictive in a wonderful way, which is a good thing because learning to get specific results doesn't come easily. But even unexpected concoctions can be amazing and useful. According to Neumann, compared to Turbosynth, "Metasynth is a little more intuitive. You can do a lot of what Turbosynth did in MetaSynth, but the approach is very different." To hear audio files Drew Neumann created with Turbosynth and MetaSynth, direct your Web browser to **www.oup.com/us/thesynthesizer** (OUP *The Synthesizer* **website**).

Premier Softsynths for Discriminating Enthusiasts

When did pro-level softsynths that you could play in real time via MIDI finally appear? In January 1997, when Propellerhead Software introduced ReBirth and Seer Systems released Reality. They were very different applications.

Reality ran within Windows 95, required an audio card, and was a highly programmable, sixteen-channel multitimbral application that could do subtractive and additive synthesis, sample playback, **four-op FM**, and physical modeling with models of plucked, struck, and sustained acoustic instruments. Every Reality patch provided multimode filters, four LFOs, and four loopable envelope generators. Although Seer Systems—founded by Stanley Jungleib with synth pioneer Dave Smith serving as president—stopped doing business in 2003, Smith founded Dave Smith Instruments later that year to make hardware synths again.

> *four-op FM:* linear frequency-modulation synthesis based on four operators, any of which can serve as a carrier or modulator; four-op FM is less flexible than the Yamaha DX7's six-op FM

Based in Stockholm, Sweden, Propellerhead Software initially put its name on the map in 1994 with ReCycle, a cross-platform utility for dividing samples of rhythmic loops into individual slices that could then be triggered via MIDI or a sequencer, allowing the loop's playback tempo to be varied without affecting the pitch of each slice. For their second product, Propellerhead founders Ernst Nathorst-Böös, Marcus Zetterquist, and Peter Jubel developed a different cross-platform application that allowed users to create computer music with softsynths that emulated vintage hardware instruments from Roland. ReBirth RB-338 modeled simulations of the TR-808 and TR-909 drum machines and the TB-303 Bass Line synth. When the company discovered users were surreptitiously customizing ReBirth's appearance and sound with software alterations called "Mods," instead of suing them Propellerhead embraced and encouraged the practice, thus making ReBirth even more popular. By the time Propellerhead discontinued ReBirth in 2005—before reintroducing it again in 2010 for Apple's iPhone and iPad—they already had a far more potent replacement in the form of Reason.

Reason developed to provide exceptional, superb-sounding, and flexible virtual music-making tools including modeled analog, graintable (a combination of granular and wavetable synthesis), and "polysonic" (multiple types of synthesis) synthesizers, flexible sample and loop players, a sample-triggering drum machine, audio and control-signal mixers and splitters, an analog-style step sequencer, an arpeggiator, and excellent and wide-ranging effects processors—all in a compositional environment consisting of a virtual rack of gear and a player piano-style linear sequencer that allows intricate manual and automated editing. Included with Reason are loads of patches, samples, and loops; Propellerhead and third-party sources sell tons more for expanding your compositional landscape. Reason's back-panel patchability for both audio and control signals seriously escalates its fun and flexibility.

> *DAW:* digital audio workstation
> *ReWire:* a software protocol developed by Propellerhead and Steinberg that allows direct interaction, audio exchange, and synchronization among different music applications, with one main program hosting client programs

Shown in this screenshot of a Propellerhead Reason 5 file are Rack (*left*) and Sequencer windows for the same song, "EQed Jan Hammer short.rns." Included at the *bottom* of each window (*left to right*) are meters for audio input and output levels and DSP and computer calculation activity, metronome settings, a tap button for tempo entry, playback marker location by measure and time above the current tempo and time signature settings, transport controls, and the measure locations of the L and R markers along with the loop-engage button. In the Rack (*top to bottom*) are the lower portion of a BV512 Vocoder switched to 16-band Equalizer mode, a Kong Drum Designer, and the upper portion of a Thor Polysonic Synthesizer. Control lanes for BV512 parameters mostly fill Reason's Sequencer window to the *right*, plus two note lanes for a Subtractor analog-style polyphonic synth. (Courtesy of Propellerhead Software AB)

Since Propellerhead introduced Reason in 2000, many users pleaded for audio recording capabilities similar to those offered by **DAW** software from other companies. Instead of immediately adding recording capabilities to Reason, Propellerhead developed a stand-alone yet complimentary application called Record, within which Reason could run via **ReWire**. By the end of 2011, Propellerhead had folded the two applications together as Reason 6, which included new functions like pitch-correction, physical modeling, and user sampling. Unleashed during the summer of 2012, Reason 6.5 added the ability to use virtual plug-in devices separately available from Propellerhead and other companies. In April 2013 came Reason 7, which for the first time allows MIDI output for mixing sounds from external hardware synths with Reason-generated material and controlling other MIDI-based products. As with previous updates, Reason 7 also includes new modules and functionality such as ReCycle-style sample-division capabilities, further extending its music-making powers. I've taught Reason to students ranging in age from ten to eighteen since 2002, finding it incredibly useful for classes that otherwise would require loads of hardware, cables and other accessories, storage space, and maintenance.

DIY Softsynth Apps and Their Potent Offspring

The year 1997 also witnessed the initial product from the German company Native Instruments (NI), which engineer Stephan Schmitt founded the previous year. With

The Synthesizer

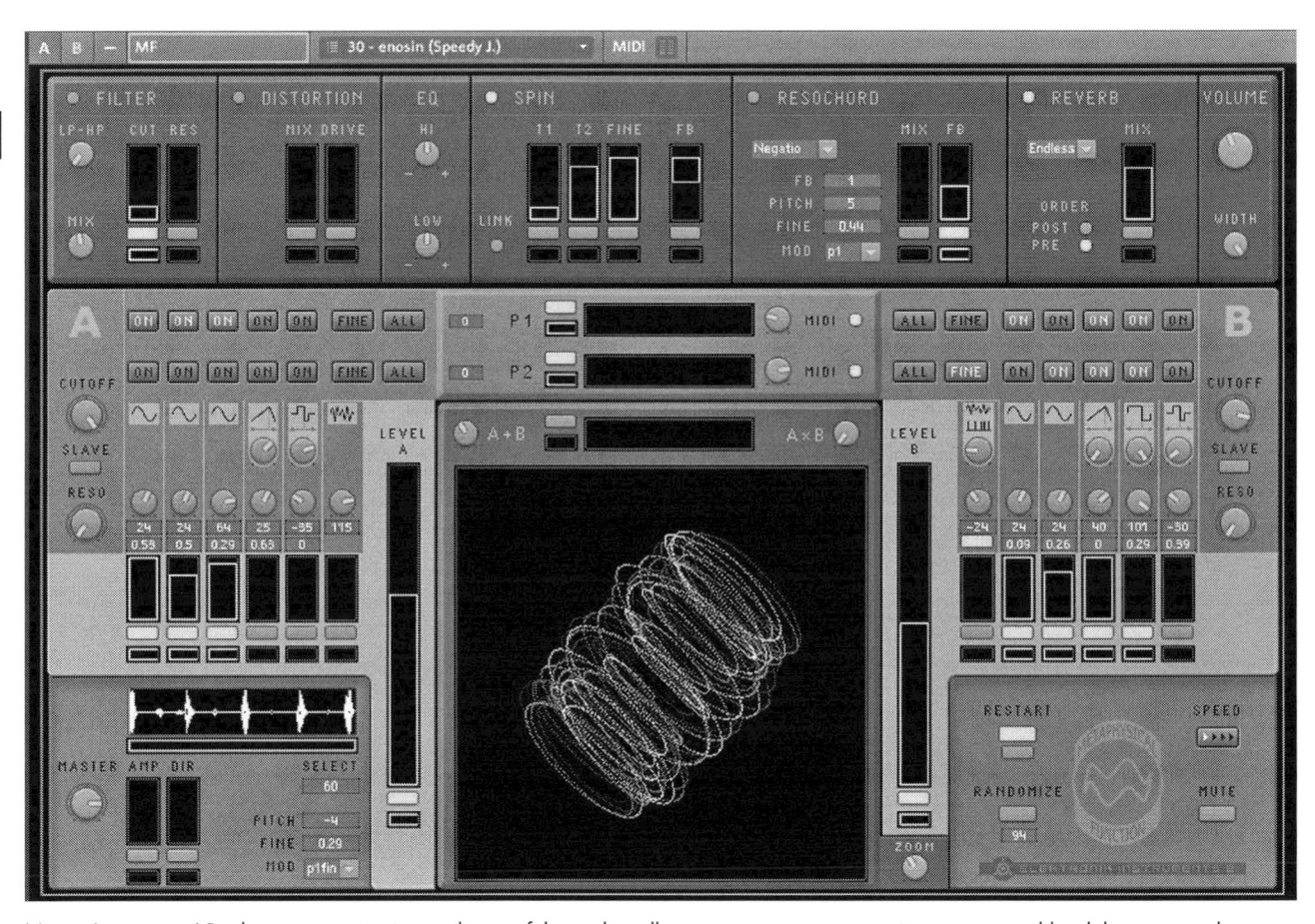

Native Instruments' Reaktor is a captivating and powerful app that allows you to create custom instruments and load those created and distributed by others. This is Hannes Strobl's "exx," a fascinating drone ensemble. With "exx"—part of the Metaphysical Function collection in Komplete 7 Elements—and other Reaktor ensembles and instruments, you can map MIDI controllers to parameters of your choice and extensively guide the sound that's produced. (Courtesy of Native Instruments GmbH)

programming assistance from Volker Hinz, Schmitt created Generator, a Windows 95 application that simulated a modular analog synthesizer. Users could select individual sound-generating and audio-processing modules from menus and connect them on-screen via virtual patch cords. You could also customize an instrument's user interface by creating controllers and assigning them to specific parameters. Along with subtractive synthesis, Generator could do FM and sample-playback, and it came with a selection of ready-to-play emulations of popular hardware synths.

The cross-platform Reaktor replaced Generator in 1999, providing a complete, complex, and advanced DIY synthesizer toolkit with an open-engine architecture. Reaktor 5, released in 2006, performs totally modular real-time synthesis, sampling, and effects processing; includes over sixty virtual synths, samplers, drum machines, and effects devices with tons of patches for all; and allows custom instrument creation ranging from low-level micro to assisted macro levels based on NI-designed building blocks.

Programmers have used Reaktor to create plenty of virtual stand-alone and plug-in instruments. While many are re-creations of popular vintage instruments including the Hammond B-3, Prophet-5, and DX7, others are original—such as Absynth and Massive, both of which can produce timbres ranging from serene to earth-shattering. Absynth provides a patchable design with simulated analog, FM, and sample-playback synthesis, waveshaping, waveform morphing, four multimode filters and three LFOs per voice, ring modulation, processing of external sound sources, and totally configurable sixty-eight-breakpoint envelopes. While you can relegate Absynth to simple pads and lush, evolving environmental soundscapes, thanks to its extensive envelopes it can also produce wicked rhythmic patterns.

As for Massive, its control panel reminds me of the Minimoog's, but sonically it goes far beyond the Mini with wavetable-scanning oscillators, multimode filters, real-time parameter morphing, and envelope functions like Absynth's. While it's perfectly capable of doing wild loops, Massive got its name due to a proclivity for pounding out beefy basses and striking solo timbres.

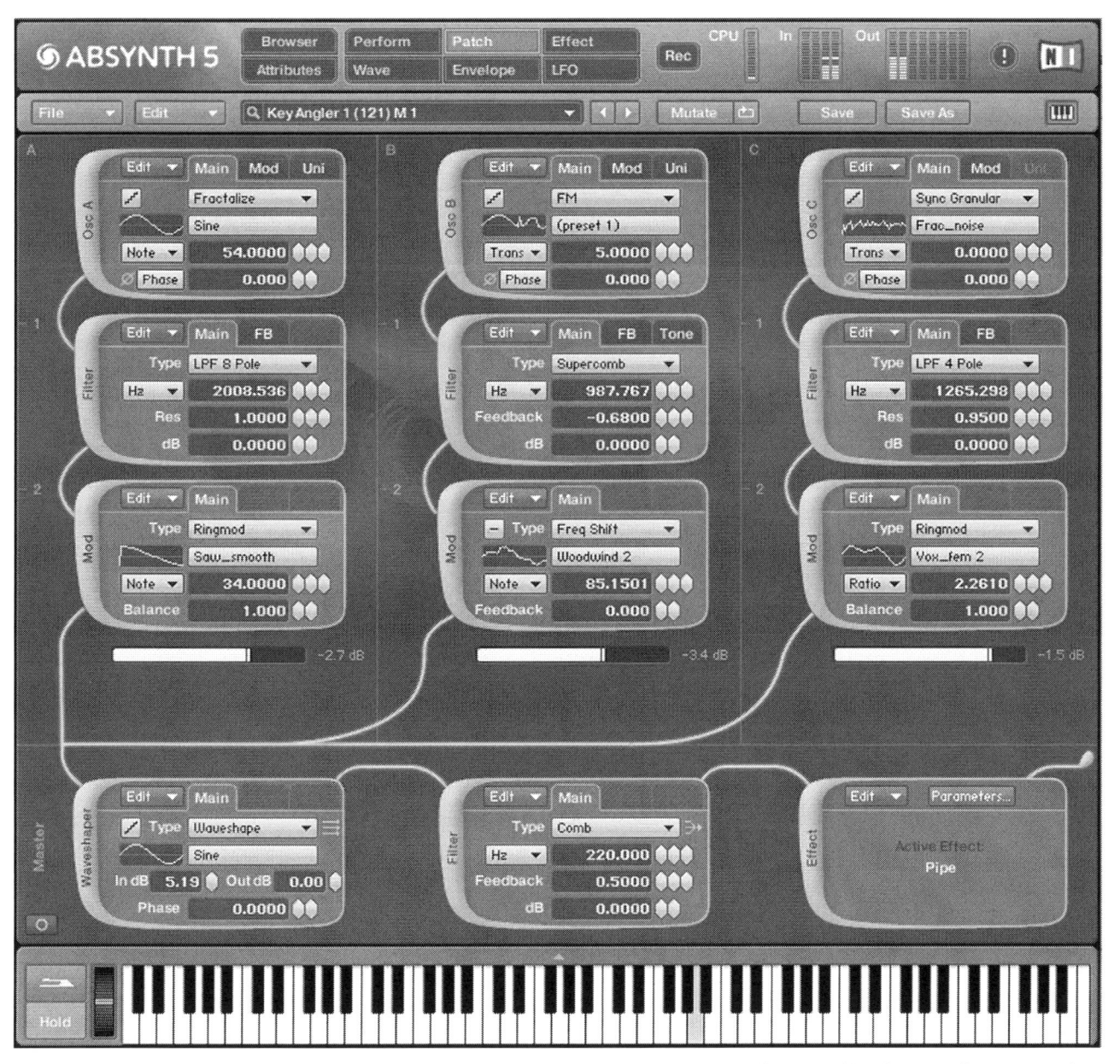

Native Instruments Absynth 5's Patch window provides three voice channels, each with an oscillator capable of seven different types of synthesis or serving as an audio input, a multimode filter, and a multipurpose audio modulator. Although audio routing is fixed within each channel, you can independently disable the filter and modulator in each channel, or disable the entire channel. The mixed channels' outputs continue to the master section, where you can route audio through a waveshaper, ring modulator, or frequency shifter; a multimode filter; and then a delay line or other effects. You can trigger a note from the virtual eight-octave keyboard across the bottom and selectively hold the note by activating the button to the *right*. (Courtesy of Native Instruments GmbH)

The Synthesizer

Given its three oscillators, dual filters, built-in effects, two insert channels, controller possibilities, and other ammenities, Native Instruments' Massive is a flexible and potent softsynth. (Courtesy of Native Instruments GmbH)

Reliable Softsynth Platform for the Road

Software synthesizers have come a long way since their inception, as have personal computers. However, many synthesists avoid using a Mac or PC onstage and in the studio because of reliability issues. There's always a potential for crashes, lock-ups, and other types of failure, especially when you're dealing with a general-purpose, consumer-oriented unit loaded with dozens of nonmusic and utility apps. There's also the issue of ever-evolving operating system updates and resulting plug-in incompatibilities.

The latest in Muse Research's lineup of Receptors as of 2012 is the VIP model, which comes with loads of software—including Native Instruments Komplete 8 and Ivory—pre-installed and already authorized, which makes it ready to roll right out of the box. Although Receptor components change every few years, it maintains about 95 percent compatibility with the plug-ins that run on the original model. (Photo © 2002–2012 Muse R&D Inc.)

Distributed by Peavey Electronics, the Muse Research MuseBox costs considerably less than the top-of-the-line Receptor, making certain plug-ins running on a robust, dedicated system available to a wider range of musicians. (Photo © 2002–2012 Muse R&D Inc.)

Since 2003, Muse Research has addressed those who thirst for the convenience and power offered by virtual synths and effects with an essentially bulletproof, road-worthy machine called the Receptor, a rugged 2U rackmount module that entirely replaces the computer and runs a plethora of **VST plug-ins**.

> *VST plug-ins:* Virtual Studio Technology software developed by Steinberg and licensed to other developers to produce softsynths and effects processors that can be used within most DAW environments

The original Receptor featured a single-core 1.5GHz AMD CPU, 256MB of RAM, and a 40GB hard drive. Muse Research focused on making it compatible with Windows-format VST instruments and effects and developed key relationships with major plug-in developers. For example, they partnered with Native Instruments to offer a model with NI's Komplete bundle pre-installed and authorized so buyers could unpack it and quickly make music. Besides offering Receptors packed similarly with plug-in bundles from IK Multimedia and East/West, Muse Research tweaked the Receptor to support virtual instruments from companies including Synthogy, Applied Acoustics Systems, Spectrasonics, UVI Sounds & Software, XLN Audio, Project SAM, and Big Fish Audio. While Receptor reached its fourth generation in 2012 in the form of the Receptor VIP, Muse Research also teamed with Peavey Electronics to produce the MuseBox, a more affordable tabletop model capable of running select VST plug-ins.

Composition

Not only have synthesizers designed primarily for composition been plentiful, but they've also greatly extended composers' capabilities in terms of both timbre and style. Some came astonishingly early and others introduced wildly unique methods. Among the recurring composition schemes are: algorithmic, based on mathematical processes; sto-

Electro-acoustic music historians acknowledge the instrument Edouard E. Coupleaux and Joseph A. Givelet made during the late 1920s as the first actual synthesizer. (Courtesy of Tom Rhea)

chastic, random-selection procedures; and manually playing notes into a sequencer for subsequent editing.

The First Synthesizer

What some experts consider the first true synthesizer appeared at the end of the 1920s. The Frenchmen Edouard E. Coupleaux (sometimes spelled Coupleux) and Joseph A. Givelet demonstrated their "Automatically Operating Musical Instrument of the Electric Oscillation Type" at the 1929 Paris Exposition. It was the first electronic instrument to allow automated control of pitches produced by four vacuum-tube oscillators, their output amplitude, and filtering of the sound to vary its timbre. The Coupleaux–Givelet incorporated a paper-tape reader with a pneumatic tracker bar like a player piano. Holes punched in specific rows of the tape varied the instrument's parameters, allowing the sequencing and articulation of predetermined notes and control of the overall sound.

Coupleaux and Givelet went on to build and install organs that generated sound from hundreds of vacuum tubes in French churches and radio stations during the 1930s, but their synthesizer apparently disappeared.

Room-Filling Automated Composition Machine

The earliest instrument actually called a synthesizer was developed primarily for composition, and its introduction came with some pretty impetuous claims: "Composers don't

The RCA Mark II synthesizer, ca. 1955. (Courtesy of Tom Rhea)

need to be able to play an instrument because our synthesizer will allow them to create any kind of music they want" and "Musicians aren't required if you have our synthesizer." David Sarnoff, chairman of RCA during the 1950s, and his associates made such claims in press releases about the RCA Synthesizer Mark I, developed and built at RCA's David Sarnoff Laboratories in Princeton, New Jersey.

The nonmusical electronic engineers Harry F. Olson and Herbert Belar began developing the duophonic Mark I during the late 1940s with the intent of making a machine for composing pop music. It took them until 1955 to complete the instrument, which generated sounds using analog circuits under digital control. It was before the arrival of solid-state circuitry, so the developers depended on vacuum tubes. The machine was huge, filling a studio with 19" racks. Since it was modular, operators could route signals as they wished.

Tuning-fork oscillators generated the RCA Synthesizer's tones. Based on the original designs of German physicist Hermann von Helmholtz during the 1860s, the oscillators produced sawtooth waveforms with lots of harmonic content that could be filtered, as with any subtractive-synthesis instrument. In addition, the RCA incorporated a method of control borrowed from the past: punched paper-tape readers. Rolls of about 15" wide punched paper contained as many as thirty-six columns of binary code, with a group of four columns designated to each parameter. Two mechanically synchronized paper-tape readers controlled a series of relays, or electro-mechanical switches, to produce two independent parts. Composers input and edited control data using keyboards similar to a typewriter, except they—like everything else in the system—were manufactured from scratch and the key arrangement bore no resemblance to your computer's familiar QWERTY keyboard.

A dual-platform turntable lathe, mechanically synchronized to the tape readers, captured Mark I recordings on a 16″ disc. One disc could contain six three-minute tracks, typically different parts of the same song. Composers could then combine the individual tracks using a six-stylus pickup arm on the upper platform to route signals through a mixer, which allowed volume control of the separate parts to the lower platform lathe to cut a mixdown track. Subsequent passes allowed multiple overdubs using the same process.

RCA's engineers designed the Mark II with the intent of mass-producing them for universities. Numerous composers tried to influence Olson and Belar in the design of the Mark II, which inhabited the Columbia-Princeton Electronic Music Center in 1959. Among them were Vladimir Ussachevsky and Otto Luening, but it was Milton Babbitt (1916–2011) who most prominently worked with the Mark II. At the time he specialized in composing complex and demanding scores, and he discovered the paper-tape control afforded possibilities that would have been extremely difficult, if not impossible, to accomplish using other methods available at the time.

Besides having twice as many voice channels as the Mark I, the quadraphonic Mark II provided access to multiple variable-frequency oscillators to augment the twelve mas-

Composer Milton Babbitt sits at an input station for the RCA Mark II Synthesizer sometime during the late 1960s. Babbitt passed away at ninety-four years of age on January 29, 2011. (Courtesy of Milton Babbitt)

ter tuning-fork oscillators, as well as a white-noise generator, highpass and lowpass filters with variable resonance, a bank of resonators, programmable glissando between notes, and much more. It also featured a disc-cutting lathe and playback turntable so that sequences could be captured and combined with others onto subsequent discs. Babbitt eventually convinced RCA to install several three-track Ampex tape recorders, a great improvement over the lathe and turntable.

During the 1960s, the Mark II was retrofitted with an optical scanner that could read continuous lines drawn with a felt-tip pen so that composers could manually input control data instead of using the paper-tape readers. In addition, the Mark II had an input for a microphone and other audio sources, allowing external sounds to be processed within the system.

Photo-Optic Instrument from Russia

Loads of creative technologies were developed inside the Soviet Union of which people outside the Iron Curtain were unaware. One example was a synthesizer called the ANS in honor of the Russian composer/pianist Alexander Nikolayevich Scriabin (1872–1915). The inventor Eugeniy Murzin (1914–70) secretly designed the ANS beginning in 1938 and finally assembled a team to build it in 1958. The only existing ANS resides at M.V. Lomonosov's Moscow State University under the care of composer Stanislav Kreychi (sometimes spelled Kreitchi), who joined Murzin's team and began working with the ANS in 1961.

The ANS is a photo-electronic additive synthesizer that generates sound from a bank of sine waves existing as rings of concentric optic phonograms on glass discs. There are five discs in the ANS's photo-optic generator, each containing 144 phonograms. The discs rotate at different speeds and produce 720 sine waves.

A piano-roll-like interface—the "coding field"—allows the composer to select which sine waves sound in any combination. An opaque, non-drying black mastic covers the coding field's glass plate. Scraping off parts of the mastic allows light from an optic phonogram—the sound track—to penetrate into the reading device, a narrow aperture containing multiple photo-electric cells. When the score moves past the reading device, the aperture detects the length of the scraped-off part of the mastic and controls the duration of the sound. The coding field, or score, has a pitch scale like a piano keyboard and a duration scale designated in measures. However, unlike a piano, instead of being limited to twelve-notes-per-octave equal-temperament, the ANS is microtonal, capable of sounding intervals as small as one-sixth of a semitone.

The score functions much like a sequencer and, although it's possible to code the envelope of every sound on the score, the ANS includes an additional electronic ADSR envelope for playing the whole vertical scale of the score like a bell or gong. Drawing freehand graphic structures on the ANS's score can result in fantastic timbres. While it's possible to code a number of different timbres simultaneously, recording different parts on separate tracks of a multitrack recorder and synchronizing them in that environment results in more interesting music. You can view numerous ANS photos, see a video of Kreychi working on and performing with the instrument in 2011, and sharpen your Russian-language skills at http://snowman-john.livejournal.com/23137.html.

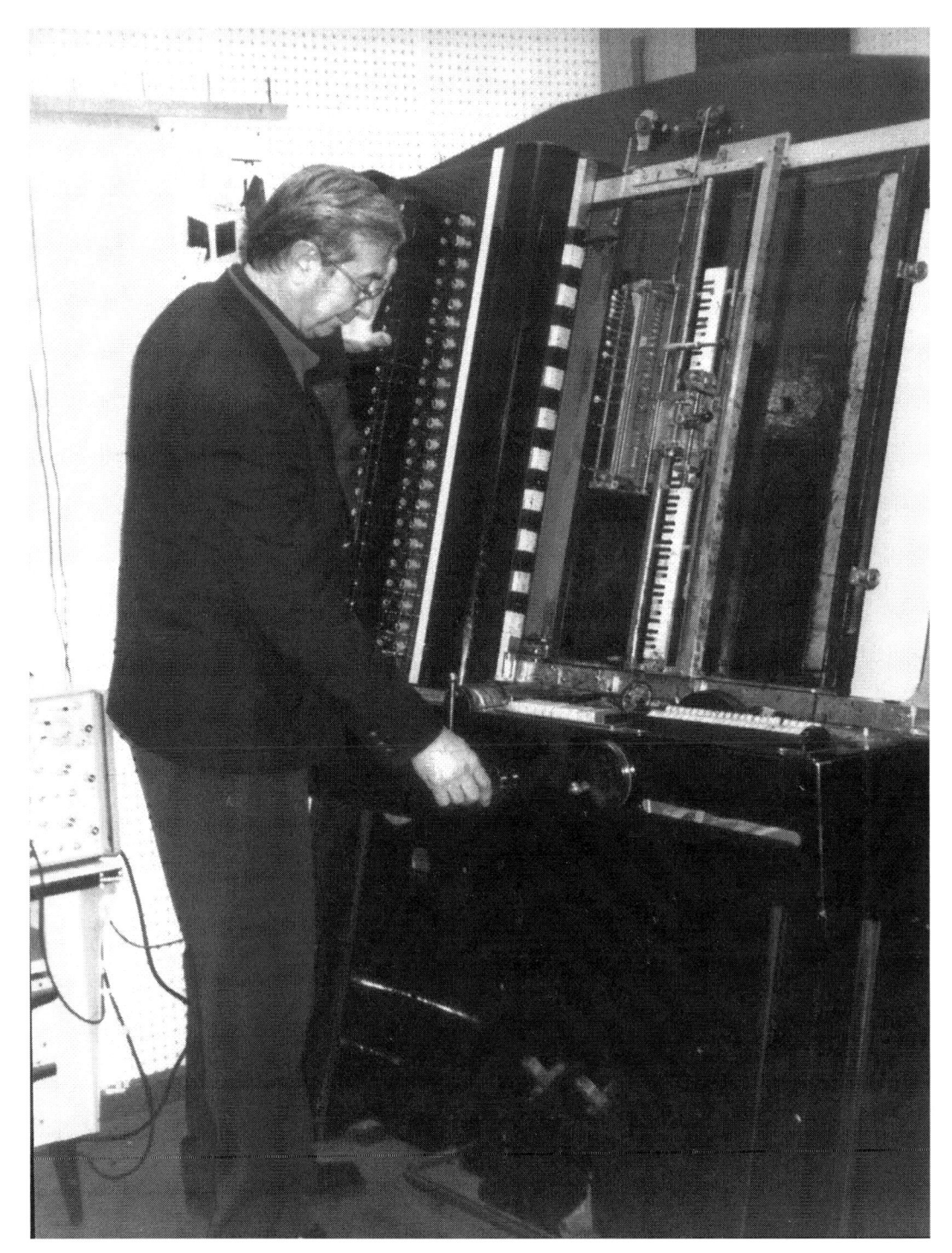

Composer/curator Stanislav Kreychi works with Eugeniy Murzin's one-of-a-kind ANS synthesizer in 2002. (Julia Murzin, courtesy of Stanislav Kreychi)

Instantaneous Composing/Performance Machine

Few in the music industry could boast of more extensive credentials than Raymond Scott (1908–94), whose given name was Harry Warnow. At the peak of the Big Band era in the 1930s, he began his professional career as the leader of the Raymond Scott Quintet, playing radio dates and recording for films and albums in New York City and Los

Raymond Scott poses with some of his magical music-making tools in his Manhattan Research studio in 1955. (Courtesy of Tom Rhea)

Angeles. In 1939 he formed an orchestra that toured extensively until the mid-'40s. Scott then started writing commercial jingles for a wide range of consumer products, such as Sprite, Bufferin, Auto-Lite, and Hostess Twinkies. Throughout most of the '50s he was the conductor for NBC's *Hit Parade* radio and TV shows. In 1966 and '67 he composed all-electronic filmscores in collaboration with the Muppeteer Jim Henson for IBM, Montreal's Expo 67, and a special TV presentation called *Limbo: The Organized Mind*.

Meanwhile, in the electronics workshop at his Manhattan Research Inc. facilities, Scott developed some of the earliest multitrack tape recorders along with a variety of musical instruments. One of these was a multitimbral, automatic composition machine called the Electronium—the Instantaneous Composing/Performance Machine—based on relay switches designed for telephone companies. Begun in 1959 and completed in May 1970, it had a control panel covered with switches and buttons, an internal electro-mechanical drum memory, and sequencing functions. It worked much like artificial intelligence processes developed much later for computers and functioned as a user-controlled stochastic music generator capable of pumping out rhythms and melodies with multiple sonorities in many different styles.

Hybrid Music Workstation that Arrived too Late

The designer/composer/engineer/visionary David McLey (1947–2010) imagined quite a music system during the late 1970s. After hot-wiring modules in his ARP 2500 for computer control, he envisioned a computerized workstation for composing and recording in his Toronto-based Nimbus 9 studio as well as for use in live performance. Funded by the Canadian entrepreneurial team Hazelcom Industries, McLey and his associates

Knobs and switches were used to program Raymond Scott's Electronium, shown here in 1965. In his "Electronic Perspectives" column in the February 1981 issue of *Contemporary Keyboard*, synth historian Tom Rhea quoted Scott as saying, "The Electronium is not played; it is guided." (Courtesy of Tom Rhea)

developed the McLeyvier, a machine that combined fifteen analog-synth voice cards, 128-voice polyphony, built-in voice editing, patching, mixing, and music notation—all under the control of a computer running a proprietary integrated operating system. Thanks to a voltage meter installed on each voice card, the master computer auto-tuned and calibrated the analog components.

According to electronic-music composer Laurie Spiegel, who joined the McLeyvier development team in 1982, each voice card was loaded with fifty or more DACs and a multitude of computer-control relays. In total, the McLeyvier had about 800 DACs connected to a DEC PDP11/23 that had 512K of memory, a pair of 5MB hard drives, a floppy drive for backup, and a Hewlett-Packard plotter for scoring. The khaki-colored McLeyvier weighed about three hundred pounds.

Regrettably, the emergence of digital signal generation and sampling had squelched analog's popularity, and Hazelcom produced only eight McLeyviers before shutting down the project in 1983. By then the McLeyvier team had developed a digital synthesis board,

One of the eight Hazelcom McLeyviers ever made. (Mark Vail, courtesy of the Audities Foundation)

which proved to be such an excellent multiprocessor that Hazelcom decided they could make more money selling it as a parallel-processing computer for hundreds of thousands of dollars rather than as the basis for a high-end computer-music instrument for $40,000 at the most.

Gigabuck Digital Audio System

In the beginning, the makers of the New England Digital Synclavier conceived of it as a computer-controlled Moog Modular synthesizer. The seeds for the Synclavier were originally sown at Dartmouth College in 1971, when the composer Jon Appleton met with Sydney Alonso at Darmouth's School of Engineering with the goal of developing an electronic instrument for real-time performance. Alonso wasn't crazy about Appleton's computerized-Moog plan and thought it would be easier to build a mini-computer-addressed digital oscillator bank for instant sound creation. At the time it took hours for a large mainframe to generate audio from computer code.

After the programmer Cameron Jones joined the team, he and Alonso founded New England Digital (NED). Instead of becoming a partner, Appleton signed on as a consultant and arranged with Alonso and Jones to always have the newest Synclavier.

In 1975, NED introduced the Synclavier I, a sixteen-channel synthesizer with a thirty-two-track digital sequencer and a list price of $13,000. The Synclavier II appeared in 1980 and cost considerably more: $35,000 to $70,000. By the time the third generation—generally recognized as *the* Synclavier, the high-end DAW capable of synthesis, sampling, hard-disk recording, sequencing, synchronization, and music notation—rolled out in 1985, the price of a well-endowed Synclavier system had ballooned exponentially. Frank

The Synthesizer

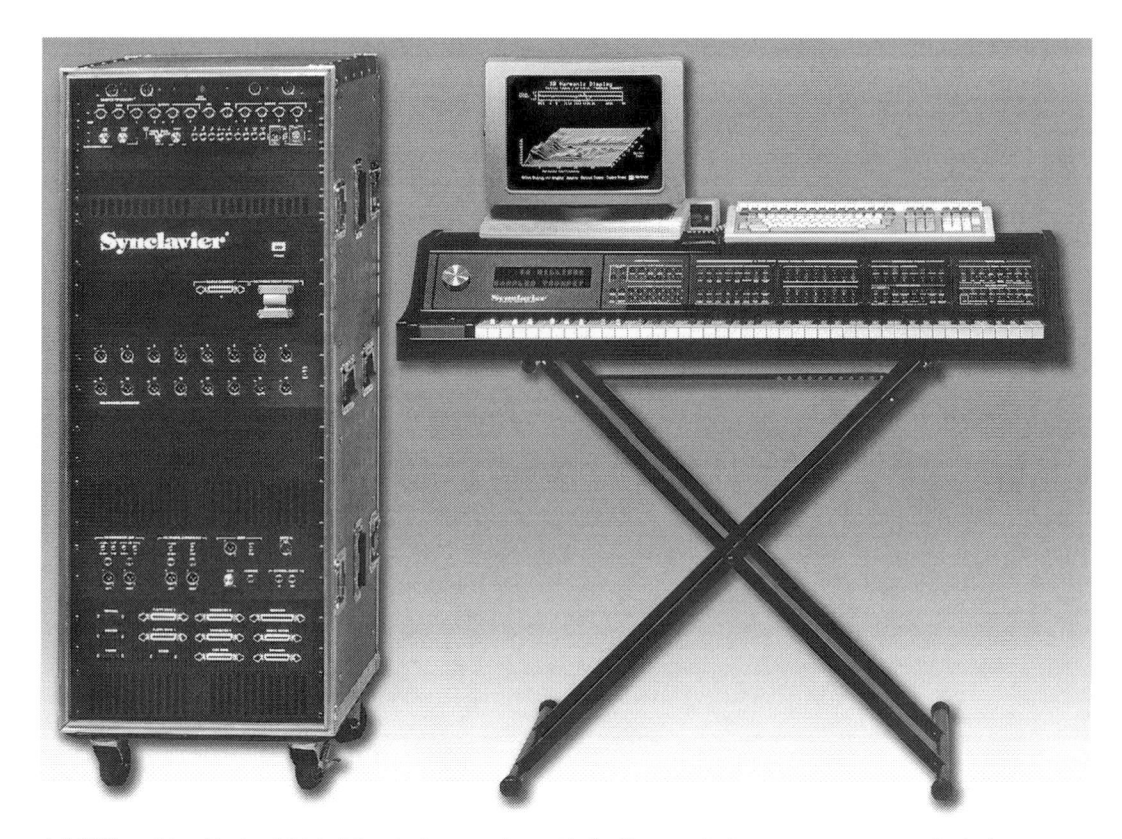

A 1987-era New England Digital Synclavier complete with the Direct-to-Disk system, a majority of which is mounted in the big Anvil case on the *left*. Among the Synclavier keyboard's amenities were a thirty-two-track sequencer, a sixteen-character by two-line display, pitch-bend and mod wheels, and a seventy-six-note velocity and poly-aftertouch sensing keyboard. Resting on *top* of the Synclavier keyboard cabinet are a CRT monitor showing its 3-D harmonic display and an ASCII keyboard. (© 1987 Jonathan Sa'adah)

Synclavier co-designer Jon Appleton plays an early model during the late 1970s. (Courtesy of the Electronic Music Foundation)

Zappa's cost $300,000; Michael Jackson had two on the *Bad* tour in 1987, tagged at $300,000 and $500,000; Sting used a similar setup and performed at NED's anniversary party in 1991, when there were 150 employees and offices in New York, Chicago, London, and LA.

Market pressure and other factors sunk NED in 1992. By then numerous companies offered far less expensive alternatives for digitally recording and editing music. Proprietary hardware also became a handicap. For a time the company was able to hold its control over the Synclavier thanks to its exclusive processor and hardware configuration, and by never making the system code public. But as they added more features and capabilities, the Synclavier's processor proved too slow and inadequate.

Economical Multitimbral Sequencing Synth

Way at the opposite end of the price scale is the Ensoniq ESQ-1, which provides considerable musical firepower for a very reasonable price. Unveiled in 1986, this affordable ($1,395 list), eight-voice, multitimbral synth has three digital oscillators per voice, **four-pole analog lowpass filters**, unusual envelope generators with three level and four time parameters, and a velocity-sensing keyboard. The ESQ-1's versatile and intuitive built-in eight-track MIDI sequencer can be particularly useful for composition and its memory is battery-backed, so everything's ready to roll as soon as you turn on the ESQ-1.

Perhaps its biggest claim to fame, however, is its implementation of **dynamic voice allocation** with **polytimbral** operation. Thanks to Ensoniq's design team—Bob Yannes, John Senior, Bill Mauchly, Alex Limberis, and Mats Myrberg—the ESQ-1 was the first synth that could automatically assign voices as needed without making disturbing pops and clicks. You don't have to specify the number of voices needed for each track, something required by most competing multitimbral instruments of its day.

Good-sounding digital wavetable synthesis, analog filters, multistage envelopes, dynamic voice allocation, and a built-in multitrack sequencer made the affordable Ensoniq ESQ-1 a hit. This one belongs to David Battino, who applied the Fairlight label and a reference chart showing a variety of tempos matched with LFO rates to produce different rhythms. Jim Johnson created this and other tables and numerous ESQ-1 tips for the August 1987 edition of *Transoniq Hacker*. (Courtesy of David Battino, www.batmosphere.com)

> *four-pole analog lowpass filters:* VCFs with a 24dB-per-octave cutoff slope
> *dynamic voice allocation:* whereas users of early multitimbral synths had to assign a specific number of voices to each timbre, dynamic voice allocation could automatically reassign voices as required by different parts—provided the instrument's maximum polyphony wasn't exceeded, in which case some notes would either be stolen before their entire duration passed or notes might not be sounded at all
> *polytimbral:* synonymous with multitimbral, capable of producing more than one timbre at one time and providing independent control of the individual timbres

Other innovative capabilities the ESQ-1 introduced were (1) a voice with a slow release will sustain after you select and begin playing a different patch (unless you overshoot the eight-voice polyphony limit); (2) when you assign different patches to play on opposite sides of a keyboard split point, you can play an eight-note chord on one side immediately followed by an eight-note chord on the other, and you'll encounter no sonic glitches; and (3) you can bend pitches of only physically held notes while the pitches of those sustained with a pedal remain static.

Musical Playstation for the Masses

Toward the end of the 1980s, many synth players were in search of an affordable-yet-capable synthesizer for composition and performance. It was Korg that bundled the goods into what became the best seller in synth history: the M1. It combined digital playback of sampled sounds with a built-in sequencer and effects, serving as a cornerstone in many a composer's home studio as well as the model for a new type of electronic instrument made by many manufacturers: the workstation. Korg released the widely beloved M1 in 1988 at a retail price of $2,665 and manufactured it until 1995—a lengthy production cycle in the synth industry. At an estimated 250,000 units sold, the M1 holds the record as the most popular synth of all time.

The M1's ROM contains four megabytes of musically useful and stunning sixteen-bit PCM sounds, including samples of exotic acoustic instruments that many in the mainstream hadn't previously heard. You can categorize M1 samples into four groups: sampled attack transients followed by single- and multicycle loops or lengthier **multisampled** loops; sustained single-cycle waveforms that lack attack transients; percussive attack samples; and rhythmic loops. Among the timbres are an acoustic piano, luscious strings, respectable acoustic guitar, eerie woodwinds, exotic sitar and kalimba, a wind-chime pattern, a vibrant hammered metal pole, notable drums, and percussion hits—a first for a sample-playback synthesizer.

Among the M1's onboard effects are **reverb**, **early reflections**, stereo delays, **chorusing** and **flanging**, tremolo, two-band **shelving EQ**, **distortion**, an **exciter**, a **Leslie speaker** simulator, and numerous multi-effects combinations. Like the ESQ-1, the M1 provides dynamic voice allocation and a built-in eight-track MIDI sequencer with battery-backed memory. Its sequencer might not be as user-friendly as the ESQ-1's, but it's enhanced by the inclusions of pattern-construction tools and drum machine–style loop recording. In addition, the M1's keyboard senses both velocity and aftertouch.

> *multisampled:* recording numerous samples across extended pitch and volume ranges from a single source so that the sound developer can flexibly arrange samples across several keys to avoid unrealistic pitch and/or vibrato changes that happen when a sample gets transposed too far, and into different velocity ranges to simulate how much force was used to play the samples
>
> *reverb:* abbreviation for reverberation, the complex reflections of sound waves in an acoustically active environment, perceived by human ears as a multitude of echoes—a wash of sound—that arrive continuously for a certain period of time before subsiding, but can't be heard as individual echoes; natural reverb can be simulated using an echo chamber, a plate of sheet metal, springs, and digital signal processing
>
> *early reflections:* waves of sound reflected by nearby surfaces and possibly heard as individual echoes before the wash of reverberated sound waves swell in volume
>
> *chorusing:* a delay-based, sound-thickening effect that simulates the sound of a musical ensemble or choir by combining the original audio signal with a duplicate that's delayed by a slowly modulating amount of time ranging from 10ms to 25ms and around 25 percent positive-phase feedback
>
> *flanging:* a delay-based, sonically whooshing effect accomplished by mixing the original audio signal with a duplicate delayed from 3ms to 20ms, modulated 100 percent at a slowly varying rate of about 0.2Hz, with 50 percent or more feedback and either positive or negative feedback phase
>
> *shelving EQ:* equalization that boosts or attenuates frequencies above (high) or below (low) a specific cutoff frequency
>
> *distortion:* the typically purposeful addition of harmonics to and otherwise changing an audio signal by overdriving circuitry such as the filter, modulating the signal's amplitude and/or frequency at audio rates, or feeding the signal back on itself; a common form of unintentional distortion occurs when you overdrive input levels of a digital device
>
> *exciter:* a type of distortion that typically adds high-frequency overtones to an audio signal
>
> *Leslie speaker:* beginning in the late 1930s, the organist and inventor Don Leslie (1911–2004) crafted speaker cabinets with rotating speaker components to enhance the sound generated by Hammond tonewheel organs; simulators attempt—with varying degrees of success—to electronically or digitally imitate the Doppler effect with virtual rotors directing sound toward and away from your ears, sound waves reflecting off of walls and other physical objects in the virtual space, and speeding up and slowing down the rotors with believable changes in motorized momentum characteristics between slow and fast rotation speeds

Following the M1's success, Korg continued to refine their workstations from the T-series (1989) through the 01/W (1991), X-series (1993/94), Trinity (1995), N-series (1996), Triton (1999), Karma (2001), OASys (2005), M3 (2007), M50 series (2008), Kronos (2011), and beyond. Over the years, Korg has progressively improved the feature sets and sound quality of their workstations.

Instrument that Launched Hip-Hop

If ever an instrument deserved credit as the catalyst of a music genre—in this case hip-hop—it would be the Akai MPC60. Turntable and scratch artists contributed in major ways, but the MPC60 clicked with hip-hop producers, as it did with those doing rap and R & B.

Not that these were the goals of its designer, Roger Linn. Before his own original company went under, Roger had introduced the LM-1 Drum Computer, LinnDrum, and Linn 9000. The 9000 was a monstrous device, both in terms of capabilities and its lack of reliability, and it played a part in the failure of Linn Electronics in February 1986. Within months, Linn teamed with Akai to develop Linn Electronics–like products, beginning with the MPC60 in 1988. While Roger was developing the MPC60's software in Santa Cruz, California, British engineer David Cockerell implemented its hardware in London.

Advertised as a MIDI production workstation, the MPC60 is a sampling drum machine with sixteen-bit **ADC**s and DACs, twelve-bit sample memory, a 40kHz sampling rate, sixteen velocity- and pressure-sensitive pads, and a built-in ninety-nine-track MIDI sequencer. As with Linn's earlier drum machines, the MPC60 had a Hi-Hat Decay slider for simulating how a drummer varies the hi-hat's response depending on how far he or she depresses the hi-hat pedal.

Akai's MPC60 music production studio—prized by producers of hip-hop, rap, and other music styles—was a collaboration between Roger Linn and David Cockerell. (Courtesy of Roger Linn)

Roger Linn designed his second drum machine, the LinnDrum, in 1982—before the LM-1 ceased production. The LinnDrum sported many of the same features but at a significantly lower price. Roger was somewhat surprised to discover that many musicians preferred the original. "We were horribly afraid that, when we brought out the LinnDrum, nobody would buy the LM-1," he recalls. "So we tried to keep it secret. I always thought, 'Who would want the older technology when the new one's cheaper and better?' But a lot of people liked certain things about the LM-1, like the individual voice tunability." (Dominic Milano)

ADC: analog-to-digital converter

After working with Akai, Linn founded Roger Linn Design in 2001 and introduced the AdrenaLinn beat-synced filter effects stompbox with integrated guitar-amp models and a drum machine. Linn announced in 2007 that he was working with Dave Smith to make the LinnDrum II—originally known as the BoomChick—an analog/digital drum machine and live performance instrument for beat-oriented music. This collaboration led to two new products: the Tempest analog/digital hybrid drum machine/synthesizer, announced in January 2011 and focused toward Dave's analog customers, and the Linn-Drum II, an all-digital instrument focused toward Roger's customers.

Multipurpose Environment for Composition and Performance

A rather obvious axiom: All sequencers aren't created equal. What began as an analog module with eight or so note-triggering steps eventually morphed into an astounding range of digital music-making extensions. Perhaps no music application set the music industry more cattywampus than Ableton Live.

Ableton AG's cofounder Gerhard Behles and its conceptual advisor, Robert Henke, introduced the perfectly named Live in 2001 as a convenient and synchronized method

The Synthesizer

The Tempest analog/digital hybrid drum machine/synthesizer from Dave Smith Instruments. It's extremely cool—extremely!—perhaps enough to convince a drummer to take up synthesis and a synthesist to take up drum-machine programming. At least that's the way it made me feel upon witnessing its co-creator, Roger Linn, put it through its paces at its introduction in January 2011 at NAMM. (Courtesy of Dave Smith)

of triggering different loops and samples in performance. As David Battino and Kelli Richards eloquently describe it in *The Art of Digital Music*, Live is "an audio sequencer you can play like an instrument." Not only do musicians use it onstage, but Live has also become an astoundingly creative and powerful environment with a potent array of tools for composition and recording in the studio; thus its placement here in the Composition section instead of within the Performance category.

A comprehensive look at what's going on in the Session View window of a song from Ableton Live version 8. Its creators have established Live as a potent and expressive music-making tool for both onstage and studio environments. In Session View, you trigger audio clips, one from any of the columns at a time—essentially playing the Live sequencer as if it were an instrument. Live can time-stretch clips to synchronize with the current tempo. (Courtesy of Ableton AG)

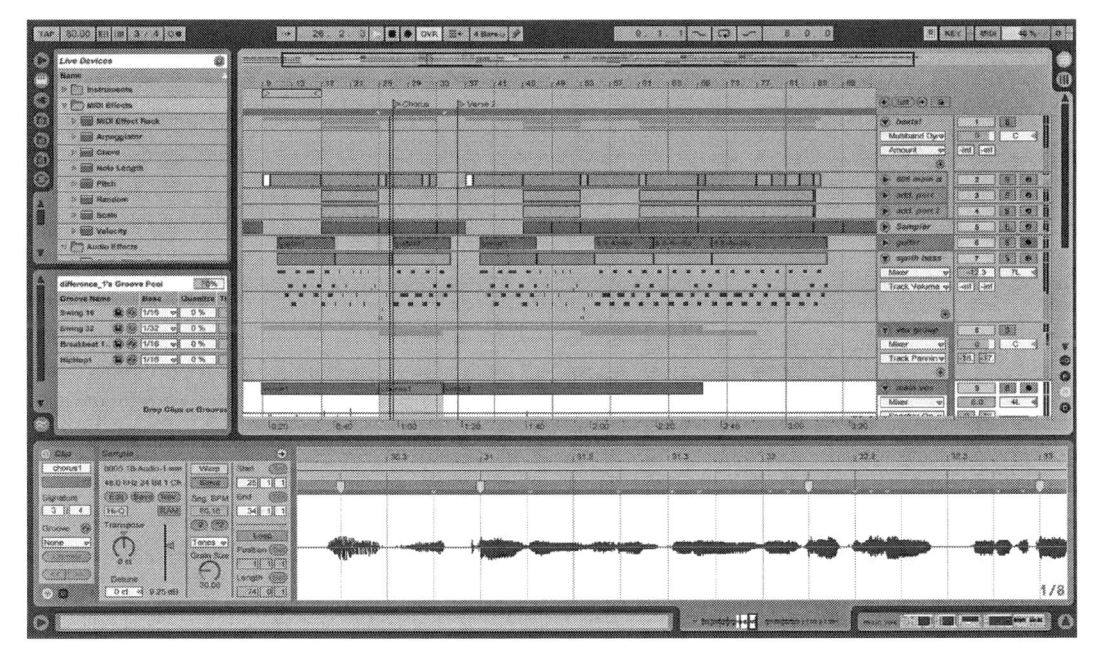

Arrangement View, shown here, is the second of Ableton Live's two main windows, this one part of the same song shown in Live 8's Session View. Here the composer can arrange sequences of both audio and MIDI events as he or she deems fit. (Courtesy of Ableton AG)

"Ableton Live was originally intended for DJs," notes the synthesist and composer Gary Chang, "but it has evolved into a much more extensive and creative tool. Together with [Cycling '74] Max for Live, it can record everything—audio and control data—and it will replicate any movements that you've made. We're after the gestures, not just the 'freeze.' We don't want snapshots; we're actually after capturing human information interactively." Chang uses Live extensively with his modular synthesizers and other instruments.

Beyond

With this chapter serving as a foundation, a rundown of those synthesizers, electronic instruments, and software that excelled—technologically, if not financially—and extended the music-making capabilities of electronic musicians, we're ready to proceed to the next step: descriptions and explanations of all of the components that make the synthesizer the most flexible, expressive, and powerful man-made instrument on Earth.

2

Acoustics and Synthesis Basics

Innovative electronic engineers and instrument makers have made astounding achievements in synthesis technology over the years, and they'll certainly continue to do so in the future. To enjoy the best experience and be efficiently productive in making music with a synthesizer, it's essential that you understand what's going on under its hood in the production of sounds.

In no way do I discourage experimentation. You can have lots of fun and get a long way in just playing with a synth: twist its knobs, throw its switches and faders, route signals through different modules with patch cords in a **modular synthesizer**, and explore parameters through a programmable synth's multilayered menu system. Such explorations can prove educational and are therefore highly recommended.

Still, a basic understanding of the process can make the experience much more satisfying and fruitful. Fear not that this will be an intensely technical dissertation. A degree in electrical engineering isn't a prerequisite to this endeavor.

> *modular synthesizer:* an electronic instrument consisting of a variety of components from one or more manufacturers mounted according to the user's wishes in a cabinet that provides power; for the instrument to generate sound, the user must patch multiple components or modules together so that audio, control-voltage, **gate**, and **trigger** signals are routed through the modules; see ch. 3 for much more about modular synthesizers
>
> *gate:* an analog timing-pulse control signal generated by activity such as a note played on a keyboard or a step reached by an **analog step sequencer**, which causes a voltage to jump to a high level and stay there until the keyboard note is released or the sequencer step ends
>
> *analog step sequencer:* a source of control voltages, gates, and triggers that repeats a pattern over a specific number of steps or stages and provides user controls to alter aspects of the entire sequence as well as each step/stage; an internal or separate clock provides periodic signals for analog sequencers to proceed from step to step
>
> *trigger:* an analog timing-pulse control signal generated by activity such as a note played on a keyboard or a step reached by a sequencer, which causes a voltage to jump to a high level for a brief, fixed duration before dropping to the previous level

First, let's take a brief look at acoustics and how they apply to sound synthesis.

A Eurorack modular synthesizer system containing modules from Synthesis Technology. Modular users can rearrange and swap in/out modules as they see fit. (Mark Vail)

Real-World Acoustics

For there to be sound, an event needs to happen within some type of medium. Typical media include air, water, and a solid object that can vibrate. That's what actually produces acoustic sound: vibration. Anything that vibrates in our normal environment—air—induces variations in air pressure. These variations spread like waves expanding on the surface of a pond after you toss in a rock, only they travel in three dimensions, not just two.

> *sound waves:* periodic alterations of pressure—typically in the air, but also occurring in liquids and solid objects—that results in an audible sound upon reaching the eardrums of cognizant creatures such as humans
> *Hertz (Hz):* a measurement of periodic frequency in cycles per second; named for German physicist Heinrich Hertz (1857–94)
> *decibel:* a measurement of loudness on a logarithmic scale of intensity

In order for us to hear **sound waves**, they need to occur at a rate—or frequency—between 20 and 20,000 cycles per second, or **Hertz** (Hz). A quicker way to say it is 20Hz–20kHz. We're most sensitive to frequencies between 250Hz and 3kHz because that's the typical range of human speech. Not all humans can hear sounds over the entire

20Hz–20kHz frequency spectrum. Along with the natural aging process that degrades our hearing, adverse health conditions and senseless activities can accelerate the deterioration of hearing. For example, subjecting yourself to continuously loud sound over extended periods or briefly being exposed to an intensely loud sound can be temporarily or permanently detrimental to your hearing, impairing your ability to detect high-pitched sounds or those within certain frequency ranges.

Besides frequency, we measure sound in amplitude using the logarithmic **decibel** (dB) scale. The lowest threshold of hearing is 0dB. Someone whispering quietly three feet from you measures about 30dB, a typical conversation is 60dB, amplified rock six feet away is 120dB, and a jet plane at a distance of one hundred feet measures 130dB. As you might imagine, the louder the sound you subject your ears to, the greater the chance of damaging your ability to hear accurately. Particularly dangerous are sounds around 4kHz at 120dB, which could leave you deaf after five to ten minutes.

Those who play in rock bands often finish a rehearsal or gig with ringing ears. That's bad. Prolonged exposure to constantly loud sounds may not make you totally deaf, but it could lead to tinnitus, a ringing in your ears that could be a permanent condition. Since hearing is important to us, we need to be cautious and protect our ears whenever possible. Products and recommendations to help you preserve your hearing, as well as additional information, can be found on the Hearing Education and Awareness for Rockers (HEAR) website at www.hearnet.com. The House Research Institute (www.houseresearch.org) is another hearing-health organization.

Types of Synthesis

During the early 1960s, the standard model of analog synthesis became **subtractive**. Audio signals from one or more oscillators generating waveforms containing lots of overtones pass through a filter to shape the sound by suppressing—subtracting—certain frequencies and exaggerating others, then through an amplifier to vary the sound's volume.

> *subtractive synthesis:* the use of oscillators that generate richly harmonic waveforms and routing their signals through voltage-controlled filters to attenuate specific harmonics and contour the resulting timbre
>
> *additive synthesis:* creating complex timbres using multiple oscillators that generate less complex waveforms, traditionally sine waves
>
> *sine waves:* oscillator-generated, periodic voltages that rise and fall smoothly and symmetrically, following the trigonometric formula for the sine function; at audible frequencies a sine wave produces only the fundamental frequency and no harmonics, sounding similar to a flute; at sub-audible frequencies, the sine wave excels at producing **vibrato** by modulating oscillator pitch and tremolo by modulating amplitude
>
> *vibrato:* periodic variations in pitch, typically at a rate of around 7Hz

> *envelope generator (EG):* a circuit that simulates the audible progression of an acoustic sound—which has a beginning, middle, and end—by generating a control voltage or digital signal whose level changes over time according to specific parameters; a common ADSR EG provides time variables called attack, decay, and release and a sustain level between the decay and release stages
>
> *linear frequency modulation:* a type of audio synthesis in which changes in the amount of modulation don't affect the center frequency of the carrier oscillator, which remains constant

The opposite, **additive synthesis**, actually existed earlier. Although the Hammond tonewheel organ—epitomized by the popular B-3—and its pipe-organ ancestors are beyond the scope of this book, they actually use additive methods. Traditional additive synthesis uses multiple **sine waves**, which produce only fundamental frequencies and no overtones. All of the sine waves sound at various harmonic frequencies, and you combine them to generate complex timbres. Depending on the additive synth, there are different techniques to modify the frequency and amplitude of every partial generator as sounds play. In the Digital Keyboards Synergy, for example, each partial generator is paired with a multistage **envelope generator** that you can loop and synchronize with other envelope generators. As potent as additive synthesis can be, it's challenging to program and thus hasn't been as popular as subtractive synthesis—as illustrated by the relative rarity of additive synths on the market.

Synthesists in search of new and unique timbres eagerly awaited digital synthesis during the 1970s and early '80s, but the technology was very expensive at first. Then in 1983, Yamaha unleashed the DX7 and changed the whole synthesis ballgame. Using the **linear frequency-modulation** (FM) synthesis technique John Chowning developed at Stanford University in 1973, the company offered the DX7 at a reasonable list price of $1,995. As implemented in the DX7, linear FM uses sine waves—somewhat like additive synthesis but in a totally different configuration. Inside the DX7 are six operators, each consisting of a digital sine-wave oscillator, an envelope generator, an amplifier, pitch and modulation inputs, and an output. Modulating a carrier operator with a signal generated by a modulator operator results in frequency modulation and the generation of harmonics a sine wave doesn't produce on its own. Thirty-two algorithms—arrangements of modulator and carrier operators—allow the generation of complex timbres without the need for all of the oscillators required in an additive synthesizer. Additive synthesis and linear FM do a more credible job of synthesizing acoustic-sounding timbres than analog synthesis, but their clean, precise, and edgy quality eventually left many synthesists craving the warmth of analog.

Digital sampling and polyphonic sample playback arrived with the original Fairlight CMI at the end of the 1970s, but few musicians could afford its price: up to $36,000. But the technology—digitally recording acoustic instruments, playing them back at different pitches and editing them, and composing music by sequencing their playback—proved enchanting. As other sampler manufacturers got involved, bit resolution expanded from eight to twelve and then sixteen bits and beyond to improve the sound quality. Other improvements evolved and instrument prices dropped to ranges that were truly affordable, making sampling dominant. It remains widespread today and, although considerable progress has made sample playback more expressive, there's no way to avoid the truth about sampling: it's essentially the audio equivalent of a snapshot. With filtering and processing you can vary sonic qualities of the sample, but the sample waveform itself is fixed.

> *aperiodic:* irregular and nonrepeating

Somewhat related to sampling is the microsound practice of granular synthesis. Theorized by Dennis Gabor in the 1940s and introduced as a synthesis technique by Iannis Xenakis in the late '50s, granular synthesis involves very brief snippets—1 to 100 milliseconds (ms) in length—of sound. Each snippet, or grain, comprises an **aperiodic** waveform that you contour using differently shaped amplitude envelopes. You arrange grains in sequences to build sound objects, but the grains are so brief it takes thousands of them to create the equivalent of a note. Granular synthesis is rare because it takes a lot of user effort, computer-processing firepower, and storage space to execute. Among the instruments capable of doing it are Symbolic Sound's Kyma and computer applications including Csound, SuperCollider, Cycling '74 Max/MSP, and Native Instruments Reaktor. The Malström softsynth in Propellerhead Reason does what's called Graintable Synthesis, a combination of granular and wavetable synthesis.

With wavetable synthesis, oscillators scan through digitized waveforms stored in ROM. Wavetables can be samples or generated using mathematical equations, and they're typically much more complex than average analog waveforms. Early wavetable synths include the Rocky Mount Instruments Keyboard Computer and the PPG Wave 2.2, introduced in 1974 and 1982, respectively. One dynamic and expressive technique Wave designer Wolfgang Palm developed is the ability to sweep through digital wavetables using enve-

Malström, Propellerhead's Graintable Synthesizer, was the second virtual synth introduced to Reason. Thanks to its two flexible modulator sections, Malström patches can evolve and move almost as if an arpeggiator or sequencer were involved. (Courtesy of Propellerhead Software AB)

A second-generation Rocky Mount Instruments Keyboard Computer, officially known as the RMI KC-II, rests on its chrome stand above multiple foot controllers. The wavetable-synthesis soundset loaded at the factory into the original Keyboard Computer—mostly borrowed from Allen's digital theater organ in what Clark Ferguson, who began working for RMI at about the time of the KC's introduction, describes as "a shotgun wedding"—didn't appeal to the customers RMI was after. Although users could load alternative wavetables into the first KC from punched cards via an optical reader, the company later developed the KC-II with new sounds and an extended feature set. (Photo courtesy of Allen Organ Company, LLC)

lope generators. The linear-arithmetic (LA) synthesis technique Roland engineers developed for the D-50, released in 1987, combined sample playback, wavetable synthesis, and built-in effects, but it was a joke originally played by one of the Japanese engineers that resulted in some of the D-50's most memorable sounds. The engineer programmed a digital sequencer that would rhythmically cycle through waveforms in an uncontrolled but hilarious-sounding manner. The D-50 programmers Eric Persing and Adrian Scott enjoyed the results so much that they convinced Roland to make the capability a permanent part of the synth's factory soundbank. Kurzweil later incorporated a similar technique in a more controllable fashion in their K2000 and K2500 series of synths.

A few years earlier, Chris Meyer at Sequential Circuits developed vector synthesis, which allows dynamic cross-fading among signals coming from four oscillators using a dedicated envelope and a joystick. Sequential introduced the technique in their Prophet-VS, which could generate sounds Meyer describes as "struck attacks that faded into shimmering flutes, clarinets that opened up into raw sawtooth waves, and much more." Sadly, the Prophet-VS—which entered the market in 1986—didn't sell well, and its production ceased when Yamaha purchased Sequential Circuits in 1988. Vector synthesis later appeared in Yamaha's SY22 and TG33 and Korg's Wavestation, all developed under the direction of Sequential's founder Dave Smith. Vector synthesis, however, wasn't the only magic that went into the Wavestation. Korg's engineers also improved on the wave-

Vector synthesis went with Dave Smith post Sequential Circuits first to Yamaha and later to Korg, represented here by the powerful and popular Wavestation. (Courtesy of Korg)

cycling techniques that appeared earlier on Roland and Kurzweil synths to develop a spinoff technique called wave sequencing, which allows the user to select, arrange, and loop through brief sampled waveforms to create complex rhythmic patterns.

During the mid-1990s, the next big thing in synthesis became physical modeling (PM), which involves the use of mathematical equations to represent physical laws and actions. When applied to sound synthesis, PM algorithms allow the simulation of acoustic musical instruments. You can use a wave equation to model a vibrating violin string, including the tension it's under, the density of its linear mass, and its air displacement. To model the entire violin, you also need wave equations for its body, bridge, catgut strings, bow, and the like. The computation of these details is CPU intensive. Julius O. Smith of Stanford University's Center for Computer Research in Music and Acoustics (CCRMA) devised the digital waveguide filter, which significantly decreases the number of functions described in the wave equation and reduces the PM computation load required from computers. The technique has appeared in numerous synths, including the Yamaha VL1, E-mu Morpheus, and Korg Kronos. However, creating great sounds using physical-modeling synthesis isn't by any means easy. While all of the details in the wave equation models are ripe for expressive control in performance, they actually demand such control. Otherwise the synthesized sound will suffer—as will listeners. If you decide to go down the physical-modeling synthesis path, be prepared to incorporate as many different controllers as you can and practice, practice, practice.

During all of the initial PM excitement, many musicians lamented the virtual disappearance in new synths of good analog tone and an interface blessed with front-panel knobs as opposed to a few buttons and a deep menu system. For years manufacturers

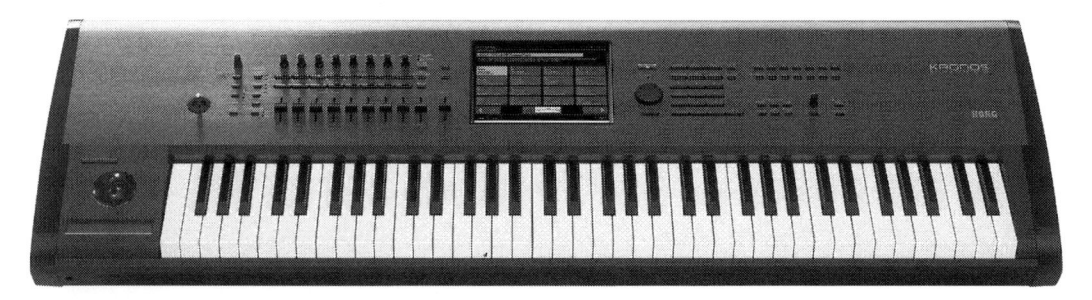

Introduced at NAMM in January 2011, the Kronos continues Korg's tradition as a prominent manufacturer of state-of-the-art synth workstations. This is the seventy-three-key model. (Courtesy of Korg)

tried to make sample-playback sound analog, to no avail. It was Hans Nordelius of Clavia in Sweden who initially found the right digital and hardware ingredients for many synthesists. He delivered the first of his distinctive crimson-red synths, the original Nord Lead, in 1995. Not only does it sport more knobs than we'd seen on a new synth in over a decade, but it also generates a convincingly analog sound thanks to the digital signal processing (DSP) synthesis method Nordelius and his team developed.

Audio Sources: Oscillators, Noise, and More

Analog synthesizers produce pitched tones using one or more oscillators, although most oscillators can generate frequencies beneath and beyond the perceptible 20Hz–20kHz spectrum. An analog **voltage-controlled oscillator** (**VCO**) typically produces a **waveform** or **waveshape** that generates timbres containing diverse frequency components. For example, oscillators 1 and 2 on a Minimoog produce **triangle**, **sawtooth**, **triangular sawtooth** (tri-saw), and three **pulse** waves: square, wide rectangle, and narrow rectangle. Since the Mini's third oscillator serves as both an audio and a **low-frequency oscillator** (**LFO**), Bob Moog, Jim Scott, Bill Hemsath, and Chad Hunt replaced the tri-saw with a **reverse sawtooth** wave, which is more useful for modulation purposes. Common VCO waveforms found on analog synths other than the Minimoog include sine and **variable pulse-width**. **Pulse-width modulation** continually alters the timbre in ways subtle to extreme. Because the sine wave lacks frequencies beyond the fundamental, it produces a flute-like sound.

> *voltage-controlled oscillator (VCO):* an analog circuit that generates cyclic and repeating signals at frequencies that can be varied using control voltages
>
> *waveform:* a repeating cyclic, aperiodic, or sampled audio or control signal
>
> *waveshape:* another term for waveform
>
> *triangle wave:* an oscillator-generated, periodic voltage that rises and falls smoothly at equal and linear rates, with sharp corners at its apex and lowest point; at audible frequencies, a triangle wave doesn't generate strong harmonics, mostly just the fundamental frequency
>
> *sawtooth wave:* an oscillator-generated, periodic voltage that rises in a linear fashion to its peak, then falls immediately to the lowest point before repeating the ascent; at audible rates, the sawtooth wave generates all of the overtone harmonics of the fundamental frequency
>
> *triangular sawtooth wave:* a fusion of triangle and sawtooth waveforms that produces an overtone series of harmonics between their extremes
>
> *pulse wave:* also called rectangular, a periodic voltage that instantly alternates between low and high values, with duty cycles determining the harmonic overtones that are created; whereas the Minimoog's square wave produces exclusively odd-numbered harmonics, both the narrow and wide pulse waves generate more harmonically complex overtones

The Synthesizer

> *low-frequency oscillator (LFO):* a signal generator that produces waveforms at sub-audible rates for controlling parameters such as the pitch of audio-frequency oscillators to produce vibrato using a triangle or sine wave or trills using a pulse or square wave; many LFOs can oscillate at audio rates, extending synthesis capabilities when applied to modulate VCO frequency, filter parameters, or other destinations
>
> *reverse sawtooth wave:* also referred to as an inverted sawtooth wave; an oscillator-generated, periodic voltage that rises immediately to the highest point before falling in a linear fashion to its lowest point before repeating the cycle; at audible rates, the reverse sawtooth wave—similar to the sawtooth wave—generates all of the overtone harmonics of the fundamental frequency; it's particularly useful at sub-audio rates for producing effects such as repeated notes by modulating amplitude level or falling oscillator-pitch dive-bombs
>
> *variable pulse-width wave:* a pulse wave that allows the user to change its duty cycle manually or using automated techniques
>
> *pulse-width modulation:* using control voltages or digital automation to vary the duty cycle of a pulse waveform

Shown here are the Minimoog's primary waveforms and their associated harmonics produced at 100Hz. As Tom Rhea explains in *The Minimoog Model D Operation Manual* (Moog Music, Inc., 1974), "Complex sounds consist of various frequency components referred to as partials. Most pitched sounds consist of a first partial, or principal sound called the fundamental, and upper partials of higher frequency and less intensity (loudness). When the frequencies of the upper partials are integer (whole-number) multiples of the frequency of the fundamental, all the partials are called harmonics."

Moog's iconic Minimoog Model D was the best-selling American-made analog monosynth of the twentieth century. (Courtesy of Moog Music Inc.)

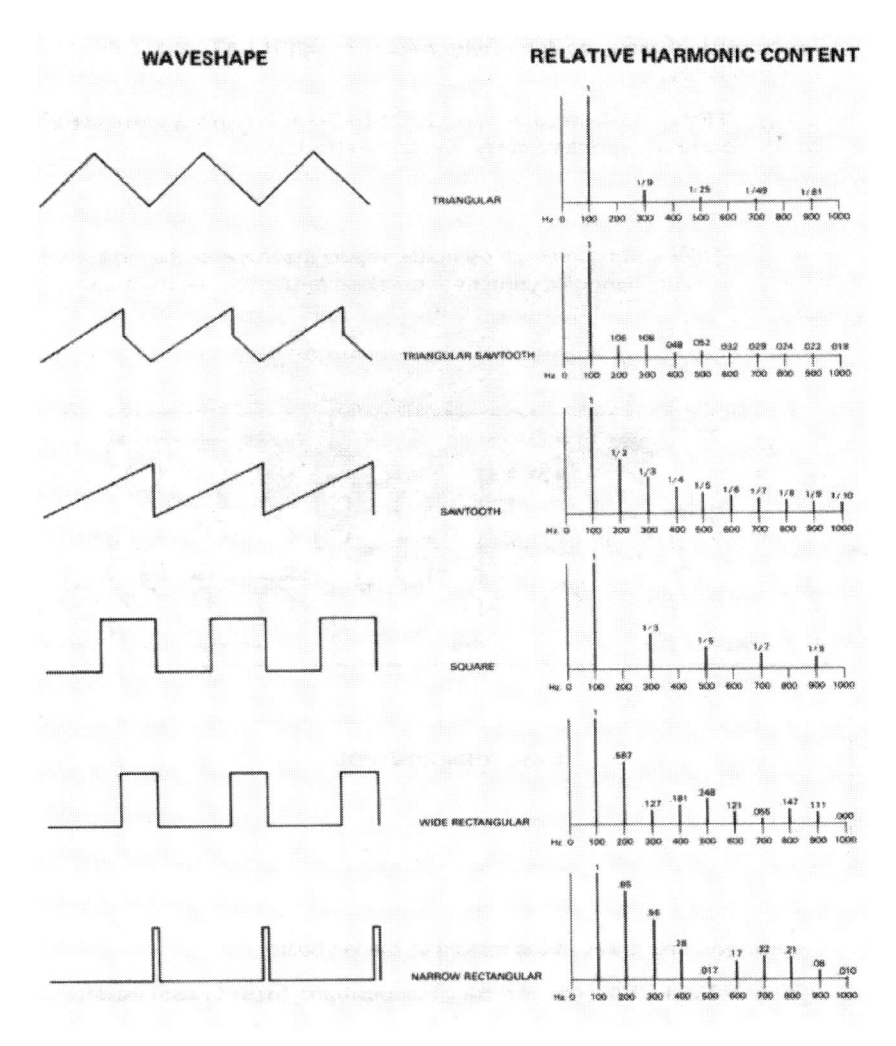

Borrowed from Tom Rhea's educational *The Minimoog Model D Operation Manual*, this page of graphics illustrates the first ten partials in the harmonic spectra of the waveforms generated at 100Hz by a Minimoog VCO. (Courtesy of Tom Rhea)

Components in early analog synthesizers tended to be unstable, uncontrollably drifting in operation when temperature, humidity, or other conditions changed in the environment. Fluctuating VCO pitches are perhaps most obvious, but considerable progress made over the years has led to the design of VCOs that once they've warmed up do a better job of staying in tune. Another interesting debate in the early years involved oscillator scaling. Most prevalent has been the one-volt-per-octave (1V/octave) scale, but early on some manufacturers—including Korg and Yamaha—used a Hertz-per-volt scale.

One method conceived to improve oscillator stability was the digitally controlled oscillator (DCO). While the oscillator itself still generates analog sound, digital control keeps it in tune. Two synths that have DCOs are the Roland Juno-106 (1984) and Oberheim Matrix-1000 (1987), both six-voice polyphonic synths. While the Juno-106 offers a five-octave keyboard and one DCO per voice, its built-in chorus effect fattens the sound; the 1U rackmount Matrix-1000 module sports two DCOs per voice. Both synths wield lots of analog punch.

VCOs often generate multiple waveforms simultaneously. Such is the case with the Minimoog's three oscillators, but you can select only one waveform per oscillator at a

The Synthesizer

Roland's Juno-106 was one of the first synthesizers to sport DCOs, or digitally controlled oscillators. (Courtesy of Roland Corporation)

time because there isn't space to conveniently squeeze controls onto the Mini's front panel for mixing and adjusting the relative volumes of the waveforms together. Most manufacturers have repeated this practice on pre-patched subtractive synthesizers, although Arturia broke the trend in 2012 with the MiniBrute, a single-oscillator monosynth with independent faders for each of its waveforms—sawtooth, pulse, and triangle—plus a noise source, a **sub-oscillator**, and an external audio input. Oscillators on modular and **patchable synthesizers** often provide separate outputs for each waveform produced by its VCOs so you can route the signals through a variety of processing components to create more complex timbres.

> *sub-oscillator:* an analog or digital audio source that typically produces frequencies one or two octaves below a master VCO or digital oscillator
> *patchable synthesizer:* an electronic instrument whose maker installed and wired components together in fixed positions behind the control panel, but also installed

Oberheim's 1U rackmount Matrix-1000 module generates analog tones, but its oscillators are of the digitally controlled variety. (Photo courtesy of Gibson Guitar Corp.)

Acoustics and Synthesis Basics

The Zeroscillator from Cyndustries is capable of synthesizing sound using exponential FM, linear through-zero FM, linear FM dynamic depth modulation, bi-phasic waveform morphing in quadrature, pulse-width modulation, variable oscillator sync, and time reversal. It comes in five different formats: MOTM, Blacet/FracRak, Synthesizers.com, Eurorack, and Modcan A—the format shown here. Not only does the Zeroscillator have sine, triangle, pulse, sawtooth, and reverse sawtooth outputs, but it sports an additional five audio outputs, four of which allow you to morph through a variety of waveshapes manually or using voltage control. (Courtesy of Cynthia Webster of Cyndustries.com)

> patch-point jacks on the control panel to allow the user to override internal wiring for more flexible signal routing for control and sound-generation purposes
>
> *normalled circuits:* internally wired components that can conduct signals to other components without the need for patch cords, but the internal wiring can be overridden by plugging patch cords into associated jacks

The main difference between synthesizers classified as modular or patchable (sometimes referred to as "semi-modular") is that the former refers to systems assembled from a variety of individual modules, often from multiple manufacturers, which can be installed and freely arranged in a cabinet, case, or rack as the synthesist sees fit. In the latter

Korg introduced the original, patchable, analog MS-20 monosynth in May 1978, and it continues to be a very popular item on the used synth market. In 2007 Korg introduced a USB controller that looks almost exactly like the MS-20, except on a slightly smaller scale. Complete with knobs, 3.5mm patch points, a pitchbend wheel, and three-octave mini keyboard, it serves as the front end to Korg's Legacy Collection bundle of softsynths. Included in Legacy is a virtual MS-20, which registers patches made on the controller's front panel. Korg also introduced a new MS-20 Mini, a fully functional synth that looks and sounds almost identical to the original but is a bit smaller, at the 2013 Winter NAMM show. (Courtesy of Korg)

case, the positions of components in a patchable or semi-modular synth are fixed in place and can't be rearranged without serious reconstructive surgery. Another difference with modular is that, unless the synthesist interconnects modules beneath the surface, components must be patched together by plugging cables into front-panel jacks to route control and audio signals. In contrast, most patchable synths have **normalled circuits**, which are interconnected internally to allow signals to be routed without patching components together, but inner connections can be overridden by patching on the front panel to open up wider ranges of timbral and control possibilities. Patchable synths include the vintage ARP 2600, Korg MS-20 (both the original and new Mini models), and EML Electrocomp 101, and current Doepfer Dark Energy II, Tom Oberheim's SEM, Cwejman S1-MK2, MFB-Kraftzwerg, Moog Minimoog Voyager XL, and Analogue Solutions Red Square, Telemark, and Vostok.

Analog waveforms can be warped in pleasing, effective, and extensive ways using various **modulation** techniques. By modulating the frequency of one VCO with another at audible levels, you can create interesting distorted and clangorous sounds. It's called frequency modulation (FM), but it's much simpler than the linear FM technique Yamaha uses in the DX7 and other FM synths. Another method is called **oscillator sync**, wherein a slave oscillator's waveform restarts whenever the master oscillator's waveform repeats from its beginning, which results in the slave oscillator generating a more complex waveform.

> *modulation:* the use of control voltages in an analog circuit or computer-generated signals in a digital environment to vary synthesizer parameters such as oscillator pitch,

Acoustics and Synthesis Basics

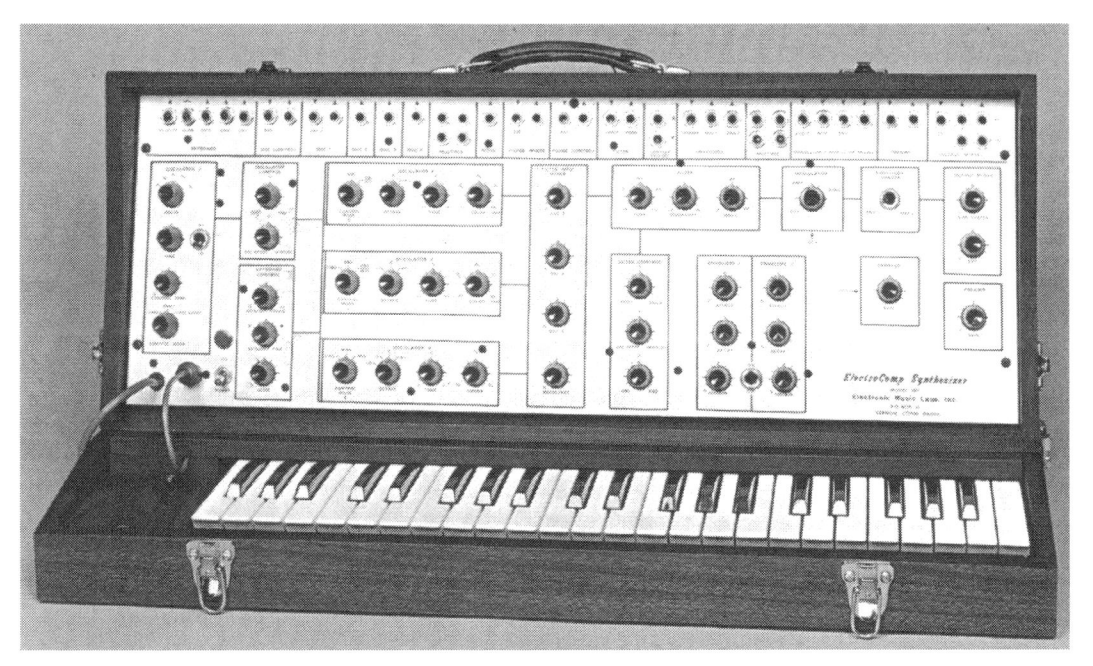

Manufactured by Electronic Music Laboratories (EML) throughout the 1970s, the potent Electrocomp 101 was an affordable alternative to the Minimoog and ARP 2600. It was fairly popular, too, with around a thousand of them being produced. Like the ARP 2600, the 101 has normalled internal connections, allowing the user to override them using 1/4" patch cords. (Courtesy of Norman Milliard, Electronic Music Laboratories)

Released in 2009, Doepfer's Dark Energy offers normalled connections with 3.5mm patch points to open it up for alternative signal-routing explorations. Doepfer discontinued the original Dark Energy when supplies of the Curtis ElectroMusic (CEM) 3394 synth-voice chip ran dry. The Dark Energy II, introduced in 2012, sounds a bit different from the original because it has new VCO, VCF, and VCA chips. (© by Doepfer Musikelektronik GmbH)

The Synthesizer

The Analogue Solutions Red Square is a patchable monophonic analog synth module and effects processor with 1/4" jacks for convenient interface with other music gear. The Red Square includes a MIDI input and is capable of converting MIDI data into control voltages and gates. (Stephi Clendinen, courtesy of Big City Music)

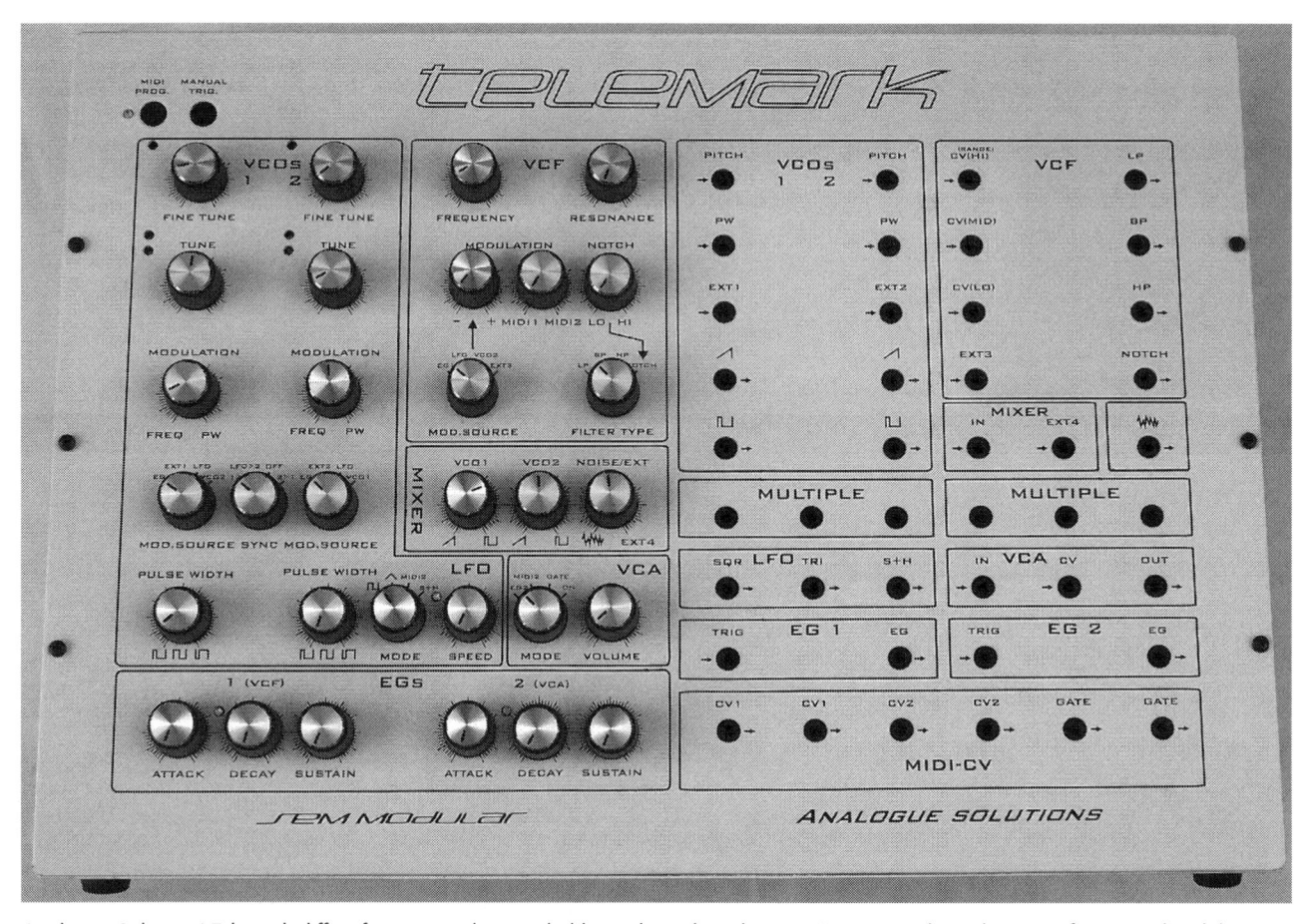

Analogue Solutions' Telemark differs from most other patchable synths in that plugging 3.5mm patch cords into its front-panel jack bay doesn't override internally wired connections. Instead, incoming signals are summed with those inside. (Stephi Clendinen, courtesy of Big City Music)

Acoustics and Synthesis Basics

About the size of a small suitcase, the Vostok from Analogue Solutions is a patchable synth that provides 3.5mm jacks as well as a small 22 × 22 matrix patch panel. Like a modular synth, you have to connect its modules using either patch cords or patch pins in the matrix. The Vostok's removable lid provides adequate clearance to leave pins and cords plugged in as long as they don't extend too far from the control panel. MIDI in and thru jacks are provided, as are MIDI-to-CV conversion, an eight-step analog CV and gate sequencer, and an analog VU meter. (Stephi Clendinen, courtesy of Big City Music)

> filter cutoff frequency, and audio signal level, thus allowing the performer to musically control the instrument
>
> *oscillator sync:* two oscillators connected so that one oscillator forces the second to begin its waveform cycle simultaneously with the first's waveform, creating a differently shaped waveform in the second oscillator and generating a timbre that has different harmonics than it otherwise would have had
>
> *sampled sound:* a digital recording of audio that may, for instance, happen acoustically in a real-world environment
>
> *modeled-analog synthesizer:* a digital instrument that generates analog-like electronic sounds using digital circuitry

Digital waveforms can be much more complex than those produced using analog circuitry, and they can also be **sampled** sounds. Likewise, thanks to the years of work and experimentation synth developers have spent, digital can convincingly model analog waveforms, which is where **modeled-analog** synths such as Clavia's Nord Lead and the

Tom Campbell of Analogue Solutions poses at the January 2010 NAMM convention with (*clockwise* from *lower left*) his Leipzig-ks monosynth keyboard, Telemark synth module, Oberkorn v3 sequencer, and Europa MIDI step sequencer/drum computer. Standing *back-to-back* with Tom is synthesizer pioneer Don Buchla, sharing space in the Big City Music booth. (Mark Vail)

Access Virus series started. Many digital oscillators are available in various forms for modular synthesizers, even further expanding their sonic capabilities.

Not to imply that digital oscillators can't produce simple waveforms as well, including the sine. One cool Eurorack-format oscillator module is the Synthesis Technology E340 Cloud Generator, which contains eight digital oscillators. Paul Schreiber, head of Synthesis Technology and mastermind behind the popular series of MOTM modules, ran with a technique developed by synthesist Robert Rich, who used twenty-four separate MOTM modules to create a "buzzing, swarming cloud of sine waves." While the E340 can behave like an analog VCO that generates sine wave and sawtooth waveforms, when you engage varying levels of its Spread function using the knob and control voltages from an external source, you begin detuning all of the oscillators. Likewise, the E340's Chaos and Chaos bandwidth (BW) knobs and CV inputs induce varying degrees and rates of modulation to the oscillator detunings, allowing you to create buzzing and swarming clouds of sounds.

Equally fascinating is Synthesis Technology's E350 Morphing Terrarium, a wavetable oscillator packed with three banks of sixty-four wavetables. Within each bank, wavetables appear in an 8 × 8 matrix and the E350 scans the matrix to morph among the wavetables and generate two independent output signals. You control the timbre exiting the XY Out jack using the E350's Morph X and Y knobs and by routing control voltages into its Morph X and Y CV inputs; likewise, there's a Morph Z knob and CV input to

Acoustics and Synthesis Basics

Along with buzzing and swarming clouds of synthesized sound you can create using the Synthesis Technology E340 Cloud Generator's Spread, Chaos, and Chaos BW functions on its eight sine- and sawtooth-generating oscillators, there are also a density switch to enable two, four, or all eight oscillators and an FM input jack and level control for modulating oscillator frequencies at adjustable levels with an exponential response. (© 2012 Synthtech Inc., used by permission)

Remember the sound of vintage wavetable synthesizers, epitomized by the PPG Wave 2.3? Synthesis Technology's E350 Morphing Terrarium goes far beyond the PPG in terms of its sonic prowess, and it's a small module available for Eurorack and FrakRak modular synth systems. (© 2012 Synthtech Inc., used by permission)

vary the Morph Z timbral output. The sonic magic happens as the E350 scans through the waveforms glitch-free thanks to its proprietary smoothing/anti-aliasing DSP algorithm to generate a boggling range of tones—unless you want old-style wavetable glitchiness, in which case you can insert a jumper on the E350's circuit board to get that sound.

Both the E340 and E350 have FM inputs with an attenuator, so you can create even more sonic chaos by pumping in any kind of audio you choose for a bit—or a lot—of exponential frequency-modulation fun. In addition, the E350 sports a three-way Range switch, which allows it to produce frequencies anywhere from a high of 10kHz to a stunning low of one cycle per thirteen minutes, converting it into a unique low-frequency oscillator.

Can't decide between these two extraordinary oscillators? Remember, they're modular synth modules, and that means you can have them both, or several of both, in a Eurorack modular system.

If you prefer FracRak modular, Blacet Research sells both the Cloud Generator and Morphing Terrarium in that form, respectively the F340 and F350. BugBrand also offers the E350 Morphing Terrarium in that flavor. As with other BugBrand modules, their E350 is FracRak sized but has banana jacks instead of those measuring 3.5mm, and—like other BugBrand modules—theirs provides attenuators on all of its inputs.

A different type of synthesizer sound generator makes noise, which is actually a good and useful commodity. A noise source is a great starting point in the synthesis of wind, waves crashing on the beach, spinning helicopter blades, and booming thunder, or for adding a percussive "chiff" at the beginning of notes. Unlike an analog waveform, noise

Paul Schreiber's E350 Morphing Terrarium is available from BugBrand for its FracRak-size format with banana connectors. (Courtesy of BugBrand)

is aperiodic: irregular and nonrepeating. In addition, there are different types of noise. White noise consists of all frequencies in equal amounts, much as white light consists of all of the colors in the visual spectrum. Pink noise, which generates an equal amount of energy per octave as opposed to across the entire frequency range, sounds darker than white noise. Digital synths such as the Clavia Nord Modular and the Subtractor softsynth in Propellerhead Reason provide a virtual knob for sweeping through various types of noise.

Some filters can create tones on their own. While in no way their raison d'être, they can oscillate given certain parameter settings and/or signal routings. The Minimoog's **lowpass filter** (**LPF**) will self-oscillate. Crank up its Filter Emphasis—often referred to as **resonance** or Q (quality factor, the sharpness of the filter)—tweak the **Cutoff Frequency** and Amount of Contour (filter envelope generator response level), and soon you'll add a whistle-like sound to the mix. It's a pure sine wave and will either track the keyboard or follow the filter envelope, depending on switch and knob settings. At the same time as you crank up the resonance, audio from the oscillators will get slightly quieter.

A Serge Creature, one of the M-class modules currently manufactured by Sound Transform Systems (STS). Besides generating sound with the Creature's VC Timegen Osc, you can drive its variable-Q multimode filter into self-oscillation by patching together the band output and input. Instead of offering individual Serge modules as in the past, STS president Rex Probe has grouped them into different and useful combinations in the M-class and Shop Panels series. (Mark Vail)

The Synthesizer

Many analog step sequencers, such as the eight-by-two model to the *left* in this STS Serge M-class Sequencer-A module, can oscillate when driven by a timing clock or pulse generator at audible rates. You can adjust the pitch by varying the clock speed and truncating the number of steps. To create complex waveforms, adjust individual step levels. The Sequencer-A includes a Time Generator/Clock module, which runs well up into the audible range, as well as an ACPR Active Processor for control voltages. (Mark Vail)

---

lowpass filter (LPF): a filter that attenuates higher frequencies above an adjustable cutoff frequency

filter resonance: a narrow band of frequencies near a filter's cutoff frequency that a synthesist can boost to a peak, often to the point of self-oscillation (depending on the filter design); also called Q, emphasis, regeneration, and feedback

cutoff frequency: the frequency point at which a filter begins attenuating or boosting frequencies

---

Don't confuse the classification of a filter as being "resonant" to mean that it will self-oscillate. Not all resonant filters can generate sound by self-oscillating.

VCAs, Envelopes, and LFOs

VCA is the acronym for **voltage-controlled amplifier**. What's its function? First you have to understand one important quality inherent in music: things change—or, at least, they should. As a singer, I learned you can't just belt out a note and let it hang static, regardless of how good you think it sounds. The note must evolve in some way to maintain listeners' interest. One such way is to vary its volume or intensity over time. In other words, its **amplitude**.

> *voltage-controlled amplifier* (*VCA*): a circuit or module that varies the volume or amount of gain of an incoming audio signal by responding to changes in voltages or digital values that arrive at its control input before passing along the audio signal
>
> *amplitude:* the volume or level of a signal measured by the amount of fluctuation in air pressure created acoustically by a sound, the voltage level of an electrical signal, or the range of numerical data in a digital environment; the amplitude of a signal in the audible range is perceived as loudness

The VCA is much more than a manual volume control. A beautiful aspect of voltage-control—and MIDI as well—is that you can program or patch physical or virtual modules together and program controllers to automatically vary aspects such as a voice's amplitude. Instead of playing notes with one hand while you tweak the volume knob with the other, you can program a module such as an envelope generator or an LFO to vary the volume for you, leaving your free hand to adjust another controller that varies filter cutoff or some other parameter. If your synth allows it, you can assign one controller—such as the **modulation wheel**—to modulate multiple destinations to, perhaps, vary filter cutoff frequency, pulse-width modulation, and a single oscillator's amplitude all at the same time.

> *modulation wheel:* a circular, free-turning (i.e., not spring-loaded, but restricted in range) performance controller mounted to roll toward and away from the performer, the upper part protruding a fraction of an inch above a synth's surface, typically to the left of the music keyboard—although sometimes above the left end of the keyboard to reduce the instrument's length; sometimes abbreviated as "mod wheel"
>
> *envelope:* a shape that changes aperiodically as a function of time, controlled by a set of rate or time and level parameters; it can serve as a control signal that can be applied to various aspects of a sound, such as pitch, filter cutoff frequency, and overall amplitude

To understand what an envelope generator is, let's start with the **envelope** part: Imagine the sound of a single piano note. First there's the initial striking of a piano key and the subsequent hammer contact with piano strings, followed by a near-immediate burst of tone produced by the vibrating strings. If you keep the key depressed, as the strings lose their vibrating energy, the volume of the tone will gradually decrease until it finally disappears. If you drew a representative plot of this sequence of sonic events on a two-dimensional graph with the x axis indicating time in seconds and the y axis the

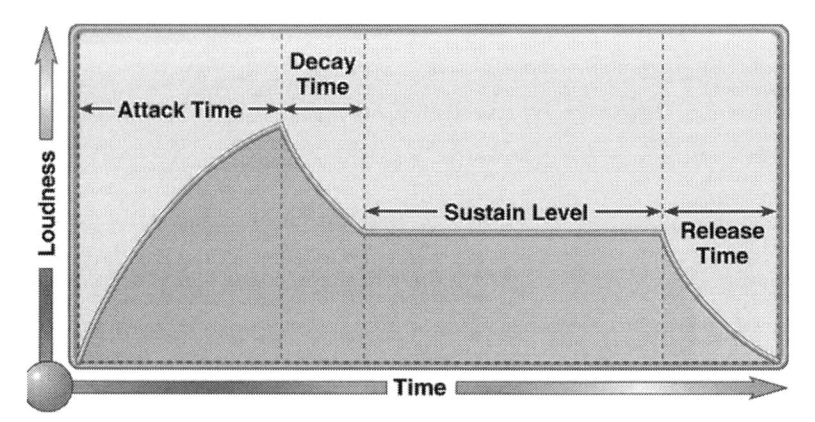

One of the most familiar types of envelopes is the ADSR, which stands for Attack, Decay, Sustain, and Release. (Illustration by Richard D. Eberly)

sound's amplitude in dB, there would be a brief moment at the beginning where the plotted line would quickly rise up from zero to a fairly high level on the amplitude scale, where it would briefly flatten out before gradually sloping back down to zero. Such a graph of a tone's volume over time is what's known as an envelope. Envelopes of other sound sources—such as a snare drum, flute, cannon, or dog bark—would look quite different. We identify the initial part of the envelope as the "attack," the fairly flat amplitude section as "sustain," and the drop as "release."

In 1863 the German physicist Hermann von Helmholtz wrote about the envelope concept in *Die Lehre von den Tonempfindungen als physiologische Grundlage für die Theorie der Musik*—which Alexander J. Ellis translated into English in 1870 as *On the Sensations of Tone as a Physiological Basis for the Theory of Music*. Helmholtz referred to the envelope as an "amplitude contour" and its segments as "attack," "steady state," and "decay." This three-part envelope description isn't far from the standard we use today.

When Bob Moog began designing his early synthesizer modules in 1964, Vladimir Ussachevsky of the Columbia-Princeton Electronic Music Center asked him to make—among numerous modules—a four-part envelope generator (EG) with control parameters called **attack, decay, sustain, and release** (**ADSR**). One difference between this and our piano envelopes is that the attack portion goes to a higher level than the sustain segment, and the decay stage comes before sustain. Whereas attack, decay, and release are time-based, sustain is a level.

> *attack, decay, sustain, and release (ADSR):* parameters found in one of the most familiar types of envelope generators; whereas the attack, decay, and release parameters are measurements of time, sustain is a level measured in voltage within an analog environment and a numerical value in the digital world

While there are more simple envelope generators—the AR is popular—the ADSR is perhaps the most common type of EG. Over the years there have been many improvements and extensions to the ADSR EG, such as:

- the Casio CZ-101's eight-stage envelope generators, with programmable rate and level parameters for each stage;
- Kurzweil's K1000 Series looping envelopes, essentially converting them into complex LFOs;
- the DADSR (delay plus ADSR) EGs on the Dave Smith Instruments Prophet 12 and other DSI instruments, which allows one EG to attack later than others for effects such as double-attack notes and auto-delayed vibrato;
- the Serge Modular Extended DADSR, which allows voltage control of the timing of each envelope stage; and
- the sixty-eight-stage envelopes in Native Instruments' Absynth for creating intricate and astounding grooves and extravagantly animated textures.

Other sophisticated EG enhancements found on a variety of synths include a Hold function to extend the peak level reached by the attack segment, making the EG an AHDSR; a Start Level parameter so the EG can begin from a value other than zero; the ability to insert negative values within bipolar envelopes, which is useful—among

The Envelope page in Native Instruments' Absynth. Few synths are as flexible as Absynth when it comes to envelopes. Not only do you get multiple stages—up to sixty-eight—to work with, but you can also draw curves within each stage to control how the level changes during that stage. Powerful and brilliant! (Courtesy of Native Instruments GmbH)

numerous techniques—for VCO pitch modulation; and the addition on many Korg synths of an extra stage called the Break Point & Slope, which follows the decay stage and allows a dip in the sustain level at a user-defined rate.

By applying EG control to a VCA, you can simulate the envelopes of many acoustic instruments and natural sounds. You can also create sounds with envelopes that wouldn't occur acoustically, especially with multisegment and loopable EGs.

VCAs can actually do more than attenuate an incoming signal; they can also alter or add some quality to the audio. Synthesist Gary Chang likes to overdrive the MetalBox tube VCA in his FracRak modular system to get a nasty snarl out of his oscillators, one of the many ways he manipulates audio. According to the MetalBox website, their tube VCA utilizes Cold War–era Soviet vacuum-tube technology in the form of a Russian-made 1J24B tube that originally appeared in MiG-29 fighter jets.

Which brings us to the LFO. Any VCO capable of oscillating at rates below 20Hz qualifies as an LFO. Typical LFO waveforms include sine, triangle, sawtooth, reverse sawtooth, pulse, and **sample-and-hold** (**S/H**) or random. Instead of serving as a sound source, an LFO typically modulates other components, such as a VCA for amplitude modulation effects such as tremolo or a VCO for vibrato or trills using, respectively, a triangle or sine wave and a pulse wave.

---

sample-and-hold (S/H) or random: a synthesizer circuit that captures an incoming control voltage or digital value when triggered by a pulse coming from an internal or external source and transmits the value to another component in the synthesizer

Among the many control functions tucked inside Moog Music's CP-251 Moogerfooger Control Processor is sample-and-hold with stepped (quantized) and smooth outputs. The CP-251 also provides a noise generator, a CV mixer, a lag processor with adjustable rise and fall rates, an LFO with oscillation rates from 0.2 to 50Hz and both triangle and square waveform outputs, a CV pedal input, two adjustable CV attenuators, and a one-in/three-out multiple. All connections are 1/4" jacks. (Courtesy of Moog Music Inc.)

How an S/H waveform is created depends on whether you're in the analog or digital domain, and whether you want independently stepped coordinates or a smooth glide between them. An analog S/H module provides two inputs and a single output. One input accepts a signal from a source of continually changing voltages, which could be a VCO, LFO, EG, sequencer, or noise generator. The second input needs a trigger of some sort from a clock or some kind of timing source. Whenever the trigger arrives, the module grabs the current value coming into the voltage input and stores it until the next trigger arrives. Between triggers the stored voltage won't change, and the module transmits the voltage through it's output. Some S/H modules have a built-in trigger clock, some provide a front-panel button for manually grabbing a sample voltage, and some don't require that you worry about all of the variables—you just enable sample-and-hold as the LFO's waveform. As for a glide between sampled voltage levels, it requires either a separate module or a built-in function called **slew** or **lag**, which induces a gradual change between voltage levels for an effect such as **portamento**.

---

slew or *lag:* a circuit that slows or smoothes instant and stepped changes in voltage at a specified rate

portamento: a function in which the pitch slides smoothly at an adjustable rate from one note to the next instead of jumping instantly to the new pitch; sometimes referred to as *glide*

LFOs can get particularly interesting and flexible in modular-synth land. Take, for example, Pittsburgh Modular's Voltage-Influenced Low Frequency Oscillator (VILFO) for Eurorack systems. At its simplest level, it's an analog LFO with a triangle-wave output along with a variable waveform output that ranges from triangle to nearly a square wave. The VILFO's two CV inputs and attenuators, however, allow transformations into other realms. Whereas the CV input on a traditional LFO module controls the oscillator frequency—the higher the voltage, the faster the oscillation—the VILFO's Influencing CV input attenuates the oscillator frequency and routes a percentage of the voltage to the module's feedback circuit, resulting in the production of anything from tremolo to wild fluctuations in the oscillating frequency. Simultaneously, using the Variable Control Voltage (VCV) knob in combination with a CV source feeding the VCV input, you can modulate the VILFO waveform between its triangle and pseudo-square shapes. Richard Nicol of Pittsburgh Modular added one extra oddity: you can use the VCV jack as an output, too, in which case you'll get a version of the variable output signal that leans toward a triangle wave. The VILFO's frequency ranges from minutes in length for slowly evolving control changes to the low end of the audible spectrum for very fast modulation speeds, switchable between the low and high ranges. A separate LFO works with the VILFO to perform effects such as clocking an analog sequencer so the sequencer occasionally skips a step and synchronization so the VILFO wave resets when its threshold level peaks, allowing syncopated and complex rhythm patterns.

Pittsburgh Modular's VILFO, an 8hp Eurorack module, may look simple, but it's capable of unusual modulation functions that synthesists have described as "quirky but musical" and "spookey." (© 2012 Pittsburgh Modular)

Don't confuse an LFO with a sub-oscillator, which is typically a slave to a master audio VCO, pitched an octave or two lower for increased bottom-end response. In contrast, a dedicated LFO is typically used to modulate a controllable parameter on another module at frequencies ranging from really slow up into the lower range of the audible spectrum. Although there's no set definition of what frequency range an LFO should cover, the most extensive and quantifiable I've found appears within the Clavia Nord Modular's selection of LFO modules, which can be set to oscillate anywhere from 699 seconds/cycle (11 min. and 39 sec., or 0.0014306Hz) to 392Hz through three independent ranges. In contrast, each of the Minimoog's three VCOs can generate frequencies from 0.1Hz to 20kHz through six overlapping ranges.

Envelope Followers and Pitch-to-Voltage Converters

In contrast to the envelope generator, the envelope follower—or envelope detector—tracks the amplitude of an incoming signal and outputs a proportional control voltage. It's simple but very useful as it allows sound generated by acoustic and electro-acoustic instruments to be involved in the electronic synthesis process.

A pitch- or frequency-to-voltage converter tracks incoming frequencies to generate a CV output. This synthesizer component attempts to detect the fundamental of the incoming signal, which can be a tricky process depending on the harmonic content, note durations, tempo, and frequencies of the signal. Such a converter doesn't handle chords well, unless you'd like a random output. Analogue Systems' RS30 combines both envelope-following and pitch-to-voltage functions in a single unit called the Frequency-to-Voltage + Envelope module. As of late 2013, Big City Music still had the RS30 in stock, but Bob Williams of Analogue Systems tells me this module has been replaced by the RS35 External Processor because the RS30 has a limited range of tracking and is more suited to converting Hz/V for early analog Korg and Yamaha synths. The RS35 is compatible with the industry-standard 1V/octave, plus it provides extra features such as trigger output and voltage hold. It also has a built-in pre-amp for boosting low-level signals from external sources.

Filters

A filter can alter incoming sounds in ways ranging from subtle to so outlandish you wouldn't recognize the original source. Most common is the lowpass filter (LPF), a circuit that attenuates higher frequencies while allowing frequencies lower than the adjustable cutoff frequency to pass. LPFs come in different flavors. One of the most sonically definitive factors in a filter is the angle of its **rolloff slope**, also referred to as a response curve and typically measured in decibels per octave. The steeper the slope, the quicker frequencies above the cutoff are attenuated by an LPF. The number of **poles** within the filter determines the rolloff slope. The more poles, the steeper the slope. Each pole adds 6dB per octave to the slope. Most common are two-pole (12dB per octave, as in the Oberheim SEM) and four-pole (24dB per octave, as in the Minimoog and ARP 2600) filters. Regardless of the rolloff slope, close the cutoff frequency all the way and no frequencies will pass.

> *rolloff slope:* the rate, usually measured in dB per octave, beginning at the frequency cutoff point at which a filter attenuates an audio signal's frequency components
> *poles:* attenuation circuits within a filter

Beyond the lowpass come highpass (HPF), bandpass (BPF), and band-reject (notch) filters. As you might expect, the HPF does the opposite of the LPF, curtailing low frequencies with a slope determined by its number of poles and passing through higher frequencies. A BPF squelches lows and highs. By patching low- and highpass filters that have the same rolloff slopes in series, you can make a bandpass filter. The notch or band-reject filter works in an opposite fashion to the bandpass: high and low frequencies pass through while the notch filler attenuates those in the middle. A resonance control on either a bandpass or notch filter allows you to adjust the peak or dip amplitude level, with the slopes on either side of the cutoff frequency getting steeper the higher or lower the resonance level. Whereas a BPF works very well to boost specific midrange frequencies in a mix, a notch filter might be perfect for quelling overly aggressive midrange frequencies.

Multimode filters provide numerous response types. For example, the Clavia Nord Lead's filter provides five modes: two- and four-pole lowpass, four-pole highpass, bandpass, and a combination notch-plus-two-pole lowpass. Multiple filter modes aren't uncommon on modular synths, either. Lowpass, highpass, bandpass, and notch output jacks appear on filters from such elder modular modules as those from E-mu and Aries, the Serge Variable Q VCF within the still-in-production Creature, Dual "Q" Filter, and MultiFilter M-class modules and certain Shop Panels from Sound Transform Systems, and many others.

Earlier I explained how a self-oscillating filter such as the Minimoog's could generate a whistle-like tone, a process that decreases the audible amplitude of its oscillators the higher you crank the **resonance**. In contrast, the Steiner-Parker Synthacon—manufactured from 1975 to 1979—sports a multimode resonant filter that not only can self-oscillate, but its designer Nyle Steiner also incorporated a positive-feedback filter rather than a negative-feedback filter like that in the Minimoog and most other analog synths. On the Minimoog, when you turn the resonance up, the oscillator audio level drops because a negative signal is being fed back. With the Synthacon's filter, the overall signal either stays constant or increases when you crank up the filter resonance. The Synthacon's filter isn't unique; Arturia successfully implemented—under Steiner's guidance—this type of filter in the MiniBrute analog monosynth (2012). You can also duplicate this positive-feedback response with any synth that allows you to route the filter's output back into its input.

> *resonance:* a circuit that routes the output of a filter back to its input at adjustable levels; increasing this level creates a peak in a narrow band of the frequency range, the exact frequency determined by the filter's cutoff frequency control; at adequately high levels, many filters will self-oscillate; also known as regeneration, Q, and feedback

Manufactured from 1975 to 1979, the Steiner-Parker Synthacon was an inexpensive rival to the Minimoog and ARP Odyssey. One way the Synthacon differs from the Minimoog is the manner in which their filters self-oscillate. "The Synthacon has a positive-feedback filter rather than a negative-feedback filter," explains its maker, Nyle Steiner. "On the Minimoog, when you turn the resonance up the output level drops because a negative signal is being fed back. With my filter circuit, the overall signal either stays constant or increases along with the filter resonance." (Courtesy of Nyle Steiner)

Among the many notable features of Arturia's affordable MiniBrute monosynth is a new version of the positive-feedback self-oscillating resonant filter Nyle Steiner created for the Steiner-Parker Synthacon. To assure they did it right, Arturia engaged Nyle himself to approve the MiniBrute's multimode filter. Yves Usson designed its analog circuitry, and Axel Hartmann arranged the layout of its controllers. (Courtesy of Arturia)

You can apply signals from various components to modulate parameters of a typical synth filter. For example, connect an EG to vary filter cutoff frequency and add harmonic motion to the filtered tone. Doing the same with an LFO or looped envelope repeats the effect over and over instead of once via a single note event. Many synths provide keyboard tracking for the filter so the filtering process differs from one end of the note range to the other. To simulate many acoustic instruments, you'll want the filter cutoff frequency to rise as you play higher-pitched notes on the keyboard. If the filter is self-oscillating, full keyboard tracking allows the resulting pitch to track the keyboard along with the oscillators—although you'll probably need to make adjustments to get perfect tuning.

Quite a few analog synths provide an audio input into which you can route signals from external sound sources and process them with the synth's filter(s), and possibly other built-in functions as well. "Since about 1994, filters and synthesizers have found a home in mixing," explains the producer/synthesist Jeff Fair.

> A lot of engineers use filter banks and synthesizers to create the textures that they're looking for. Not so much as an instrument per se, but almost as an effects device as a way of creating the overtones and clamping down on the frequency spectrum that they're dealing with. Being able to put sounds in a frequency space

of their own using lowpass, highpass, or bandpass filters and resonance to peak frequencies exactly where they want, or to take energy away from another part of the sound, is a great and wonderful thing.

Numerous filters do more than alter the harmonic content of an audio signal, purposely affecting the audio quality as well. Consider the Flight of Harmony Plague Bearer (PB), a Eurorack module also produced for a time in FracRak form and as a stand-alone, battery-powered Quad processor containing four PBs. Although it's generically classified as a voltage-controlled resonant bandpass filter, the PB has also been called a waveshaper, distortion unit, and audio mangler. It's definitely all of the above in good and sonically potent ways, it can self-oscillate with a few knob twists, and it provides plenty of CV input jacks to control much of what it does.

Among current Eurorack offerings, there are a multitude of filter modules from which to choose, some of them originating in another format. One example is Malekko Heavy Industry's licensed Eurorack version of the Wiard Boogie Lowpass filter, which sports the gamut of 6, 12, 18, and 24dB/octave output jacks. Each cutoff slope has its own particular sonic characteristics, and it's useful to be able to mix the outputs in combination or further process individual slope outputs as you see fit.

A rev3.3 Flight of Harmony Plague Bearer Eurorack module. Not only can it process audio signals, but it can self-oscillate and serve as a noise source. Its High and Low knobs don't actually function as you might expect. As spelled out in the PB documentation, "Okay, a confession: The controls are technically labeled incorrectly. *High* actually controls the cutoff frequency (f_c) of the lowpass portion . . . while *Low* controls the f_c of the highpass section." In addition, the High, Low, and Gain knobs vary filter resonance. It's a potent combination that can lead to scalding timbres, or soothing ones if you treat the PB with tender, loving care. (Mark Vail)

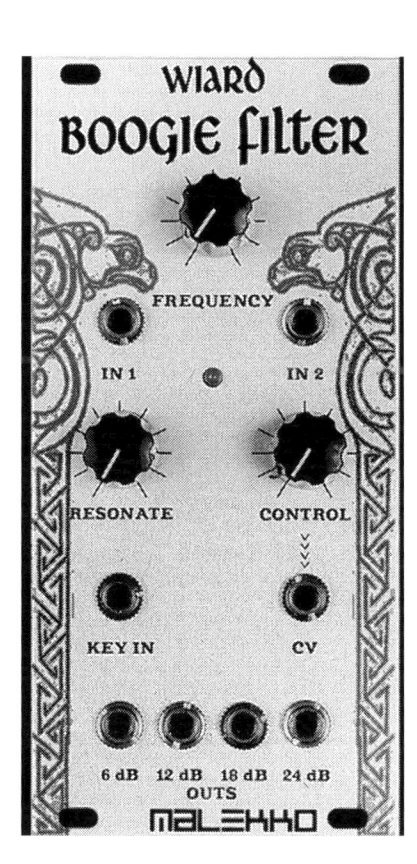

Malekko Heavy Industry's version of the Wiard Boogie Filter will take up 12hp of horizontal space in a Eurorack cabinet. The acronym *hp* stands for horizontal pitch and is a standard measurement of Eurorack module width where one hp equals 0.2" (5.08mm). (© 2012 Malekko Heavy Industry Corp.)

You can find quite a selection of stand-alone filters and processors that not only work really well with a variety of instruments, but also are equipped with patch points for synth-style CV control. Within the stompbox/tabletop realm, Moog Music offers the analog Moogerfooger MF-101 Lowpass Filter, which bestows Minimoog-like filtering and much more. It provides both two- and four-pole slopes along with self-oscillation for producing tones ranging from the song of a humpback whale to a squealing banshee when you crank up the Resonance. Along with an internal envelope follower that responds to the loudness of incoming audio, you can select either smooth or fast triggering of the envelope. The smooth setting creates more of a **wah effect**, but fast mode works better for brief events such as a snare hit. On the MF-101's back panel, you'll find 1/4" jacks for audio I/O, envelope follower CV output, and CV inputs for filter cutoff frequency, resonance level, wet/dry mix, and envelope amount. Along with Moog-style knobs for setting the envelope amount, wet/dry mix, and filter cutoff frequency and resonance, there's a Drive knob for adjusting input gain up to and beyond a sweet overdrive effect. If you're after the legendary Moog filter sound, the MF-101 delivers.

> *wah effect:* the sound of a filter's cutoff frequency going up and down or opening and closing, creating a sort of vocal-like "wow" or "wah" tonal change

Another tone processor that's been popular with electronic musicians since 1996 is the Sherman Filterbank (FB). Available in tabletop and rackmount forms, the FB excels

The Synthesizer

Trickled down from synth modules Bob Moog designed during the 1960s, the Moogerfooger MF-101 Lowpass Filter can self-oscillate to produce a whistle-like tone. Pump a digital synth through the MF-101 to create a ballsy vintage analog sound, or imprint the Moog filter sound on drum tracks, guitar, vocals, or whatever. (Courtesy of Moog Music)

at messing up and distorting audio with its analog circuitry, which includes twin two-pole, resonant, multimode filters that allow you to smoothly sweep from lowpass through bandpass to highpass characteristics. This is very uncommon; not only can you route audio through the filters in series for a 24dB/octave response and formant-like filtering or in parallel for stereo filtered sweep effects, but you can also dial up continuously variable combinations of both configurations. Among the FB's other circuits are an LFO capable of oscillating at frequencies up into the audible spectrum for beefy modulation effects; amplitude and frequency modulation; and MIDI control of filter cutoff frequencies and resonances, FM and AM depth, envelope attack and release times, ADSR decay time, and output volume. The FB has multiple 1/4" inputs—audio, FM, AM, ADSR trigger, AR trigger, link for a multi-FB system, and, introduced on version 2, a bypass footswitch—and outputs—main, filter 1, LFO, ADSR, and link. Signs of FB maker Herman Gillis's intent: Sherman's lesson-oriented FB user booklet is called the "Abuser's Manual," and one of their logos includes phrases such as "Dangerous Frequency Range" and "Watch Your Speakers" encircling a contemporary rendition of the face and hands from Edvard Munch's painting *The Scream*.

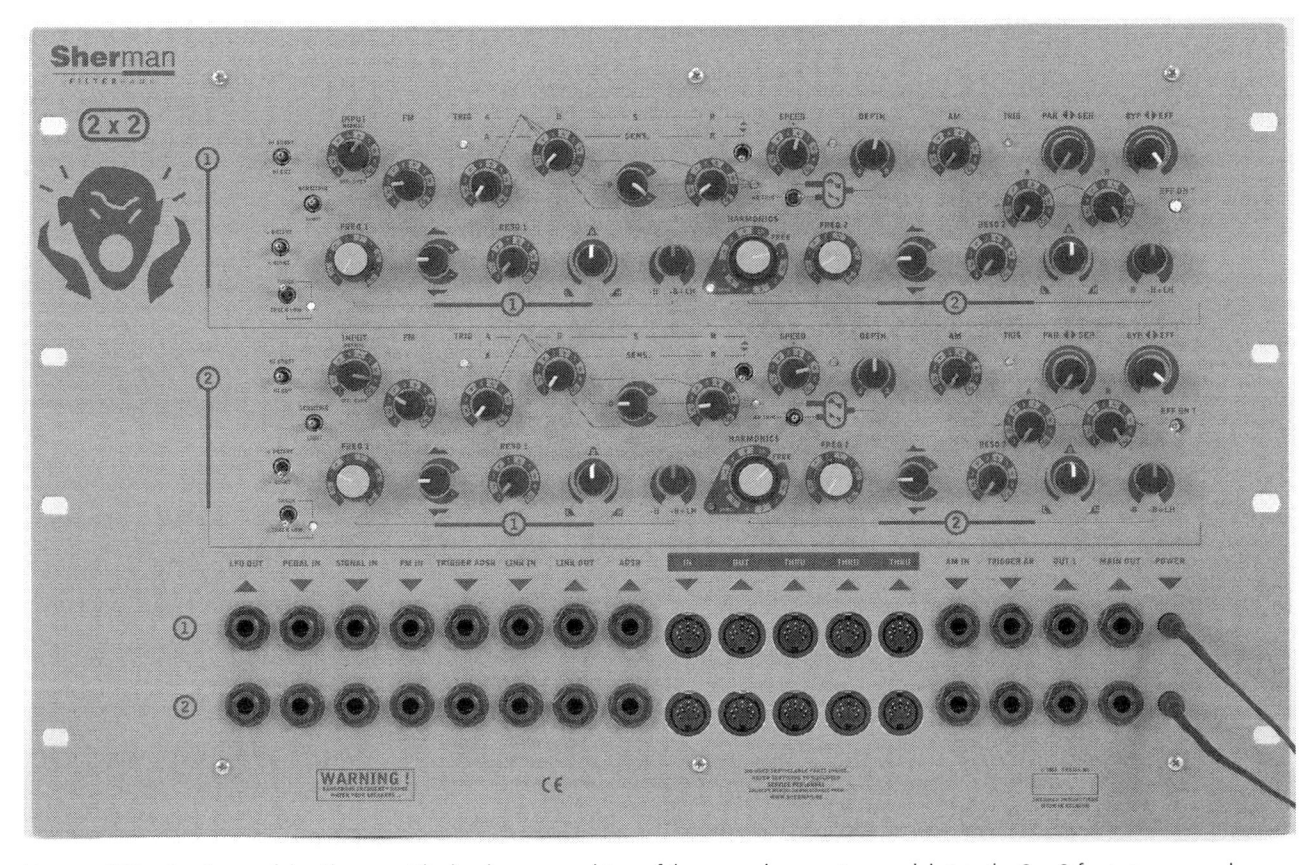

Herman Gillis, developer of the Sherman Filterbank, squeezed two of the second-generation models into the 2 × 2 for twice as much filtering fun. Among the improvements over the original Filterbank are: a Hi Boost/Cut switch that in the Hi mode adds considerable virility to high-frequency content; a switchable transpose function that can shift the filter range up an octave or, for a particularly aggressive result, a fifth; and a new pitch-tracking feature that attempts to tune the filters to incoming audio, which can lead to entertaining effects when the source sound features lots of harmonics. (© 2012 Sherman Productions B.V.B.A.)

Herman Gillis also teamed with Rodec, a veteran manufacturer of DJ gear, to create the Restyler, another filtering audio processor. Sporting a stereo multimode filter and a flexible envelope follower, the tabletop Restyler also packs three short-throw (20mm) sliders for adjusting the output levels of its low-, band-, and highpass filter ranges; independent two- and four-pole cutoff-slope pushbuttons for each range, allowing quick timbral transformations; and LED-encircled encoder knobs for adjusting the envelope follower's trigger frequency and the filter's master cutoff frequency. You adjust the envelope follower's trigger sensitivity, trigger speed, and transient response from smooth to abrupt using one set of three knobs, as well as the filter's resonance peak using a fourth knob. In unique Sherman fashion, the Restyler can perform FM on incoming audio as well as AM on the individual filter bands. The Restyler is a real-time-only processor with no MIDI or CV facilities for automation. It sports RCA audio I/O jacks for the DJ crowd, as well as balanced Neutrik Combo input jacks that accept either XLR or TRS 1/4″ plugs. Balanced TRS 1/4″ output jacks also come standard; optionally available are XLR output jacks, which you can install with a screwdriver, no soldering required. The Restyler works exceptionally well in converting meek tones into some that are quite aggressive, subtly coloring digital timbres, and doing practically anything in between.

Audio mangling is also a forte of the Schippmann Ebbe und Flut (EUF), German for "ebb and flow." This 2U rackmount analog processor contains two slightly different

The Restyler, developed in collaboration by Sherman Productions and Rodec, contains a multimode filter, an envelope follower, and other functions for bending audio. As advertised, it specializes in processing dynamics, punch, groove, and the sound of individual instruments and complete mixes. The Restyler works particularly well on drum and percussion tracks. (©2012 Sherman Productions B.V.B.A.)

four-pole multimode VCFs, each under control of an independent attack/hold/release EG, with continuously variable envelope-tracking. Also available for modulating the filters are an LFO that offers triangle, sawtooth, and pulse waveforms; sample and hold; an envelope follower with linear and logarithmic response modes; and a trigger input that dynamically responds to incoming signals. Each filter provides a choice of twelve filter modes, including LPF, BPF, and HPF, band-reject, and **allpass**. The EUF's filters can impart oomph, character, and energy to sounds by making them brittle, smooth, or aggressive. The EUF features abundant 1/4" jacks for CV and trigger I/O.

> *allpass filter:* while all frequencies advance unabated, cutoff frequency and resonance settings cause changes in the **phase** of some frequencies
> *phase:* the current point in a waveform cycle, measured in degrees
> *ADCs:* analog-to-digital converters
> *DACs:* digital-to-analog converters

Expressive filters also dwell within digital signal processors, one of which kindled Gary Chang's creative enthusiasm in 2010: the OTO Machines Biscuit. Along with a stereo, multimode, four-pole analog filter, the Biscuit has eight low-resolution eight-bit **ADCs/DACs** that can transform pristine audio into different levels of '80s-vintage digital grunge, and it will step through the convertors using its built-in sequencer, which you can sync to a drum machine or external sequencer via MIDI. You can vary the Biscuit's sampling rate all the way down to 250Hz to deliciously crunch a sound and process it with a waveshaper to introduce harmonics that weren't there before, a MIDI-synced or

Flexible and powerful analog filtering and signal processing are possible thanks to the Schippmann Ebbe und Flut. (Courtesy of Dipl.-Ing. Carsten Schippmann, Schippmann Electronic Musical Instruments, www.schippmann-music.com)

tap-tempo digital delay, a variable pitch-shifter, a pitch-harmonizer, a tube saturation simulator, step-sequenced filtering, or vibrato. The Biscuit is fully MIDI compatible, allowing you to capture, edit, and replay knob adjustments and button selections with a sequencer, as well as back up your sixteen patches from internal memory. You can download Biscuit designer Denis Cazajeux's software upgrades via the Internet and transfer them into the unit via MIDI sys-ex. New firmware released in November 2011 allows the Biscuit to alternatively function as a two-oscillator monosynth with a sixteen-step sequencer. Chang values the Biscuit because it offers multiple processing functions in an integrated package, and he enjoys running drum tracks through it to get more variety in the beats.

The OTO Biscuit packs lots of processing power—and now even a monophonic synthesis mode—in a small metal box that weighs less than 1.5 pounds and measures a mere 7.48" × 2.36" × 4.60". The backlit buttons glow different colors according to the Biscuit's processing activity. (Alex Gopher, courtesy of OTO Machines)

EQs and Filter Banks

While you'll find an equalizer (EQ) more often in a mixing console, as stand-alone hardware, or as plug-in software than in a synthesizer, it's a type of filter that you typically use to subtly adjust the frequency content in an audio signal—although you can push an EQ's response to extremes, such as boosting the bass too high because a cheap sound system doesn't reveal what's actually going on down in the low end well enough for you to hear.

Representing EQ in its simplest form are bass and treble boost/cut knobs on a car stereo, guitar amp, or boombox. That is what's known as two-band shelving EQ for two reasons: first because it divides the entire frequency spectrum into only two segments—low and high; and second because it cuts or boosts all of the frequencies below or above a specific frequency—known as the shelf, hinge, or corner frequency—with cutoff slopes followed at either end by essentially flat lines, the actual "shelves," at amplitudes determined by the parameter settings. Slightly more sophisticated is three-band EQ, with level controls for bass, midrange, and treble frequencies. Since consumer hi-fi-oriented EQ has fixed bandwidth and corner frequency components, it's only useful for general adjustments of frequency levels.

A graphic equalizer breaks down the frequency spectrum into multiple fixed bands, with individual controls to boost or cut the amplitude level—perhaps within a range of ±15 to ±18dB or more—in each band. A common graphic EQ guitar stompbox might provide ten bands with center frequencies chosen to enhance harmonics generated by an electric guitar. More serious rackmount or plug-in graphic EQs for onstage or studio use typically have two separate channels of twelve to thirty-two bands. In a live situation with open mics, a graphic EQ might help you avoid unwanted feedback from onstage monitor speakers.

Parametric EQs don't usually provide as many individual bands as a graphic EQ—four or five is common, but BIAS SuperFreq allows up to ten—but it's far more flexible. For each parametric band, you typically get controls for selecting a center frequency, varying the cut or gain with ranges similar to what you get with a graphic EQ, and the "Q" or bandwidth, which allows you to dial the equalization curve somewhere from flat through a roundish hill/valley to a mountain peak/deep gully.

In the synthesizer realm, there's a specialized filter that's somewhat similar to a graphic EQ and typically doesn't allow voltage-control. It's called the fixed filter bank or formant filter. Bob Moog designed an early version, the Model 907A module, which provides ten independent filters. At the low end is a four-pole LPF, at the top is a four-pole HPF, and in between are eight BPFs with fixed center frequencies of 250Hz, 350Hz, 500Hz, 700Hz, 1kHz, 1.4kHz, 2kHz, and 2.8kHz. Each of the 907A's BPFs has a fixed bandwidth of half an octave and each filter has a single knob for boosting or cutting frequencies within its particular range. The specific frequency centers assist in simulating the harmonic content of certain acoustic instruments. As Dan Wyman wrote in the 907A's owner's manual for Moog Music in 1981, "completely different timbres can be set up for different ranges of the same tone, if the output of the filter is recombined with unfiltered frequencies at different levels."

There are quite a few fixed filter banks in the modular-synth sector. Eurorack users can, for example, choose the fifteen-band Doepfer A-128—with manufacturer-provided

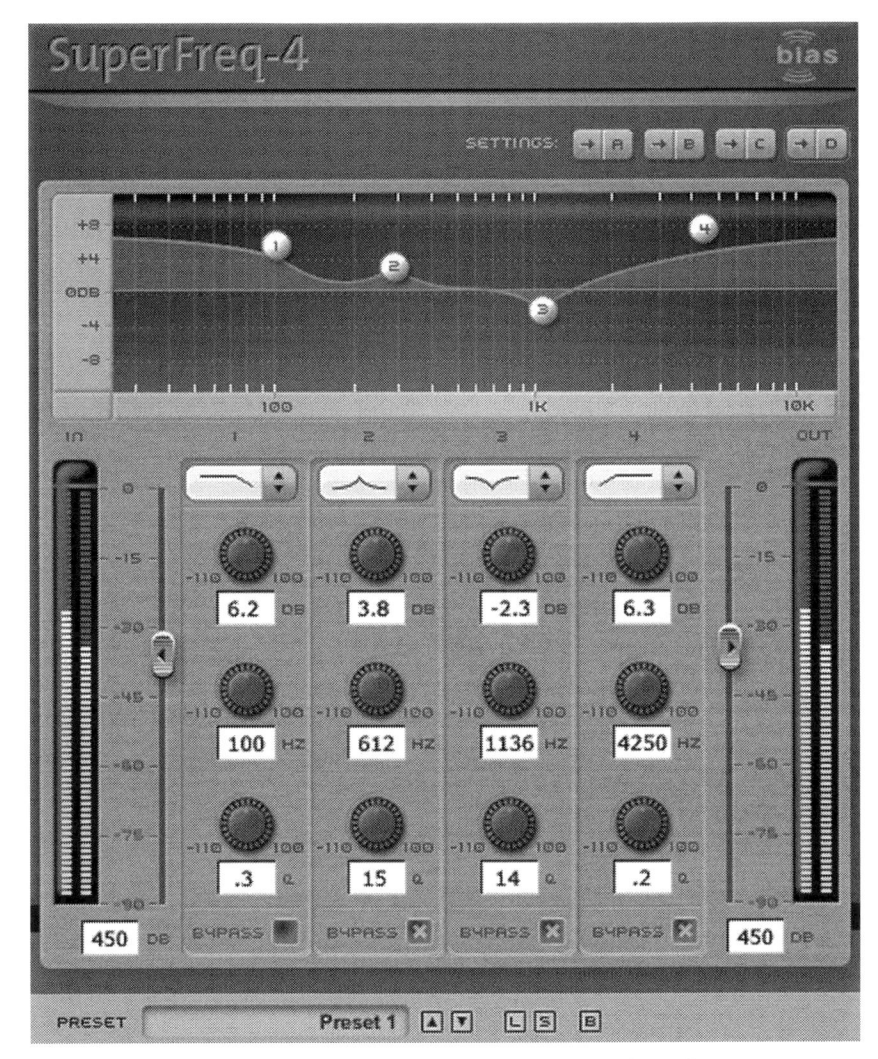

A screenshot of the four-band BIAS SuperFreq-4 parametric equalizer plug-in. SuperFreq also provides six-, eight-, and ten-band plug-ins. You can select an EQ shape, dB cut or boost, center frequency, and bandwidth for each band; you can also bypass any band using a virtual button. The graphic display at the top indicates the EQ curve, and meters on either side indicate the incoming and processed output levels. (Reprinted with permission from owner © 2012, Marin Audio Technology, LLC)

directions to build a separate breakout-box module that provides an individual output for each band—and the Analogue Systems RS215 Eight-Band Octave Filter. Long available in the Serge lineup of modules—and currently found in the EQ Shifter and Audio Interface M-class modules and Soup Kitchen 1 panel from Sound Transform Systems—is the ten-band Resonant Equalizer. Its eight middle bands are spaced at major-seventh intervals to avoid, according to Serge documentation, "the very common effect of an accentuated resonance in one key, as will be the effect from graphic equalizers with octave or third-octave spacing between bands. . . . The Resonant Equalizer's band spacing [produces] formant peaks and valleys that are similar to those in acoustic instrument sounds."

Don Buchla has designed two of the most unusual filters within the modular-synth realm. The first appeared within his vintage Series 200 as the Model 296 Programmable Spectral Processor, and the second is currently available in the Series 200e as the Model 296e Spectral Processor. Both are sixteen-channel filter banks that allow voltage-control.

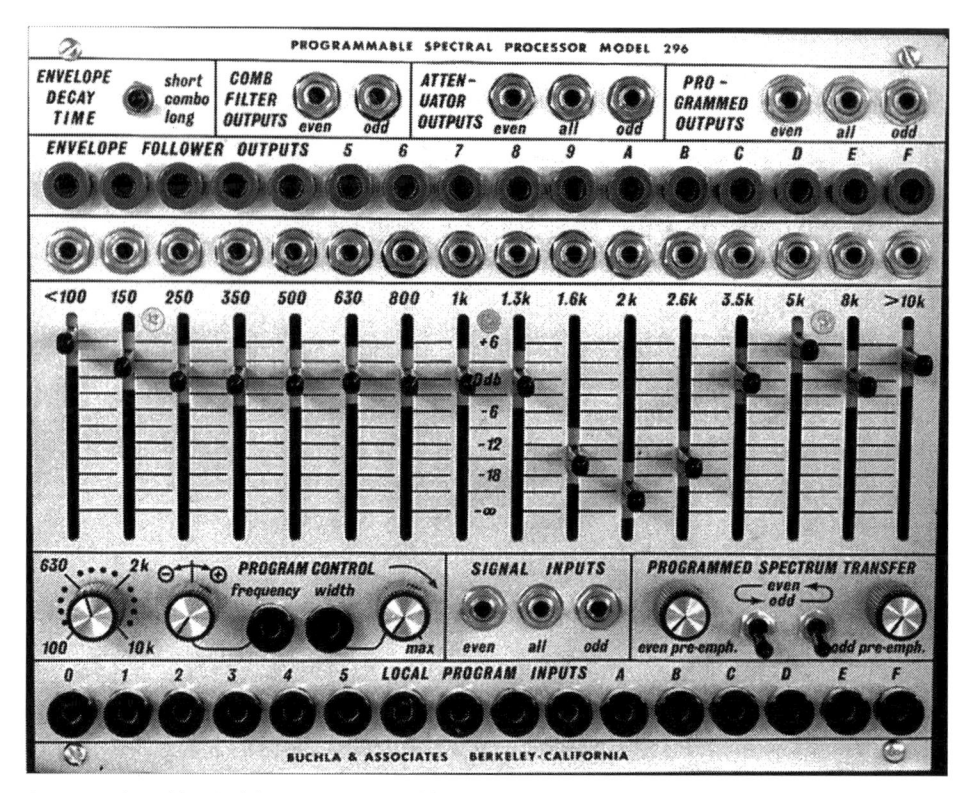

An original Buchla Model 296 Programmable Spectral Processor module. It does sixteen channels of Constant Bark. (Photo courtesy of Buchla Electronic Musical Instruments)

Buchla selected their bandpass center frequencies to complement the human ear's discrimination curve. As Don describes the original module, "It has 16 channels of filtering, but they cover the same frequency range of a 24-channel third-octave filter because they're Constant Bark filters and the channels are wider in the areas where you have more frequency confusion and less frequency perceptual separation."

The bark scale relates to human perceptual frequency discrimination. Bark units are smaller in the midrange and considerably wider at the bass and treble ends. Every channel on the original 296 Spectral Processor has a VCA and an envelope detector for which you can adjust the channel's decay time and response. You can set all sixteen channels to have the same response and make them short or long. You can base them on the frequencies so that the high ones are shorter and the low ones much longer. It also has gating, so you can connect the envelope outputs from one Spectral Processor to the gated inputs of another and transfer spectrums "from your voice to a sawtooth, a cement mixer, or any raucous-sounding contraption you like," says Don.

This process differs from what a **vocoder** does, although it can sound similar. In a traditional sense, vocoding describes a range of techniques for encoding or camouflaging the voice, including the Bell Labs–invented triple-filter process that models the human vocal tract (the larynx inside the laryngeal cavity, followed by the pharynx, the oral cavity, and the nasal cavity). Vocoding also requires fewer parameters to function. Since sixteen is a lot of interconnections to make on the Spectral Processor, it has a provision that allows eight channels to use their envelope detectors to gate the alternate channels so that you can analyze the signal with eight odd channels and then transfer it to the eight even channels, which forms a displacement.

Acoustics and Synthesis Basics

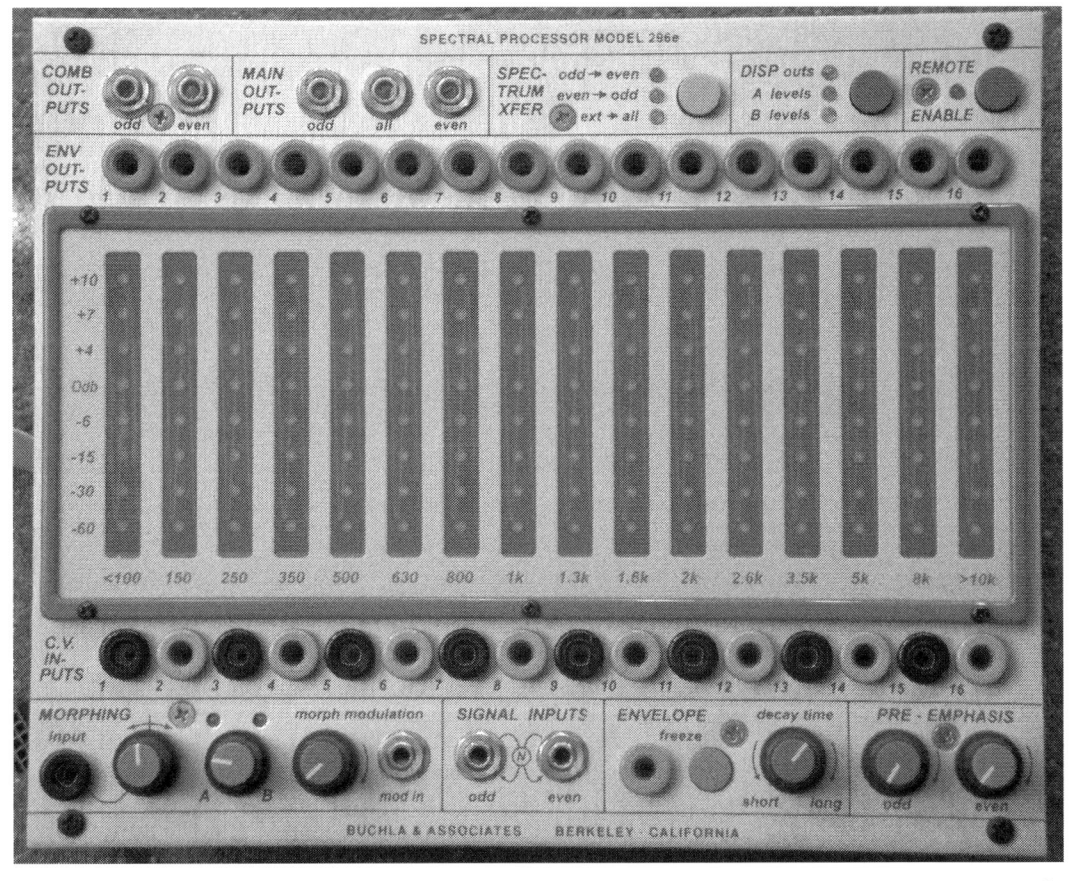

The twenty-first-century version of Buchla's Constant Bark filter, the Model 296e Spectral Processor. (Courtesy of Buchla Electronic Musical Instruments)

Synthesizer pioneer Don Buchla, wearing his favorite chapeau, takes a walk at the 2012 Winter NAMM show. (Mark Vail)

vocoder: an electronic device that analyzes the varying tonal characteristics of one source and applies them to another

The twenty-first-century Model 296e works in much the same way, except that it has multiple touch ribbons with memories on top of LEDs instead of the original's analog sliders. You touch a 296e ribbon to change the amplitude level, which is illustrated by LEDs. There are two response memories, allowing you to set up different EQ curves and morph between them manually or using CV control and even an audio signal. The ribbon LEDs change to indicate the current levels of all sixteen bands. Alternatively, the LEDs can display the envelope decay rates in real time. To see Niklas Winde's 296e demonstrations, direct your Web browser to **www.oup.com/us/thesynthesizer (OUP *The Synthesizer* website)**.

Filter banks aren't confined to modular synths. You'll also find stand-alone versions in stompbox and tabletop forms. Moog Music has produced a flexible collection of filter banks in their Moogerfooger line bearing the name MuRF—the Multiple Resonance Filter array. The original, Bob Moog-developed MF-105 MuRF arrived in 2004. Squeezed inside it are eight resonant BPFs with their own vertical level sliders, along with a sine wave LFO and a sequencing envelope generator that steps through envelope-controlled filter settings at a chosen tempo, imparting a striking rhythmic pattern to incoming audio. Not only can you adjust the envelope amount, input/drive, and output levels using front-panel knobs, but 1/4" CV inputs also allow you to vary the sequence speed, wet/dry mix level, envelope amount, and LFO sweep range using external CV sources. Besides a footswitch tap-tempo input, there are mono audio input and left/mono and right audio outputs—all 1/4" jacks.

Two revised MuRFs followed the original: the MF-105B specifically addresses bass players with a different set of center filter frequencies, and you can switch the current MF-105M MIDI MuRF between the original and bass filter frequencies. The MF-105M—introduced in 2009—provides MIDI input for syncing the MuRF's sequencer to MIDI clock and controlling MuRF parameters using MIDI and CV signals.

Another flexible filter bank comes from Roger Linn, the drum-machine pioneer, but it does way more than that. Roger introduced the AdrenaLinn stompbox in 2001. He may have intended it for electric guitar, but it's far too versatile and potent to limit its bundle of sonic-altering functions to that instrument alone. The AdrenaLinn provides hundreds of editable, four-part drum patterns complete with different varieties of kick, snare, hi-hat/ride cymbal/shaker/tambourine, and shaker/claps/tom-tom/triangle/conga/cowbell. It also offers virtual models of forty vintage guitar and bass amps that impart different and adjustable levels and types of overdrive/distortion to the signal. There are also signal-processing effects including delay, stereo reverb, auto wah, flanging, **talkbox**, **compression**, auto pan, and an arpeggiator sequence function with which you'll hear a two-measure pattern emphasizing certain notes that you've programmed into the preset or select live via MIDI notes. You can order these effects to your liking. But what specifically applies to this discussion is the AdrenaLinn's beat-synchronized filter processing. A two-bar sequencer can step through thirty-two filter cutoff-frequency settings—sixteen steps per measure, divisible into timings of sixteenth, swing, half-swing, eighths, and eighth-note triplets—adding unique resonance changes in sync with the drum patterns or an external MIDI clock. Not only does the AdrenaLinn filter provide a bandpass mode, but it will also do two- and four-pole lowpass, highpass, notch, and comb (flanging) filtering. All delays and swept modulations—tremolo, flanging, swept filters, random filtering, etc.—are synced to the drum patterns or MIDI clock. The AdrenaLinn sports dozens of parameters and a challenging programming interface, but it's easier to program using SoundTower's AdrenaLinn III SE—an affordable cross-platform editor—and a USB-to-MIDI interface.

> *talkbox:* traditionally an electro-acoustic process that incorporates a speaker sealed in a box and a flexible plastic tube that conducts the speaker's output directly to the performer's mouth, where changes in the shape of the mouth cavity filter the sound and a microphone picks up the results for amplification; notably used by guitarists Peter Frampton and Joe Walsh, respectively, in "Do You Feel Like We Do" and "Rocky Mountain Way"
>
> *compression:* a process that reduces the amplitude range of an audio signal by diminishing peaks and increasing low levels

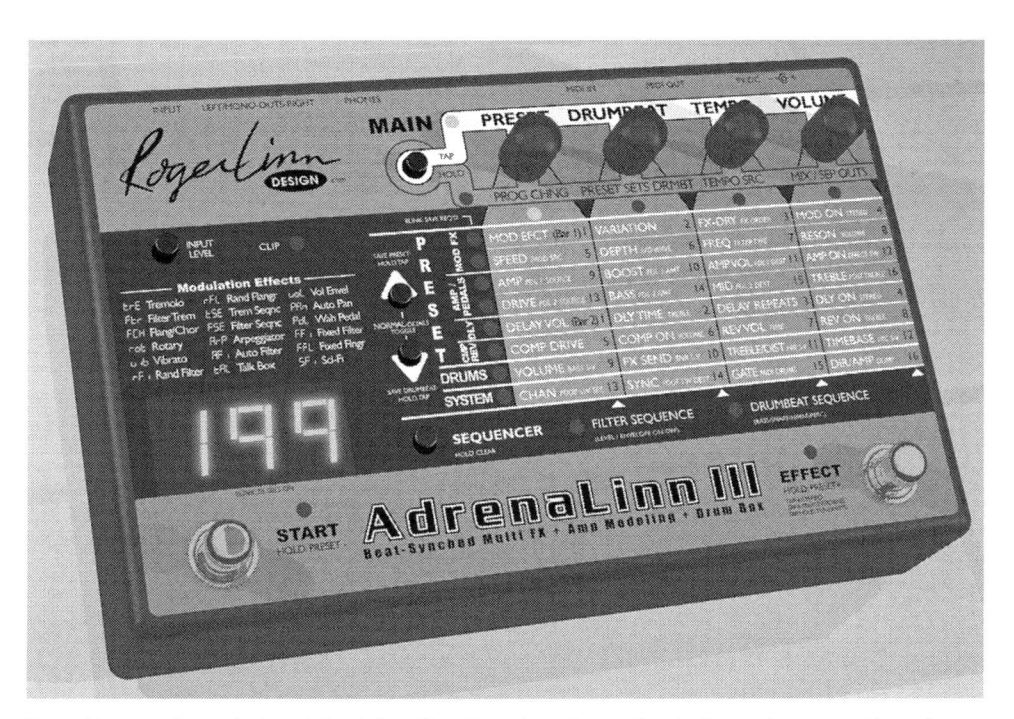

Roger Linn may have designed the AdrenaLinn for guitar players, but it also works great with synths and other sound sources. The major hardware differences between the original AdrenaLinn and versions II and III are a more powerful main computer chip and larger flash memory—plus AdrenaLinns prior to serial number A02200 lack the 1/4" headphone jack. To upgrade either the original or AdrenaLinn II to version III functionality, you simply swap the existing chips with newer ones and replace the front-panel adhesive overlay. (Courtesy of Roger Linn Design)

Roger Linn appears in his booth at the January 2005 NAMM show, when he introduced the AdrenaLinn II. Roger is mostly known for his programmable drum machines, but he's an outstanding guitar player and multi-instrumentalist, played lead guitar with Leon and Mary Russell on *Saturday Night Live* in May 1976, composed hit songs for Eric Clapton and Mary Chapin Carpenter, and won the Technical Grammy Award in 2011. (Mark Vail)

Analog Sequencers

Born in the original heyday of analog modular synthesizers, an analog step sequencer typically has knobs or sliders arranged in one to three rows of eight or sixteen columns. It traditionally scans from left to right across the columns, transmitting gates or triggers and control voltages based on the knob positions. You apply the sequencer's CV outputs to control VCO pitch, VCF cutoff frequency, VCA amplitude, or any destination you find useful, and gate/trigger outputs to EG inputs. After you make the appropriate module connections, the sequencer repeatedly plays an **ostinato** pattern while you tweak its knobs or others elsewhere in the system.

> *ostinato:* a repeating melodic pattern or succession of notes that might continue through an entire piece of music

You'll hear step sequencing in many pieces and styles of electronic music, and sometimes it even shows up in a rock song. One of the most effective and memorable examples of the latter is the brilliantly blippy, repetitively self-oscillating filter melody starting at

2:54 in Joe Walsh's "Life's Been Good" on *But Seriously, Folks....* Joe created it with an ARP Odyssey and a sixteen-step ARP Sequencer. While the Odyssey's oscillators play a subtle A note on every step, control voltages change the cutoff frequency of the self-oscillating filter to play Walsh's clever melody over and over again.

Taking up prime real estate alongside multiple VCOs, filters, and other modules in a 1974-era Moog Synthesizer 55 modular system is a Moog 960 Sequential Controller. Each of its eight stages has three knobs for dialing CV output levels; a three-way rotary switch to play or skip the stage, or stop there when the sequence arrives; a light to indicate the active stage; a pushbutton to manually jump to that stage; and 1/4" trigger I/O jacks. The 960's built-in clock will run at frequencies ranging from 0.1Hz to 500Hz—controllable and extendable via CV input—over six switchable ranges. Directions for using the 960 as a complex audio oscillator appear in the Moog Modular Owner's Manual. You can split and run each of the 960's three rows independently or string them together for up to twenty-four steps of single CV output. Each row has two 1/4" CV outputs for routing flexibility, and you can separate the third row so its knobs act as timers for stage durations, allowing you to create intricate rhythm patterns. You can route a patch cord from a trigger output on any stage to fire off events on other modules, and you can connect a white noise source to randomly sequence through the 960's eight stages.

Thanks to the revival of modular synths, many analog step sequencers are now available and their capabilities have progressed in fascinating ways. The first analog-style MIDI

A 1975 photo of synth pioneer Bob Moog playing a Minimoog keyboard while adjusting a knob on a Moog Modular. (With the permission of Ileana Grams-Moog)

The Synthesizer

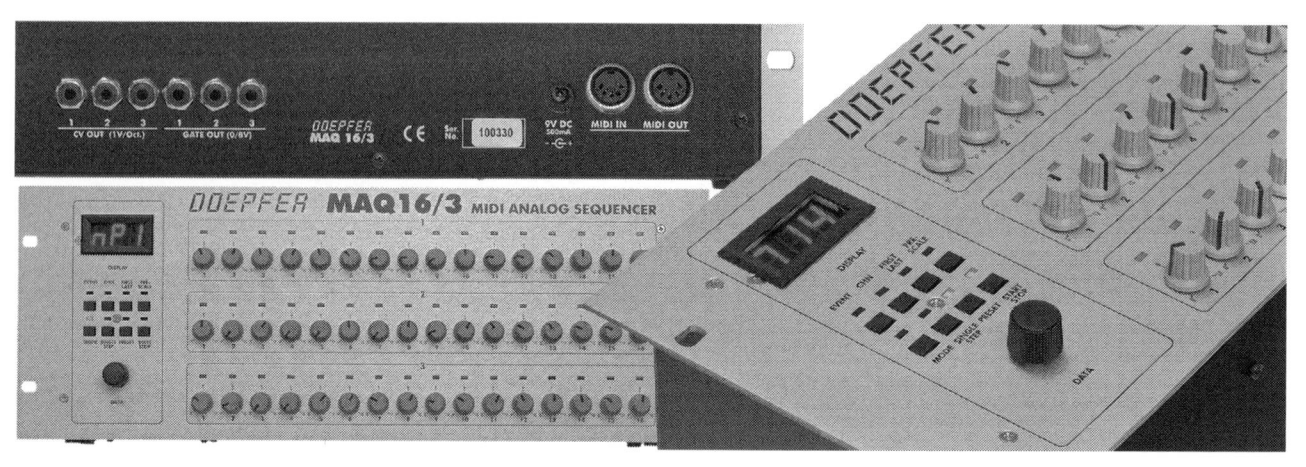

Three views of the Doepfer MAQ16/3 MIDI Analog Sequencer, which includes functions that go far beyond those of a traditional analog step sequencer. (© by Doepfer Musikelektronik GmbH)

sequencer was Doepfer's MAQ 16/3 (MAQ is a pseudo-acronym for MIDI-Analog-seQuencer). Introduced in 1993, the MAQ is a 4U rackmount, sixteen-stage by three-row sequencer with memory slots for sequence storage. Given its forty-eight real-time knobs, it's much more interactive than many MIDI sequencers. Surprisingly, manufacturing of the MAQ 16/3 continues today with a considerably expanded feature set. The original model had four sequencer memories, but it now provides thirty of them and—along with MIDI I/O—3.5mm CV and gate outputs on the back panel. For a reasonable price, Doepfer can upgrade the original MAQ 16/3 to the new version. Not many companies offer such support for twenty-year-old gear.

Another unit that in ways works like the Moog 960 yet goes much farther is the Analogue Solutions Oberkorn mk3, a potent, sixteen-step, 3U rackmount analog sequencer with three independent CV output channels, CV inputs for independently transposing each output channel, two independent gate output channels, MIDI-in for synchronization and step selection, forty-eight CV knobs, sixteen gate switches, and seventeen blue LEDs.

Doepfer's A-155 is an eight-stage CV and trigger sequencer that takes up 50hp of horizontal space in a Eurorack system. Each stage has two CV knobs plus two switches

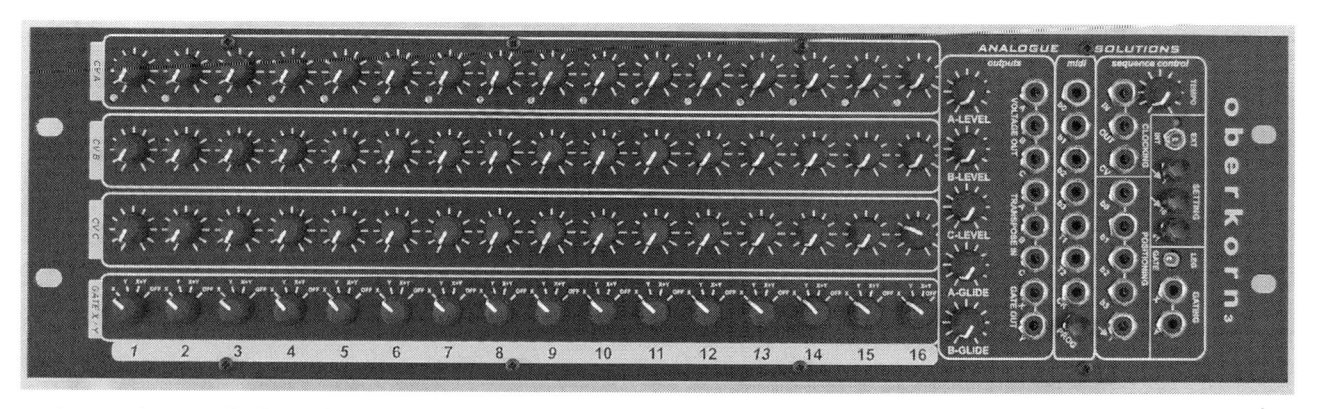

Analogue Solutions' Oberkorn Mk3 3U rackmount analog sequencer provides 16 stages with three independent control-voltage channels, sixteen gate switches, two independent gate channels, and MIDI control of various functions including internal clock tempo—which you can also vary under CV control. Each CV channel has its own CV input for independent transposition of the three CV channels. (Stephi Clendinen, courtesy of Big City Music)

for determining whether the stage transmits a trigger, gate, or neither, and to which of three outputs a trigger is routed. The A-155 also includes sample-and-hold and glide functions. Each CV row has pre and post outputs; while the pre output avoids sample-and-hold and glide functions, both are included in the post output. Along with the bottom row of knobs are inputs for CV or audio signals to control the voltage level of each stage. What the A-155 lacks is an internal clock, which isn't unusual for sequencers in the modular world. You can drive the A-155 with an LFO, pair it with Doepfer's A-190 MIDI-to-CV/Gate/Clock Interface module for MIDI control, or use any module that can generate timing pulses. To considerably extend the A-155's capabilities, you could add an A-154 Sequencer Controller, which can serve as a clock source; adds forward, backward, random, CV control, and one-shot (one time through the sequence) playback capabilities; and—with the addition of an A150 Dual VCS voltage-controlled switcher—can simultaneously control two A-155 sequencers for sequences of up to sixteen steps.

Another sequencer from Doepfer is the stand-alone, tabletop Dark Time. Although it has digital components, the Dark Time works like an analog step sequencer, transmitting MIDI data, control voltages, and gates; serving as the master or syncing to external clocks in a multisequencer environment; and allowing transposition via MIDI or CV input. It also provides two switches per step, allowing you to skip the step, stop there when the sequence arrives, transmit signals or be muted, and "jump"—a function that works in different ways depending on whether jump is enabled for multiple steps. There's even a USB jack for communication with your computer.

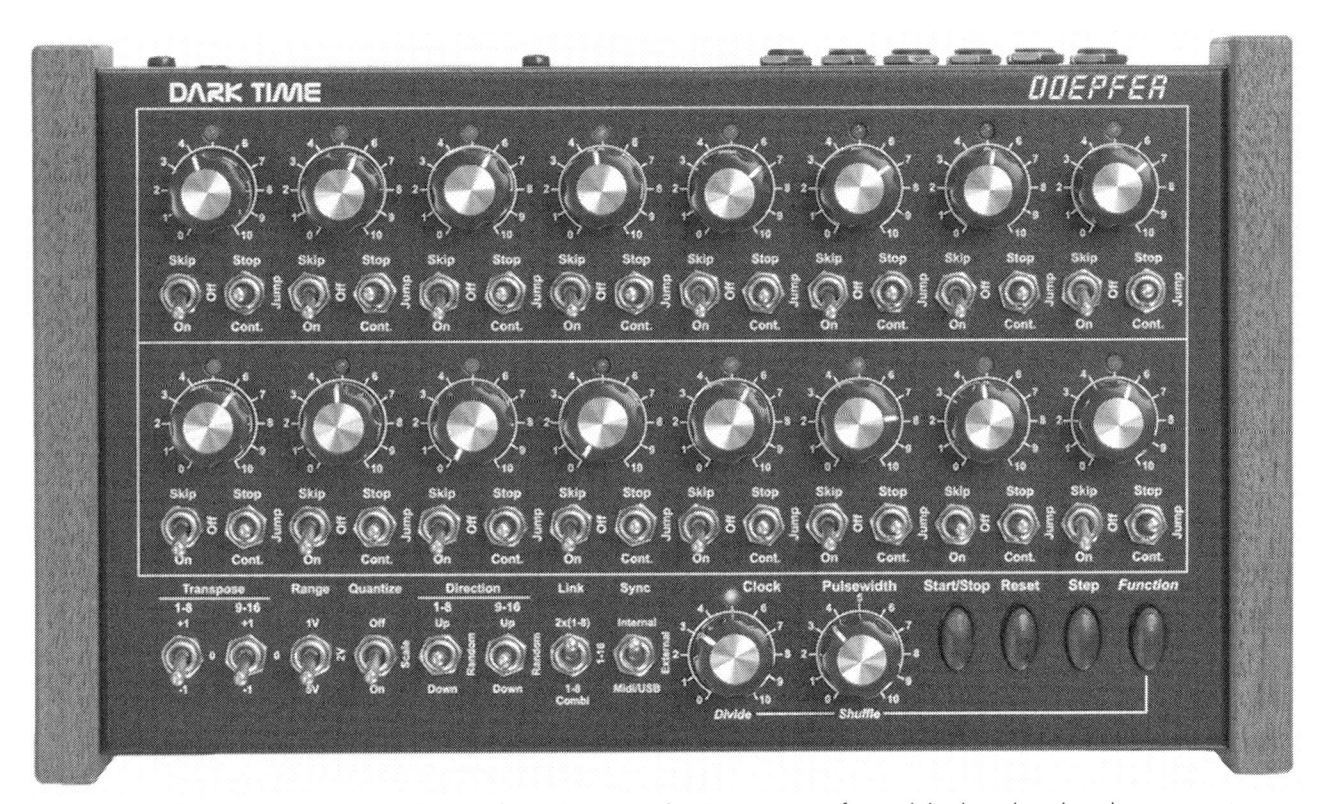

Among the playback modes provided by the Doepfer Dark Time Analog Sequencer are forward, backward, and random progression through stages. You get to choose from three different playback modes: 2 × 8 sequencing transmits up to an eight-step pattern with control over two knobs per step, 1 × 8 combi mode allows you to set the gate length of each step using knobs in the lower row, and 1 × 16 mode daisy-chains both rows of knobs together for a pattern of up to sixteen steps. (© by Doepfer Musikelektronik GmbH)

The Synthesizer

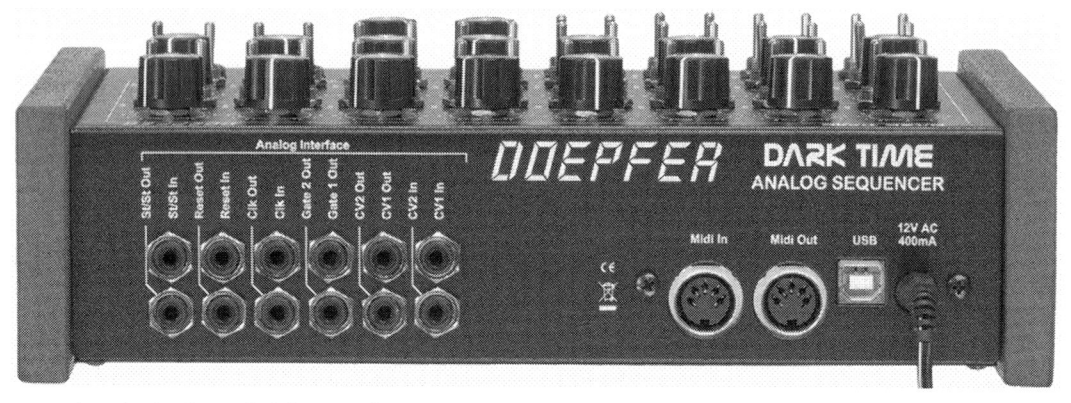

Located on the back panel of the Doepfer Dark Time are (*left to right*) twelve 3.5mm input and output jacks for gate, CV, clock, and control, MIDI in and out, a USB jack, and power in. The USB jack transmits and receives data precisely like the MIDI in and out jacks, but users should connect only MIDI or USB to avoid, as detailed in the manual, "unpredictable and undesirable effects." Still, it's very cool that the Dark Time has USB. It can transmit data on two MIDI channels simultaneously, so you can sequence two MIDI synths at the same time as you drive an analog synth. In addition, you can transpose the sequence using a MIDI controller or one or two stepped CV signals from an external source. (© by Doepfer Musikelektronik GmbH)

BugBrand offers an eight-stage CV/gate sequencer called the SEQ1, which is FracRak-sized and has banana jacks like other BugBrand modules. While its internal clock allows it to sequence on its own, it excels in sequencing capabilities when driven with clocks from other sources. When clocked at rates within the audible range, the SEQ1 can oscillate and generate complex waveforms determined by its knob settings. Throw it into random mode to generate digital noise. Whether they're internally or externally generated, clock signals pass to an output that allows other sequencers, drum machines, and devices with clock inputs to synchronize with the SEQ1. An internal pulse-stretching circuit allows manual control of the gate length of all stages and you can connect the gate output to externally synchronized devices to control gate lengths on those devices as well. Each stage can selectively route the gate to either of two outputs, useful for selectively triggering two different envelope generators. You can switch each of the main gate outputs to transmit a high voltage throughout each stage or to a variable gate length. BugBrand's SEQ1X slave module extends the SEQ1's capabilities with eight additional CV knobs, eight more gate switches, and extra CV and gate outputs.

Available in Eurorack and Mattson Mini Modular formats, the Mattson/Division 6 SQ816 sequencer can generate eight- and sixteen-stage patterns and transmits both CV/gates and MIDI data. It has a built-in clock as well as an input for external clock. A tap-tempo mode allows you to input instant tempo changes and set gate lengths with a few finger taps. You can group stages and mute them alone during playback. While the Division 6 Eurorack version is a complete 52hp module, the Mattson-format version consists of two modules: the main sequencer, which sports twenty-four CV level knobs within a matrix of three rows by eight columns, stage LEDs that change colors in sixteen-step mode between the first and second eight steps, a playback direction switch, main CV and gate outputs, and a mysteriously labeled "Lots of Stuff" button that randomly alters what the SQ816 is doing; and the SQ816 Expansion Module, which provides MIDI out, a USB port, sixteen gate outputs, and a footswitch input for starting and stopping playback. There are also assorted interface connections for combining multiple systems to work together in series or parallel.

Acoustics and Synthesis Basics

BugBrand's SEQ1 analog step sequencer and companion SEQ1X slave pack flexible and potent sequencing capabilities in small packages. If this photo were in color, you could enjoy BugBrand's beautiful blue module finish, contrasted nicely with lighter blue input and red output jack sockets and black knobs with orange or red direction indicators. (Courtesy of BugBrand)

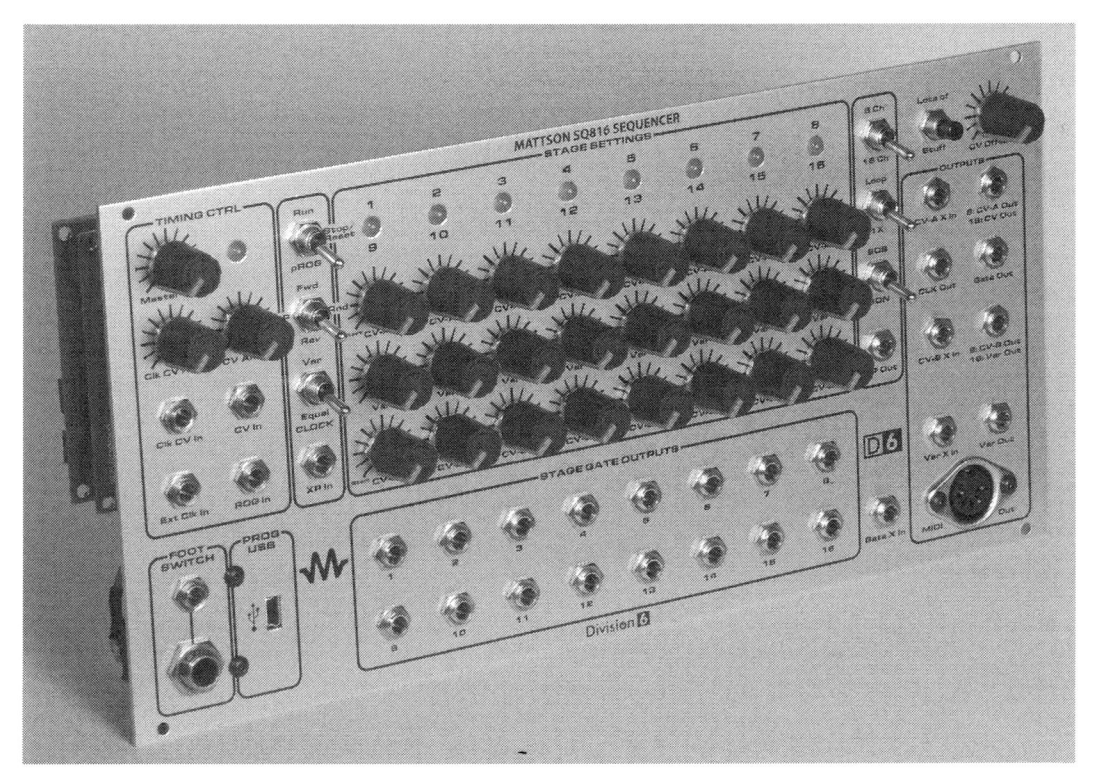

Division 6 makes the Eurorack version of the Mattson SQ816 analog sequencer, which only has eight physical columns but indicates which of its sixteen stages is active with multicolored LEDs across the top. (Scott Rise, ©2012 Mattson Mini Modular and Division 6)

The Synthesizer

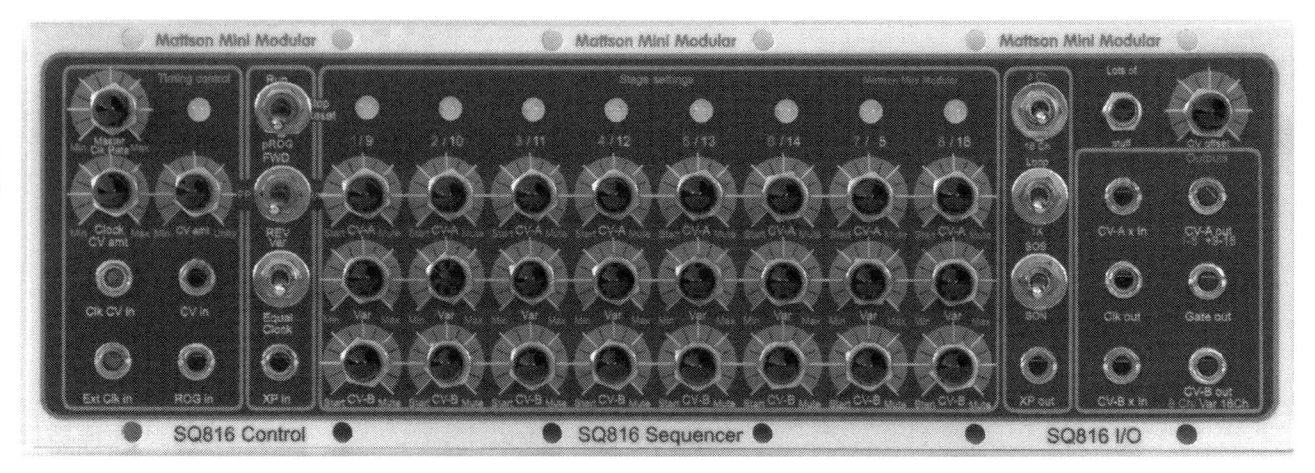

Knobs, switches, LEDs, and numerous 3.5mm jacks cover the main sequencer module of the Mattson Mini Modular SQ816. (Scott Rise, ©2012 Mattson Mini Modular and Division 6)

Also in the Eurorack format are two notable digital step sequencers. Gur Milstein's Z8000 Matrix Sequencer from Tiptop Audio has a 28hp front panel covered with a 4 × 4 matrix of knobs alongside associated multicolor LEDs and multiple 3.5mm jacks. Hidden underneath the panel are ten independent sequencers. Eight of them have four stages, four running in the horizontal direction and four that run vertically. The other two are sixteen-step sequencers, one running horizontally and the other vertically. The Z8000 has no built-in clocks, so external clock sources are required to run the Z8000's separate sequencers. Not that you'll need ten separate clocks, however, because each group of four sequencers can sync to a single clock, or three sequencers in a group can sync to one clock while the fourth tracks to another, and so on. You control the direction and number of steps for each Z8000 sequencer by routing CVs to the independent direction and reset inputs. As you might imagine, the Z8000 specializes in polyrhythmic patterns.

Equally out of the ordinary is Tony Rolando's René from Make Noise Music. Covering the lower two-thirds of René's 34hp front panel are two 4 × 4 matrices: one matrix

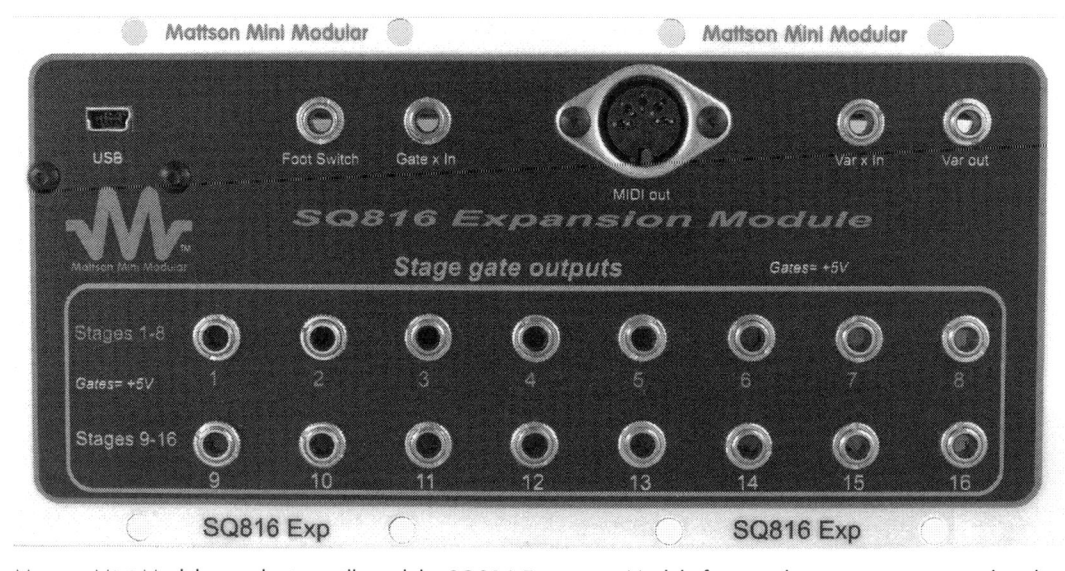

Mattson Mini Modular synthesists will need the SQ816 Expansion Module for complete sequencing control and MIDI transmission from the MMM SQ816 sequencer module. (Scott Rise, ©2012 Mattson Mini Modular and Division 6)

George Mattson (*left*) of Mattson Mini Modular poses with his brother, Scott Rise of Division 6, behind racks of MMM modules and a skiff of Division 6 Eurorack modules in July 2012. The MMM version of the SQ816 sequencer, which George and Scott developed together, is mounted at the top of the rack on the *right*. Out front for MIDI output is a Hand Roll Piano K-61. (Mark Vail)

of multicolor backlit knobs, and the other of rectangular touchpads. Toward the top are six CV inputs and four CV outputs. According to the Make Noise website, René is "the world's first and only Cartesian Sequencer for music synthesizers. Named for the French philosopher and mathematician René Descartes, it uses his Cartesian coordinate system to unlock the analog step sequencer from the shackles of linearity." René has four clock inputs and two CV inputs that you can use simultaneously to create complex musical patterns with quantized voltages, non-quantized voltages, and two gate/pulse output streams. While it provides the equivalent of sixteen stages, rather than sequentially step-

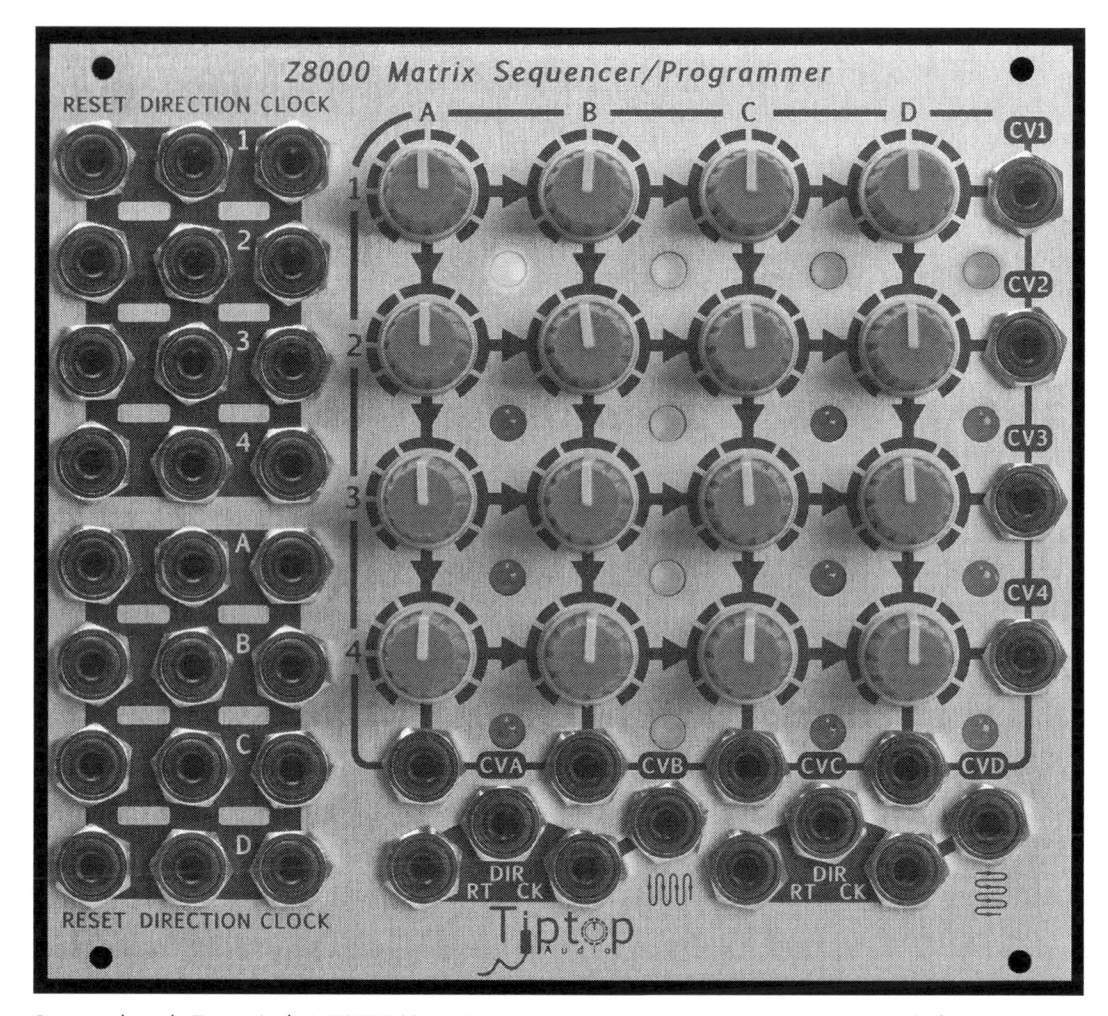

Squeezed inside Tiptop Audio's Z8000 Matrix Sequencer are ten separate step sequencers, eight four-stage sequencers and two sixteen-stage sequencers. There's an impressive amount of sequencing power in this moderately sized Eurorack Module. (Courtesy of Tiptop Audio)

ping through them one by one, René maps coordinates to grid locations (the Make Noise term for stages or steps) and can play the same sequence in an infinite number of ways. Independent clock, modulation, and CV inputs appear for both the x and y axes, and René chooses its next location based on the signals arriving at these inputs. In play mode, René's backlit knobs indicate the sequence's direction through the grid, and you can touch plates in the grid to grant or deny access to any of the sixteen grid locations, stop and hold the sequence at a grid location, and choose a new starting location.

These are just a handful of analog step and coordinate-mapping sequencers that are available; there are many more to choose from and more appearing all the time. Also available are loads of clock/pulse dividers, logic processors, quantizers, envelope and function generators, and other modules that can add more flexibility to step sequencers.

Arpeggiators

Play and sustain a chord on a keyboard that has a built-in arpeggiator or is connected to one and, instead of the chord, you'll hear individual notes playing back one at a time at

Acoustics and Synthesis Basics

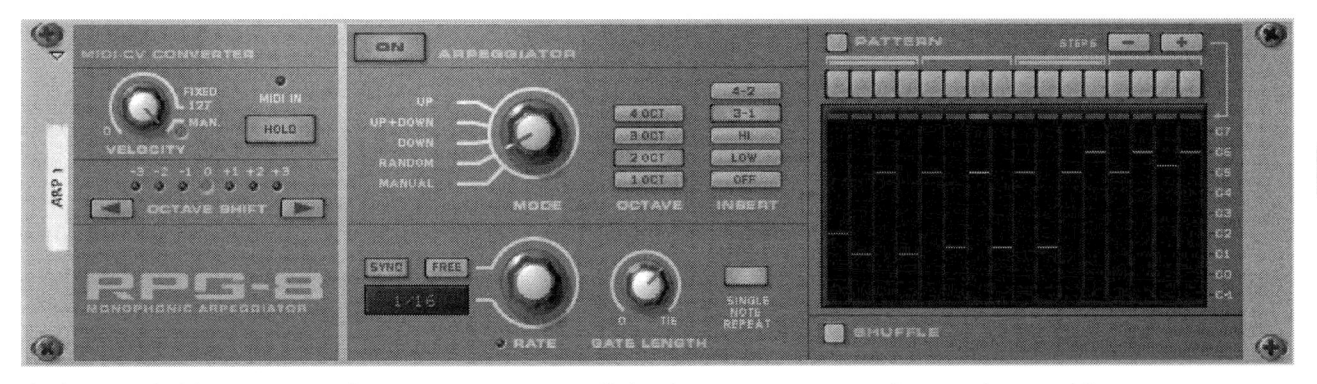

The front panel of the RPG-8 monophonic arpeggiator in Propellerhead Reason. Among your choices within its middle section are a five-position switch to select the playback order of notes you manually sustain, which can be up, up and down, down, random (currently chosen), or the order in which you played the notes; note playback rate in Herz if you select Free or, if synchronized to song tempo (currently selected) by note values such as sixty-fourth, sixteenth (as set here), sixteenth triplet, eighth duplet, quarter, and whole; repeated arpeggios in higher octaves up to four (two, in this case); and note duration (gate length). (Courtesy of Propellerhead Software AB)

a tempo determined by a system clock. Depending on the arpeggiator's capabilities, the notes may play in ascending or descending order, both ascending and descending, sequentially in the order that you played the keys, randomly, repeated an octave, two, three, or more higher, and sequencing through different sounds on successive notes. An arpeggiator can be inspiring to work with and often is more interactive than a typical sequencer.

At least two arpeggiators exist in the Moog Modular–inspired 5U format. One is the Synthesis Technology MOTM-650 4-Channel MIDI-CV Converter, which includes two separate arpeggiators. Another is the C951 Arpeggiator from Club of the Knobs. Oddly, the C951's MIDI in port is a 1/4" TRS jack, but included with the module is an adapter cable for connection with a common MIDI out port on a controller.

Stephen Kay of Karma Lab LLC developed a very sophisticated arpeggiator called KARMA, the Kay Algorithmic Realtime Music Architecture, which first appeared in early 2001 in the Korg Karma and subsequently in Korg's OASys, M3, and Kronos synths. Kay also developed KARMA extensions for the Korg Triton and M50, and released a version for Yamaha's Motif workstation series in July 2012. While most arpeggiators—

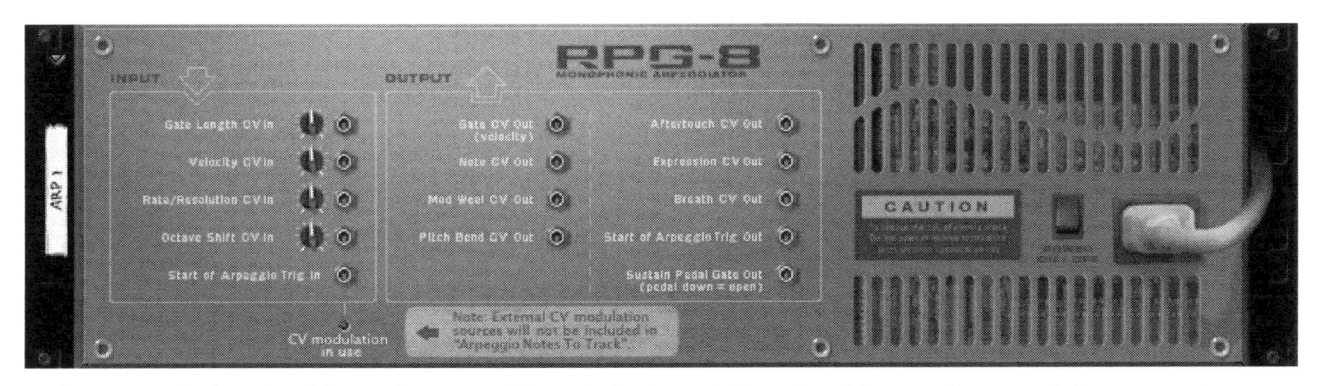

Hit the computer keyboard's Tab key and Reason will flip to the back panel of virtual modules currently in its rack. Here we see the backside of the RPG-8 monophonic arpeggiator, which currently isn't connected to another module, but revealing the RPG-8's controller routing possibilities. Unless you hold the Shift key when creating a device, Reason will automatically connect it to another module in the rack. For example, if a Subtractor synth module were selected when you create an RPG-8, Reason would route four of the arpeggiator's outputs—Gate CV Out with velocity response, Note CV Out, Mod Wheel CV Out, and Pitch Bend CV Out—to appropriate input jacks on the Subtractor. (Courtesy of Propellerhead Software AB)

Synthesis Technology's MOTM-650 module in 5U format not only works as a MIDI-to-CV converter, but it also sports arpeggiator functions. (© 2012 Synthesis Technology, used by permission)

unless you adjust some parameters—repeat the same pattern for as long as you hold the same keys, KARMA varies phrases, grooves, and patterns, and it reacts interactively with the performer in randomly controlled ways.

Reverb

As beautiful and powerful as synths can sound, effects processing can often extensively improve and enhance their timbres. While a completely dry and claustrophobic atmosphere is perfectly fitting on occasion—perhaps in the soundtrack to *Night of the Living Dead*—sometimes it's good to virtually locate your sounds in an acoustic environment, be it the Room of Requirement, the Chamber of Mazarbul, or Carnegie Hall. To do so you'd typically use reverb.

In a physical environment, reverb is a wash of reflected sound waves that reach your ears for a time following a sonic event. The length of time reverb continues is determined by numerous factors, most critically the size of the space and the reflective nature of surfaces in that space. Imagine being on the court with a basketball in Madison Square Garden, all by yourself. Throw the ball down as hard as you can on the court surface and it will take a matter of seconds for the resulting sound waves to traverse the arena and bounce back around you until silence returns. *That's* reverb, of the acoustic kind. It's like a wave of echoes, except that you can't hear the individual echoes, only wisps of what began as the smack of the basketball on the wooden court floor.

Many techniques can simulate natural reverb. For example, hidden away through the doors at the back of Studio Two at Abbey Road Studios and past another door in a small storage room is Abbey Road's Echo Chamber Two. This dank, claustrophobic space—measuring about 12 × 21 feet—houses a variety of objects that have reflective and non-reflective surfaces. Tall sections of massive sewer pipe stand here and there on end, stretching up about six feet but falling far short of the high ceiling. Various sorts of speaker cabinets lie about, and there are patchbays that connect to Studio Two's control room. While one wall is tiled, others are gloss-painted concrete. It doesn't smell very good in there, and it's definitely creepy, but Echo Chamber Two has created a wonderful wash of reverb for many recording projects and plenty of hit songs over multiple decades.

Don't have a basement to spare for your own echo chamber? How about a tiled bathroom or a long hall with a wooden floor? Given a guitar amp, a mic or two, and some imagination, you can simulate an acoustic echo chamber. Or how about a big sheet of stainless steel? Hang it from the ceiling, attach an amplified electromechanical transducer—essentially the driver component of a loudspeaker—and position a mic or two near different areas of the plate or else tape a contact mic to the opposite end from the transducer. Pump audio through the transducer and—*voila!*—you've got reverb. This is considerably more portable than Abbey Road's Echo Chamber Two, and you can have hours of fun designing electro-acoustic sounds as you find different positions for the transducer and mics, and experiment with different sound sources. Don't forget to whack the plate to

In spite of its appearance, this isn't a secretive section of a late '50s Cold War-era bomb shelter. It's actually Echo Chamber Two at Abbey Road Studios, which contributed reverb effects to the best works of the Beatles and many other bands who've recorded there. The combination of curved and diversely-coated surfaces with precisely positioned speakers and microphones creates natural-sounding reverbs. (Johanna Hanno, courtesy of Propellerhead Software AB, © 2007; Abbey Road Studios is a registered trade mark of EMI [IP] Limited and is used with kind permission)

get impressive thunder. Plenty of recording studios have used plate reverbs over the years, and still do.

Perhaps you're in search of a reverb that's more portable. What about springs? If Laurens Hammond—inventor of Hammond tonewheel organs including the famous B-3, as well as many other innovative products—didn't invent spring reverb, he at least made it popular by using it to enhance the sound of his instruments. Early versions used two 3'-long springs, some immersed in nonevaporating oil. They were minimally effective but a definite improvement over no reverb at all. As time passed, engineers and designers dispensed with the oil, discovered that three springs give a smoother response than only two, and improved the electrical components—a transducer at one end to induce vibrations into the springs and a pickup at the other end to gather the spring vibrations for amplification.

While there have been vast improvements in the design of digital reverb processors, spring reverb never totally went away. Not only do many guitar-amp manufacturers install spring-reverb tanks in their products, but you can also find them for modular synthesizers and as stand-alone processors. For example, Doepfer's A-199 SPRV works in Eurorack modular systems and allows you to feed its output back to its input to the point of self-oscillation of the springs. For the 5U format, there's Synthesizers.com's Q115. Both come with a separate reverb tank, which installs inside the modular cabinet and connects via cables to the input/output/control modules. For kit and DIY makers, there are the Paia 6740K Hot Springs Reverb Kit and the MOD 4AB3C1B reverb tank from Amplified Parts. And don't overlook the peculiar Knas Ekdahl Moisturizer, which exposes

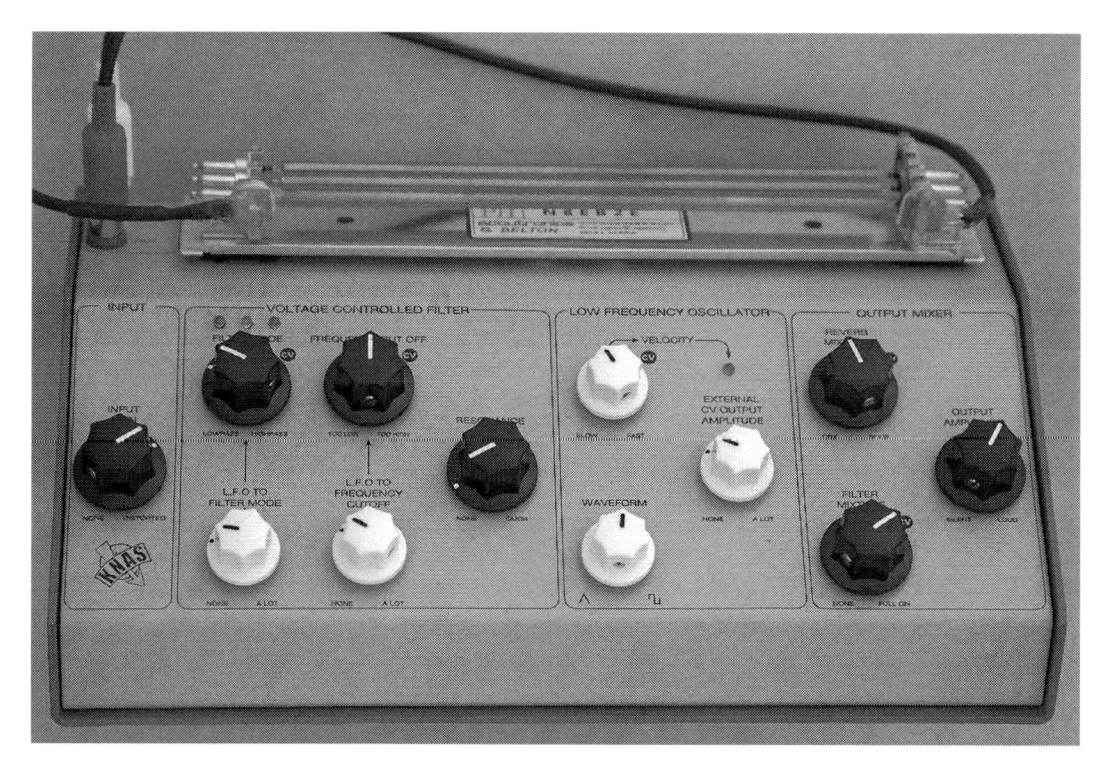

The Knas Ekdahl Moisturizer isn't your typical, run-of-the-mill spring reverb. Not only does it provide a built-in continuously variable multimode VCF, LFO, and audio mixer, but it also exposes its springs for hands-on manipulation and sonic devastation. Other spring reverbs—if they're of manageable size—merely allow you to create thunderous sounds and blow speakers by vigorously shaking their enclosures, or just add reverb to the input audio. (Roger Cordell, courtesy of Big City Music)

its springs for manipulation and torture, and includes a built-in multimode filter and an LFO. Thanks to the unique quality of their sound, spring reverbs will probably never go away. Besides, you can create all kinds of electro-acoustic mayhem—and potential ear and speaker damage—by giving them a good shake when they're plugged in.

Digital reverb is the most popular and flexible type these days, using DSP in either hardware processors or as software running on a computer. With digital reverb, you can typically customize the effect in many ways. Choose among **algorithms** for the simulation of environments including small rooms, medium-sized concert halls, or arenas. Adjust the **damping** parameter to control how quickly high frequencies die away. Tweak the **early reflections** characteristics to vary the apparent size of the space you're in. Fine-tune pre-delay to virtually position the audio source in relation to your ears. Change the **diffusion** anywhere from hearing individual echoes to more of a wash of sound. Digital reverbs commonly have a reverse mode, which makes the reverb wash come before you hear the original sound, and a gated process that begins with a big reverb wash immediately after a sound, such as a snare hit, before quickly shutting down to no reverb at all. Many digital reverb processors can also simulate the sounds of plate and spring reverbs.

---

algorithms: programming code for a microprocessor, in this case to perform different types of reverb processing on incoming audio signals

damping: a decrease in the apparent acoustic energy in a virtual reverb space

early reflections: distinct echoes that arrive before a wash of reverb

diffusion: the characteristics of sound waves distributed in an acoustic or virtual space

---

You'll find hardware digital reverb processors in formats including rackmount and stompbox. While stompboxes mainly appeal to guitar players, there are quite a few floor-ready digital reverbs that work outstandingly well for synths, too, and in general they're less expensive than the rackmount variety. Eventide's Space stompbox is great for enhancing synth sounds in ultracreative ways. Beyond the expected hall, room, plate, and spring reverbs, Space delivers such effects as reverse and dual reverbs, echoes, distortion, and various modulation processing. Along with a flexible MIDI implementation for controlling parameters, Space provides inputs for expression pedals and footswitches, nine knobs for adjusting parameters, and a data-entry knob for preset selection.

Many software developers offer stand-alone applications and plug-ins that do reverb. The latest form of digital reverb to evolve is based on convolution, a mathematical process. It's a bit like digital sampling, which explains why some people refer to it as sampling reverb. If you're starting from scratch, you typically need a lively acoustic space, which is the model for the type of reverb you'd like to simulate. Inside it you record an audible event. Whereas early convolution-reverb practitioners used something like a starter pistol, later they discovered a sustained burst of broadband noise or the sweep of an amplified sine wave from sub- to superaudible frequencies led to more satisfactory results. This process creates an impulse response (IR), an audio file that includes early reflections and the reverb tail, as well as all of the frequency content that resonates in the

The Synthesizer

Spectacular reverb algorithms are squeezed into the knob-laden black brick of a stompbox called the Eventide Space: Reverb and Beyond. Adding zing to reverb presets are delays, pitch-shifting, gating, tremolo, flanging, chorusing, distortion, and more. (© 2012 Eventide, Inc.)

space. Using a convolution engine to apply an IR to an audio file or in real time, you get a processed version of the original sound in the IR-influenced reverb space.

You don't have to create your own IRs because they're included with most convolution reverb applications. These IRs don't always come from real acoustic environments, either, and you can create IRs by sampling audio routed through existing reverb units.

Using the virtual sliders at the bottom of the main page of McDSP's Revolver Flexible Convolution Reverb plug-in, you can independently regulate the wet and dry signal levels, adjust the reverb pre-delay and attack times, and vary low- and high-frequency shelving EQ ("color") levels and their central frequencies. The big knob to the *upper left* allows you to adjust the total reverb time in terms of both the percentage of the reverb length and the TR60 value, which defines the amount of time it takes for the reverb to decrease to a level 60dB below the original sound's volume. Shown to the *upper right* is a depiction of the current preset's impulse response space, in this case captured in a reverberant stairwell. It's one of hundreds of IRs that come with Revolver, which also allows you to capture IRs of your own favorite reverb environments. (Courtesy of McDSP)

Depending on the convolution engine, reverb isn't all you can do. For example BIAS Peak Pro 6 provides a convolve DSP function that allows you to morph one audio file with another. The results may not be what you'd expected, but you might be surprised and have fun with this alternate form of non-real-time digital synthesis.

Analog Delay

While reverb apparently puts audio into a natural—or not-so-natural—acoustic space, an echo/delay effect repeats a sonic event as many times as the repeats are audibly fed back to the delay input, with the time between repetitions determined by parameters depending on the delay technique in play. Natural echo occurs when a sound reflects off of a surface and returns to ears at the source of the sound. If you're between parallel flat and reflective surfaces, echoes can bounce back and forth for a matter of seconds. In order for a delayed sound to qualify as echo, by definition it must happen at least 50ms after the original sound. Routing synths through a delay processor allows you to play along with what you did previously. By synchronizing delays to a song's tempo, you can dynamically enhance the rhythm.

The creation of a delay effect has undergone considerable technological advancements over the years. Beginning in the early 1960s, magnetic recording tape provided a workable means to create delay effects. At the time, composers including David Tudor, Pauline Oliveros, and Terry Riley looped tape between two or more **reel-to-reel decks** or bought tape heads in bulk and arranged them in series and ran tape through them, the first head recording the incoming sound and subsequent heads repeating the recorded sound like echoes.

> *reel-to-reel deck:* a tape recorder on which recording tape runs between two separate metal or plastic wheels rather than being enclosed in a plastic case like a cassette; alternatively referred to as an open-reel tape recorder

At about the same time, Mike Battle was perfecting the Echoplex—the most familiar dedicated tape-delay processor of its day. Inside it a tape loop runs across record and playback tape heads. You move the Echoplex's Echo Delay Control lever to vary the playback head's position and adjust the length of the echo period. Adjusting the feedback amount varies the number of repeated echoes. Roland's Space Echo RE-201 is another popular tape delay. While tape saturation can enhance the echoed repeats, dealing with magnetic tape is problematic in many ways: it's relatively fragile, the technology suffers from undesired noise buildup in the audio signal, tape heads require frequent maintenance to keep them clean and free of magnetism, and some vintages of tape deteriorate to the point of being unusable. Even so, there are plenty of tape-delay enthusiasts who wouldn't use anything else.

The development of analog **bucket-brigade delay** (**BBD**) chips at the end of the 1960s provided an electronic alternative to magnetic tape. The more stages in a BBD, the

Roland unveiled the Space Echo RE-201 tape-echo processor in 1973, and it eventually became a prized vintage-era unit. For a used one in pristine condition and perfectly functional today, you might have to shell out $500 to $900. (Courtesy of Roland Corporation)

longer the available delays—although analog delay time is typically limited to one second or less. As Barry Klein wrote in *Electronic Music Circuits* (Blacksburg Continuing Education Series, 1982), "Devices with at least 512 stages can be used for vibrato, **chorus**, and flanging effects. Echo usually requires devices with more stages."

> *bucket-brigade delay (BBD)*: an integrated-circuit chip containing a series of analog sample-and-hold circuits used to delay an audio signal
> *chorus*: an audio-thickening effect created with a delay of around 10 to 25ms, a feedback amount of about 25 percent, and an even mix of wet and dry signals
> *through-hole*: traditional electronic components with metal leads that poke through predrilled holes in printed circuit boards, where they're soldered to exposed copper signal traces

Through-hole BBD chips went out of production some years ago, resulting in dedicated analog delay processors becoming relatively rare for a time. Thankfully at least one company is manufacturing surface-mount technology (SMT) BBD chips because—despite impressive digital delay advantages such as a broader bandwidth, superior signal-to-noise ratio, and better sound quality—many musicians prefer the analog-delay sound. CoolAudio manufacturers numerous SMT audio chips, including several BBD analog delay lines. As explained in the sidebar starting on page 189, SMT circuitry requires different assembly techniques than through-hole components. Richard Nicol of Pittsburgh Modular says he's happy with the performance he gets from the CoolAudio chips, although he's disappointed they don't make a 512-stage BBD chip that's needed for good analog chorus and flanging effects. Dieter Doepfer, another CoolAudio customer, laments

Like many electronic products on the market today, the Radikal Technologies Accelerator synth depends on a combination of SMT and through-hole circuitry, but mostly the former. Its maker, Jörg Schaaf, switched to SMT because through-hole components are getting more difficult to source and, once he'd found a good assembly company, he deemed the SMT production process more reliable and the audible differences between SMT and through-hole circuitry insignificant. The Accelerator generates an aggressive, analog-like sound using DSP. It provides eight voices of polyphony standard, but you can increase it by adding one or two twelve-voice expansion boards. Each voice consists of three complex oscillators, six envelope generators, three LFOs, two multimode filters, three-band parametric EQ, and a noise source with its own multimode filter, amplifier, and envelope generator. Other Accelerator features include programmable matrix modulation, four effects buses, polyphonic arpeggiators, thirty-two-step sequencers with chord memory, a sixty-one-note keyboard that responds to velocity and aftertouch, and memory for five hundred patches, three hundred performances, and one hundred performance chains. The Accelerator is a powerful and sonically outstanding synth that deserves more recognition than it's been getting. (© Radikal Technologies, Inc.)

that, whereas there are 1024-, 2048-, and 4096-stage SMT BBD chips, there aren't 128-, 256-, and 512-stage chips for shorter delay effects that don't require so many stages.

Through-Hole vs. SMT

Those who've assembled electronic kits from Heathkit, Paia, Southwest Technical, Dynaco, and many other sources that required soldering components onto a printed circuit board (PCB) have dealt with through-hole components such as resistors, transistors, capacitors, and diodes. These individual parts are being absorbed into tiny, complex devices in the realm of surface-mount technology (SMT), which has been around since the 1960s. Its assembly usually takes place in automated machinery, but brave souls with steady hands, good eyes, and the proper tools may be able to work on the tiny technology themselves. Not me. I've already ruined an electronic device trying to replace its surface-mount device (SMD).

Many synth manufacturers continue to use through-hole PCB construction and discrete components, but others have chosen the SMT path. Among the latter is Dave Smith, who uses it in all DSI products because SMDs are much smaller and allow more component density. SMDs also sit on the top of PCBs and don't require holes to be drilled. "Holes cost money," he explains. "Not much, but it adds up. Also, the parts themselves cost a lot less. . . . Having small parts allows shorter signal traces, which often helps reduce noise and crosstalk in both analog and digital circuits. In general, keeping circuits smaller usually gives you better performance."

While Dieter Doepfer mostly continues to use through-hole components, he incorporates SMDs in a few modules. Their small size allows him, for example, to fit a

> complete synth voice inside a single Eurorack module, the A-111-5. He still, however, prefers through-hole construction mostly because it simplifies serviceability should a single component fail. If an SMD fails, in most cases the entire PCB gets scrapped, resulting in yet more dangerous materials ending up in a landfill. If specific components are only available in SMD form, Doepfer uses piggyback adapters that convert the device into a through-hole part.
>
> Plenty of consumers are less than thrilled about the through-hole-to-SMT movement. "Some people are really upset that Paul Schreiber of Synthesis Technology isn't making kits any more because he's gone to the less-expensive option of using SMT circuits," reports synthesist John L. Rice, who often beta tests Schreiber's Eurorack modules. "Many people like to build their own modular synths." Fortunately these folks aren't entirely out of luck: Although Schreiber no longer sells MOTM kits and modules, Scott Deyo of the Bride Chamber has taken over their distribution.
>
> "There are a lot of people out there who are just on the musical side of the fence and want a big, flexible modular synthesizer," asserts synthesist, multi-instrumentalist, music journalist, and instrument designer Marvin Jones. "Buying modules in kit or DIY format is a convenient way to save money."
>
> In the end, synth manufacturers may not have a choice. "A lot of through-hole components are going away," concludes Marvin. "You can't get some of the individual components any more."

One analog delay processor based on out-of-production through-hole BBD chips is Moog Music's Moogerfooger MF-104, which has gone in and out of production since 2000 and offers delay times from about 50 to 800ms. Moog scored a small supply of more BBD chips in 2012 and released the MF-104M analog delay with some features that didn't appear on earlier MF-104s. Not only does it sport knobs and 1/4" CV inputs for varying delay time, feedback level, and wet/dry mix, it also has a six-waveform LFO with knobs and CV inputs as well as a tap-tempo switch, which you can apply separately to vary delay time and LFO rate. In addition, there's a feedback insert jack so you can route delays to external effects such as a distortion box, so subsequent delays get grungier as they loop. There's also a delay output, which allows you to create stereo effects or you can connect it to a keyboard amp that's separate from your main amp; if you decrease the delay level in the main output, delays will come from a different location. Finally, the MF-104M has a spillover function that allows you to switch on bypass mode without truncating delays that are already happening, as well as a MIDI in for parameter control, LFO sync, and delay-time sync to an external clock.

In the Eurorack world, Doepfer makes two analog delay modules, the A-188-1 BBD and A-188-2 Tapped BBD. Along with two standard versions of the A-188—A-188-1B with 1,024 stages and A-188-1C with 2,048 stages—Doepfer will offer 128-, 256-, 512-, and 4,096-stage versions of the A-188-1 as long as quantities of the respective BBDs last. Besides delay, the A-188-1 can do flanging and **doubling**. With the A-188-2, you

Acoustics and Synthesis Basics

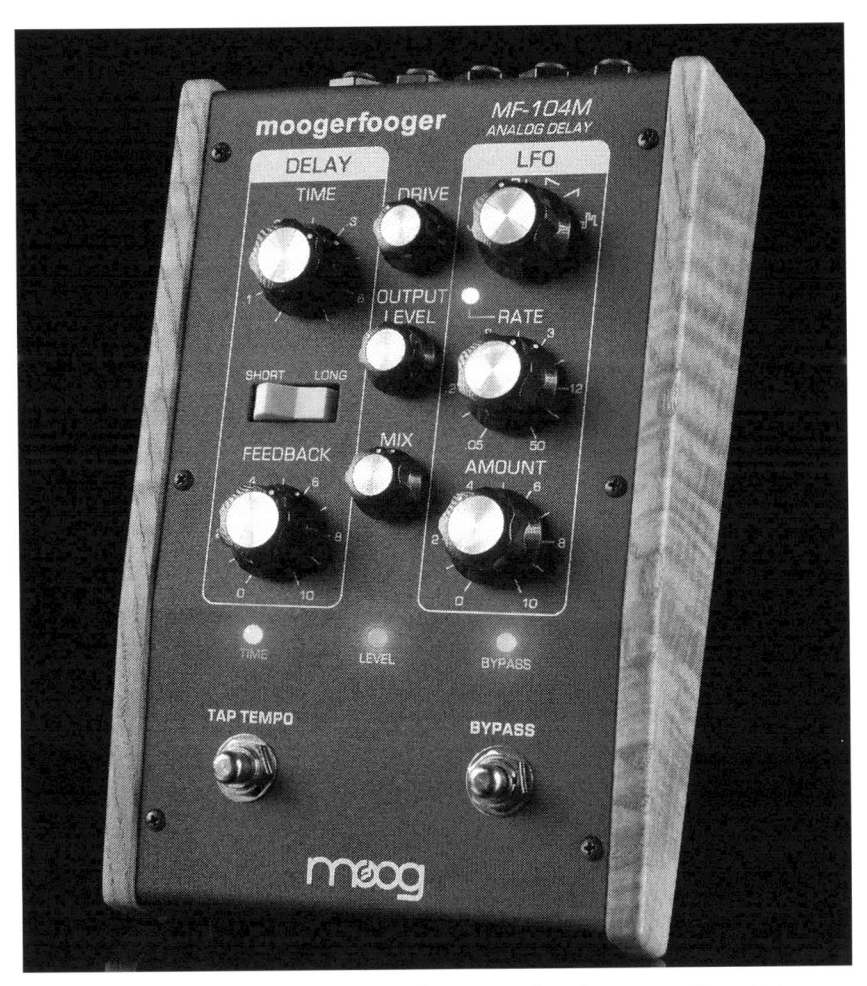

Bucket-brigade delay chips in through-hole form are a dwindling commodity, which explains why Moog Music has manufactured the Moogerfooger MF-104 analog delay in several limited production runs over the years. This is the latest, the 2012-era MF-104M, which includes improvements over previous versions of the MF-104, including delay sync to MIDI clock—a first for an analog delay. (Courtesy of Moog Music)

get independent audio outputs from the BBD taps at stages 396, 662, 1,194, 1,726, 2,790, and 3,328, opening up a mind-boggling array of signal-routing possibilities. Flanging was originally a manual technique that required two identical reel-to-reel tape recorders, both recording the same audio and simultaneously recording a mix of their outputs via the recorders' playback heads to a third recorder. Occasionally slowing one of the two recorders by dragging a thumb on the edge, or flange, of the feeding reel on one of the two first decks would put the two decks slightly out of phase and result in an animated, shwooshing effect. Now we have technology to make flanging much easier. It takes anywhere from zero to 20ms of delay, about 50 percent feedback, 50/50 wet/dry mix, and a slow modulation of the delay time—around 0.2Hz, or once every four or five seconds. The sweeping delay causes the cancellation of certain frequency components in the sound as the wet and dry signals go out of phase from each other. Flanging differs from **phase-shifting**, which sounds dissimilar. In phase-shifting, you equally modulate the center frequencies of numerous narrow-band notch filters across the spectrum to create a subtle, jet-like effect.

The Synthesizer

For the Eurorack modular synth format, Doepfer offers two bucket-brigade delay modules. This is the A-188-2, which offers six independent delay outputs from its multitap BBD chip, along with two separate output channels to which you can assign varying levels of each delay tap. (© by Doepfer Musikelektronik GmbH)

> *doubling:* in the traditional sense, a musician in the studio overdubs nearly the same part twice to add depth; it's simulated electronically using a delay of about 25ms, modulating the delay about 20 percent at a moderately slow rate, no feedback, and a 50/50 wet/dry mix
>
> *phase-shifting:* a process of delaying an audio signal at adjustable and varying rates and mixing the delayed signal with the original so that frequencies in the signals go in and out of phase, creating an audible sweep in the sound; adjusting the signal feedback level varies the sound's resonance

Among Pittsburgh Modular's selection of Eurorack modules is the Analog Delay (AD), which provides a maximum out-of-the-box delay time of 0.9 second. Tweak a couple of trim pots connected to one of the AD's two 4096 BBD chips and you can extend delay time up to two seconds, although you'll get grainier echoes. Along with knobs for adjusting and CV inputs for varying the delay time and feedback and wet levels, the AD provides knobs for attenuating their modulation response. In addition to input and mix output jacks you get an output jack for the feedback signal alone, which allows more flexible audio routing for additional processing.

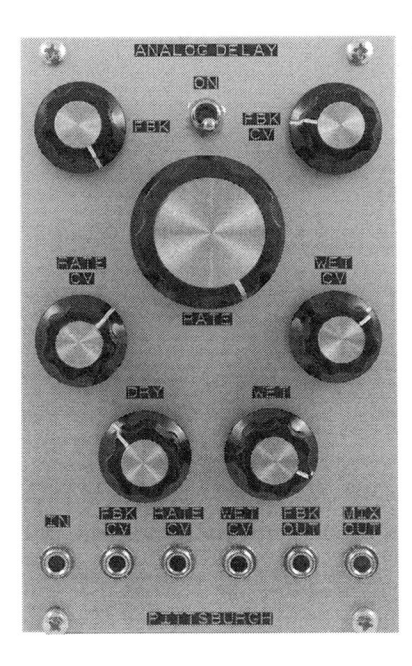

A pair of 4096 bucket-brigade chips provide echo effects in Pittsburgh Modular's Analog Delay module. In spite of appearances, those aren't actually plastic Dymo labels on the 16hp Eurorack module's front panel; they're purposely silkscreened to look that way. (©2012 Pittsburgh Modular)

Serge modular synthesists swear by the Wilson Analog Delay (WAD), currently available in two of Sound Transform Systems' M-class modules—the Wilson Analog Delay and the Klangziet—and in the Soup Kitchen 1 Shop Panel. Serge Tcherepnin designed the WAD to allow internal processes such as filtering, feedback, and delay to be determined by the user as a patch-programmable function. Its maximum delay time of around half a second won't excite many users, but those with WAD experience rave about its propensity to warp, deconstruct, and transform audio, smear harmonic content, and leave more of a shadowy, dissolving vapor trail than distinct echoes.

BBD processors in FracRak form are very rare, perhaps the one and only being the discontinued Blacet Research Time Machine 2050. Not only can it produce great flanging and chorusing effects, but the 2050 also provides CV ins for modulating delay time, regeneration, and built-in LFO modulation rate and depth. Along with an input for using an external modulation source, there's also a delay cancel jack that allows gated and tempo-driven delay effects. To compensate for BBD's notoriously noisy reputation, John Blacet installed a companding network that compresses incoming audio to avoid distortion-prone amplitude peaks prior to reaching the analog delay line, then filters the delayed output to squelch unwanted noise and expands the results in an attempt to give the echoes as much harmonic energy as the original signal.

In the 5U realm, Club of the Knobs makes the C1680 Voltage-Controlled Analog Delay, with delay times ranging from 20 to 1,200ms within three switchable ranges, manual and CV modulation of delay time and feedback level, send and return jacks for exclusively processing delays externally, and a built-in cross-mix audio enhancer that creates a quasi-stereo signal.

Digital Delay

Digital-delay processors trickled into the market beginning in the early 1970s at very expensive prices. It took time for engineers to develop analog-to-digital and digital-to-

The C1680 voltage-controlled analog delay from Club of the Knobs in 5U modular format has a big delay-time knob and delay times up to 1.2 seconds. (@club.of.the .knobs.com)

analog converters that sounded decent, but DSP opened the doors to processing capabilities that previously weren't possible, such as feeding back a repeating echo as many times as you'd like with no loss of audio quality and delay times measured in multiple seconds rather than fractions of them.

These days the most prevalent digital delays come in stompbox/tabletop form, although there are plenty of rackmount digital delay lines (DDLs) to choose from as well. I've gotten years of good delays and reliable service out of a Boss DD-5 stompbox. Boss now makes the DD-7, which provides up to 6.4 seconds of delay, mono/stereo I/O, analog-delay modeling, a CV input for control of the delay time, feedback level, or wet/dry effect level, and a sound-on-sound function that allows you to record new material on top of what you'd previously done for a duration up to forty seconds.

Even with digital circuits, musicians and developers strive for re-creations of what used to be. John L. Rice champions the Strymon El Capistan dTape Echo stompbox, specifically for its accurate and flexible simulations of Roland's Space Echo and the Echoplex. It has a sound-on-sound function for creating tape-style overdubs with virtual tape splicing, bulk erase, and your choice of double virtual tape speed for higher fidelity or

Simulations of vintage tape-delay machines—the Echoplex and Roland Space Echo—come complements of Strymon's El Capistan dTape Echo processor. (Courtesy of Strymon Engineering)

normal speed for longer delay times. The El Capistan also offers adjustable Wow & Flutter to simulate pitch fluctuations of material recorded on tape and Tape Age, which can range from "new and full-magnetic-tape-spectrum nice" to "ought-to-be-retired crummy and suffering from diminished high-frequency response and audible dropouts."

Eurorack enthusiasts have the broadest selection of DDLs from which to choose for modular synths. Analogue Systems makes the 12hp RS390 Echo module, which delivers a mono input and stereo outputs for ping-pong echoes, along with three ranges of delay times from a minimum of 1.75ms to a max of three seconds. CV inputs allow modulation of delay time and dry/wet mix. Flight of Harmony's the Sound of Shadows (SOS), also a 12hp module, allows knob and voltage control of delay time from 31.3 to 342ms, feedback level, and the built-in VCA. The SOS's third-of-a-second maximum delay may not sound impressive, but it's capable of sonic mutilation and signal-routing flexibility that more than make up for that limitation.

Synthesis Technology's E580 Resampling Mini-Delay is a 14hp Eurorack DDL module with a twist: It incorporates a resampling algorithm to mimic analog BBD and tape delays, or you can set it to output clean and unprocessed echoes. In BBD mode, a lowpass filter attenuates higher frequencies with a response curve that depends on the delay time—up to 750ms—and the circuit adds a bit of BBD-like noise to the echoes. In tape-delay mode, you get some nonlinear distortion to simulate tape saturation, along with wow and flutter to simulate an unsteady tape-drive motor. Along with a pure delay output, there's a tap output whose delay time is an adjustable percentage of the main delay time.

Owners of FracRak modular systems who can't find a Blacet Research Time Machine 2050 BBD module might satisfy their delay needs with Blacet's FracRak version of Synthesis Technology's Resampling Mini-Delay, which goes by model number F580.

The Eurorack-format E580 Resampling Mini-Delay from Synthesis Technology can provide clean, BBD-like, or tape-simulation delays and allows CV control of four parameters. (© 2012 Synthtech Inc., used by permission)

Bruce Duncan of Modcan offers a DDL module in both his A and B Series formats. Both the 59A and 59B provide delay times from 50ms to 5.8 seconds, a mono input and stereo outputs with a ping-pong mode for bouncing echoes back and forth, a loop mode for use as a sampling function, a tap tempo button for quickly adjusting delay time to a specific rhythm, and switchable lowpass filtering for emulating analog delay processors. Inputs allow CV modulation of delay time, feedback level, and wet/dry mix, as well as a trigger input for synchronizing delay time to an LFO or external clock.

One of the more affordable hardware DDLs is Wooster Audio's Space Baby, available in kit and assembled forms. Considering its twelve-bit resolution and 14kHz sampling rate, this open circuit-board device definitely doesn't qualify as a hi-fi processor, and its maximum delay time is limited at around half a second. Still, the nine-volt battery-powered Space Baby offers some intriguing features that aren't run of the mill, such as variable delay-time modulation and adjustable ring modulation based on the fed-back delay signal—although you need to watch levels because the effect really elevates the volume.

Another inexpensive DDL is the Korg Monotron Delay (MD), which includes a sawtooth-waveform VCO processed by a built-in VCF modeled after the one in Korg's vintage MS-20 analog patchable synth of the 1970s. While you coarsely control oscillator pitch over a roughly six-octave range with a 3.25″ ribbon, you can use the MD's knobs to adjust LFO rate and depth of modulation, filter cutoff frequency, delay time of up to about three-quarters of a second, and feedback level. You have the choice of triangle or pulse wave for the LFO and you can adjust its waveform shape with a trim pot accessible from the rear. The Monotron Delay runs on two AAA batteries, has a little built-in speaker, is great for creating crunchy, lo-fi delay-processed effects, and provides a 1/8″ stereo headphone output alongside a 1/8″ auxiliary input for processing externally generated sounds with its filter and delay.

The inexpensive Wooster Audio Space Baby does more than digital delay. Not only does it allow subtle to deep delay-time modulation and ring modulation based on feedback echoes, but the Space Baby also can synchronize delays via an ingenious infrared I/O system to Andromeda Space Rockers-series devices from Wooster Audio and other manufacturers based in Austin, Texas. (© Nathan Wooster)

Loopers

Spinning off from the DDL are loopers, which offer lengthy delay times—typically measured by the minute, but sometimes by the hour!—for recording licks, phrases, patterns, and whatever noises you make on the fly, then repeating them under your control while you play along without recording or overdub new material on top of what you've already recorded. Some loopers allow you to separately record and play different parts, so you can do real-time mixing. Adding a looper to your rig can be like gaining an entirely new instrument that requires you to practice for optimal musicality, optimize setup for looping the right material, and learn some alternative performance techniques. Loopers are a boon for live performers and improvisers.

There's a wide variety of hardware loopers on the market, each with a particular collection of capabilities. A series of units that have been popular since the mid-1990s come from Boomerang Musical Products, whose current model is the Boomerang III Phrase Sampler—introduced in September 2009. With it you can record up to four different stereo loops, overdub onto existing loops, undo and redo the last overdub to bring it in and out of the mix, erase one loop while others are playing or erase them all at once, drop a loop an octave to play at half speed, play a loop in reverse, trigger a loop to play once,

The Synthesizer

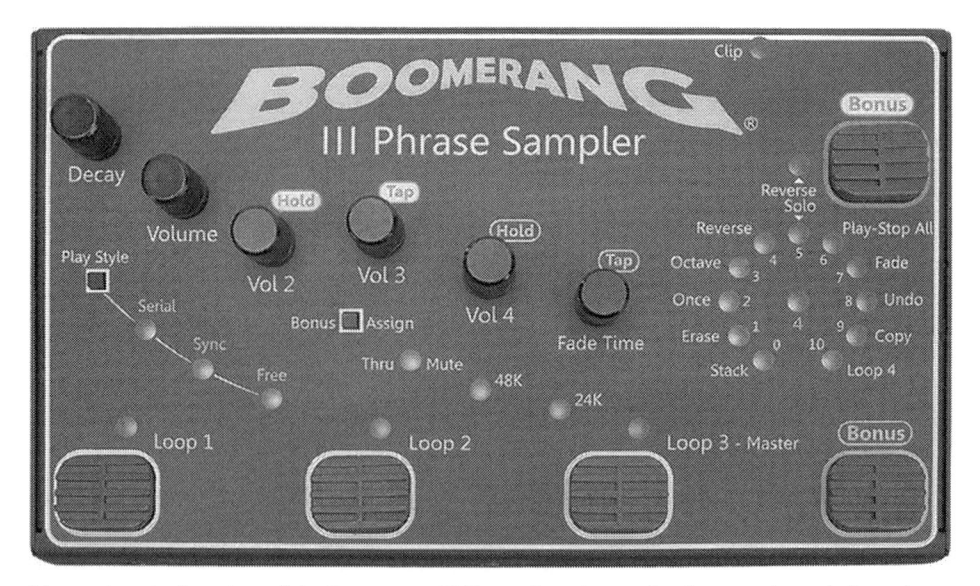

Mounted on the faceplate of the Boomerang III Phrase Sampler are five buttons, three dedicated to record and play loops 1 through 3, and two Bonus buttons that you can easily reassign to functions including stack new audio on top of an existing loop, erase or reverse the playback of a loop, and record and play a fourth loop. Knobs allow you to adjust the rate at which earlier recorded audio decays as you record new parts on top of it, the Boomerang III's overall output level and the volume of individual loops, and the overall fade-in or fade-out time—if any—from three to forty-five seconds. Multiple LEDs indicate the Boomerang III's current operational state, and two buttons allow you to select the Play Style looping mode and assign alternative functions to the Bonus buttons. (Courtesy of Boomerang Musical Products, Ltd.)

stutter-start a loop to sound like DJ scratching, and use an expression pedal to adjust the overall playback volume or decay rate. If you record the master loop first, subsequent slave loops can be longer in a multiple of the master's length. You can program the Boomerang III to play one loop at a time for different parts of a song, as many as four loops in sync with each other or independently without sync, or one slave loop at a time to accompany the master loop. The Boomerang's buttons respond with a good tactile feel and the unit is quite forgiving if your switching isn't perfectly on the beat. It's strictly a real-time device, though, with no memory or facility to keep audio you've recorded. As of software version 3.0, Boomerang III can sync to MIDI clock and allows MIDI Start and Stop functionality of loop playback.

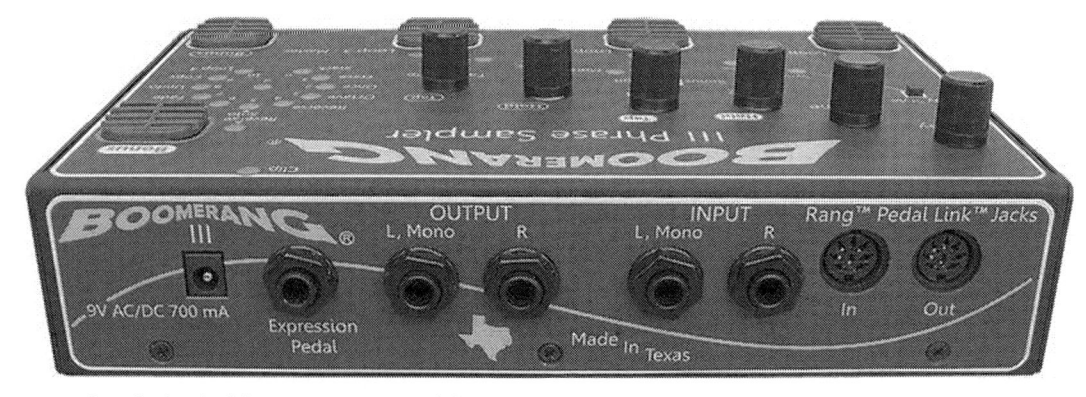

Located on the back of the Boomerang III pedal are its power input, 1/4" jacks for an expression pedal, left/mono and right outputs and inputs, and multipin connectors for the optional Boomerang Side Car. Once you've loaded version 3 of the Boomerang III software, the multipin connectors serve as MIDI in and out jacks, allowing the III to sync to an external MIDI clock. (Courtesy of Boomerang Musical Products, Ltd.)

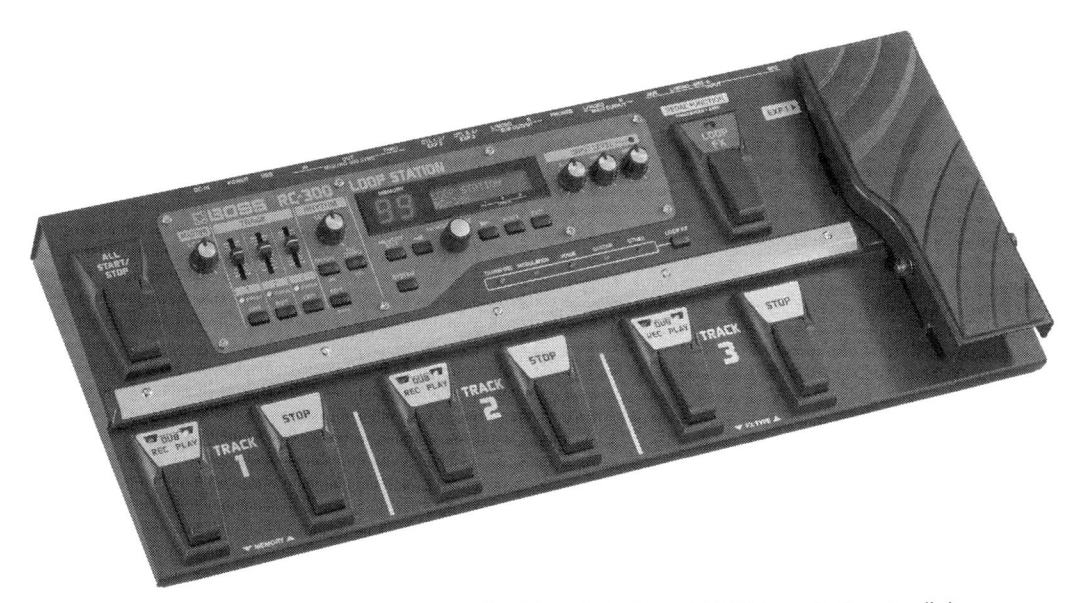

Phrase looping in the hardware domain gets very flexible with the Boss RC-300 Loop Station. It will, however, eat up a good portion of floor space, measuring over twenty-one inches across and nine inches front to back. That seems reasonable considering all of the controls are nicely spaced instead of being cramped. (Courtesy of Roland Corporation)

Boss's RC-300 looper provides three hours of recording time for three syncable stereo tracks of independent lengths and assignable to the main or sub outputs so guitar players don't ask too much from their amps for bass lines, vocals, and drum parts. Also resident in the RC-300 are a conveniently mounted, assignable expression pedal, a USB port for directly transferring WAV files between the RC-300 and a computer, MIDI I/O with sync-to-clock capability, and generous audio I/O including an XLR mic input with switchable **phantom power**. You can also assign the onboard effects—including reverb; delay; transposition up or down as much as an octave without affecting tempo; pitch bends with or without delayed vibrato; vocal processing to make a voice sound male, female, or robotic; flanging; phase-shifting; and distortion—independently to process your loop tracks.

> *phantom power:* DC power, typically 48 volts, required by many condenser microphones and active direct boxes in order for them to work properly

If you'd prefer a software-based looping experience, try the possibilities provided by Ableton Live. Its Looper Device is a plug-in simulation of a multitrack hardware looper with extra bells and whistles. You can import audio to be looped, record unlimited overdubs on top of it, export audio you've recorded, and assign MIDI controllers to enhance the looping experience. Live's Looper can analyze what you've recorded to determine its tempo and length in number of bars, reverse a track, and route overdubs to be independently processed by other Live effects. You can also run and synchronize multiple Looper Devices.

Other Effects

When is a filter not a filter? When it's a **comb filter**. If its an analog comb filter, it's yet another device that depends on BBD. The effect requires a mix of the original signal with a briefly delayed—around 2 or 3ms up to 10ms—version to create an altered tone, producing an audible quality that can range from hollow to phase-shifted and adds automation if you modulate the delay time. If you graphically plotted the results, it would look like a bunch of valleys between peaks, which is why it's referred to as a "comb." Most comb filters provide a resonance or **feedback** knob, which boosts or attenuates the peaks to make the sound vary between brighter and mellower. One example of an analog comb filter in Eurorack format is the Analogue Systems RS120.

> *comb filter:* a circuit or algorithm that passes the entire frequency range minus a group of extremely narrow and deep notches that are typically spaced at equal distances from each other on a linear, logarithmic, or harmonic scale; mixing a delayed audio signal with the original signal creates a comb-filter effect, which is used to create phase-shifting; modulating the delay time adds animation to the results
> *feedback:* another term for filter resonance

Any 5U modular synthesists interested in an effect that sounds like a cross between flanging and phase-shifting—plus what John L. Rice describes as similar to comb filtering—should consider the C1660 Phase Processor from Club of the Knobs. Its designer, Kazike, says the C1660 is a twenty-stage phase-delaying allpass filter.

One of the most innovative ideas in dedicated hardware DSP comes in the form of the Z-DSP VC-Digital Signal Processor from Tiptop Audio. A 28hp Eurorack module, the Z-DSP allows open-source programming, which means you can program it via the computer language of your choice to function as DDLs, filters, oscillators, and more. You can also take advantage of Z-DSP programs others have created. As many as eight Z-DSP programs are stored per removable cartridge. Included with the module is the Dragonfly Delay cartridge, which provides eight delay programs. Optionally available are the Bat Filter cartridge, a collection of eight voltage-controlled digital filter programs, and the Broken Silicon cartridge, which includes a dual comb filter, a digital noise generator, the Bit Eater audio destroyer, and a Wave Shaver—all voltage-controllable. Tiptop Audio sells blank cartridges for storage of your own Z-DSP algorithms.

Perhaps the simplest description of a vocoder is "the thing that makes an instrument talk." Many first heard vocoding in Stanley Kubrick's 1971 film *A Clockwork Orange*, where Wendy Carlos made her Moog Modular sing in "March from *A Clockwork Orange*," an abridged reworking of the "Choral Movement" from Beethoven's Ninth Symphony. Two sound sources are required to make a vocoder work. It analyzes the varying tonal characteristics of one source and applies them to the other. As traditionally used, the first source would be a microphone into which a person speaks, and the second source would be a musical instrument. The miked voice would be the **program** and the instrument the **carrier**. The more frequency bands in a vocoder, the more intelligible its

Among numerous effects, synthesist John L. Rice uses a Club of the Knobs C1660 Voltage-Controlled Phase Processor to create a cool, whispery, vocal-bell drone. He also takes advantage of its voltage-control capabilities—linear and exponential modulation of phase-shift amount, regeneration level, and waveshape processing—in combination with an analog sequencer to produce exciting, dynamic timbral-shifting effects. (© club.of.the.knobs.com)

vocoded output. The BV512 module in Propellerhead Reason functions as either a vocoder or a graphic EQ. You can choose four, eight, sixteen, or thirty-two bands for each application, or switch it to FFT (Fast Fourier Transform) mode, which breaks the spectrum into 512 bands but might induce a slight delay in processing the signal.

> *program:* a source of modulation, also known as a modulator
> *carrier:* the signal to be modulated by the program

To subtly or dramatically alter acoustic or electronic sounds, try a **frequency shifter**. Harald Bode made one of the first and most musical, the Bode 735. A frequency shifter has an internal **quadrature oscillator** for adjusting the amount of shift, either manually or under voltage control. They're particularly good for **barber-pole effects**; detuning

The Synthesizer

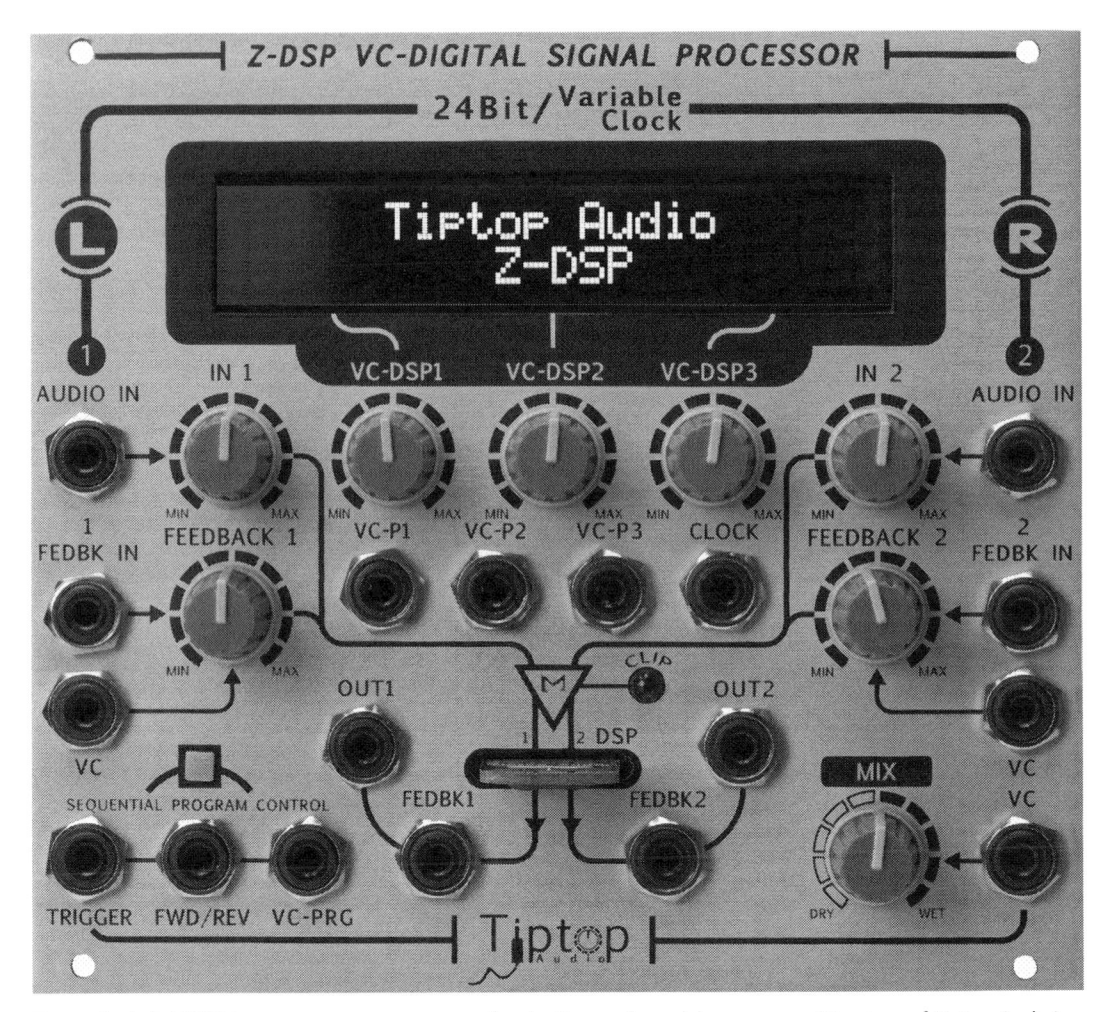

Tiptop Audio's Z-DSP is an open-source processor for the Eurorack modular segment. (Courtesy of Tiptop Audio)

Harald Bode introduced his Model 7702 sixteen-channel Vocoder in 1977. Norlin subsequently took over production in 1978, manufactured a hundred at a cost of $1,500 apiece, slapped on the Moog moniker, and put them on the market at a suggested retail price of $6,600. As you might imagine, they didn't sell too many—at least at that price. (Courtesy of Tom Rhea)

Korg introduced the nifty VC-10 vocoder in September 1978. It includes a twenty-band analyzer and twenty-band equalizer, a built-in polyphonic tone source, a thirty-two-note keyboard with a pitchbend wheel, and a boom for an optional mic. Asking price upon its introduction was $1,299, not including the microphone. A VC-10 sold on eBay for $1,399 in August 2013. (Courtesy of Korg)

Few if any manufacturers have offered vocoding in as many different packages as Roland. This is a VP-330 Vocoder Plus, which came out in 1979 and combined a vocoder with an ensemble-style keyboard that produced string and choir timbres. (Courtesy of Roland Corporation)

The Synthesizer

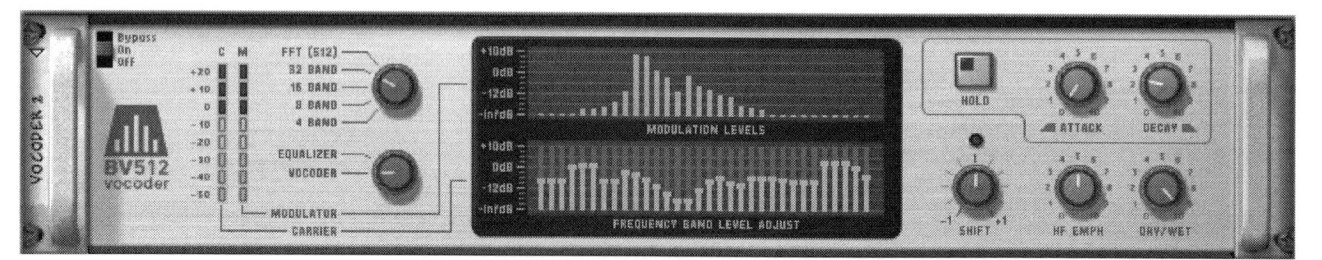

The BV512 vocoder in Propellerhead Reason offers four-, eight-, sixteen-, and thirty-two-band vocoding, along with Fast Fourier Transform (FFT) analysis and processing of audio. The BV512 can also be used as a graphic equalizer, providing the same number of frequency bands as in vocoder mode. (Courtesy of Propellerhead Software AB)

sources such as drums and percussion instruments, ring tones, glockenspiel, and voice; or creating unique timbres from familiar analog waveforms. Drew Neumann is a fan of the Encore Frequency Shifter, which is available in MOTM, FracRak, and Eurorack formats.

> *frequency shifter:* a circuit that multiplies 90 degree-phased versions of incoming audio with oscillator-generated quadrature signals to shift all of its frequency components by an equal number of Hertz, creating two separate outputs composed of upward- and downward-shifted sum and difference frequencies that can be summed to produce subtle to intense stereo phase-shifts, vibrato, a Leslie speaker simulation, and inharmonic and clangorous effects
>
> *quadrature oscillator:* a sine-wave generator that outputs two signals that are out of phase with each other by 90 degrees at frequencies as low as 0Hz and far up into the audible frequency range
>
> *barber-pole effects:* an audible impression of frequencies continuously rising or falling but never reaching the upper or lower threshold of hearing
>
> *pitch shifter:* a circuit or algorithm that lowers or raises the frequency of an incoming audio signal while preserving its harmonic relationships

You might think sounds processed with a **pitch shifter** would be similar to what you get from a frequency shifter, but that's not the case. While a frequency shifter alters the source's pitch purely to change the timbre, a pitch shifter alters the pitch without changing the timbre because it preserves the ratios of the harmonics in the sound.

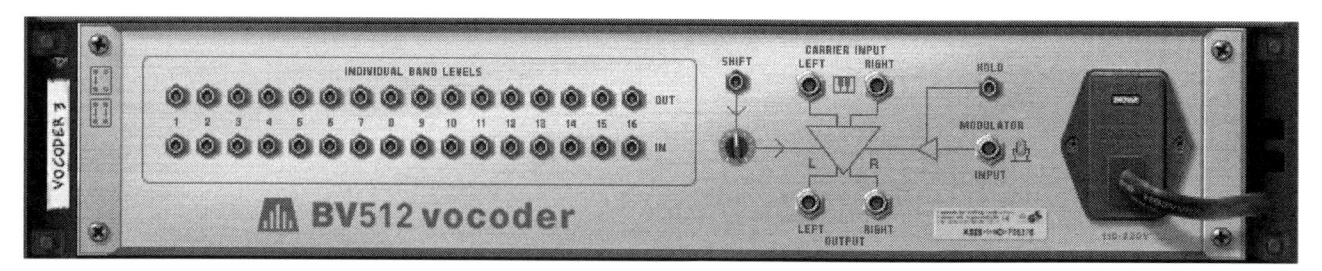

Looking at Propellerhead Reason's BV512 vocoder, you get a clue as to the flexible signal-routing possibilities offered by Reason's virtual modules. For example, if you really wanted to get creative, connect any of the BV512's individual band level outputs to differently numbered inputs and see what happens with the audio content. Don't worry, you'll never run out of cables. (Courtesy of Propellerhead Software AB)

Acoustics and Synthesis Basics

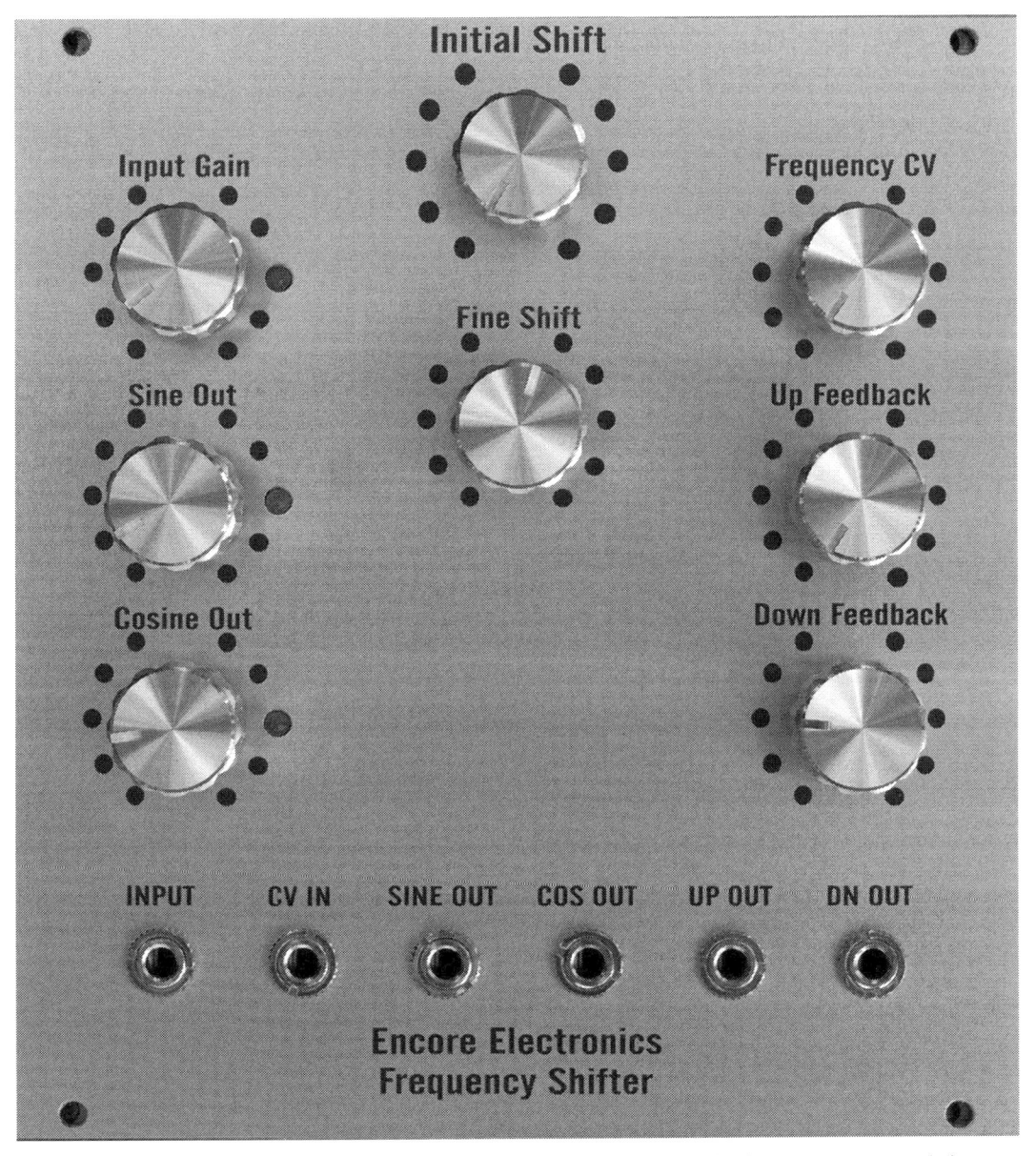

The 20hp Eurorack version of the Encore Electronics frequency shifter uses a hybrid processing approach that, according to Encore's website, combines a RISC (reduced instruction set computing) microprocessor-generated quadrature oscillator "with analog multipliers to generate the frequency-shifting effect." Tony Karavidas of Encore also offers the frequency shifter in MOTM and FracRak formats. (Tony Karavidas)

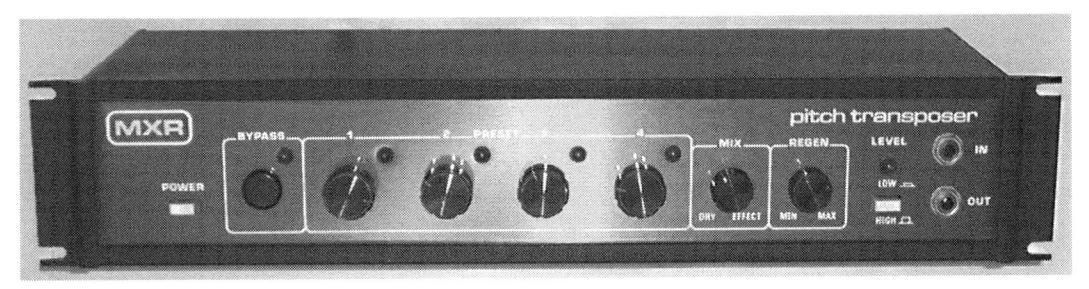

One of the coolest pitch transposers I ever saw came from MXR. A 2U rackmount processor developed by engineer Tony Gambacurta, the MXR Pitch Transposer (PT) originally appeared in 1978 and enjoyed quite a lengthy production cycle into 1987—after ART assumed production in 1984. It features a unique interface with four pitch-shift preset knobs on its front panel. Touch one and the PT toggles to that preset's pitch offset. (Roger Cordell, courtesy of Big City Music)

For something completely different, there's ring modulation. Two sound sources are required by a ring modulator (RM)—although some come with a built-in carrier oscillator that can serve as one source. The RM multiplies both sources together and outputs only the sum and difference frequencies, none from the original sounds. The results are often clangorous and inharmonic. Ring-modulated timbres can get very interesting with more complex source and carrier signals.

I'm a big fan of the Moog Music Moogerfooger MF-102 Ring Modulator, a stompbox that includes an LFO and a carrier oscillator. The LFO modulates the pitch of the internally generated carrier tone using either a sine or square waveform at varying frequencies. With a sine wave at slower frequencies, you can hear the sum and difference tones sweep toward and away from each other. Increase the LFO rate into the audio range to get more complex, clangorous timbres. Engage the LFO's square wave to create an even more intense tone. The higher you raise the MF-102's internal carrier oscillator frequency, the more pronounced the bell-like timbre and the less in-tune the resulting notes. You can make astonishing timbres and sound effects by plugging an external source into

My ring modulator of choice is the Bob Moog-designed Moogerfooger MF-102. It provides a built-in sine-wave oscillator, which you can use instead of an external carrier audio source. It also sports an LFO that produces either a square or sine wave for modulation, and CV inputs for controlling the wet/dry mix, LFO rate and modulation amount, and internal oscillator frequency. (Mark Vail)

Eurorack synthesists can create subtle to extreme frequency-shifting, phase-shifting, and ring-modulation effects with Synthesis Technology's E560 Deflector Shield. (© 2012 Synthtech Inc., used by permission)

the MF-102's carrier input. Combining a static tone with a sequenced or arpeggiated synth timbre can lead to extraordinary patterns. Connect a CD player to the audio input, insert a spoken-word CD, and ring modulate the text with the Moogerfooger's carrier oscillator or another external sound source in order to produce alien voices. Words won't be nearly as intelligible as a vocoder would create, but the results can be fascinating and sometimes terrifying.

For Eurorack enthusiasts, Synthesis Technology makes the E560 Deflector Shield, a 14hp digital processing module that can do frequency-shifting, eight-stage phase-shifting, and ring-modulation effects—one at a time. (FracRak modular synthesists can get the Deflector Shield in that format from Blacet Research as the F560 module.) It has eight different carrier waveforms, which you can continuously cross-fade among to create effects not possible with processors that only have sine-wave carriers. The Deflector Shield's carrier waveforms range from those that create simple frequency shifts to one that generates sixty-four-note patterns and another that produces extreme harmonics. Applying these carrier waveforms in ring-modulation mode allows the creation of effects ranging from tremolo to audio gating to radical distortion. While there's a mono audio input, the E560 has two audio outputs that transmit sound depending on the chosen effect. For example, with phase-shifting and the sixty-four-random phase waveform engaged, processed sounds will bounce all around a stereo field.

Among the great multi-effect processors—those that can generate more than one effect at a time—is Korg's Kaoss Pad series. The original KP1, released in 1999, provides reverbs, delays, flanging, distortion, tremolo, step-modulated phase-shifting, filters, ring modulation, looping, and panning, many of them available simultaneously in preset combinations. Ten of the fifty presets can sample up to five seconds of audio, although you'll lose the sample if you subsequently choose a reverb preset or turn the unit off. The KP1's two-dimensional pad allows you to control parameters of the presets in real time, and the

For hands-on, realtime control of an effects processor, you can't beat the Kaoss Pad series from Korg. The original came out in 1999. This is the Kaoss Pad Quad, introduced in January 2011. Whereas other Kaoss Pads provide multiple memory locations for different types of effects, the Quad delivers four different effects sections—looping, modulation (distortion, flanging, phasing, and ducking compression), filtering/pitch-shifting, and delay/reverb—that you can enable, disable, and freeze independently. It's really quite fun, powerful, and great-sounding. (Courtesy of Korg)

unit transmits MIDI control change (CC) data generated by your interactions with its pad. There's a 1/4" mic input, but the KP1's line-level inputs and outputs are all on RCA jacks—not including the 1/8" headphone jack. RCAs are typically what DJs deal with, but that's actually the market Korg meant to address with the original and subsequent Kaoss Pads.

In 2007 Korg introduced the miniKP, a small processor that has ninety-nine different effects, a tap-tempo button, a three-digit LED display, and one hundred presets. It's missing MIDI output and the mic input, but it does an excellent job of processing sounds as you control what it's doing from the pad, the tap-tempo feature works effectively, and you can use it anywhere since it will run on batteries.

The Korg Kaoss Pad Quad (KPQ) arrived in 2011. It lacks MIDI and presets and requires AC power, but it has a 1/4" mic input along with RCA I/O. One aspect that makes the Quad special is that you can independently engage any of four types of effects at once, and you can independently freeze a pad position for any of them to maintain what that particular effect is doing. Available effects are a looper, a modulator, a filter, and a delay/reverb—each of which can produce five different effects. Among the outstanding effects are reverse loop, which allows you to vary the loop length by moving your finger vertically on the pad; the loop slicer and grain shifter, both of which repeat part of the incoming audio and break it down into different sections as you move your finger around the pad; the decimator, which reduces the sampling frequency and the length of the data bit to make the audio grungy and lo-fi; the pitch-shifter; any of the filters—low-, high-, and bandpass; and tape echo, which simulates different anomalies of tape-echo machines as you touch different parts of the pad. Another effective KPQ feature is auto BPM detection, which does a reasonable job of sensing a tempo and synchronizing its clock to beats per minute—a convenient function when you're focusing on performance, and it's relatively easy to click a few times on the KPQ's tap button if auto-sync strays too far from the true tempo.

While you can certainly accomplish much of what the Kaoss Pads do using other devices and technologies plus a considerable amount of thought and work, Korg's already done all of that for you and served up the functionality in reasonably economical forms.

3
Choosing Your Synthesizer(s)

Diversity is key in the synthesizer universe. Within each of the two main categories—hardware and software—are a dozen or so often overlapping subclasses. Of the hardware variety, there are modular, patchable, normalled, fixed-architecture, analog, virtual analog, subtractive, additive, digital, hybrid, FM, sampler or sample-player, specialized vs. do-it-all workstation, drum machine, programmable with patch memory or nonprogrammable, voltage-controlled, with or without MIDI, knob-laden, menu-driven, physically modeled, noise toys, do-it-yourself (DIY) homemades, circuit-bent, assembled from a kit, keyboard-based, wind-controller driven, alternatively controlled, and so on.

On the software side come another bevy of subgenres: virtual analog, emulations of famous hardware synths, FM, sampler or sample-player, stand-alone, plug-in, assemble-your-own from scratch, audio-editing environments with synthesis capabilities, digital voltage-control generators (i.e., Expert Sleepers Silent Way and MOTU Volta), and for different platforms: Macintosh, Windows PC, or both (cross-platform); Linux; iOS apps for Apple's iPhone, iPod Touch, and iPad—a category that's seen explosive growth since 2008—and other platforms either existing or to come.

The decisions to consider within the synth market are vast. Here are some thoughts that may prove helpful.

If you're in the market for a high-end digital synthesizer, consider the Solaris from John Bowen Synth Design. Besides having flexible oscillators and filters that allow you to mimic vintage sounds and create new timbres, the Solaris provides complex, modular-like signal routing and modulation mapping along with extensive programming and performance functionality. It has six backlit LCDs matched with knobs and buttons for immediate parameter access, as well as wheels, a joystick, lengthy ribbon, a velocity- and pressure-sensing five-octave keyboard, a four-row by sixteen-step sequencer, and an arpeggiator for performance control. (Courtesy of John Bowen Synth Design)

John Bowen poses with a prototype of the Solaris at the January 2008 NAMM show. (Mark Vail)

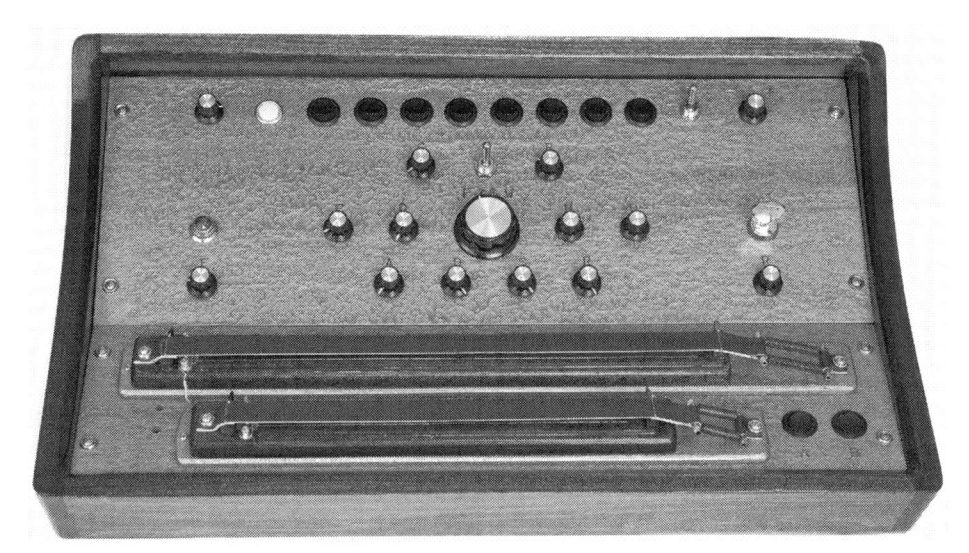

Representing the experimental wing of synthesizers is the Dewanatron Swarmatron, an eight-oscillator analog instrument with a span control that can expand oscillator tuning from nearly equal to widely diverse, ribbons for controlling the overall pitch and oscillator tunings, multiple control knobs, CV inputs for controlling and sequencing the Swarmatron from external sources, beautiful wood cabinetry, and a control surface worthy of a steampunk scene. (© 2011, courtesy of Joshua Sarner)

The Synthesizer

Arturia's ARP 2600V2 softsynth. Relatively few musicians ever got a chance to own or even play an ARP 2600 synthesizer, a highly desirable vintage analog synth that allows users to override its normalled internal signal routing using patch cords. If you can't find or afford one of the real things but you have a good Mac or Windows computer, you can virtually live the experience with the Arturia's 2600V2. Not only does it provide polyphony beyond ARP's Model 3620 keyboard duophony, but the virtual Arturia version also includes a re-creation of the much sought-after ARP Model 1601 sixteen-step sequencer. (Screenshot courtesy of Arturia)

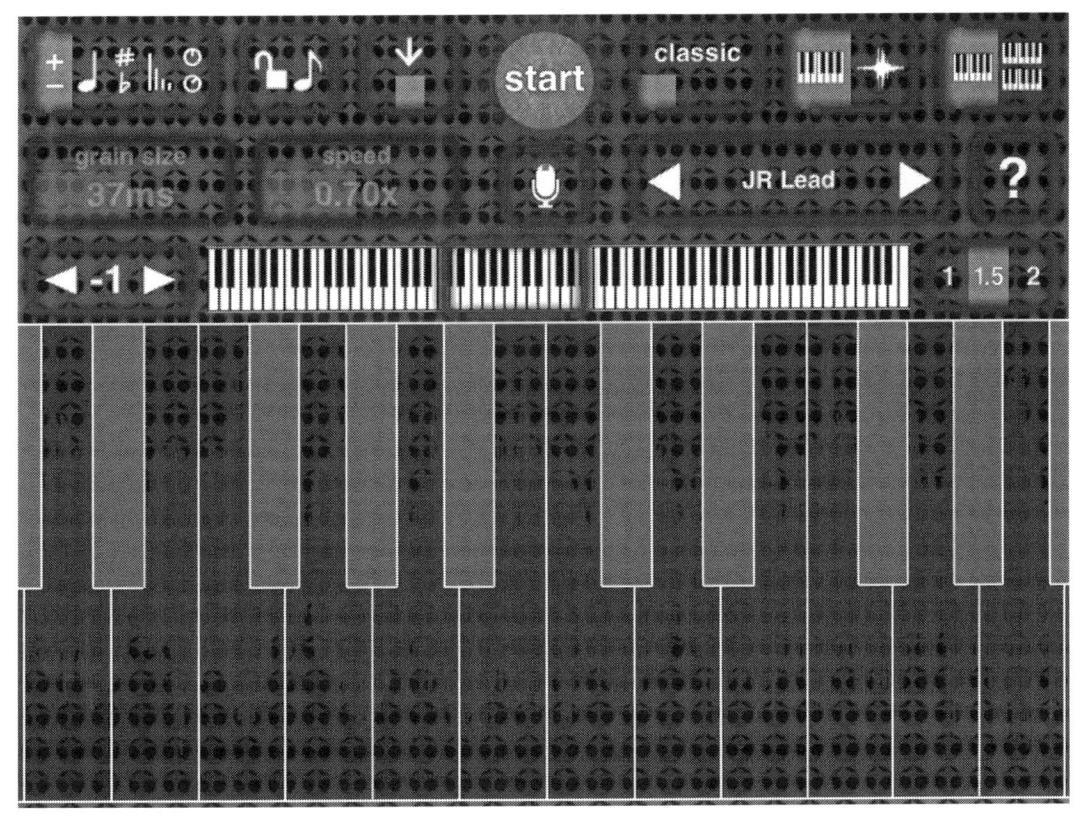

SampleWiz, from the Jordan Rudess company Wizdom Music, LLC, runs on an iPad, iPod Touch, or iPhone; allows you to sample your voice or other sounds; and lets you have loads of polyphonic fun with the sample. (© Wizdom Music)

Options

What's Your Budget?

Obviously you want to get the most bang for your buck. You may not be able to afford as much if electronic music is a hobby as opposed to a business venture in which the synth could pay for itself over time used for studio sessions, scoring films, composing songs, creating patches for sale to others with the same synth, designing unique sound effects and instrumental timbres for theater and video, touring with a popular band, performing live shows locally or globally, or teaching synthesis to others.

Musical Tastes and Goals

What kind of music do you want to make and how will you use a synthesizer to make it? Do you want an instrument for composition, performance, improvisation, recording, scoring to picture, reeking sonic havoc, or what? Find out what instruments and gear your favorite artists use, and see if any of them might suit your needs and fall within your financial constraints. Not to say that by having the same instruments you'll be able to sound similar or even come close to your heroes, but it will give you an idea of what synths you might like. When the time comes to make a final decision, do all that you can to actually play the synth(s) you're considering for as long as possible. The single most important aspect when you're making a choice is what you think of an instrument's sound.

The Synthesizer

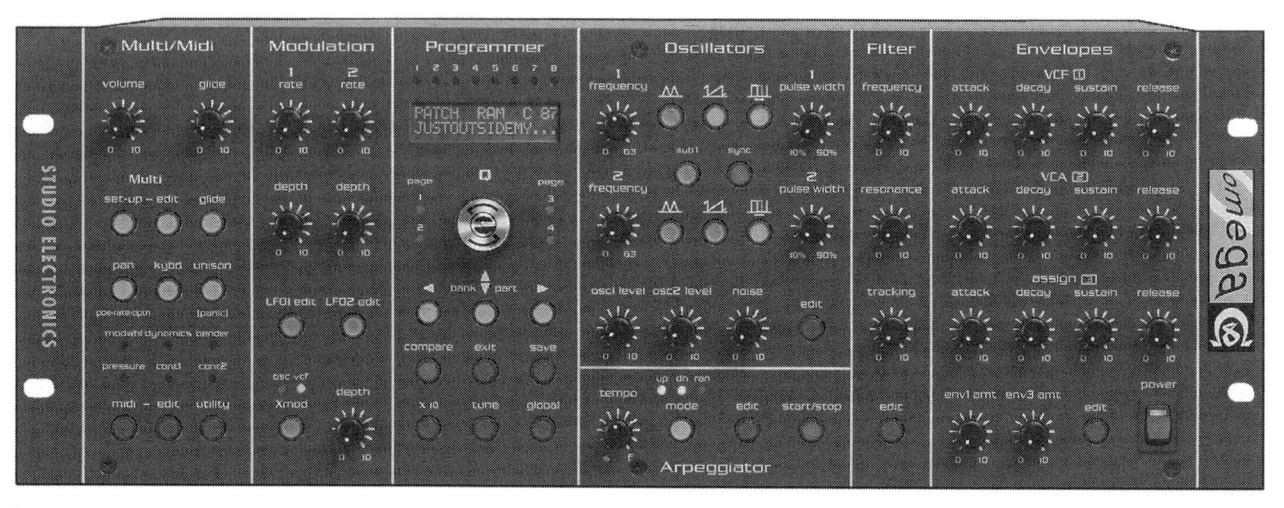

This is an eight-voice Omega8G polyphonic analog synth module from Studio Electronics. Founded in 1981, Studio Electronics earned a reputation for converting vintage synths such as the Minimoog, Sequential Circuits Prophet-5, and Oberheim OB-8 into top-notch rackmount modules—including the addition of MIDI control and whatever fortifications and modifications were necessary to keep them working and sounding great. When the well of refurbishable vintage synths began to dry up, the SE team took on the design and development of their own superb analog synth modules. (Courtesy of Studio Electronics)

Modular synthesizers have strongly rebounded since their near disappearance during the 1980s and '90s. Today there are many more modular makers than ever before. This two-panel Eurorack system consists primarily of Make Noise modules, but also represented are 4ms Pedals and the Harvestman. (Mark Vail)

If you don't like what you hear, chances are you'll never be able to make it sound the way you want, and you'll be dissatisfied with it from the outset.

Also consider how the instrument responds to you. If you dislike the way its knobs turn, its sliders feel, its keys—if it has them—play, the look of its display, the flow of its menu system, and the positions of its real-time controls, look elsewhere.

Before you shop, spend enough time with every instrument you already have in order to learn it as well as you can. When you buy a new instrument, set aside time—two weeks, two months, or however long it takes—to become intimately familiar with it. If other instruments might distract you, pack them away during your familiarization process. Once you've grasped as much as possible on one synth, tuck it away and work with another in the same way. The rewards will be immense.

If you won't be able to devote the time necessary to take full advantage of a new purchase, consider devoting time to what you already have in your possession. The urge to buy new things can be extremely difficult to resist. A new purchase might renew and ignite creativity, as can discovering previously untried techniques and unknown capabilities on gear you already have.

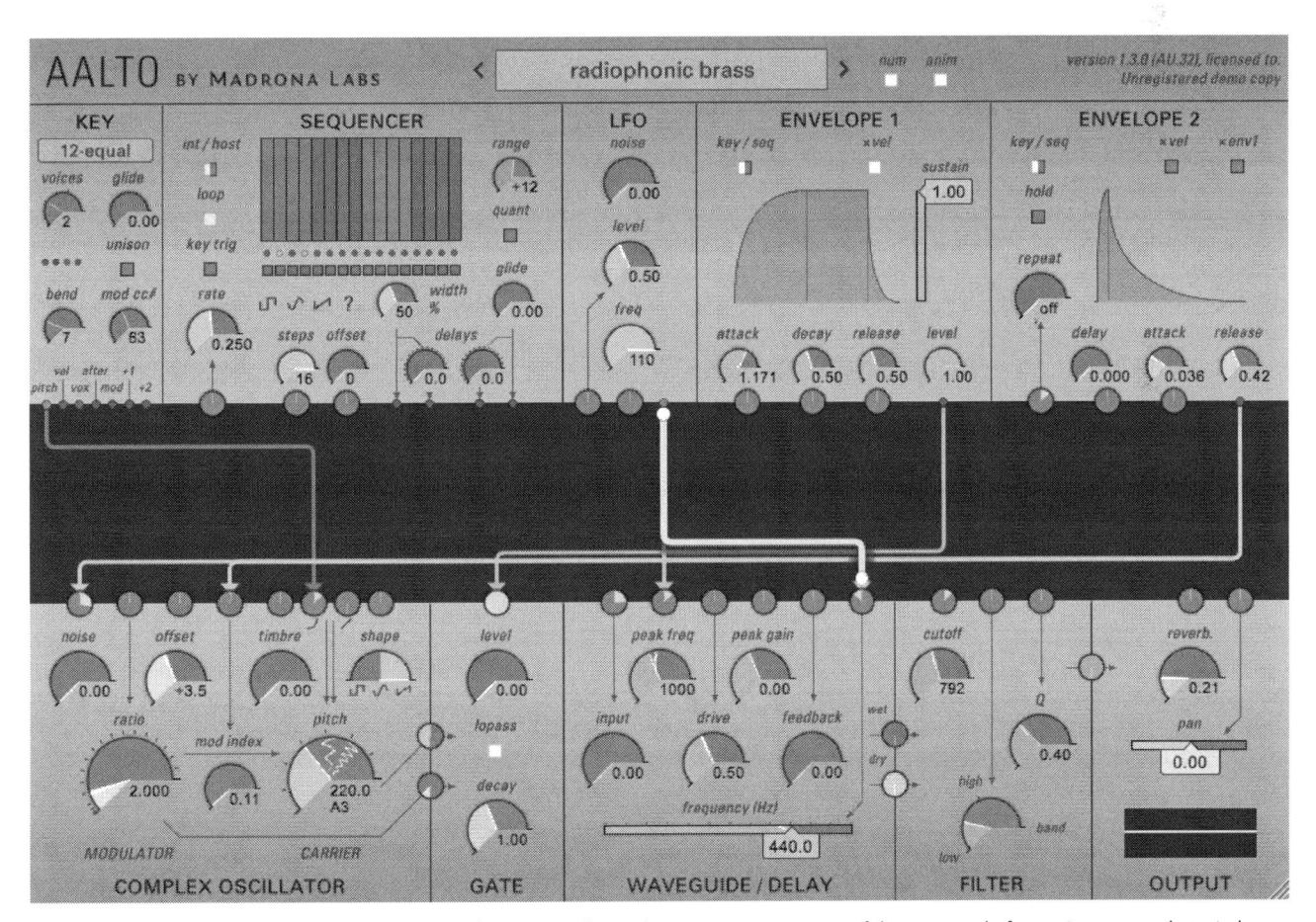

Hundreds of software synthesizers are available for Mac and Windows computers, many of them cross-platform. One example is Aalto, Madrona Labs' first softsynth. Aalto is totally patchable, allowing you to freely route signals between its control generators across the top—key, sixteen-step sequencer, LFO, and dual envelope generators—and audio generators on the bottom—complex oscillator, gate, waveguide/delay, multiband filter, and output. (Courtesy of Madrona Labs)

Owners of an iPhone, iPad, or iPod Touch who are looking for iOS music applications should check out the Xenon Groove Synthesizer from iceGear. It's an environment that provides hybrid, virtual analog, and sample-playback synthesizers; rhythm, pattern, and song sequencers; and a mixer page. You can export Xenon songs as files that are compatible with Apple Garageband and Intua Beatmaker. Xenon also supports CoreMIDI input and comes with drivers for the Akai SynthStation25 keyboard controller. (© iceGear)

You might be tempted to buy a bunch of new gear all at once, but that could be counterproductive. "Our technology now is probably like it was for us as kids when we got a few more toys than we needed for Christmas," offers Don Lewis, the incomparable pop/gospel-singing organist/synthesist who first blew me away at the Hungry Tiger in San Francisco in 1980 while performing with the Live Electronic Orchestra. LEO isn't a band; it's the incredible performance system Don assembled during the mid-1970s to perform inspiring one-man shows. LEO now spends most of its time on display in Carlsbad, California, at the Museum of Making Music (www.museumofmakingmusic.org), although Lewis refurbished it at the end of 2012 for performances at the January 2013 NAMM convention in Anaheim, California. "The biggest frustration I had as a kid," Don recalls, "was trying to get all of the toys to work at one time and enjoy them. Some of the most memorable Christmases were when we didn't get a lot of toys, maybe only one that we could really sink our teeth into, and we would play with that toy in so many imaginative ways."

Hardware vs. Software

Do you prefer to stay within the hardware realm or is software an attractive alternative? Scores of affordable, productive, and exciting music applications await those who buy a computer or tablet device such as an iPad, iPhone, Kindle Fire, Android, and the like. Many outstanding softsynths are available for amazing deals, and some are even free. However, price alone isn't the only consideration. The platform on which you run softsynths—

Gospel/pop/jazz/classical organist, vocalist, and synthesist Don Lewis plays LEO, the Live Electronic Orchestra, in 1977. The console was in a previous life a Hammond Concorde organ. LEO also includes four Oberheim SEMs, two ARP 2600s, an ARP Pro Soloist, a custom-built ARP LFO, and a Tapco mixer. (Phil Toy, courtesy of Don and Julie Lewis)

To the *right* is the three-manual performance console with which Don Lewis plays and controls LEO, the Live Electronic Orchestra. While the dual-pier chrome pedestal came from a Hammond X-66 organ, he pirated the two lower manuals, drawbars, organ voice circuits, and chrome pedals from a Hammond Concorde. Lewis helped Armand Pascetta develop the polyphonic keyboard controller that serves as the upper manual. While LEO now resides in the Museum of Making Music in Carlsbad, California, Don still tours and performs with more modern gear, although nothing performs quite the way LEO did. (Courtesy of Don and Julie Lewis)

The remaining components in Don Lewis's LEO. Stacked from *top to bottom* are a Roland DC-50 Digital Chorus on top of an RE-201 Space Echo enclosed in a Plexiglas cabinet next to a Boss mixer *on the right*, a second Plexiglas cabinet containing four Oberheim SEMs flanked on the *left* and *right* by patchbays, and a third Plexiglas cabinet encasing the synthesis engines of two ARP 2600s. Not shown are the Roland CR-68, CR-78, and TR-808 drum machines and Vocoder Plus VP-330 that Don also used in performance. Controlling the whole shebang from the triple-manual console, a few supplemental keyboards, and a drum machine, Don alternately used LEO to churn up his audience with rousing barn-burners and soothe them with soft ballads and classical-tinged instrumentals. Not only could Don produce the sounds of full-on symphony orchestras and cathedral pipe organs, but he could back his tremendous lead vocals with a choir of angels . . . or heathens and robots. (Courtesy of Don and Julie Lewis)

unless it's a Muse Research Receptor—is most likely intended for consumer rather than professional use. The manufactured lifespan of consumer products is typically far shorter than that of most pro-quality musical instruments. Technological advancements come fast and often with consumer electronics. New operating systems can render software that ran perfectly well on the previous operating system nonfunctional; hopefully the maker of the software has developed an upgrade that works with the new OS—if they're still in business. If they haven't or aren't, your choice is either to maintain the platform and OS on which the software runs properly or move on.

Working with hardware is an entirely different experience. Knobs, buttons, sliders, wheels, and other controls are often single-function so they respond immediately and in predictable ways. Synth manufacturers make their instruments to do one thing—create music—and not multitask to perform nonmusical functions on the side. The instrument is what it is when you start working with it—although manufacturers may release updates that owners can easily load in if it's software or may require a visit to the store for a firmware upgrade if the user doesn't feel capable of performing the operation.

What can go wrong with a hardware synthesizer? Normal wear and tear, for one thing. Parts age, pots get scratchy, jacks corrode, critical components get discontinued, instruments get physically abused on the road—it all takes a toll. With diligent care, a properly designed electronic instrument that gets routine servicing can last a very long time, much like an acoustic instrument. Provided a synth hasn't suffered major trauma, it can usually be repaired and even totally refurbished.

The Lead-Free Solder Blues

Gary Chang points out that lead-free solder, which became a requirement in 2006, degrades over time. Drew Neumann agrees. "Search on Google for 'tin whiskering.' There are a lot of theories about long-term reliability of electronics as they're soldered together now post-RoHS [Restriction of Hazardous Substances]. From what I've heard, Texas Instruments swears their new formulations of solder are longtime reliable, but there has been evidence, for example, of satellites that conformed to these rules failing. What happens is, if there isn't lead in the formulation, the tin—according to the second law of thermodynamics—wants to grow together and form stalactites and stalagmites and micro-shorts start popping up. The question is, what do they put in the formulation now that will make up for that? I think in the 1940s they discovered about lead that balancing the mix—what was it, 60/40?—keeps the tin from getting nasty. Lead's not a real good thing to have in the environment, so it's understandable that they want to do something about it, but I try to keep a lifetime supply of the old, good solder around so that I can fix my gear. . . . I'm sure this room probably would be rated a HazMat zone given all of the years I've been restoring and building electronics in here with lead-based solder."

From the manufacturer's standpoint, the hardware-vs.-software situation becomes even more interesting. Eric Persing, who runs Spectrasonics and has helped in the development

Spectrasonics founder Eric Persing, who's actively participated in the development of both hardware and software synthesizers, sits before a Moog Modular, Sequential Circuits Prophet-VS, and Roland JP-8000 in his studio. Above the VS to the *right* is an oversized poster of a screenshot of the Visualizer window from Spectrasonics' Omnisphere. (Courtesy of Spectrasonics)

of hardware synths including the sensationally popular Roland D-50 (1987), shares his perspective on designing instruments in both domains. "The design process is similar," he says, "although in software you have a lot more flexibility to dramatically change aspects of the instrument along the way because you aren't as committed. I love that you can always keep changing and tweaking software. I don't like the idea of getting a product to a certain point where you can't touch it any more."

Eric then points out a major difference in the manufacturing process: With a software synth, you don't need a hundred-million-dollar factory to make it. Anyone with an idea and coding experience can create a software instrument, which is why there are so many softsynth companies. "The downside," he adds, "is that just because you can develop a softsynth so easily doesn't mean you should release it. It should be the very best thing you've ever done as far as its capabilities are concerned, and it should be something that will last a long time."

Unlike manufacturers of digital synthesizers, softsynth developers don't need to make DSP chips for their instruments. Persing explains that it can take about five years for a manufacturer to design and produce a processing chip for a digital synth, and by the time the instrument exists the DSP chip is already outdated because it's underpowered. Eric believes this disadvantage may eventually result in digital synthesis moving almost exclusively into the computer domain, leaving analog synthesizers as the prominent hardware instruments.

In addition, softsynth companies don't require big production teams as do major hardware manufacturers, which need developers, engineers, assembly-line workers, qual-

This fabulous instrument, dubbed the OMG-1, is a unique synthesizer Eric Persing designed for a giveaway to benefit the Bob Moog Foundation. He combined a Moog Little Phatty analog synth with a Mac Mini, two iPads, two iPods, and an Airport Express wireless network from Apple; an Akai LPF-25 mini-keyboard controller; and Daniel Auon's beautiful, handcrafted curly-maple cabinet. Eric and Michelle Moog-Koussa, Executive Director of the Bob Moog Foundation, introduced the OMG-1 at the January 2011 NAMM show. Judges auditioned over four hundred entries submitted from musicians around the worldwide and, in September 2011, awarded Torley Wong with the coveted OMG-1 based on fifteen songs he recorded using mostly Spectrasonics Omnisphere sounds from the Bob Moog Tribute Library. (Courtesy of Amin Bhatia)

ity-control testers, and so on. Software delivery is far easier and much less expensive as well, especially when it can be distributed via the Internet.

There are pros and cons to hardware and software, as well as advocates who lean one way or the other. Perhaps the best approach is to acknowledge the benefits of each and take advantage of both. It's truly a wonderful age in which to be a synthesist!

Portability and Power

Is portability important for transportation and onstage use, situations in which your gear will face the perilous rigors of the road? If your new synth is going to stay in one place, its size and weight won't matter as much as it would if you plan on taking it elsewhere for gigs and jams. If you aren't a VIP with roadies, not only will you need a properly sized vehicle but you might want to avoid anything too big and cumbersome. You also should invest in proper cases to protect your synth(s) and other gear from getting beat up during transit.

Likewise, consider set-up time. The more separate devices, stands, and cables in your rig, the longer it will take you to put the pieces together for a show and take them apart afterward. If you have racks of gear, permanently patch as much as possible together inside each rack and minimize the number of cables needed to run between the racks and the synths and/or controllers you actually play during performance.

> **Power to the Pieces**
>
> Power delivery to your synths and other electronic music-making gear is an important consideration. Attached power cords are good in the sense that you won't ever lose them, but they potentially lengthen set-up and tear-down times. Grounded, three-conductor IEC power cords are preferable because they're readily available and, during set-up, you can first arrange your instruments on their stands and then plug in all of the cords; after the show, unplug and store the cords before packing your instruments in their cases—and yes, road cases, even if they're soft-shell, are necessary to protect your valuable investments.
>
> As for the pesky wall-wart power supplies that come with so many electronic devices these days, sometimes you just have to live with them. External power supplies save manufacturers quite a bit in production costs because they might otherwise have to install different power supplies for each country they ship their products to—although thankfully the number of universal supplies is growing. Lump-in-the-middle supplies are more convenient than wall warts, but they're far less common. If you're surrounded by too many wall warts, consider a multioutput, multivoltage supply such as the Voodoo Lab ISO-5.
>
> Here's an important tip: Whenever you receive a new electronic device with a wall wart or proprietary power supply, as soon as you unpack them and before you set them up in your rig, apply some kind of ID label to indicate which device it goes with. There are so many different voltage standards and positive-versus-negative and AC/DC variations that the last thing you want to do is plug the wrong supply into an important piece of gear and inadvertently fry it. Believe me, it's worth the effort to label everything so that nothing goes awry.
>
> If you have space, rackmount power supplies are wonderful items, both for the road and in the studio. There are a variety of styles from which to choose, ranging from surge protectors to sequenced-switchers to power conditioners to uninterruptible power supplies. Among those who manufacture such products are Furman, Monster, Juice Goose, SurgeX, PS Audio, Tripp Lite, and Equi=Tech. Surge-protected power strips also come in handy. In the studio, its useful to arrange switchable power supplies so that you can turn on and off specific banks of gear as needed.
>
> A word of warning about inexpensive surge protectors: One nasty surge might knock out the protection circuitry, and you would never know about it. I had to replace a power supply once because I depended on a failed surge protector. If you want to save money by buying cheap surge protectors, it might be a good idea to occasionally replace them. But considering the potential for serious damage to your valuable gear, it pays to pay more and get good-quality power distributors.

Will AC power always be available where you perform, or will there be important occasions where battery power would be essential? Along with your synth(s), this also applies to mixers, effects, and amplification. While there are generators that run on gasoline or solar energy and DC-to-AC converters for twelve-volt car batteries, consider the extra hardware involved with such a proposition compared to battery-powered gear.

Programmability: Pros and Cons

Is a programmable, fixed-architecture synth with patch memory what you need, or would you prefer the freedom and flexibility of audio and control signal routing provided by a modular or patchable synth? Whereas the former can provide instant gratification from a memory full of professionally programmed patches and the ability for you to modify those patches and create your own, the latter prove much more challenging when it comes to repatching to create entirely different sounds. Working with either type of system can be exciting, frustrating, inspirational, humbling, and time-consuming.

When you begin evaluating a programmable synth, devote time to audition as many of its factory patches as you can—or those stored by its previous owner. This should introduce you to the instrument's range of sonic capabilities; when you start tweaking patches to satisfy your own needs, you've begun the familiarization process for that instrument.

Programmability in itself is a thorny issue. There's no doubt that when it arrived during the late 1970s, the use of synthesizers in live performance surged dramatically because access to different sounds became nearly immediate. It proved a boon to session players in busy studios as well. However, there are downsides to programmability. For instance, players who don't make their own sounds avoid taking the time to learn all of the features and capabilities of their instrument(s).

The composer/synthesist Gary Chang, who has scored many of Steven King's productions for television, points out a telling analogy: "It's like the difference between a Line 6 guitar amplifier versus a professional guitarist's rig," says Gary. "For example, the Line 6 Spider IV Jam allows anyone to select a 1965 Fender Twin Reverb or a Mesa/Boogie Dual Rectifier preset and get very close to that sound. On the other hand, if you actually have the real gear, it takes experience and skill to know exactly what settings and conditions you need to make to create the real sound." Chang stipulates that synthesizer programmability has "minimized and even negated a lot of the creativity that was basically implied in modular and patchable instruments."

Making music with a nonprogrammable instrument such as the Minimoog forces you—unless you're the rumored rock-star keyboardist who had the wherewithal to buy a dozen Minimoogs, turned the knobs and threw switches on one until he had a sound he liked, taped the knobs and switches in place, and then moved on to the next Minimoog—to constantly interact with its controls to shape the sound as you play, reinforcing your intimate knowledge of the instrument. Perhaps due to the connection such synths forge with their owners, numerous instruments that aren't programmable have appeared during the past decade, including the Doepfer Dark Energy, Arturia Minibrute, Moog Minimoog Voyager Old School, Studio Electronics' Boomstar series, and Tom Oberheim's resurrected SEM.

Expandability

Is expandability important in considering your next purchase? This applies in particular to modular synths, for which you'd like to start with a cabinet that's large enough to contain what you need and still have extra space for more. It can also make a difference if you prefer to stay within the MIDI realm or are looking for gear that will transmit and respond to control voltages, triggers, and gates for analog devices. The more products that

The Boomstar 5089 from Studio Electronics, like the Minimoog, doesn't have patch memory. It does, however, provide plenty of knobs, switches, and jack I/O for synthesis fun. Inside the Boomstar 5089 is a re-creation of the classic Moog four-pole ladder filter. (Courtesy of Studio Electronics)

will interface together in your rig, the more flexibility you'll have in composing and performing music.

As Others Have Done

With any of the above thoughts that apply to you in mind, consider another asset that might help you decide which synths would work for you: experiences of professional synthesists. Take, for example, Drew Neumann, who initially hit it big by composing the captivating music and creating sound effects and voices for Peter Chung's *Aeon Flux*, launched on MTV's critically acclaimed *Liquid Television* animation series in 1991. Its success led to Neumann composing music for all eighty-four episodes of Nickelodeon's *The Wild Thornberrys* and fifty-two episodes of *Aaahh!!! Real Monsters*, both developed at the Klasky/Csupo studio, along with episodes of *The Grim Adventures of Billy & Mandy* and *Evil Con Carne* on the Cartoon Network. Drew also created and designed sound effects for Disney's *Beauty and the Beast*, *Rollercoaster Rabbit*, and *Off His Rockers*, and composed music for Disney Television Animation, E! Entertainment Television's *Talk Soup*, and major advertising agencies worldwide.

As you can see from the pictures here, Neumann has a stunning synth collection—plus all of the software you don't see, including MOTU Digital Performer, Apple Logic

Choosing Your Synthesizer(s)

Drew Neumann may look bewildered, but he's just posing. Directly in *front* of him are two Moog Music Minimoog Voyagers, twenty-first-century editions of the classic Minimoog, the most popular American-made analog monophonic synthesizer from the twentieth century. To the *lower right* you can see a pair of Moog Music Moogerfooger processors—an MF-103 12-Stage Phaser and MF-105 MuRF—alongside a Crumar-made, pre-MIDI Electronic Valve Instrument (EVI) designed by Nyle Steiner. (Courtesy of Amin Bhatia)

Scanning to the *right* of the vantage point from the previous photo in Drew Neumann's studio, you get to see more of his synth collection. To the *right* of the Korg Wavestation keyboard on the rolling table are a modular synth, various rackmount synths, and other devices we'll focus on shortly. Identifiable on the *far right* are a Jomox Sunsyn eight-voice polyphonic synth module and four keyboard synths (*top to bottom*): a Waldorf Q virtual modeled-analog synth, a Yamaha VL1 physical-modeling synth, an Alesis Andromeda A6 polyphonic analog synth, and an Ensoniq TS-10 sample-playback synth/workstation. (Courtesy of Amin Bhatia)

Studio, Celemony Melodyne, Ableton Live, and Gigastudio, and plug-ins such as the entire Arturia V-collection, Native Instruments Komplete, and a variety of softsynths from Steinberg, MOTU, BIAS, and Waldorf. When you buy your first synth, you might dream of having a studio filled with synths like Drew has.

If you want to make good music with this many synths—or only one—it takes practice and a lot of time and work. Experimentation often plays an important role as well. Drew is indeed capable of not only handling all of his marvelous musical toys and know-

An overhead view of the Waldorf Q, Yamaha VL1, and Alesis Andromeda A6 in Drew Neumann's studio. (Mark Vail)

A formidable six-panel 5U modular synth consumes a wide birth and scores of patch cables in one corner of Drew Neumann's Droomusic studio. Dubbed the Knob Grotto by Drew's wife Leslie, it consists of modules from Synthesis Technology, Synthesizers.com, Oakley Sound Systems, Encore Electronics, Blacet, Paia, STG Soundlabs, Magic Smoke Electronics, Yusynth, and Digisound—some of which Drew handcrafted himself. To the *left from the top* are a pair of Kenton Pro 4 MIDI-to-CV converters, Drew's custom-made patchbay, a Mackie 1604 VLZ mixer, and a Korg Wavestation. In the rack to the *right* of the Knob Grotto are (from the *top down*): two Alesis 3630 compressors, a dbx 266 compressor/limiter, Line 6 Delay and Modulation modeler processors, an MXR 1500 delay line, two Deltalab Effectron II ADM1024 delay processors, another dbx 266 compressor/limiter, a Vermona PH-16 analog phaser, a Tascam patchbay, two MacBeth Studio Systems M3X analog synth modules, a Jomox Sunsyn (*on a shelf extending out of the front of the rack*), two MOTU MIDI Express XT MIDI interfaces, and a Mackie 1202 VLZ Pro mixer (*also on a shelf*). (Courtesy of Amin Bhatia)

ing to which he should turn for specific types of sounds and music, but he also often tinkers with their innards to make them even better than they were to start with. He's a busy guy, which makes it even more remarkable that he knows all of his gear so well. "How did I find the time?" he poses. "Sometimes in cartoons you have down time; other times it's just a matter of doing something for fun. It's very satisfying to use things you built on TV shows, even if nobody else knows it."

Neumann is a big fan of the Arturia Origin, comparing it to the PPG Realizer. At the 1986 Frankfurt Musikmesse, PPG founder Wolfgang Palm demonstrated a prototype of a visionary instrument that could emulate a variety of synthesizers via different types of synthesis. Sadly, PPG went out of business before Palm could complete the Realizer. Drew appreciates the Origin because it allows him to do things like create a patch with eight oscillators and a mixture of ARP, Roland, and Moog filters, and route signals in novel ways. Origin provides simulations of a Minimoog filter, something closer to a Moog Modular filter, a Yamaha CS-80 highpass filter, and much more—even a Bode Frequency Shifter—then allows you to arrange them with other virtual modules as you can with a hardware modular synth. But instead of a monophonic voice, you get up to thirty-two

Standing before Drew Neumann's 5U Knob Grotto modular system, which only had a few patch cords plugged in at the time, and over a Korg Wavestation is Morbius, the patchable synth Neumann designed and built using synth components from Paia and E-mu while attending CalArts during the early 1980s. He named it after Dr. Morbius (played by Walter Pidgeon) in MGM's classic 1956 sci-fi movie *Forbidden Planet*, which featured an unforgettable electronic filmscore by Louis and Bebe Barron. (Mark Vail)

voices of polyphony. With the Origin, Arturia created a digital instrument capable of many extraordinary synthesis operations.

Like many other manufacturers and developers of digital synths and audio gear, Arturia incorporates Analog Devices' SHARC DSP processor chips in the Origin (SHARC is an acronym for Super Harvard ARchitecture single-chip Computer). Denis Labrecque

Looking down the line from above the Minimoog Voyagers in Drew Neumann's Droomusic studio, you can see in the background a pair of Oberheim SEMs in the rack above an Arturia Origin module. Farther back in the racks to the right are Waldorf Q, Microwave II, and original Microwave modules, alongside a pair of Akai Z8 samplers. Peaking out beneath the closer Minimoog Voyager at the *bottom right* is the keyboard of a Waldorf Wave. Hanging on the wall to the *upper left* are a Fender Toronado electric guitar, a Spector Electric Bass, and a five-string Fender Jazz Bass. (Courtesy of Amin Bhatia)

Drew Neumann's Morbius synth also appears in this photo on the *left*, supporting a pair of Moog Music Moogerfooger CP-251 Control Processors. In front of Morbius is an M-Audio Oxygen 8 MIDI/USB keyboard controller. Past these items are (from *left to right*): a tall Eurorack/FracRak modular system containing modules from Analogue Systems, Doepfer, Blacet, Bananalogue, and Cyndustries; a Modcan A Series/Cyndustries modular system; and a six-panel Serge Modular system. *Beneath* the Modcan is a Clavia Nord Lead, *above* the Serge is a balalaika, and on the *right* is a Steinway 1917 Model M grand piano. (Courtesy of Amin Bhatia)

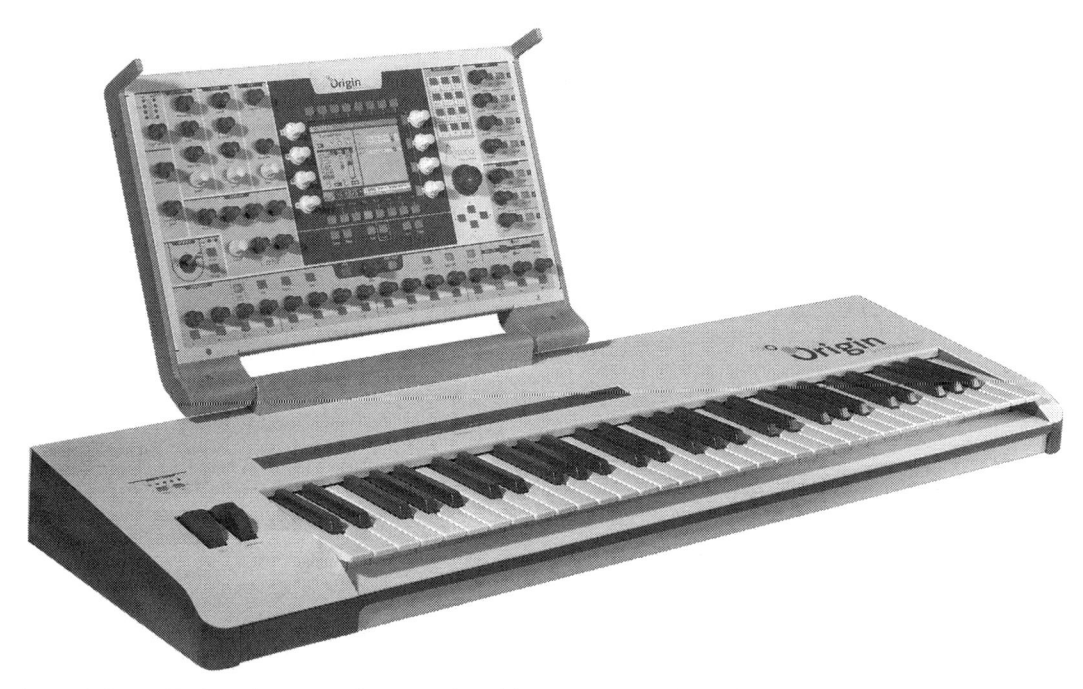

Arturia's Origin Keyboard is essentially a virtual modular system in hardware form, and it delivers digitally modeled re-creations of vintage components such as Moog and ARP filters and the Bode Frequency Shifter. Some might find its display—which, unlike the tabletop Origin module, lacks a contrast control—a bit small, and it's a shame the flip-up control panel doesn't lock in its closed position, making the instrument somewhat of a challenge for an individual to carry. Then again it sports an outstanding multitimbral synth engine, an excellent sixty-one-note keyboard that senses velocity and aftertouch—and even a form of polyphonic aftertouch—along with Moog-style wheels and a nearly 16"-long ribbon controller, and lots and lots of buttons and knobs. (Courtesy of Arturia)

Axel Hartmann's Gambit bears a striking resemblance to the Arturia Origin Keyboard, for good reason: He designed both of them. One of the main differences between them is that the Gambit makes no sound because it's a prototype. It was Axel's graduation work in industrial design in 1989. The software screenshots shown on the Gambit display were from Steinberg Avalon and Cubase. (Courtesy of Hartmann Music)

of Analog Devices explains that the Harvard architecture physically separates storage and signal pathways for instructions and data, which works outstandingly well for audio processing.

Arturia's Origin reminds me of the Clavia Nord Modular (1997–2009), except for at least two significant differences. First, while the Origin allows you to program it entirely from its front panel, you need a computer to create Nord patches. Another differ-

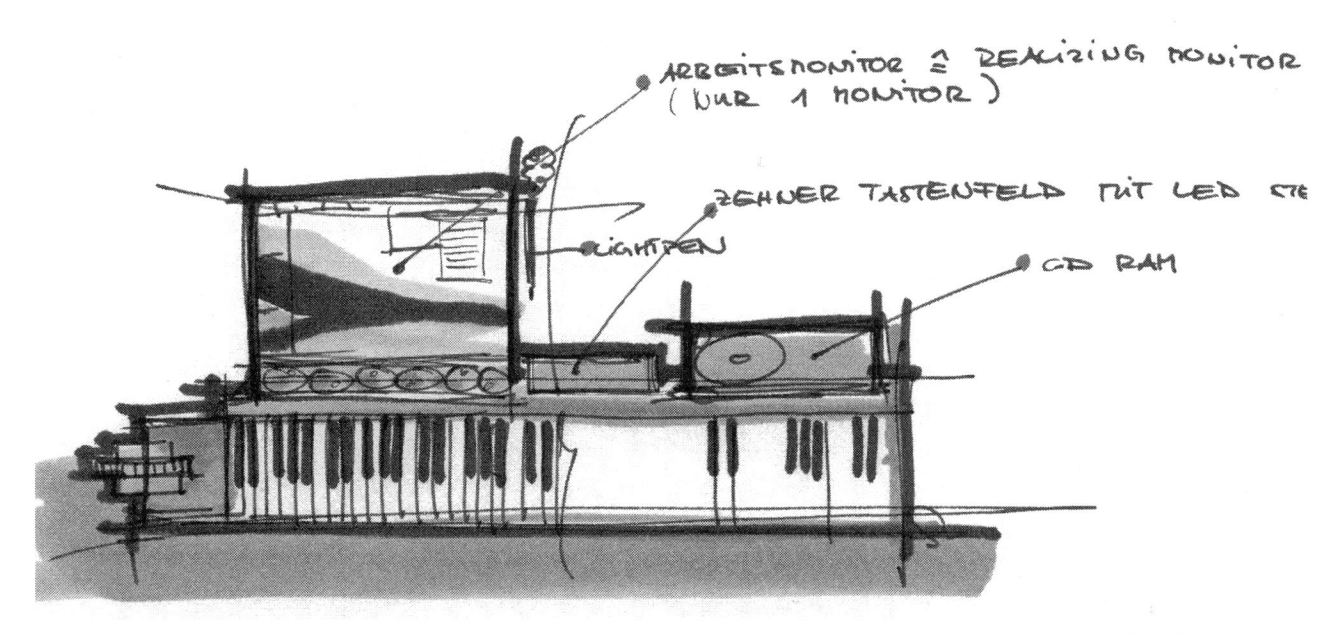

The original scribbles that led to Axel Hartmann's Gambit synthesizer prototype and, eventually, the Arturia Origin Keyboard. Hartmann has contributed to the designs of dozens of synthesizers, including the Waldorf Wave and Blofeld, Access Virus, Alesis Andromeda, and Moog Minimoog Voyager. He also designs medical products, dishwashers, and devices for other industries that prove more lucrative, but designing synths is his favorite occupation. (Courtesy of Hartmann Music)

Although it never went into production, the PPG Realizer (1986) could be considered the first virtual instrument. PPG founder Wolfgang Palm designed the Realizer to digitally replicate different types of synthesis—he successfully modeled the Minimoog (as shown here) and Yamaha DX7—but its development ended along with PPG as a manufacturer in 1987. (Courtesy of Wolfgang Palm)

ence that's less obvious is that, as Neumann points out, where the Nord Modular provides a variety of virtual filter, oscillator, envelope generator, LFO, and other modules, they aren't modeled on specific synthesizer components as they are in the Origin. For example, the Origin includes an emulation of ARP's 4075 filter, which was in the Odyssey II, Axxe II, Quadra, Omni, Omni 2, and Avatar. It purposely smothers high frequencies and sounds toy-like—in all the right ways to Drew's ears.

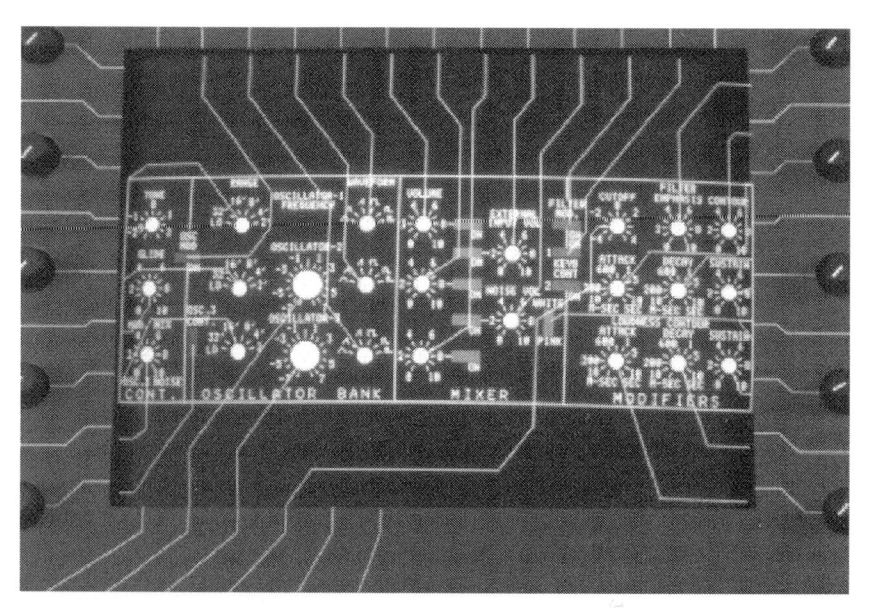

A close-up view of the PPG Realizer-modeled Minimoog, complete with lines indicating which Realizer knobs addressed the virtual Minimoog's knobs. (Courtesy of Wolfgang Palm)

Choosing Your Synthesizer(s)

Clavia's Nord Modular, released in 1997, is a hybrid hardware instrument with computer programming. Illustrated on a computer display are modules—oscillators, envelope generators, filters, and more—that you interconnect with virtual patch cords. The computer, however, doesn't generate sound. Instead, you transfer patches conceived there to the hardware component, which generates the sound. Once loaded with patches, the Nord Modular hardware functions on its own. (Courtesy of Hans Nordelius and Clavia DMI AB)

ARP released the Quadra in 1978. It consisted of circuitry from an Omni, an Axxe, a Solus, and other synths, all under the control of a microprocessor and strapped together in one box with a sixty-one-note keyboard. Both the Arturia Origin and Origin Keyboard provide a simulation of ARP's 4075 filter, which appeared in the Quadra, Omni, Axxe, and other ARP synths. (Courtesy of Alan R. Pearlman)

Virtual-analog synthesis is certainly effective and potent, but true analog synthesis has returned strong after nearly disappearing during the 1980s and '90s. One of the most exciting developments in the synth industry in recent years is Tom Oberheim's return to making the Synthesizer Expander Module (SEM), which served as the guts of the Oberheim Four Voice and Eight Voice polyphonic synths of the late 1970s. Drew Neumann has directly compared two variations of the new-and-improved model—the MIDI SEM and SEM Pro—with his two original SEMs, and he's quite complimentary of the reincarnated versions. He says they sound better in some ways, perhaps due to their modern components. The Tom Oberheim SEM is "a really ballsy-sounding synth with earth-shaking bottom end and a really clean, crisp signal path," he reports. "Tom has done a really good job."

Analog synths are Neumann's personal favorites, mostly because they respond in ways similar to members of an orchestra who play the same piece of music differently each time with varying degrees of expression. Likewise, the temperamental drift and fluctuations in an analog synth's oscillator tuning, filter components, and LFO frequencies due to changes in temperature and humidity result in the instrument playing the same sequence slightly differently each time. Drew turns to the analog synthesizers in his studio to add randomness, warmth, and life to music that is inherently sample-driven. While he maintains absolute control over his digital instruments in a predictable and repeatable manner, he's happy to add an element to the mix that isn't 100 percent predictable. "It's very important to squeeze every bit of expression you can out of an instrument because human ears respond better to that," says Drew. "I also think it's okay to let the instrument contribute a bit of its own life to the performance."

As epitomized by the original Two Voice shown here, early Oberheim synthesizers were based on the SEM, or Synthesizer Expander Module. The Two Voice, which Tom introduced at the June 1975 NAMM show, includes a thirty-seven-note keyboard, an eight-step analog sequencer, and a two-channel mixer, all enclosed in its own touring case. As of late 2013, Tom Oberheim hopes to soon release a new Two Voice Pro Synthesizer that has a twenty-first-century mini-sequencer. (Photo courtesy of Gibson Guitar Corp.)

Tom Oberheim reintroduced the SEM under his own name in 2009. He offers three different versions: one with MIDI input via a built-in MIDI-to-CV convertor, another with CV control via a patchbay panel of thirty-three 3.5mm jacks that can override normalled internal circuit connections, and the third—the SEM-Pro, shown here—with the MIDI-to-CV converter and twenty-one 3.5mm patch points. (Courtesy of Tom Oberheim)

A Yamaha CS-80. Scott Rider says this CS-80 (serial number 1408) is in such beautiful condition because it never went on the road. To augment Yamaha's twenty-two factory presets, CS-80 users programmed their own patches with four miniaturized versions of the control panel, revealed by opening the hatch to the *upper left*. Lots of great additional CS-80 info is available on Rider's website "Old Crow's Synth Shop: Maintaining the Yamaha CS-80." In addition, Mac and Windows users can experience much of the CS-80's best qualities via Arturia's brilliant CS-80V software synth. (Scott Rider, www.cs80.com)

The Synthesizer

In February 2011, a friend of Drew Neumann's dropped off a pair of thrashed CS-80s that had been in storage for a decade. Drew could keep one in trade for repairing both. The pair of super analog polysynths dwarf Drew's 1917-vintage Steinway Model M grand piano. By early September he'd successfully rebuilt both synths and installed MIDI in the nicer-looking one. Drew has refurbished a few CS-80s during his hard-to-find spare time, but he isn't interested in doing it too often. (Drew Neumann, Droomusic)

Take a peek at the thousands of wires revealed after Kent Spong opened up this misused Yamaha CS-80 during its restoration and you can imagine why the synth tends to suffer from reliability issues. Kent has had plenty of experience fixing many CS-80s. (Kent Spong)

To address the perfect stability of digital synthesis, many makers of virtual-analog and plug-in synths intentionally build in subtle randomness to simulate that analog quality. Dave Smith added an "oscillator slop" factor to the DCOs in the DSI Prophet '08 and Arturia implemented complex analog drift settings in the Origin and the CS-80V plug-in. Drew also points out that Yamaha's physical-modeling VL1 may be the most chaotic and expressive digital synth ever made, which makes it extremely useful to him because it never plays a sequenced line exactly the same way twice.

Amin Bhatia is another successful TV and film composer/synthesist who, like Drew Neumann, faces production deadlines while confronting a plethora of music-making gear. Bhatia—who over the years has consulted and programmed for numerous synth and audio companies, including Roland, QSound, Arturia, and Spectrasonics—currently shares scoring duties with Ari Posner for the CBS/CTV drama *Flashpoint*, for which they won a Canadian Screen Award for Best Music Score in 2013. Both depend on combinations of hardware and software synths. They often work in the Native Instruments Kontakt environment with a variety of percussion and orchestral libraries. Bhatia also is a fan of Arturia plug-ins, working with their entire V2 collection—ARP 2600 V, Minimoog V, CS-80V, Jupiter-8V, Moog Modular V, and Prophet-V2—because it's "absolutely excellent for the job," Bhatia raves.

Fully functioning Yamaha CS-80 polysynths are rare, but Arturia has replicated the CS-80's timbral and control capabilities with CS-80V2. Since all of the sliders, buttons, ribbon, knobs, and keyboard are so readily accessible, it's very easy to sit entranced as you work with the CS-80V2 on your computer. CS-80V2 also provides matrix patchability that goes beyond the original's scope of operation. Play it from a keyboard that senses polyaftertouch and you'll be pleased to discover CS-80V2 also responds to that marvelous control capability. (Screenshot courtesy of Arturia)

The Synthesizer

Re-creating the Sequential Circuits Prophet-5 for the twenty-first century, Dave Smith Instruments released the Prophet '08 in . . . guess what year. You got it, 2008. Thanks to a purely analog audio signal path and Doug Curtis's analog lowpass filters, the new edition can sound very much like the original, plus it can do a whole lot more. (Courtesy of Dave Smith Instruments)

Amin also "religiously" uses the trio of Spectrasonics Omnisphere, Trilian, and Stylus RMX. "For a cop show like *Flashpoint*, they form a very large part of my sound palette," he says. "Spectrasonics' organization of the sounds is unbelievable and I love the fact that I can customize things. Having grown up in the days of analog synths, to just use a preset? I can't do it." He appreciates that Kontakt and the Spectrasonics apps enable him to quickly

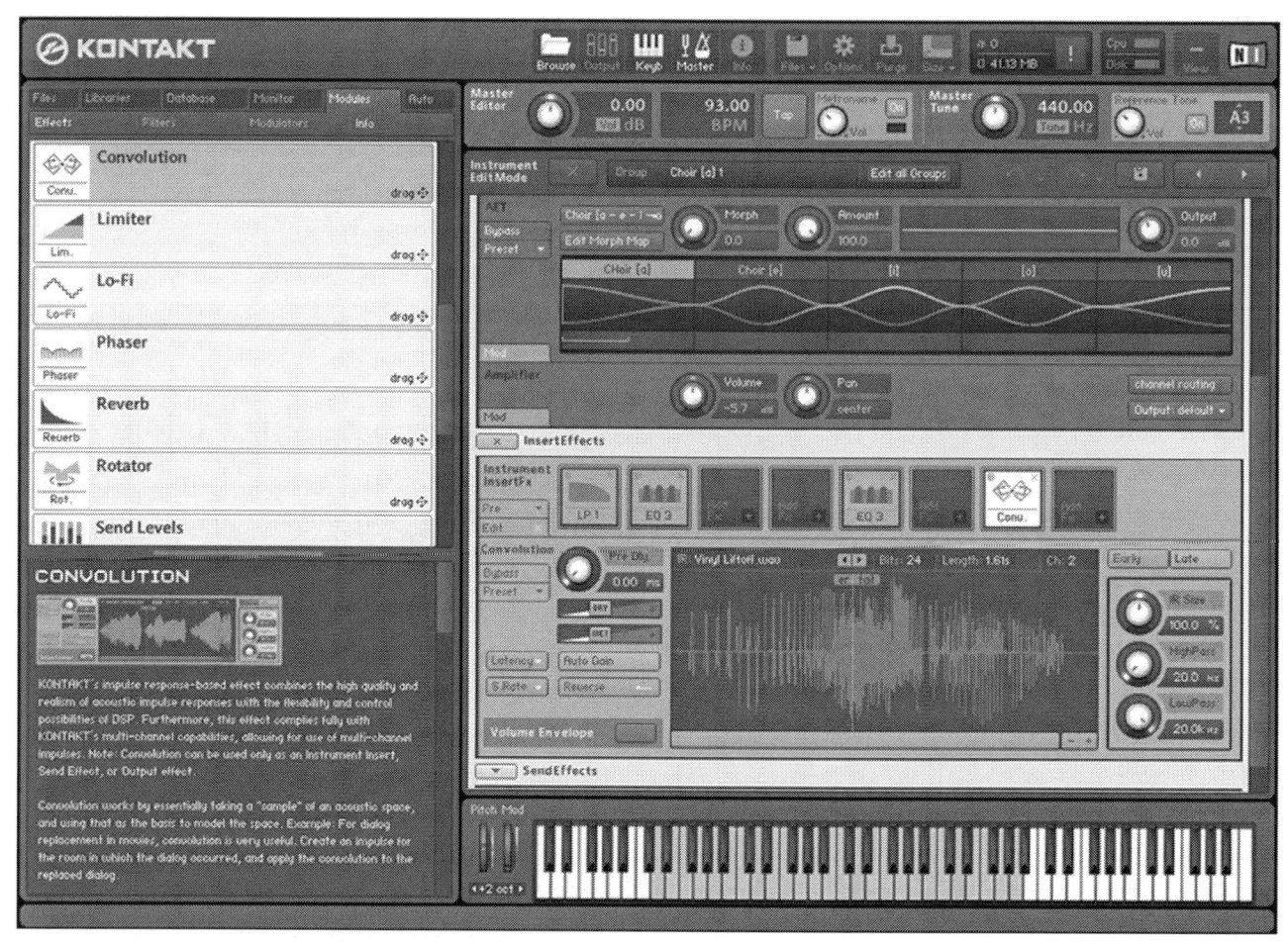

Among the multitude of effects available in Native Instruments Kontakt—version 4 shown here—is a Convolution process that allows you to capture the acoustic characteristics of an environment and then subsequently model the sound of that space algorithmically. (Screenshot courtesy of Native Instruments GmbH)

Choosing Your Synthesizer(s)

This is a screenshot of version 2 of Arturia's Minimoog V. Don't freak out, but I sold my Minimoog—which I purchased in Miami, Florida, in 1976, brought it cross-country to the Bay Area in 1977, and played the heck out of it for over two decades—in 2010 because I wanted to finally satisfy a longtime craving for a modular synth system. In truth I felt I could do this thanks to Arturia's Minimoog V softsynth. Besides its sound coming awfully close to the real deal, it's capable of many tricks I could never do on the original. By opening up the Minimoog V as shown here, you get access to a motion recorder, a vocal filter, a modulation matrix, an arpeggiator, and chorus and delay effects. (Screenshot courtesy of Arturia)

find a sound, shape and tweak it, give it a character of its own, and then layer it with the analog warmth provided by the Arturia plug-ins.

To satisfy his preference for hardware gear, Bhatia has a pair of classic analog synths—a Minimoog and ARP 2600—both of which he sequences via a vintage Roland MPU-101 MIDI-to-CV interface. In addition, there's a pair of rackmounted sample-playback synths: a Roland XV-5080 that contains sixty-four of Amin's favorite samples ready to go when needed—"I spent so much time organizing them," he explains, "that I wasn't going to throw them out as the whole world started to go into the Mac"—and a Korg TR-Rack packing outstanding tom and bass sounds.

Also in Amin's arsenal are two virtual-analog synth modules: a Clavia Nord Rack and a Roland JP-8080. "For virtual analog," Amin observes, "both are amazing. Their sound quality is excellent. You'd swear there's a vacuum tube inside the 8080. What the Roland doesn't have the Nord does, and vice versa. I can probably get larger, more lush

Floating in front of Spectrasonics Omnisphere 1.5's Granular Zoom window is the Orb screen, which users can address via the computer's mouse or wirelessly from an iPad to adjust multiple Omnisphere parameters on the fly. (Screenshot courtesy of Spectrasonics)

sounds out of the 8080 if I want to go galactic, but if I want a killer bass line that spits and buzzes along, sixteenth notes flying around, there are few synths that can match the Nord Lead and the Nord Rack."

Bhatia is also a longtime fan of Yamaha synths. The oldest in his current lineup is the TX816, a 4U rackmount modular FM machine in which you can pack up to eight TF1 modules, each essentially the equivalent of a DX7 with improvements including assignable key ranges and independent balanced XLR audio outputs. "The Yamaha sound has always had a unique high-frequency character," says Amin, "whether you're talking about the Motif, the CS-80, or their whole FM line. It adds an extra bite to all of the analog timbres that I use." To fortify the FM sound, he uses Native Instruments' FM8 plug-in, of which he reports 80 percent of the patches are identical to what he gets out of the TX816, but in the rest algorithms and distortion "aren't quite right, and the original module sounds much cleaner."

Another mid-'80s module Bhatia still depends on for sonic impact is an Oberheim Xpander, particularly appreciating its unique tonal character. He has tried to sample it,

Choosing Your Synthesizer(s)

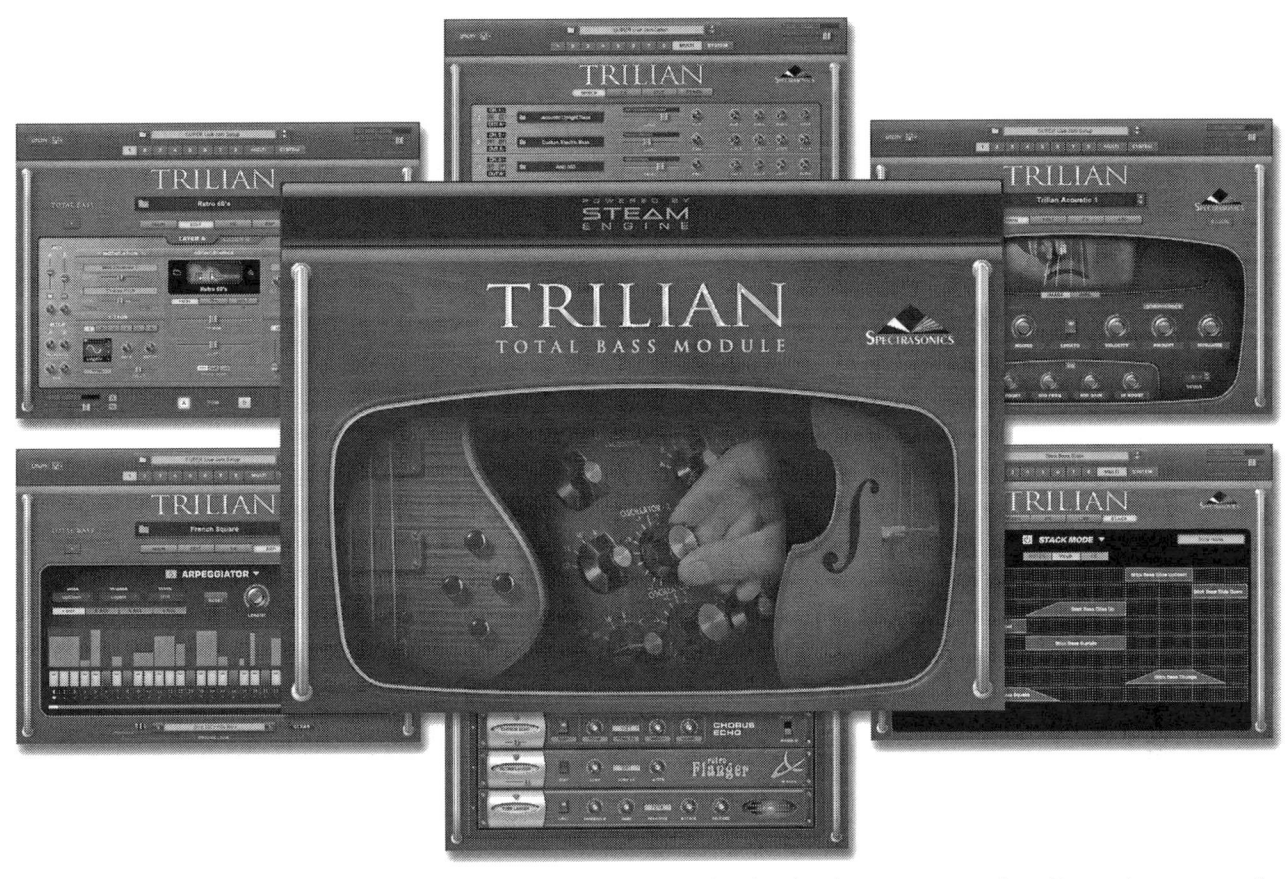

An extensive universe of sampled and synthesized bass sounds is the specialized realm of Spectrasonics' Trilian. (Screenshot courtesy of Spectrasonics)

Thousands of looped patterns and sounds—7.4GB worth—come with Spectrasonics' Stylus RMX, the realtime groove module. Stylus RMX is based on the Spectrasonics Advanced Groove Engine, or SAGE, and it allows you to control groove playback in real time with capabilities that are absolutely sick. (Screenshot courtesy of Spectrasonics)

Among the purely vintage synths and those fast approaching that status in Amin Bhatia's studio are (*left, top to bottom*) an ARP 2600 synth cabinet, a Minimoog, and an Oberheim Xpander. Progressing downward from the top at the *lower right* are a Clavia Nord Rack, a Drawmer 1960 Mic Pre/Vacuum Tube Compressor (see the Outboard Processing section in chap. 5), and rackmount Roland V-Synth XT and JP-8080 synth modules. (Courtesy of Amin Bhatia)

but the digital conversion doesn't capture the Xpander's analog bite, so he keeps the synth handy. But there's a hidden function—unless you look at its back panel—that's uncommon, at least beyond modular synths: The Xpander has six channels of CV and gate inputs, so it interfaces with synths that sport those outputs. Not only can you play the Xpander's six voices from CV sources, but also the converted data gets transmitted through the MIDI out for controlling other MIDI devices.

Amin relies on Apple Logic to compose and sequence his music:

Logic is my sequencer of reluctant choice because I grew up with it since version 4, and I've been a reluctant beta tester on every single bug they've had with

Yamaha's TX816, released in 1985, is the rackmount equivalent of eight DX7s. (That's the plural of DX7, not to be confused with the FM keyboard synth that preceded the DX7II series.) You can insert up to eight TF1s into the TX frame. If there were only two, you'd have a TX216; four TF1s would make a TX416. Since you can't program a TF1 from its front panel, you'll need a DX7-era synth or a software editor. (Courtesy of Yamaha Corporation of America)

the program. For someone new to Logic, Apple has worked out most of the bugs and it's a fun sequencer to use, but for those of us who've grown up with it and have had to find where they've hidden something with every upgrade, it's been a challenge. It's undoubtedly the most powerful and the most annoying piece of equipment in my studio. I absolutely loved Opcode Studio Vision and if it hadn't gone down—and if the last versions weren't so buggy—I would have stayed with it.

Of Logic's sound generators, Bhatia is a big fan of the ES2 virtual synthesizer due mainly to its Sculpture synth engine. "It's a modeling synth that has some gorgeous sounds in it. Logic's Sculpture is a very creative and beautiful thing." For sample playback, he prefers Native Instruments' Kontakt to Logic's EXS24 because of Kontakt's ease of programming, allowing him to quickly tweak and organize samples, easily access modulation and controller parameters, and assign different knobs and skins to each module. "Between all of that and its **scripting language**, I think it's a very powerful system."

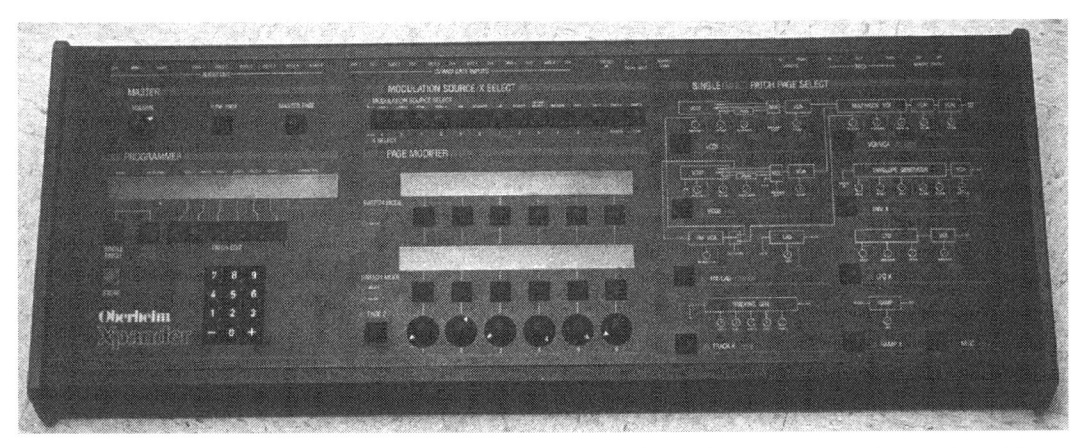

Oberheim introduced the MIDI-compatible Xpander—an absolutely killer tabletop synth module—in 1984. (Photo courtesy of Gibson Guitar Corp.)

> *scripting language:* a facility that allows users to program commands that alter sample-playback parameters and MIDI data in real time

Along with his musical work on the CBS/CTV series *Flashpoint*, Bhatia has scored an impressive share of feature movies and TV shows and contributed to numerous albums for other major artists. However, he's particularly renowned for two fabulous synth albums. First came *The Interstellar Suite*, a synthesis treasure originally released as an LP in 1987, remastered and rereleased on CD in 2004, and—as of mid-2013—Amin and his crew are working with the twenty-four-track analog master tapes to create a surround-sound version. In 2005 the Irondale High School Marching Knights of New Brighton, Minnesota, performed their own live versions of selections from *The Interstellar Suite*, which has become standard repertoire in many drum corps and marching band competitions across the United States, performed by groups ranging from Spirit of Atlanta to the Blue Devils.

Amin released his second synthesizer masterpiece, *Virtuality*, on May 23, 2008, in honor of what would have been Bob Moog's seventy-fourth birthday. Prior to his death on August 21, 2005, Bob had agreed to record voiceovers for *Virtuality*'s pivotal piece, "Bolero Electronica." In orchestrating Maurice Ravel's tour de force, Bhatia incorporated a wide array of historical instruments dating back to the Ondes Martenot and Theremin, and progressing through contemporary electronic instruments. Among the dozens of synths represented are the Moog Modular and Memorymoog, ARP 2600, Roland TR-808 and D-50, E-mu Modular and Emulator-II, Korg Wavestation and Triton, Yamaha TX802 and Motif, Access Virus, Alesis Andromeda A6, Spectrasonics Stylus and Trilogy Bass, Roger Linn's Linndrum, Dave Smith Instruments Evolver, Casio CZ-101, Arturia Moog Modular V, Oberheim Xpander, and Ensoniq Mirage. Virtuosos who contributed include Patrick Moraz and Steve Porcaro on synths, Kevin Kissinger on Theremin, and Thomas Bloch on Ondes Martenot.

During production, Bhatia traveled to Calgary, Alberta, Canada, to take advantage of the vast vintage-synth collection housed at the National Music Centre (nmc.ca). Vintage expert technician extraordinaire John J. L. Leimseider maintains the wealth of electronic instruments there, and it's worth any synthesist's effort to go see and, in many cases, play them.

Perspective

Mortal musicians confronted with as many synths as Drew Neumann and Amin Bhatia have might suffer brain lock. However, both know the ins and outs of each instrument after dedicating thousands of hours overall—surely hundreds on individual synths alone—to learn about them. Every musical instrument requires a lot of practice for anyone to be competent and productive with it. And even though you won't have to master appropriate embouchure for trumpet, fingering and bowing techniques for violin, or breath and soft-palate control to sing, getting the most out of any synthesizer will take loads of patience, work, experimentation, and practice.

> "It's very easy to use a push-button preset approach to making music with our current technology. There are tens of thousands of GarageBand and Live users cranking out hours of music that all sounds the same. Unless you find a way to harness the beast of electronic music in a personal and uniquely expressive way, there's nothing in it worth listening to." Drew Neumann

As the synthesist/producer Jeff Fair articulates, "Synthesizers that allow you to perform with and change their parameters in real time are in many ways like acoustic instruments. They take practice to master. You can't just be a pianist and walk up and master a Minimoog. You have one part of it down, but part of the mastery is on the front panel; it isn't totally on the keyboard."

It's critically important that synthesists work with gear that functions as needed and doesn't lure them away from doing the job that needs to be done. The challenge is to choose gear to which you'll devote a great deal of your time to master. Where do you start in collecting instruments that will work best for you? Perhaps precisely where the modern era began in the early 1960s: a modular synthesizer. Let's further investigate that universe and what it might mean to you.

Modular Synthesizers in the Twenty-first Century

An Overview

The modern synthesizer era began with Don Buchla designing electronic modules for Morton Subotnick and others at the San Francisco Tape Music Center in 1963. At about the same time, Bob Moog started working on electronic components with Herb Deutsch in Trumansburg, New York. Buchla's and Moog's design approaches and the components they used were very different, but both were making modular synthesizers—although they didn't necessarily call them by that name at the time.

> ### Vintage Modular Warning
> Due to experience gained from years of refurbishing and rebuilding modular synths, Steve Masucci offers valuable advice to anyone with a modular-synth jones—especially of the vintage variety. "A lot of people buy something like a Moog Modular and, if it isn't working correctly, they get frustrated," Masucci explains. "It may be making noise, but there's a huge difference between just making noise and it actually behaving like a predictable and useable piece of studio gear that allows you to make your music without interruption. The difference is a huge chasm. Once you cross it and the instrument has been fully restored, then the machine becomes much more pleasurable to use. You aren't working around a bunch of problems. I think for a composer, it's usually a good investment to get the thing up and running because then the time in

> using it is much more rewarding. A lot of old modulars need work. It gives you a misleading picture of exactly what one is like to work with if too much of it doesn't work properly.
>
> "Another thing to consider with a lot of the stuff from the '60s is that it wasn't meant for a home environment. Bob Moog's clientele wasn't someone down the street or a guy in a private studio—with very rare exceptions. It was an institution or a college or, more likely, a recording facility that had a Moog Modular, and in that facility were technicians who did maintenance. Someone was there to maintain the recording console, the patchbays, and any outboard gear, align the tape decks, and tweak the Moog—all of which was part of a standard studio maintenance program. All of the regular maintenance was taken care of before a session. I think Bob built his modulars with that same criteria. They were well-made and incredibly robust given what they were, but he also knew they would occasionally need to be aligned and maintained.
>
> "Now people are getting this stuff at home and there's no maintenance guy to come in and look at it, so it becomes another layer of difficulty for them. That's why when people ask me what they should buy, I say, 'Buy something new,' because if you're buying a collector's piece, you also now have to do all of the maintenance for it. If you buy new machines—from sources such as Bruce Duncan of Modcan, Roger Arrick at Synthesizers.com, Don Buchla, Rex Probe at Sound Transform Systems, Paul Schreiber at Synthesis Technology, and Dieter Doepfer—you really won't have that requirement any more. They're much more stable and predictable. They don't sound exactly the same, but all machines sound different."

A modular synthesizer consists of one or more cases or cabinets into which you install individual modules that serve different purposes. Unless you wire some of them together behind their front panels, they need to be externally patched together with cords to make anything happen. Modular synths virtually disappeared during the 1980s, but the industry has seriously expanded since the '90s. While there were only a handful of modular synthesizer manufacturers during the '60s and '70s, today there are scores of them. Common formats, from tallest to shortest, include:

- Technosaurus
- Roland Model 700
- Wiard
- CMS
- Aries, Digisound, Cyndustries, and Modcan A Series
- 5U, which includes Moog, Synthesizers.com, Synthesis Technology/MOTM (loosely the acronym for Mother of All Modulars), Club of the Knobs (COTK), Mos-Lab, Moon Modular, Oakley Sound Systems, Encore, and Modcan B Series
- ARP 2500
- Buchla and Serge
- Eurorack

- FracRak, currently supported by Paia, Blacet Research, Metalbox, and numerous other module makers
- Mattson Mini Modular

> *mult:* a multiple junction module that contains numerous jacks wired together for the distribution of one input signal to multiple destinations

Some of the module heights are similar, but they may not be compatible if they're in different formats and come from different manufacturers. There have, however, been successful efforts to standardize many module designs within some formats.

Chronologically speaking, first came the Buchla. After creating plentiful and unique modular systems and instruments over the years, Don Buchla reintroduced his favorite modular format in 2004. Originally known in 1970 as the Series 200, it's now called the Series 200e. Another proprietary modular format that first saw the light of day during the '70s is Serge Modular, manufactured since 1992 by Sound Transform Systems.

Numerous modular manufacturers make systems that conform to the standards Bob Moog introduced with his Moog Modular systems—or at least they come close. The height of a Moog module measures 8.75" and is called "5U" because it conforms to the professional rackmount standard wherein 1U equals 1.75". Companies that make 5U modules—as well, perhaps, as those in other formats—include Modcan (B Series), Synthesizers.com, Synthesis Technology/MOTM, COTK, Mos-Lab, Moon Modular, Oakley Sound Systems, Krisp1, Grove Audio, MegaOhm Audio, STG Soundlabs, Synthetic Sound Labs (SSL), and Cyndustries. Drew Neumann points out that even though modules from these companies are technically 5U, they might vary a bit, but with minor modifications they can work together in the same cabinet. All but MOTM, Oakley, and Modcan B Series conform to the old Moog look and format.

Ten modules illustrate common modular-synthesizer formats. From the *left*: Mattson Mini Modular Phoenix Series VCO-J, Malekko Heavy Industry Wiard Oscillator (Eurorack), Blacet Research Klang Werk (FracRak), STS Serge Modular Creature, Buchla Complex Waveform Generator Model 261e, Synthesis Technology MOTM-300 Ultra VCO (5U), Synthesizer.com Q106 Oscillator (5U), Modcan Oscillator 01A, Cirocco Modular Systems (CMS) V.C. Oscillator Module, and Wiard Synthesizer Company Model 341 Classic VCO. (Photo collage assembled by John Loffink; permission to publish module images granted by George Mattson of Mattson Mini Modular, Josh Holley of Malekko Heavy Industry, John Blacet of Blacet Research, Rex Probe of Sound Transform Systems, Don Buchla of Buchla Electronic Musical Instruments, Paul Schreiber of Synthesis Technology, Roger Arrick of Synthesizers.com Modular Analog Music Synthesizers, Bruce Duncan of Modcan Modular Synthesizers, Phil Cirocco of CMS, and Grant Richter and Cary Grace of Wiard Synthesizer Company)

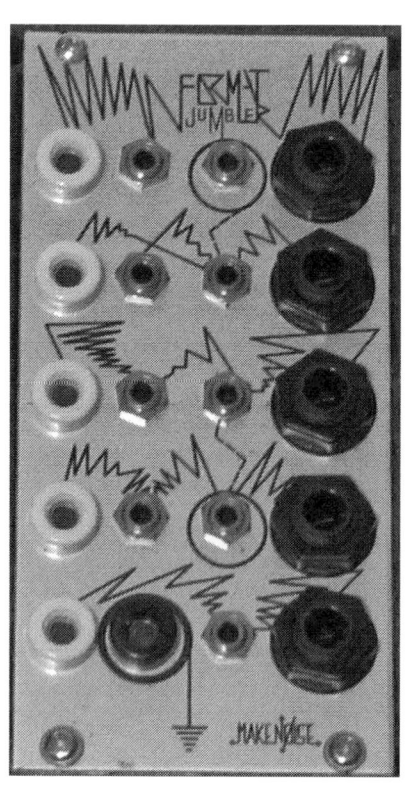

Unlike a typical **mult**, which provides similar-sized jacks—1/4", 3.5mm, or banana, depending on the particular modular-synth format—for distributing an input signal to multiple destinations, the Make Noise Format Jumbler simplifies interfacing of different-format synth modules by sporting a combination of all three types of jacks. It routes signals to certain jacks depending on how they're connected and includes a common ground for multiple systems. The Format Jumbler is a passive Eurorack module. (Mark Vail)

A respectably large, mostly 5U modular synth system assembled by John L. Rice. Among the components are modules from Synthesis Technology, Synthesizers.com, Moon Modular, Oakley Sound Systems, STG Soundlabs, Music from Outer Space, Modcan, Rob Hordijk Designs, Grove Audio, Encore Electronics, Flight of Harmony, Cyndustries, Club of the Knobs, The Bride Chamber, MegaOhm Audio, Mos-Lab, Tellun Corp., and Thomas White. Among the synth modules at the *bottom left* are a Novation Supernova, Roland Fantom XR, and a Yamaha RM1x. (Courtesy of John L. Rice, ©2010, www.imjohn.com)

The synthesist John L. Rice explains that MOTM modules use the same U dimensions for width and height, so a 1U module is 1.75″ wide, a 2U is 3.5″ wide, and so on—although widths are a hair narrower to allow space between modules to compensate for manufacturing variances. Besides those from Synthesis Technology, Oakley and the Modcan B Series modules conform to the MOTM spec for width and mounting-hole spacing. Manufacturers that support the traditional Moog-module width standard of 1U (2.125″) include Synthesizers.com, COTK, Mos-Lab, Moon Modular, Grove Audio, MegaOhm (most modules), STG (most modules), SSL, Krisp1 (the source for Tony Allgood's Oakley modules), Corsynth, Marienberg, Happy Nerding, Analog Craftsman, Synthetic Sound Labs, Zerosum Inertia, Voltergeist, and SoundMachines. (See appendix B for a list of manufacturer websites.)

Although he still designs and supports MOTM modules, Synthesis Technology's Paul Schreiber suspended their in-house production in early 2012. Scott Deyo of the Bride Chamber is now the source of MOTM products, which come assembled or as kits.

During the early 1970s, Paia's John Simonton (1943–2005) introduced the 4700 series of modules, establishing the FracRak (short for Fractional Rack) standard. In fact, Paia has returned to making modular synth kits with their current 9700 series. FracRak is a 3U format, its module panels measuring 5.25″ in height. John Blacet adopted the same format, and the popularity of his modules helped FracRak become its own standard.

John L. Rice appears with a significantly scaled-down performance system in the Synth Petting Zoo room at the March 2013 Mostly Modular Trade Association (MMTA) Synthfest in the Shoreline Community College Music Building near Seattle, Washington. While the left rack consists of synth modules, stuffed in the case on the right are three stompboxes—a Hall of Fame Reverb and a Flashback Delay and Looper from TC Electronic, and an MXR SF01 Slash Octave Fuzz—along with an Alesis NanoPiano MIDI synth module, a Mackie 802-VLZ3 mixer, and power adapters plugged into a Furman Plug Lock power strip at the top. (Mark Vail)

Rackmounted beneath a custom-made attenuating patchbay of 1/4" jacks in John L. Rice's mobile modular-synth rack are rows of Synthesis Technology Eurorack and a variety of 5U modules. Synthesis Technology's E340 Cloud Generator, E350 Morphing Terrarium, E355 Morphing Dual LFO, E560 Deflector Shield, and E580 Resampling Mini-Delay represent the Eurorack contingent. Rice plans to fill the open gap with an E440 LP VCF when Paul Schreiber of Synthesis Technology releases it. The Modcan B modules across the third row are a Dual Quantizer 55B, Reverb 35B, Dual Lag 18B, Touch-Sequencer 72B, Quad Envelope 60B, and 4VCA 31B. Across the *bottom* are a HexInverter sympleSEQ, Moon blank panel, Moon 526 Reversible Mixer, Happy Nerding Fun VCF, COTK C946 LFO, Moon 551 MIDI-to-CV Interface, and a Moon blank panel that John converted into a power-inlet module with three attenuating mults. (Mark Vail)

Blacet also offers FracRak versions of numerous modules produced by Eurorack manufacturers. Other companies that support the FracRak format include Ad Infinitum, Bananalogue, BugBrand, Cyndustries, Encore Electronics, Future Sound Systems, Metalbox, STG Soundlabs, Synthasonic, and the Wiard Synthesizer Company.

Given the number of companies within the Eurorack realm—approaching sixty in January 2009, according to "The Synthtopia Guide to Eurorack Modular Synthesizers" (www.synthtopia.com/content/2009/01/31/eurorack-modular-synthesizers), and an unofficial tally conducted in August 2013 climbed to 118 Eurorack manufacturers—it's clearly the most popular modular format and, surprisingly, some of the most advanced ideas in electronic-music technology are happening there. Dieter Doepfer of Doepfer Musikelektronik introduced the Eurorack format to the synth market in 1996, although the spec existed before he adopted it—albeit by a different name: DIN 41494 (DIN is the acronym for Deutsches Institut für Normung e.V. [German Institute for Standardization]). Dieter chose this standard while designing the Doepfer A-100 series because information about specifications such as front-panel dimensions, positions of mounting

Four Paia Electronics 9700 Series modules—a 9700 MIDI2CV8 MIDI-to-CV converter, a 9720 VCO, a 9730 VCF, and 9710 VCA/Mixer—mounted inside a rack in Marvin Jones's studio. Paia founder John Simonton entered the modular synthesizer market during the early 1970s, selling entire systems in kit form for hundreds of dollars. Paia offered an extensive range of analog modules within the 2700 and 4700 series, as well as a 6503 microprocessor-based computer/controller called the 8700 from 1976 to 1980. The company stopped making module kits soon after Simonton passed away at the age of sixty-two in November 2005, but Paia continues and, thanks to Scott Lee and Brad Martin, introduced a new line of FracRak-format module kits within the 9700 Series in 2006. (Mark Vail)

Dieter Doepfer poses with a Doepfer Musikelektronik Eurorack system at the January 2010 NAMM convention in Anaheim, California. Not only did Dieter adopt what became the Eurorack standard in 1996, but he also played a big role in rekindling worldwide interest in modular synthesizers. (Mark Vail)

holes, and module depth were so well defined. DIN 41494 instrumentation appears in many nonmusical, industrial applications, such as in trains to control electronic equipment.

Two proprietary formats have surfaced relatively recently. The year 2007 saw the introduction of the Mattson Mini Modular, whose modules measure a tiny 3.5″ across by 3.5″ high. In July 2012 Andrew Kilpatrick—who already makes several Eurorack modules—introduced a format called the Kilpatrick Format Modular Synthesizer. Kilpatrick Format modules are available in complete systems or as individual modules. Like Serge and Buchla modules, the new Kilpatrick Format modules are 7″ high, otherwise defined as 4U—but that doesn't mean they're completely compatible with those other formats.

Along with module size disparities among the different modular formats, there are considerable differences in the types of connectors, voltage levels, and other attributes among the systems. Where patching connections are concerned, 5U and vintage modular synths from Moog, EML, E-mu, Polyfusion, and Roland (System 700) feature 1/4″ jacks; those from Mattson, Aries, Paia, and Roland (System 100)—as well as a vast majority of Eurorack and FracRak modules—have 3.5mm jacks; Serge, Modcan Series A, BugBrand, Synton, and Kilpatrick Format modules have banana jacks, as do otherwise FracRak-format modules from BugBrand and Metalbox; Buchlas have 3.5mm jacks for audio and banana jacks for control voltages, triggers, and gates. One of banana's advantages is the ability to stack plugs and route signals from a single output jack to multiple input jacks without the need for a mult. Until 2010 synthesists patching modulars with 3.5mm jacks had to rely on mults in their systems; thanks to Tiptop Audio's Stackcables,

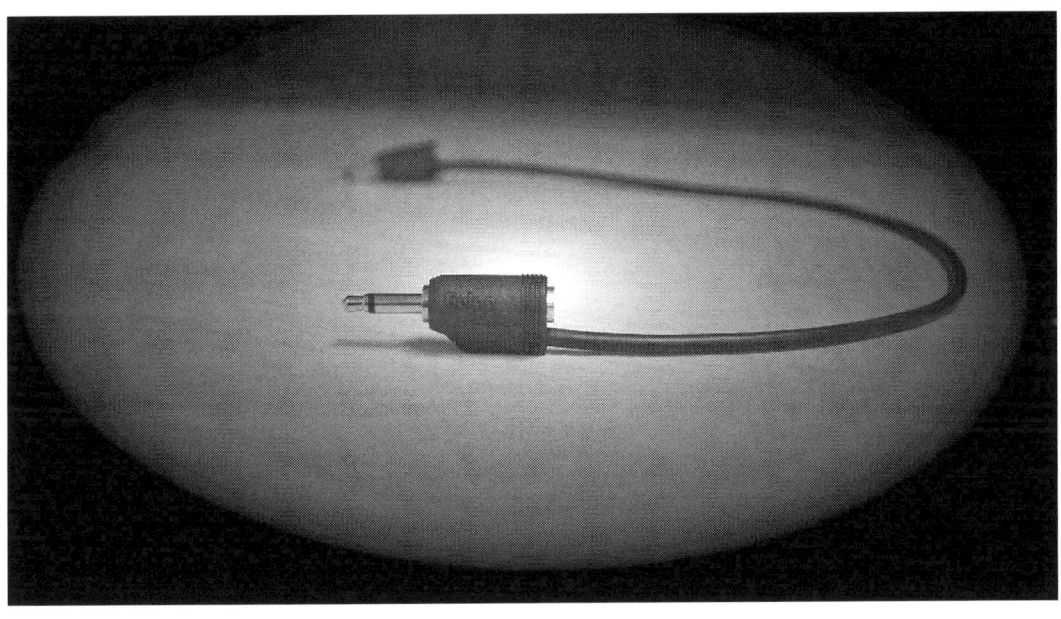

Tiptop Audio's Stackcable allows Eurorack synthesists to stack 3.5mm plugs for routing signals from an output to multiple inputs, obviating the need for a mult. (Courtesy of Tiptop Audio)

3.5mm plugs can be stacked like banana plugs. It's doubtful anyone will make stackable 1/4" plugs because they're too long and bulky.

The contemporary world of modular synths is truly vast and the buying decisions many, both in the format you choose and the number of individual modules available within each format. Before committing to one format in particular, it's wise to consider the pros and cons of each by doing plenty of research. Roger Arrick of Synthesizers.com has posted the helpful Modular Form Factors chart (www.synthesizers.com/formfactors.html), which includes enough information about module heights, widths, connector types, and power requirements to get newcomers started. Not only does the outstanding Modular Grid (www.modulargrid.net) serve as a database for many of the modular formats, but after you register you can also access online planners and fit specific modules into racks of sizes that you define. You'll also find plenty of lively discussions about modular synths, electronic-music technology and artists, music software, video synthesis, DIY hardware and software, and much more on Muff's Modules & More (www.muffwiggler.com) and Electro-Music (electro-music.com). Likewise, four synth blogs that will keep you up to date on important synth-related developments are Synthtopia (www.synthtopia.com), Sonicstate (sonicstate.com), Matrixsynth (matrixsynth.blogspot.com), and Create Digital Music (createdigitalmusic.com). For a great online source of info about vintage synthesizers, don't miss Vintage Synth Explorer (www.vintagesynth.com). Twenty excellent sources of DIY module kits, schematics, loads of information, and more are:

- Blacet Research (www.blacet.com)
- the Bride Chamber (www.bridechamber.com)
- CGS (www.cgs.synth.net)
- Chameleon (www.chameleon.synth.net)
- Doepfer Musikelektronik GmbH (www.doepfer.de)
- Elby Designs (www.elby-designs.com)

- Electric Druid (www.electricdruid.net)
- 4ms Pedals (www.4mspedals.com)
- GetLoFi (www.getlofi.com)
- Jürgen Haible (1964–2011, www.jhaible.de)
- Magic Smoke Electronics (www.magsmoke.com)
- Mattson Mini Modular (www.mattsonminimodular.com)
- Music from Outer Space (www.musicfromouterspace.com)
- Mutable Instruments (mutable-instruments.net)
- Natural Rhythm Music (www.naturalrhythmmusic.com)
- Oakley Sound Systems (www.oakleysound.com)
- Paia Corporation (www.paia.com)
- SynthDIY.com (www.synthdiy.com)
- Synthrotek (www.synthrotek.com)
- Yves Usson's Yusynth (yusynth.net)

For a more complete and up-to-date list, search the Internet for "synth DIY."

Modular Synth Shopping

Why buy a modular synth? For one thing, in the current market it can be far more economical to assemble a system than it was in the distant past—although you can still pay tens of thousands of dollars for large systems in some modular formats. In addition, rather than settling for components that are fixed, you can choose any modules that interest you. If you can afford it, you could have ten different oscillators, five types of filters, four flavors of envelope generators, a handful of flexible and syncable LFOs, three very dissimilar analog sequencers, and exotic effects processors that don't exist outside of the modular environment.

Buying modules for a modular system isn't as simple as buying a stompbox or a MIDI synth module, for many reasons. Before you decide on a format, do as much research as possible so that you understand what's available and get ideas about what might work for you. Modular synthesizer components exist within a niche market, so you'll rarely find them for sale in a typical music store. Many modular manufacturers are tiny—some as small as a one-person operation—and each company handles orders differently. While dealers and some makers have inventories of modules ready to go, other makers may wait to assemble products after you've made a deposit. The wait time for delivery of modular gear can range anywhere from a week or two to a year or longer for a truly special item. Surf the websites mentioned earlier to see what experienced modular synthesists have to say about their dealings with different companies and you should be able to get a good idea about how your experience will be. Don't hesitate to get directly in touch with a modular maker or dealer, either; they want to help you get precisely the modules you'll enjoy making music with as soon as possible. Dealers might have a better chance of filling orders more quickly because they have inventory, and they typically post availability of specific items on that item's web page. A few manufacturers, however, only sell direct and you have no choice.

On the other hand, you might really prefer to play with something before you buy it. While still rather rare, the number of physical stores that carry modular gear is on the

Other than two Malekko Heavy Industry Wiard Envelator's tucked toward the *bottom right* and a handful of Doepfer modules sprinkled here and there, this modular Eurorack synth case is mostly loaded with Livewire Electronics modules. Represented are the Vulcan Modulator, Dalek Modulator, Audio Frequency Generator, Dual Cyclotron, FrequenSteiner, Dual Bissell Generator, and Chaos Computer. (Mark Vail)

upswing. You'll find a list of sixteen stores that focus mainly on synths and devices for making electronic music in appendix B. Many thanks to Chuck Oken Jr. of Noisebug (www.noisebug.net) for helping me assemble this list.

If you can't make your way to any of the stores listed, the Internet might help you find other modular enthusiasts in your area who share your interests. Keep an eye out for modular conferences, meetings, and events that happen near you. A specific wing of the Muff's Modules forum called Gatherings, Events and Meets shares info about such occasions. If you go, you'll meet kindred spirits, have a look at and perhaps try a bit of patchwork on modulars you'd rarely encounter, and maybe even find some gear to buy. And at least you'll find discussions about what others have discovered and what they like

Shown at the January 2010 NAMM show with one of his Eurorack systems is Mike Brown, the man behind Livewire Electronics synth modules. Sadly, Mike passed away in March 2012. (Mark Vail)

A closeup of the Livewire Electronics well-endowed analog VCO, the Audio Frequency Generator—or AFG for brevity. (Stephi Clendinen, courtesy of Big City Music)

Low-, band-, and highpass modes are available with Livewire Electronics FrequenSteiner multimode filter module. (Stephi Clendinen, courtesy of Big City Music)

Ken MacBeth of MacBeth Studio Systems sits at the January 2011 NAMM with George Mattson and a pair of Mattson Mini Modular cabinets. You can install MMM components in cabinets vertically or horizontally, and the cabinets interlock for a sturdy setup. MMM systems may be small, but they're potent. A three-cabinet MMM system consisting of the right compliment of thirty-six modules is essentially the equivalent of a classic Moog Modular Synthesizer 55. George formerly worked as an independent factory representative for Electronic Music Laboratories (EML), invented the first self-contained, strap-on keyboard synth—the Performance Music Systems Syntar—in 1978, and has developed the smallest-format modular synthesizer system to date. MacBeth, who's based in Edinburgh, Scotland, makes his own line of analog synthesizers and modules. (Mark Vail)

and dislike. Everyone has his or her own tastes, and modular formats differ enough that—even though different formats can work together—your life will be easier if you stick with one format to begin with.

Settling on a format is only the beginning of a complex decision path. Before you start ordering modules in a particular format, you'll need hardware in which to mount them. Numerous manufacturers—including Monorocket, Gorillabox, Analogue Solutions, Livid Instruments, J9K, Doepfer, Goike, Analogue Systems, Tiptop Audio, Synthesizers.com, Buchla, Pittsburgh Modular, and Sound Transform Systems—offer a variety of pre-assembled cases, cabinets, and rackmount enclosures with built-in or external power supplies and mounting hardware, which can get you started without too much hassle. Several of these companies also make module-ready 19″ inserts that allow you to use portable rackmount and mixer cases from SKB, Gator, Odyssey, and other companies—provided they're deep enough for all of your modules—or any 19″ rack hardware, portable or otherwise. If it's important that your modular stay patched on the move, make sure the closeable case you're considering allows clearance for patch cords on the front and space behind for anything that plugs into the back of your modular. Don't overlook rack furniture and hardware from Omnirax, KK Audio, Middle Atlantic, Raxxess, Samson, and other companies.

For a personal touch, you might choose to convert an adequately sized vintage suitcase—provided you're your own roadie and don't need ATA-quality protection (the Air Transport Association long ago developed standards for air-cargo cases designed to protect fragile and valuable contents)—or even build your own case/cabinet. Plenty of synthesists prefer the DIY approach, which should be less expensive (although much more time consuming).

A Eurorack modular system contained in two portable cases. Among the components are modules from Doepfer, Tiptop Audio, the Harvestman, and Cwejman. (Mark Vail)

Choosing Your Synthesizer(s)

Two types of cases contain this expanded Eurorack system. Whereas the top case holds modules from Make Noise, the Harvestman, and Cwejman, the base case is replete with modules from Make Noise, Malekko Heavy Industry, Synthwerks, Flight of Harmony, Intellijel Designs, and 4ms Pedals. (Mark Vail)

Properly encased Eurorack modular synths can be very portable, such as with a Tiptop Audio Station 252 Case like the one shown here. Folded for travel, the 252 will fit inside the overhead compartment on most commercial airliners. (Courtesy of Tiptop Audio)

Tiptop Audio mastermind Gur Milstein poses with a prototype of the company's Station 252 case filled with Tiptop modules at the January 2010 NAMM show. (Mark Vail)

How big does your modular case need to be? It depends on the modules you decide to buy, but you don't want to paint yourself into a corner by buying or making a case that runs out of room before you have all of the modules you need. Even after you think you've chosen exactly the modules you want, once you start working with them you might discover alternatives that you might want instead or that you want to add to your existing system. Although it isn't the norm where other formats are concerned, Eurorack modules typically are relatively inexpensive compared to the cost of the case, so better to

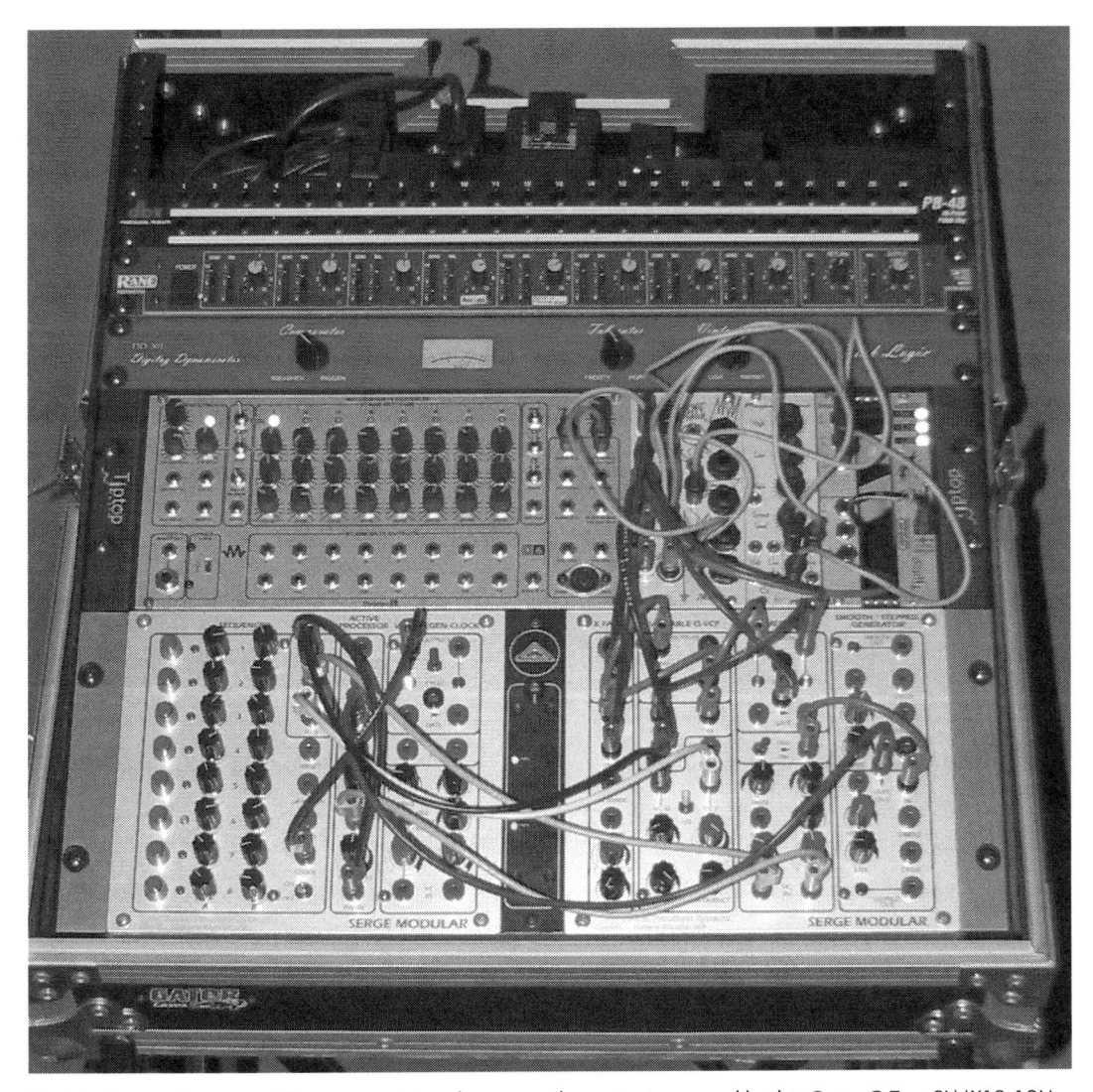

Provided none of your modules or gear is too deep, a rackmount mixer case like this Gator G-Tour-SLMX12 12U slant-top unit can serve as a convenient and protective vessel to get your modular synth rig to a gig. After securely mounting necessary power supplies inside the cabinet where space allowed, I stuffed in (*top to bottom*) a dbx PB-48 patchbay, Rane SM 82 mixer, Funk Logic DD-301 Digilog Dynamicator (a fancy, nonfunctional panel that leaves a bit of cooling space inside for the power supplies), several Eurorack modules mounted in a Tiptop Audio Happy Ending Kit, and a pair of STS Serge M-class modules. One of the SLMX12's benefits in this application is that I can leave most of the patch cables in place when I put the top of the case on. (Mark Vail)

get a case that offers extra room than too little, even if there are a few unsightly gaps that you'd eventually like to fill. Be patient, try to avoid serious bouts of gear-lust, work to learn and get the most out of the modules you have, and don't waste time craving those you wish you had. But consider this caveat: Adding, swapping, and selling modules might become a lifetime adventure.

"I'll encounter guys who say, 'I'm going to collect synth modules for the next five years and, as soon as I get 67 modules, I can start recording music.' And I'll reply, 'I can create music with just three oscillators and a mixer. You can

> do plenty with four modules or six modules. Get something going now so you can start gaining experience, and it might actually enlighten you to purchases you may not want to make later on, stuff that you don't need.' That's a better way to get into modular synthesis so that you don't buy stuff and then not use it." Steve Masucci

When you order modules, most of which require power from a regulated source at specific voltages, confirm that they come with necessary cables to connect to the system's power supply. Most modules do, but you don't want to get stuck waiting for anything once your case(s) and modules are at hand, ready for assembly.

You also need to verify the rack works with all of the modules you want, in terms of both power and mounting requirements. There can even be inconsistencies within specific formats. For example, according to Bob Williams of Analogue Systems, his systems are Eurorack-compatible. His RS10 and RS15 cases have 1.5-amp power supplies delivering +12V, +5V (as standard), and –12V, which Eurorack modules require. On each power supply board are fourteen sockets for plugging in Analogue Systems modules because he hasn't adopted the Doepfer-style sockets in his design, but there are also eight Doepfer-style sockets so that users can mix and match modules.

Next you'll need an adequate supply of cables to patch modules together. Be sure to get cords in different lengths and colors to assist in the patching process. Also remember that you must be able to get to these cables without any hassle so that patching is always fun and constructive. Pomona Electronics makes sturdy metal test lead holders for different-sized cables and plugs. Mount as many holders as you need in close proximity to your synth(s) for patching sessions, and make sure they're high enough on a wall or cabinet so the cables hang freely and don't tangle. You'll find plans for Scott Juskiw's great DIY cable tree at www.tellun.com/motm/diy/cabletree/cabletree.html.

More on Eurorack Modular

A majority of the current activity in modular synths occurs within the Eurorack realm, which is supported by the most manufacturers. It's very common to see Eurorack systems made up of modules from many different companies, resembling Dolly Parton's "Coat of Many Colors." Some Eurorack owners may not feel their modular synth functions like a finished instrument, which happens less frequently with systems consisting of modules produced by the same maker.

When Dieter Doepfer wanted to display his first Eurorack modules at the 1996 Frankfurt Musikmesse trade show, his German dealers were leery about the modular-synth concept, doubting that anyone would be interested in seemingly ancient electronic-music technology. They therefore insisted on having Doepfer's MIDI keyboard controllers prominently positioned at the front in their booth and reluctantly devoted space in the back of the booth for Dieter to set up his modular systems. From opening day onward, while the keyboard zone remained mostly empty, crowds constantly surrounded the modular synths at the back. Thus began the Eurorack modular craze.

Paul Schreiber of Synthesis Technology prepares one of his new Eurorack modules for introduction at the January 2012 NAMM show. (Mark Vail)

Over the years, many other modular-synth companies began offering Eurorack modules. How does Dieter Doepfer feel about these newcomers? "At first we thought it would drop our sales," he acknowledges, "but in fact it's been quite the opposite. We are not really competitors. They offer modules that we don't, and vice versa. If I see that someone offers a certain function, we won't design one like it because it doesn't make sense. It's such a small community, it doesn't make sense to make too much competition. It's better to say, 'Okay, you make this module, you make that module, and we'll make the other modules.' Our sales rose as the other companies offered their own modules. So we're all lucky."

In exchange for the portability factor of Eurorack systems and others in small format, sometimes getting at knobs and jacks situated in confined spaces and hidden by numerous cables can be challenging. Another consideration is inconsistent module width among manufacturers. For example, whereas the width of all Analogue Systems modules are divisible by 6hp (horizontal pitch; a single hp unit equals 0.2″ or 5.08mm), some Eurorack companies make modules measuring 8hp, 10hp, and in other sizes, which can make spacing an issue. Eurorack shoppers will find the Modular Planner (www.modularplanner.co.uk) invaluable in sizing and choosing modules for specific modular cabinets.

Within his Eurorack system, Drew Neumann has many favorite modules. He likes Doepfer oscillators because they're very lively in a good way, and he says Doepfer's A-120 VCF1 Moog-style filter is tremendous for bass lines. There are numerous Analogue Systems modules in his collection, too, including an RS240 Bode Frequency Shifter that

Dann Green of 4ms Pedals demonstrates some of his Eurorack modules at a July 2012 Bay Area Synth Meet in San Francisco. Not only does 4ms offer a variety of Eurorack modules, but there are also inexpensive kits and complete instruments, effects processors, and controllers for creating alternative and experimental electronic music. (Mark Vail)

gives him everything from clangorous effects to—when set up with feedback paths—barber-pole phase-shifting that generates up and down harmonic sweeps.

Drew is also a fan of Analogue Systems' RS500E, a licensed and legitimate version of the EMS Synthi filter. It offers slow and fast slewing speeds and provides both pre- and post-1974 cutoff slopes, which sound quite different from each other.

Neumann also has Analogue Systems' RS310 Reverb/Chorus, a bucket-brigade device with analog-delay chips, and he's particularly excited about their RS360 Vocal Phase Filter Bank: "It's a bit like Jürgen Haibel's and Synthesis Technology's triple bandpass filter," says Drew, referring in the latter case to the MOTM-410 Triple Resonant Filter with DualVCLFO, "except it doesn't use **vactrols**. They're standard analog chips, but you can control each filter separately and you get a variety of different outputs plus the sum of those outputs. The RS360 is great for creating vocal formants and shifting textures."

> *vactrols:* photo-resistive opto-isolator devices that combine a light source such as an LED with a light detector like a photocell; see ch. 4 for more details

More on FracRak Modular

While FracRak and Eurorack modules are nearly the same height, one difference is the way they mount in a cabinet. Another? Not all of their front panels induce claustrophobia. "Blacet modules provide quite a lot of room to move around in," Drew Neumann points out about these FracRak modules, "and they keep jacks—and therefore any connected cables—separate from where the knobs are."

Among the Blacet FracRak modules Neumann enjoys using are the VCO2100, which he says creates "a really deep, rich, rude kind of sound," and the Klang Werk KW2010 ring modulator. "It has its own internal oscillator that doesn't really track a keyboard, but it's there or you can use an external oscillator. It's a really great-sounding ring modulator, very flexible."

Marvin Jones, the founding editor of *Polyphony* and *Electronic Musician* magazines and designer of many electronic instruments and related gear, is another big fan of Blacet modules. "I really admire John Blacet's designs," says Marvin. "He has a tendency to try to put as many functions as possible under voltage control—every knob and switch that's possible, and I really like that. As an electronics engineer who's designed electronic-music devices, I've always strived to put as much controllability as possible into the circuits."

More on Serge Modular

During the early 1970s, professor Serge Tcherepnin and some of his students at the California Institute of the Arts in Valencia (CalArts, calarts.edu)—Randy Cohen, Richard Gold, Naut Human from Rhythm And Noise, Will "Stonewall" Jackson with Ether Ship, and Rex Probe—decided they should build powerful yet affordable modular synthesizers of Tcherepnin's design. The results were the birth of the Serge Modular synthesizer, which lives on today.

Rex Probe founded Sound Transform Systems (STS) in Oakland, California, in 1984 and took over Serge production and intellectual property in 1992. In 2000 he relocated the operation to Wisconsin. There's no official Serge website, but you can contact Rex Probe directly by writing to him at Sound Transform Systems, 151 E. Capitol Drive, Hartland, WI 53029; calling him at 262-367-3030 (he'll usually answer during business hours

Marvin Jones sits at the keyboard synths and controllers in front of his modular-synth system in December 2010. He worked for Paia Electronics founder John Simonton from 1974 to 1981, developing a series of kits and later serving as the founding editor of *Polyphony* magazine, which later became *Electronic Musician*. (Mark Vail)

and you'll be in for a very entertaining and informative conversation); or faxing him at 262-367-3434. While individual Serge modules are no longer available, STS sells complete panels and M-Class modules, which are a confluence of function blocks designed by Tcherepnin and Probe.

While some Serge components are classified in familiar synth terms such as oscillator, filter, VCA, and envelope generator, many are capable of functions that exceed such classifications—depending on how the synthesist patches the components together. For example, as Ken Tkacs explains in *The Serge Modular Creature: An Unauthorized User's Manual* (downloadable at www.carbon111.com/creature_manual.html), the Serge Universal Slope Generator can serve as an envelope generator, slew processor, LFO, VCO, frequency divider, lowpass VCF, trigger/gate delay, or envelope follower. Such component flexibility provides considerable synthesis power within a relatively compact space.

Connectivity

Convincing Analog and MIDI Synths to Coexist

Beginning in 1963, the synthesizer pioneers Don Buchla and Bob Moog developed methods of using analog voltages to control parameters such as the pitch produced by an oscillator, the frequencies passed by a filter, and the volume output by an amplifier. During the '70s, manufacturers began incorporating microprocessors to digitally control analog

Since witnessing synthesist Paul Young demonstrate a huge Serge Modular in San Francisco in 1980, I've wanted one. I had to start small, though. On the *left* is an STS Serge Sequencer A and on the *right* a Serge Creature, both from the M-class series. It's a small, single-panel system, but extremely flexible and potent in creating timbres and patterns. Shown above the Serge is an OTO Biscuit. (Mark Vail)

CVs for purposes such as generating sequences of notes and storing multiple parameter settings and signal routings to make an instrument programmable.

Prior to 1983, some manufacturers used proprietary digital interfaces to transfer control data among CPUs in their instruments and synchronize time-based events. To convince a digitally controlled device from company A to play nicely with one from company B, synthesists had to incorporate a variety of converters and techniques. Thanks to the pioneering efforts of Dave Smith and Chet Wood of Sequential Circuits and Ikutaro Kakehashi of Roland, along with collaboration from Korg, Yamaha, and Kawai, the Musical Instrument Digital Interface (MIDI) appeared and proprietary interfaces faded away. Eventually electronic instruments from all manufacturers could function together as one system, and the industry expanded exponentially as it never had before.

Although analog synthesis receded to the background for a time, it never disappeared and came back strong during the 1990s. Since a lot of analog gear doesn't have MIDI, the need for converters returned. There are many MIDI-to-CV converters on the market, as well as some for CV-to-MIDI conversion. Since many synthesists are or soon will be working with both analog and MIDI instruments, the converters themselves deserve consideration.

MIDI-to-CV Conversion

Control voltages, triggers, and gates arrived in the synthesizer universe long before MIDI, and today there are many options for those who want to convert MIDI data into analog

Composer Edmund Eagan refers to this massive twelve-panel Serge Modular as "the Beast." He designed it so that as many modules are accessible as possible from a sitting position. It took about ten years to collect all of the modules and assemble the Beast, which includes a custom seven-input, quadraphonic-output voltage-controlled mixer as well as a touch-envelope generator. (© Edmund Eagan)

signals to control analog synthesizer components. Kenton has been active at this for years and provides several solutions in tabletop, rackmount, and Eurorack varieties. Drew Neumann has long favored the Kenton Pro 4, introduced during the mid-'90s, because of its stable operation; it has dedicated outputs for CV, gate, and expression; it allows him to use it with a tuner; and it provides a hardware tuning potentiometer for calibrating its volt/octave operation. Drew depends on a pair of Pro 4s and several newer Kenton Pro-2000 tabletop/rackmount units, which require a more extensive set-up process than the earlier units and handle calibration in software. He also drives his original Minimoog Model D via a single-channel Pro-Solo MkII MIDI-to-CV converter, a tabletop version of Kenton's Modular-Solo Eurorack module.

IEC: International Electrotechnical Commission

S-trigger: an abbreviation for "switch trigger"; on vintage Moog synths such as the Minimoog and on certain Moog Modular modules including the 911 Envelope Generator and 921 VCO, you'll find an S-trigger input jack that accepts a two-prong "cinch-Jones plug." Whereas the voltage level at an S-trigger input remains nominally positive, closing the switch by playing a key on the Minimoog—in which case the S-trigger connection happens internally—or by connecting an inverted-gate (aka switch-to-ground) signal to the cinch-Jones input (which causes the nominal voltage at the input to drop to zero, or switch to ground when triggered) the voltage level will stay at zero as long as the key is held or the trigger signal is present at the input. A typical use of the S-trigger is to start the attack and release segments of an envelope generator that could—depending on how it's patched—subsequently open and close a VCA or a VCF cutoff frequency; here the term "trigger" differs from what's used for most other analog synths, such as those from ARP Instruments, in that a trigger in this context isn't a momentary, near-instantaneous change in the signal level but is a latched signal that might more accurately be

The Pro-2000 MkII, Kenton's top-of-the-line MIDI-to-CV converter, is tabletop ready, but you can buy optional ears to rackmount it. It has two programmable LFOs for modulating CV outputs, each of which can produce any of nine waveforms including sample-and-hold, and you can sync the LFOs to MIDI clock. In its polyphonic mode, the Pro-2000 MkII can output up to five channels of CVs and gates. Around back are a standard **IEC** grounded AC input for the built-in power supply; MIDI in, out, and thru; a DIN Sync 24 jack for synchronizing pre-MIDI Roland drum machines and the TB-303 Bass Line; and eleven 3.5mm jacks. The latter break down into two channels of CV and gate/**S-trigger** jacks, clock out, and six auxiliary outputs that can transmit CVs or gates. You can independently program the main CV outputs for one volt-per-octave, Hertz-per-volt, or 1.2 volts-per-octave scaling. An output expansion port can accommodate one of two optional interfaces: a DCB interface for Roland's Juno-60 and DCB-equipped Jupiter-8s, or a KADI/Wasp interface to drive specially modified Roland TR-606 and TR-808 drum machines and the Electronic Dream Plant Wasp monosynth. (Courtesy of Kenton Electronics Ltd.)

Kenton's Pro Solo MkII is an affordable tabletop MIDI-to-CV converter with a built-in, multi-waveform LFO that will sync to MIDI clock. It can transmit pulses to drive pre-MIDI drum machines, arpeggiators, and sequencers or CVs of zero and +5 volts. Kenton sells a special cable for controlling the accent and slide inputs on a Roland TB-303 Bass Line that's been retrofit with Kenton's optional upgrade kit. Alongside the MIDI thru on the Pro Solo MkII's back panel are the MIDI in, 9V DC power input for the external power supply, and three 3.5mm output jacks: auxiliary/clock, gate/S-trigger, and CV, the latter of which you can assign to either the more common one volt-per-octave tuning scale that works for most pre-MIDI synths, or the Hertz-per-volt arrangement for old Yamaha and Korg synths. Other niceties worth mentioning are the Pro Solo's adjustable portamento, which you can set to glide only during **legato playing** and at either fixed rate or fixed time, and note priority of lowest, highest, or last. (Courtesy of Kenton Electronics Ltd.)

---

described as an inverted-gate. One of the advantages of an S-trigger system is that no active electronic elements are required; in fact, according to Moog Music veteran and electronic music historian Tom Rhea, Bob Moog used a doorbell as the first S-trigger generator on his 911 Envelope Generator.

legato playing: engaging a new key before completely releasing the previously played key

---

Another affordable tabletop interface is Doepfer's Dark Link, which can convert signals from MIDI and USB sources into CVs and gates. Alongside its dedicated 3.5mm gate output are 3.5mm CV outs for note on/off, pitchbend, velocity, and a variable controller. The Dark Link also features a MIDI learn function and a portamento rate knob.

Eurorack owners interested in MIDIfying their systems have numerous options. Doepfer makes three converter modules. Their A-190-1 provides two CV outputs—one that converts MIDI notes with twelve-bit DAC resolution for VCO pitch and the other assignable to different MIDI CCs with seven-bit resolution. It also includes a built-in LFO and a clock output with sync to MIDI clock and onboard division circuitry for different

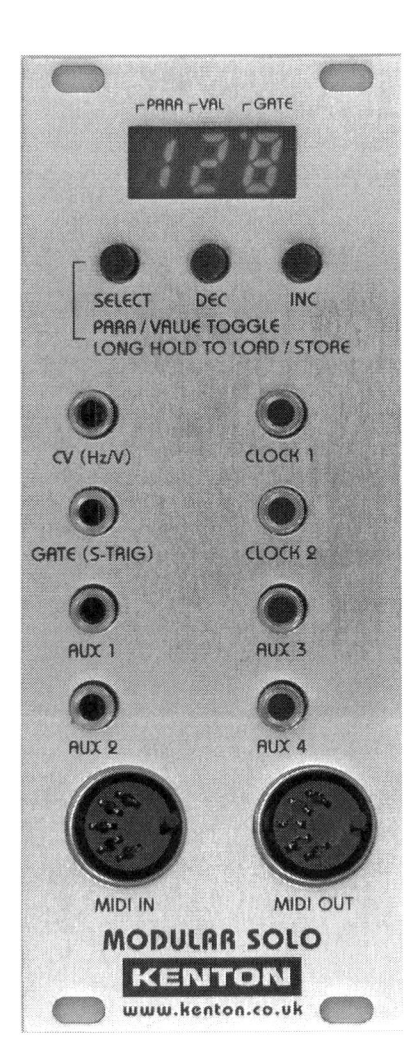

Not only has Kenton squeezed all of the functionality and nearly all of the guts of their Pro Solo MkII MIDI-to-CV converter into the Modular Solo, a module for Eurorack systems, but it also provides four continuously variable outputs instead of only one. It comes with a ribbon cable for connection to a standard Eurorack system bus. (Courtesy of Kenton Electronics Ltd.)

timing resolutions. Slightly less expensive and missing the LFO and clock output are Doepfer's A-190-2 and the MIDI- and USB-in equipped A-190-3. All have adjustable-rate portamento for the CV1 output; while portamento is a programmable function on the A-190-1, it's under knob control on the other two modules.

With Kilpatrick Audio's K1600 MIDI Converter—which has two CV, two gate, and four trigger outputs—you can transmit two-note polyphony via the two CV-and-gate

The Doepfer Dark Link converts MIDI and USB input to four channels of control voltages and +5-volt gate in a little black metal box. (© by Doepfer Musikelektronik GmbH)

pairs or split your MIDI keyboard to send two different CV-and-gate note signals. It also has clock and reset outputs for interfacing with analog sequencers and drum machines. You program the K1600 with a single Setup switch in combination with its MIDI learn function.

Three additional Eurorack MIDI-to-CV modules run the financial gamut from the affordable Atomosynth Koneko to the highly programmable Analogue Systems RS140, with the four-channel Vermona Quad MIDI Interface (QMI) coming in slightly less expensive than the RS140. Others in this format have likely appeared by the time you read this, so a search of the Internet will reveal new models.

For the FracRak segment, Paia offers the 9700K MIDI2CV8. Owners of a Buchla 200e modular system can turn to the Model 225e MIDI Decoder/Preset Manager, which does double-duty for MIDI-to-CV conversion and storage and recall of 200e patches.

There's even a MIDI-to-CV converter module for the smallest modular synth format on record, the Mattson Mini Modular. Mattson's MIDI-to-CV controller module—the PE/MIDI-SR1—features 3.5mm gate, CV, and modulation outputs. Scott Rise of Division 6 designed its CV out to drive a VCO at the one-volt-per-octave standard, although you can adjust the scaling with a recessed trim pot on the front panel. You can switch envelope triggering between single and multiple modes for legato play, vary the portamento rate with a front-panel knob, and use two switches—one with three positions—to select among the portamento modes: smooth or quantized steps between notes, a normal glide time that's equal per octave, a fixed-time glide rate that takes the same amount of time regardless of how far apart the original and subsequent notes, and no portamento at all. You can also program the Mattson MIDI-to-CV module so that portamento happens only in one direction or both ways. For bending pitch, you can independently program the up and down directions by ranges up to a full octave. Note priority can be your choice of highest, lowest, or last-played, and you can program the gate to open only on ascending or descending keys and for anywhere from the first to the eighth key you press instead of for every newly played note. You can also transpose the note range by redefining MIDI Middle C. You can change the MIDI channel the PE/MIDI-SR1 responds to or disable MIDI response entirely. You can also lock the gate, which is convenient for creating drones.

Drew Neumann feels the Encore Electronics Expressionist is one of the more flexible MIDI-to-CV converters out there. A 1U rackmount device that's gone in and out of production since 1997, the Expressionist has a two-line by twenty-character backlit LCD for programming—a process that Drew Neumann refers to as "kludgy" because of its lack of a data knob, forcing you to use buttons both to navigate through its fairly deep menu system and to adjust parameters. Its complement of seventeen 1/4" jacks—eight CV outputs, eight gate/S-trigger outputs, and a footswitch input—along with a DIN sync out, MIDI in and out connectors, and 9V AC power input, consume the Expressionist's back panel. Among its added attractions are three LFOs, each capable of generating any of six waveforms; volts-per-octave and Hertz-per-octave scaling, the former for Moog, ARP, and most other analog synths and the latter for ancient Korgs and Yamahas; independent offsets for tracking and tuning adjustments per channel; and memory for one hundred user patches. While Drew says the Expressionist has a hard time addressing extremely large systems—perhaps due to impedance issues—he also discovered it could

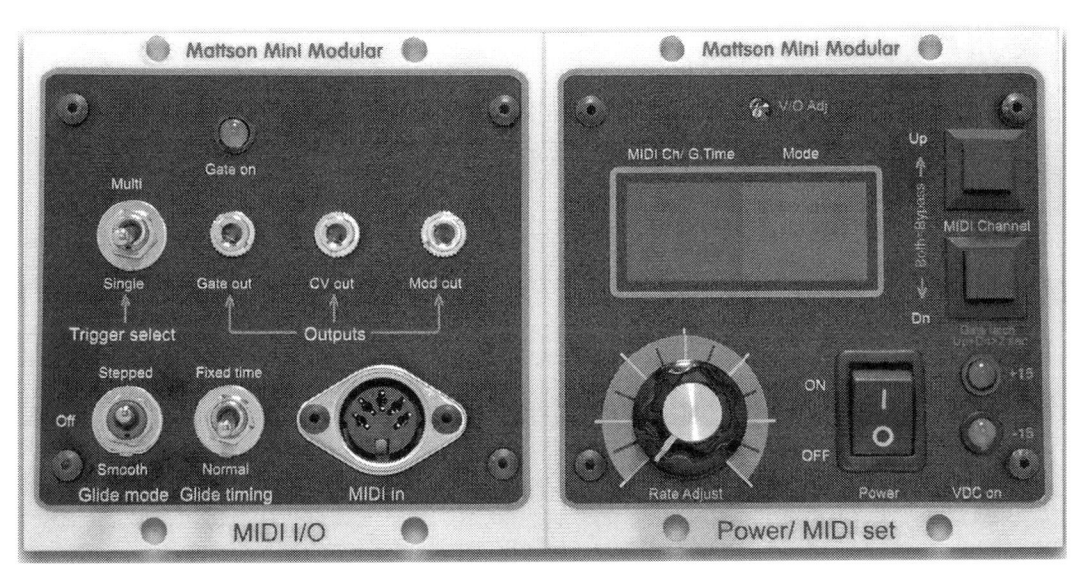

Lots of capabilities are hidden within the tiny Mattson MIDI-to-CV converter module, which allows you to drive gear that has CV and gate inputs from your favorite MIDI controller. It's a double-wide Mattson module, measuring a mere 7" across and 3.5" high. (© 2007 Scott Rise)

trigger notes and envelopes on a borrowed Moog 15 modular, which he couldn't get to work with any of his other MIDI-to-CV converters.

On the used market, you might look for a Roland MPU-101—which is what Amin Bhatia uses to MIDI-control his Minimoog and ARP 2600. Manufactured in 1985, the MPU-101 was one of the earliest commercially available MIDI-to-CV converters. It provides four channels of CV, gate, and "dynamics" (note velocity) outputs, along with outputs for pitchbend, modulation wheel, aftertouch, and volume. There are buttons for polyphonic modes, knobs for selecting the MIDI channel and tuning, a three-way transposition switch, and more.

In addition, there are two sources of software that will adapt certain audio interfaces for MIDI-to-CV conversion: Expert Sleepers' Silent Way and MOTU's Volta. Both companies also produce hardware to make the conversion happen.

CV-to-MIDI Conversion

Stand-alone CV-to-MIDI converters are rare, but there is a respectable number of them in modular form, particularly for the Eurorack segment. One example is the Analogue Solutions CVM, a dual-channel unit with one gate and two CV inputs per channel. It will translate outputs from an analog step-sequencer into MIDI notes with velocity data on MIDI channels 1 and 2. Analogue Solutions also makes the CVQ02, a dual-channel CV-to-MIDI converter that will transform two CVs and one gate into MIDI note data, with the second control voltage determining note velocities. The CVQ02 also provides two channels of quantized CV output to produce specific note voltages, as well as CV and gate thru connectors to drive other analog modules along with data transmitted from the MIDI out jack.

Doepfer's A-192-1 CVM16 converts sixteen channels of control voltages into MIDI data, and its memory contains 128 presets to define what MIDI control change (CC) messages the CV-to-MIDI conversion generates. In case none of the presets does precisely what you want, you can download a free Windows editor for creating your own presets. Three simple preset examples: (1) the transmission of volume or pan data over sixteen MIDI channels, (2) volume and pan data over eight different MIDI channels, or (3) filter cutoff frequency and resonance level data over eight MIDI channels. Along with the sixteen CV inputs, the A-192-1 provides a snapshot button to transmit the current sixteen CV levels, a red control activity LED, and a MIDI input through which incoming data is merged with CC data generated within the unit. Note that the A-192-1 won't convert control voltages into MIDI notes.

The Analogue Systems RS300 may have only half as many CV channels as the Doepfer A-192-1, but it can generate more types of MIDI messages. You can assign its eight channels of CV-to-MIDI conversion to generate MIDI notes with fixed or dynamic velocity levels, pitchbend or aftertouch data, or any MIDI CC from zero to 127. To program, edit, and store up to forty presets in the RS300, you work from its front panel using an edit knob/enter pushbutton and cancel button while navigating through a menu system displayed on a two-line by twenty-character backlit LCD. The composer/synthesist Gary Chang is a big RS300 fan, calling it "a really wild module that allows you to do all sorts of whacky stuff." To demonstrate how accurate the RS300 is, he routes a random CV output from a sample-and-hold module into the RS300's CV1 input, makes a few additional connections, and assigns the module to quantize the CV1 signal into MIDI notes. Gary routes the MIDI data into an Access Virus virtual-analog synth, which obediently tracks what he's doing with the S/H module. You can use an RS300 to convert the CV, gate, and trigger outputs from an analog step-sequencer into MIDI data to drive MIDI synths or capture with a MIDI sequencer. Using the RS300 with modules

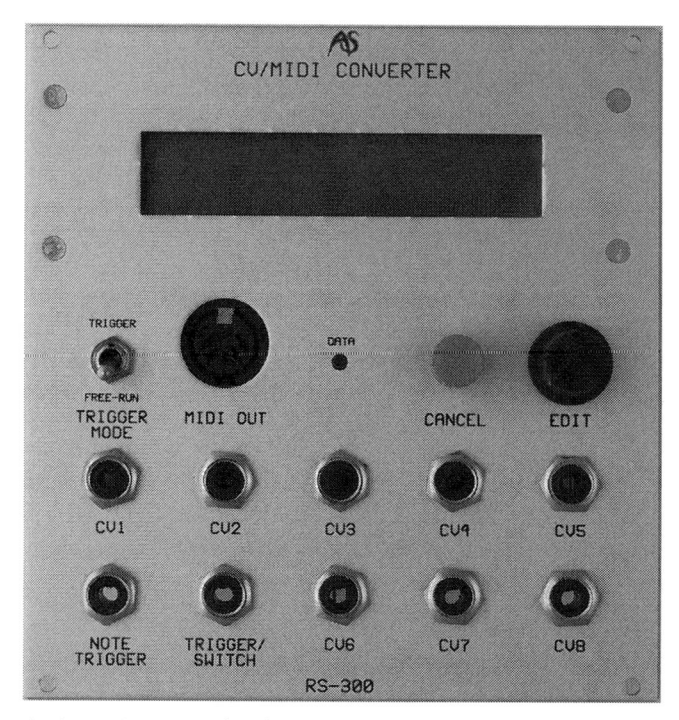

Analogue Systems makes the RS300 CV/MIDI Converter for the Eurorack format modular systems. CV-to-MIDI converters are rarer than the MIDI-to-CV type. The RS300 provides eight CV inputs and can be programmed to generate note-on/off, velocity, aftertouch, and a wide variety of MIDI CC data. (Stephi Clendinen, courtesy of Big City Music)

The 5U Moon Modular 552 module can convert four channels of analog CV and gate signals into a bevy of MIDI messages for output over one to four MIDI channels. Among its many flexible control functions is the ability to transpose MIDI note output under CV and MIDI control, which you can selectively enable or disable for each of the transmission channels. (© 2012 Lunar Experience)

in your modular synth, you can add extra LFOs, sample-and-holds, and control signals from other sources to extend the capabilities of a typical MIDI synth.

For the 5U modular enthusiast, Moon Modular offers the 552 CV-to-MIDI converter, which provides four channels of CV and gate inputs and rotary switches for selecting the type of MIDI output data for each channel. There's a list of twelve, including note, note with velocity, mod wheel, volume, pan, program change, sustain, and aftertouch. You choose among eight fixed MIDI-channel transmission configurations using another rotary switch. There's also a toggle switch for enabling or disabling each note-on channel to respond to a transposition input, the source of which can be either CV or MIDI for all channels together.

FracRak modular synthesists can turn to the Paia 8031 CV-to-MIDI converter, which is part of two different Paia kits. With Paia's 9201FK MIDI Fader Kit, the 8031 will convert eight zero to five-volt signals into CC, pitchbend, and aftertouch data. As part of Paia's 9201DK MIDI Drum Brain Kit, the 8031 converts trigger pulses from eight sensors into MIDI note on/off and velocity data. Piezo disks, force-sensing resistors, or electret mics can serve as sensors.

The Synthesizer

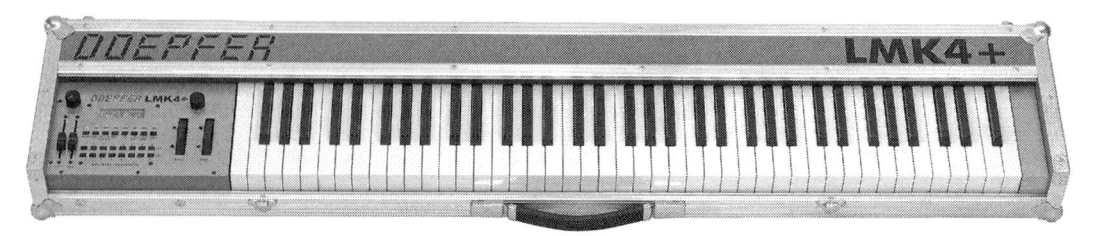

Doepfer's LMK4+ represents the epitome of the programmable controller keyboard thanks to its flexibility, MIDI and USB connectivity, and top-notch portability. It's available with either seventy-six or eighty-eight hammer-action keys, allows up to eight splits zones, provides 128 memory locations, and sports two performance wheels, two sliders, a rotary encoder, two footswitch jacks, two footpedal jacks, velocity and channel aftertouch response, and a two-line by sixteen-character backlit LCD—all housed in a protective ATA-approved flight case with a detachable lid. Windows-compatible editing software is available for free. (© by Doepfer Musikelektronik GmbH)

Controllers

Synths and Controllers with Keyboards

If you've got your mind set on a keyboard instrument, how many keys do you need and what kind of action do you prefer? If you're a pianist, you might want a complete complement of eighty-eight full-size keys with a piano-like hammer action. Manufacturers of full-fledged workstation keyboard synthesizers—Korg, Yamaha, Roland, and Kurzweil—offer eighty-eight-key models with hammer-action keyboards. Most synths with twenty-five to seventy-six full-size keys have an organ-like, "semi-weighted" action.

Alternatively, you'll find a lot of dedicated keyboard controllers that don't have built-in sound generators but allow you to play synth modules via MIDI and softsynths via USB. Since 2009 Doepfer has produced three eighty-eight-key controllers with both USB and MIDI ports and hammer actions. They're built inside flight cases for on-road protection. Akai, M-Audio, Fatar/Studiologic, and CME also make eighty-eight-note keyboard

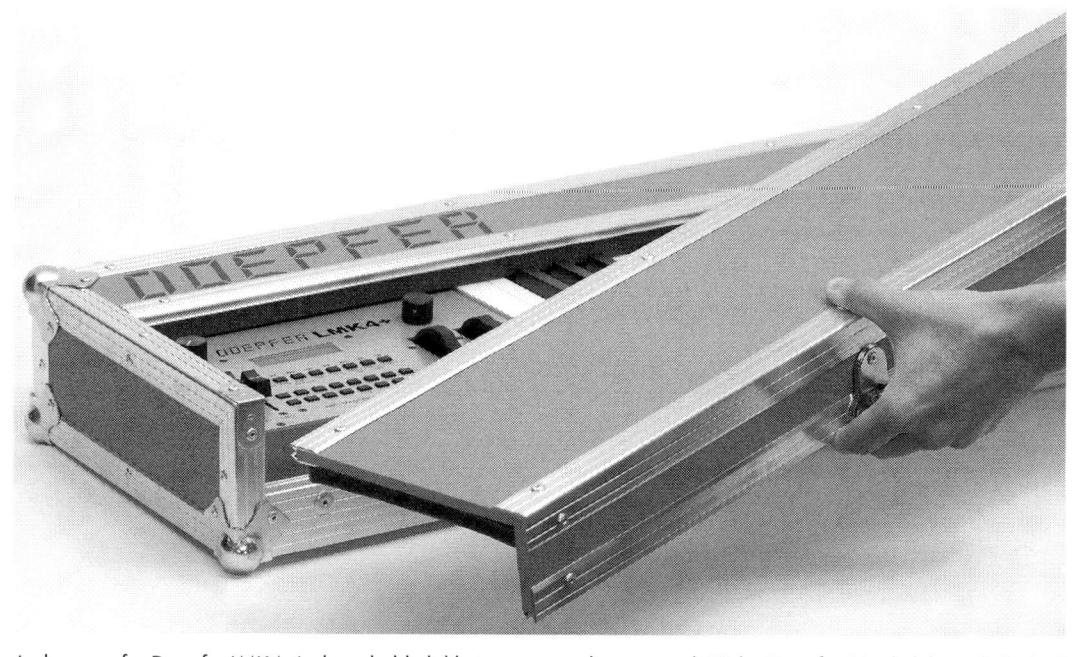

A closeup of a Doepfer LMK4+'s detatchable lid being removed or secured. (© by Doepfer Musikelektronik GmbH)

Choosing Your Synthesizer(s)

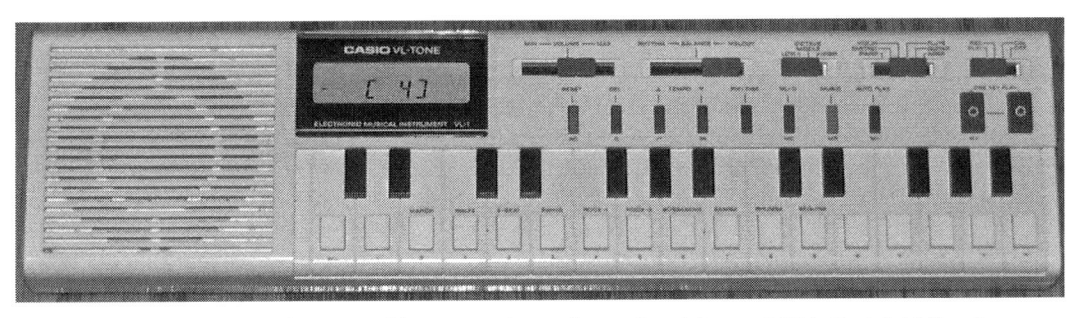

Introduced in June 1979 at a list price of $69.95 and manufactured until August 1984, Casio's VL-Tone has twenty-nine calculator-button keys (G to B), a three-position octave switch, one programmable and five preset sounds, ten built-in rhythm patterns, an eight-character LCD, a one-hundred-note sequencer, and a multifunction calculator mode. It measures a mere 11-3/4" by 3" by 1-3/8", weighs less than a pound, and plays the cheesiest demo—a German folk song called "Unterlanders Heimweh"—you've ever heard. (Mark Vail)

controllers—all with MIDI and USB connections, some with hammer actions. Note that true hammer action adds weight and bulk due to the physical mechanisms involved.

Many manufacturers of keyboard synthesizers and controllers offer them with twenty-five, thirty-seven, forty-nine, sixty-one, seventy-six, or eighty-eight keys, with a few variations. The feel of keys tends to vary from one manufacturer to another, and not all of them are full-size; you'll find quite a few inexpensive synths, portable keyboards, and controllers with minikeys and sometimes even simple pushbuttons. Consider Casio's VL-Tone VL-1 from 1979 and the contemporary Teenage Engineering OP-1, both of which sport calculator-style buttons arranged like a keyboard. Not to directly compare them, only their keys: The OP-1 isn't inexpensive, but it's a really small instrument with rotary encoders (unlimited 360-degree rotation), multiple function keys, and a tiny, marvelous color display. Given all of its synthesis engines—FM, subtractive, physical modeling, phase distortion, eight-bit sampling, and more—plus effects processing and recording functions, the OP-1 is certainly fun, potent, and inventive. So was the VL-Tone—in a kitschy, late-'70s way.

Relatively few mass-produced keyboard synths and controllers have supported poly-aftertouch, among them the Yamaha CS-80, Sequential Circuits Prophet-T8, Kurzweil Midiboard, and Ensoniq EPS-16+ and TS-10. Of these, only those from Sequential, Kurzweil, and Ensoniq have MIDI; whereas the T8 and Midiboard retain high resale

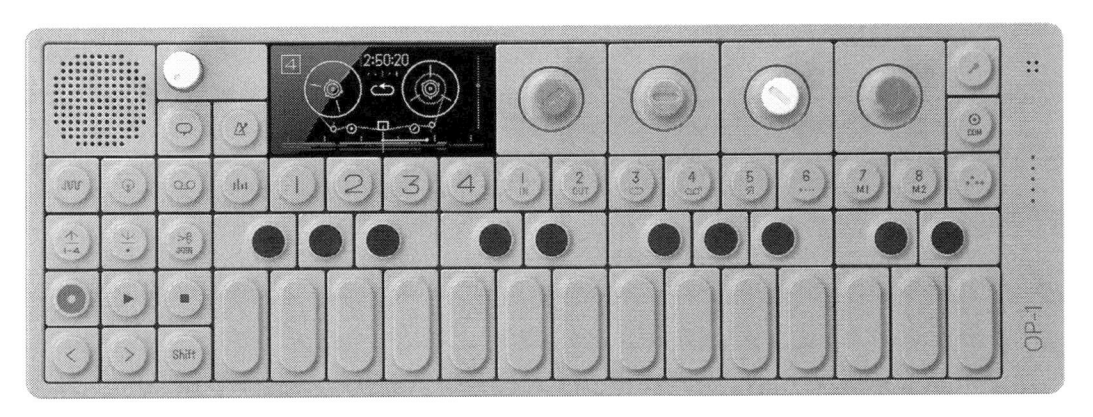

Loads of twenty-first-century technology have been squeezed into the tiny Teenage Engineering OP-1, including eight synth engines, multi-effect processing, sampling, a modeled four-track tape recorder with variable speed, USB connection for file transfers, four rotary encoders and gobs of buttons—including twenty-four laid out like a piano keyboard—and a minuscule but gorgeous color LCD. (Ola Bergengren, courtesy of Teenage Engineering)

values, Ensoniqs generally can be had for a song. Some players keep them just for their poly-aftertouch keyboards. Prefer to buy new? As of late 2013, I'm aware of only two MIDI/USB keyboard controllers with full-size keys and poly-aftertouch response still in production. One is the seventy-six-key Infinite Response VAX77, which is not only notable for that feature, but also because it supports release velocity and folds in half for improved portability.

As for the other keyboard with full-size keys and poly-aftertouch, refer back to chapter 1 to the discussion of the Multiple-Touch-Sensitive Keyboard that Bob Moog and John Eaton started working on beginning in 1968 (see page 24). While Eaton has a functioning unit, it's never been commercially available. However, the Perfect Fretworks

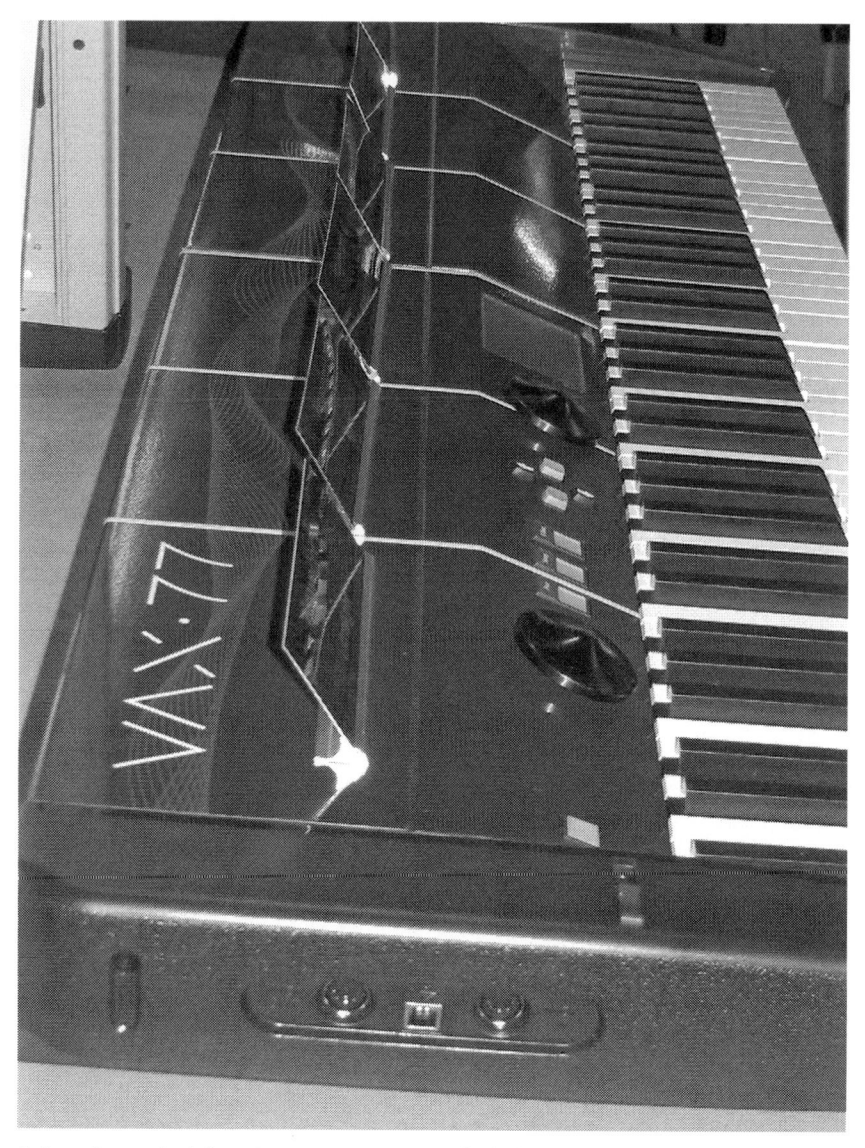

At first glance, the Infinite Response VAX77 may look like a typical seventy-six-note keyboard controller or even a digital piano. Not only does it possess great features such as poly-aftertouch and release-velocity response, a backlit touchscreen color display, and both MIDI and USB connectivity, but it's also available with either a standard or heavy action to satisfying players who respectively prefer organ- or piano-like touch and its pitchbend and modulation controllers are different and uniquely positioned. Undetectable from this view, however, is the VAX77's unequaled trait: It folds in half for portability. (Mark Vail)

This shot indicates how the Infinite Response VAX77 keyboard controller folds in half, successfully making it more manageable to transport than any other seventy-six-note keyboard without compromising its feel and playability. (Mark Vail)

Hyperkeys—which Jeff Tripp developed—offers similar control functions with both MIDI and USB outputs and thirty-seven full-size keys that not only go up and down as you'd expect, but they also travel in and out. Synthesist, teacher, and author Don Muro had a chance to play Jeff Tripp's original "3D keyboard" and heard a demonstrator play a piece in four-part polyphony while doing independent expression on each key. "It was the most expressive live polyphonic electronic music I'd ever heard!" Don recalls. "Considering it was performed by fingers on a clavier, it was unbelievable. If only I could take six months of my life to learn the proper technique!"

Perhaps the smallest and most flexible keyboard controller you can imagine comes from Keith McMillen Instruments. Although it doesn't have full-size keys, the QuNexus provides twenty-five backlit "smart sensor" keys that respond to velocity, pressure, and location. It will generate poly-aftertouch, you can transpose the keys over a seven-octave range, and it has a pitchbend pad and an arpeggiator. Most surprising is that along with USB and MIDI I/O and compatibility with Mac, Windows, iOS, Android, and Linux, it sports two CV/gate inputs and three CV and one gate output. In combination with the optional KMI MIDI Expander, it can convert MIDI data into analog CV and gate signals and—amazingly for a device that measures merely $3.5'' \times 10'' \times 0.5''$ and weighs fourteen ounces—will convert incoming control voltages and gates into MIDI data.

Although the manufacturing of modular synthesizer components has exploded since the mid '90s, there aren't a lot choices for keyboards that function directly with modulars. Three come from Analogue Systems: the Demon, the Sorceror, and the French Con-

Bob Moog (*left*) and John Eaton pose with the Multiple-Touch-Sensitive Keyboard, on which Bob worked with and for composer John Eaton beginning in 1968. By the time they finished making it in 1991, it could generate so much MIDI CC data that they found it difficult to find enough suitable parameters in synths of the early '90s for expressive performance. In 2006, John Eaton returned to using it with softsynths. (With the permission of Ileana Grams-Moog)

nection. Each has a forty-nine-note keyboard that transmits CVs, triggers, and gates via 3.5mm jacks and is enclosed in a beautiful wooden cabinet. The Demon and Sorceror keyboards respond to aftertouch by transmitting CVs and MIDI data. They also transmit notes polyphonically via MIDI. Per customer order they're either fitted with the RS220 Joystick module, which provides two CV outputs for both the x and y axes along with bipolar range pots for each axis, or the RS600 Performance Wheels module, which sports

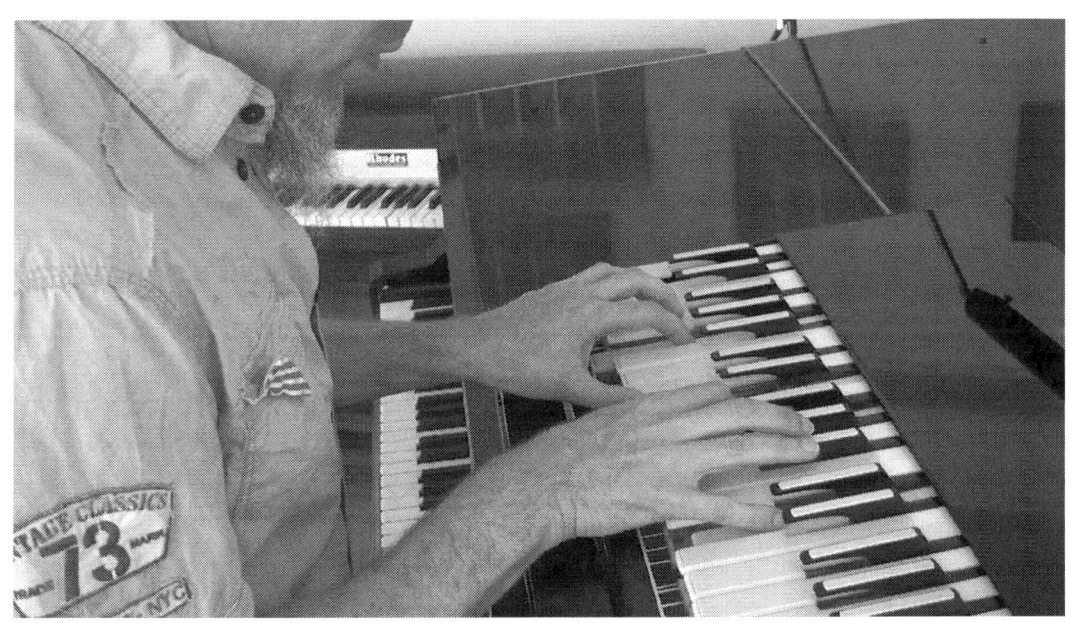

Putting Jeff Tripp's Hyperkeys controller through its paces is Jordan Rudess. Notice how Jordan is pulling some keys toward himself while pushing others away. As Jeff wrote to me in July 2011, "What I have found important for mechanisms like this is that they be balanced to support articulation anywhere in the plane in which the key is free to travel. This is not 'feels like a piano.' Why bother? If you want to play a piano, do it. . . . The frontier now is between notes and not-notes, and different tools are called for. We are at, in my opinion, the dawn of the Age of Controllers." (Richard Lainhart, courtesy of Perfect Fretworks)

clear Moog-style modulation and pitchbend wheels backlit with LEDs that change colors as you move the wheels. Other RS600 features: a built-in LFO that pulses the LEDs to indicate its rate; CV outputs for bend, mod, and a mix of both; and an external input for CV or audio signals. The Sorceror's cabinet is oversized to provide room for 168hp of Eurorack and Analogue Systems modules. As for the French Connection, it's a little bigger than the Demon and, although it lacks MIDI output, beneath its four-octave keyboard you'll find a special type of controller: a re-creation of the Ondes Martenot's ring-on-a-wire suspended over an etched chromatic fingerboard, allowing you to glide from note to note and naturally induce vibrato with a wiggle of your finger.

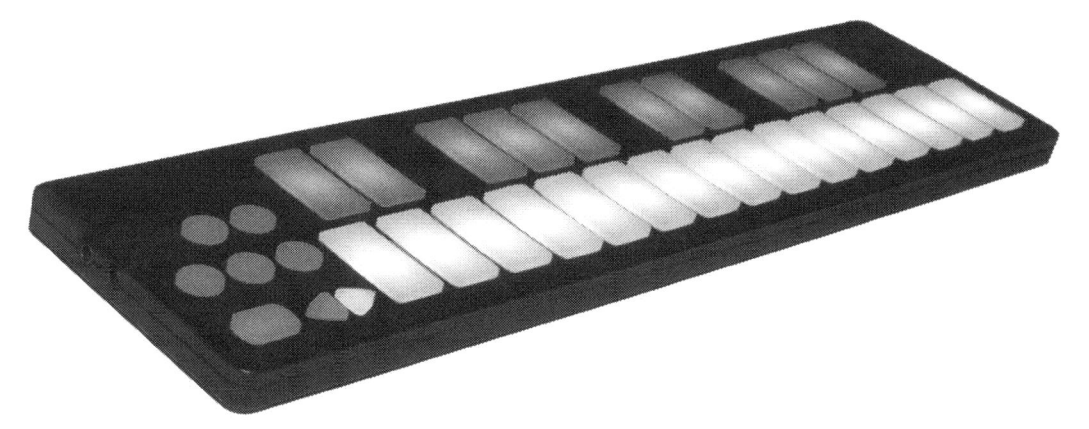

Keith McMillen's QuNexus controller provides twenty-five multiresponse keys that light in blue or white depending on what's happening. (Tom Ferguson, courtesy of Keith McMillen Instruments)

Introduced in early 2013, the Roli Seaboard Grand provides a soft, three-dimensional surface consisting of ridges arranged like the eighty-eight notes on an acoustic piano keyboard along with flat, ribbon-like bands that stretch across above and below the "keys." Each segment responds to velocity, pressure, and location, allowing the Seaboard Grand to transmit control data for pitch, volume, and timbre through its USB connector. It also provides an input jack for footswitch control. (Juan Trujillo)

Available from Synthesizers.com is the QKB15S Five-Octave Walnut Studio Keyboard. This one has some impressively flexible functionality, including the transmission of CVs, gates, and triggers via 1/4″ jacks along with MIDI, as well as built-in MIDI-to-CV conversion. Marvin Jones enjoys the QKB15S's ability to transmit MIDI notes polyphonically so he can play softsynths on his computer at the same time that he plays one or two voices from his modular synth. While in dual-voice mode the QKB15S outputs CVs and gates for two notes simultaneously, in single-voice mode it outputs CV and gate monophonically along with velocity and trigger so you get a short trigger in addition to an extended gate. That's very useful if you're working with a complex modular patch. The QKB15S also offers a keyboard split at octave 1 or 2. One drawback, however, is the QKB15S's lack of lefthand controls; there are no wheels or a joystick. Jones solves this issue with a Kurzweil ExpressionMate ribbon controller/MIDI processor (released in 1999) to add pitchbend and modulation output to his softsynths.

The French Connection from Analogue Systems physically models some of the performance characteristics found on the Ondes Martenot of the early twentieth century. (Stephi Clendinen, courtesy of Big City Music)

The newest keyboard among this arrangement of controllers and synths on a stand in Marvin Jones's studio appears at the *bottom*; the remainder are pure vintage. From the *top* down, there are an ARP Sequencer, a Paia model 6780 Organtua, a Sequential Circuits Prophet-5, and a Synthesizers.com QKB15S MIDI and CV keyboard controller. (Mark Vail)

Alternative Controllers

A keyboard isn't the only way to play a synthesizer. Synthesist/multi-instrumentalist/composer Kevin Fortune enjoys using alternative controllers. He believes the kind of controller you use not only directly influences the type of music you create, but it also can lead to "something less habitual and more spontaneous" than you'd otherwise play on a standard keyboard. Kevin is grateful that manufacturers and individuals are actively

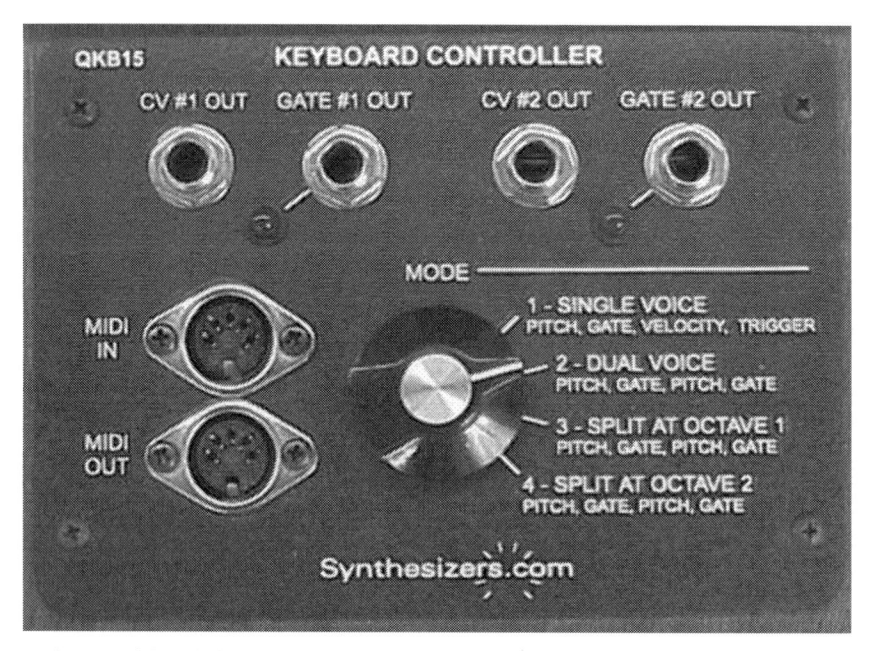

A closeup of the Synthesizers.com QKB15S keyboard's control panel, complete with two channels of 1/4" CV and gate outputs, MIDI in and out, and four-way mode selector. (Courtesy of Synthesizers.com)

creating more kinesthetic controllers because they lead to music that is different and more expressive.

The universe of alternative controllers is vast, and the following list is nowhere near comprehensive. It's intended to get you started on a path of discovery to find the alternative controller(s) with which you'll enjoy making music. And don't forget to explore the DIY controller market. Among the great resources are Electrotap, Eowave Electronic Arts & Sensor Systems, I-CubeX, and Livid Instruments, all of which offer plenty of tools for exploration in this field.

Wind Controllers

One of the most popular wind controllers, Nyle Steiner's Electronic Valve Instrument (EVI), has been around since the 1970s, is favored by many brass players who want to

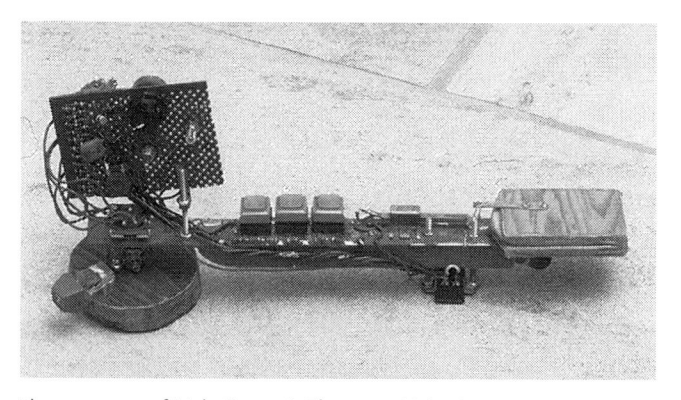

The prototype of Nyle Steiner's Electronic Valve Instrument, or EVI, which he assembled in 1973. It took a few years before he started making them to sell to others. (Courtesy of David Kean/The Audities Foundation)

play electronic sounds, and is still available in refurbished and occasionally new forms from Patchman Music. Nyle has handmade many EVIs himself and, in 1987, Akai manufactured the EVI1000 controller and EWV2000 synth module, which were based on a custom EVI and synth-in-a-briefcase system called the EVI Steinerphone.

Steiner's goal was to create an electronic instrument that would play as expressively as a solo acoustic instrument like the violin, trumpet, or oboe, allowing the performer to produce human-influenced vibrato and breath-controlled dynamics. The pre-MIDI EVI functioned so well at translating the performer's expressions into CVs and gates to drive analog synthesizers that Steiner was initially reluctant to rely purely on MIDI, considering it "an absolutely absurd idea because of the resolution of MIDI," he admits. "There are only 127 steps, and when you do a crescendo you can hear it zipper. But numerous manufacturers of current sound modules have been able to smooth the response by interpolating between steps, so now I totally embrace the idea of playing using MIDI alone."

Besides hosting the Nyle Steiner Homepage (www.patchmanmusic.com/NyleSteiner Homepage.html) and a comprehensive wind-controller website (www.patchmanmusic.com), Patchman Music's Matt Traum has played, collected, repaired, and programmed synth patches for EVIs since nearly the beginning. He's quick to share his enthusiasm about the EVI: "In addition to providing a huge pallet of sound possibilities for any brass player, Nyle's EVI has been a blessing to brass players who simply can't or don't want to play its acoustic counterparts."

Since 1987 Akai has manufactured several versions of another Nyle Steiner creation, the Electronic Wind Instrument (EWI), designed for woodwind players who want to explore the electronic-music universe. As of 2013 Akai offers two models: the EWI USB, which supports plug-and-play functionality on Mac and Windows computers; and the EWI4000S, which has MIDI output and a built-in analog-modeling synth engine.

Martin Hurni of Softwind Instruments has been producing a more traditional-looking woodwind controller, the Synthophone MIDI sax, for decades. He converts a Yamaha YAS-275 alto sax into a beautifully expressive and potent MIDI controller by hiding all of the electronics inside the instrument.

Although now you'll only find them on the used market, Yamaha used to make a line of woodwind-style MIDI controllers, including the WX5, WX7, and WX11. Their design

The original production version of the Steiner EVI was the first synthesizer controller built specifically for trumpet players. While Nyle Steiner designed a model for Akai to produce, those he's made himself are hand-built and each is in some way unique. Nyle also designed the Electronic Wind Instrument (EWI) for woodwind players. (Courtesy of David Kean/The Audities Foundation)

To provide an expressive voice for his Electronic Wind Instrument, Nyle Steiner designed a portable, two-oscillator, analog synth module during the mid-1980s. Kevin Fortune assembled five prototypes in attaché-sized flight cases for Nyle in 1984, including this one and the EWI that Kevin built for himself. (Courtesy of Kevin Fortune, © 2004 Heartcall Music)

was inspired by the pre-MIDI Lyricon. Not only can you buy refurbished WX controllers from Patchman Music, but Matt Traum also programs and sells wind-controller-specific patches for a wide range of synths. He recommends wind-controller players and those interested in taking it up check out the Wind Controller forum at groups.yahoo.com/group/windcontroller.

Touch Controllers

Some of the earliest alternative controllers came from Don Buchla, who has mostly avoided implementing standard organ-style keyboards on his synthesizers. Beginning with the first modular synthesizer he developed for the San Francisco Tape Music Center, Don incorporated some form of touchplate—two on the original 100 Series. "The input devices were an important aspect to that system," he explains. "They were all capacitance-sensitive touchplates, or resistance-sensitive in some cases, organized in various sorts of arrays."

Morton Subotnick, co-founder of the San Francisco Tape Music Center with Ramon Sender in 1961, describes Buchla's original touchplates as being "pressure-sensitive. One had 12 keys and you could tune it straight across the board. You could get a chromatic scale if you chose to. It had three control voltages per position. The other one had ten keys and one output per key. We often used this one to control the amplitudes of *musique concrète* tapes during playback. You could literally play ten loops with your fingers."

Serge's TKB, the Touch Activated Keyboard, serves as both a sequencer and analog programmer. Multipurpose module capabilities is a common theme within the Serge Modular universe, where modules typically function like Swiss Army Knives. This TKB belongs to Drew Neumann, whom you can witness demonstrating some of its capabilities with his six-panel Serge and massive Modcan A/Cyndustries modular systems at www.youtube.com/watch?v=AXgv7lidBcI. (Mark Vail)

Serge Tcherepnin, who began designing Serge Modular systems in 1974, also avoided organ-style keyboards. The Touch Activated Keyboard Sequencer (TKB) is the biggest and most complicated Serge module. Along with a matrix of sixteen columns by four rows of knobs, the TKB sports a couple of switches, thirty banana jacks, and a strip of sixteen touchplates along the bottom of the panel. Not only will the TKB function as an analog step sequencer, but you can also select a specific column by touching one of these sixteen buttons, making it a voltage programmer for triggering different notes or selecting a different arrangement of knob settings. Drew Neumann often turns to the TKB in his vintage six-panel Serge Modular system. He finds that not only is its touchplate pressure sensitive, but it's also unpredictably mood-sensitive. Its response can vary depending on the humidity, how dry your skin is, or the static-electricity and grounding conditions determined by whether you're wearing socks or going barefooted. "Sometimes," says Drew, "if you touch two TKB plates you'll get different intervals depending on which plates you touch; other times you'll get a garbled response. It depends on your overall resistance, the mood of the machine that day, or whatever."

Numerous touch-activated controllers have appeared in the Eurorack modular format. Pressure Points from Make Noise is a four-column controller with each column providing a pulse-wave-like squiggle of copper at the bottom that senses finger pressure. There are three knobs to set CV levels to be output by each step. You can chain up to four Pressure Points together and with Make Noise's Brains module you can convert one or two Pressure Points into a four- or eight-step analog sequencer. Tony Rolando of Make Noise also created René, described as "the world's first and only Cartesian Sequencer." René features two 4 × 4 matrices on its front panel, one of touchplate buttons and the other of knobs. It has four clock inputs, two CV inputs, and outputs for quantized voltages, non-quantized voltages, and two gate/pulse streams.

Synthwerks offers several varieties of force-sensing touchplate controller modules for Eurorack. The smallest is the FSR-1N, with a single finger-size pad; the equivalent of four of these make up the FSR-4, available in Classic (through-hole circuitry) and MkII (SMT and thus shallower) versions. Four larger force-sensing squares appear on one of the two modules in Synthwerks' FSR-4C/B package. You can touch the squares with your fin-

A potent pair of Eurorack-format controllers from Make Noise: The touchplate half of the René Cartesian Sequencer on the *left* and the Pressure Points touchplate controller on the *right*. (Mark Vail)

Tony Rolando of Make Noise poses with a Eurorack modular system containing some of his noise toys and controllers at the January 2010 NAMM show. (Mark Vail)

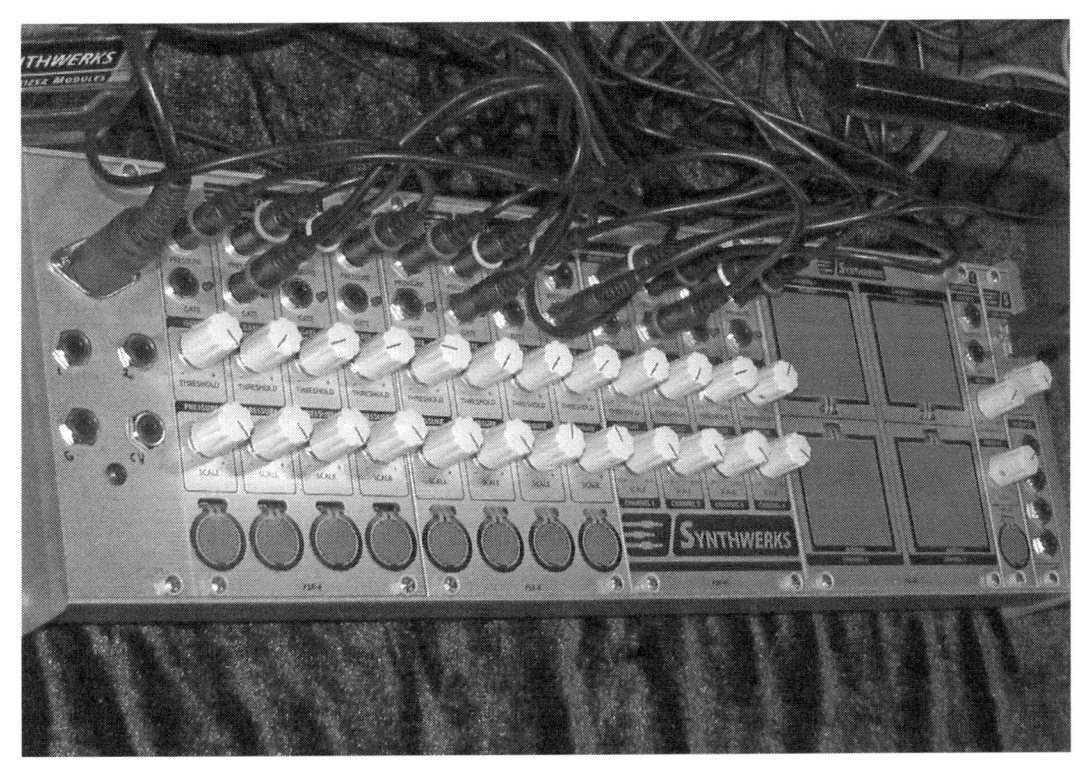

On display at the January 2011 NAMM was this tabletop Eurorack controller panel filled with Synthwerks modules. Synthwerks designer James Husted and engineer Steve Turnidge both refer to the package as a "skiff" and tell me its enclosure consists of scrap Plexiglas and spare Schroff rails. From *left to right* you see a custom module that connects via a seven-pin DIN connector to the main modular cabinet for power and to conduct four busses of CV and gate signals; two FSR-4 MkII force-sensing touch-plate modules, clearly the newer version made with surface-mount technology for a shallower profile, not the Classic version with through-hole components and socketed ICs because it would be far too deep to fit in this enclosure; a dual-component FSR-4C/B combo, comprising the output section and a four-pad sensor module; an FSR-1N single-channel Force-Sensing Resistor module; and a Lamp-1 module, which combines a four-way mult with a dimmable gooseneck LED lamp that isn't visible here. (Mark Vail)

gers or cover them with included rubber pad overlays and strike them with drumsticks without damaging them.

Within BugBrand's version of the FracRak universe—banana connectors instead of 3.5mm jacks—comes the BugBrand CTL1 Touch Panel. It combines four touchplate "keys" with four-step sequencing and Tom Bugs's special approach to clock-sync, which involves combining clocking signals from multiple sources to create a clock train that's synced to a master yet avoids repeating a 4/4 pattern ad nauseam. Tom admits his interest in metric variety comes from his drumming background and says he loves odd polyrhythms.

Beyond modular-specific controllers, there's a wide range of touch-activated alternative controllers from which to choose. Don Buchla extended his application of touchplates in 1990 with Thunder, which offers serious performance programmability and twenty-five touch-sensitive performance pads, some of which can be split into two or three different response sections. Its configuration of touchplates also appears within the Buchla Series 200e as the Model 222e Multi-Dimensional Kinesthetic Input Port. Since Thunder, Buchla touchplates have not only been pressure-sensitive, but many of them also track the position of a finger across their surfaces.

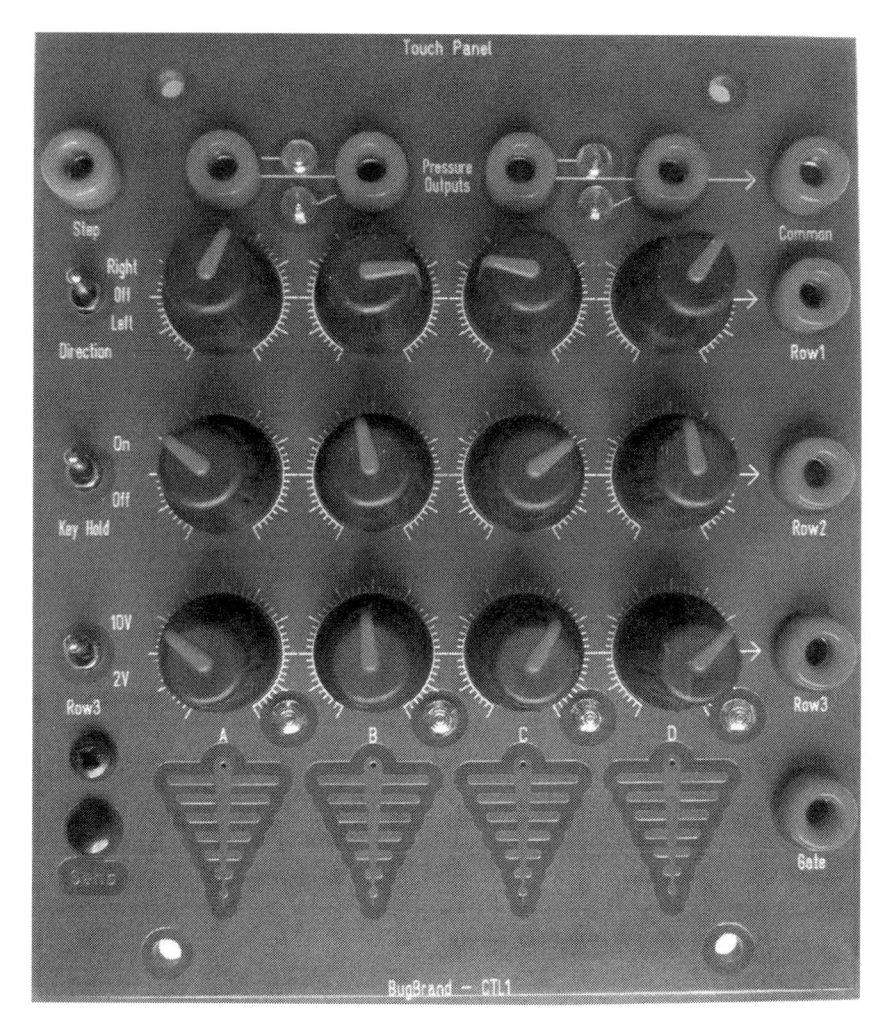

The BugBrand CTL1 Touch Panel is a FracRak-format module that combines touchplate and sequencing capabilities. Its four tactile "keys" generate CV output signals whose voltage levels depend on how much skin comes into contact with the keys themselves, also commonly referred to as "pressure." Touching a key also results in the CTL1 transmitting gate and CV signals to common outputs and activating one of the CTL1's four stages—identified as Columns A through D. Each stage transmits three CVs out of independent Row 1 through 3 outputs, their voltage levels determined by the corresponding knob in that row. A two-way switch allows you to set Row 3's knobs to cover a range of either two or ten volts. Pipe in a clock signal and the CTL1 becomes a four-step sequencer, allowing you to switch to left or right playback direction, or stop sequencing altogether. If you touch a stage key while the sequencer is engaged, the CTL1 will stay on that column as long as you keep touching the key. It exclusively bears banana jacks, which is common for nearly all audio, CV, and gate connections throughout the BugBrand module range. (Courtesy of BugBrand)

If you'd prefer a surface that's stretched much farther, consider the Haken Continuum Fingerboard. Its control surface feels like silk and looks like a wide ribbon with alternating scarlet and maroon stripes. Designed by Lippold Haken, the Continuum goes beyond two dimensions. Its low-friction surface responds to finger positions from side to side (x-factor) and front to back (y-factor), as well as the exerted pressure (z-factor)—polyphonically for up to sixteen fingers! The Continuum is available in two sizes—about as broad as four- and eight-octave keyboards—and later models come with a built-in synth chip for stand-alone operation. All Continuums have MIDI I/O. Optionally available is the Continuum Voltage Converter (CVC), which outputs gate and control voltages for

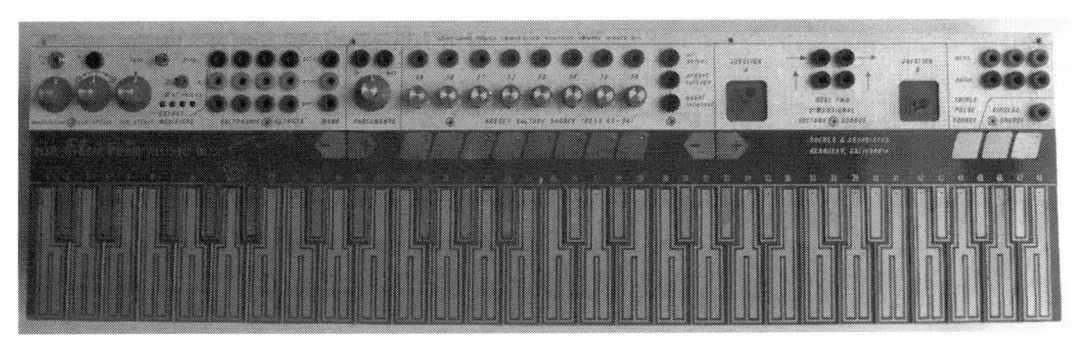

The 1970s-era Buchla Model 219 Compound Touch-Controlled Voltage Source has forty-eight touch-sensitive surfaces configured like keys on a piano. It can generate control voltages monophonically and polyphonically—up to four voices—and the key pads respond to pressure. The 219 also has a separate eight-key section of independently tunable keys, two joysticks for single-point control of two variables each, three keys with independent pulse and pressure outputs, adjustable portamento, a bipolar CV output applicable for pitchbends and vibrato, and a buffered digital output to interface with external digital processors. (Rick Smith, Buchla Restorations, www.electricmusicbox.com)

the x, y, and z coordinates over four voice channels, allowing you to control analog synths that have CV and gate inputs.

Gary Chang is a devoted Continuum user who finds it a very expressive controller that's easy to play in monophonic mode, but more challenging to control polyphonically when all three axes are simultaneously active. Disabling one of the axes makes its response more manageable. Chang also reports that traditional keyboard fingerings can feel

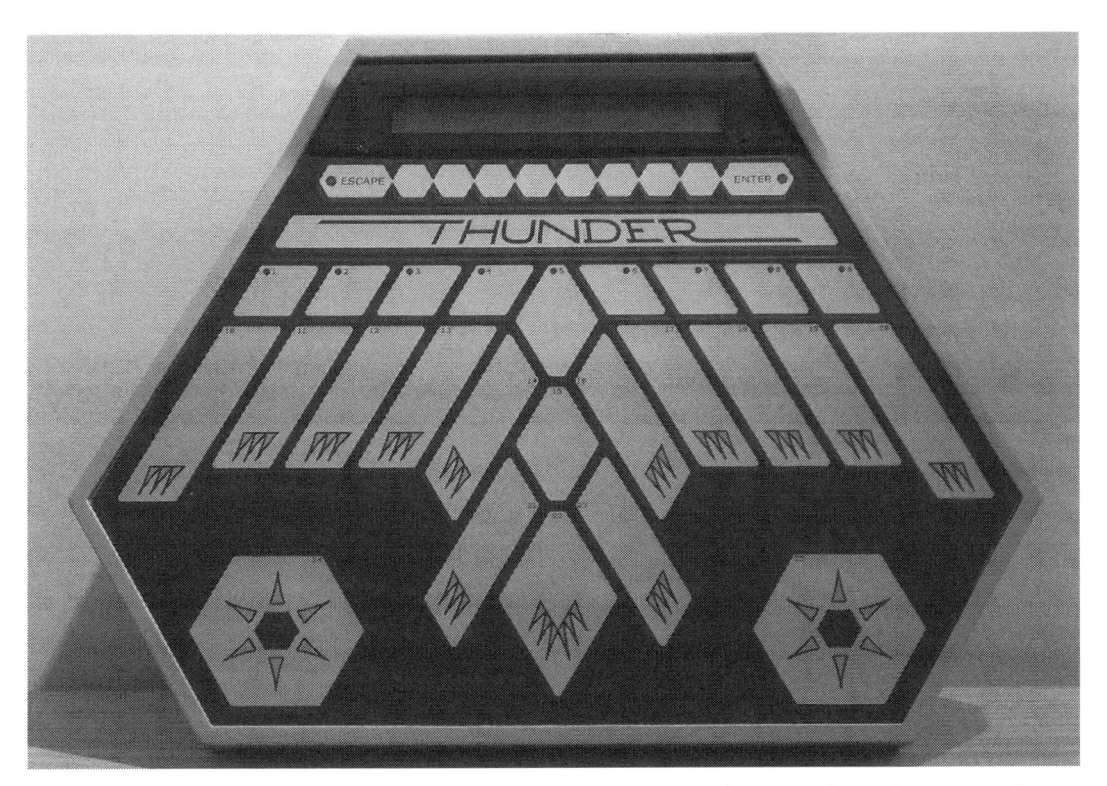

Buchla's Thunder MIDI controller came out in 1990. You can split thirteen of its twenty-five performance pads to transmit two independent MIDI notes per pad, and you can split another pair three ways, allowing a total transmission of forty-two different notes. Every performance pad senses both velocity and pressure and can transmit MIDI control change commands and other data along with a specific note on any of the sixteen MIDI channels. There's internal memory for eight Thunder configurations, and its built-in "riff" function allows the storage of ninety-nine notes divisible into eight riffs. You can create riff sequences ahead of time or capture and loop them improvisationally during performance. (Courtesy of David Kean/The Audities Foundation)

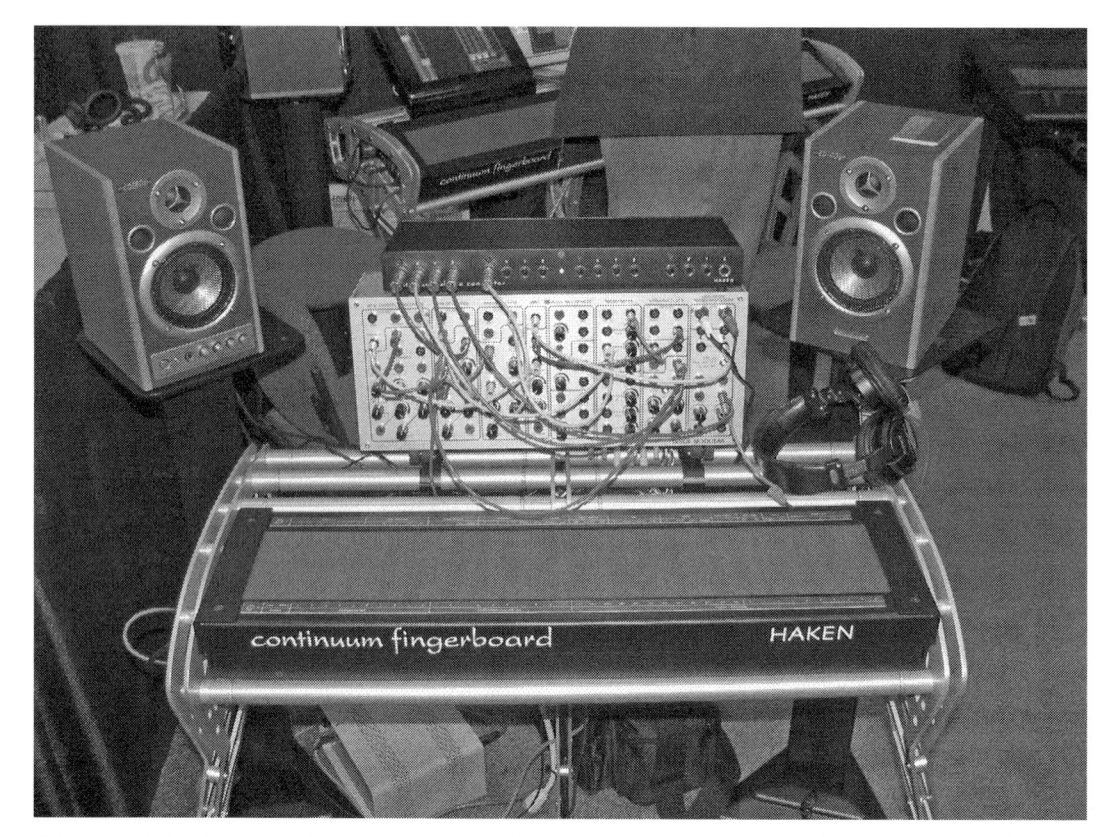

A half-size Haken Audio Continuum and its Control Voltage Converter (*top*) set up with an STS Serge Modular Blue Fun Station panel on top of a prototype of the Continuum Stand—designed by Sarah Dobbin of Fathom Labs and Edmund Eagan of Twelfth Root—at the January 2007 NAMM show. (Mark Vail)

awkward since such gestures on a flat surface offer no physical feedback like a mechanical keyboard does. However, he says the Continuum's Rounding function, which quantizes the initial pitch, can help. "I especially appreciate the Continuum's build quality," Gary adds. "It's built for the ages, which is important because I see the Continuum as a lifetime commitment."

Another groundbreaking alternative controller that offers rewarding musical expressivity is the Eigenlabs Eigenharp. There are three Eigenharp models to choose from: the original, full-size Eigenharp Alpha, the mid-sized Eigenharp Tau, and the smaller, educational-oriented Eigenharp Pico. Performers can carry any of them around during performance. The larger Alpha and Tau each come with a supportive neck strap and have a "cello spike" if you'd rather stay in place and play the instrument like a double bass. As for the Pico, it's small enough to hold like a clarinet. One of the Eigenharp's controllers is a breath pipe with an interchangeable mouthpiece for shared use. Another is at least one ribbon, depending on the model. You play notes using the Eigenharp's keys, each of which senses velocity, side-to-side finger movements, and pressure. Pressure sensing is polyphonic for individual note expression. The Eigenharp Alpha and Tau connect via a multiconductor cable to a Basestation interface, which comes in Standard and Pro versions. The Basestation is where you'll find all of the interfacing connections.

A host computer—Macintosh or Windows PC—generates sounds for the Eigenharps, each of which comes with physical models of cello and clarinet, synthesis and sample-playback engines, a 6GB collection of multisampled Steinway grand piano and Rhodes

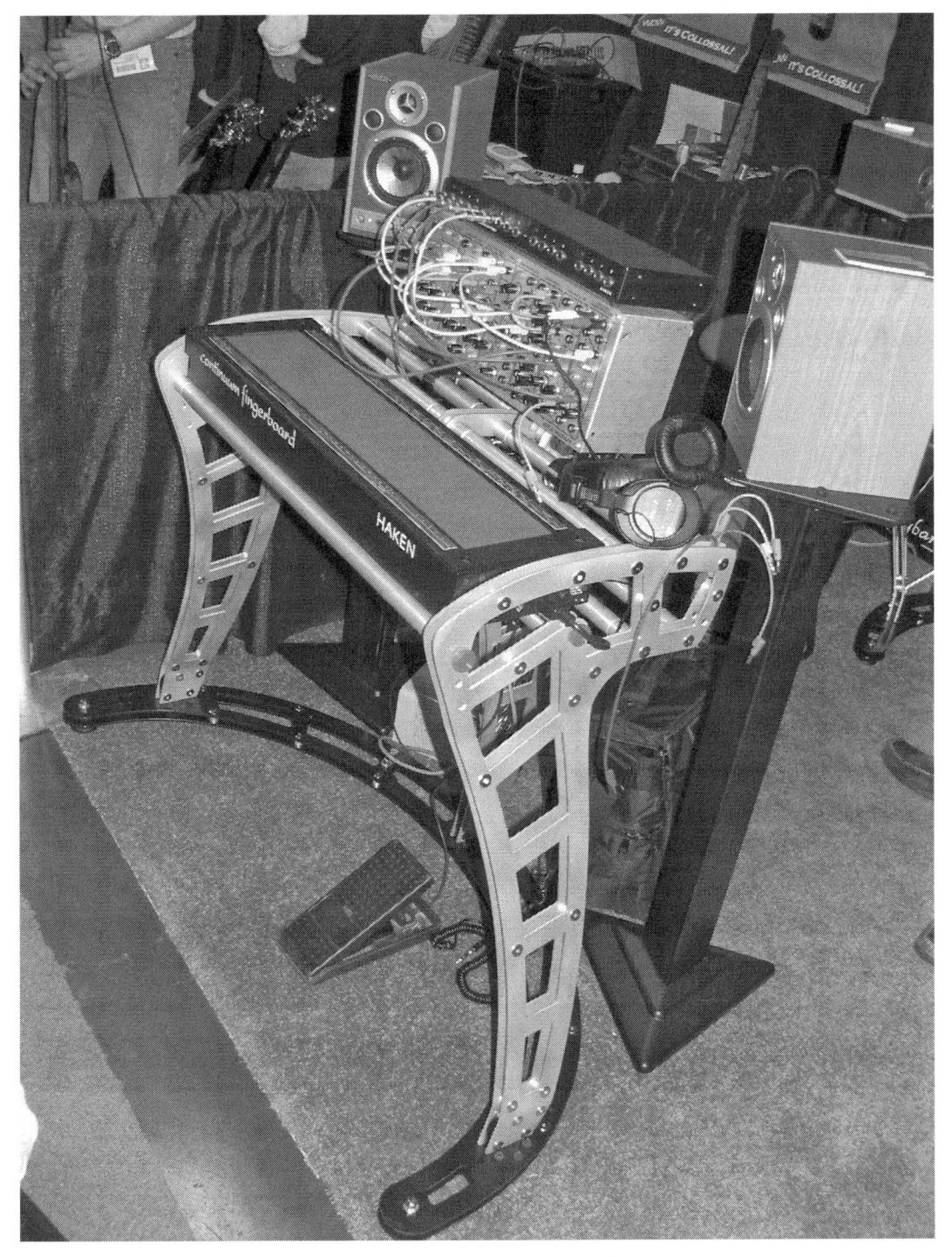

The same Haken Audio Continuum setup viewed from the side. (Mark Vail)

and Wurlitzer electric pianos, and 1,500 drum and percussion loops. An Eigenharp can also trigger user sounds and software instruments. According to Eigenharp designer John Lambert, most of its players use Ableton Live, Steinberg Cubase, Apple Logic, or another host for AU and VST plug-ins. The Eigenharps allow extensive MIDI control and provide a routing matrix to eke the best out of the MIDI protocol. Lambert has been working with Steinberg so that the Eigenharps can drive their Note Expression feature via MIDI as well, supporting numerous ways of dealing with individual note expressivity

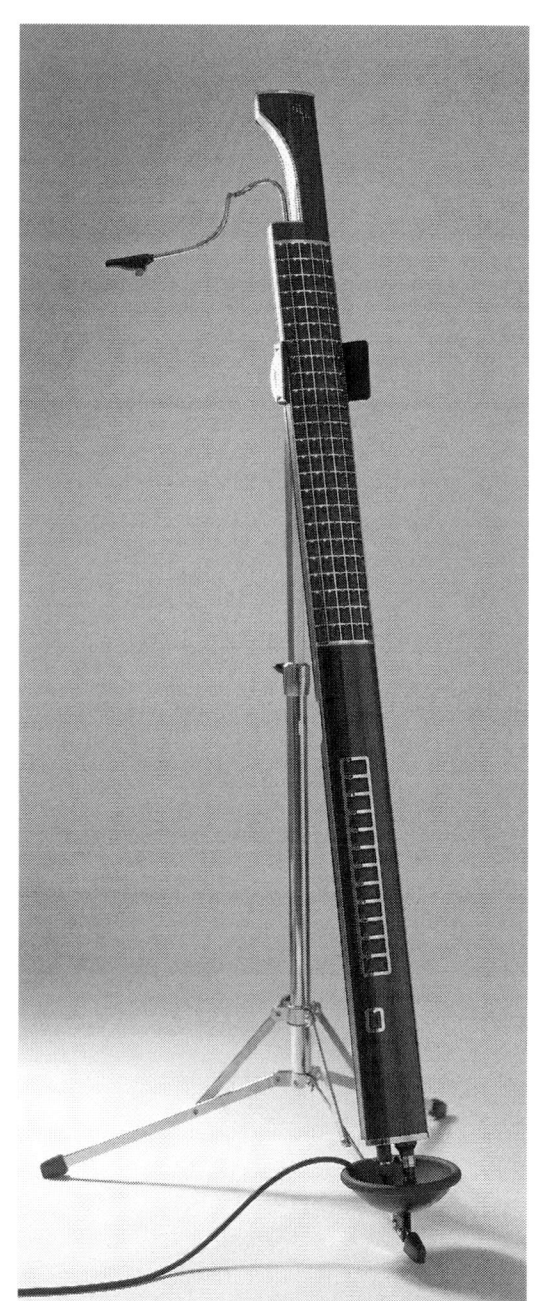

Eigenlabs's flagship Eigenharp Alpha, shown resting on its optional stand. The Alpha sports 120 note keys, twelve percussion-trigger keys, and two ribbons. (Courtesy of Eigenlabs.com)

including polyphonic aftertouch and channelized notes. Eigenlabs is also working on an extensive Open Sound Control (OSC) networking implementation to go with MIDI I/O. Jordan Rudess raves about Eigenharps, pointing out that they have the most responsive keys of any instrument he's played and a lightening-fast touch response.

Another beautiful and powerful touch controller, this one featuring 150 rectangular walnut keys arranged in a five-row by thirty-column matrix laid within a 29" × 8" × 1-1/4" block of Washington alder and weighing 4.6 pounds, is the Madrona Labs Soundplane Model A. Each key senses velocity, position, and pressure, and the controller, which has a USB jack for direct connection to a computer, scans the playing surface with high bandwidth at a rate of 975 samples per second for precise control. Separate modes allow

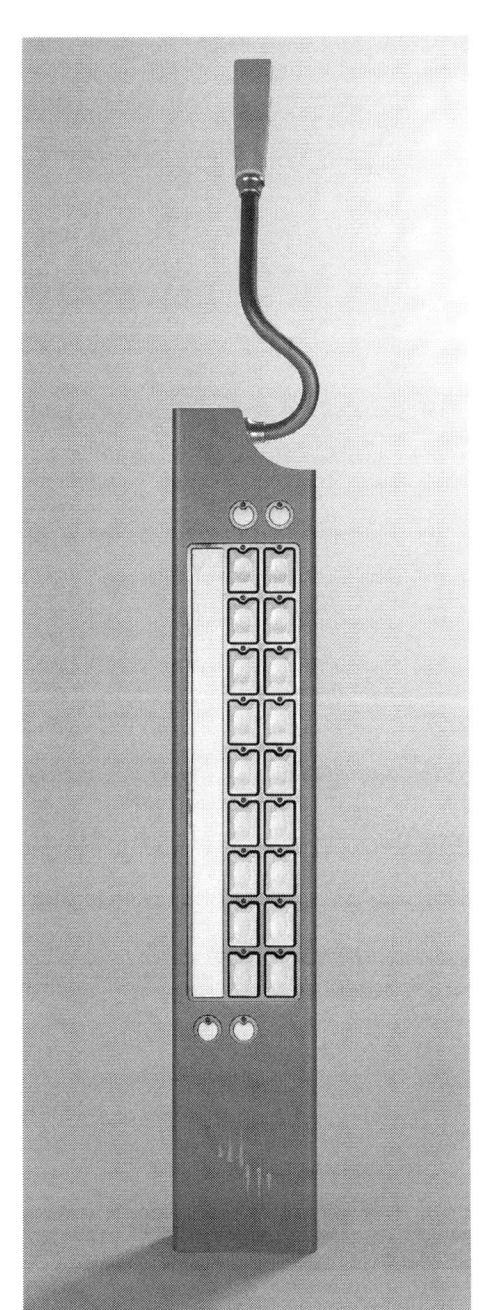

The most affordable Eigenlabs instrument is the Pico, which has eighteen keys, four mode buttons, and a ribbon. Although you can't tell from the photo, this is a Pink Pico, which costs a bit more than those with silver or black finishes. (Courtesy of Eigenlabs.com)

the Soundplane to sense individual key activity or the entire surface as a continuous controller. The Soundplane comes with Mac software that converts performance data into MIDI and OSC, Madrona's Aalto patchable softsynth, and Max/MSP objects. Software for Windows and Linux are in the works.

Drum-machine pioneer Roger Linn's LinnStrument is a pressure-sensitive, multi-touch USB controller that comes with different overlays that have raised tactile ridges between note regions. The Piano Overlay has virtual upper and lower manuals that stretch over three octaves. Choose the Guitar/Grid Overlay and you'll have eight virtual strings along a virtual fretboard on which you can finger chords. Other overlays include the Drum Pad with larger squares and the Hex with hexagonally shaped keys. Once you touch the

The Synthesizer

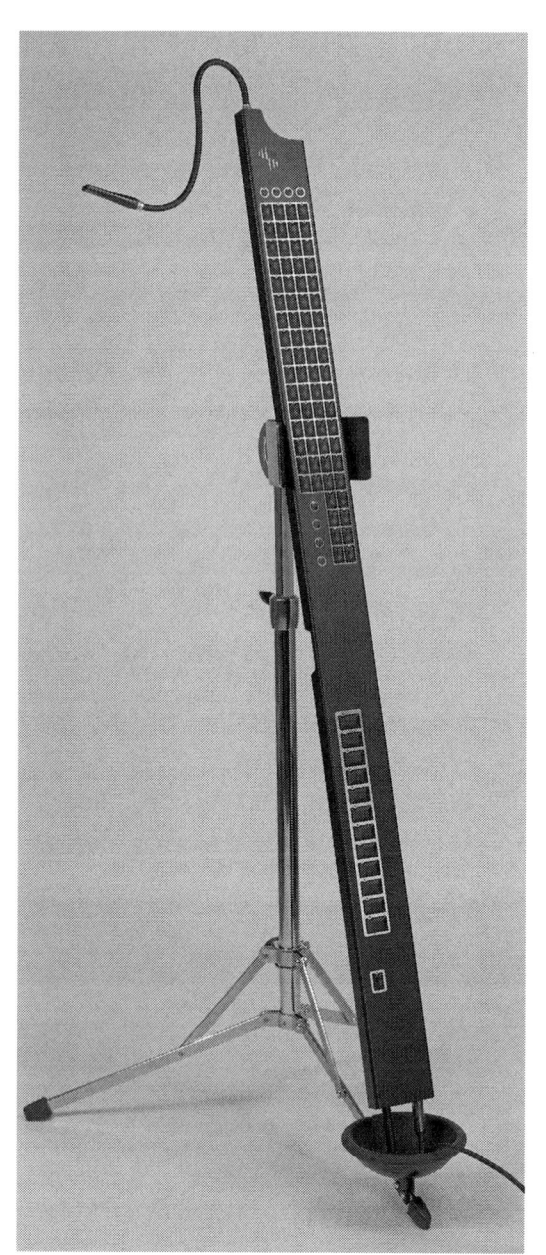

Eigenlabs's Eigenharp Tau represents the midrange of their instrument lineup, having seventy-two note keys, twelve percussion-trigger keys, and one ribbon. The stand shown here is optional. (Courtesy of Eigenlabs.com)

A view of the connection panel of an Eigenlabs Basestation Pro, revealing multipin jacks for the Eigenharp and an Extension, MIDI in and out, a USB 2.0 jack for connection to a computer, two 1/4" input jacks for footswitches, two sets of 1/4" jacks to serve as inputs and outputs for foot pedals, and a grounded IEC AC power jack. (Courtesy of Eigenlabs.com)

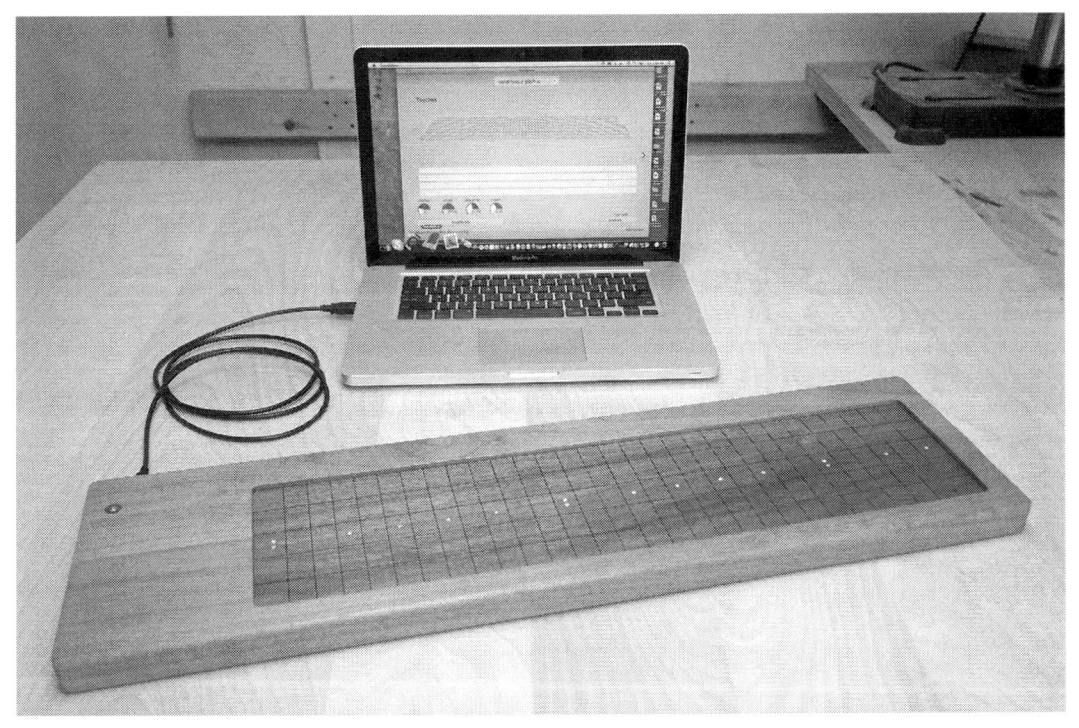

Other than its high-speed pressure sensor, high-bandwidth DSP computer, and related electronic hardware, Madrona Lab's Soundplane Model A USB controller—shown here connected to a MacBook Pro running calibration software—is made of wood to give it the feel of an acoustic instrument. (Courtesy of Madrona Labs)

LinnStrument's surface, you can move your fingers horizontally to polyphonically add vibrato to individual notes and bend their pitches, move them vertically to vary the timbre of individual notes, and vary how hard you press each finger to vary the volume of notes independently. Each overlay also provides special performance capabilities. For example, in Guitar/Grid Overlay mode, your initial touches trigger notes at the pitches you'd hear according to the frets on a guitar, but then the virtual frets disappear and you can slide your fingers to new positions to make a new chord.

Front-panel buttons allow you to change sounds, transpose by octaves, vary the output volume, and more, and there are two assignable 1/4" pedal inputs. The LinnStrument

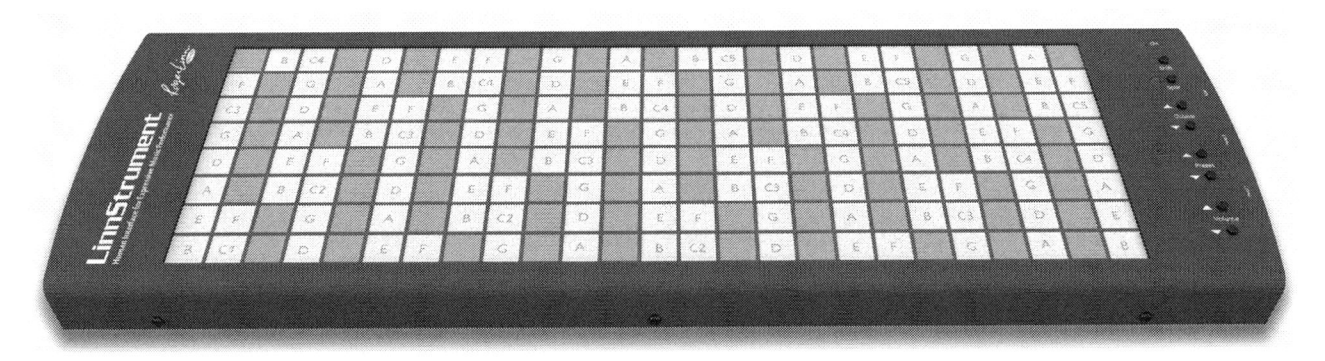

Roger Linn's LinnStrument comes with six overlays—clear, thin plastic sheets with raised, silk-screened ridges between the note regions—to match the controller's display modes. Shown here is the Note Grid overlay, with notes laid out in a guitar neck-like configuration except that there's equal spacing between each semitone and the notes overlap in two octaves. Other overlays mimic a guitar fretboard, two overlapping forty-three-note virtual keyboards (C to F#), a 12 × 4 drum-pad matrix, and two hexagonal configurations turned ninety degrees from each other. The multitouch LinnStrument independently tracks movements of numerous fingers on its surface in three dimensions: pressure, left-right, and forward-backward. These motions are typically assigned to control volume, pitch, and timbre, respectively, providing expressive manipulation for each note independently. (Permission to copy freely granted by Roger Linn Design)

requires a Mac or Windows computer to generate sounds, connecting to either platform via USB. It comes with sound-generating software that will also generate MIDI data and OSC messages, and allow you to customize the LinnStrument's organization of virtual keys, configure custom scales, create a virtual pitchbend ribbon, and assign a space that you can rhythmically touch to retrigger guitar strums or arpeggiate notes in a chord.

Another ultraflexible USB pad controller comes in the form of the QuNeo from Keith McMillen Instruments. Equal in size to the original Apple iPad, the QuNeo has a controller surface covered with a variety of sensors, each illuminated with an LED capable of glowing in 251 different colors. There are sixteen square trigger pads capable of sensing 127 velocity levels along with pressure and location on an x/y axis. Two rotary sensors measure the angle and pressure of touch. Nine touch-sensitive ribbons function like sliders for controlling fader levels or effects parameters, and each is lit with multiple LEDs to make them work as level meters. Seventeen pressure-sensitive buttons that serve as switches are intelligently located around the other surface controllers. You can program all of the QuNeo's controllers to respond according to your needs, and it comes with presets, templates, and scripts for applications including Ableton Live, Serato Scratch Live, Native Instruments Traktor and Battery, Apple Logic Pro, and Propellerhead Reason. Add the Rogue, which attaches to the QuNeo's underside, and you now have a wireless controller with a sixty-meter range. It also powers the QuNeo for six to eight hours of continuous operation.

The 2010 release of Apple's iPad, its popularity, and certain iOS applications may have resulted in the JazzMutant Lemur being discontinued. Lemur is a programmable, multitouch, touchscreen device with multitasking capabilities and a gorgeous display, and it complies with the OSC networking protocol. It works really well with Ableton Live, Symbolic Sound's Kyma, Native Instruments Reaktor, Cycling '74 Max/MSP, Super-Collider, and many other applications. Fortunately, Liine introduced an iOS version of Lemur for the iPad in late 2011.

Within the multitude of alternative controllers developed over the years, one of the more deceptively simple but potent for creating step sequences (among many activities,

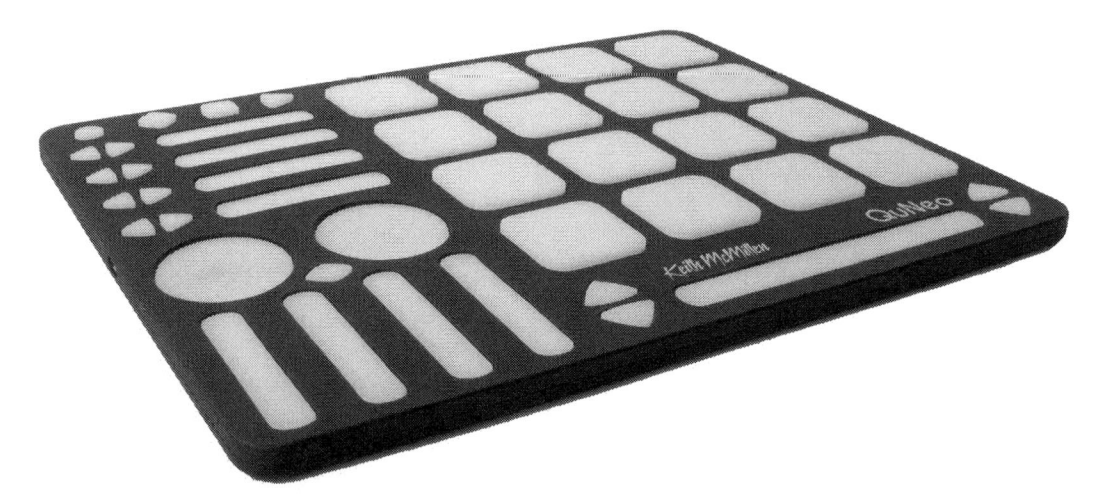

The QuNeo from Keith McMillen Instruments measures a mere 9.45" across by 7.28" deep by 0.39" high and weighs only fourteen ounces. (Tom Ferguson, courtesy of Keith McMillen Instruments)

Choosing Your Synthesizer(s)

Although it's been discontinued, the JazzMutant Lemur introduced touchscreen capabilities similar to those later provided by the Apple iPad. (Courtesy of Stantum Technologies)

including lighting control, gaming, and whatever task you want to create via open-source software) is the Monome. It's a tabletop box that typically has a grid of sixty-four or more backlit silicone-rubber buttons—"keypads" in Monome-speak—and a USB port for connection to a computer. Brian Crabtree made the original prototype in 2001 as a controller for Cycling '74's Max/MSP. He teamed with his wife, Kelli Cain, a year later to begin production of Monomes, including models with 128, 256, and 512 keypads and one containing an accelerometer for motion detection.

A variety of Monome clones has also appeared, sometimes fortified with continuous controllers such as LED-encircled rotary encoders that also serve as pushbuttons. Some were specifically designed for Ableton Live. For example, Livid Instruments offers a lineup that includes the Code, Block, Ohm64, and Builder DIY. In 2008, Yamaha introduced the Tenori-On, which combines a Monome-like matrix of light-flashing buttons with

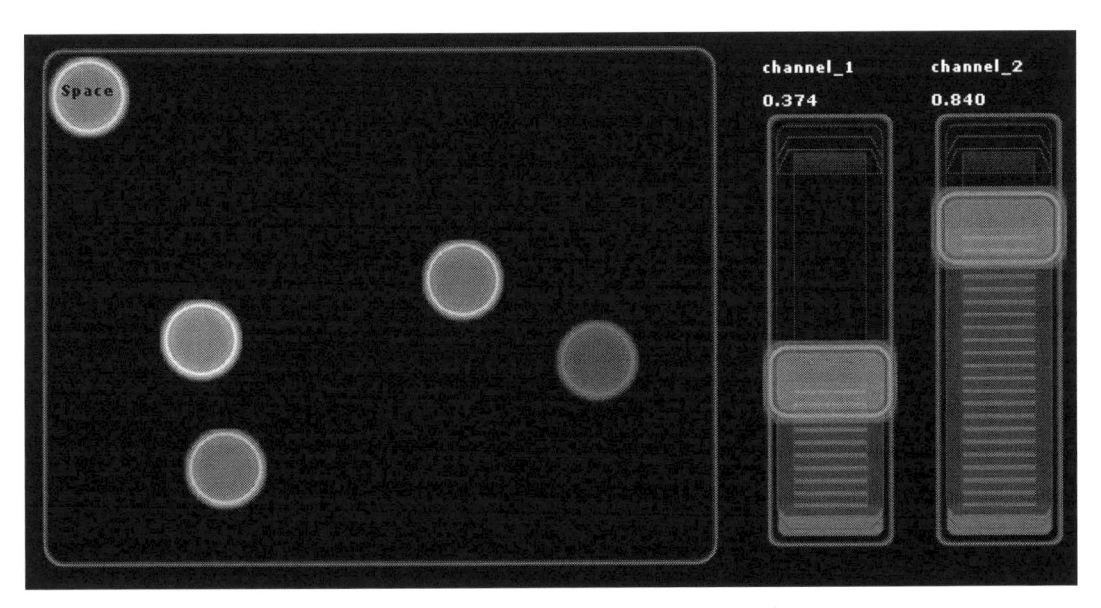

A screenshot from the JazzMutant Lemur. (Screenshot courtesy of Stantum Technologies)

Gary Chang demonstrates a 16-x-16 Monome. (Mark Vail)

built-in sound generation, sampling, and transmission of MIDI data for controlling external gear. There's now an iOS version for iPad, iPhone, and iPod Touch called the TNR-i.

Not only has Ableton encouraged other companies to design Live controllers with similarities to the Monome, but they've even collaborated with two manufacturers to design and make them. Novation's Launchpad combines a multifunction sixty-four-keypad grid, eight assignable buttons, and eight fixed-function buttons—all of them backlit—on the compact surface of a device that weighs less than two pounds and measures 9.45″ × 9.45″ and only 0.79″ deep. It's USB-powered, and there are modes specifically for Live plus two user memories for custom keypad assignments. You can combine as many as six Launchpads to work together simultaneously, and the Launchpad supports Novation's Automap function for controlling softsynths and other programs besides Live.

The second manufacturer is Akai, which makes two Live-focused controllers: the APC20 and APC40. Measuring 11.61″ × 13.11″ × 2.24″ and weighing 3.8 pounds, the APC20 is slightly bigger and heavier than the Launchpad. While the latter has a bigger grid—eight rows by eight columns to the APC20's five rows and eight columns—the APC20 includes nine faders, one for each column plus a master level fader, along with a Cue Level knob and significantly more function buttons. The APC40 offers a five-by-eight grid of backlit keypads alongside gobs of knobs, buttons, sliders, and a DJ-style fader. It measures 16.88″ × 13.13″ × 2.62″ and weighs 5.8 pounds.

Numerous other controllers have emerged for Ableton Live. For example, the Faderfox LV3 is smaller than many other Live controllers, yet it squeezes eight sliders, four rotary-encoder/buttons, twenty-four programmable buttons, two joysticks, and more onto

An Akai APC40 controller connected to an Apple MacBook Pro running Ableton Live software in Gary Chang's studio. (Mark Vail)

its calculator-sized control panel. It measures 7.1″ × 4.1″ × 2.8″, weighs about three-quarters of a pound, and connects to a computer and draws power via USB. The LV3 will function with other programs and Faderfox offers a variety of similarly sized controllers geared for different applications.

Hand-Held Controllers

Electronic controllers that you hold in your hands and shake or move about to make music date back to 1986. That was the year Palmtree Instruments introduced Airdrums, a tabletop MIDI controller wired to two tubes that contain sensors for detecting motion in any of six directions. The control box transmits six triggers per tube for playing notes, starting sequences, and generating other MIDI data depending on user assignments. Airdrums started the ball rolling in the development of controllers such as the Nintendo Wii, which some contemporary performers use as a softsynth controller.

Also in 1986, computer-music pioneer Max Mathews (1926–2011) introduced the Radio Baton, which consists of a pair of mallets with built-in radio transmitters and a table surface beneath which are five antennas. As a computer loaded with Max's conductor software follows movements of the mallets above the table, it generates MIDI output for controlling the volume, timbre, and rhythm of a sequencer playing music.

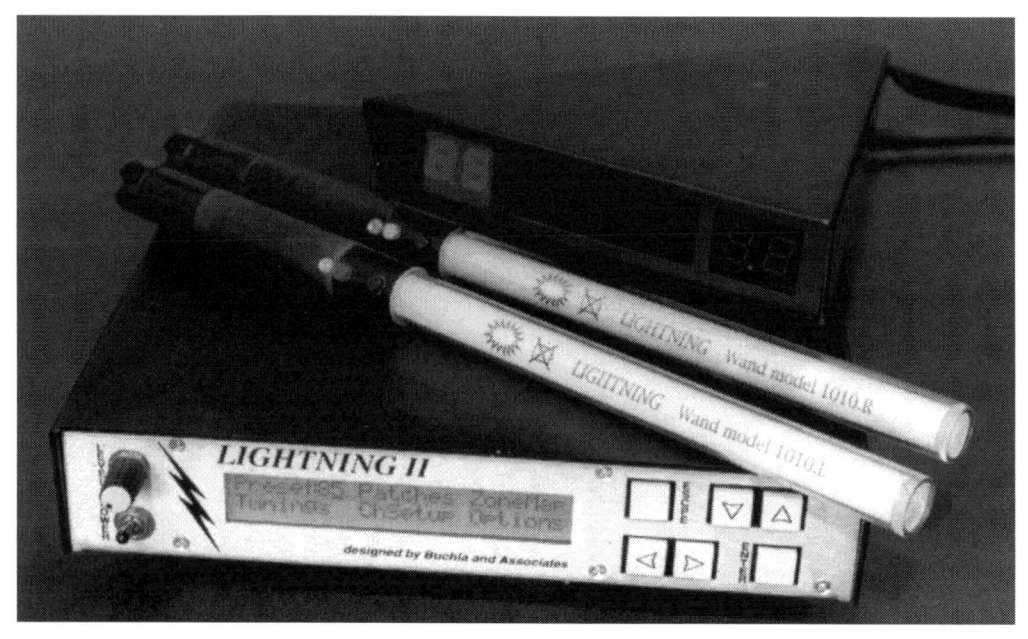

Imagine if the batons held by a member of the ground crew to safely direct an aircraft into a gate at an airport controlled the pitch, timbre, and other aspects of sound generated by a synthesizer. That's essentially what Don Buchla's Lightning does. This is the Lightning II system, complete with the triangular, optic-sensing head, a pair of wireless, infrared-transmitting wands, and the half-rack control module, which housed a thirty-two-voice synthesizer. Lightning II was introduced in 1996, later to be replaced by the Lightning III. (Courtesy of Buchla and Associates)

Don Buchla introduced Lightning in 1991. It has two wireless wands that contain infrared transmitters, a remote infrared-tracking head that can be mounted on a mic stand and senses positions of and gestures made with the wands, and the third component, a half-rack-sized box that contains electronic circuits. You can program the receiver that tracks wand movements to perform actions such as note selection, pitchbends, stereo panning, and volume. Originally Lightning only transmitted MIDI, but the current version—the Buchla Lightning III—transmits MIDI and also has a built-in thirty-two-voice synthesizer.

Struck Controllers

Numerous individuals and companies have made electronic controllers and instruments for drummers and percussionists since Joe Pollard developed the Syndrum in 1977. Soon to follow were the U.S.-built Star Instruments Synare series from 1975 to 1983 and the British-made Simmons pads and sound generators.

Plenty of drum and percussion controllers and systems have come and gone since MIDI arrived in 1983. Among the manufacturers to develop full-fledged electronic kits are Alesis, 2Box Music Applications, Roland, and Yamaha. All of them make modules to go with the drum pads and related controllers—cymbals, too—but of course since they're MIDI controllers you can trigger any MIDI sound generator(s) of your choice.

Drum controllers don't have to look like drum sets. Over the years there have been many great percussion controllers and instruments, whether you hit them with sticks—Roland's Octapad series and the Korg Wavedrum come to mind—or your hands—i.e., Roland's Handsonic HPD-15. One manufacturer has been making percussion controllers since the mid 1980s in Chicopee, Massachusetts, originally as Kat and now as Alter-

Choosing Your Synthesizer(s)

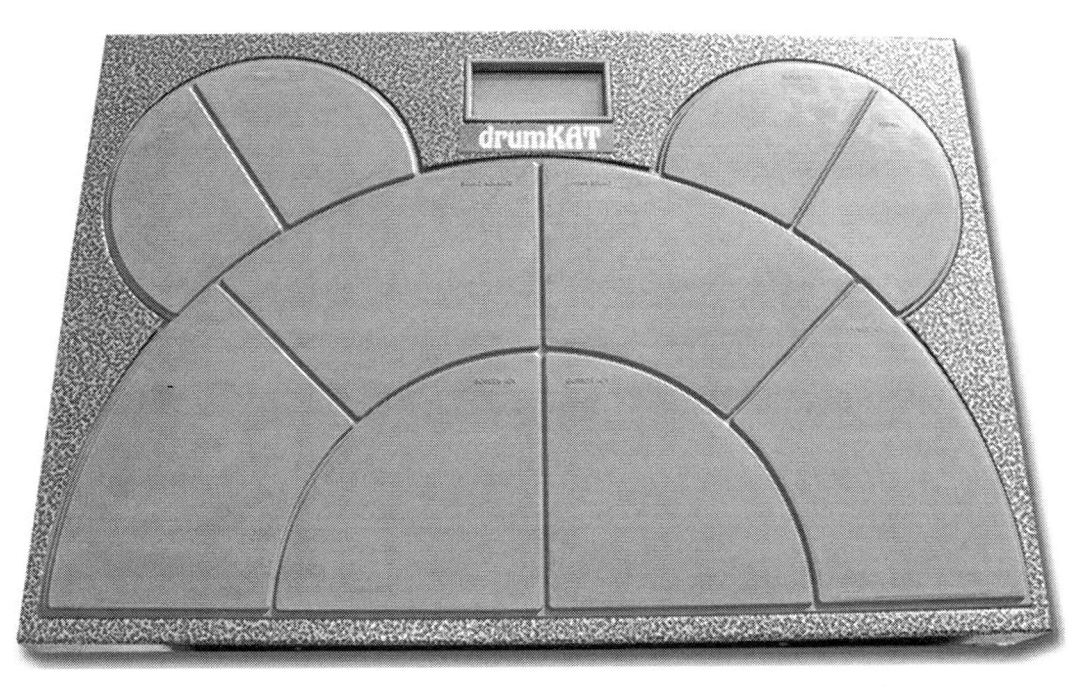

Alternate Mode's programmable drumKat controller allows you to trigger MIDI synths to play drum, percussion, or whatever sounds you choose. You can program individual pads to transmit single notes, melodic lines, or up to eight notes at a time. If you'd prefer a complete instrument, there's the drumKat Turbo KS, which has a built-in Kurzweil synthesizer. (Courtesy of Alternate Mode, Inc.)

nate Mode. Their ten-pad drumKat is an expressive controller that has gone through numerous updates since its early '90s introduction. The bigger and more extensive trapKat provides twenty-four trigger pads across its 41.5" × 19" surface. Both supply user memories and lots of programmability in a single unit that's far easier to tear down, transport, and set up than an entire electronic drum kit.

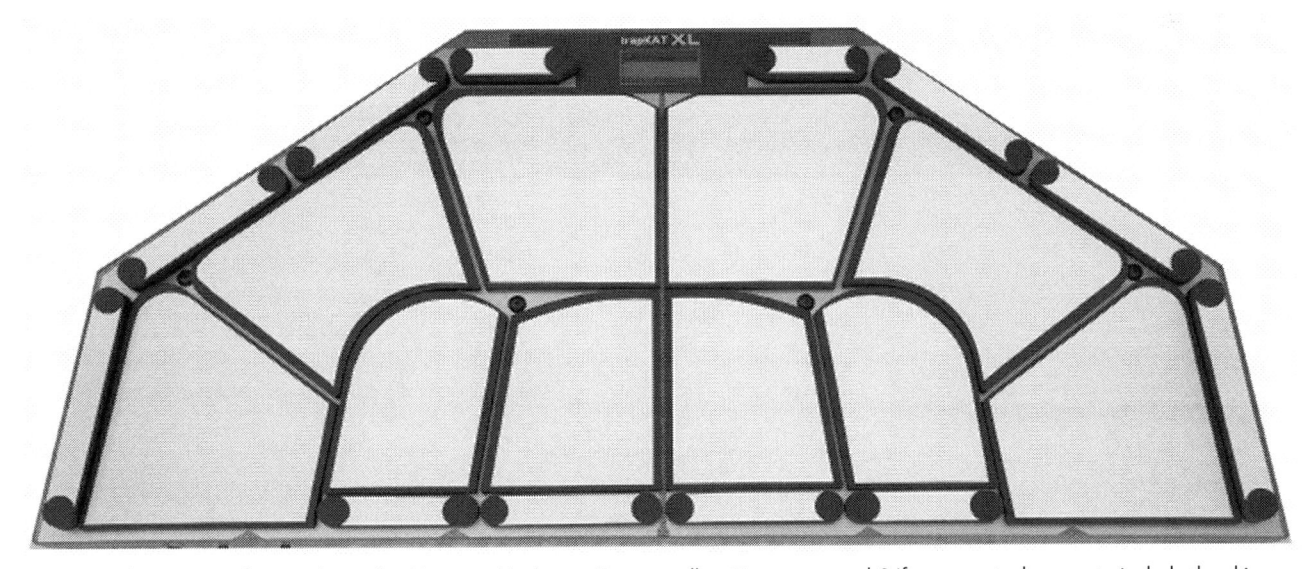

Trigger pads are spread out wide on the Alternate Mode trapKat controller. How many pads? If you count—be sure to include the skinny ones around the perimeter and across the front—you'll get up to twenty-two, but there are actually twenty-four. The skinny pads to the *extreme left and right* are actually spit in half to serve as two pads each. Connected to one or more capable MIDI sound generators, you can assign up to sixteen sounds to each pad and trigger them individually by velocity switching among them, layer them all together, or sequence through them one at a time. Also available is the trapKat 5KS, which includes a built-in Kurzweil synth engine. (Courtesy of Alternate Mode, Inc.)

The Synthesizer

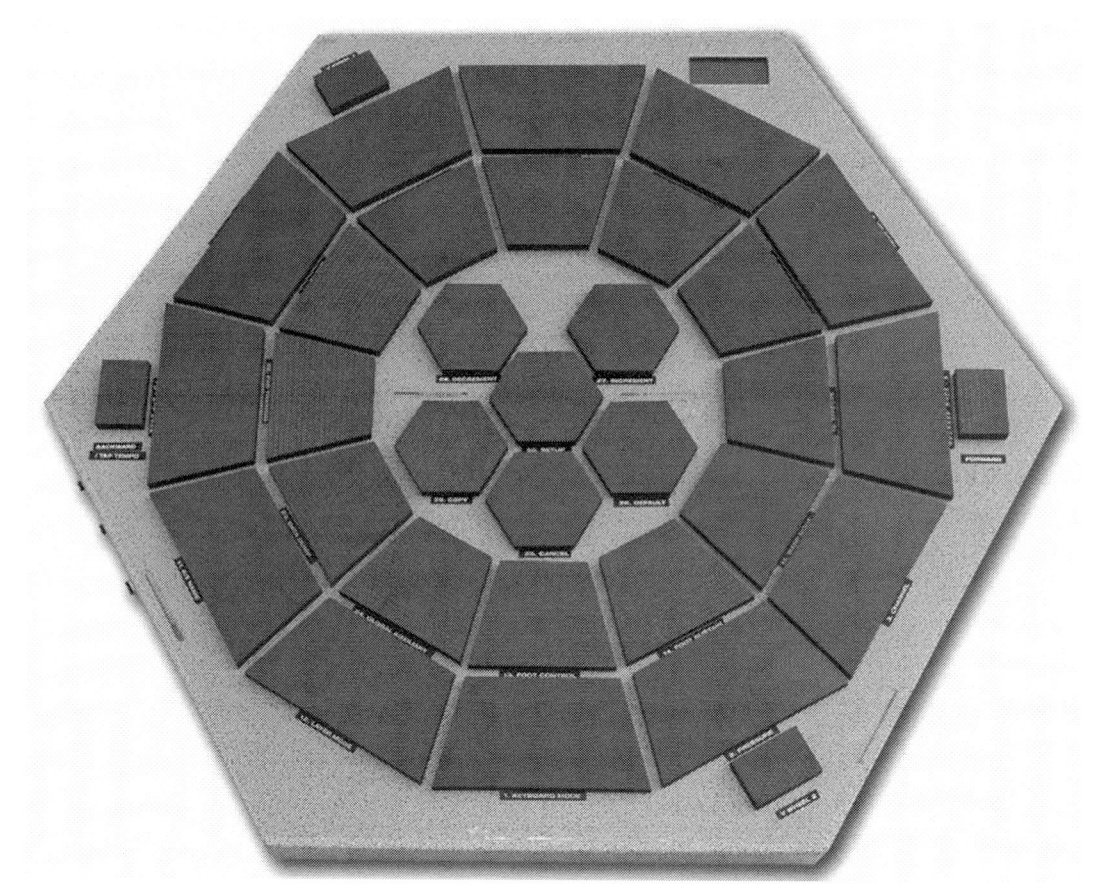

Steel drums have always fascinated me, as well as the music played on them. How would you like to have one that you can play any sounds you'd like on? Introducing the panKat MIDI controller from Alternate Mode. It gives you 128 memory locations to store your assignments of its thirty trigger pads. (Courtesy of Alternate Mode, Inc.)

Alternate Mode's panKat has thirty pads primarily arranged in a circular pattern like the playing surface of a steel drum, only on a flat plane instead of being concave. Alternate Mode also offers the malletKat—in versions with two or three octaves of pads—for xylophone, vibe, or marimba players interested in using MIDI. The malletKat 7KS has a built-in Kurzweil synthesizing soundcard, making it a stand-alone instrument.

Alternative Mode's malletKat Express provides two octaves of trigger pads arranged like the bars of a marimba. The malletKat is also available in three- and four-octave models—the Pro and Grand, respectively—and you can get any of them with a built-in Kurzweil synth engine. You can also buy a single-octave pad expander to increase the note range of any malletKat. (Courtesy of Alternate Mode, Inc.)

Another marimba-style controller comes from Don Buchla, who teamed with percussionist/programmer Mark Goldstein and marimbist/sound designer Joel Davel to create the Marimba Lumina mallet MIDI controller/instrument—Buchla's final twentieth-century product. It's available in two sizes, responds independently to as many as four different mallets for gestural control, and features a built-in synth engine for stand-alone performance.

Controllers for Microtonal Tunings

The twelve-notes-per-octave equal-tempered scale we're accustomed to hearing in Western music is in truth a compromise in tuning, adopted during the early nineteenth century mostly to allow easy transposition into different keys. Whereas such a division of the octave results in unnatural tuning beats in intervals such as a major third or fifth because frequency ratios between the low and high notes are sharp or flat, tunings based on frequency ratios such as 5:4 for a major third and 3:2 for a perfect fifth in just intonation result in pure, beat-free interactions between the low and high notes. Explorations of just intonation and other microtonal tunings—including equal-tempered scales in which the octave is divided into increments such as fifty-three, forty, thirty-one, or seven—can be fascinating, rewarding, and potentially never-ending.

Not only are just intonation and other non-equal-tempered and microtonal tunings infinitely easier to do with synthesizers—many of which support different tunings, some more flexibly and easier to program than others—than with acoustic instruments, but there's also a variety of controllers and instruments specifically tailored for playing microtonal parts. The widest variety appears among the offerings in the Tonal Plexus lineup from H-Pi Instruments. These complex, colorful instruments are available in ranges covering two, four, and six octaves in blue, green, red, or yellow highlighting. A Tonal Plexus can have either MIDI I/O or a USB connector, and some are available with built-in General MIDI sound generation and a stereo sound system with internal speakers and a headphone jack. Every Tonal Plexus instrument comes with cross-platform editing software and features a 1/4" sustain pedal input jack.

H-Pi Instruments also offers numerous computer applications, including microtonal notation, tuning, ear-training, and scale-editing software for Mac and Windows; a scale

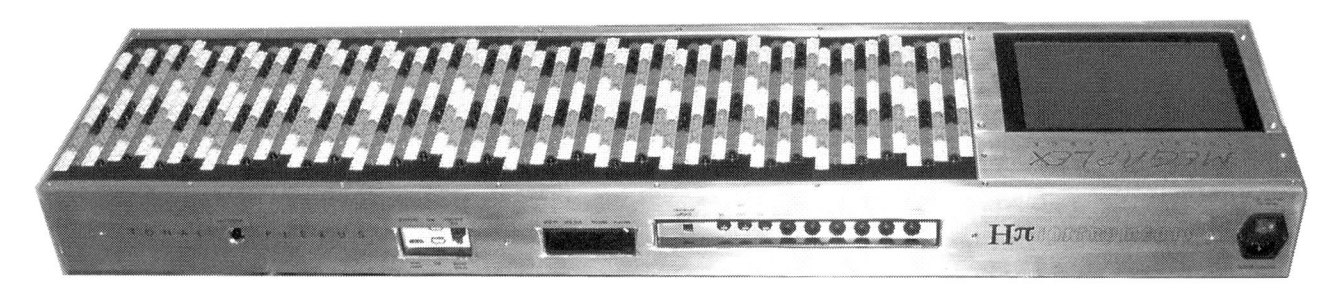

The MegaPlex from H-Pi Instruments is a version of the Tonal Plexus series with 256 velocity-sensing keys per octave covering six octaves. Built-in are a Mac Mini with all of its connections—HDMI, Ethernet, mic input, two USB ports, and Firewire 800—accessible on the back panel, a 1,024 × 768 TFT LCD singletouch screen, and a built-in stereo sound system with line-level input and output and a headphone jack. Alongside the MIDI in, out, and thru connectors are six 1/4" jacks for foot controllers. Although you can run the Macintosh music applications of your choice, H-Pi's microsynth comes installed on the MegaPlex's internal Mac Mini, which requires a USB keyboard and mouse to boot up, but the built-in touchscreen works directly with the Mac. (© 2012 H-Pi Instruments)

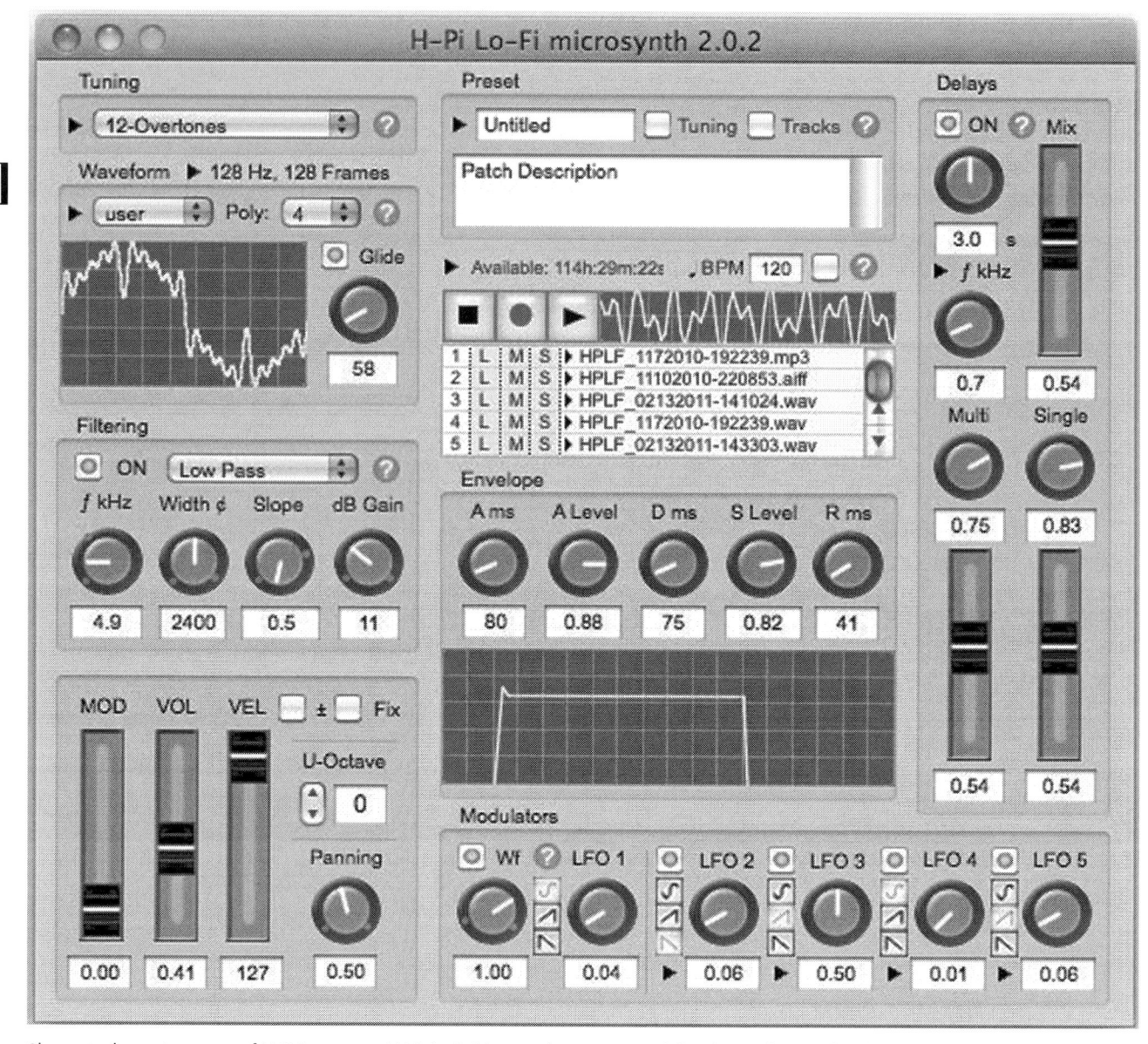

Shown in the main screen of H-Pi Instruments' H-Pi Lo-Fi Microstudio are a user-defined waveform with a lowpass filter, five LFOs, a delay, and five tracks of recorded audio in the mixer. (© 2012 H-Pi Instruments)

browser that includes an archive of over 3,800 scales; H-Pi Lo-Fi Microstudio, a microtonal softsynth and audio recording/editing app for Mac; and microsynth, a microtonal soundfont synth that's available from the Mac App Store.

If microtonal tunings interest you, note that John Loffink maintains the extraordinary Microtonal Synthesis Web Site (www.microtonal-synthesis.com) with tips, links, and information about working with microtonal scales on different synthesizers, a recommended listening list, and coverage of microtonal composer Harry Partch (1901–74).

Noise Toys

This category includes a myriad of electronic devices. Many make outrageous sounds and can be interesting and fun to play with, but don't expect them to allow you to make music that a majority of others will enjoy. Some come as kits, others assembled. Most are battery-powered, and many are inexpensive enough that you won't lose too much should you destroy them while trying some circuit-bending. There's a whole movement of noise-music enthusiasts to whom many of these devices will appeal. I've worked with some of the devices myself, but in the end I prefer instruments that provide more precise control, predictability, and repeatability.

Of the kits I've purchased since 2007, my favorites are: the 4ms Pedals Autonomous Bassline Generator (ABG), which plays a subtly changing sequence that you can influence using the ABG's buttons, data knob, and light sensor; and two from Bleep Labs, the ThingamaKit and the Nebulophone. Bleep Labs original Thingamagoop came assembled and has a blinking LEDacle on a flexible stalk, a light sensor, two knobs, two switches, and a base-mounted speaker that's perfect for holding to your mouth for acoustic cavity filtering. The ABG and Nebulophone belong to the Andromeda Space Rocker series of kits that sync to each other via infrared emitters and sensors. The Wooster Audio Space Baby delay detailed in chapter 2 (see pages 196 and 197) also fits into this category.

Two ready-to-play, nine-volt battery-powered noise toys that I've enjoyed working with are a 2009-vintage BugBrand Board Weevil and a Flower Electronics Little Boy Blue. The Board Weevil is an open circuit-board device festooned with three syncable oscillators, seven pots, nine switches, fourteen touch points, two light sensors, a small

The relatively easy-to-assemble Autonomous Bassline Generator from 4ms Pedals will voice a sequence twice before subtly varying it. Using the ABG's buttons and knobs, you can transpose the sequence, slightly vary note selection, alter the attack and decay characteristics of the filter, and manually modulate the oscillator's pulse width. There's a tap-tempo button for setting tempo or, as one of numerous devices among the Andromeda Space Rocker infrared I/O protocol, the ABG will sync with or serve as the master clock for other ASR devices. Blocking light from the LED received by the sensor adjusts the filter cutoff frequency. (Mark Vail)

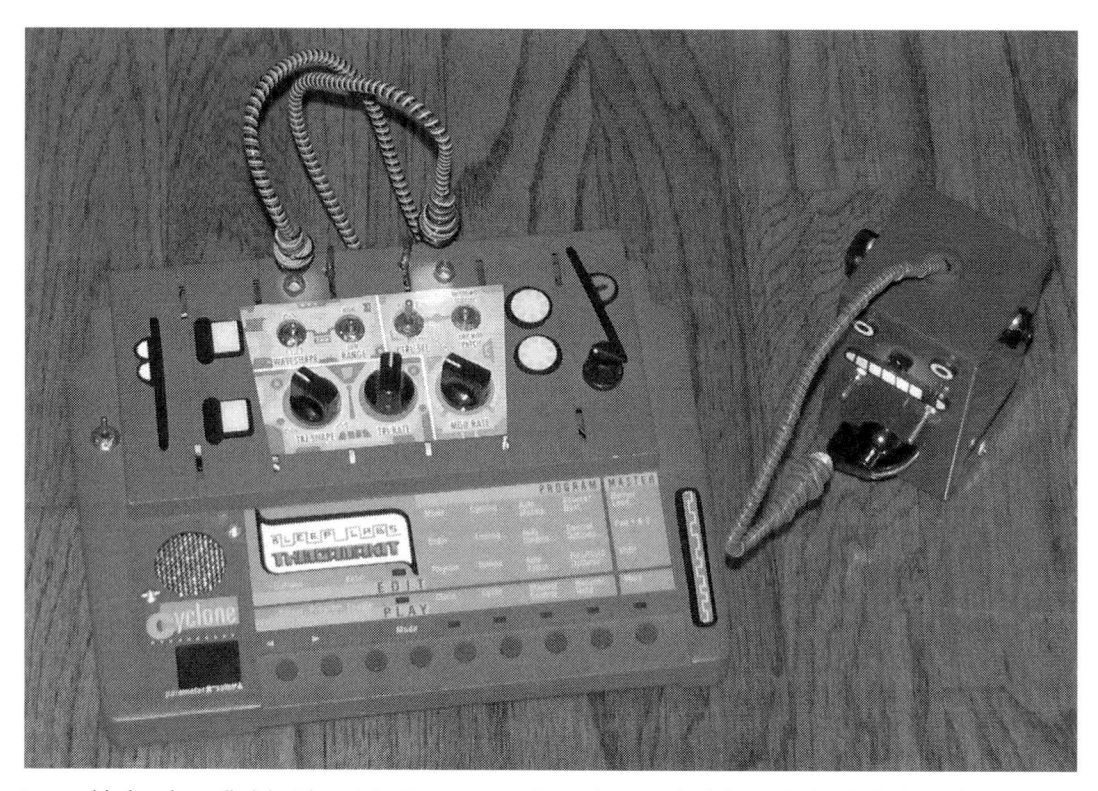

I assembled and installed the Bleep Labs ThingamaKit, shown here on the *left*, inside the shell of an Oberheim Cyclone MIDI sequencer prototype from the late 1980s. Its two LEDacles—LEDs on flexible wire stalks—function like LFOs, with knobs and switches for adjusting how the LEDs flash. By directing these lights into the two sensors, you can convince the ThingamaKit to make Morse code-like blips and beeps or screaming digital noise. The ThingamaKit followed the original Thingamagoop, shown on the *right*. Not that either is musical in a traditional sense, but they make interesting sounds and interacting with their LEDacles, light sensors, and manual controls can be entertaining for both the performer and his or her audience. (Mark Vail)

No longer available except on the used market, the 2009 version of the BugBrand Board Weevil allows you to control the whistles, squeaks, swooshes, chirps, beats, screams, and buzzes it generates using its knobs, touchpads, and light sensors. BugBrand founder Tom Bugs designs and builds limited quantities of stand-alone sound devices and effects processors as well as modular synthesizer components that are popular due to their sonic and interactive capabilities and, therefore, quickly consumed by his worldwide clientele. (Mark Vail)

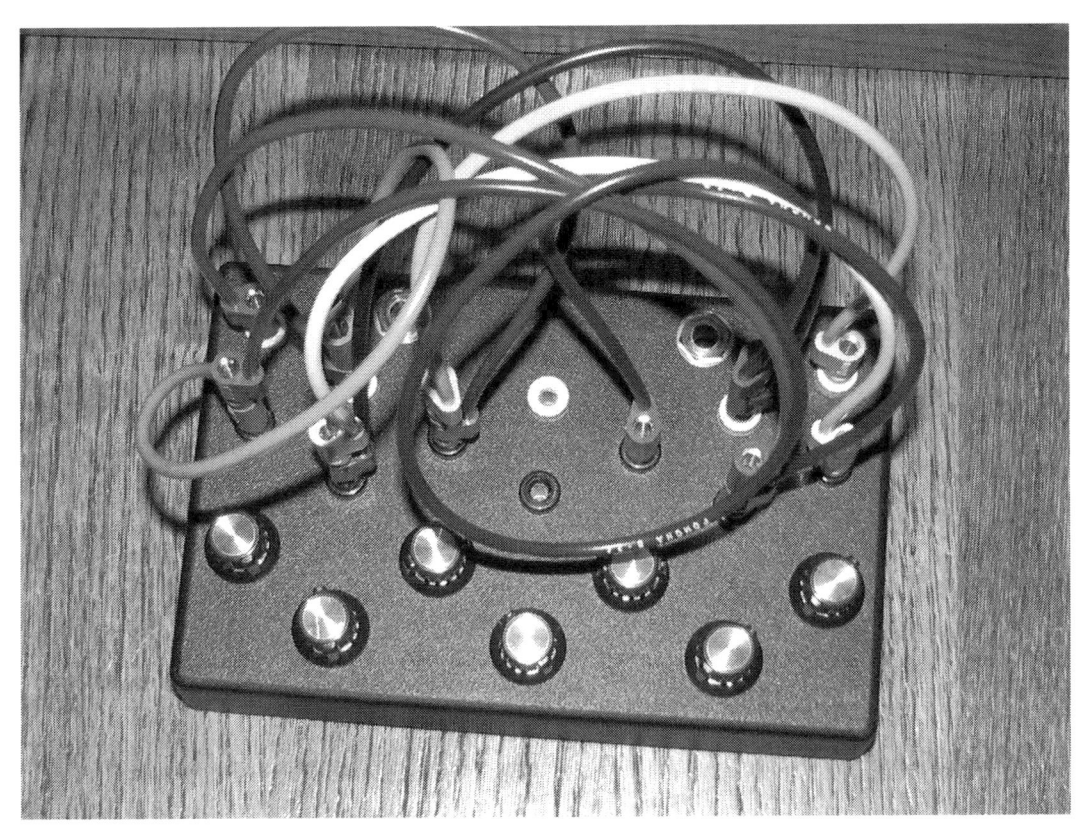

Thanks to its patching flexibility—which is extended by stackable banana-plug connections that allow you to patch different types of feedback loops—the Flower Electronics Little Boy Blue is capable of generating wickedly rude sounds. Pomona banana cables are shown here with the LBB; it comes with cables that allow the plug at one end to be stacked. (Mark Vail)

speaker (see Thingamagoop filtering comment above), and a 1/4″ audio output. It produces a wide range of clicks, shuffles, and whistle-like sounds and is highly interactive thanks to all of its controllers. As for the Little Boy Blue (LBB), you have to connect patch cables to its twelve banana jacks before it generates sounds. It has two sawtooth oscillators, an envelope follower, a two-channel mixer, an intermodulating output stage, seven knobs, and 1/4″ audio I/O. An aluminum enclosure finished in light blue or black houses its components. Thanks to the LBB's signal-routing flexibility and potent sound-generation circuitry, it's capable of producing outrageous timbres, and it can brutalize sounds from external sources.

Noise toys aren't for everyone, but they're fun for letting off steam and annoying others.

Composition, Programming, and Performance Techniques

Considering how much you've paid for your synthesizer(s), you might like some ideas about how to get maximum return for your investment. The discussions below reveal successful techniques practiced by some of my favorite synthesists.

Composition

Scoring to Picture

From 1989 to 1994, one of the best reasons to turn on *The Arsenio Hall Show* was to catch a glimpse of the stand-up keyboardist Starr Parodi in the house band, the Posse. The beautiful musician wasn't, however, only there for her looks; she's an outstanding pianist, synthesist, and composer.

These days Starr and her husband Jeff Fair mainly produce soundtracks for TV shows, movies, and movie trailers. When they take on a new project, first they focus on creating a musical palette of sounds that will enhance the picture for a particular show or movie.

Starr Parodi and Jeff Fair in their home studio in 2009. (Rich Schmitt, courtesy of Parodi/Fair)

They often use analog-synth timbres as a glue between existing sounds—something that moves back and forth like a connecting thread—to pull the listener in.

They record audio as they perform and simultaneously capture MIDI data with Steinberg Cubase for subsequent editing and playback. Later they can adjust the tempo of the MIDI tracks and play other parts on top of them. While composing music for orchestras and acoustic instrumentalists, Parodi and Fair write parts out by hand and enter whatever is necessary into Sibelius notation software to print parts for other musicians. When they compose all-synth soundscapes for movie trailers, however, they don't notate the music but perform and produce the work from conception to final product. They have also orchestrated MIDI tracks with their hardware synths for people who have composed music for films and trailers using softsynths that emulate the hardware.

One of their biggest challenges is dealing with demanding filmmakers when they are preparing mockups for new projects. "You have to create something that producers and directors are going to understand and sounds almost finished," says Starr. "And it has to move them emotionally," Jeff adds.

The animated-film and TV composer/synthesist Drew Neumann occasionally enjoys a bit of ostinato-and-drone jamming but, he asserts, "Once you have all of this gear, you realize how easy that is to do. What's beautiful about the works that Wendy Carlos and Isao Tomita have done is that they did it the hard way, layering and developing sounds in very complex ways."

Drew's orchestrations rely heavily on sampling, "the meat-and-potatoes of scoring these days," he affirms. "For most of the music I'm asked to do, film and TV producers understand and can tell me what they want as far as sampled content is concerned. Syn-

Drew Neumann relaxes in front of his favorite banana modular system, a Modcan A that he enjoys working with because it's relatively easy and quick for him to get fantastically complex sounds out of it. (Mark Vail)

thesizers are a bit more abstract to them and they rarely ask specifically for something synthesized—with the notable exception of Adam Burton, aka Maxwell Atoms, creator of *The Grim Adventures of Billy & Mandy*, who is a longtime synth-music fan.

"Where I find synthesizers do a great job is in gluing the photos together," Neumann continues. "If you think about sampling as a bunch of snippets or Polaroids—like a David Hockney photomontage—they play out like a deck of cards. If you play the same note of a clarinet sample over and over again, listeners will notice that it isn't a real clarinet, so you have to adjust the phrasing so that you can avoid that."

He's discovered that one of the most subtle uses of synthesizers is to back up monophonic parts such as woodwinds or a clarinet sample with something like the Nord Lead playing legato lines so that it has a sense of a continuous phrase. It can also give the phrase more of a stereo fullness and a bit of bottom-end depth. Neumann also believes that the random factor that analog components add when they drift gives the music life that otherwise wouldn't be there.

Drew has covered the gamut from using synths to back up sampled material all the way to scoring entirely with analog synthesizers—such as for *The Grim Adventures of Billy & Mandy*, on which he strictly used synths to define the Grim Reaper character with timbres that were cold and death-like.

He spends most of his time composing on the Macintosh. Although he truly enjoys playing around with modular synths, he's usually working under very tight deadlines and can't indulge in much experimentation. Time permitting, Drew will patch a modular to double lines, which adds more bass, drama, randomness, and fidelity to give the music extra life. "Sampled sounds don't always have a nice, high-end sizzle to them," he explains, "and they don't have a really pure, deep, earth-shattering bottom end. Sometimes it makes for a good mix to blend samples and analog synthesis together."

While scoring to video, Neumann strives to give his music a narrative flow that supports the picture. Often he has to audibly smooth animated action when visual elements don't quite flow, forcing him to somehow glue them together. On shows like the *Shnookums and Meat Funny Cartoon Show* for Disney, Drew would get five short episodes and, in transcribing what he wanted to do musically for them, it turned out to be six hundred pages of score. That's why he mostly works directly with MIDI data while composing such scores.

Neumann initially hit it big by composing the music and creating sound effects and voices for Peter Chung's *Aeon Flux*, launched on MTV's *Liquid Television* animation series in 1991. *Aeon Flux*'s success led to Drew composing music for all eighty-four episodes of Nickelodeon's *The Wild Thornberrys* and fifty-two episodes of *Aaahh!!! Real Monsters*, both developed at the Klasky/Csupo studio, along with episodes of *The Grim Adventures of Billy & Mandy* and *Evil Con Carne* on the Cartoon Network. Between graduating from CalArts in 1982 and beginning his scoring-for-animated-films career, he wore numerous hats. In fact, his BFA isn't even music-related: He has a degree in Visual Effects and Experimental Animation.

No doubt this education came in handy when Drew began scoring animated films. He explains the difference in composing for two-dimensional (2D) animated films versus those in three dimensions (3D), which creates new challenges and opportunities for composing synthesists. "When you're scoring to 2D animation," he says, "things move

Gary Chang appears before his huge Wiard modular system in 2010. (© 2012, Gary Chang Music, Inc.)

based on the traditional concept of Antic and Take. That means to make the drawings pop in motion, animators will actually squash the character (blink and squash) before the Take, which is the extreme stretch position. Tex Avery and Chuck Jones used this technique, and it appears a lot in *Who Framed Roger Rabbit?* Most cartoons use squash and stretch to overemphasize actions."

This forces the composer to musically exaggerate the animated movement. Whereas some of that happens in soundtracks for 3D, it's more constrained so that it's closer to natural physics where characters have weight, which allows the composer to slow the score's tempo a bit. The music can have more depth and reverb in the mix instead of being dry and up front. If it's a 2D picture, animators prefer the music to feel very dry, light, and bright because it better matches the visual quality. The richer visual texture of 3D animation requires a deeper, more layered and nuanced score.

Scoring for live action productions is totally different. Besides doing loads of album sessions over the years, Gary Chang has scored many live-action movies and TV shows. He varies the use of reverb in stereo versus surround-sound environments. "In 5.1 surround where there are speakers all around you," he explains, "the reverb has to be much cleaner than when it's in stereo. Stereo reverb seems to come from behind the speakers, so it needs to be more opaque. You don't want that kind of frosty sound all the way around you when you're sitting in a room with surround-sound. You want the sound to be really clear and have a completely different quality."

Chang began composing movie scores in a generation when he could get away with making the music electronic as long as it didn't offend anybody:

There's a ton of electronic music in all of my filmscores, but if someone complains—"Nope, nope, that's electronic!"—the next thing you know the producer or director says, "Yeah, can we do away with the synthesizer parts?" Ultimately, the better you get at it the less that happens. People can also change their minds. After hearing one score I did years ago, the producer came up and said, "You know, usually I can't stand electronic-music scores, but this one is really emotional." In other words, it was music, he heard it, and he didn't notice the fly in the soup.

Gary chooses instruments and themes with which he can create an emotional connection with the audience. When he first began composing music, he started with the simplest metaphors—happy is major, sad is minor—then progressed to exploring with more sophistication. These days he's an avid user of Ableton Live alongside a humongous Wiard 300 modular system, a small Eurorack system for live performance, many rackmount and software synths, and an NED Synclavier. He uses Live to either control an analog synth with MIDI or to synchronize it, record elements, and edit those elements in a digital environment. Live is especially valuable to Chang because of its Session Page, which he uses like a mixer. He puts down tracks, plugs in a modular synth, and synchronizes it so that when he hits "play," the analog instrument plays in sync. He can record and immediately play back two, four, eight, twenty-four, or thirty-two bars. Live allows him to compile performance information in real time and intuitively format the results. Live can also record gestures and performance actions he makes with a variety of MIDI controllers, then store the data as automation. Instead of sequencing in a linear fashion, Gary can record events into Live and then chop them up as he sees fit.

Amin Bhatia uses a blend of old and new technologies in composing music with Ari Posner for the CBS/CTV drama *Flashpoint*. Bhatia thinks anyone starting out in the

Gary Chang's enormous Wiard 300 modular synthesizer takes up considerable space in his home studio. (Mark Vail)

Amin Bhatia in his studio in 2011. (Courtesy of Amin Bhatia)

film- and TV-scoring business might be able to work purely within a computer environment instead of collecting a ton of outboard gear, but he also believes the most important thing is to know precisely what you're working with and let it become a sound that you know in your head. He finds that such a deep understanding of your tools is the secret to good orchestration for film and television. While Amin will occasionally let a preset sound inspire him, he much prefers to judge what a scene needs, pre-produce an idea in his head, and consider precisely what he'll need to create the sound, melody, or texture he has in mind. Then he selects the synths he'll use for that particular piece of music and—almost equally important—which ones he won't use to avoid getting bogged down by the temptation to keep adding parts. "By far the best music I've created comes after I've decided, 'I'm just going to use these three particular sounds,'" he says. "'From limitations come freedom.' I don't know who said that, but it's a great line."

Flashpoint scores are approximately 95 percent electronic. Sometimes Bhatia and Posner will bring in a solo instrument or a vocalist, but short production schedules dictate whether it's possible. Amin and Ari split up their work at the spotting session, where they sit down, look at the story, and decide who covers what before going away and separately writing music. Generally, Ari handles the ballad-like parts because he's more the songwriter, and Amin usually handles the chase music. Between them they can cover any kind of music the director requests.

While choosing sounds for *Flashpoint*, Bhatia and Posner don't focus on what frequency range those sounds are going to be in or how up front or far away they're going to be in the mix; instead they decide which of four stereo stems they're going to be in. A stem is like a submix. The lead stem usually contains the main melody and solo lines. The second stem contains all of the pads—strings and warm surround timbres. The third stem is for all of the rhythm parts: loops, the kick drum, the snare, and so on. The fourth stem is the bass. When the re-recording mixing engineer receives those four stems, he has what's needed to carve out a particular sound by raising or lowering the level of any part. If a melody line gets in the way of dialog, it's in the lead stem and can be muted if necessary.

Ari and Amin maintain a database to keep track of all of the cues, including the start and end keys of each cue. Sometimes one of them will phone or email the other to confirm what key they're composing in so parts will mesh seamlessly. Organization is vital to their successful partnership.

Their music editor, Joe Mancuso, also works with stems when editing an existing track. He can cut it up or remix it. Joe can convert a two-minute cue into a four-minute cue by muting certain stems; he'll start with only rhythm and bass, loop it adding the melody, and then loop it again to add the pads. After Joe has finished his manipulations, he can hand the results back to Amin and Ari to add new material.

Bhatia and Posner have programmed a Logic template so that as soon as they're finished writing a cue and are happy with it, the template enables four stereo tracks to be recorded in a single pass to immediately create an archive. They've set up signal routings so they can hear the audio in stereo as they feed different sets of stem recording tracks with separate reverbs and other processing. In this way they've addressed potential technical problems before they start writing and they have a master template they start with on every cue. It's crucial to have the organization complete and ready so your creative energies aren't squelched when you get creative. Bhatia acknowledges Steve Porcaro and David Greene as mentors who taught him how to be so organized in the studio.

Composing for Living Art

One of the recurring projects Jeff Fair and Starr Parodi undertake seems particularly intriguing: Composing orchestral music for Pageant of the Masters, part of the Festival of Arts series that takes place every July and August in Laguna Beach, California (www.foapom.com). Jeff calls it "*tableau vivant*, which is French for 'living pictures.' They re-create classical and contemporary art masterpieces—paintings, statues, and sculptures—with real people playing the part of humans in the portraits."

What's special about this re-creation is that the actors and the actresses appearing within the scene are painted to look two-dimensional when the lighting hits them at a certain angle. "They look three-dimensional until they turn a certain way and all of a sudden they look flat!" Jeff exclaims. "It freaks you out a little bit."

The Festival of Arts has a different theme every year. Its organizers assign paintings to Parodi and Fair so they can compose music to be played by a live orchestra that includes two synthesists. Besides composing the music, Starr and Jeff create and choose sounds for the synthesists to play. Sometimes they provide patches for specific synths, other times they record samples to trigger with the orchestra. "Every year we try to find something different for the synthesists to do," says Jeff, "something unique."

Laguna Beach's Irvine Bowl plays host to the Pageant of the Masters and seats about 3,000 people. The Festival of Arts began in 1932 and averages about 200,000 attendees each year. It isn't easy to get tickets. "They've told us Starr is the first woman composer ever to work there," says Fair. "It's something that everybody should see at least once in their lives."

Jeff Fair and Starr Parodi in 2008. (Courtesy of Parodi/Fair)

"It's like going to a really cool museum," Starr explains. "You're sitting and looking at a painting, only it's on a huge stage and it's alive!"

Following Through on a Thought

Larry Fast, the man who released his first great rock-driven synth album—*Electronic Realizations for Rock Orchestra*—under the name Synergy in 1975, has long used a productive method in composing: "Snippets." It may begin when he's noodling around on a piano, playing riffs onstage during a soundcheck, drifting off to sleep, or during a period that's been specifically blocked out because he needs to create something for a project that has a deadline, such as the work he's done over the years for XM Satellite Radio, Tribune Broadcasting, Disney, and Filmscore. "For me," Larry explains, "it all starts with finding some little hook, melodic structure, or sonic effect if it's a non-musical piece, and working from there."

Fast collects his musical ideas by notating them on paper or recording them, and he keeps these ideas in an easily accessible library that he can refer to for inspiration in the creation of longer musical works. He then refines, polishes, and edits until he's happy with the results: "I take advantage of the experiences I've had as a producer for other people, which makes it easier to tell myself, 'That's not so good. Get rid of that part. What were you thinking?' or 'That one could be really good, but you haven't put enough time into expanding it.' Those are the little voices in my head as I wear the producer hat, the musician hat, the composer hat, or the engineer hat. They all fight for dominance at given times."

A promo shot of Larry Fast for the release of his *Sequencer* album under the name Synergy in 1976. (Courtesy of Synergy® Electronic Music. Inc.)

Sage Advice from a Master

Wendy Carlos encourages synthesists to put in the time and effort to learn the flexibility of "the deliberately open-ended tools we have at our disposal" to allow them to communicate. "We need the ABCs, but how you use them—to form words, sentences, thoughts,

Larry Fast, who recorded and performed under the name Synergy, in his studio in 1984. (Bernhard J. Suess, courtesy of Synergy® Electronic Music. Inc.)

compelling arguments, passion—that's what you want." Wendy also encourages musicians to edit their work and toss out what isn't working.

"The technology of electro-acoustic music," she continues, "is to serve in the communication of a creative, expressive art, not just to copy what's already there." While she believes it's okay for students to copy the work of others, that's only a starting point. Once you've grasped the techniques, use them to say something in your own voice, based on your own life's experiences, your desires, and your point of view. Carlos insists there's no shortcut to developing the knowledge and skill necessary to be able to communicate that voice to your audience.

After you've learned how to make your instruments express your ideas, Wendy wants musicians to "Speak! Communicate! Say something! Make your own statement, don't just parrot back what everyone already has heard countless times."

Scoring with Intent, Even When Intimidated

Kevin Fortune composes music and works on synthesizer patches with the intent of transforming listeners. "When you listen to something," he explains, "your emotions change, your state of mind changes, and you may feel different physically." While he's working, he challenges himself by asking, "What do you want it to do? What are you feeling? What's your intent of doing this in the first place? Where do you want to go with it? What's the outcome?"

Kevin agrees with Gary Chang, who's said that synthesists' "instrument is the speaker." "The very act of playing an instrument and the gestures you use to play it are important,"

Kevin Fortune poses in 2011 with his Mighty Serge. (Mark Vail)

Fortune points out. "If you pick up a saxophone, the instrument is the speaker. With a synthesizer, the flow of electrons expresses emotions through a speaker and into the air. Rex Probe [of Sound Transform Systems, maker of Serge Modular synthesizers since 1993] says, 'We make amusement parks for electrons.' I love that! Under the synthesist's control, electrons are moving in an expressive direction toward the listener and creating a sonic environment, so it's all part of the instrument. The studio itself is an instrument. I don't distinguish between pieces of gear, I concentrate on what I'm doing."

Like many synthesists, Kevin is surrounded in his studio by multiple instruments and, therefore, faces many choices and paths to take in making music. He focuses on his intent when selecting tools to create a new piece, which inspires him "because any choice works if it fulfills the intent." He usually turns to his Serge because he knows it so well, but sometimes he'll reach for something different and focus in an entirely new way. "That's a great, almost Buddhist approach," says Kevin. "You do something the same way every day, but one day you wake up and see it differently. Fantastic! Now something creative can happen because we're moving beyond our tendency to be habituated to comfort—including composing, playing, and everything else."

It's easy to become overwhelmed by choice. When Fortune assembled his Mighty Serge modular system, all of his energy went into creating as many choices for himself

Kevin (Braheny) Fortune designed and built the Mighty Serge in 1977. It's a fifteen-panel modular system with multiple patchbays enclosed in a Chas Smith-fabricated framework that conforms to Kevin's reach and allows the system to be separated and folded for transport. Kevin designed and customized many of the Serge modules; he began working with Serge Tcherepnin in 1975 and occasionally travels to Wisconsin to work with Rex Probe on M-class modules and Shop Panels at Sound Transform Systems. (Courtesy of Kevin Fortune, © 2004 Heartcall Music)

as possible. He hardwired some modules together and made numerous connections with switches so he could quickly make changes during performance rather than by repatching cords. But after he'd finished assembling the instrument, it intimidated him. "It seemed to be sitting there with its arms folded on its chest, saying, 'Okay, you built me. Now what are you going to do with me?' I had to leave the room right then! But I came back the next day with the attitude that I was ready to work with it, and then I really got into it. I was also really pleased with all of the modifications and choices I'd made."

Patching, aka Programming

Encouraging Synthesists' Creativity

Eric Persing of Spectrasonics is a man on a mission. His company's popular softsynths—including the current lineup of Omnisphere, Trilian, and Stylus RMX, as well as the legacy applications Atmosphere, Stylus, and Trilogy—come with killer patches that he and his team have programmed to demonstrate the possibilities. Eric doesn't, however, want his customers to stop there. He wants them to create their own sounds with the tools he's supplied. He reluctantly admits, though, that the percentage of Spectrasonics customers who actually program their own sounds seems to be very small.

Could it be that Spectrasonics' programmers are doing too good of a job with the presets they create and ship with the apps—although realistically they must do so in order to sell the products? Many of Spectrasonics' customers are apparently music producers who rely more on sample libraries as opposed to approaching their synthesizers as adaptable instruments that can be customized and optimized for users' needs. While Persing hopes his customers find the presets inspirational, he also encourages them to create their own sounds.

To facilitate this approach, in January 2011 Spectrasonics introduced a new sound-manipulation feature within Omnisphere and a performance interface application for the Apple iPad. Omni TR (Touch Remote) is a wireless iPad app that allows gestural control of user-specified Omnisphere parameters within the "Orb" feature. By tracing a finger across the iPad's touchscreen, you can tweak filters, activate voices, and seriously alter the current Omnisphere patch—or switch to an entirely different patch among eight that are active within Live Mode.

The Omni TR and Orb are a combination patch editor and alternative controller. Control data generated by the Orb address meaningful parameters for each patch, whether it's based on multisamples, granular synthesis, or whatever. If you don't like the results, you can engage the dice function to get a bunch of new assignments and possibilities. Eric hopes these features will serve as an entryway for musicians to experiment with sound creation.

Persing admitted in 2003 to being the unknowing source of a popular sound used in trance music. He'd heard about the "Hoover sound," and described it as

> a really annoying sound with a lot of pulse-width modulation. I'd see people refer to it online: "Hoover this" and "Hoover that" and "Who's got the best Hoover?" I started doing some research because I'm thinking we should probably include the "Hoover sound" in our current instruments. I find a website dedicated to

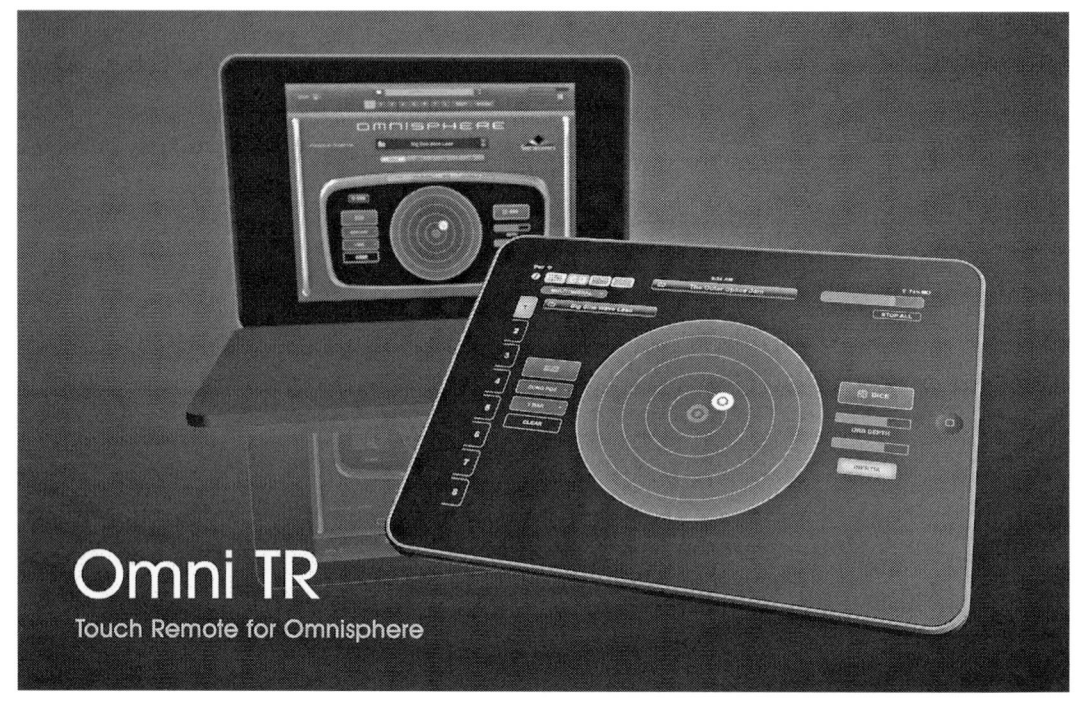

Spectrasonics created Omni TR to allow wireless control and sound programming of Omnisphere from an Apple iPad. (Courtesy of Spectrasonics)

"Hoovers" and posted there is a big picture of Roland's Alpha Juno-2, the coveted "Hoover" machine in Europe for trance and rave music because it can make this annoying sound. As I dug further I discovered that the "Hoover sound" comes from a factory preset in the Alpha Juno-2 called "WhatThe." Then I realized that I'd programmed the WhatThe patch for Roland as a joke! There's only one envelope in the Alpha Juno-2, and when you trigger WhatThe the envelope goes "Raaa" [upward pitchbend] and when you release it goes "Raaaah" [downward pitchbend]. It sounds sort of like a vacuum cleaner. The original sound wasn't intended to be anything but a joke and it ended up in the Alpha Juno-2's factory patch set!

Lesson to be learned: Be careful with your jokes or else they may come back to haunt you as a fresh, groundbreaking synthesizer sound in some new form of electronic music.

When and How to Experiment with Sounds

Amin Bhatia's synthesizer arsenal includes an ARP 2600, which has internally normalled circuitry that you can override by patching cables among its front-panel jacks. Amin never does that to get new sounds while he's composing music for *Flashpoint*. "Not for the TV series," he explains. "The 2600 is here because whenever I have time, I love to make a whole new sound with the instrument. But for television work, external patching is simply not practical because of the tight deadlines."

Drew Neumann also refrains from patching and programming his synths to create new timbres while facing a deadline. During that time he concentrates on the composi-

Spectrasonics founder Eric Persing shown recording sounds from a Tibetan bowl for the "Psychoacoustic" soundset in Omnisphere. He was swinging the Rode NT-4 mic to capture the sound in stereo. (Courtesy of Spectrasonics)

tion process and relegates experimentation to the back burner because he has to stay practical and focused. Patching his Modcan and Serge modulars is a three- to four-day job to get thirteen voices out of them, so he uses the results for a story arc within a series or a season of shows so he can come back to certain signature sounds again and again. But in the process of coming up with sounds, he will often invest time in modifying the patches to create a family of certain types of sounds and effects.

When he's pursuing a specific sound, Neumann doesn't need to experiment because he's worked with synths since the 1970s and he knows his instruments so well that he understands precisely how to get what he needs from them sonically. There's an initial phase of experimentation when he first adds or builds a new module so he can determine what it sounds like, what he can get out of it, how he might circuit-bend it, what

"The Bridge," as he calls it, is where Amin Bhatia composes music and controls all of his synths. Shown on the computer monitor is Apple Logic and Plogue Bidule running on a Mac Pro Quad-Core. Among the hardware controllers on the Bridge are a Euphonix MC Control, Novation Remote Zero SL, and Kurzweil PC1x Performance Controller keyboard. (Courtesy of Amin Bhatia)

feedback paths work well, and what breaks it. Then he focuses on being productive with what he decides is the best modular synth for that particular project. Once he's finished a project, he evaluates the end product, and sometimes the outcome surprises him. "'That's not what I really had in mind,' I might tell myself, 'but it's not bad. Let's go with it.' That's part of dealing with these beasts: You may envision something, but you have to accept that it's going to take you here and land you there."

Drew prefers to sequence analog synthesizer parts when recording so their sounds are fresh and hot, straight out of the boxes. On occasion he'll sample a monophonic voice generated by a modular synth and layer the polyphonic results with the original's raw sound at the mixing board. On top of the plug-in processed polyphonic voices, he can add a monophonic lead with a bit of uneven lag processing where glides are slow going up and fast coming down or vice versa, allowing him to articulate lines almost like a violinist—jumping directly between some notes and gliding between others for more expression.

While Starr Parodi and Jeff Fair use some software instruments—Native Instruments Absynth and Kontakt, Korg's MS20:Legacy, and a few additional Legacy plug-ins—they mostly depend on a combination of vintage and approaching-vintage synths, including a Roland MKS-80 Super Jupiter, Access Virus, and Waldorf Pulse Plus. "Not only does the Pulse Plus have built-in MIDI-to-CV conversion and CV/gate I/O for working with non-MIDI analog gear," Jeff enthuses, "but it also provides an audio input and really good filtering. You can process external sound sources with the Pulse's filter to change the spectral fingerprint of piano, organ, guitar, drums, and other acoustic instruments."

Composition, Programming, and Performance Techniques

Arranged across one corner of Drew Neumann's studio are (*left to right, top to bottom*): the Morbius synth Drew designed and built from E-mu and Paia components while attending CalArts during the early '80s, an M-Audio Oxygen 8 keyboard, and a rack containing a Fostex 3180 dual-channel spring reverb; a rack containing an Encore Electronics Expressionist MIDI-to-CV converter, a panel of Analogue Systems Integrator Eurorack modules, three panels of FracRak modules from Blacet Research, four panels of mostly Doepfer Eurorack modules, a Powertran Digital Delay Line that Drew assembled from a kit during the early '80s—and fixes as needed—an Alesis Quadraverb, and a Mackie 1202 VLZ mixer; the Modcan's spring reverb and three Kenton Pro-2000 mkII and one Pro4 MIDI-to-CV converters on top of the Modcan/Cyndustries modular system, a Clavia Nord Lead 2X, and a rack containing an MAM Chorus/Flanger, a DeltaLab ADM 1024 DDL, and a Synthesis Technology MOTM adapter panel that contains a few modules; and, at *far right*, a balalaika hanging on the wall alongside a 1949 vintage Shure Model 55 C microphone that rests—"for good luck," says Drew—on top of a six-panel Serge Modular system. (Drew Neumann, Droomusic)

Composing mainly in the studio, Jeff and Starr use synthesizers to either augment orchestral pieces or create soundscapes. They purposely avoid trying to re-create acoustic instruments with synths. "What I love about the synthesizer most is when it makes you feel emotion that's unlike any earthly sound," says Parodi.

They frequently run audio through an old bass vacuum-tube amp or a Leslie speaker and set up mics to get specific results. Since they work to picture so often, much of what they do requires them to sonically create a mood or emphasize certain emotions in a scene. "It depends on whether we're playing the environment or the emotion or the relationship on-picture," says Fair. "We tend to not use the synthesizer in a static way. It has to have movement and it has to have emotion."

Their Minimoog is a favorite tool because it helps them create the emotion needed to enhance a scene. Fair finds the real-time control provided by its knobs equates to the physicality of the vibrations of strings and the wood of an acoustic piano. For Jeff, with one hand on the Minimoog's keyboard and the other on its knobs, it feels almost like a complete circuit. "It isn't necessarily about what's going on on the keyboard," he explains, "it's about what's happening on the front panel of the instrument in real time and

Starr Parodi and Jeff Fair in a promo shot taken in 2002. (Ron Taft, courtesy of Parodi/Fair)

doing things that can't be programmed on the instrument itself; it has to be played in real time. Even though there isn't a physical resonance coming out of the instrument, you're connected with the performance of that instrument in ways that you aren't with softsynths."

Although Jeff enjoys many of Absynth's programmable features, he laments its lack of real-time control functionality. He also takes advantage of the arpeggiator on the Access Virus, working with its knobs during pattern playback.

Synthesizer manufacturers have long used different terminology for similar features. They also configure components in their instruments differently, which synthesists need to consider when working with unfamiliar gear. For example, Gary Chang points out that the mixers in Waldorf synths provide independent level controls for audio signals such as those coming directly from oscillators. If you crank them up beyond a value of eight out of the possible ten, you'll overdrive the mixer's input as well as the synth's filter—which can be very desirable traits. In contrast, most Japanese synths—such as Roland's Jupiter-8—provide a mixer fader parameter to adjust relative oscillator volumes, which keeps you from overdriving anything. The Waldorf gives you more range, but not everyone realizes that. "A friend of mine who was used to programming Japanese synthesizers called one day to tell me he was trying to make a string sound with his new Waldorf Microwave XT," says Chang. "He said, 'I can't seem to get it.' He'd turned up the XT's oscillator levels so high the timbre was coming out as a square wave because the waveforms were getting clipped."

During the 1970s Chang studied with Morton Subotnick at CalArts, where they had Buchla 200 Electric Music Boxes in the studios. Subotnick taught Gary how to use gestures to control multiple layers of expression on a Buchla 200. "He'd route CV outputs from a joystick to VCAs," Gary recalls.

> Then, using oscillators, he'd record the gestures as amplitude onto tape. He'd play them back through envelope detectors that converted them back into voltages. Buchla's Model 295 ten-channel comb filter has one input, summed outputs, and individual band outputs. Mort would tune sine waves to only output through each of the comb bands. He could put ten oscillators on one track, play them back through the comb filter, take the individual outputs into envelope detectors, and get ten control voltages to play back at once. As a performer played, Mort would run the tape through that system to control location, amplitude modulation, and other parameters. This was before computers were available to mortal men, but since then no one has duplicated an equivalent technique that's as direct and viscerally controllable.

The Good and Bad of Non-Programmability

Before synthesists could program and digitally store patches in memory for instant recall, they had to use some type of diagram or notation if they wanted to re-create or come close to reproducing a synthesized sound on the same instrument. Moog Music shipped the Minimoog with a pad of sheets with a blank front-panel illustration on which you could document a patch by inking in knob and wheel positions and switch settings—although it wasn't always possible to get an exactly identical timbre by dialing in those settings again. Analog circuits like those in the Minimoog and factors such as the room and synth's internal temperatures, humidity, static electricity, and the length of time the synth has been on can cause slight to significant deviations in the results.

Even analog synths from the same manufacturer often sound different, whether you're manually re-creating sounds from patch sheets or digitally loading memory from a card or MIDI system-exclusive dump from a computer. For example, Drew Neumann has two versions of the Moog Minimoog Voyager: the Performer Edition and Moog Music's 50th Anniversary Edition. He reports they actually sound different and he doesn't bother to transfer patches from one to the other because, for one reason or another, the results won't sound the same. This is both a blessing and a curse of analog.

Due to the number of patch cords required to make a modular synth function, the notation issue gets far more complicated. Consider, for example, keeping track of all of the cord routings and knob and switch settings on a Moog Modular. In working with a large Moog to create her early albums, Wendy Carlos became very familiar with the challenges. Inside *Book One: New Notes* of her *Switched-On Boxed Set* are several diagrams, each labeled "Patch Sketch." The drawings appearing there are "Bass Drum," "Basic Vocal," and "Half-Speed Snare Drum." Sadly, these are the only such scribbles that have surfaced. Wendy usually didn't notate her patches and, when she did, she'd refer to the

The Synthesizer

Beyond the pair of Moog Music Minimoog Voyagers (original and 50th Anniversary Editions) and the Waldorf Wave Shadow Edition immediately beneath them, we can make out one rack that contains (*top to bottom*) a Studio Electronics Midimini, two original Oberheim SEMs, a Studio Electronics Omega 8, an Arturia Origin, and a Yamaha TX802; another rack loaded with Waldorf Micro Q, Microwave IIXT, Microwave II, and original Microwave I modules, an Access Microwave Programmer, two MOTU MIDI Express interfaces, and Line 6 DL4 and Modulation Modeler stompboxes; and, in the rack farthest to the *right*, a MOTU 828 audio interface, a Lexicon MPX100, a Kurzweil K2000R, two Akai Z8 samplers, and two E-mu E4XT Ultra samplers. (Amin Bhatia)

slips of paper once before setting them aside and they'd subsequently disappear. Something like a snare drum or heartbeat patch could be quite intricate so she wrote those down, but she understood the Moog so thoroughly that she could create a basic timbre within a few minutes.

As Wendy did then, she focuses today on her intent and the needs of a piece when she creates synthesized sounds. She approaches the creation of a sound by selecting an appropriate waveform and then methodically reworking it. She talks herself through her thinking process: "'I need four or five bright waves, low-pitched, 16' or 32', then let's tune them slightly apart from each other.'" Carlos explains. "You make your choices, patch modules together, and keep trying it out. 'Hmm, I need to envelope the filter here,' so you patch in a lowpass or bandpass filter, set up the ADSR for it, and do the same thing for the voltage-controlled amp with a different set of knobs. Then maybe you decide to modulate several of the waves with a touch of pink or red noise to roughen it up more."

Drew Neumann never notates his modular patches. If he creates something that he likes and later needs to get it back again, he relies on his experience to get something similar—unless it's ridiculously complex. For fairly simple emulations of an ARP 2600 or a Moog Modular, he can patch it up on any of his modular systems in minutes. If it's a complex, multilayered feedback loop going on in his Serge that will only happen once, Drew records the audio before repatching the synth.

> Notating anything is a pain. What are you going to do, take a picture of all those cords and write, "The orange one goes here, the blue one goes there," and so on? Also, the Serge doesn't always behave the same way from one day to the next. I might find that the Frequency Shifter feeding back with the Wilson Analog Delay in a loop works a certain way one day and then—because of changes in tuning, humidity, and any number of other factors—the next day I find myself saying, "I liked it yesterday, but I don't like it today!" Then I'll go back and listen to the recording and realize, "Yeah, I liked it better yesterday."

Programming for Progress

While her initial success came with *Switched-On Bach*, many synthesists admire Wendy Carlos even more for her brilliant original compositions. Consider "Timesteps" from *A Clockwork Orange*, "The Rocky Mountains" from *The Shining*, and anything from *Digital Moonscapes, Beauty In the Beast, Tron*, and *Tales of Heaven & Hell*. These aren't simple improvisations or noodlings on top of repetitive Berlin-school four-on-the-floor sequences. The intricacies of the timbres and the progressions of events are astounding works of pure genius!

Carlos has for the most part left modular analog synthesizers to her past. While her old Moog Modular still behaves itself to an extent, its potentiometers, switches, and jacks have oxidized over time and need to be cleaned or replaced to ensure the integrity of its sound. Wendy found analog synthesis a quick and convenient way to get in the ballpark of many families of sounds, which was essential to doing all of her early recordings without patch memory. Wendy thinks she would never have finished those albums if she'd had to contend with deep menu systems like those found in many contemporary digital synthesizers.

The Synthesizer

Many synth experts credit Kurzweil's Variable Architecture Synthesis Technology—as delivered by this K2661 and Kurzweil synths since the K2000 arrived in late 1991—as being the best implementation of sample-playback synthesis to date. Wendy Carlos is a fervent fan of VAST. (Courtesy of Ray Kurzweil)

Wendy's current work with synthesizers returns her to the past, recalling passions for many acoustic instruments. It began with a Kurzweil 2600 she acquired in 2001. She enjoys being able to stack multisamples over multiple pitches and dynamics, getting rid of most of the static quality inherent in sample playback. She finds that Kurzweil's Variable Architecture Synthesis Technology (VAST) permits a generous degree of sound-shaping, which allows her to program expressive sounds. Most of her *Tales of Heaven & Hell* album demonstrates VAST's power. She's a big fan of Kurzweil's 2600 series—the last she purchased was the 2661 (2004)—even though they've been discontinued. Carlos also misses the frequency modulation that VAST used to have. FM, she believes, would enrich basic waveforms in a convenient and fast way to get another family of more complicated and interesting timbres.

Carlos found early samplers disappointing due to their lack of expressive control, every note playing the same sample every time with no variations. Brass and string samples in particular frustrated her. As many synthesists have discovered, instruments such as solo violin and trumpet are next to impossible to convincingly simulate using a sampler. For any chance of success, they must layer multisamples and meticulously program patches to respond to various controllers, and then practice to develop first-rate performance skills. Wendy's personal favorite is Gary Garrison's family of solo instrument emulations. "The solo Stradivarius violin and Gofriller cello Gary and his team have created are amazing," she enthuses. "They're sample-based, but the model they used is extremely elaborate and subtle. You need to practice on them to sharpen your chops and use more than the usual number of controllers, as with any fine musical instrument. But once you do, it becomes a moot point that this isn't a live, wonderful-sounding, traditional acoustic instrument being played really well. That surely breaks down the barrier we're talking about, and I certainly expect to use these new replicas in my future music."

Wendy is inspired now that synthesis technology has caught up with what has been the most interesting aspect to her: sophistication in musical timbre. Early electro-acoustic instruments weren't promising until Bob Moog's synthesizer modules opened a door for her. Carlos finds contemporary synthesizers useful because they allow her to

> create subtle complexities that take away analog's flatness and limited palette. Analog sounds so thick, fat, and muddied when you mix four or five timbres together.

Soon all of the ear-space is used up and you can't jam anything else in there with a trowel. With the newer synthesis tools, you can program sounds ranging from wiry to delicate, running from a razor's edge to a bit of acoustic "dirt"—on the pitch, on certain harmonics, on expression and volume, or on various other functions. When you think about it, it's the same way acoustic instruments contain interesting, subtle, acoustic dirt. Think of the gristle of a bow and rosin on violin strings, the buzz of a wind player's lips on a brass instrument's mouthpiece, the variations from how a woodwind reed is shaved and if it's moist or dry, even the different yarns wound around percussion instrument mallets. The often random elements add extremely important expression and life to musical sounds and we shouldn't ignore them in electro-acoustic music. It needs nuance and a careful touch, and it needs to be more complicated than just a cartoon—unless you're aiming for deliberate cartooniness. Our earlier electronic sources were far too simple compared to the rich things we can do now. It makes the future look bright and promising, and much more interesting. It's the way I'd like to work from now on.

Fun with Modular Synths

Simulating acoustic instruments isn't typically Drew Neumann's goal, but he reveals an exceptionally effective technique you can use with any kind of patch—provided your synth allows it. To simulate an overblown flute using two oscillators, tune one oscillator an octave higher than the other, choose a pulse wave for the lower oscillator, and assign an ADSR envelope to control the oscillator's pulse-width modulation so that it's silenced as the duty cycle goes to 100 percent or 0 percent. The result is a sub-octave blip followed by what sounds like an overblown flute harmonic. He acoustically demonstrates the effect for me with a Hungarian harmonic flute, first playing the fundamental pitch and then increasing his blowing pressure until the instrument's pitch suddenly jumps up an octave. He explains that the wind feeds back on itself because of the chaos model generated by the increased air pressure, resulting in pitches that cycle through the harmonic series as you blow harder. There's too much air pressure to go through the instrument because it's such a thin, long, sealed tube. You can electronically simulate this process to create a harmonic series by setting up a second oscillator that plays the fundamental frequency, and then pulse-width modulation kills its sound.

Drew has a vast array of synthesizers, including four large modular synthesizer systems: a Serge, a Modcan/Cyndustries, and two really tall systems: the 5U "Knob Grotto" and a combination Eurorack/FracRak modular. Among the hundreds of modules are many that Drew crafted and modified himself. There's also the patchable Morbius synth Drew made out of Paia and E-mu components as a CalArts student during the early '80s.

With so many modular synths in his studio to choose from, Neumann considers the sound qualities of each when reaching for a tool to attain specific goals. The Serge has a unique sound, but the Modcan and Knob Grotto overlap territory in certain ways. His choices depend on whether a sound needs to be abstract or imitative, or just a bass timbre. Neumann develops a sense of what voice architecture he wants for certain kinds of sounds. If he wants something reedy, ethereal, and not brash and in-your-face, he might

Drew Neumann looks rather proud—and rightfully so—of the patch he's created on his Knob Grotto, comprising modules from Synthesis Technology, Synthesizers.com, Encore Electronics, Blacet, Oakley, Paia, Bridechamber, Juergen Haible, Buchla (via Thomas White's licensed design), and Drew himself. Contained in the rack are (*from top to bottom*) two dbx 266 compressors, Line 6 Delay Modeler and Modulation Modeler, MXR 1500 DDL, two DeltaLab Effectron II DDLs, dbx 166X compressor, Vermona 12-Stage Phaser, Tascam patchbay, two MacBeth Studio Systems M3X analog synth modules, and a Jomox SunSyn tabletop synth. (Amin Bhatia)

A close-up of the front panel on Drew Neumann's custom Morbius patchable synth. He used components from E-mu and Paia, and made the front panel and wood cabinet himself in a workshop on the CalArts campus. (Mark Vail)

select an ARP filter. If he wants a big, brash, full sound, he uses the Moog ladder filter. To get a sound that's edgy and distorted, the Modcan Diode Filter 23A or the Cyndustries Synthesis Filter might work best. For a couple of seasons of *The Grim Adventures of Billy & Mandy*, he created a tuned analog feedback loop with the Modcan flanger, feeding white noise into a flanging, comb-filtering effect and making the pitch track the keyboard over a few octaves. He used this sound—which he describes as, "a little dusty and out there, not of this world"—for the Grim Reaper character.

He compares individual Serge modules to Swiss Army knives because you can patch them to perform functions for which they normally wouldn't be used. For instance, he can use a Serge envelope generator as a wave shaper or the Dual Transient Generator as a subharmonic generator, an envelope generator, an audio processor, or a lag processor.

Although Neumann doesn't have a Buchla modular synth, there are modules based on Buchla lopass gates in his Modcan and Knob Grotto systems. Don Buchla designed lopass gates using vactrols, or photoresistive opto-isolators, each consisting of an LED and a photocell sensor in an analog signal path. The Buchla lopass gate can function as a VCA, a filter, or a combination of both. Feed audio into a lopass gate and you'll get a spongy sound because there's a bit of sloppiness in a vactrol's response. If you tune two of them together in series and feed the output back to the input, you can also get the lopass gate to resonate. Thomas White's Resonant Lopass Gate—approved by Don Buchla and sometimes available as a PCB from Natural Rhythm Music (www.naturalrhythmmusic.com)—has this feedback path built into it. Gary Chang likes to route a pulse wave into a lopass gate to open it up without a snap or glitch because of the vactrol's slow response, performing the equivalent task of an envelope generator opening a VCA.

Layering Synth Sounds

During the mid to late 1980s, a popular technique was to layer combinations of analog, digital, and sample-playback synthesizers for the best of their attributes. Thanks to MIDI, it's easy to connect instruments that produce sounds in different ways so that each note consists of multiple voices.

After you've gained intimate knowledge of all of your synths, you can begin working with them together, which will be a learning experience as you discover ways of successfully integrating their voices together in your music. You may occasionally encounter discords among instruments you're controlling simultaneously. If you enjoy working with pitchbend and modulation wheels and other controllers as you play, you should coordinate what these do to each synth's voice so that they all perform nicely together. Bending the pitch of one synth up a fifth while another only goes up a second can lead to discordant results. Avoid this problem by equalizing the pitchbend ranges of all of your layered instruments—unless you want to create certain chords in a controllable fashion with your favorite bender.

David Rosenthal—perhaps best known as Billy Joel's musical director, arranger, and synthesist—is an ardent practitioner of layering because it gives such depth to his synth patches. He likes to combine voices that have cascading attack and release times, which gives the sound more character. Rosenthal also melds different elements in layers so they become one timbre. This requires the use of multiple synthesizers because voices from the same multitimbral instrument retain the same character since they're coming out of the same DACs and have the same envelope response times. Even if it's a powerful, state-of-the-art, flagship, workstation synth, David finds working with only one instrument one-dimensional in comparison to layering sounds from different synths and tailoring the filters and envelopes to all work together. "If I were to create everything on the same synth," he explains, "it would be like painting with ten shades of red. I want the whole palette. Yes, you can still do some miraculous artwork with that, but it isn't the whole picture to me."

Layering is also crucial to Amin Bhatia. Just as people who work with a single synthesizer use different oscillators to create a certain sound and then route it through different filters and different amplifiers, Bhatia likes to use different synths as partials of a larger sound. He's very fond of MIDIing a Nord Lead sound with a Roland sound, a Yamaha sound, and some strange thing in Kontakt, and then playing them all at once as a single hybrid instrument. Amin uses components of different synthesizers as opposed to expecting one synth to produce the be-all, go-to sound.

By taking the time to combine sounds from different synths into a hybrid, you create a unique texture or timbre. Bhatia, however, has noticed that sounds are becoming more important than the melody line. He feels this has gone too far, and he'd like to see melody's return to prominence.

David Rosenthal, who loves to layer synth timbres, appears in May 2007 with Billy Joel in concert in St. Paul, Minnesota. David's onstage synthesizer arsenal is huge because he has to re-create sounds that have appeared in Joel's songs throughout the 1970s, '80s, and '90s. Rosenthal is in the process of sampling and converting as many synth sounds as possible into NI Kontakt patches that he'll play from a Muse Receptor. (Tomohiro Akutsu)

Living in Amin Bhatia's studio are (*top to bottom*) the synth cabinet from an ARP 2600, a Minimoog next to a Roland MPU-101 MIDI-to-CV interface, and an Oberheim Xpander. (Courtesy of Amin Bhatia)

Much of the voice layering Amin Bhatia conducts comes from synth modules in this rack, including Roland's XV-5080, D-550, and MKS-70; a Korg TR-Rack; and a Yamaha TX816. (Courtesy of Amin Bhatia)

Programming for Expression

Gary Chang loves polyphonic synthesizers, but he considers using them only for pads a waste of great resources. He uses the Waldorf Wave to double movement in an orchestral piece. It doesn't matter how quietly he turns down the music volume, he still hears the Wave parts because they sound so opaque.

While attending CalArts during the mid 1970s, Chang was drawn to the Buchla 200 because it had ten sine-wave oscillators. He enjoyed frequency-modulating them to create sidebands that he could manipulate and vary the resulting harmonics, which he preferred over filtering square waves to erase harmonics. Practicing what Gary calls "sinusoidal audio phenomena" allowed him to use fewer filters, or none at all.

A pair of Waldorf rackmount synth modules—a Q and Microwave XT, spinoff synths from the Wave—add to the sonic resources in Gary Chang's studio. Gary points out that, unlike some synths that have a balance control to adjust the relative volume between two oscillators, Waldorf synths provide volume controls for individual oscillators, which allows them to overdrive subsequent circuits in ways that might be desired or unexpected. (Mark Vail)

A Buchla 259 Programmable Complex Waveform Generator from the original Series 200. (Courtesy of David Kean/The Audities Foundation)

Chang points out that the original Buchla Series 200 is a Fourier additive synth with which he would stack harmonics and independently control their amplitudes using the modular's multitude of envelope generators and gates. It can also do FM and subtractive synthesis. Buchla's 259 Programmable Complex Waveform Generator houses two oscillators, one the main oscillator and the other an oscillator for modulating amplitude, frequency, or balance (ring modulation). Gary has composed pieces with his huge Wiard modular using only sine-wave oscillators because the combination of sine waves and distortion sounds much more musical to him. "The harmonic spectra is more natural," he says, "more of what our ears are able to understand."

Performance

Tools of the Trade

Playing synths live nearly always proves challenging, although not as much as during the early days when drifty analog modulars and monosynths were the norm or before programmable instruments became available. Synthesists with lots of experience sometimes consider the old days not so bad, or at least some of the vintage technology they used that has since become rare or extinct.

The Synthesizer

Don Muro performs on his monster setup in 1979. *Above his left arm* are an Eventide HM80 Baby Harmonizer resting on the synth cabinet of an ARP 2600. Directly *to the right* is a Mutron Bi-Phase above a Sequential Circuits 700 Programmer, with a Roland SVC-350 vocoder and Roland CR-78 drum machine beneath that, *to the left*. Underneath an Oberheim DS-2 digital sequencer is an ARP Pro DGX, which Don is playing, and under that is an ARP Omni mk II that ARP customized by adding aftertouch response to its keyboard along with some other features. At the *bottom* of the photo are an ARP Odyssey *to the left* of an ARP mult box and an MXR Phase 100 stompbox. (Photo courtesy of Don Muro)

The synthesist, teacher, and author Don Muro has long been a huge fan of Nyle Steiner's Masters Touch, a breath-to-voltage converter with a built-in lowpass filter. When you blew through its tube, it opened the filter's cutoff frequency. Don used it for the first time with a Korg Trident mkII, which came out in 1982 and provided three synthesis sections: synth, brass, and strings. Each section had an independent audio output. He routed the brass section through the Masters Touch and then to a separate amp and speaker in the back of the room. While he was playing, he would occasionally blow into the Masters Touch tube and the horn sound would appear from silence in the back of the room. People at first jumped up out of their chairs because the sound was fairly loud, and nothing had come from behind them until then. Muro recalls the Masters Touch as being a great effect that enabled him to play more expressively because it forced him to phrase lines differently.

Upon hearing Wendy Carlos's *Switched-On Bach* in 1969, Muro—a trained concert organist—was anxious to play Bach in real time on synthesizers. To do so properly, however, required a concert organ-style pedalboard. In 1977, Don and his father commissioned

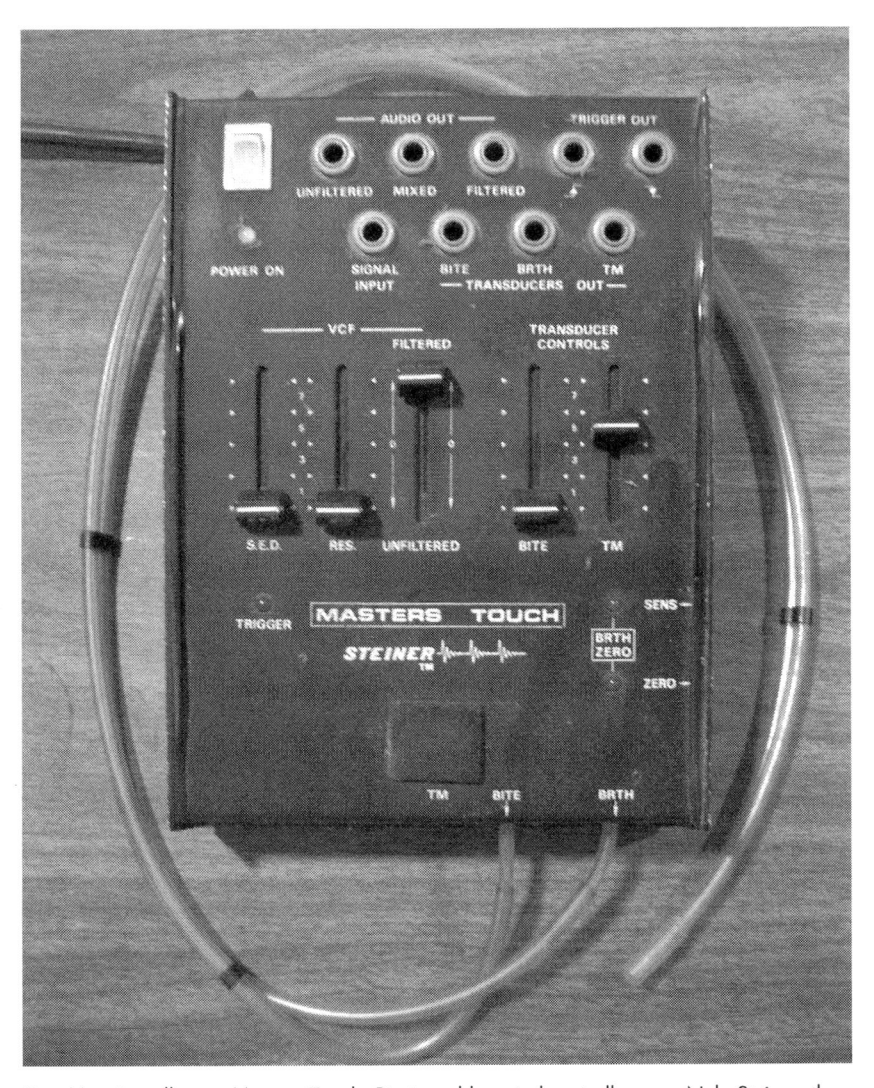

Don Muro's well-worn Masters Touch. Designed by wind-controller guru Nyle Steiner, the Masters Touch provided powerful control capabilities before the advent of MIDI. (Photo courtesy of Don Muro)

An original Korg Trident, predecessor to the Trident mkII Don Muro found particularly potent for live performance when teamed with a Steiner Masters Touch. Like the mkII, the Trident offers three different voices: synth, brass, and string sections. (Courtesy of Korg)

ARP technician Mark Smith to adapt a Reisner standard AGO (American Guild of Organists) thirty-two-note pedalboard with ARP's 3620 keyboard controller to drive an ARP 2600. Muro's initial composite performance instrument comprised this pedalboard; ARP 2600, Pro-DGX, Odyssey, and Omni II synthesizers; an Oberheim DS-2 digital sequencer; a Yamaha mixer; dbx 154 noise reduction; an SAE power amp; a Roland 201 Space Echo; and an Eventide Harmonizer—plus volume and CV pedals and footswitches galore. He first performed a concert with this setup "for the conference of the Pennsylvania Music Educators association on January 12, 1979, at the Hershey Convention Center," Muro wrote in his "Synthesizers in Performance" column in the April 1985 issue of *Keyboard* magazine. Of course he played Bach.

Over the years, Don has continually refined his concert setup, including the pedalboard. In the spring of 1984, he hired Jim Wright—an engineer who helped design Korg's Polysix and Mono/Poly synths—to develop a second-generation thirty-two-note AGO pedalboard with MIDI output. It has a strange interface—a device that started out as a polyphonic metronome—but it worked flawlessly, and it included analog CV and gate outputs so Don could still use it with older analog instruments.

Before the end of the 1980s, Wright built Muro another MIDI pedalboard controller with a simpler interface. In the early '90s, they modified the pedalboard to do splits and be more portable. By the mid-'90s, they added a JLCooper MIDI retrofit kit and enclosed all of the electronics inside the pedalboard itself, further improving its portability. Today, virtually all pipe organs and electronic church organs output MIDI.

Dependence on the Tried and True, but Moving Forward

Even as he strives to incorporate the newest of musical technologies in his onstage and studio rigs, David Rosenthal has had to depend on out-of-production hardware and software that are nearing or past two decades in age. Until recently he continued to use Opcode StudioVision software and Studio 5 MIDI interfaces. Rosenthal also still has

Don Muro's May 1981-era monster setup, beginning from the *upper left*: Sequential Circuits 700 Programmer above ARP 2600 and ARP 3620 keyboard controller beneath cables for the pedalboard; Roland TR-808 drum machine on top of Roland SVC-350 vocoder and Roland SRE-555 Chorus Echo; ARP Pro DGX above Oberheim OB-X, and below them multiple foot pedals and switches above a thirty-two-note AGO pedalboard with custom-built monophonic CV and gate outputs; and Oberheim DS-2 digital sequencer and customized ARP Odyssey at the *far right*. (Photo courtesy of Don Muro)

three Mac PowerBook G3 laptops running System 8.6. He's been relying on this rig for around twenty years, and he attributes this longevity to Opcode's innovators, who understood what musicians needed and wanted, and created products that were always ahead of the curve. David laments that the company no longer exists because, sooner or later, the hardware is going to fail, and he won't be able to find any more spares. He has five Studio 5s; they almost never die, but it's the laptops he's worried about because all of the Opcode hardware is pre-USB. That and the fact SCSI hard drives are getting harder to come by indicate this system's days are numbered. Therefore, David's in the process of switching over to Apple MainStage.

Surprisingly, the Opcode system isn't the oldest technology Rosenthal continues to use. A pair of Lake Butler MIDI Mitigator RFC-1 Foot Controllers, introduced in 1987, share onstage floor space beneath his synths, and he has eight spares in case one quits working. Each Mitigator enables him to send program changes, currently, to the Opcode Studio 5, but soon MainStage, and then the Studio 5/MainStage will change the whole rig. The Mitigator has five definable MIDI footswitches that allow settings to be saved as a song. Rosenthal can put all of the enclosed songs in alphabetical order, but the Mitigator's most unique feature allows him to program three different set lists and step through them during the show. On tours with Billy Joel, one of David's Mitigators contains programs for the show in the song order that the band is going play that night, and the other has all of the songs in alphabetical order in case Billy calls a song that isn't in the set list.

In a November 2007 performance with Billy Joel, David Rosenthal plays a Roland JD-800 and Yamaha Motif ES7, with a Kurzweil K2661 above a Hammond Suzuki Xk-3c in the background. On the floor behind him is one of David's two Lake Butler MIDI Mitigator RFC-1 Foot Controllers. The pedalboard is a Fast Forward Designs MIDIstep. (Tomohiro Akutsu)

Bear in mind that Joel's immense song catalog stretches back to the 1970s and, over the years, he incorporated many different synths in his music, depending on what was popular and available at the time. When the Minimoog and Yamaha DX7 were hot in their respective periods, Billy was using and featuring them a lot. There's been an ever-changing landscape of synth technology during Billy Joel's long career, and Rosenthal—Billy's musical director—has to replicate all of it live, requiring a lot of different synths from various eras and diverse ways of reproducing all of those sounds.

Not only does Rosenthal need to know all of the songs by heart, but he also must have immediate access to all of the appropriate synth sounds within seconds. It simply isn't possible for him to remember all of the patches required for every song. What he's been working with for so long—a very complex system of old and new synthesizers, effects, computers, interfaces, and controllers—seems the only reliable way to execute what needs to be done.

After many years of touring with Billy Joel and other major acts, David decided to scale back his touring rig from lots of hardware to softsynths and less hardware. In late 2010, he began converting sounds from some of his hardware synths into softsynths using Redmatica AutoSampler (AS). Apple Inc. purchased Redmatica in May 2012, and as yet there's been no indication whether AS and other Redmatica applications will ever become available again. A current alternative to AS would be the cross-platform Sound-lib Samplit.

AutoSampler provided tools to simplify the process of converting sounds from hardware synths into software instruments, doing the process unattended after you'd set its parameters. You could choose from one to sixteen velocities per voice, and AS would sequentially transmit MIDI notes at those velocities one at a time to the synth being sampled—actually, up to sixty-four synths at once if you have enough MIDI ports. David discovered the sixteen-velocity setting resulted in samples that played and sounded the same way they had from the original instrument, which was critical. He also programmed AS to sample every minor third so that each sample needed only to stretch up or down a half step. After David programmed AS and set up his audio routing and levels, the application ran through the process and created sample sets and instruments for Logic EXS24, Native Instruments Kontakt, Pro Tools Structure, Reason NN-XT, and Redmatica Keymap. It could also auto-loop samples.

The first synth Rosenthal ran through the AS process was the Roland JD-800. He quickly learned that the character of the JD-800 sounds and those from a lot of other synths of that era came from their built-in effects. You can't sample with reverb, chorus, or delay activated because they ruin the samples when you transpose them. He therefore had to disable all of the effects, run AutoSampler to get the samples, and then replicate the effects in MainStage. Copying the effects was the most time-consuming part because David needed to confirm that the MainStage effects responded the same way that they did in the source instrument.

Once Rosenthal found the parameter set that worked, he was able to import the collection of multisamples as an EXS24 instrument that he then loaded into a Muse Research Receptor for live performances. He's found the Receptor to be very stable, which is crucial because Billy Joel doesn't rehearse, and his band has to play everything live onstage. Thus, David can't experiment in that situation and almost never has an opportunity to try out new things. Stability is therefore his number one concern—even if he has to stay behind the curve because he has to go onstage and everything has to work flawlessly.

He replaced the JD-800 before Billy Joel's three-month tour with Elton John in 2010, so he used MainStage as a module—not controlling his whole rig. He created an EXS24 instrument out of his Redmatica AutoSampler JD-800—twenty-two patches that he absolutely couldn't live without—and it held up fine. When they go out on tour again, David plans to give MainStage control of his entire setup, getting rid of individual hardware modules and shrinking his whole setup down in favor of softsynths. He wants to capture the thousands of hours of programming he's put into Billy Joel's complete catalog of songs and transfer it into the modern technology. That way he can create software instruments in software samplers using streaming and maintain the integrity of the sound. Rosenthal reported in February 2013 that he had switched everything over to MainStage and the Receptor in time for an upcoming gig with Joel, the first time he'll perform with the converted rig. David said at first the whole system choked and couldn't deal with the massive amount of streaming sounds and instruments that he was using, but after he transferred everything from hard drives to solid-state drives "it became a new world. Everything is working great now."

Modular Apparitions

If awards were handed out to honor the all-time most impressive onstage appearances of a single synthesizer, one would definitely go to the monstrous Moog Modular that loomed

Inspirational prog-rock keyboardist Keith Emerson plays a Yamaha GX-1 in rehearsal with Emerson, Lake & Palmer in 1977. Behind him are a Hammond C-3 supporting the keyboard and ribbon controller connected to Keith's monster Moog Modular synth *at far right*. (© Dominic Milano. All rights reserved.)

over Keith Emerson and his Hammond C-3 organ for years at countless Emerson, Lake & Palmer concerts. Will Alexander, who with Gene Stopp refurbished Emerson's Moog during the early 1990s, called it "the world's most dangerous synth."

Moog modules established a format called "5U," which continues to be used by numerous modular manufacturers today, including Bridechamber (now selling and supporting Synthesis Technology/MOTM modules), Moon Modular/Lunar Experience, and Synthesizer.com. Although 5U modules aren't the tallest, they're considerably larger than those within the Eurorack, FracRak, Mattson, and other small-format realms. I doubt a comparably equipped Eurorack modular would have had the same impact as Keith's big Moog.

Although 5U systems are larger and less portable than their smaller brethren, they offer several benefits—both onstage and in the studio. Since the modules are bigger, the surface of a 5U system spreads out to cover an impressive amount of space. In a performance environment, smaller systems such as a Eurorack or FracRak might be overlooked—especially from a distance—and movements a performing synthesist makes are at a relatively smaller scale. With a 5U system that's so spread out, the synthesist has to reach far up to adjust a knob and swim through overhanging cables like a waterfall, and such large-scale interaction is more interesting for an audience to watch. Even if it isn't a one-to-one relationship such as someone hitting a drum, strumming a guitar, or blowing a horn, it's more entertaining than observing someone work on a small scale with a Eurorack modular or a laptop computer.

Bob Moog poses with Keith Emerson and Keith's Moog Modular—which stands 4-1/4' tall, spans 4' across, and weighs 550 pounds—and Hammond C-3 organ in the mid-1970s. Few if any synths at the time could compare in stage presence with "the World's Most Dangerous Synth." (With the permission of Ileana Grams-Moog)

That being said, you can certainly expand a small-format modular system until it's quite large. Serge Modular panels lie halfway between the heights of 5U and Eurorack modules, but I've seen two huge and remarkably well-configured Serge systems that, while they may not be nearly as big as Keith Emerson's Moog Modular, are absolutely dazzling with eye appeal more than equal to that Moog. First there's the Beast, a twelve-panel Serge that belongs to the Canadian composer Edmund Eagan. He explains that its structure was designed to make as many modules accessible as possible from one sitting position. I agree with him that it looks like something out of *Star Wars*, but that wasn't his intent. It took Eagan ten years to acquire and make the Beast.

Kevin Fortune created the second system of note, the Mighty Serge. He was inspired to create an instrument that allowed him to perform live electronic music while entertaining his audience with significant movements that would draw their interest. He wanted to avoid the visually boring experiences he recalled from early electronic music concerts, when musicians stood still and did nothing that was interesting to watch. Audiences want to be part of an experience where they can somehow interact with the performing musicians. That's why Kevin designed the Mighty Serge to conform to the arc of his arms, so that when he reaches for something it has visual appeal that connects with the audience.

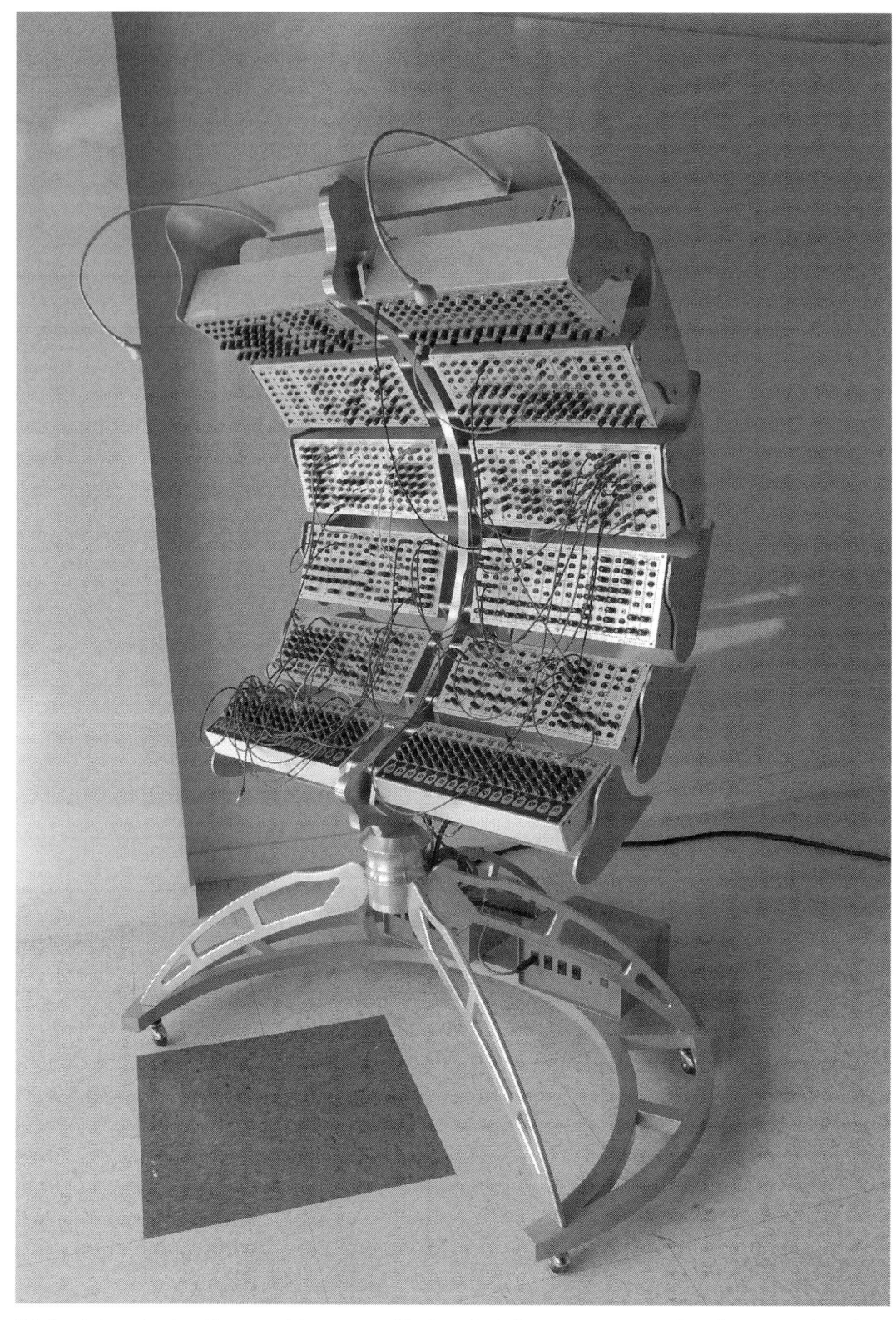

This futuristic and unique Serge modular system—"the Beast"—belongs to composer Edmund Eagan and resides at Twelfth Root Studio in Ottawa, Canada (www.twelfthroot.com). The custom-designed aluminum structure houses its dozen Serge panels such that a sitting synthesist can reach every one from that position. Among the modules is a rare TEV, a Touch Envelope Voltage Source, and a custom seven-into-four quad-channel voltage-controlled mixer designed by Sound Transform Systems. Eagan reports that the latter has an amazingly wide signal-to-noise ratio. While he regrets not having more than two DSG modules—Dual Universal Slope Generators—and that the system isn't very portable, Ed says the Beast sounds awesome and he enjoys the experience of sitting in front of and working with the beautiful system. (© Edmund Eagan)

Kevin Fortune designed and assembled his impressive Mighty Serge in 1977 for ease of patching and performance, as well as synthesis power and flexibility. (Mark Vail)

Defying the Dependence on Visuals

Maintaining a connection with the audience during live performance is crucial to many of the best musicians. Wendy Carlos maintains that "We tend to lose sight of outer-directed communication, expression, humanity, the very reasons we're involved with the art-form of music—why anyone is an artist, isn't it?"

The gospel performer Don Lewis echoes the thoughts about communication. "The idea of music to me is that there should be an underlying passion for wanting to communicate," says Lewis.

Don Muro addresses the pitfalls of technology's use in performance and entertainment. "We have a whole generation of people who think music and video are one and the same," Muro offers. "That's a loss, but there's nothing we can do about it. We're part of the last generation that can really listen to music without seeing something."

Don Lewis appears at the January 2013 NAMM convention in Anaheim, California, to perform with and explain the Live Electronic Orchestra (LEO), which he originally finished during the mid-'70s and refurbished toward the end of 2012. (Mark Vail)

Four Oberheim SEM modules and a Roland Space Echo are part of Don Lewis's LEO, on which he performed during the late '70s and early '80s, for a few days in January 2013, and perhaps on tours to come. (Mark Vail)

Composition, Programming, and Performance Techniques

Tucked into the vintage corner of Don Muro's studio as of 2011 are (counterclockwise from the *upper left*) a Steiner Master's Touch next to an ARP Odyssey, a Korg Wavestation EX, a Korg CX3 organ, a Fender Rhodes 73 electric piano, and a rare, giant Korg MS-20 known as "the blackboard." "It's a heck of a conversation piece," Muro says of the supersized MS-20, which was designed for educational purposes. While its keyboard and jacks are standard size, everything else is proportionally larger, so all of the teacher's knob adjustments could be seen by the whole class. Korg made about twenty blackboards. (Derek Muro, courtesy of Don Muro)

5

Recording the Synthesizer

Given the nature of synthesis, recording typically happens entirely in an electronic environment. Unless you're after certain types of effects, you won't need to worry about special miking techniques as you would with most acoustic and electro-acoustic instruments. Still, there are numerous choices to make when you record your synthesizers, including whether you can simply plug an instrument directly into a mixer that feeds audio into your recorder or should consider running the signal through some type of processor beforehand; what type of media you should record on; which conventional tools can enhance and simplify the recording process and how experienced composers use them; and what kinds of economical choices can still result in good recorded sound.

As It Was and How It's Become for the *Switched-On* Innovator

Master synthesist Wendy Carlos threw down the gauntlet with her 1968 release *Switched-On Bach*, proving that music created with synthesizers could be emotional, articulate, spellbinding, expressive, joyful, dynamic, mysterious, forceful, harmonic, and—most importantly in this context—very well recorded. The work she and her colleagues did in making that album and those that followed was immense and difficult, and many of the tools they used bear little resemblance to those we have today. Wendy had to contend with early analog oscillators and other components that would continuously drift in and out of skew during every session, recording monophonic tracks one at a time on multitrack open-reel magnetic tape with complex synchronizers, Dolby noise reduction for each track, and much more that's hard to fathom in this advanced digital age.

In comparison, it's much easier and simpler for synthesists to record their music today. Or is it? If it is, is everyone taking advantage of what he or she actually has access to or can get?

Let's consider—from numerous perspectives—many of the variables that go into recording the synthesizer, including where and through what to route synths' audio, what to record with, and how recording media may or may not become obsolete.

While producing *Switched-On Bach*, *The Well-Tempered Synthesizer*, *Switched-On Bach II*, and *Switched-On Brandenburgs*, Carlos recorded on either 1″ eight-track or 2″ sixteen-track reel-to-reel decks because the head gaps were wide and, with Dolby processing, she could get a very clean sound. When she remastered these masterpieces for re-release on CD by East Side Digital, she was surprised and delighted by the sound quality of her early recordings. "I probably never heard them properly until I got into my new studio, which has a Faraday cage around the whole room, so it's a very quiet environment. We get a clean sound and I don't listen too loudly because I don't want to hurt my hearing."

A Faraday cage is an electromagnetic shield consisting of wire mesh implanted in the walls, ceiling, and floor and tied to a common ground. It greatly reduces—and may totally eliminate—interference caused by the radio signals and electric fields that are prominent where Carlos works, in downtown New York City.

In 1995, Wendy worked with an Akai A-DAM (Akai Digital Audio Multitrack) twelve-track deck to produce *Switched-On Bach 2000*. The A-DAM recorded to 8mm videotapes and mostly worked well for her, although she found it a bit slower and less convenient than reel-to-reel tape. She was particularly fond of the A-DAM's control box, using its memory storage and cache to save pointers and jump to specific locations as quickly as the tape mechanism could respond. Her mixdown system was more problematic, "a kludged-together system made by an English company," she recalls. "It was basically two PCM 701 processors tied together with a high-band video deck. It worked pretty well, but most of those tapes are unplayable any more."

Some of the tapes she refers to are no longer playable because of obsolescence due to their extremely proprietary nature and because Carlos has moved on to newer technology. She also points out a dilemma faced by anyone who depended on magnetic recording tape produced during the 1970s and '80s, when many manufacturers incorporated polyurethane binding. The binding breaks down over time and makes the tape sticky and unplayable unless it's baked using delicate and precise procedures—a temporary fix that at best makes the tape playable for a short time.

Wendy's early non-tape-based digital audio recording required two computers, one of which drove multiple MIDI synths and played audio tracks. She used SMPTE (Society of Motion Picture and Television Engineers) Time Code to synchronize the computer to video and fed all of the audio into a mixing console—working as she previously did with multitrack tape—to the second computer, which ran Digidesign Sound Designer software to record the music. This system allowed her to make fine-quality recordings, edit and mix them within the computer, and create new audio tracks onto which she could add more layers.

These days Carlos uses MOTU Digital Performer running on a single Mac to sequence her MIDI gear and record audio directly onto hard disks, a much simpler system with which to work. Her audio interfaces of choice also come from MOTU, which she calls very good. She swaps in new interfaces once the older models become outdated. She's also fairly impressed with the audio quality she gets while recording with a small handheld recorder, and even accepts the audio quality of her Mac's I/O, saying it "doesn't sound too bad. It has a little bit of leakage from the digital into the analog circuits, so there's a low-level buzz that's down far enough that it doesn't bother me. But for simple captures and a lot of mixes, it's remarkable how well the Mac holds up."

Serial vs. Random-Access Media

The Alesis ADAT proved revolutionary in the early 1990s by introducing multitrack digital tape recording that mortal musicians could afford. With an ADAT, you can record nearly forty-one minutes of eight-track, sixteen-bit audio at a sampling rate of 44.1 or 48kHz onto a standard S-VHS tape cassette. You can synchronize up to sixteen ADATs for as many as 128 recording tracks with an Alesis Big Remote Control (BRC). The original ADAT has unbalanced 1/4″ input and output jacks at the consumer-standard −10dBV level, as well as a fifty-six-pin Elco connector for professional +4dBu audio I/O. Its proprietary Lightpipe fiber-optic digital input and output ports for eight-track transfers have become standard connectors on many digital audio products.

There's a word in the previous paragraph that many musicians choose to avoid now: tape. Magnetic tape recorders have been around since the 1930s and certainly served the music industry well. However, one of their major disadvantages is the maintenance required to keep tape heads clean, demagnetized, and properly aligned. Another is its purely serial means of audio access. To hear music recorded two minutes and fifty-five seconds from a song's beginning, you have to fast-forward or reverse the transport to the correct tape location.

Other digital recorders besides the ADAT deal with audio in a linear manner. So do DAT recorders and the Sony MiniDisc, which survived from its introduction in 1992 until Sony stopped production of MiniDisc machines in early 2013.

Much more convenient is random-access digital recording, as is done with hard-disk technology that's been around about as long as the ADAT and newer solid-state conveniences such as a USB flash drive and SD memory card. Not only does random-access technology allow you to immediately zero in on specific spots in a recording, but it's also crucial for cut/copy/paste editing, volume normalization, and swift transfers of audio files from a machine such as a portable digital recorder to a computer in which you can edit the audio.

Not everyone has signed off on the use of magnetic tape. There are plenty of advocates of the qualities inherent in recording analog audio to tape, even to the point of mixing multitrack digital recordings to analog tape. If you'd prefer to forgo the tape, you can find audio processors that simulate the analog-tape sound. One is the AnaMod Audio ATS-1 Analog Tape Simulator, which can process stereo audio to sound as if it's been recorded by one of four different tape machines at 7.5, 15, or 30 inches per second using any of four formulations of tape. This processing happens entirely in analog with no latency, and there are controls for adjusting tape bias, low and high frequency EQ, and tape hiss. The ATS-1 is but one tape simulator on the market; there are others in hardware and plug-in software forms.

For those who want to digitally record their synthesizers on affordable machines, there are currently many alternatives. I've gotten good results recording stereo tracks with a handheld Edirol R-09 and multiple tracks on a Zoom R16, both of which record audio on an SD card that I can slip into a USB adapter and plug into my MacBook Pro for quick file transfers and extensive editing. In the studio, I record with the Mac running Propellerhead Reason or Ableton Live using an RME Fireface 400 audio interface and a Glyph GT050 hard drive to capture the audio.

Strategies for Recording Film and TV Scores

When Amin Bhatia composes for film, he has to keep in mind that his music is only one of three different elements in the soundtrack. There are also sound effects and dialog, and there's no way he can predict how his music is going to fit with those other elements. Sometimes a melody might conflict with a new line of dialogue that wasn't in his work tape.

In composing and recording music for films and TV series such as *Flashpoint*, Amin Bhatia works with old and new, analog and digital gear arranged and connected for maximum efficiency. (Courtesy of Amin Bhatia)

Rarely does Amin create pieces of music where the final result is a stereo mix. He and co-*Flashpoint*-composer Ari Posner have set up systems by which they record to stems, a series of components that can subsequently be mixed together (see chap. 4). A group of stems all have the same start and end points so, if you assign each stem to a track and merge them all to the same output, you'll get a stereo mix.

While some composers deliver a completed 5.1 mix for a film project, unless it's a live orchestral recording Amin isn't a fan of that approach. Instead, he provides his mix engineers with more flexibility by giving them a group of calibrated stems so they can decide how far back in the mix the strings should sit or how far forward the percussion should be. Bass is always on a separate stem because bass management works differently on film and TV than it does on an album.

Bhatia and Posner create interleaved stereo, 48kHz WAV files that they share with each other and the music editor via an online FTP site. Bhatia credits producer/engineer David Greene for teaching him how to imagine the final stereo master and then work backward to create its multitrack elements. Greene taught him to organize his tracks, pans, and reverbs in advance so that the process of playing and mixing them is much more coherent. Amin will spend weeks honing the perfect template for a particular show by pre-assigning the level for every possible instrument he plans to use, which allows him to forget about the engineering task and focus on composing the music.

Since a single computer can't handle Amin's softsynth and recording requirements, as of June 2011 he incorporated three in his studio—affectionately referred to as "Father," "Mother," and "Daughter." Father is an old Mac G5 Power PC that runs Pro Tools Digi 003, which functions as a multitrack recorder. For filmscore projects, it serves as a master "tape recorder," capturing all of the different pieces of music that he can check any time.

The Synthesizer

Accompanying a few rackmounted hardware synth modules in Amin Bhatia's studio are three Macintosh tower computers—dubbed Mother, Father, and Daughter—at the *lower left*. (Courtesy of Amin Bhatia)

Mother is one of two Mac Pro Quad-Core Intel machines. Running on this computer are Logic and an application called Plogue Bidule, which translates from French into English as "plug-in gadget." Bidule is a plug-in host program that sits in the background and allows the user to patch into it using the computer's virtual MIDI Setup. It's somewhat like Propellerhead ReWire, but Bhatia finds it less restrictive than ReWire in regard to host, slave, and which of them has to boot first. Bidule is a lot more flexible and Amin can get "under the hood to play with its nuts and bolts," as he explains:

Bidule is a little nugget of virtual modules inside the computer. In some ways it resembles an analog modular synthesizer and in other ways it's like the Max programming language. It has all kinds of MIDI and audio modules, it hosts plug-ins, it can reassign MIDI controller numbers, it has random MIDI and audio generators, it has granular generators, and it has metering. But most importantly it allows you to run several plug-ins in the background, inside the same computer.

So your sequencer can occupy one portion of memory and Bidule can occupy another portion of memory. If a large plug-in like Kontakt starts to choke the sequencer, I can put another instance of Kontakt inside Bidule and internally transfer MIDI data back and forth between the two.

Plogue Bidule is very useful, but it isn't unique. KVR Audio (www.kvraudio.com) is a superb online source of information about everything related to plug-ins and hosts.

Daughter, Bhatia's second Mac Pro, also runs Bidule, along with Kontakt plug-ins, the Vienna Ensemble library, and other orchestral libraries from EastWest. Daughter is essentially a large sample player that Amin uses as his stock orchestral ensemble, waiting as a virtual host for incoming MIDI data. He uses Musiclab's MIDIoverLAN CP to send MIDI data via Ethernet. He's loaded orchestral sounds into the Daughter computer because latency is less of an issue in orchestral music as opposed to a bass line locked to a rhythm groove. Daughter's orchestral parts might seem a bit lazy, but they work for his purposes.

Amin's main audio interface is a MOTU 424 PCI card inside Mother with four external MOTU interfaces: an HD192, two 2408MKIIIs, and a 24io. This system provides him with sixty input channels into which he feeds audio from all of his different synths. Bhatia directs audio from Daughter via an M-Audio Lightpipe ProFire Bridge, which gives him eight ADAT channels from that computer. He routes audio from the interfaces and Lightpipe back to the MOTU interface on the main computer. The 424 system uses Audio Wire—which is similar to Firewire cable, but with a different proto-

Bhatia runs Apple Logic, shown here with open *Flashpoint* video and Spectrasonics Omnisphere windows, on the Macintosh Pro Quad-Core computer known as Mother. (Courtesy of Amin Bhatia)

The Synthesizer

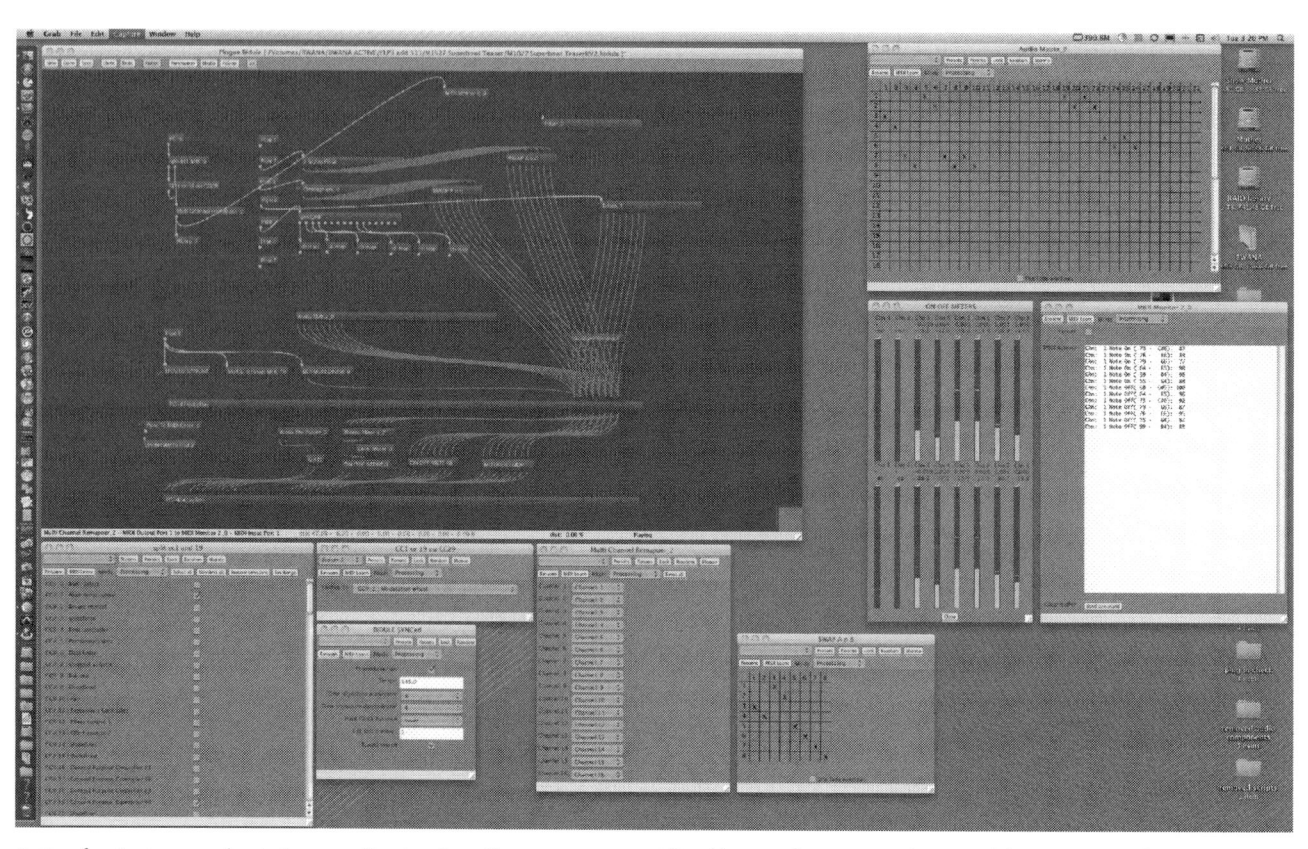

Acting for Amin as a plug-in host application that allows extensive and flexible signal routing is Plogue Bidule. (Courtesy of Amin Bhatia)

Bhatia also relies heavily on Native Instruments Kontakt, shown here running EastWest's Vienna Ensemble on the computer Amin has dubbed Daughter. (Courtesy of Amin Bhatia)

col—to feed all of his different MOTU interfaces. This technology is aging, but it works for Amin and he's reluctant to change anything—especially in the middle of composing for a season of *Flashpoint* episodes.

When his schedule allows, Bhatia plans to make major changes, including the purchase of new Mac computers and upgrading to the latest version of Pro Tools. Then he imagines he'll treat Logic like a plug-in that sits in the background, loaded with thirty-two of his favorite sounds.

Harnessing the Power of Modular Synths with Ableton Live

Gary Chang combines a monstrous Wiard 300 Series modular synthesizer, several Eurorack and FracRak modular systems, a Waldorf Wave, an NED Synclavier with its mainframe system tucked into its own isolation room, racks filled with synth modules and hardware processors, and Ableton Live running on an Apple MacBook Pro laptop computer to compose soundtracks for TV shows and movies, and to contribute synth parts to projects done by other recording artists. He runs Live fortified with Cycling '74's Max for Live supplement on the computer, which is connected to a TC Electronic Studio Konnekt 48 for audio and MIDI I/O interfacing to all of the hardware in his studio. Along with a Doepfer LMK4+ master keyboard controller, Chang uses an Akai APC40 and a 16 × 16 Monome to control Live. Among his plethora of external hardware processors is an OTO Machines Biscuit, which he incorporates into his music quite often.

Not only is Gary Chang's huge Wiard modular system impressive from the front, but it's also striking from the side and back thanks to its uniquely shaped metallic blue cabinet. Gary is a huge fan of the modules designed by Wiard's Grant Richter. (Mark Vail)

Gary Chang poses in June 2010 with his beautiful living-room drum/coffee table, which was made out of a tree trunk. (Mark Vail)

Both audio and MIDI interconnect all of Chang's musical gear. This allows him to record and process audio coming from Live tracks and internal VST and Audio Unit plug-ins—such as Drone Maker from Michael Norris's SoundMagic Spectral freeware suite, one that Gary's particularly fond of—as well as external sound modules, and to capture not only the audio but also all of his knob twirls, fader adjustments, keyboard performances, and button pushes he makes on the LMK4+, APC40, Monome, and Biscuit as MIDI data for subsequent editing and playback.

Automated Mixing

Don Muro was thrilled when he got his first programmable digital mixer, a Yamaha ProMix 01. He was blown away when he discovered he could finally store and recall every aspect of a mixdown and automate functions such as precise EQ changes in the middle of a song. He'd waited many years for such functionality. He later upgraded to Yamaha's 03D, which allows 48kHz/24-bit ADC and DAC resolution—specs that have long since been eclipsed, but they were fine for Muro's needs at the time. These days Don routes all of his analog signals straight into an RME Hammerfall DSP audio interface, which has eight analog inputs and outputs and ADAT Lightpipe I/O. From there all of the digitized audio goes directly into his computer.

Outboard Processing: Preparing Audio for Recording

Synthesists with a long history of recording develop preferences: i.e., ways of working, how to set things up for the process, and which external devices to incorporate. As you might expect, opinions and practices vary widely.

One tool synthesists often overlook is the direct box—also commonly referred to as a DI, the acronym for direct-insert or direct-injection. Recording engineers often use a direct box to route audio from an electric guitar or bass directly to a mixing board or recording deck because, otherwise, the instrument's level, impedance, and other characteristics would work very poorly. Not only does a direct box balance the electrical signal coming from the guitar or bass and allow the signal to be efficiently and effectively transmitted over longer cables, but it also converts the instrument's high-impedance output to a low impedance for the input on a mixing board or recorder. A direct box also preserves the instrument's frequency spectrum and timbral characteristics, which would be degraded in the DI's absence. It can equally be applied to synths and other instruments that output weak and high-impedance signals.

Another hardware utility select synthesists often use in recording is a preamplifier, which can typically add gain to a signal without inducing noise and distortion. Better preamps may also add sonic qualities that enhance an instrument's sound.

Whether he's working onstage or in the studio, David Rosenthal always routes his synth signals through direct boxes and preamps to ensure the sound he delivers for recording or amplification is optimal. Merely satisfactory audio quality won't do, so David is very particular about the components he chooses because he feels they color the sound as substantially as anything else. Rosenthal recommends synthesists avoid plugging their instruments directly into a mixer because they won't sound as full as they potentially can.

The DI of Rosenthal's choice is the Countryman Type 85, which he's directly compared to virtually everything else on the market and concluded it's hands down the best for recording synths. He has a rack of Type 85 DIs in his studio connected to a patchbay so he can patch instruments through them as he sees fit. He also has a rack of them on the back of his live rig to send signals from all of his synthesizers to the house mixer.

For his preamp, Rosenthal prefers the Shep SN8 module. He has a pair of them housed in a rack with a power supply. The SN8 is a four-band EQ/mic pre, a knockoff of the classic Neve 1073. David thinks it sounds amazing because it opens up the whole frequency range for him. When he uses it on a piano sound or a Rhodes electric piano, he says the overtones "get sparkly." David also reports that the SN8 doesn't color the sound, it only enhances what's already there.

When he's composing and recording, Rosenthal keeps everything virtual until he finalizes his decisions. Then he records in stereo, routing the mix of all of his instruments through the Shep SN8s into Pro Tools.

Amin Bhatia uses a Drawmer 1960 Mic Pre/Vacuum Tube **Compressor**, a stereo rackmount unit that he keeps connected to a dedicated set of inputs and outputs in his mixer. When he wants to warm the sound of a particular synth or a final mix, he can go outboard to the Drawmer and bring the processed audio back in again.

> *compressor:* an electronic circuit that reduces loud levels and increases the volume of quieter sonic events within an audio signal to minimize the dynamic range, sort of an automatic gain control

Bhatia also fights the impulse to categorize anything that's still useful and functional as "obsolete," proven by the presence of a Studer A80 1/4" two-track reel-to-reel deck in his studio. Sometimes he uses it to resurrect projects he worked on in the 1980s and '90s, transferring audio from tapes in his archive into the digital realm. Other times he'll run digital audio to tape and bring it back purely to get the actual tape sound. "Why go through a Pro Tools plug-in tape emulator or buy a tape-simulation box when I actually have a working tape machine here?" Amin rhetorically asks.

Amin Bhatia still relies on magnetic audio tape at some points in the recording process, and to resurrect recordings he made before going digital. This is his well-maintained Studer A80 1/4" two-track reel-to-reel deck. (Courtesy of Amin Bhatia)

I can't help but ask about the dull job of cleaning and demagnetizing the A80's tape heads on a regular schedule. "True," Bhatia admits, "but cleaning and demagnetizing heads takes far less time than chasing down tech support when a plug-in has failed."

Starr Parodi and Jeff Fair rely on yet another processing device during crucial synth recordings: a Great River MP-2NV. It's a dual-channel mic preamp that also has line-level inputs. According to Jeff, it's very similar to a Neve 1073. "One of the beauties of this particular piece," he explains, "is that it has independent input and output volume controls, so if you don't want to overdrive it but you want to turn up its output a little bit, it has the ability to stay very clean, but still with a little bit of the high-quality transformer sonics."

Instead of routing the outputs of their synthesizers into a mixer before the MP-2NV preamp, Jeff and Starr usually record only one synth at a time. Whenever they record their Minimoog, they connect its low-level output to its audio input, crank up the input

Starr Parodi and Jeff Fair shown backstage prior to performing for President Bill Clinton's inauguration at the Kennedy Center in January 1993. (Courtesy of Parodi/Fair)

level until it adds to the tone's girth and harmonic content, then use the results as an element in the mix stage—an old-school technique all Minimoog players should try.

Recording Direct and Expanding for Surround-Sound

Drew Neumann records his synths without using direct boxes or preamps. Although numerous twenty- and thirty-foot balanced and unbalanced audio cables run around his studio from synths to a Mackie 8-Bus mixer, he makes sure their signals are of such a high level that DIs and preamps aren't necessary. He's also modified some of them to improve their sonic characteristics, and his studio is wired with dual-phase power, which cancels any potential hum at the mixing board.

While studying at CalArts during the early 1980s, Neumann began learning interesting details about specific electronic components, such as the effects different capacitors and op amps have on audio signals that pass through them. In working with engineers on various projects and experimenting with circuits over the years, he's learned how to improve the audio qualities and extend the frequency bandwidth of electronic instruments by swapping in better components. His capacitor modifications go a long way in doing that, as do IC and passive filtering changes when necessary.

If Drew were to route a synth through any of the DIs or preamps in his studio, it wouldn't be one that incorporated vacuum tubes. "I don't put synth signals through anything that has tubes in it," he asserts. "I don't like the coloration tubes add to synth sounds. Don't get me wrong, I *love* guitar and Chapman stick through tubes, and some-

The LEDs, jacks, and cables shine eerily from the Modcan A Series/Cyndustries and Serge modular synths under a black light in Drew Neumann's studio after he turned off the overhead lights and kept his camera's shutter open for a few seconds. Although he doesn't route his synth signals through direct boxes or preamps, he does use balanced audio cables with certain synths, and he's wired the studio to minimize RFI and electric noise problems. (Drew Neumann, Droomusic)

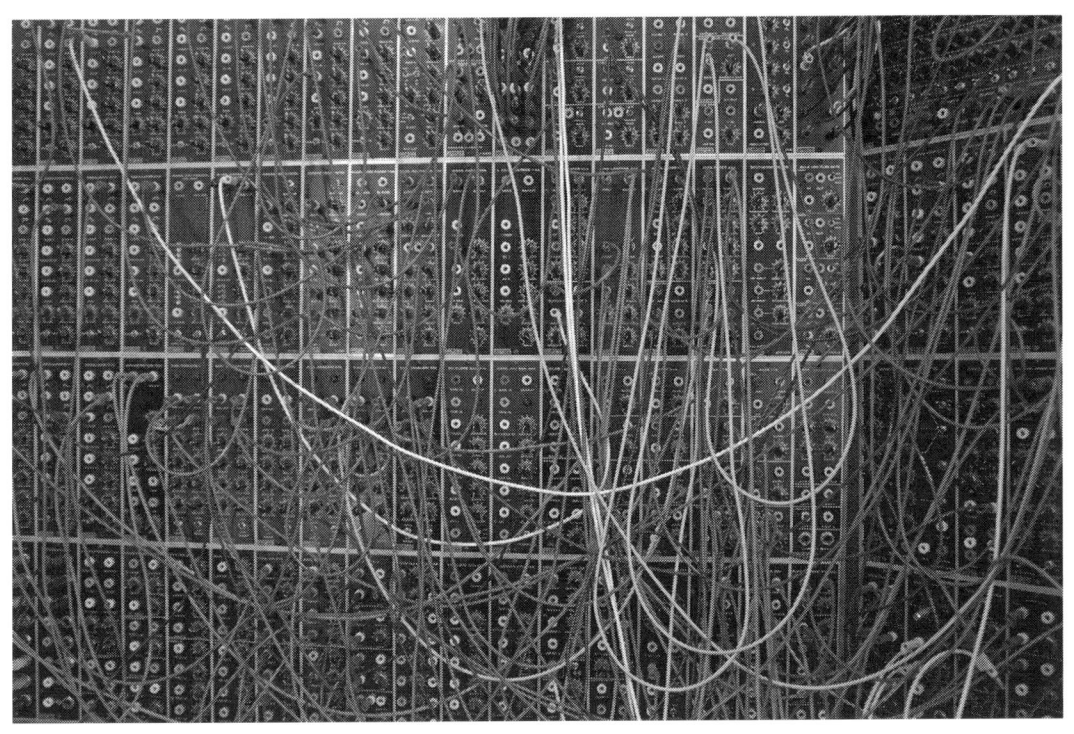

A web of patch cords obscures the many modules in Drew Neumann's Modcan A Series/Cyndustries modular system. (Amin Bhatia)

times even vocals. Even a cheap tube preamp can add just the right kind of dirt to those sounds, but not for synths. That's just my personal taste."

Neumann readily confesses that his aging fifty-six-channel Mackie 8-Bus mixer isn't optimal and someday, given time, he'll work on it like he's done his synths. "If I had the bucks, I'd dump the Mackie and get a Trident or a Neve, although I've heard good things about Toft Audio mixers," he proclaims. "High-end gear sounds great for a reason. My motto is, 'Use what you can afford and go make music.' Otherwise you'll drive yourself crazy and go broke."

As a film and television composer, Drew has, however, come to an important realization. "I will probably have to upgrade to full 5.1 surround recording eventually," he admits, "if I want to stay employable."

APPENDICES

APPENDIX A   Selected Bibliography, Films, and Museums

You'll find an extensive discography of music featuring synthesizers of all sorts on the companion website for *The Synthesizer*. Unless indicated otherwise, all URLs appearing on these pages begin with the prefix "http://".

Books

Aikin, Jim. *Power Tools for Synthesizer Programming: The Ultimate Reference for Sound Design.* San Francisco: Backbeat Books, 2004.

Anderton, Craig. *The Digital Delay Handbook.* New York: Amsco Publications, 1985.

Anderton, Craig. *Home Recording for Musicians.* Saratoga, CA: Guitar Player Books, 1978.

Anderton, Craig. *MIDI for Musicians.* New York: Amsco Publications, 1986.

Anderton, Craig, Bob Moses, and Greg Bartlett. *Digital Projects for Musicians.* New York: Amsco Publications, 1994.

Appleton, Jon, and Ronald C. Perera. *The Development and Practice of Electronic Music.* Upper Saddle River, NJ: Prentice Hall, Inc., 1975.

Austin, Larry, and Douglas Kahn. *Source: Music of the Avant-Garde, 1966–1973.* Berkeley: University of California Press, 2011.

Battino, David, and Kelli Richards. *The Art of Digital Music: 56 Visionary Artists & Insiders Reveal Their Creative Secrets.* Milwaukee: Backbeat Books, 2005.

Benade, Arthur H. *Fundamentals of Musical Acoustics.* Mineola, NY: Dover Publications, Inc., 1976, 1990.

Bernstein, David W., ed. *The San Francisco Tape Music Center: 1960s Counterculture and the Avant-Garde.* Berkeley: University of California Press, 2008.

Bode, Harald. "Sound Synthesizer Creates New Musical Effects: New Frontiers in Electronic Music." *Electronics*, December 1, 1961, available for download from haraldbodenews.wordpress.com/2010/08/31/123.

Borgo, David. *Sync or Swarm: Improvising Music in a Complex Age.* New York: Continuum International Publishing Group Inc., 2007.

Cann, Simon. *Becoming a Synthesizer Wizard: From Presets to Power User.* Boston, MA: Course Technology, a part of Cengage Learning, 2010.

Chadabe, Joel. *Electric Sound: The Past and Promise of Electronic Music.* Upper Saddle River, NJ: Prentice Hall, 1997.

Chamberlin, Hal. *Musical Applications of Microprocessors.* Hasbrouck Heights, NJ/Berkeley, CA: Samsung Semiconductors, 1980; Hayden Book Company, 1985.

Cipriani, Alessandro, and Maurizio Giri. *Electronic Music and Sound Design: Theory and Practice with Max/MSP.* Vol. 1. ConTempoNet s.a.s., Rome, Italy, 2010.

Colbeck, Julian. *KEYFAX: The Definitive Guide to Electronic Keyboards.* New York: Amsco Publications, 1985.

Colbeck, Julian. *KEYFAX 2: The Guide to Electronic Keyboards.* Suffolk, Great Britain: Virgin Books Ltd., 1986.

Colbeck, Julian. *KEYFAX 4: Synthesisers, Samplers & Controllers.* London: Making Music Ltd, 1993.

Colbeck, Julian. *KEYFAX: Omnibus Edition.* Ann Arbor, MI: MixBooks, 1996.

Collins, Nicolas. *Handmade Electronic Music: The Art of Hardware Hacking.* New York: Routledge/Taylor and Francis Group, 2006, 2009.

Collins, Nick, and Julio d'Escrivan, eds. *The Cambridge Companion to Electronic Music.* Cambridge: Cambridge University Press, 2007.

Cope, David. *Computers and Musical Style.* Middleton, WI: A-R Editions, Inc., 1991.

Coryat, Karl. *Guerrilla Home Recording: How to Get Great Sound from Any Studio (no matter how weird or cheap your gear is).* Milwaukee: Backbeat Books, 2005.

Countryman, Dana. *Passport to the Future: The Amazing Life and Music of Electronic Pop Music Pioneer Jean-Jacques Perrey.* Everett, WA: Sterling Swan Press, 2010.

Crane, Larry, ed. *Top Op: The Book About Creative Music Recording.* Venice, CA: Feral House, 2000.

Crombie, David. *The Complete Synthesizer: A Comprehensive Guide.* London: Omnibus Press, 1982.

Darter, Tom, comp. *The Whole Synthesizer Catalogue.* Milwaukee: Hal Leonard Publishing, 1985.

Darter, Tom, comp., Greg Armbruster, ed. *The Art of Electronic Music: The Instruments, Designers, and Musicians Behind the Artistic and Popular Explosion of Electronic Music.* New York: GPI Publications, 1984.

Davis, Gary, and Associates. *Dictionary of Creative Audio Terms.* Framingham, MA: CAMEO (Creative Audio & Music Electronics Organization), 1979.

De Furia, Steve. With Joe Scacciaferro. *The MIDI Book: Using MIDI and Related Interfaces.* Rutherford, NJ: Third Earth Productions, Inc., 1986.

Delaney, Martin. *Laptop Music.* Thetford, UK: PC Publishing, 2004.

Demers, Joanna. *Listening Through the Noise: The Aesthetics of Experimental Electronic Music.* New York: Oxford University Press, 2010.

Deutsch, Herbert A. *Electroacoustic Music: The First Century.* Miami, FL: Belwin Mills, c/o CPP/Belwin, Inc, 1993.

Deutsch, Herbert A. *Synthesis: An Introduction to the History, Theory, & Practice of Electronic Music.* Port Washington, NY: Alfred Publishing Co., Inc., 1976.

Devarahi. *The Complete Guide to Synthesizers.* Englewood Cliffs, NJ: Prentice Hall, Inc., 1982.

Eiche, Jon F. *What's a Synthesizer?* Milwaukee: Hal Leonard Books, 1987.

Friend, David, Alan R. Pearlman, and Thomas D. Piggot. *Learning Music with Synthesizers.* Milwaukee: Hal Leonard Publishing, 1974.

Forrest, Peter. *The A-Z of Analogue Synthesisers.* Part One, A–M. Exeter, UK: Susurreal Publishing, 1994, 1998.

Forrest, Peter. *The A-Z of Analogue Synthesisers.* Part Two, N–Z. Exeter and Devon, UK: Susurreal Publishing, 1996, 2003.

Fryer, Terry. *A Practical Approach to Digital Sampling.* Milwaukee: Hal Leonard Publishing Corporation, 1989.

Gallagher, Mitch. *Acoustic Design for the Home Studio.* Boston: Cengage Learning, 2006.

Ghazala, Reed. *Circuit Bending: Build Your Own Alien Instruments.* New York: Wiley Publishing, Inc., 2005.

Glasser, Brian. *In a Silent Way: A Portrait of Joe Zawinul.* London: Sanctuary Publishing Limited, 2001.

Glinsky, Albert. *Theremin: Ether Music and Espionage.* Urbana: University of Illinois Press, 2000.

Gorges, Peter, and Len Sasso. *Nord Modular: Introduction, Modular Sound Design, Virtual Assembly Instructions.* 2nd ed. Bremen, Germany: Wizoo, 2000.

Haus, Goffredo, ed. *MusicProcessing.* Vol. 9. Middleton, WI: A-R Editions, Inc., 1993.

Helmholtz, Hermann. *On the Sensations of Tone.* New York: Dover Publications, 1954.

Holmes, Thom. *Electronic and Experimental Music: Technology, Music, and Culture.* 4th ed. New York: Routledge, 2012.

Horn, Delton T. *Music Synthesizers: A Manual of Design & Construction*. Blue Ridge Summit, PA: Tab Books Inc., 1984.

Jacobson, Linda, ed. *Cyberarts: Exploring Art & Technology*. San Francisco: Miller Freeman Inc., 1992.

Jenkins, Mark. *Analog Synthesizers: Understanding, Performing, Buying*. Oxford: Focal Press, 2007.

Jones, Marvin. *The Source: Book of Patching and Programming from Polyphony*. Oklahoma City: Polyphony Publishing, 1978.

Kakehashi, Ikutaro, with Robert Olsen. *I Believe in Music: Life Experiences and Thoughts on the Future of Electronic Music by the Founder of the Roland Corporation*. Milwaukee: Hal Leonard Corporation, 2002.

Kehew, Brian, and Kevin Ryan. *Recording The Beatles: The Studio Equipment and Techniques Used to Create Their Classic Albums*. Houston: Curvebender Publishing, 2006.

Kirn, Peter. *Real World Digital Audio*. Berkeley: Peachpit Press, 2006.

Klein, Barry. *Electronic Music Circuits*. Blacksburg, VA: Blacksburg Continuing Education Series, 1982.

Kurzweil, Ray. *The Age of Spiritual Machines: When Computers Exceed Human Intelligence*. New York: Penguin Books, 1999.

Landy, Leigh. *Understanding the Art of Sound Organization*. Cambridge, MA: MIT Press, 2007.

Lehrman, Paul D., and Tim Tully. *MIDI for the Professional*. New York: Amsco Publications, 1993.

Lloyd, William, and Paul Terry. *Music Sequence: A Complete Guide to Midi Sequencing*. London: Musonix Publishing, 1991.

Lovelace, David C. *The Packrat Sampler: A Collection of Synthy Comics*. David C. Lovelace, privately published, 2012.

Loy, Gareth. *Musimathics: The Mathematical Foundations of Music*. Vol. 1. Cambridge, MA: MIT Press, 2006.

Loy, Gareth. *Musimathics: The Mathematical Foundations of Music*. Vol. 2. Cambridge, MA: MIT Press, 2007.

Manning, Peter. *Electronic and Computer Music*. New York: Oxford University Press, 2004.

Manzo, V. J. *Max/MSP/Jitter for Music: A Practical Guide to Developing Interactive Music Systems for Education and More*. New York: Oxford University Press, 2011.

Massey, Howard. *Behind the Glass: Top Record Producers Tell How They Craft the Hits*. San Francisco: Miller Freeman Books, 2000.

Massey, Howard. With Alex Noyes and Daniel Shklair. *A Synthesist's Guide to Acoustic Instruments*. New York: Amsco Publications, 1987.

Metzler, Bob. *Audio Measurement Handbook*. Beaverton, OR: Audio Precision, Inc., 1993.

Miller, Paul D., ed. *Sound Unbound: Sampling Digital Music and Culture*. Cambridge, MA: MIT Press, 2008.

Moog, Robert A., and Thomas L. Rhea. "Evolution of the Keyboard Interface: The Bösendorfer 290 SE Recording Piano and The Moog Multiply-Touch-Sensitive Keyboards." *Computer Music Journal* (Summer 1990), download from www.media.mit.edu/resenv/classes/MAS960/NewReadings/moog_evolution.pdf.

Nachmanovitch, Stephen. *Free Play: The Power of Improvisation in Life and the Arts*. New York: Jeremy P. Tarcher, Inc., 1990.

Newell, Philip, and Keith Holland. *Loudspeakers for Music Recording and Reproduction*. Oxford, UK: Focal Press, 2007.

Nyman, Michael. *Experimental Music: Cage and Beyond*. New York: Schirmer Books, 1974.

Perry, Megan. *Wired: Musician's Home Studio: Tools and Techniques of the Musical Mavericks*. Milwaukee: Backbeat Books, 2004.

Petersen, George, and Steve Oppenheimer. *Tech Terms: A Practical Dictionary for Audio and Music Production*. Milwaukee: Hal Leonard Publishing Corp., 1993.

Pierce, John R. *The Science of Musical Sound*. Rev. ed. New York: W. H. Freeman and Co., 1983, 1992.

Platt, Charles. *Encyclopedia of Electronic Components*. Vol. 1, *Power Sources and Conversion: Resistors, Capacitors, Inductors, Switches, Encoders, Relays, and Transistors*. Sebastopol, CA: O'Reilly Media, 2012.

Platt, Charles. *Encyclopedia of Electronic Components*. Vol. 2, *Signal Processing: Diodes, Transistors, Chips, Light, Heat, and Sound Emitters*. Sebastopol, CA: O'Reilly Media, 2013.

Platt, Charles. *Make: Electronics: Learning Through Discovery*. Sebastopol, CA: O'Reilly Media, Inc., 2009.

Pressing, Jeff. *Synthesizer Performance and Real-Time Techniques*. Middleton, WI: A-R Editions, Inc., 1992.

Preve, Francis. *Power Tools: Software for Loop Music: Essential Desktop Production Techniques*. San Francisco: Backbeat Books, 2004.

Rhea, Thomas Lamar. "The Evolution of Electronic Musical Instruments in the United States." PhD diss., Peabody College for Teachers of Vanderbilt University, 1972; AAT 7234209, available for download from www.proquest.com/en-US.

Roads, Curtis, ed. *Composers and the Computer*. Los Altos, CA: William Kaufmann, Inc., 1985.

Roads, Curtis. *Microsound*. London: MIT Press, 2001.

Roads, Curtis, and John Strawn, ed. *Foundations of Computer Music*. Cambridge, MA: MIT Press, 1985.

Robair, Gino. *The Ultimate Personal Recording Studio*. Boston: Thomson Course Technology, PTR, 2007.

Robinson, Keith. *Ableton Live 8 and Suite 8: Create, Produce, and Perform*. Oxford, UK: Focal Press, 2010.

Rona, Jeffrey. *MIDI: The Ins, Outs, & Thrus*. Milwaukee: Hal Leonard Books, 1987.

Rona, Jeffrey. *The MIDI Companion: The Complete Guide to Using MIDI Synthesizers, Samplers, Sound Cards, Sequencers, Computers and More!* Milwaukee: Hal Leonard, 1994.

Rona, Jeffrey. *Synchronization from Reel to Reel: A Complete Guide for the Synchronization of Audio, Film, & Video*. Milwaukee: Hal Leonard Publishing Corp., 1990.

Rowe, Robert. *Machine Musicianship*. Cambridge, MA: MIT Press, 2001.

Sasso, Len. *The Wizoo Pro Guide to MetaSynth 2.5*. Cologne, Germany: 1998.

Sonnenschein, David. *Sound Design: The Expressive Power of Music, Voice, and Sound Effects in Cinema*. Studio City, CA: Michael Wiese Productions, 2001.

Stewart, Dave. *The Musician's Guide to Reading and Writing Music*. San Francisco: GPI Books, 1993.

Strange, Allen. *Electronic Music: Systems, Techniques, and Controls*. 2nd ed. Dubuque, IA: Wm. C. Brown Co. Publishers, 1983.

Strawn, John, ed. *Digital Audio Signal Processing: An Anthology*. Los Altos, CA: William Kaufmann, Inc., 1985.

Thompson, Art. *Stompbox: A History of Guitar Fuzzes, Flangers, Phasers, Echoes, & Wahs*. San Francisco: Miller Freeman Books, 1997.

Tompkins, Dave. *How to Wreck a Nice Beach: The Vocoder from World War II to Hip-Hop*. Brooklyn, NY: Stopsmiling Books, 2010.

Toole, Floyd E. *Sound Reproduction: Loudspeakers and Rooms*. Oxford, UK: Focal Press, 2008.

Truax, Barry, ed. *The World Soundscape Project's Handbook for Acoustic Ecology*. Burnaby, BC, Canada: A.R.C. Publications, 1978.

Vail, Mark. *The Hammond Organ: Beauty in the B*. San Francisco: Backbeat Books, 1997, 2002.

Vail, Mark. *Vintage Synthesizers*. San Francisco: Miller Freeman Books, 1993. Reprint, San Francisco: Backbeat Books, 2000.

Welsh, Fred. *Welsh's Synthesizer Cookbook*. 3rd ed. Fred Welsh, 2006.

Welsh, Fred. *Welsh's Synthesizer Cookbook*. Vol. 2, *Harmonic Catalog*. Fred Welsh, 2010.

White, Paul. *Basic MIDI*. London: Sanctuary Publishing, 2006.

Whitney, John. *Digital Harmony: On the Complementarity of Music and Visual Art*. Peterborough, NH: Byte Books, 1980.

Wierzbicki, James. *Louis and Bebe Barron's "Forbidden Planet": A Film Score Guide*. Lanham, MD: Scarecrow Press, Inc., 2005.

Wilkinson, Scott R. *Tuning In: Microtonality in Electronic Music*. Milwaukee: Hal Leonard Books, 1988.

Wilson, Ray. *Make: Analog Synthesizers: A Modern Approach to Old School Sound Synthesis*. Sebastopol, CA: O'Reilly, 2013.

Winkler, Todd. *Composing Interactive Music: Techniques and Ideas Using Max*. Cambridge, MA: MIT Press, 1998.

Yelton, Geary. *The Rock Synthesizer Manual: A Revised Guide for the Electronic Musician*. Woodstock, GA: Rock Tech Publications, 1986.

Periodicals

Computer Music, www.musicradar.com/computermusic

Computer Music Journal, www.mitpressjournals.org/loi/comj

Electronic Musician: Record, Produce, Perform, www.emusician.com

Future Music: Technique and Technology for Making Music, www.futuremusic.com

Keyboard, www.keyboardmag.com

Leonardo Music Journal, leonardo.info/lmj

Make: Technology on Your Time, makezine.com

MusicTech: The Magazine for Producers, Engineers and Recording usicians, www.musictechmag.co.uk

Nuts and Volts: Everything for Electronics, www.nutsvolts.com

Servo Magazine, www.servomagazine.com

Signal To Noise: The Journal of Improvised & Experimental Music, signaltonoisemagazine.org

Sound On Sound: The World's Best Recording Technology Magazine, www.soundonsound.com

Tape Op: The Creative Recording Magazine, www.tapeop.com

Films

Deconstructing Dad: The Music, Machines and Mystery of Raymond Scott, www.scottdoc.com

I Dream of Wires, idreamofwires.org

Jean-Jacques Perrey: Life, Laughter & Loops, www.jjpdvd.com

Mellodrama: The Mellotron Movie, www.mellodramadvd.com

Modulations: Cinema for the Ear, musicvideodistributors.com

Moog: A Documentary Film by Hans Fjellestad, www.moogmovie.com

Morton Subotnick, Vol. 1: Electronic Works; Vol. 2: Electronic Works, www.moderecords.com

An Overview of Electronic Instruments with Don Muro, www.jdwallpublishing.com

Theremin: An Electronic Odyssey, www.mgm.com/dvd

Synthesizer Museums

The Bob Moog Foundation
2 Wall Street, suite 212
Asheville, NC 28801
www.moogfoundation.org

National Music Centre
formerly Cantos Music Foundation
134 11th Ave. SE
Calgary, Alberta, Canada, T2G-0X5
(403) 543-5115
Fax (403) 543-5129
www.nmc.ca

Museum of Making Music
5790 Armada Drive
Carlsbad, CA 92008
(760) 438-5996
Fax: (760) 438-8964
Toll Free: (877) 551-9976
www.museumofmakingmusic.org

APPENDIX B Manufacturers, Forums, Blogs, Dealers, and Stores

You'll find web links for all of the following organizations on the companion website for *The Synthesizer*, along with additional ones that go online after the publication of this book. Unless indicated otherwise, all URLs appearing on these pages begin with the prefix "http://".

Ableton AG, www.ableton.com
Access Music Electronics GmbH, www.access-music.de
Acoustic Image, www.acousticimg.com
Adam Professional Audio, www.adam-audio.com
ADDAC System, www.addacsystem.org
Ad Infinitum, adinfinitummusic.com
Akai Professional, www.akaipro.com
Alesis, www.alesis.com
All Electronics Corporation, www.allelectronics.com
Allen & Heath, www.allen-heath.com
Altec Lansing LLC, www.alteclansing.com
Alternate Mode Kat, www.alternatemode.com
Alyseum, www.alyseum.com
Amplified Parts, www.amplifiedparts.com
AMSynths, www.amsynths.co.uk
Analog Craftsman, analogcraftsman.com
Analog Devices, www.analog.com
Analog Metropolis, www.amsynths.co.uk
Analogue Solutions, www.analoguesolutions.com
Analogue Systems Synthesis Equipment, www.analoguesystems.com
AnaMod Audio, www.anamodaudio.com
Aphex, www.aphex.com
Apogee Electronics, www.apogeedigital.com
Apple, www.apple.com
Applied Acoustics Systems, www.applied-acoustics.com
ART (Applied Research and Technology), www.artproaudio.com
Arturia Musical Instruments, www.arturia.com
Ashly Audio, www.ashly.com
Atomosynth, www.atomosynth.com/koneko.html
Audiobro, audiobro.com
Auralex, www.auralex.com
Avid/Digidesign, www.avid.com
Bag End, www.bagend.com
Bananalogue (see Big City Music)

Barbetta Electronics, www.barbetta.com
BBE Sound Inc., www.bbesound.com
Big Blue Wave, www.bigbluewave.co.uk
Big Fish Audio, www.bigfishaudio.com
Blacet Research, www.blacet.com
Bleep Labs, bleeplabs.com
Blue Sky International, abluesky.com
Boomerang Musical Products, www.boomerangmusic.com
Bose, www.bose.com
Boss, www.rolandus.com
The Bride Chamber, www.bridechamber.com
Bubblesound, www.bubblesound-instruments.com
Buchla Electronic Musical Instruments, www.buchla.com
BugBrand, www.bugbrand.co.uk
Carvin, www.carvinguitars.com
Casio, www.casio.com
Casper Electronics, casperelectronics.com
Cerwin-Vega, www.cerwinvega.com
CGS, www.cgs.synth.net
Chameleon, www.chameleon.synth.net
Chicken Systems, www.chickensys.com
Circuit Abbey, www.circuitabbey.com
Clavia DMI AB, www.clavia.se
Club of the Knobs (COTK), www.cluboftheknobs.com
CME, www.cme-pro.com/en/news.php
CMS (Cirocco Modular Synthesizers), www.discretesynthesizers.com
CoolAudio International Limited, www.coolaudio.com
Coresynth, corsynth.com
Countryman Associates, Inc., www.countryman.com
Crate Amplification, www.crateamps.com
Create Digital Music, createdigitalmusic.com
Crown Audio, www.crownaudio.com
Cwejman, www.cwejman.net
Cyndustries, www.cyndustries.com
Cycling '74, cycling74.com
Dave Jones Design, www.jonesvideo.com
Dave Smith Instruments (DSI), www.davesmithinstruments.com
Delptronics, www.delptronics.com
Dewanatron Electronics, www.dewanatron.com
Digi-Key Corporation, www.digikey.com
DinSync, www.dinsync.info
Division 6, www.division-6.com
Doepfer Musikelektronik GmbH, www.doepfer.de
Drawmer, www.drawmer.com
D16 Group, www.d16.pl

Dutch Instruments Fenix, www.dutchsynth.nl
Dynaudio Professional, dynaudioprofessional.com
Eardrill, www.eardrill.com
Ebtech, www.ebtechaudio.com
Eigenlabs, www.eigenlabs.com
Elby Designs, www.elby-designs.com/panther/panther.htm
Electric Druid, www.electricdruid.net
Electro-Harmonix, www.ehx.com
Electro-Music, electro-music.com
Electronic Music Works (EMW), www.electronicmusicworks.com
Electronotes, electronotes.netfirms.com
Electrotap, shop.electrotap.com
Elektron ESI AB, www.elektron.se
Electro-Voice, www.electrovoice.com
E-mu Systems, www.creative.com/emu
Encore Electronics, www.encoreelectronics.com
Endangered Audio, smashingguitarsasheville.com/endangered-audio
Endorphin.es, endorphin.es
Eowave, www.eowave.com
Equi=Tech Corp., www.equitech.com
Event Electronics, www.eventelectronics.com
Expert Sleepers, www.expert-sleepers.co.uk
Faderfox, www.faderfox.de
Fatar/Studiologic, www.fatar.com/scegli.htm
Fender Musical Instruments Corporation, www.fender.com
Flame, flame.fortschritt-musik.de/start.htm
Flight of Harmony, www.flightofharmony.com
Flower Electronics, www.flowerelectronics.com
Focal Professional, www.focalprofessional.com
Focusrite, us.focusrite.com
Fonitronik, www.fonitronik.de
4ms Pedals, 4mspedals.com
Furman Sound, www.furmansound.com
Future Apps, future-apps.net
Future Sound Systems, www.futuresoundsystems.co.uk
Garritan Instruments, www.garritan.com
Gator Cases, www.gatorcases.com
Genelec, www.genelec.com
Genz Benz, www.genzbenz.com
GetLoFi, www.getlofi.com
Goike, www.goike.com
Gorillabox, gorillabox.bigcartel.com
Gotharman, www.gotharman.dk
Great River Electronics, www.greatriverelectronics.com
Groove Tubes, www.groovetubes.com

Grove Audio, www.groveaudio.com
Jürgen Haibel, www.jhaible.de
Haken Audio, www.hakenaudio.com
Happy Nerding, www.happynerding.com
Hartke, www.samsontech.com/hartke
The Harvestman, www.theharvestman.org
HexInverter, cv.hexinverter.net
Hinton Instruments, hinton-instruments.co.uk
HK Audio, hkaudio.com
H-Pi Instruments (Hπ Instruments), www.h-pi.com
Hybrid Cases, www.hybridcases.com
iceGear, iphone.icegear.net
I-CubeX, infusionsystems.com
IK Multimedia, www.ikmultimedia.com
Infinite Response, www.infiniteresponse.com
Intellijel, www.intellijel.com
Jameco Electronics, www.jameco.com
Jawbone, jawbone.com
JazzMutant, www.jazzmutant.com
JBL Professional, www.jblpro.com
J9K, www.jninek.com
John Bowen Synth Design, www.johnbowen,com
Jomox, www.jomox.de
Juice Goose, www.juicegoose.com
Karma Lab LLC, www.karma-lab.com
Keith McMillen Instruments, www.keithmcmillen.com
Kenton, www.kentonuk.com
Kilpatrick Audio, www.kilpatrickaudio.com
KK Audio, www.kkaudio.com
Klipsch, www.klipsch.com
Knas, www.knasmusic.com
Koma Elektronik, www.koma-elektronik.com
Korg, www.korg.com
Krisp1, www.krisp1.com
KRK Systems, www.krksys.com
Kurzweil Music Systems, kurzweil.com
KVR Audio, www.kvraudio.com
Lexicon, www.lexiconpro.com
Liine, liine.net/en
Line 6, line6.com
Livewire Electronics, www.livewire-synthesizers.com
Livid Instruments, lividinstruments.com
Logitech, www.logitech.com
Low-Gain Electronics, www.lowgain-audio.com

LZX Industries, www.lzxindustries.net
Macbeth, www.macbethstudiosystems.com
Mackie, www.mackie.com
Madisound Speaker Components, www.madisound.com
Madrona Labs, madronalabs.com
Magic Smoke Electronics, www.magsmoke.com/magsmoke.asp
Make Noise, www.makenoisemusic.com
Maker Shed, www.makershed.com
Malekko Heavy Industry Corporation, www.malekkoheavyindustry.com
Marienberg Devices Germany, marienbergdevices.de
Marshall Amplification, www.marshallamps.com
Matrixsynth, matrixsynth.blogspot.com
Mattson Mini Modular, www.mattsonminimodular.com
M-Audio, www.m-audio.com
MegaOhm Audio, www.megaohmaudio.com
MetalBox, www.metalbox.com
Metasonix, www.metasonix.com
Meyer Sound, www.meyersound.com
MFB, www.mfberlin.de
Middle Atlantic Products, www.middleatlantic.com
MIDI Solutions, www.midisolutions.com
Modcan, www.modcan.com
Modular Grid, www.modulargrid.net
Monome, monome.org
Monoprice, www.monoprice.com
Monorocket, monorocket.com
Monster Cable Products, www.monstercable.com
Moog Music, www.moogmusic.com
Moon Modular, www.lunar-experience.com
Mos-Lab, www.mos-lab.com
Motion Sound, www.motionsoundamps.com
MOTU (Mark of the Unicorn), www.motu.com
Mouser Electronics, www.mouser.com
Muff's Modules & More, www.muffwiggler.com
Muse Research, www.museresearch.com
Music from Outer Space, www.musicfromouterspace.com
Musiclab, www.musiclab.com
Mutable Instruments, mutable-instruments.net
MXR/Dunlop Manufacturing, Inc., www.jimdunlop.com
National Music Centre, www.nmc.ca
Native Instruments, www.native-instruments.com
Natural Rhythm Music, www.naturalrhythmmusic.com
Neve, ams-neve.com
Michael Norris, www.michaelnorris.info

Novation, us.novationmusic.com
Oakley Sound Systems, www.oakleysound.com
Oceanhouse Media, www.oceanhousemedia.com
Odyssey, www.odysseygear.com
Omnirax Technical Furniture, www.omnirax.com
Optigan, optigan.com
OTO Machines, www.otomachines.com
Paia Corporation, www.paia.com
Parts Express, www.madisound.com
Patchman Music, LLC, www.patchmanmusic.com
Pea Hicks, www.optigan.com
Peavey Electronics, www.peavey.com
Pelican, www.pelicancasesusa.com
Perfect Circuit Audio, www.perfectcircuitaudio.com
Perfect Fretworks, www.hyperkeys.com
Peter Vogel Instruments (formerly Fairlight), petervogelinstruments.com.au
Pignose Gorilla, www.pignoseamps.com
Pigtronix, www.pigtronix.com
Pinnacle Speakers, www.pinnaclespeakers.com
Pittsburgh Modular, pittsburghmodular.com
Plogue, www.plogue.com
PlugIn Guru, pluginguru.com
Pomona Electronics, www.pomonaelectronics.com
PreSonus, www.presonus.com
Project SAM Cinematic Sampling, www.projectsam.com
Propellerhead Software, www.propellerheads.se
PS Audio, www.psaudio.com
QSC, www.qsc.com
QSound, www.qsound.com
Radikal Technologies, www.radikaltechnologies.com
Ramsey Electronics, www.ramseyelectronics.com
Rane Corporation, www.rane.com
Raxxess, www.chiefmfg.com
RCF, www.rcf.it
RME, www.rme-audio.de
Roger Linn Design, www.rogerlinndesign.com
Roland, www.rolandus.com
Rupert Neve Designs, rupertneve.com
Samson Technologies Corp, www.samsontech.com
Schippmann Music, www.schippmann-music.com
Sequentix Music Systems, www.sequentix.com
Shep Associates Ltd., www.shep.co.uk
Sherman Productions, www.sherman.be
Signal Arts, www.signalarts.ca
SKB, www.skbcases.com

Softwind Instruments, www.softwind.ch/synthophone.html
Somatic Circuits, somaticcircuits.com
Sonicstate, sonicstate.com
Soundcraft, www.soundcraft.com
Soundlib, www.soundlib.com
SoundMachines, soundmachines.wordpress.com
SoundTower, www.soundtower.com
Sound Transform Systems Serge Modular, www.serge-fans.com and www.carbon111.com/serge_index.html
Sound Trends LLC, www.soundtrends.com
Speck Electronics, www.speck.com
Spectrasonics, www.spectrasonics.net
Steinberg Media Technologies GmbH, www.steinberg.net
Steinway & Sons, www.steinway.com
Stewart Audio Inc., www.stewartaudio.com
STG Soundlabs, www.stgsoundlabs.com
Strymon, www.strymon.net
Studio Electronics, www.studioelectronics.com
SuperCollider, supercollider.sourceforge.net
SurgeX Electronic Systems Production, Inc., www.surgex.com
Symbolic Sound, www.symbolicsound.com
Synovatron, postmodular.co.uk/synovatron
Synthasonic, www.synthasonic.com
SynthDIY.com, www.synthdiy.com
Synthesis Technology/MOTM, www.synthtech.com
Synthesizers.com, www.synthesizers.com
Synthetic Sound Labs (SSL), steamsynth.com
Synthogy, synthogy.com
Synthrotek, www.synthrotek.com
Synthtopia, www.synthtopia.com
Synthwerks, www.synthwerks.com
SynthWise/The Sonic Workshop, synthwise.com
Tannoy Limited, www.tannoy.com
Tascam, tascam.com
TC Electronic, www.tcelectronic.com
Teenage Engineering, www.teenageengineering.com
Tellun, www.tellun.com
TestPath, www.testpath.com
ThumbJam, thumbjam.com
Tiptop Audio, www.tiptopaudio.com
Toft Audio Designs, toftaudiodesigns.com
Tom Oberheim, www.tomoberheim.com
Toppobrillo, www.sdiy.org/toppobrillo
TouellSkouarn, www.touellskouarn.fr
Trident Audio Developments, www.trident-audio.com

Tripp Lite, www.tripplite.com
Trogotronic, trogotronic.com
2Box Music Applications, www.2box.se
U&I Software, www.uisoftware.com
U-He, www.u-he.com
UVI Sounds & Software, www.uvi.net
VBrazil, www.vbrazil.eng.br
Velleman Inc., www.vellemanusa.com
Velodyne, velodyne.com
Vermona, www.vermona.com
Vintage Synth Explorer, www.vintagesynth.com
VirSyn Software Synthesizer, www.virsyn.net
The Voice of Saturn, www.recompas.com
Voltergeist Synthesizer Modules, voltergeist.org
Voodoo Lab, www.voodoolab.com
Vox Amplification, www.voxamps.com
Waldorf Music GmbH, www.waldorfmusic.de
Waves Audio Ltd., www.waves.com
Wiard Synthesizer Company, www.wiard.com
Wizdom Music, wizdommusic.com
WMD, www.wmdevices.com
Wolfgang Palm Plex 2 Restructuring Synthesizer, plex.hermannseib.com
Wooster Audio, woosteraudio.com
XLN Audio, www.xlnaudio.com
Yamaha, www.yamahasynth.com
Yorkville Sound, www.yorkville.com
Yusynth, yusynth.net
Zerosum Inertia, zerosuminertia.com
Zerotronics, zerotronics.com

Dealers and Stores

Analogue Haven, www.analoguehaven.com
Big City Music, bigcitymusic.com
Control, www.ctrl-mod.com
Control Voltage, controlvoltage.net
Equinoxoz, equinoxoz.com
Escape From Noise, escapefromnoise.com
Foxtone Music, foxtonemusic.com
Lunchbox Audio, lunchboxaudio.com
MeMe Antenna, www.memeantenna.com
Modular Square, www.modularsquare.com
Noise Android, www.noiseandroid.com
Noisebug, www.noisebug.net
Post Modular, postmodular.co.uk

Rhythm Active, www.rhythmactive.com.au
Robotspeak, www.robotspeak.com
Schneidersladen, www.schneidersladen.de
Squiggletronics Module Library, squiggletronics.com
Switched-On Music Electronics, www.switchedonaustin.com

INDEX

Aaahh!!! Real Monsters, 224, 312
Abbey Road Studios Echo Chamber Two, 183, 183*f*
Ableton AG, 300
    Live, 127, 128*f*, 129, 129*f*, 199, 226, 293, 298, 299, 300, 301*f*, 314, 354, 359
    Live Looper Device, 199
AC/DC power adapter issues, 222
Access Music Electronics GmbH, 64
    Microwave Programmer, Waldorf, 328*f*
    Virus modeled-analog polysynth, 65*f*, 67, 146, 231*f*, 244, 274, 324, 326
    Virus TI Polar WhiteOut Special Edition modeled-analog polysynth, 65*f*
Ace Electronics, 82
    Rhythm Ace, 82
acid music, 85
acoustic environments
    Carnegie Hall, 182
    the Chamber of Mazarbul, 182
    Echo Chamber Two at Abbey Road Studios, 183, 183*f*
    Madison Square Garden, 182
    Room of Requirement, 182
    See also reverb
Acxel (ACoustics and ELements), 99–100
acxelization, 100
Adams, Mike, 23*f*
additive synthesis, 41, 60, 61, 72, 97, 100, 101, 102, 107, 117, 132 (definition), 133, 210, 339
Aeon Flux, 106, 224, 312
aftertouch, 22, 24 (definition), 26, 28, 40*f*, 49, 82, 101, 122*f*, 125, 189*f*, 230*f*, 237, 273, 274, 274*f*, 275, 276*f*, 277–280, 278*f*, 294, 340*f*
aggregate synthesis, 60
Akai Professional, 13, 90*f*, 91, 127, 276, 285, 285*f*, 300
    A-DAM (Akai Digital Audio Multitrack) twelve-track recorder, 353
    APC20 controller, 300
    APC40 controller, 300, 301*f*, 359
    EVI1000 wind controller, 285
    EWI4000S (Electronic Wind Instrument), 285
    EWI USB, 285
    EWV2000 synth module, 285
    LPF-25 mini-keyboard controller, 221*f*
    MPC (MIDI production workstation), 90*f*
    MPC60 MIDI production workstation, 40, 91, 126, 126*f*, 127
    S900 sampler, 40
    SynthStation25 keyboard controller, 216*f*
    Z8 sampler, 229*f*, 328*f*

Alesis, 13, 302
    ADAT (Alesis Digital Audio Tape) multitrack recorder, 353, 354, 357, 361
    Andromeda A6 polyphonic analog synthesizer, 67, 225*f*, 226*f*, 231*f*, 244
    Big Remote Control (BRC), 353–354
    NanoPiano MIDI synth module, 249*f*
    Quadraverb effects processor, 325*f*
    3630 compressor, 227*f*
Alexander, Will, 346
aliasing, 45, 46 (definition), 56, 148
Alles, Dr. Hal, 42, 42*f*
allpass filter, 164 (definition), 200
Alonso, Sydney, 121
alpha microtonal tuning scale, 44, 45 (definition)
Alternate Mode (Kat), Inc., 13
    drumKat MIDI controller, 303*f*
    drumKat Turbo KS synthesizer/controller, 303*f*
    mallet Kat Express, Pro, and Grand MIDI controllers, 304*f*
    malletKat 7KS synthesizer/controller, 304
    panKat MIDI controller, 304*f*
    trapKat MIDI controller, 303*f*
    trapKat 5KS synthesizer/controller, 303*f*
alternative controllers, 13–14, 283–306
    breath, 30 (definition), 31, 285, 292, 341
    handheld/wand, 301–302
    microtonal tuning, for, 305–306
    Radio Baton, 40, 301
    struck, 302–305
    touchplate/pad/ribbon, ix, 6, 11, 13, 14*f*, 21, 22, 28, 87–88, 91, 94, 99*f*, 100, 170, 178–180, 179*f*, 205*f*, 207–209, 208*f*, 213*f*, 214*f*, 268*f*, 286–301, 287*f*, 288*f*, 289*f*, 290*f*, 291*f*, 292*f*, 293*f*, 294*f*, 295*f*, 296*f*, 297*f*, 298*f*, 299*f*, 300*f*, 301*f*, 307, 308*f*, 321, 348*f*
    wind, 30, 31, 210, 284–286
American Guild of Organists (AGO) pedalboard, 342
Amplified Parts MOD 4AB3C1B reverb tank, 184
amplitude, ix, 4 (definition), 10, 12, 20, 24, 25, 33, 41–42, 46*f*, 54, 66, 78, 100, 102, 105, 114, 125, 132, 133, 134, 138, 151 (definition), 152, 154, 156, 157, 158, 162, 166, 170, 171, 172, 193, 286, 327, 339
amplitude contour, 152
amplitude modulation (AM), 41 (definition), 42, 154, 327
AM synthesis, 60
analog delay (AD), 187–193
analog/digital hybrid, 56 (definition), 127, 128*f*

Index

analog modeling, 46 (definition), 47, 285
analog sequencer, 15, 16 (definition), 20, 130, 155, 172–180, 201, 234, 254, 272, 287
analog-to-digital converter (ADC), 126, 127, 164, 361
analog tuning scales, one-volt per octave vs. Hz per volt, 157
Analogue Solutions, 146f, 258, 273
    CVM and CVQ02 CV-to-MIDI converter modules, 273
    Europa MIDI step sequencer/drum computer, 146f
    Leipzig-ks monosynth keyboard, 146f
    Oberkorn Mk3 rackmount analog sequencer, 146f, 174, 174f
    Red Square patchable rackmount synth, 142, 144f
    Telemark patchable tabletop synth, 142, 144f, 146f
    Vostok patchable suitcase synth, 142, 145f
Analogue Systems, 157, 195, 230f, 258, 262, 263, 279
    Demon analog/MIDI keyboard controller, 279–280
    French Connection analog keyboard/Ondes Martenot controller, 279–281, 282f
    Integrator modules, 325f
    RS10 and RS15 modular cases, 262
    RS30 Frequency-to-Voltage + Envelope Hz/V converter module, 157
    RS35 External Processor 1V/octave converter module, 157
    RS120 analog comb filter module, 200
    RS140 MIDI-to-CV converter module, 272
    RS215 Eight-Band Octave Filter module, 167
    RS220 Joystick module, 280
    RS240 Bode Frequency Shifter module, 263
    RS300 CV/MIDI converter, 274, 274f
    RS310 Reverb/Chorus module, 265
    RS390 Echo module, 195
    RS500E EMS Synthi filter module, 264
    RS600 Performance Wheels module, 280–281
    Sorceror analog/MIDI keyboard controller/modular cabinet, 279–281
AnaMod Audio ATS-1 Analog Tape Simulator, 354
Andromeda Space Rockers, 197f, 307, 307f
animation, scoring to, 312, 313
ANS (Alexander Nikolayevich Scriabin) synthesizer, 117, 118f
aperiodic, 134 (definition), 137, 149, 151
Apple, Fiona, 71
Apple Inc., 344
    Airport Express Wi-Fi base station, 221f
    II home computer, 103
    IIe personal computer, 29
    EXS24 sampler plug-in, 80, 345
    Garageband recording studio application, 216
    iPad, iPhone, and iPod Touch iOS devices, 22, 47, 49, 60, 88, 102, 103f, 108, 210, 298, 299f, 321, 322f
    Logic music production application, 224, 242–243, 293, 298, 316, 324f, 345, 356, 357f, 359
    Macintosh computer, 58, 61, 79, 101, 102, 104, 106, 107, 210, 301, 324f, 343, 353, 356, 357f, 359
    MainStage live performance software, 343, 345
Appleton, Jon, 121, 122f
Aries Music Inc. modular synthesizers, 158, 246, 252
ARP Instruments, 29, 29f, 76, 80, 81, 91f, 92f, 93, 93f, 94, 227, 230f, 233f, 269, 272, 342
    Avatar prototype guitar synth, 29, 232
    Axxe analog monosynth, 233f
    Axxe II analog monosynth, 232
    Centaur prototype polyphonic synth, 29
    Electronic Piano, 29
    LFO (custom), 217f
    Model 1601 Sequencer, 173, 212f, 283f
    mult box, 340f
    Odyssey analog monosynth, 29, 158f, 173, 340f, 342, 343f, 351f
    Odyssey II analog monosynth, 232
    Omni analog polysynth, 28, 29, 232, 233f
    Omni mk II analog polysynth, 232, 340f, 342
    Pro DGX analog monosynth, 340f, 342, 343f
    Proportional Pressure Controllers (PPCs), 81
    Pro Soloist analog monosynth, 29, 217f
    Quadra analog polysynth, 232, 233f
    Solus analog monosynth, 233f
    2500 modular synth, 91, 91f, 119, 246
    2600 patchable synth, 26, 38, 92f (Blue Meanie/Blue Marvin), 93f, 142, 143f, 157, 212f, 217f, 218f, 239, 242f, 244, 273, 322, 329, 336f, 340f, 342, 343f
    3620 duophonic analog keyboard controller, 212f, 342, 343f
    4075 filter, 232, 233f, 334
arpeggiators, 52, 53, 87, 88, 170, 180–182
Arrick, Roger, 246, 247f, 253
The Arsenio Hall Show, 310
The Art of Digital Music, 128
artificial intelligence, 119
Arturia Musical Instruments, 41, 56, 67, 140, 158, 159f, 228, 235f, 237, 239
    Arturia V-collection, 226
    CS-80V softsynth, 235f, 237
    CS-80V2, 237f
    Jupiter-8V softsynth, 237
    Minibrute analog monosynth, 67, 140, 158, 159f, 223
    MinimoogV softsynth, 237, 239f
    Moog ModularV softsynth, 237, 244
    Origin modular DSP synth module, 67, 227–228, 231, 232, 233f, 237, 328f
    Origin Keyboard modular DSP synth, 67, 230f, 231f, 233f
    ProphetV softsynth, 56

Index

ProphetV2 softsynth, 57*f*, 237
SEMV softsynth, 41
Spark hardware-and-software drum machine, 67
2600V softsynth, 237
2600V2, 212*f*
assemble-your-own software, 210
assembly-language subroutines, 102
Atoms, Maxwell, 312
attack (initial portion of a sound), 4 (definition), 8, 11, 20, 37, 39, 51, 53, 54, 55, 69, 72, 100, 106*f*, 124, 133, 135, 152, 152*f*, 153, 162, 164, 186*f*, 269, 307*f*, 334
attack, decay, sustain, release (ADSR) envelope generator, 20, 104 (brief definition), 106*f*, 117, 133, 152–153 (definition), 152*f*, 162, 329, 331, 162, 329, 331
attack, hold, decay, sustain, release (AHDSR) envelope generator, 153, 164
attack, release (AR) envelope generator, 152
attack, sustain, release (ASR) envelope generator, 39
attack transient, 53, 54 (definition), 69, 72, 100, 124
Audio Interchange File Format (AIFF) digital sound file, 66, 106
audio morphing, 60, 63, 105*f*, 110, 111, 141*f*, 146
auto pan, 170
Auon, Daniel, 221*f*
Automatically Operating Musical Instrument of Electric Oscillation Type (first true synthesizer), 114
Avery, Tex, 313

Babbitt, Milton, 116–117, 116*f*
Bacon, Francis, 33, 34
Balinese pelog microtonal tuning scale, 44, 45
ballad, 218*f*, 315
banana cables, connectors, jacks, modular systems, and plugs, 148, 148*f*, 176, 248*f*, 252, 253, 287, 289, 290*f*, 309, 309*f*, 311*f*
Bananalogue, 230*f*, 251
bandpass filter (BPF), 18, 37, 38 (definition), 39, 157, 158, 160, 162, 168, 171, 209, 265, 329
bandwidth (BW), 21, 146, 166 (fixed and "Q"), 167*f*, 188, 294, 297*f*, 364
barber-pole effects, 201, 204 (definition), 264
bark scale, 168
Barr, Jay, 94
bass and treble equalization, 166, 168
bass management, 355
Battino, David, 123*f*, 128
Battle, Mike, 187
BBC's Radiophonic Workshop, 89, 91
beat boxes. *See* drum machines and beat boxes
Beauty and the Beast, 224
Beck, Ken, 95
Beethoven's Ninth Symphony, 200
Behles, Gerhard, 127
Belar, Herbert, 115–116

Bell Labs, 31–33, 42, 102, 168
beta microtonal tuning scale, 44, 45
Bhatia, Amin, 237–244, 273, 314–316, 322, 324*f*, 335, 354–359, 362–363
BIAS Inc. (Berkley Integrated Audio Software), 226
Peak Pro 6 audio editor software, 187
SuperFreq parametric equalizer plug-in, 166, 167*f*
Big Band era, 118–119
Big Bladder Simulator, 74*f*
Big Briar, 17, 22
Big Briar/Moog Music Etherwave Theremin, 7*f*, 23*f*
Big City Music, 146*f*, 157
The Birds, 8–9
bit-reducing decimator, 66, 67 (definition)
Blacet, John, 193, 247*f*, 249, 265
Blacet Research, 141*f*, 148, 227*f*, 230*f*, 247, 247*f*, 251, 253, 265, 325*f*, 332*f*
F340 Cloud Generator module, 148
F350 Morphing Terrarium module, 148
F560 Deflector Shield module, 207, 250*f*
F580 Resampling Mini-Delay module, 195
Klang Werk KW2010 ring modulator module, 265
Time Machine 2050 analog delay module, 193, 195
VCO2010 oscillator module, 265
Bleep Labs, 307
Nebulophone, 307
Thingamagoop, 307, 308*f*, 309
ThingamaKit, 307, 308*f*
blessing and curse of analog synths, 327–329
Bloch, Thomas, 244
Blue Meanie/Blue Marvin, 92*f*
Bob Moog Foundation, ix, x, xii, 221*f*, 374
Bode, Harald, ix, 17, 201, 202*f*
Bode Model 7702 Vocoder, 202*f*
"Bolero Electronica," 244
books, selected bibliography, 369–373
Boomerang III Phase Sampler, 197–198, 198*f*
Borovec, Richard, 94
Boss
DD-5 and DD-7 digital delay stompboxes, 194
mixer, 218*f*
RC-300 Loop Station, 199, 199*f*
Bowen, John, 81, 210*f*, 211*f*
Bradley, Frank, 68–69
Bradley, Leslie, 68–69
Bradley, Norman, 68–69
breath controller, 30 (definition), 31, 285
Bride Chamber, 253, 332*f*, 346
Briefel, Dennis, 42
Briefel, Ernie, 42
Bristow, Dave, 49
Brown, Mike, 256*f*
Buchla, Don, xv, 13–17, 146*f*, 167–170, 169*f*, 245, 246, 247, 247*f*, 266, 286, 289, 302, 305, 334

Index

Buchla and Associates, now dba Buchla Electronic Musical Instruments, 15, 17, 93, 246, 247, 252, 258, 289, 302, 302f, 332f, 334
    Lightning wireless wand controller, 17, 302, 302f
    lopass gate, 334
    Marimba Lumina mallet MIDI controller/instrument, 305
    100 Series modular synth, 14f, 286
    106 Six-Channel Mixer module, 14f
    110 Dual Voltage-Controlled Gate module, 14f
    111 Dual Ring Modulator module, 14f
    112 Touch-Controlled Voltage Source module, 14f, 286
    123 Eight-Stage Sequential Voltage Source module, 14f
    146 16-Stage Sequential Voltage Source module, 14f
    Piano Bar, 17, 23f
    200 Series Electric Music Box modular synth, 15, 15f, 327, 338–339
    219 Compound Touch-Controlled Voltage Source analog controller, 291f
    259 Programmable Complex Waveform Generator module, 247f, 339, 339f
    295 Ten-Channel Comb Filter module, 327
    296 Programmable Spectral Processor module, 167–168, 168f
    200e Series modular synth, 15, 16f, 272
    219 Compound Touch-Controlled Voltage Source, 291f
    222e Multi-Dimensional Kinesthetic Input Port, 289
    225e MIDI Decoder/Preset Manager module, 272
    296e Spectral Processor module, xv, 167–170, 169f
    300 Series modular synth, 15
    400 Series modular synth, 15
    500 Series modular synth, 15
    700 Series modular synth, 15
    Thunder pad controller, 17, 289, 291f
    WIMP (Wideband Interface for Music Performance), 17
bucket-brigade delay (BBD), 187–193, 188 (definition), 192f, 193f, 195 (digital simulation), 196f, 265
budget considerations, 213–224
    product lifespan, 219
BugBrand Ltd., 148, 176, 251, 252, 289, 290f, 308
    Board Weevil (2009 version), 307, 308f
    CTL1 Touch Panel module, 289, 290f
    E350 Morphing Terrarium module, 146, 146f
    SEQ1 CV/gate sequencer and SEQ1X slave modules, 176, 177f
Bugs, Tom, 289, 308f
Burton, Adam, aka Maxwell Atoms, 312

But Seriously, Folks…, 173
buying modular synthesizer components, advice from experienced enthusiasts, 254

cabinets and cases for modular synthesizers, 16, 130, 131f, 141–142, 161, 184, 223, 246–247, 248f, 249f, 252f, 255f, 257f, 258f, 258–265, 259f, 260f, 261f, 268f, 281, 286f, 289, 314f, 318f, 319f, 320f, 325f, 346f, 348f, 349f, 359f, 364f
cables, jacks, and plugs, 24, 40f, 41, 88, 94, 95f, 100–101, 109, 140–142, 144f, 145f, 146, 147f, 148, 154f, 155, 158, 160, 161, 163, 164, 170, 173, 176, 176f, 177f, 178, 178f, 181, 181f, 184, 190, 192, 193, 198f, 204f, 208, 219, 221, 222, 224f, 227f, 228f, 252–253, 235f, 236f, 247, 248f, 249f, 250f, 252–253, 253f, 258, 261f, 262, 263, 265, 269, 269f, 270f, 272, 273, 276f, 280, 282, 282f, 287, 289, 290f, 296f, 305, 305f, 309, 309f, 322, 329, 346, 351f, 352, 354, 361, 364, 364f, 365f
    banana jacks, 148, 176, 252, 287, 290f, 309f
    cinch-Jones input, 269
    computer connectivity (USB, Ethernet, Firewire), 49, 52, 59f, 58–61, 74, 142f, 171, 175, 176, 176f, 199, 270, 271, 271f, 276–279, 276f, 277f, 278f, 282f, 285, 294, 295, 296f, 297–301, 297f, 301f, 305–306, 305f, 342–343, 354
    mult, 247 (definition), 248f, 250f, 252–253, 253f, 289f, 320f
    patch cords, 16, 21, 22f, 93, 94, 100–101, 110, 130, 141, 143f, 144f, 145f, 173, 212f, 228f, 233f, 258, 327, 365f
    patch cord tree, 22f, 262
Cahill, Thaddeus, ix, 3
Cain, Kelli, 299
Campbell, Tom, 146f
capacitors, 38, 189, 364
car stereo, bass and treble equalizer, 166
Carlos, Wendy, xi, 18, 41–45, 200, 311, 318–319, 327–329, 329–331, 341, 349, 352–353
    Beauty in the Beast, 44, 329
    Book One: New Notes, from *Switched-On Boxed Set*, 327
    A Clockwork Orange, 200, 329
    Digital Moonscapes, 329
    "The Rocky Mountains," 329
    The Well-Tempered Synthesizer, 352
    The Shining, 329
    "Timesteps," 329
    Tales of Heaven & Hell, 329, 330
    Tron, 329
Carpenter, Mary Chapin, 172f
carrier, as used in vocoding and modulation, 18, 41, 50, 108, 133, 200, 201 (definition), 206–207, 206f
Cartesian Sequencer, 178–180, 287, 288f
Cary, Tristram, 89

Index

Casio, 50–52, 277
    AZ-1 strap-on MIDI keyboard controller, 52
    Cosmo Synth System, 50
    CZ-101 phase-distortion synth, 50–51, 50f, 153, 244
    CZ-1000 phase distortion synth, 50
    FZ-1 sampling keyboard, 51
    phase distortion, 50–53
    RZ-1 sampling drum machine, 51, 51f
    VL-Tone VL-1 calculator synth, 277, 277f
    VZ-1 digital synth, 51, 51f
    XW-G1 groove synth, 52, 52f
    XW-P1 performance synth, 52, 52f
Cazajeux, Denis, 165
CBS
    CBS/CTV *Flashpoint*, 237, 244, 314
    Rhodes division, 29
CCRMA (Center for Computer Research in Music and Acoustics at Stanford University), 30, 136
Cecil, Malcolm, 26
celluloid
    Mattel Optigan discs, 69–71
    ring worn on a finger (Ondes Martenot), 35
central processing unit (CPU), 26
Chamberlin, Harry, 69
Chamberlin
    Rhythmate, 69
    Riviera, 69f
Chang, Gary, 129, 154, 164, 219, 223, 274, 291–292, 300f, 301f, 313f, 313–314, 314f, 319, 326–327, 334, 338–339, 338f, 359–360, 360f
Charpentier, Al, 75
chase music, 315
Chicken Systems, 31
Chidlaw, Bob, 78
Mr. Chorus, 54
chorusing effect, 31, 33 (definition), 53, 124, 125 (definition), 139, 186f, 188 (definition), 193, 218f, 239f, 265, 325f, 343f, 345
Chowning, John, 41, 47, 48, 133
Chroma synthesizer, 29, 29f
Chung, Peter, 224, 312
circuit-bent/bending, 210, 307, 323–324
Cirocco, Phil, 247f
clarinet sound, 12, 55, 135, 292, 312
Clapton, Eric, 172f
the Clash, 71
Claude, Jean, 91, 93
Clavecin Electrique/Electric Harpsichord, 3
Clavia DMI AB, 64, 65f, 100–102, 137
    Nord Lead, 63–64, 64f, 137, 145, 158, 230f, 312, 325f, 335
    Nord Micro Modular, 101, 101f
    Nord Modular, 100–102, 101f, 149, 156, 231–232, 233f
    Nord Modular G2, 101–102
    Nord Rack, 239–240, 242f

Clinton, Bill, 1993 inauguration at Kennedy Center, 363f
Close Encounters of the Third Kind, 91, 93
Club of the Knobs, 181, 193, 194f, 200, 246, 248f
    C951 Arpeggiator module, 181
    C1660 Phase Processor module, 200, 201f
    C1680 Voltage-Controlled Analog Delay module, 193, 194f
CMS (Cirocco Modular Systems), 246, 247f
"Coat of Many Colors," 262
Cockerell, David, 88–91, 90f, 126, 126f
coding field (score), 117
Cohen, Marvin, 92f
Cohen, Randy, 265
collectors' pieces, warning, 245–246
Columbia-Princeton Electronic Music Center, 116, 152
comb filter, 200 (definition), 327, 334
Commodore Business Machines, 75, 104
    Commodore 64 personal computer, 75, 103f, 104
    Sound Interface Device (SID) chip, 75, 104
composing/composition, 3, 113–129, 133, 213, 224, 310–321, 322, 325, 355, 355f, 359, 362
    algorithmic composition schemes, 113, 181
    do-it-all computer-music system, 95–99, 97f, 98f
    early composition instruments, 113–121
    economical multitimbral sequencing synth, 123–124
    editing, importance of, 73, 108, 133, 311, 317, 319, 360
    first synthesizers, 114–117
    gigabuck digital audio system, 121–123
    hip-hop, 126–127
    hybrid music workstation, 119–121
    instantaneous composing/performance machine, 118–119
    intention of composition, 319–321
    living art, composing for, 316–317
    multipurpose environment for composition and performance, 127–129
    musical playstation for the masses, 124–126
    photo-optic instrument, 117, 118f
    random-selection composition schemes, 114
    soundtrack production, 310–316
    stochastic composition schemes, 114
    techniques of experienced synthesists, 310–321
compounding digital-to-analog converter (ComDAC), 85
compression, 66, 78, 106f, 170, 171 (definition), 208f
compressors, 227f, 242f, 332f, 362 (definition)
Computer History Museum, 98f, 99
Computer Music Journal, 42
computers, historical uses for creating electronic music, 102
Con Brio ADS (Advanced Digital Synthesizer), 95–99, 97f, 98f
    ADS 100, 97, 97f
    ADS 200 and 200-R, 97, 97f, 98f, 99

Index

conductivity matrix interface, 94
Constant Bark filters, 167–170, 168f, 169f
consumer vs. professional equipment, 216, 219
control voltage (CV), 13, 20, 30, 41, 56, 94, 130, 133, 137, 138, 142, 144f, 146–148, 150f, 154, 155, 156, 157, 161, 172–173, 174f, 175, 223–224, 252–253, 267, 279, 286, 290, 291f, 292f, 327
    CV-to-MIDI conversion, 273–275, 274f, 275f, 279
    MIDI-to-CV conversion, 41, 144f, 181, 267–273, 269f, 270f, 271f, 273f, 274f, 279
    pitch/frequency-to-CV conversion, 157
    See also voltage control
controllers and controlling sound, ix, 3–33, 276–306
    alternative controllers, 13–14, 283–306
    foot controllers and pedals, 22, 31, 32f, 43, 51, 64, 71, 124, 126, 135f, 154f, 162, 170, 176, 185, 198, 198f, 199, 217f, 272, 276f, 282f, 296f, 297, 305, 305f, 341–342, 343, 343f, 344f
    keyboards, ix, 10–13, 18, 22, 23f, 24, 25, 25f, 26–27, 28, 29, 31, 35, 39, 39f, 40f, 43, 52, 52f, 68–69, 73–74, 82, 89, 91, 99, 101, 111f, 122f, 130, 159, 180, 217f, 230f, 237f, 245, 257f, 265, 272, 276–283, 276f, 277f, 278f, 279f, 280f, 282f, 283f, 284f, 291–292, 325, 325f, 334, 340f, 359–360
        See also keyboards
    mallet, 40, 301
    microtonal tuning, for, 305–306
    Radio Baton, 40, 301
    ribbon, 11, 13, 20, 21 (definition), 28, 35, 78f, 81, 170, 196, 210f, 211f, 230f, 237f, 282, 282f, 290, 292, 294f, 295f, 296f, 298, 346f
    speech, finger-controlled, 31–33, 32f
    struck controllers, 302–305
    timbral shaping, 11–13
    touchplate/pad/ribbon, ix, 6, 11, 13, 14f, 21, 22, 28, 87–88, 91, 94, 99f, 100, 170, 178–180, 179f, 205f, 207–209, 208f, 213f, 214f, 268f, 286–301, 287f, 288f, 289f, 290f, 291f, 292f, 293f, 294f, 295f, 296f, 297f, 298f, 299f, 300f, 301f, 307, 308f, 321, 348f
    untouched instruments, 4–7
    waggling keyboard, 10–11
    wand, 17, 302, 302f
    wind, 30, 31, 210, 284–286
convolution reverb, 185–187, 186f, 238f
CoolAudio International Limited (SMT BBD chips), 188–189
coordinate-mapping sequencer, 179–180
Corea, Chick, 21
corner frequency (equalization), 166
Costello, Elvis, 71
Countryman, Dana, 10f
Countryman Type 85 direct box, 361
Coupleaux, Edouard E., 114, 114f

Coupleaux-Givelet Automatically Operating Musical Instrument of Electric Oscillation Type (first true synthesizer), 114
Crabtree, Brian, 299
Create Digital Music, 253
Creative Labs/Creative Technology Ltd., 74, 76
Create Music Web link, 253
Crockett, Bruce, 75
Cromophonic mode, 66
cross-fading/fade, 55, 55f, 56 (definition), 61, 63, 135, 207
cross-platform software, 41 (definition), 60, 101f, 108, 110, 171, 210, 215f, 305, 344
cross-switching, 43 (definition), 303f
Crumar, 42, 42f, 43f, 225f
csGrain (Csound for the Apple iPad), 102
Csound, 102, 134
Curtin, Steven, 94
Curved Air, 91
CV. *See* control voltage
Cwejman, 258f, 259f
    S1-MK2 patchable synth, 142
Cycling '74, 104, 105f
    Max for Live (Ableton), 129, 359
    Max/MSP graphic music programming environment, 104, 105f, 134, 298, 299
Cyndustries, 141f, 230f, 246, 247, 248f, 251, 287f, 325f, 331, 364f, 365f
    Synthesis Filter, 334
    Zeroscillator, 141f

damping (acoustic energy in reverberation), 185 (definition)
dance music production, 85
dancer, control by, 6, 6f
Danner, Gregory, 94
Danziger, Alan, 97, 97f
Darmouth's School of Engineering, 121
DAT recorders, 354
"Daughter, Mother, Father," 355–359, 356f, 357f, 358f
Dave Smith Instruments (DSI), 56, 108, 153, 238f
    Evolver analog/digital hybrid monosynth module, 56, 244
    Mopho analog monosynth module, 56
    Mopho x4 analog polysynth, 56
    Poly Evolver Keyboard synth, 58f
    Prophet '08 analog polysynth, 56, 238f
    Prophet 12 hybrid polysynth, 56, 153
    Tempest hybrid drum machine/synth, 56, 128f
    Tetra analog polysynth module, 56, 57f
Davel, Joel, 305
decibel (dB), 4 (definition), 39, 104, 105, 124, 131 (definition), 132, 152, 157, 160, 162, 166, 167f, 186f, 354
deafness, 132

Index

dealers and stores, list of, 382–383
decay (portion of a sound), 20, 74, 104, 126, 133, 152, 152*f*, 154, 162, 168, 170, 198, 198*f*, 307*f*
Déchelle, François, 104
delay, 31, 33 (definition), 53, 59*f*, 66, 100, 105, 105*f*, 111*f*, 124, 125, 165, 170–171, 185, 186*f*, 187–197, 188*f*, 191*f*, 192*f*, 193*f*, 194*f*, 195*f*, 196*f*, 197*f*, 199, 200, 201, 207, 208*f*, 209, 215*f*, 227*f*, 239*f*, 249*f*, 250*f*, 265, 306*f*, 307*f*, 325*f*, 329, 332*f*, 345
    analog delay, 187–193
    digital delay, 193–197
delay plus ADSR (DADSR) envelope generators, 153
Descartes, René, 179
Deutsch, Herbert A., 17, 18, 245
Devo, 71
Dewanatron Electronics Swarmatron, 211*f*
Deyo, Scott, 190, 249
DI (direct-insert or direct-injection), 361, 364
diffusers (Ondes Martenot speakers), 34*f*, 35*f*, 36, 36*f*
diffusion, 185 (definition)
Digidesign, xv, 104–106, 106*f*, 107, 353
    Pro Tools computer-based digital audio workstation, 104, 345, 359, 362
    Pro Tools Digi 003 Firewire audio interface, 355
    Sound Designer virtual modular synthesizer and processor software, 353
    Turbosynth, xv, 104–106, 106*f*, 107
Digisound, 227*f*, 246
digital in history of electronic musical instruments, 133–137
digital audio workstations (DAWs), 108, 109, 113, 121
digital control, 94, 115, 139
digital delay, 105, 165, 188, 193–197, 325*f*
Digital Equipment Corporation (DEC) PDP-8 minicomputer, 89
Digital Keyboards Synergy, 41–45, 43*f*, 133
digital oscillators, 43, 46, 97, 121, 123, 140, 146
digital signal processing (DSP), 58, 61, 67, 74, 76, 79*f*, 100–101, 107, 109*f*, 137, 148, 185, 187, 189*f*, 194, 200, 220, 228, 297*f*
digital-to-analog converter (DAC), 75, 76, 85 (compounding), 102, 120, 126, 164, 193–194, 270, 335, 361
digital-to-analog-to-digital conversion, 54
digitally controlled oscillator (DCO), 139, 140*f*, 237
DigitalNativeDance patch (Roland D-50), 54
direct box (DI), 199, 361, 364, 364*f*
direct computer connectivity
    Ethernet, 49, 59*f*, 60, 305*f*, 357
    Firewire, 49, 59*f*, 60, 305*f*, 357
    USB, 49, 52, 59*f*, 60, 74, 142*f*, 175, 176, 176*f*, 199, 230*f*, 270, 271, 271*f*, 276–279, 276*f*, 277*f*, 278*f*, 282*f*, 285, 294–301, 296*f*, 297*f*, 305, 305*f*, 343

direct memory access (DMA), 99
distortion, 50–51, 66, 72, 87, 94, 105, 106*f*, 124, 125 (definition), 160, 170, 185, 186*f*, 190, 193, 195, 199, 207, 208*f*, 240, 277, 339, 361
    distorter, 37 (control tube), 38 (definition)
    exciter, 124, 125 (definition)
    phase distortion, 50–51, 277
    waveshaper, 94 (definition), 101, 105, 106, 106*f*, 111*f*, 160, 164
Divilbiss, James, 94
Division 6, 176, 177*f*, 179*f*, 272
    SQ816 analog sequencer module, 176, 177*f*
do-it-yourself (DIY) hardware, 184, 189–190, 210, 253–254 (modular synths), 258, 262, 284, 299
do-it-yourself (DIY) software, 253
    Cycling '74 Max/MSP, 104–105, 105*f*, 295, 298, 299
    IRCAM Jmax, 104
    Native Instruments Generator/Reaktor, 109–111, 110*f*, 134, 298
    Miller Puckette/IRCAM Patcher/Pd (Pure Data), 104
    Barry Vercoe's Csound/Boulanger Labs csGrain, 102, 134
DJ turntable and hip hop/scratch artists, 52*f*, 82, 84*f*, 126, 126*f*, 129, 163, 164*f*, 198, 208, 300
Doctor Who, 91
Dodds, Philip, 29, 91–93
Doepfer, Dieter, 188, 189–190, 246, 251–252, 252*f*, 262–263
Doepfer Musikelektronik GmbH, 13, 142, 143*f*, 174, 175, 188–190, 192*f*, 230*f*, 246, 251–252, 252*f*, 253, 255*f*, 258, 258*f*, 262–264, 270–271, 276, 276*f*, 325*f*
    A-100 series Eurorack modular systems, 251–252
    A-128 fixed filter bank module, 166–167
    A-150 Dual VCS voltage-controlled switcher module, 175
    A-154 Sequencer Controller module, 175
    A-155 sequencer module, 174–175
    A-188-1 BBD analog delay module, 190
    A-188-2 Tapped BBD analog delay module, 190–191, 192*f*
    A-190 MIDI-to-CV/Gate/Clock Interface module, 175, 270–271
    A-190-2 MIDI-to-CV/Gate Interface module, 271
    A-192-1 CVM16 CV-to-MIDI converter module, 273–274
    A-199 SPRV spring reverb module, 184
    Dark Energy, 142, 143*f*, 223
    Dark Link MIDI/USB-to-CV and gate converter, 270, 271*f*
    Dark Time, 175, 175*f*, 176*f*
    LMK4+ MIDI/USB master keyboard controller, 276*f*, 359–360
    MAQ16/3 MIDI Analog Sequencer, 173–174, 174*f*

Index

do-it-all systems
  Con Brio ADS, 95–99
  Fairlight CMI, 72–73
  Korg M1, T-series, 01/W, X-series, Trinity, N-series, Triton, 124–126
  Korg OASYS/Kronos, 61–62
  McLeyvier hybrid music workstation, 119–121
  NED Synclavier, 121–123
  PPG Realizer, 47
  Propellerhead Reason, 108–109
  Roland Fantom, 54
  Yamaha Motif, 49
Dolby magnetic recording tape noise reduction, 352
Dolby, Thomas, 45, 72
Doren, Kevin, 42
doubling effect, 190, 192 (definition)
Dr. Bob's SoundSchool, the Bob Moog Foundation, ix
Dr. T's Music Software, 104
Drawmer 1960 Mic Pre/Vacuum Tube Compressor, 242f, 362 (definition)
Drone Maker, from Michael Norris's SoundMagic Spectral freeware, 360
Droomusic studio, 227f, 229f
drop/add fixed-rate sample-skipping architecture, 75
drum machines and beat boxes, 40, 51, 51f, 56, 67 (definition), 74, 82–86, 108, 110, 125, 126–127, 128f, 164, 170, 172f, 176, 210, 218f, 269f, 270f, 272, 295, 340f, 343f
  Casio RZ-1 sampling drum machine, 51, 51f
  classic beat boxes, 82–86
  Dave Smith Instruments Tempest analog/digital hybrid drum machine/synthesizer, 56, 127, 128f
  E-mu Drumulator sample-playback drum machine, 74
  E-mu SP12 and SP1200 sampling drum machines, 74
  hip hop, 82, 84f, 126
  hip-hop and techno music, rhythm machine of choice, 82, 84f
  Linn Electronics LM-1 Drum Computer, 73, 84, 85–86, 86f, 126, 127f
drum tracks, processing, 162, 165
DSI. *See* Dave Smith Instruments
dual-manual keyboard controller/configuration, 19f, 39, 71f
Dudley, Homer W., 31, 33
Duncan, Bruce, 196, 246, 247f
Dunnington, Steve, 23f
duophonic, 30 (definition), 89, 115
dynamic voice allocation, 123, 123f, 124 (definition)

Eagan, Edmund, 268f, 292f, 347, 348f
early reflections, 124, 125 (definition), 185 (definition)

EastWest Communications, Inc., 113, 357, 358f
  Vienna Ensemble, 357, 358f
Eaton, John, ix, 24–25, 25f, 278, 280f
Eaton-Moog keyboard, ix, 24, 278, 280f
echo, 33, 42, 51, 105, 107f (pre- and post-), 125, 183, 183f, 185, 187, 188, 188f, 192, 193, 193f, 194–197, 195f, 197f, 209, 218f, 342, 343f, 350f
  echo chambers, 125, 183, 183f
  natural echo, 187
  See also delay and reverb
Echo Chamber Two at Abbey Road Studios, 183, 183f
Echoplex, 187, 194, 195f
Edirol R-09 digital stereo recorder, 354
Edison cylinder, 69, 70 (definition)
education
  the blackboard (oversized Korg MS-20), 351f
  educational instruments, 91–95, 109, 130, 139f, 292, 295f, 351f
Eigenlabs, 13, 292–294
  Basestation Pro, 296f
  Eigenlabs Eigenharp Alpha, 292, 294f
  Eigenlabs Eigenharp Tau, 292, 296f
  Eigenlabs Pico, 292, 295f
Electric Music Box systems, 15, 15f, 327, 338–339
Electric Music Laboratories (EML), 143f, 252, 257f
  Electrocomp 101 patchable monosynth, 142, 143f
electric piano (EP), 52, 53, 292, 351f, 361
  Fender Rhodes EP, 361
  Fender Rhodes 73 electric piano, 351f
  Fender Rhodes Suitcase electric piano, 53
  Wurlitzer EP, 293
  Wurlitzer 200A electric piano, 53
electrical engineer/engineering, 29 and 91 (Alan R. Pearlman), 58 (doctorate degree, Kurt Hebel), 130 (degree unnecessary for understanding acoustics and synthesis basics)
Electro Group, 26
Electro-Harmonix, 90f, 91
Electro-Music Web link, 253
Electronic Dream Plant Wasp analog monosynth, 91, 269f
Electronic Musician magazine, 265, 266f
Electronic Perspectives, 120f
Electronic Realizations for Rock Orchestra, 317
Electronic Sackbut, 11–13, 12f
Electronium, 119, 120f
Elektron SidStation, 104
Ellis, Alexander J., 152
Emerson, Keith, 19f, 21, 72, 345–346, 346f, 347, 347f
Emerson, Lake & Palmer, 346, 346f
EMS (Electronic Music Studios), 88–91
  DK2 duophonic analog keyboard controller, 89, 89f

Index

KS capacitive touchplate keyboard, 91
Synthi A (Portabella) analog suitcase synth, 89*f*
Synthi AKS analog synth, capacitive touchplate keyboard, and digital monophonic sequencer in a suitcase, 90*f*
Synthi KB-1 analog synth, 89*f*
Synthi 100, 89, 90*f*, 91
VCS3 (Voltage-Controlled Studio, attempt #3; aka the Putney), 88, 89*f*, 91, 175
emotional music. *See* expressive sound
E-mu Systems, 39, 73–74, 75, 158, 228*f*, 244, 252, 325*f*, 331, 333*f*
　Drumulator sample-playback drum machine, 74
　SP12 and SP1200 sampling drum machines, 74
　E4XT Ultra rackmount sampler, 328
　Emulator sampler, 73–74, 74*f*, 75
　Emax sampler, 74
　ESI rackmount sampler, 74
　modular synths, 158, 244, 252
　Morpheus rackmount synth, 136
　Proteus series sample-players, 74
Encore Electronics, 205*f*, 227*f*, 246, 248*f*, 251, 332*f*,
　Expressionist MIDI-to-CV converter, 272–273, 325*f*
　Frequency Shifter module, 204, 205*f* (Eurorack)
English language phonemes, 31–33
Ensoniq, 33, 75–76, 104, 123, 277–278
　ASR-series samplers, 31, 39, 76, 99
　Digital Oscillator Chip (DOC), 75–76
　EPS (Ensoniq Performance Sampler), 31, 76, 277
　EPS-16 Plus sampler, 31, 76, 277
　ESP I DSP signal processor chip, 76
　ESQ-1 polysynth, 123–124, 123*f*
　Fizmo polysynth, 76
　Mirage sampler, 75–76, 75*f*
　OTIS DSP effects chip, 76
　OTTO DSP effects chip, 76
　OTTO-FX DSP effects chip, 76
　SDP-1 digital piano, 75
　SQ-80 polysynth, 75
　TS-10 sample-playback synth, 225*f*
　VFX polyphonic synth, 76
envelopes, 20 (definition), 37, 51*f*, 66, 89, 99–100, 99*f*, 111, 123*f*, 134, 151 (definition), 152, 152*f*, 153–154, 273, 335
　ASR envelope, 39 (definition)
　ADSR envelope, 104, 152 (definition), 152*f*, 162
envelope follower, 20 (definition), 156, 161, 163–164, 164*f*, 266, 309
envelope generator (EG), 20 (definition), 38, 39, 45–46, 50–51, 78, 97, 101, 102, 104, 108, 123, 133 (definition), 149, 151–154, 156, 170, 176, 189*f*, 215*f*, 232, 233*f*, 254, 266, 268*f*, 269, 270, 334, 339
EPROM (erasable programmable read-only memory), 78 (definition)

equalizer (EQ), 33 (definition), 109*f*, 166–171, 203*f*, 204*f*
Etherphone, 4
Ether Ship, 265
Etherwave Dance Stage (aka Terpsitone), 6, 6*f*
Eurorack modular synth format, 146, 148, 155, 160, 166–167, 174, 176, 178, 184, 189–192, 200, 204, 207, 246, 251–253, 262–265, 269, 270–272, 273–275, 281, 287–289, 314, 331, 346, 347, 359
　delay modules, 190–193 (analog), 195–196 (digital)
　filter modules, 160, 161, 166–167, 176, 178, 184, 200
　photos, 131*f*, 147*f*, 156*f*, 160*f*, 161*f*, 177*f*, 179*f*, 180*f*, 192*f*, 193*f*, 196*f*, 202*f*, 205*f*, 207*f*, 214*f*, 247*f*, 248*f*, 250*f*, 252*f*, 253*f*, 255*f*, 256*f*, 257*f*, 258*f*, 259*f*, 260*f*, 261*f*, 263*f*, 264*f*, 271*f*, 274*f*, 288*f*, 289*f*, 325*f*
　sequencers, 174–175, 177*f*, 178–180, 180*f*
　The Synthtopia Guide to Eurorack Modular Synthesizers, 251
Eventide
　Harmonizer, 342
　HM80 Baby Harmonizer processor, 340*f*
　Space stompbox, 185, 186f
Evil Con Carne, 224, 312
exciter signal processor, 124, 125 (definition)
expandability in making purchasing decisions, 223–224
expressive control of synthesized sound, 4–33, 128*f*, 129, 134–137, 164–165, 185, 234, 237, 245, 278–279, 280*f*, 283–305, 318–320, 324, 327, 330–331, 338–342, 349, 352
　See also controllers and controlling sound

Fair, Jeff, 159–160, 245, 310–311, 310*f*, 316–317, 317*f*, 324–326, 326*f*, 363–364, 363*f*
Fairhurst, Barb, 81
Fairlight Computer Musical Instrument (CMI) systems, 72–73, 73*f*, 74, 75, 75*f*, 123*f*, 133
Faraday cage, 352–353
Fast, Larry, 317, 318*f*
"Father, Mother, Daughter," 355, 356*f*, 357, 358*f*
Fender Rhodes electric pianos
　73 Stage EP, 351f
　Suitcase EP, 53
Festival of Arts, 316–317
file transfers, 49 (Yamaha Motif XF8, iPad), 277 (Teenage Engineering OP-1, USB), 354 (SD card, USB)
　FTP sharing, 355
　SCSI (Small Computer System Interface), 40, 41 (definition), 343
films
　recording film and TV scores, 354–359
　scoring to film and TV, 213, 237, 310–316
　selected "filmography," 373

Index

filters, 21 (definition), 157–172
    bandpass (BPF), 18, 37, 38 (definition), 39, 157, 158, 160, 162, 167–172, 209, 265, 329
    cutoff frequency, 28, 39, 63, 66, 81 (definition), 87, 125, 145, 149, 150 (definition), 151, 157, 158, 159, 160, 160*f*, 161, 162, 163, 164, 171, 172, 173, 196, 269, 274, 307*f*, 341
    fixed bandwidth, 166
    formant/fixed-filter bank, 8, 9 (definition), 12, 18 (definition), 100, 162, 166, 167, 265
    highpass (HPF), 20, 21 (definition), 37, 39, 134, 157, 158, 160, 160*f*, 162, 163, 171, 227, 257*f*
    key tracking, 66 (definition), 159
    lowpass (LPF), 20, 21 (definition), 37, 39, 105, 117, 123, 124, 149, 150 (definition), 157, 158, 160, 160*f*, 161, 162, 162*f*, 171, 195, 196, 238*f*, 266, 306*f*, 329, 341
    Moog four-pole lowpass ladder filter, 224, 334
    multimode, 39 (definition), 63, 66, 104, 108, 110, 111, 111*f*, 149*f*, 158, 159*f*, 162, 163, 164, 164*f*, 184*f*, 185, 189*f*, 257*f*
    negative- and positive-feedback, 158
    notch/band reject, 157, 158, 164, 171, 191, 200
    Q factor. *See* resonance *below*
    resonance (aka "Q" and bandwidth), 9 (acoustic instruments), 12 (definition), 63, 117, 149, 150 (definition), 157, 158 (definition), 158*f*, 160, 160*f*, 161, 162, 163, 164, 166, 167, 170, 171, 192, 200, 274
    rolloff/cutoff slope, 39, 124, 157 (definition), 160, 161, 163, 166, 264
    poles, 39, 123, 157 (definition), 158, 161, 162, 163, 164, 166, 171, 224*f*
    self-oscillating, 94, 150, 158, 159*f*, 172–173
filter banks, 18, 25*f*, 89, 159, 166–171, 265
fingerboard instruments, 6, 7*f*, 34*f*, 35, 281, 290–292
first synthesizer, 114
5U modular synth format, 181, 184, 193, 200, 246, 252, 275, 331
    explained, 247, 346–347
    photographs, 182*f*, 194*f*, 227*f*, 228*f*, 247*f*, 248*f*, 250*f*, 275*f*
fixed-architecture/pre-patched hardware synths, xi, 140, 210, 223
fixed-rate sample-skipping (aka drop/add), 75
flanging effect, 100, 124, 125 (definition), 170–171, 186*f*, 188, 190, 191, 193, 199, 200, 207, 208*f*, 334
Flash WAV memory, 49 (definition), 52*f*, 171*f*, 354
Flashpoint, 237–238, 244, 314–315, 322, 355–359, 355*f*, 357*f*
flight cases (ATA-approved), 71*f*, 276–277, 276*f*, 286*f*
Flight of Harmony, 248*f*, 259*f*
    Plague Bearer (PB) filter module, 160, 160*f*
    Sound of Shadows (SOS) delay module, 195
floating-point keyboard split, 43 (definition)
Flower Electronics Little Boy Blue, 307, 309, 309*f*

flute sound, 4, 12, 45, 54, 55, 68, 132, 135, 137, 152, 331
FM (frequency modulation) synthesis, 41–42, 50, 60, 61, 63, 101, 102, 107, 108, 110, 141*f*, 142, 147*f*, 148, 162, 163, 240, 243*f*, 277, 330, 339
    four-op FM, 107, 108 (definition)
    linear, 41, 47–49, 108, 133 (definition), 141*f*, 142
Foley, Paul, 104
Forbidden Planet, 107*f*, 228*f*, 373
Fortune, Kevin, 283, 286*f*, 319–321, 319*f*, 347, 349*f*
forums and blogs, list of, 375–382
Fostex 3180 dual-channel spring reverb, 325*f*
4ms Pedals, 214*f*, 254, 259*f*, 264*f*, 307, 307*f*
    Autonomous Bassline Generator (ABG), 307, 307*f*
FracRak modular synth format, 141*f*, 148, 154, 160, 176, 193, 195, 204, 205*f*, 207, 247, 247*f*, 249, 251, 252, 265, 272, 275, 289, 331, 346, 359
    photos, 148*f*, 251*f*, 290*f*, 325*f*
Francis, Joseph, 104
Franco, Sergio, 94
Franke, Christopher, 45
frequency divider, 25, 37 (definition), 266
frequency modulation. *See* FM
frequency shifter, 111*f*, 201, 204 (definition), 205*f*, 227, 230*f*, 263, 329
frequency-to-voltage converter, 157
Froese, Edgar, 45
FTP site, sharing music via, 355
Fukuda, Mark, 50
fundamental frequency, 9 (definition), 11, 12, 37, 132, 133, 137, 138, 157, 331

Gabor, Dennis, 134
Gambe, 36
gamelan, 45
Garrison, Gary, 330
Garritan Instruments, 80
gate, 14*f*, 26, 30, 87–88, 97, 130 (definition), 144*f*, 145*f*, 168, 172, 174–176, 174*f*, 175*f*, 176*f*, 179, 181*f*, 185, 193, 215*f*, 223, 242, 252, 266, 267, 269–270, 269*f*, 270*f*, 271–273, 271*f*, 273*f*, 273–275, 275*f*, 279–280, 282, 284*f*, 285, 287, 289*f*, 290–291, 290*f*, 302*f*, 324, 334, 339, 342, 343*f*
    See also trigger
Gator G-Tour-SLMX12 12U mixer case, 258, 261*f*
GigaSampler and GigaStudio, 79–80, 80*f*
Gillis, Herman, 162–163
Givelet, Joseph A., 114, 114*f*
goals, consideration when choosing synthesizers, 213–216
Gofriller cello samples, 330
Gold, Richard, 265
Goldstein, Mark, 305
gong, 36 (component in Ondes Martenot *Métallique* diffuser), 45 (gamelan instrument)

Gong, 91
gong sound, 117
Grace, Cary, 247f
Graham, Chet, 78
graintable (combination of granular and wavetable synthesis), 108
Graintable Synthesizer, 134, 134f
Grammy awards, 56, 83–84, 86, 172f
grand piano, 61 (keyboard action), 230f and 236f (1917 Steinway Model M), 292 (Steinway samples)
granular synthesis, 60, 105 (definition), 108, 134, 321, 356
Grapher, 99–100, 99f
graphic equalizer, 166, 167, 204f
graphic programming, 60, 104–107, 105f, 106f, 107f
Great River MP-2NV dual-channel mic preamp, 363
Green, Dann, 264f
Greene, David, 316, 355
grid locations (Make Noise René term for stages or steps), 180
The Grim Adventures of Billy & Mandy, 224, 312, 334
groove synthesizer, 52, 216f
GROOVE (Generating Realtime Operations On Voltage-controlled Equipment), 102
grungy quality of sound, 45, 75–76, 104, 164, 190, 209
Guilmette, Pierre, 100
guitar sounds, 36, 52, 124, 298, 324

Haibel, Jurgen, 265
Haken, Lippold, 58, 290
Haken Audio Continuum Fingerboard, 290–292, 292f, 293f
Hammer, Jan, 21, 72, 109f
Hammond, Laurens, 3, 184
Hammond Organ Company, 36, 38, 125, 133, 184
    B-3 tonewheel organ, 3, 36, 61, 110, 125, 133, 184
    C-3 tonewheel organ, 19f, 346, 346f, 347f
    Concorde electronic organ, 217f
    Novachord, 36–38, 37f
    X-66, 217f
Hammond organ sounds/simulations, 52f, 61, 68, 72, 78f, 110
Hammond Suzuki Xk-3c organ, 344f
Hand Roll Piano K-61, 179f
hard disks and hard disk technology, 61, 79–80, 102, 121, 345, 353, 354
    playing samples directly from disk, 79–80, 80f
hard oscillator sync, 63 (definition), 81, 104, 141f, 142, 145 (definition)
hardware to softsynth conversion, 344–345
hardware *vs.* software, pros and cons, 216, 219–221
harmonic tunings, 44–45

harmonics, 8, 9 (definition), 11, 12, 18, 25, 33, 37, 38, 41, 46, 54, 63, 67, 72, 78f, 86, 100, 105, 115, 122f, 125, 132–133, 137–139, 139f, 145, 157, 159–160, 163f, 164, 166, 193, 200, 204, 206–207, 264, 331, 334, 338–339, 363–364
harpsichord, 3 (*Clavecin Electrique*/Electric Harpsichord), 18 (pre-touch-sensitive synth keyboard response)
Hartmann, Axel, 65f, 66f, 67, 159f, 231f
    Hartmann synth designs, 64, 65f, 66–67, 159f, 231f,
    Gambit synth prototype, 231f
    ModelMaker Neuron patch editor, 66
    Neuron neural-modeling polysynth, 64, 66–67, 66f
    NeuronVS softsynth application, 67
    Nuke tabletop controller, 67
Harvestman, the, 214f, 258f, 259f
Haut-parleur, 34f, 36
Hazelcom Industries, 119–121
HEAR (Hearing Education and Awareness for Rockers, 132
hearing, 4 (dB scale), 33 (Francis Bacon, 1626), 88 (realtime synthesis control), 93f (Joe Zawinul inspiration), 99 (Con Brio ADS), 131–132 (preserving), 185 (reverb diffusion), 204 (barber-pole effect), 305 (tunings), 314 (reactions to electronic music), 341 (*Switched-On Bach* inspiration), 352 (preservation in the studio)
Hemsath, Bill, 21, 137
Henke, Robert, 127
Hertz (Hz), 4, 131 (definition), 204
Hertz-per-volt scale, 139, 269f, 270f, 272
heterodyning, 4 (definition), 34
Hewlett-Packard plotter for scoring, 120
Hi-Hat Decay slider, 126
Hindemith, Paul, 9
hinge frequency in shelving EQ, 166
Hinz, Volker, 110
hip hop, 82, 84f, 126–127
    Akai MPC60, 40, 91, 126–127, 126f
    Roland TR-808, 84f, 108
Hitchcock, Alfred, 9
Hockney, David, 312
Holley, Josh, 247f
Hollow, 36
Hoover sound, 321–322
Hot Springs Reverb Kit, 184
Hotop, Jack, 62f
House Research Institute, the, 132
house music, 85
H-Pi Instruments, 305–306, 305f, 306f
    Lo-Fi Microstudio microtonal softsynth, recording, and editing application for Macintosh, 306, 306f
    Tonal Plexus MegaPlex microtonal key controller, 305f

Index

Huggett, Chris, 91
human nuance in musical sound, 11, 25, 313, 319, 320, 325, 330–331
   See also controllers and controlling sound
human speech simulations, 31–33, 32*f*, 168
   talkbox, 69, 170, 171 (definition)
   See also vocoder
humidity, effects of, 82*f*, 139, 234, 287, 327, 329
Human, Naut, 265
Hunt, Chad, 21, 137
Hurni, Martin, 285
Husted, James, 289*f*
hybrid modular synth, 100–102
Hyperkeys controller, 278–279, 281*f*
Hyundai, 79

IBM computers, early electronic music applications for, 102
IBM, all-electronic filmscores, 119
IBM-PC, 29, 103
iceGear Xenon Groove Synthesizer iOS music app, 216*f*
IK Multimedia, 113
improvisation instruments, 86–88, 94–95, 213, 291*f*
impulse response (IR), 185–186
industrial sculpture, SalMar Construction, 94–95, 95*f*, 96*f*
Infinite Response VAX77, 278, 278*f*, 279*f*
instantaneous composing/performance machine, 118–119, 120*f*
Intermorph mode, 66
Internet
   companion website, explanation of, xv
   sites related to manufacturers, dealers, periodicals, etc., 253, 254, 373–382
The Interstellar Suite, 244
IRCAM (Institut de Recherche et Coordination Acoustique/ Musique), 104

Jackson, Michael, 123
Jackson, Will "Stonewall," 265
jargon, different terminology for similar features, 326
Jarre, Jean-Michel, 72, 91
JazzMutant Lemur, 298, 299*f*
Jeffery, Mark, 104
Jenny, Georges, 10–11
Jmax, 104
Joel, Billy, 334, 335*f*, 343–345, 344*f*
John, Elton, 345
John Bowen Synth Design, 210*f*
Johnson, Jim, 123*f*
Jomox Sunsyn, 225*f*, 227*f*, 332*f*
Jones, Cameron, 121
Jones, Chuck, 313
Jones, Marvin, 190, 251*f*, 265, 266*f*, 282, 283*f*
Jones, Quincy, 26

joystick, 20, 21 (definition), 43, 55, 55*f*, 66–67, 135, 210*f*, 280, 282, 291*f*, 300, 327
Jubel, Peter, 108
Jungleib, Stanley, 108
Juskiw, Scott, 262
just intonation, 44–45, 305

Kakehashi, Ikutaro, 56, 82–85, 83*f*, 267
Kakehashi, Ikuo, 84
Kaplan, Jerry, 41
Karma Lab LLC KARMA (Kay Algorithmic Realtime Music Architecture), 181–182
Kay, Stephen, 181
Kaypro computer, 43*f*, 44
Kehew, Brian, 98*f*, 99
Keith McMillen Instruments, 279, 298
   KMI MIDI Expander, 279
   QuNeo USB pad controller, 298, 298*f*
   QuNexus USB/MIDI/CV key controller, 279, 281*f*
   Rogue wireless, battery supplement for QuNeo, 298
Kenton, 269–270, 271*f*
   DCB interface, 269*f*
   KADI/Wasp interface, 269
   Modular Solo Eurorack MIDI-to-CV converter, 269, 271*f*
   Pro 4 MIDI-to-CV converter, 227*f*, 325*f*
   Pro Solo MkII MIDI-to-CV converter, 270*f*
   Pro-2000 MkII MIDI-to-CV converter, 269*f*, 325*f*
Ketoff, Paul, ix, 24–25, 25*f*
Keyboard magazine, xi, 342
keyboard splits, 26, 43, 52*f*, 74, 82, 99, 124, 272, 276*f*, 282
keyboard tracking, 66, 159
keyboards, ix, 3, 10–13, 18, 19*f*, 22, 23*f*, 24, 25, 25*f*, 26–27, 27*f*, 28, 29, 31, 35, 37, 38–39, 39*f*, 40*f*, 42*f*, 43, 46*f*, 49, 50–52, 52*f*, 53, 56, 61–62, 63, 68–69, 72, 73–74, 75, 75*f*, 78*f*, 81–82, 82*f*, 89, 89*f*, 91, 92*f*, 99, 100–101, 101*f*, 111*f*, 117, 122*f*, 123–124, 125, 130, 139, 142*f*, 146*f*, 149, 151, 159, 173*f*, 180, 189*f*, 203*f*, 210, 210*f*, 212*f*, 216*f*, 217*f*, 221*f*, 225*f*, 229*f*, 230*f*, 231*f*, 233*f*, 234*f*, 237*f*, 245, 257*f*, 262, 265, 266*f*, 272, 276–283, 276*f*, 277*f*, 278*f*, 279*f*, 280*f*, 282*f*, 283*f*, 284*f*, 286–287, 290, 291–292, 297*f*, 324*f*, 325, 325*f*, 334, 340*f*, 342, 343*f*, 346*f*, 351*f*, 359–360
   aftertouch/pressure response (monophonic, channel), 10, 11, 12, 14, 22, 24 (definition), 26, 31, 40*f*, 49, 53, 101, 125, 126, 189*f*, 210*f*, 230*f*, 273, 274, 274*f*, 275, 276*f*, 279, 280, 282*f*, 286, 287, 289, 290, 290*f*, 291*f*, 292, 294, 295, 297*f*, 298, 340*f*
   "an antiquated interface," Bob Moog, ix
   cross-switching voice response, 43 (definition), 61

Index

finger position/location, 13, 24, 279, 282*f*, 289, 290, 294, 297, 298
floating-point keyboard split mode, 43 (definition)
hammer action, 61, 62, 276, 277
keyboard-based hardware, 210
polyphonic aftertouch, 24 (definition), 28, 82, 122*f*, 230*f*, 237*f*, 277–279, 278*f*, 292, 294
release velocity response, 26 (definition), 82, 278, 278*f*
splits, 26 (definition), 82, 124
velocity response, 11, 12 (definition), 22, 25, 26, 28, 29, 31, 40*f*, 43–44, 46*f*, 49, 53, 63, 66, 75, 82*f*, 100, 101, 122*f*, 123, 125, 126, 181*f*, 189*f*, 210*f*, 230*f*, 270, 273, 274, 274*f*, 275, 276*f*, 279, 282, 282*f*, 291*f*, 292, 294, 298, 305*f*, 345
vintage keyboards, 283*f*
voice layering, 16, 38, 43 (definition), 52*f*, 63, 70, 78, 82, 99, 239, 303*f*, 311, 324, 329, 334–335, 337*f*
Kilpatrick, Andrew, 252
Kilpatrick Audio, 252, 271
  K1600 MIDI Converter module, 271
  Kilpatrick Format Modular Synthesizer, 252
KIM-1 (Keyboard Input Monitor) microprocessor, 103
King, Steven, 223
King Crimson, 91
Kissinger, Kevin, 244
Klein, Barry, 188
Knas Ekdahl Moisturizer, 184, 184*f*
knee lever, 36
Knob Grotto modular synth, 227*f*, 228*f*, 331, 332*f*, 334
knob-laden synthesizer/stompbox, 94, 186*f*, 210
Korg, 13, 55, 56, 61–62, 62*f*, 64, 86–88, 124–126, 135, 136*f*, 139, 142, 142*f*, 154, 157, 181, 196, 203*f*, 207–209, 225*f*, 267, 270*f*, 272, 276, 337*f*, 341, 342*f*, 351*f*
  CX3 digital organ, 351*f*
  iKaossilator softsynth app for iOS, 88
  Kaossilator improvisation instrument, 86–88, 87*f*
  Kaossilator Pro Phrase Synthesizer and Loop Recorder, 88
  Kaossilator 2 handheld improv instrument, 88
  Kaoss Pad KP1 multi-effects processor, 207–208
  Kaoss Pad miniKP multi-effect processor, 208
  Kaoss Pad multi-effect processor series, 207–209
  Kaoss Pad Quad (KPQ) multi-effects processor, 208–209, 208*f*
  Karma sequencing polysynth with KARMA arpeggiator, 126, 181
  Krome workstation synth, 62
  Kronos multi-synthesis workstation, 56, 62, 126, 136, 136*f*, 181
  M1 workstation synth, 124–126
  Mono/Poly analog synth, 342
  Monotron Delay (MD) handheld analog monosynth with DDL, 196
  MS20:Legacy softsynth, 324
  MS-20 patchable analog monosynth, 142, 142*f*, 196, 351*f* (giant educational version, "the blackboard")
  MS20 Mini patchable analog monosynth, 142
  M3 workstation synth, 126, 181
  M50 workstation synth, 126, 181
  N-series workstation synths, 126
  OASys (Open Architecture Synthesis System) PCI computer card, 61
  OASys prototype physical-modeling synth, 56, 61
  OASYS (Open Architecture Synthesis Studio) workstation, 56, 61–62, 62*f*, 126, 181
  Polysix analog polysynth, 342
  Prophecy physical-modeling monosynth, 61
  Trident analog polysynth, 342*f*
  Trident mkII analog polysynth, 341
  Trinity workstation synth, 126
  Triton workstation synth, 126, 181
  TR-Rack synth module, 239, 337*f*
  T-series workstation synths, 126
  VC-10 vocoder keyboard, 203*f*
  Wavedrum percussion synth, 302
  Wavestation Legacy softsynth, 56
  Wavestation vector synth, 56, 135, 136, 136*f*, 225*f*, 227*f*, 228*f*, 244, 351*f*
  Wavestation EX vector synth, 351*f*
  X-series workstation synths, 126
  Z1 physical-modeling multitimbral synth, 61
  01/W workstation synth, 126
Kreychi, Stanislav, 117, 118*f*
Kubrick, Stanley, 200
Kunimoto, Toshifumi, 30
Kurzweil, Ray, 76, 77*f*, 78–79
  Kurzweil Reading Machine, 76
Kurzweil Music Systems, 13, 76–79, 135, 136, 153, 276, 303*f*, 304, 304*f*, 330, 330*f*, 344*f*
  ExpressionMate ribbon controller/MIDI processor, 282
  K250 sample-playback synthesizer with optional sampling, 76–78
  K1000 Series sample-playback synths, 78
  K2000 VAST synth, 78, 135
  K2000R VAST synth module, 328*f*
  K2500 VAST synth, 78, 135
  K2600 VAST synth, 78, 330
  K2661 VAST synth, 330, 330*f*, 344*f*
  Midiboard MIDI controller keyboard, 277
  PC1x Performance Controller keyboard, 324*f*
  PC3K series (PC3K6, PC3K7, and PC3K8) production station synths, 79*f*
  Variable Architecture Synthesis Technology (VAST), 78–79, 330, 330*f*
KVR Audio, online information about plug-ins and host programs, 357

Index

La Borde, Jean-Baptiste de, 3
labeling proprietary AC/DC wall-wart power supplies, 222
Labrecque, Denis, 228, 231
ladder filter, Moog four-pole lowpass, 224, 334
lag processor, 154f, 155 (definition), 250f, 324, 334
Lake Butler MIDI Mitigator RFC-1 Foot Controller, 343, 344f
Lambert, John, 293
layering voices, 16, 38, 43 (definition), 52f, 63, 78, 82, 99, 311, 334–335, 337f
LCD (liquid-crystal display), 49, 51f, 61, 210f, 272, 274, 276f, 277f, 305f
Le Caine, Hugh, 11–13, 12f
Lee, Scott, 251f
Leimseider, John J. L., 244
LEO (Live Electronic Orchestra), 26, 216, 217f, 218f, 350f
Leslie, Don, 125
Leslie speaker, 124, 125 (definition), 325
Leslie speaker simulation, 204
Leuenberger, Gary, 49
Lewis, Don, 26, 84, 216, 217f, 218f, 349, 350f
LFO (low-frequency oscillator), 11, 22, 24, 31, 33 (definition), 39, 63, 66, 78, 87, 101, 104, 108, 110, 123f, 137, 138 (definition), 148, 151, 153, 154–156, 154f, 156f, 159, 162, 164, 170, 175, 184f, 185, 189f, 190, 193, 196, 206, 206f, 215f, 217f, 232, 234, 250f, 254, 265, 266, 269f, 270, 270f, 271, 272, 275, 281, 306f, 308f
  distinguished from a sub-oscillator, 156
  voltage-influenced, 155, 156f
Lieberman, Don, 95–99, 97f, 98f
"Life's Been Good," 173
Limberis, Alex, 75, 123
linear arithmetic (LA) synthesis, 53–54, 135
linear frequency modulation (FM). *See* frequency modulation
lingo, different terminology for similar features, 326
Linn, Roger, 56, 73, 84–86, 86f, 91, 126–127, 126f, 127f, 128f, 170–171, 172f, 244, 295
Linn Electronics, 56, 73, 84, 85, 86f, 126, 297f
  LinnDrum, 126, 127f, 244
  Linn 9000 multitrack MIDI sequencer with sampling, 126
  LM-1 Drum Computer, 73, 84–86, 86f, 126
Linux platform, 210, 279, 295
Liquid Television, 224, 312
Livewire Electronics, 255f, 256f, 257f, 259f
  Audio Frequency Generator (AFG) module, 256f
  FrequenSteiner multimode filter module, 257f
Loffink, John, 44, 247f, 306
loopers, 197–200
looping envelopes, Kurzweil K1000 Series synths, 153
looping functions, 87, 88 (definition), 105, 207, 208f

lopass gates, 334
Luening, Otto, 24, 116

MacBeth, Ken, 257f
MacBeth Studio Systems, 257f
  M3X analog synth module, 227f, 332f,
Mackie
  8-Bus mixer, 364, 365
  802 VLZ3 mixer, 249f
  1202 VLZ Pro mixer, 227f, 325f
  1604 VLZ mixer, 227f
Madrona Labs, 294, 297f
  Aalto cross-platform softsynth, 215f, 295
  Soundplane Model A USB controller, 294–295, 297f
Maestro, subsidiary of Chicago Musical Instruments, 38, 39
Make Noise Co., 178–180, 214f, 248f, 259f, 287, 288f
  Brains clocked sequential binary event module, 287
  Format Jumbler 3.5mm/banana/¼" mult module, 248f
  Pressure Points touch controller module, 287, 288f
  René Cartesian Sequencer module, 178–180, 287, 288f
Malekko Heavy Industry Corp., 160, 161f, 247f, 255f, 259f
  Wiard Boogie Lowpass filter module, 160, 161f
Mancini, Henry, 26
Mancuso, Joe, 316
mangling audio, 105, 160, 163
Manhattan Research Inc., 119, 119f
Mann, Aimee, 71
manufacturers' websites, list of, 375–382
Marinuzzi, Gino, 24
Marion Systems, 40
  MSR2 rackmount synth module, 40
  SCSI for Akai MPC60 music workstation, 40
  Tom Oberheim SEM analog monosynth module, 41, 223, 234, 235f
  sixteen-bit audio upgrade for Akai S900 sampler, 40
  Tom Oberheim Son of 4-Voice analog synth system, 41
  Tom Oberheim Two Voice Pro analog synthesizer, 40f, 234f
Martenot, 34–36
Martenot, Ginett, 35f, 36f
Martenot, Maurice, 35, 35f, 36f
Martin, Brad, 251f
Martirano, Dorothy, 94
Martirano, Salvatore, 94–96, 96f
Masucci, Steve, 245–246, 261–262
Mathews, Max, 40, 102, 104, 301
Matrixsynth Web link, 253
Mattel, 68–71, 70f

Index

Matthews, Mike, 91
Mattson, George, 179f, 247f, 257f
Mattson Mini Modular, 176, 178f, 179f, 247, 247f, 252, 254, 257f, 272, 273f, 346
   PE/MIDI1 MIDI/CV controller with power entry module, 272, 273f
   Phoenix Series VCO-J, 247f
   SQ816 and SQ816 Expansion sequencer modules, 176, 178f, 179f
Mauchly, Bill, 31, 75, 123
Max graphic music programming environment, 104, 105f, 129, 134
McDSP Revolver Flexible Convolution Reverb plug-in, 186f
McLey, David, 119–121
McLeyvier hybrid music workstation, 119–121
McMillen, Keith, 279, 298
Mellotron, 67, 68–69, 68f, 69f, 71
Mendes, Sergio, 26
menu systems, programming, 29, 53, 99, 110, 130, 136, 210, 215, 272, 274, 329
Mersenne, Marin, 45
MetalBox, 154, 247, 251, 252
   tube VCA module, 154
Métallique, 34f, 36
Meyer, Chris, 55–56, 135
MFB-Kraftzwerg patchable tabletop synth module, 142
Microtonal Synthesis Web Site, 44
microtonal tunings and scales, 44–45, 117, 305–306
MIDI (Musical Instrument Digital Interface), 16 (definition), 17, 22, 24, 30, 33, 47, 50, 52, 56, 103f, 104, 108–109, 173–178, 199, 267, 276–282, 285, 301–305, 311, 312, 314, 334–335, 343, 356–357, 359–360
   alternative communication protocols, 17, 26–27, 29, 40, 46f, 83, 99
   CV-to-MIDI conversion, 242, 267, 273–275
   development, 47–48, 56, 83
   MIDI-to-CV conversion, 41, 145f, 175, 181, 182f, 235f, 239, 250f, 251f, 267–273, 273f, 274f, 282, 324, 325f, 336f
   obsolescence, 27
MIDI clock sync, 40f, 164, 170, 171, 190, 191f, 198, 199, 269f, 270, 270f, 314
MIDI Solutions, 47f, 48f
   Quadra Merge MIDI processor, 48f
   T8 rackmount MIDI thru box, 47f
Mighty Serge Modular, 319f, 320–321, 320f, 347, 349f
Milstein, Gur, 178, 260f
The Minimoog Model D Operation Manual, 138, 139f
MIT Media Lab, 102
mixing, 159–160, 166, 315–316, 324, 353, 354–355, 360–364
   automated mixing, 360–361
Mixtur Trautonium, 9, 9f

mod/modulation wheel, 28, 31, 51f, 63, 66, 101, 151 (definition), 273, 275, 334
Modcan, 196, 246, 247f, 248f, 325f, 331, 334
   A Series modular format, 141f, 246, 247f, 311f, 323, 364f, 365f
   B Series modular format, 250f, 246, 247, 249, 250f
   Diode Filter 23A module, 334
   Dual Lag 18B module, 250f
   Dual Quantizer 55B module, 250f
   4VCA 31B module, 250f
   Digital Delay 59A and 59B modules, 196
   Quad Envelope 60B module, 250f
   Reverb 35A module, 325f
   Reverb 35B module, 250f
   Touch-Sequencer 72B module, 250f
   VC Flanger 38A, 334
modeled-analog synthesizer, 63, 64f, 145 (definition)
Modular Form Factors chart Web link, 253
Modular Grid Web link, 253
modular synthesizers
   database of formats, 253
   dealers and stores, Web links, 382–383
   DIY blogs and forums, 253–254
   informative Web links, 253–254
   twenty-first century, in the, 245–266
modulation, 11, 28 (definition), 41–42, 63, 142 and 145 (definition)
Mohn, Terry, 94
Moi, Wing, 41
Monome, 298–300, 300f, 359–360
monotimbral voices, 81 (definition)
Moody Blues, 91
Moog, Dr. Robert A./Bob, ix, 7f, 17–24, 17f, 18f, 19f, 23f, 77f, 85, 137, 152, 162f, 166, 170, 173f, 206f, 244, 245, 247, 266, 269–270, 274, 278, 280f, 330, 347f
Moog-Koussa, Michelle, ix–x, 221f
Moog Music, 7f, 17, 21–22, 23f, 29, 80, 93, 103f, 104, 138, 154f, 161, 166, 170, 191, 206, 225f, 230f, 269–270, 327
   Animoog iOS softsynth, 103f
   Etherwave Pro Theremin, 23f
   Guitar, 22
   Little Phatty, 22, 67
   Minimoog Model D analog monosynth, xi, 18f, 21, 22, 38, 61, 111, 137–140, 138f, 139f, 143f, 149, 156, 157, 158, 158f, 161, 173f, 214f, 223, 224f, 225f, 227, 232f, 239, 239f, 242f, 245, 269–270, 273, 325, 327, 336f, 344, 363–364
   Minimoog Voyager analog monosynth, ix, 22, 23f, 67, 142, 223, 225f, 229f, 231f, 327, 328f
   Minimoog Voyager Old School analog monosynth, 22, 67, 223
   Modular synths, ix, 17–18, 18f, 19f, 20f, 22f, 71, 88, 121, 152, 162f, 166, 173f, 181, 220f, 245–246, 269–270, 329, 345, 346, 347f
   Moogerfooger signal processors, 23f, 170, 225f

Moog Music (*continued*)
    Moogerfooger CP-251 Control Processor, 154*f*, 230*f*
    Moogerfooger MF-101 Lowpass Filter, 161, 162*f*
    Moogerfooger MF-102 Ring Modulator, 206–207, 206*f*
    Moogerfooger MF-103 12-Stage Phaser, 225*f*
    Moogerfooger MF-104 and MF-104M analog delay processors, 190, 191*f*
    Moogerfooger MF-105 MuRF (Multiple Resonance Filter array), M-105B MuRF, and MF-105M MIDI MuRF signal processors, 23*f*, 170
    Slim Phatty analog monosynth module, 67
    Sonic Six analog duophonic suitcase synth, 18*f*
    office, 22*f*, 23*f*
    Percussion Controller, 18*f*
    Taurus III synth bass pedals, 22, 67
Moon Modular/Lunar Experience, 246, 247, 248*f*, 249, 275, 275*f*, 346
    552 Quad Control Voltage-to-MIDI Converter module, 275, 275*f*
Moore, F. Richard, 102
Moraz, Patrick, 71*f*, 244
Morbius homemade patchable synth, 228*f*, 230*f*, 325*f*, 331, 333*f*
Moscow State University, 117
MOTM (loosely the acronym for Mother of All Modulars) modular format. *See* Synthesis Technology, 141, 146
MOTU (Mark of the Unicorn), 226, 353, 357, 359
    Digital Performer audio workstation with MIDI sequencing, 224, 353
    HD192 audio interface, 357
    828 audio interface, 328*f*
    424 PCI card, 357
    MIDI Express XT MIDI interface, 227*f*, 328*f*,
    24io audio interface, 357
    2408MKIII audio interface, 357
    Volta voltage-control instrument plug-in, 210, 273
Mr. Chorus, 54
Mr. K. *See* Kakehashi, Ikutaro
Mr. PCM, 54
Mr. Reverb, 54
MTI General Development System (Music Technology Inc. GDS), 41–45, 42*f*
Muff's Modules & More, 253 (Web link), 253, 255
mult (multiple junction module), 247, 248*f*
Multiple-Touch-Sensitive Keyboard, ix, 24, 278, 280*f*
multisample, 124, 125 (definition), 292, 321, 330, 345
multitimbral operation, 26 (definition), 27*f*, 29, 49, 50, 52, 57*f*, 61, 63, 75, 76–79, 97, 107, 119, 123–124, 230*f*, 335
Munch, Edvard, 162
Munchkinized, 73, 74 (definition)
Muro, Don, 92*f*, 279, 340*f*, 341–342, 342*f*, 343*f*, 349, 351*f*, 360–361

Murzin, Eugeniy, 117, 118*f*
Muse Research, 112–113, 219
    Receptor rackmount VST and softsynth platform, 112–113, 112*f*, 219, 335*f*, 345
    MuseBox, 113, 113*f*
museums of interest to synthesists, 94, 216, 217f, 244, 374
Music I, II, and V music applications, 102
Musiclab MIDIoverLAN CP, 357
musique concrète, 13, 286
MXR
    1500 DDL rackmount effects processor, 227*f*, 332*f*
    Phase 100 stompbox effects processor, 340*f*
    Pitch Transposer (PT) rackmount effects processor, 205*f*
    SF01 Slash Octave Fuzz stompbox effects processor, 249*f*
Myrberg, Mats, 75, 123

NAMM (National Association of Music Merchants) tradeshow/convention, 58*f*, 61 (definition), 62*f*, 64, 73, 73*f*, 74, 77*f*, 80, 83*f*, 103*f*, 128*f*, 136*f*, 142*f*, 146*f*, 169*f*, 172*f*, 211*f*, 216, 221*f*, 234*f*, 252*f*, 256*f*, 257*f*, 260*f*, 263*f*, 288*f*, 289*f*, 292*f*, 350*f*
Nasillard, 36
Nathorst-Böös, Ernst, 108
National Music Centre, 244, 374
Native Instruments, 80*f*, 109–112, 113, 134, 237, 238*f*, 243, 323, 335, 345, 357, 358*f*
    Absynth softsynth, 110–111, 111*f*, 153, 153*f*, 324, 326
    Battery software drum sampler, 298
    FM8 softsynth, 240
    Generator virtual modular analog synth, 110
    Komplete software library of instruments and effects, 110*f*, 226
    Kontakt software sampler, 237, 238, 238*f*, 243, 324, 335, 345, 357, 358*f*
    Massive, 110, 111, 112*f*
    Metaphysical Function softsynths for Reaktor, 110*f*
    Reaktor do-it-yourself softsynth toolkit, 110, 110*f*, 134, 298
    Traktor DJ software, 298
NED (New England Digital), 121–123
    Synclavier, 121–123, 122*f*, 314, 359
NemeSys, 79–80
Neumann, Drew, xv, 80*f*, 106–107, 106*f*, 107*f*, 204, 219, 224–237, 225*f*, 226*f*, 227*f*, 228*f*, 229*f*, 230*f*, 236*f*, 244, 247, 263–265, 269, 272–273, 287, 287*f*, 311–313, 311*f*, 322–324, 325*f*, 327, 329, 331–334, 332*f*, 333*f*, 364–365, 365*f*
    quote, 245
neural modeling, 64, 66–67
neural network-controlled adaptive sound analysis, 64, 66–67

Index

neuronal resynthesis, 64, 66–67
Neve
    mixing console, 365
    1073 mic preamp, 361, 363
The New Atlantis, 33, 34
New England Digital. *See* NED
Nicol, Richard, 155, 188
Night of the Living Dead, 182
Nimbus 9 studio, 119
noise generator, 12, 20, 21 (definition), 25*f*, 106*f*, 117, 140, 148–149, 154*f*, 155, 160*f*, 173, 176, 189*f*, 195, 200, 329
noise issues, 54, 56, 93, 187, 188, 189, 193
noise toys, 210, 306–309
non-equal-tempered tunings, 44–45, 305–306
nonprogrammable voltage-controlled synths, 210, 223
non-synthesist approach to playing the Minimoog, 223
Nordelius, Hans, 64, 65*f*, 100, 137
Norlin Corporation, 38–39, 202*f*
normalization, 105 (definition), 354
normalled/hard-wired circuitry, 21 (definition), 41, 94, 141, 142, 143*f*, 210, 212*f*, 235*f*, 322
Norris, Michael, 360
notation of patches, 327, 329
Novation, 64, 300
    Automap controller assignment software, 300
    Launchpad USB performance controller, 300
    Remote Zero SL multifunction USB controller, 324*f*
    Supernova rackmount analog-modeling polysynth, 91, 248*f*
Nyquist frequency and theorem, 46 (definition), 85
Nyquist, Harry, 46

Oberheim, Tom, 38–41, 80, 142, 223, 234, 235*f*
Oberheim Electronics
    DMX drum machine, 40
    DS-2 digital sequencer, 38, 340*f*, 342, 343*f*
    DSX digital multitrack sequencer, 40
    Eight Voice analog polysynth, 39, 80, 234
    Four Voice analog polysynth, 28, 39, 80, 234
    OB-1 programmable analog monosynth, 40
    OB-8 analog rackmount polysynth, 214*f*
    OB-X analog polysynth, 40, 343*f*
    Matrix-12 analog polysynth, 40
    Matrix-1000 analog rackmount polysynth module, 139, 140*f*
    Parallel Buss pre-MIDI synchronization, 40
    Polyphonic Synthesizer Programmer, 40
    SEM (Synthesizer Expansion Module), 26, 27*f*, 39, 142, 157 217*f*, 218*f*, 229*f*, 328*f*, 350*f*
    Two Voice duophonic analog synth, 39, 55, 234*f*
    Xpander analog synth module, 40, 240, 242, 243*f*, 244, 336*f*
oboe sound, 12, 285

obsolescence in technology, 353, 362
Octaviant, 36
Off His Rockers, 224
Oken, Chuck, Jr., 255
Old Crow's Synth Shop, 235*f*
old-school
    Minimoog patching technique, 363–364
    modular synths as seemingly ancient technology, 262
    recording techniques, 354, 362–364
    See also vintage equipment
Oliveros, Pauline, 187
Olson, Harry F., 115–116
OMG-1, 221*f*
Ondes Martenot (aka Ondes Musicales), 34–36, 34*f*, 35*f*
Ondioline, 10–11, 10*f*
one-volt-per-octave (1V/octave) scale, 139, 272
online information
    companion website, explanation of, xv
    sites related to manufacturers, dealers, periodicals, etc., 253, 254, 373–382
Opcode Systems, 104, 343
    Studio 5 MIDI interface, 342
    Studio Vision MIDI sequencing software, 243, 342
open-source programming, 200, 202*f*
opera composer, 25
operating systems
    compatibility issues, 61, 79, 80*f*, 101, 112, 112*f*, 113, 120, 219, 279
    cross-platform software, 41 (definition), 60, 101*f*, 108, 110, 171, 210, 215*f*, 305, 344
    upgrades/updates, 112, 219
optical reader for punched cards, 135*f*
optic phonogram, 117
Optigan, 69–71, 70*f*
organs and organ sounds, 3, 4, 12, 18, 19*f*, 25, 26, 36, 38, 52, 52*f*, 61, 68, 69, 70*f*, 72, 78*f*, 80, 82, 85, 110, 114, 125, 133, 135*f*, 184, 216, 218*f*, 217*f*, 218*f*, 283*f*, 324, 341–342, 344*f*, 346, 346*f*, 347*f*, 351*f*
    AGO (American Guild of Organists) pedalboard, 341–342
    keyboard instrument to supplement organ and piano, 10–11
    organ-style keyboard, 3, 13, 276, 278*f*, 286, 287
    photo-electric organ, 69
    tonewheel organs, 3, 19*f*, 36, 61, 78, 110, 125, 133, 184, 346, 346*f*, 347*f*
OSC (Open Sound Control), 60 (definition), 294
oscillator, 4 (definition), 21, 25, 37, 38, 41, 50, 51, 52, 54, 55, 58*f*, 81, 82, 89, 93, 97, 104, 121, 123, 132, 135, 137–150, 151, 154, 158, 159, 173, 206*f*, 211*f*, 247*f*, 254, 265, 266, 307, 307*f*, 309, 326–327, 335, 338, 338*f*, 339, 352
    analog sequencer as oscillator, 173, 176
    carrier, 133, 206–207

Index

oscillator (*continued*)
   Convert to Oscillator function, 106
   digital, 43, 46, 56, 61, 63, 75, 94, 97, 101, 102, 105, 106, 111, 111*f*, 112*f*, 121, 123, 133, 134, 140, 146, 147*f*, 165, 189*f*, 200, 210*f*, 215*f*, 227, 232, 233*f*
   digitally controlled (DCO), 139, 140*f*
   heterodyning, 4 (definition), 34
   low frequency. *See* LFOs (low-frequency oscillators)
   modular synth modules, 141*f*, 146, 147*f*, 148, 148*f*, 247*f*, 261–262, 263, 266, 286, 331, 339, 339*f*
   neon tube, 8
   pitch/frequency control, 21, 28, 34, 41, 66, 116, 138, 142, 155, 196, 211*f*, 234, 237
   quadrature, 201, 204 (definition), 205*f*
   resynthesis, 66 (definition)
   scaling (one-volt-per-octave vs. Hertz-per-volt), 139
   self-oscillator of spring reverb, 184
   sub-oscillator, 140 (definition), 156
   sync, 63 (definition), 81 (sweeping), 104, 142, 145 (definition)
   tuning-fork, 115, 117
   vacuum-tube, 114
   voltage-controlled (VCO), 38 (definition), 39, 137 (definition), 138, 139–142, 143*f*, 146, 154–156, 172–173, 196, 247*f*, 251*f*, 256*f*, 265, 266, 269, 270, 272
   waveform selection/generation, 139–140
ostinato, 172 (definition), 311
OTO Machines Biscuit, 164–165, 165*f*, 267*f*, 359–360
out-of-production hardware and software, 190, 342
overdriving audio circuitry, 105, 125, 154, 161, 170, 326, 338*f*, 363
overdubs, 87, 88, 116, 192, 194, 197, 199
Oxford Synthesiser Company OSCar monosynth, 91
oxidation of vintage synthesizer components, 329

Packard Bell, 69
Pageant of the Masters, 316
Paia Electronics Corporation, 55, 189, 227*f*, 228*f*, 247, 249, 251*f*, 252, 254, 266*f*, 272, 325*f*, 331, 332*f*, 333*f*
   2700 series synth modules, 251*f*
   4700 series synth modules, 251*f*
   6740K Hot Springs Reverb Kit, 184
   6780 Organtua, 283*f*
   8031 CV-to-MIDI converter, 275
   8700 6503 microprocessor/controller, 251*f*
   9201DK MIDI Drum Brain Kit, 275
   9201FK MIDI Fader Kit, 275
   9700 series synth modules, 251*f*
   9700K MIDI2CV8 MIDI-to-CV converter module, 251*f*, 272
   9710 VCA/Mixer module, 251*f*
   9720 VCO module, 251*f*
   9730 VCF module, 251*f*
   Programmable Drum Set, 82, 84*f*, 85
Palm, Wolfgang, 45–47, 134, 227, 232*f*
   Plex 2 Restructuring Synthesizer for Windows, 47
   PPG MiniMapper iOS softsynth, 47
   PPG WaveGenerator iOS softsynth, 47
   PPG WaveMapper iOS softsynth, 47
Palme diffuser, 34*f*, 35*f*, 36, 36*f*
panning, 66, 67 (definition), 94, 105*f*, 207, 302
paper-tape readers, 114–117
parametric EQ, 105, 166, 167*f*, 189*f*,
Parent, Nil, 100
Paris Exposition 1929, 114
Parodi, Starr, 310–311, 310*f*, 316–317, 317*f*, 324–326, 326*f*, 363–364, 363*f*
Partch, Harry, 44, 306
partials in harmonic spectra, 138–139, 139*f*, 335
Parton, Dolly, 262
Pascetta, Armand, 26–27
Pascetta pre-MIDI polyphonic keyboard controllers, 26–27, 27*f*, 217*f*
Passport Designs, 104
password to companion website, xv
patchable (aka semi-modular) vs. modular synths, xi, 20, 21, 140–142, 210, 223
patchbay, 22, 24 (definition), 25*f*, 41, 97, 183, 218*f*, 227*f*, 235*f*, 246, 250*f*, 261*f*, 320*f*, 332*f*, 361
patchboard/pin matrix, 88–91, 91*f*, 93, 145*f*
patch cords, 16, 21, 22*f*, 93, 94, 100, 101, 110, 130, 141, 143*f*, 144*f*, 145*f*, 173, 212*f*, 228*f*, 233*f*, 258, 327, 365*f*
patch cord tree, 22*f*, 262
patch points, 21, 41, 100, 140–141, 142*f*, 143*f*, 161, 235*f*
Patcher (application), 104
patches/programs and patching/programming, 22, 29, 31, 39*f*, 41, 43*f*, 49, 50, 53*f*, 54, 55, 58, 60, 64, 80–81, 88, 100, 101, 101*f*, 105, 105*f*, 106*f*, 108, 110, 111*f*, 120, 142, 193, 210, 213, 215*f*, 223, 227, 235*f*, 237*f*, 266, 272, 285–286, 312, 316, 321–339, 334, 335*f*, 344–345, 356–357
   creativity and experimentation, 321–327
   expression, programming for, 285–286, 319, 338–339
   modular synths, 58, 100, 101*f*, 215*f*, 246, 252–253, 258, 261*f*, 262, 266, 269–270, 272, 282, 312, 331–334, 349*f*
   non-programmability, 210, 223, 224*f*, 309, 309*f*, 327, 329
   programmable patch names, 49
   See also programmability; software/softsynths
PCI (Peripheral Component Interconnect), 61, 357
PCM (pulse-code modulation), 54, 124, 353
personal computers (PCs)
   appearance of, 102
   built-in synth chip, 103–104

reliability issues, 112–113
See also software/softsynths and Windows platform
Pd (Pure Data), 104
Pearlman, Alan R., 29, 91, 93–94
Peavey Electronics, 113, 113*f*
pedals, 22, 31, 32*f*, 43, 64, 71, 124, 126, 154*f*, 185, 198, 199, 217*f*, 276*f*, 296*f*, 297, 305, 341–342, 343*f*, 344*f*
    stompboxes, 23*f*, 38 (definition), 39, 127, 161, 166, 170–171, 171*f*, 185, 186*f*, 190, 194–195, 195*f*, 206–207, 206*f*, 249*f*, 254, 328*f*, 340*f*
pelog and slendro scales, 44–45
Pennsylvania Music Educators association conference, 342
percussion/drum controllers/instruments, electronic, 18*f*, 67, 82–88, 94, 124, 204, 237, 293, 294*f*, 296*f*, 302–305, 331, 355
Perfect Fretworks Hyperkeys, 278–279, 281*f*
performance art, 316–317
performance, 67–88, 127–129, 339–351
    audience connection, 218, 314, 319, 346–351
    noise toys, 306–309
    small-scale improvisation instruments, 86–88
    techniques of experienced synthesists, 339–351
    tools of the trade, 339–351
    visuals, listening without, 349–351
periodicals, selected bibliography of, 373
Peripheral Visions, 75
Perrey, Jean-Jacques, 10*f*, 11, 370, 373
Persing, Eric, 54, 135, 219–221, 220*f*, 221*f*, 321–322, 323*f*
phantom power, 199
phase, 164 (definition), 191, 201*f*, 204
    phase distortion, 50–51, 277
    phase modulation, 41, 97
    phase-shifting, 191, 192 (definition), 199, 200, 207, 207*f*, 264
phonemes, 31
Phonosynth, 24
physical modeling (PM) synthesis, 29, 30 (definition), 31, 30*f*, 60, 61–62, 107–108, 109, 136, 210, 237, 277
piano
    acoustic signature, 325
    ARP Electronic Piano, 29
    phases of amplitude envelope, 4, 151–152
    Buchla Piano Bar, 17, 23*f*
    calculator-key arrangement, 277*f*
    composition, 317
    digital pianos, 52, 75, 278*f*
    electric, 52, 53, 292–293, 351*f*
    fixed note frequencies, 4, 117
    grand, 230*f*, 236*f*
    keyboard for piano enhancement, 10–11
    piano-like keyboard action (or not), 61, 276, 278*f*, 281*f*, 282*f*, 291*f*, 295
    MIDI synth module, 249*f*
    player piano-roll-style sequencing, 108, 114, 117
    Piano 300: Celebrating Three Centuries of People and Pianos, 23*f*
    processing, 324, 361
    sounds/samples, 52, 79, 124, 292
    toy piano keys, 25
    Yamaha S stage-piano series, 49
    Young Chang, 78
Pink Floyd, 91
pink noise, 21, 149, 329
pitchbend, 28 (definition), 43, 51*f*, 273–275, 278, 279, 281, 282, 291*f*, 298, 302, 322, 334
    bipolar CV output, 291
    CV-to-MIDI conversion, 274–275
    equalizing bend ranges of layered voices, 334
    held-note mode, 51*f*
    "Hoover sound" components, 322
    joystick, 43
    MIDI-to-CV conversion, 270, 273
    pad, 279
    Proportional Pressure Controllers (PPCs), 81
    range, 11, 28, 334
    ribbon, 81, 282, 298 (virtual)
    spring-loaded knob, 43
    stick, 64
    unconventional bender on a fold-up keyboard controller, 278*f*
    wand-controlled, 302
    wheel, 51*f*, 81, 142*f*, 203*f*, 281
    wheels *vs.* ribbons *vs.* Proportional Pressure Controllers (PPCs), 81
pitch shifter, 106, 165, 204 (definition), 205*f*, 209
pitch-to-voltage converter, 157
Pittsburgh Modular, 155, 188, 192, 258
    Analog Delay (AD), 192, 193*f*
    Voltage-Influenced Low Frequency Oscillator (VILFO), 155, 156*f*
planned error in reading waveform data from tables, 50
Plogue Bidule, 324*f*, 356, 357, 358*f*
plug-in software. *See* software/softsynths
pneumatic tracker bar, 114
Pollard, Joe, 302
polyphonic portamento, 26 (definition), 50, 63
Polyphony magazine, 265, 266*f*
polysonic synth, 108, 109*f*
polytimbral operation, 123, 124 (definition)
polyurethane recording tape binding, 353
Porcaro, Steve, 244, 316
portamento, 26, 50, 63, 155 (definition), 270, 270*f*, 271, 272, 291*f*
Posner, Ari, 237, 314–316, 354–359
The Posse, 310
Powell, Roger, 19*f*
PPG (Palm Products Germany)
    Expansion Voice Unit (EVU), 46*f*
    PRK Processor keyboard, 46*f*

Index

PPG (Palm Products Germany) (*continued*)
   Realizer digital music machine, 47, 227, 232*f*
   Waveterm wavetable programming system, 46*f*
   Wave 2.2 wavetable synth, 46*f*, 134–135
   Wave 2.3 wavetable synth, 147*f*
   Wave wavetable synths, 45–47
Pratt-Reed keyboard, 26, 75*f*
preamplifier, 361, 363–365
processing sounds from external sources, 21, 33, 61, 111, 117, 140, 159, 196, 206–207, 309, 324, 360
Probe, Rex, 149*f*, 246, 247*f*, 265–266, 320, 320*f*
programmability, 22, 36, 40, 80, 223, 289, 303
   good and bad of non-programmability, 327, 329
   pros and cons, 223
   See also patches/programs and patching/programming; software/softsynths
Propellerhead Software AB, 107, 108–109, 134, 149, 181*f*, 201, 204*f*, 298, 345, 354, 356
   BV512 virtual vocoder/graphic equalizer module, 109*f*, 201, 204*f*
   Kong Drum Designer virtual drum machine, 109*f*
   Malström Graintable Synthesis softsynth, 134, 134*f*
   Mods, user-created software alterations to ReBirth, 108
   NN-XT software sampler, 345
   Reason computer-based music-production system, 108–109, 109*f*, 149, 181*f*, 201, 204*f*, 298, 354
   Record audio-recording software, 109
   ReBirth RB-338 virtual drum-machine-and-bass instrument, 107, 108
   ReCycle loop-editing software, 108–109
   ReWire music software host application, 108 (definition), 109, 356
   RPG-8 virtual arpeggiator, 181*f*
   Subtractor analog-style polyphonic softsynth, 109*f*, 149, 181*f*
   Thor Polysonic Synthesizer softsynth, 109*f*
Puckette, Miller, 104
pulse wave, 63 (definition), 137 (definition), 138, 154, 164, 196, 331, 334
pulse-width modulation, 63 (definition), 137, 138 (definition), 141*f*, 151, 321–322, 331
punched paper-tape readers, 114, 115–116

Q factor. *See* resonance *under* filters
quadrature oscillator, 201, 204 (definition), 205*f*
quantized (stepped) voltages, 154*f*, 179, 273, 274, 287, 292
quantizer modules, 180, 250*f*, 272, 273, 274, 274*f*, 287
quantizing sequenced event timing in drum patterns, 85, 86 (definition)

rackmount devices, 24 (definition)
   illustrations, 47*f*, 112*f*, 140*f*, 163*f*, 174*f*, 205*f*, 214*f*, 225*f*, 243*f*, 250*f*, 261*f*, 337*f*, 338*f*
   power supplies, 222

Radikal Technologies Accelerator modeled-analog synth, 189*f*
Radio Baton mallet controller, 40, 301
RAM (random access memory), 49 (definition), 60, 79, 104, 113
R & B music, 126
random-access digital recording, 354
rap music, 126
Ravel, Maurice, 244
Raymond Scott Quintet, 118–119
RCA synthesizers, 114–117
   Mark I, 115–116
   Mark II, 116–117, 115*f*, 116*f*
realtime groove softsynth, 241*f*
real-world acoustics, 131–132
recording, 13, 46, 47, 55, 61, 70, 72, 88, 104, 106, 109, 116, 117, 121–123, 127–129, 133–134, 145, 183–184, 187, 191, 197–199, 213, 261–262, 277, 306, 317, 323*f*, 324, 329, 352–365
   automated mixing, 360–361
   film and TV scores, 118–119, 310–316, 354–359
   old-school techniques, 352–353, 354, 362–364
   outboard processing, 361–364
   preparing audio for recording, 361–364
   serial *vs.* random-access media, 353–354
   surround-sound recording, 244, 313, 364–365
   techniques of experienced synthesists, 352–365
red noise, 329
Redmatica AutoSampler (AS), 344–345
reel-to-reel tape, 13, 187, 191, 352, 353, 362, 362*f*
Reisner standard AGO (American Guild of Organists) pedalboard, 342
release (portion of a sound), 4 (definition), 20, 133, 152, 152*f*, 162, 164, 269, 334
resistance-sensitive touchplates, 13, 286
Resonant Lopass Gate, 334
response curve, 157, 195
Restyler, from Sherman Productions and Rodec, 163, 164*f*
Resynator (resynthesis oscillator) sound generator, 66
resynthesis, 59*f*, 64, 66 (definition)
resynthesizers, 64, 66–67, 99–100, 123
Mr. Reverb, 54
reverb, 25*f*, 53, 66, 124, 125 (definition), 182–187, 313, 316, 345, 355
   acoustic/natural, 125, 182
   analog/BBD, 265
   built-in, 53, 66, 124
   convolution, 185–187, 186*f*
   differences in processing for stereo and surround-sound environments, 313
   digital, 125, 170, 184, 185, 186*f*, 199, 207–209, 208*f*, 249*f*, 250*f*,
   Echo Chamber Two at Abbey Road Studios, 183, 183*f*
   echo chamber, 125, 183
   long hall with a wooden floor, 183

plate, 125, 183–184, 185
reverse, 185
spring, 25f, 125, 184–185, 184f, 325f
tiled bathroom, 183
reverse sawtooth waveform, 9, 137, 138 (definition), 141f, 154
ReWire software protocol, 108, 109, 356
Rhea, Tom, 120f, 138, 139f, 269–270
Rhodes
Chroma synthesizer, 29, 29f
division of CBS, 29
electric piano, 29, 53, 292–293, 351f, 361
Rhythm And Noise, 265
ribbon controllers, 11, 20, 21, 28, 35, 170, 211f, 282, 295f, 298
pitchbend wheels *vs.* ribbons *vs.* Proportional Pressure Controllers (PPCs), 81
Rice, John L., 190, 194, 200, 201f, 248f, 249, 249f, 250f
Rich, Robert, 146
Richter, Grant, 247f, 359f
Richards, Kelli, 128
Rider, Scott, 235f
Riley, Terry, 187
ring modulation, 50 (definition), 66, 101, 104, 111, 196, 197f, 206, 207, 207f, 339
ringing ears, 132
Rise, Scott, 179f, 272
Rockwell Semiconductor's EndlessWave technology, 79
Rocky Mount Instruments Keyboard Computer, 134, 135f
RMI KC-II, 135f
Rodec, 163, 164f
Roger Linn Design, 127
AdrenaLinn stompbox, 127, 170–171, 171f, 172f
LinnDrum II (originally called the BoomChick) digital drum machine, 56, 127
LinnStrument USB touch controller, 295, 297–298, 297f
Roland, 13, 53–54, 56, 64, 80, 82–85, 108, 135, 136, 227, 237, 267, 269f, 302, 322, 335
Alpha Juno-2 analog polysynth, 322
CompuRhythm CR-68 drum machine, 218f
CompuRhythm CR-78 drum machine, 82, 83, 83f, 84f, 85, 218f, 340f
DCB Bus proprietary pre-MIDI communications protocol, 83, 269f
DC-50 Digital Chorus effects processor, 218f
D-50 linear-arithmetic polysynth, 53–54, 53f, 135, 220, 244
D-550 linear-arithmetic rackmount polysynth module, 337f
Fantom workstations, 54
Fantom XR rackmount workstation module, 248f
Gaia SH-01 analog-modeling polysynth, 54
Handsonic HPD-15 percussion pad synth, 302
JD-800 digital polysynth, 344f, 345

JP-8000 analog-modeling polysynth, 220f
JP-8080 rackmount analog-modeling polysynth module, 239–240, 242f
Juno-60 analog polysynth, 269f
Juno-106 analog polysynth, 139, 140f
Jupiter-8 analog polysynth, 54, 237, 269f, 326
Jupiter-80 analog-modeling and digital polysynth, 54, 55f, 324
MKS-70 Super JX rackmount analog polysynth, 337f
MKS-80 Super Jupiter rackmount analog polysynth, 324
MPU-101 MIDI-to-CV converter, 239, 273, 336f
Octapad MIDI percussion pad controller, 302
RC-300 Loop Station looper, 199, 199f
RE-201 Space Echo tape-delay effects processor, 187, 188f, 194, 195f, 218f, 342, 350f
SRE-555 Chorus Echo effects processor, 343f
SVC-350 vocoder, 340f, 343f
System 100M modular synth line, 54, 252
System 700 modular synth line, 54, 246, 252
TB-303 Bass Line synth module, 85, 108, 269f, 270f
TR-505 drum machine, 269f
TR-707 drum machine, 85
TR-808 drum machine, 82–83, 84f, 218f, 244, 269f, 343f
TR-909 drum machine, 84–85, 85f
VP-330 Vocoder Plus, 203f, 218f
V-Synth Elastic Audio Synthesizer series, 54
V-Synth XT rackmount Elastic Audio Synthesizer module, 242f
XV-5080 rackmount sample-playback synth module, 239, 337f
Rolando, Tony, 178, 287, 288f
Roli Seaboard Grand, 282f
ROM (read-only memory), 49 (definition), 53–54
Rosenthal, David, 334–335, 335f, 342–345, 344f, 361–362
Rossum, Dave, 39, 73–74
Rudess, Jordan, 213f, 281f, 294
Ryan, Tim, 95–99, 97f,

sackbut, 11
Sala, Oskar, 8f, 9, 9f
SalMar Construction, 94–95, 95f, 96f
sample-and-hold (S/H), 20, 21 (definition), 31, 63, 154 (definition), 154f, 155, 175, 269, 274, 275
sample libraries, 74, 237, 321, 357
sample playback/player, 30 (definition), 31, 49, 52, 53, 61, 62, 67, 68, 71–72, 76–79, 77f, 78f, 79–80, 84–87, 86f, 107, 108, 110, 124–126, 133, 134, 135, 137
sampler, 31 (definition), 33, 40, 48, 51, 51f, 56, 67, 72–76, 73f, 74f, 75f, 78, 82, 88, 90f, 91, 109, 110, 126, 277
sampling, 33, 46 (definition), 47, 49, 51, 52, 54, 60, 61, 72–76, 78, 85–86, 88, 99–100, 109, 110,

Index

sampling (continued)
  120, 121, 126, 133–134, 185–186, 277, 300, 311–312, 335f
  fixed-rate sample-skipping (aka drop/add), 75
San Francisco Tape Music Center, 13, 14f, 245, 286
Sarnoff, David, 115
sawtooth waveform, 8, 9 (definition), 36, 55, 115, 135, 137 (definition), 140, 141f, 146, 147f, 154, 164, 168, 196, 309
  reverse sawtooth waveform, 9, 137, 138 (definition), 141f, 154
Schippmann Ebbe und Flut (EUF), 163–164, 165f
Schmitt, Stephan, 109–110
Schreiber, Paul, 146, 148f, 190, 246, 247f, 249, 250f, 263f
Schulze, Klauze, 91
Scott, Adrian, 54, 135
Scott, Jim, 21, 137
Scott, Raymond, ix, 118–119, 119f
  Electronium, 119, 120f
scratch artists, 126, 198, 208
Scriabin, Alexander Nikolayevich, 117
scripting language, 243, 244 (definition)
SCSI (Small Computer System Interface), 40, 41 (definition), 343
SeaSound audio interfaces, 40
Seer Systems Reality softsynth, 56, 107–108
Sekon, Josef, 94
Sender, Ramon, 13, 286
Senior, John, 75, 123
sequencers/sequencing
  "audio sequencer you can play like an instrument," 127–129, 314
  drum machine, 67, 85–86, 170–171, 272
  4ms Autonomous Bassline Generator, 307
  granular, 107, 134
  MIDI, 16, 29, 49, 52, 56, 61, 72–73, 76, 78, 109, 121–122, 123, 124, 126, 174, 216f, 242–243, 274, 291, 301, 353, 356–357
  pre-MIDI, 38, 40, 43, 47, 74, 81, 82, 89–91, 94, 95, 97, 114, 117, 119, 121, 133, 266–267, 277f, 340f, 342, 343f
  step, 15, 16 (definition), 20, 40f, 101, 108, 130 (definition), 145f, 146f, 150f, 164–165, 170, 172–173, 174–180, 189f, 210f, 212f, 215f, 234f, 250f, 267f, 272, 273, 274, 283f, 287, 288f, 289, 290f, 298
  waveform-scanning/wave-sequencing, 54, 61 (definition), 135–136
Sequential Circuits Inc., 56, 81, 82f, 135, 136f, 267
  digital sequencer, 81
  700 Programmer, 81, 340f, 343f
  Pro-One analog monosynth, 82
  Prophet-5 programmable analog polysynth, 28, 48, 56, 80–82, 81f, 110, 214f, 238f, 283f
  Prophet-T8 programmable analog polysynth, 82, 82f, 277

  Prophet-2000 digital sampler, 56, 82
  Prophet-3000 rackmount digital sampler, 82
  Prophet-VS vector synth, 55–57, 55f, 135, 220f
Serge Modular, 230f, 246, 247, 252, 265–266, 268f, 320, 323, 325f, 329, 331, 334, 347, 364f
  Dual Transient Generator (DTG) module, 334
  Dual Universal Slope Generators (DSG) module, 348f
  Extended DADSR module, 153
  Frequency Shifter module, 329
  Resonant Equalizer module, 167
  STS (Sound Transform Systems) Audio Interface M-class module, 167
  STS Blue Fun Station panel, 292f, 293f
  STS Creature M-class module, 149f, 158, 247f, 266, 267f
  STS Dual "Q" Filter M-class module, 158
  STS EQ Shifter M-class module, 167
  STS Klangziet M-class module, 193
  STS MultiFilter M-class module, 158
  STS Sequencer-A M-class module, 150f, 267f
  STS Soup Kitchen 1 panel, 167, 193
  STS Wilson Analog Delay M-class module, 193
  Touch Activated Keyboard (TKB), 287, 287f
  Touch Envelope Voltage Source (TEV) module, 348f
  Universal Slope Generator, 266
  Variable QVCF module, 158
  Wilson Analog Delay (WAD) module, 193, 329
Serge Modular Beast, 268f, 347, 348f
The Serge Modular Creature: An Unauthorized User's Manual, 266
serial vs. random-access media, 353–354
Shapiro, Gerald "Shep," 93
shelving EQ, 124, 125 (definition), 166, 186f,
Shep SN8 module, 361–362
Sherman Filterbank (FB), 161–162, 163f
Shnookums and Meat Funny Cartoon Show, 312
shuffle-play, 85, 86 (definition)
Shykun, John, 76, 77f
signal processing, 33, 47, 50, 58, 59f, 60, 61, 67, 78, 88, 91, 101, 102, 104, 105, 106f, 110–111, 125, 134, 140, 164f, 165, 165f, 170–171, 182–197, 199, 200–209, 230–231, 242f, 246, 277, 277f, 314–316, 361–364
signal-to-noise ratio, 54, 348f
Simonton, John, 84f, 85, 249, 251f, 266f
sine waveform, 11 (definition), 41, 46f, 58, 117, 132 (definition), 133, 137, 138, 146, 149, 154, 170, 185, 204, 206, 207, 327, 338, 339
"sinusoidal audio phenomena," 338
sixteenth-note swing, 86
slew processor, 155 (definition) *See also* lag processor
Slicer module, 66
Smith, Dave, 58f, 81, 83, 108, 135, 153, 237, 244, 266
  See also Dave Smith Instruments (DSI)
Smith, Julius O., 30, 136

Smith, Mark, 342
Smith, Rick, 15*f*
Smith, William O., 24
SMPTE (Society of Motion Picture and Television Engineers) Time Code synchronization, 72 (definition), 353
snippets of musical ideas, 317
softsynths, 54 (definition), 56, 102, 107–112, 113, 134, 210, 215*f*, 216, 220–221, 306*f*, 321–322
   DIY apps, 109–110
   emulating vintage hardware, 56, 57*f*, 142, 108, 212*f*, 239*f*,
   graphically programmable computer music language, 104, 105*f*
   hardware to software conversion, 344–345
solder, pros and cons of lead-free, 219
solid-state vs. hard-disk drives, 345
Sonicstate Web link, 253
Sony MiniDisc, 354
Sound Transform Systems (STS, manufacturer of Serge Modular), 149*f*, 150*f*, 158, 167, 193, 246, 247, 247*f*, 258, 261*f*, 265–266, 267*f*, 292*f*, 293*f*, 319–321, 320*f*, 348*f*
sound waves, 131 (definition), 182, 185
Soundlib
   G-Player native Gigastudio file player, 80*f*
   Samplit Automatic Sampling Solution, 344
SoundMagic Spectral freeware suite, 360
SoundTower Software AdrenaLinn III SE cross-platform editor, 171
Sousa Archives and Center for American Music museum, 94
spectral processing, 60
Spectrasonics, 54, 113, 219, 220*f*, 221*f*, 237, 238, 321–322, 323*f*
   Atmosphere Dream Synth Module softsynth, 321
   Omnisphere softsynth for synthesis, composition, production and performance, 220*f*, 221*f*, 238, 240*f*, 321, 322*f*, 357*f*
   Omni TR (Touch Remote) wireless iPad app for Omnisphere, 321, 322*f*
   Orb performance/editing app for Omnisphere, 240*f*, 321
   Stylus Vinyl Groove Module softsynth, 244, 321
   Stylus RMX Realtime Groove Module softsynth, 238, 241*f*, 321
   Trilian Total Bass Module softsynth, 238, 241*f*, 321
   Trilogy Bass Total Bass Module softsynth, 244, 321
speech synthesizer, 31–33, 168
   talkbox, 69, 170, 171 (definition)
   See also vocoder
Spiegel, Laurie, 120
Spielberg, Steven, 91
Spong, Kent, 236
Stanford University, 30, 48, 133, 136
static electricity, 3, 287, 327
steel-guitar-style pitchbends, 51*f*

Steinberg Media Technologies GmbH, 108, 113, 226, 231*f*, 293, 311
   Avalon sample processing and resynthesis software for Atari ST computer, 231*f*
   Cubase digital audio workstation, 231*f*, 293, 311
   ReWire music software host application, 108 (definition), 109, 356
   VST (Virtual Studio Technology) plug-in software, 113 (definition)
Steiner, Nyle, 13, 158, 159*f*, 225*f*, 284–285, 284*f*, 285*f*, 286*f*, 341, 341*f*
Steiner Electronic Valve Instrument (EVI), 31, 225*f*, 284–285, 284*f*, 285*f*, 286*f*
Steiner EVI Steinerphone synth in a briefcase, 285, 286*f*
Steiner Electronic Wind Instrument (EWI), 286*f*
Steiner Master's Touch, 341, 342*f*, 351*f*
Steiner-Parker Synthacon, 158, 158*f*, 159*f*
Steinway Model M grand piano, 230*f*, 236*f*
stem audio tracks, 315–316
Sting, 123
stochastic music generator, 119
Stockell, Mercer "Stoney," 42, 44
stompboxes, 23*f*, 38 (definition), 39, 127, 161, 166, 170–171, 171*f*, 185, 186*f*, 190, 194–195, 195*f*, 206–207, 206*f*, 249*f*, 254, 328*f*, 340*f*
Strobl, Hannes, 110*f*
Stopp, Gene, 346
Strymon El Capistan dTape Echo stompbox, 194–195, 195*f*
Studer A80, 362, 362*f*
Studio Electronics, 214*f*
   Boomstar series tabletop synth modules, 223, 224*f*
   Boomstar 5089 tabletop synth module, 224*f*
   Midimini rackmount analog monosynth, 328*f*
   Omega8G rackmount analog polysynth, 214*f*
Studio Two at Abbey Road Studios, 183, 183*f*
sub-oscillator, 140 (definition), 156
Subotnick, Morton, 245, 286, 327
subtractive synthesis, 53, 54 (definition), 60, 101, 102, 107, 110, 115, 132 (definition), 133, 140, 210, 277, 339
Super-Just microtonal tuning, 44
SuperCollider, 134
surface-mount technology (SMT), 188–190, 189*f*, 287
   vs. through-hole, 189–190
surge protectors, 222
surround-sound *vs.* stereo environments, 313
sustain segment, 50, 51, 104, 152, 152*f*
swarming and buzzing, 146, 147*f*
Switched-On Bach, 18, 329, 341, 352
Switched-On Bach II, 352
Switched-On Bach 2000, 353
Switched-On Boxed Set, 327
Switched-On Brandenburgs, 352
symbolic icons, 106*f*

Index

Symbolic Sound
　products, 58–60, 134
　　Capybara, 58
　　Kyma multisynthesis and processing system, 58–61, 59*f*, 60*f*, 134, 298
　　Pacarana, 59*f*, 60
　　Platypus digital signal processor, 58
Syndrum, 302
Syn-Ket (Synthesizer Ketoff), 24–25, 25*f*
Synergy, Larry Fast, 317, 318*f*
Synth Petting Zoo, 249*f*
Synthesis Technology, 131*f*, 146, 190, 227*f*, 246, 247, 247*f*, 248*f*, 249, 250*f*, 263*f*, 265, 325*f*, 332*f*, 346
　　E340 Cloud Generator oscillator module, 146, 148, 147*f*, 250*f*
　　E440 LP VCF module, 250*f*
　　E350 Morphing Terrarium oscillator module, 146–148, 147*f*, 250*f*
　　E560 Deflector Shield effects module, 207, 207*f*, 250*f*
　　E580 Resampling Mini-Delay DDL module, 195, 196*f*, 250*f*
　　MOTM-300 Ultra VCO module, 247*f*
　　MOTM-410 Triple Resonant Filter with Dual VCLFO module, 265
　　MOTM-650 MIDI-CV converter and arpeggiator module, 181, 182*f*
Synthesizers.com, 141*f*, 184, 227*f*, 246, 247, 247*f*, 248*f*, 249, 253, 258, 332*f*, 346
　　products, 247*f*, 284*f*
　　QKB15S MIDI and CV keyboard controller, 282, 283*f*, 284*f*
　　Q106 oscillator module, 247*f*
　　Q115 spring reverb module, 184
Synthtopia Web link, 253
The Synthtopia Guide to Eurorack Modular Synthesizers, Web link, 251
Synthwerks, 259*f*, 287, 289, 289*f*
　　FSR-1N single-finger-pad force-sensing touchplate controller, 287, 289*f*
　　FSR-4 Classic (through-hole) four-finger-pad force-sensing touchplate controller, 287
　　FSR-4 MkII (SMT) four-finger-pad force-sensing touchplate controller, 287, 289*f*
　　FSR-4C/B four square-pad force-sensing touchplate controller, 287, 289*f*
　　Lamp-1 LED module with four-way mult, 289*f*

tableau vivant, 316
Talk Soup, 224
Tangerine Dream, 45, 91
Tascam, 80, 227*f*, 332*f*
TC Electronic
　　Flashback Delay and Looper stompbox processor, 249*f*
　　Hall of Fame Reverb stompbox processor, 249*f*
　　Studio Konnekt 48 audio and MIDI interface, 359

Tcherepnin, Serge, 193, 265, 266, 287, 320*f*
techno music, 82, 85
Technos Acxel Resynthesizer, 99, 100
　　Acxel 32 Master system, 100
　　Grapher programming interface, 99*f*
　　Starter-Stage playback-only system, 100
Teenage Engineering OP-1, 277, 277*f*
Telefunken Trautonium, 8–9, 8*f*
Telharmonium, 3
Termenvox, 4
terminology, different for similar features, 326
Terpsitone, 6, 6*f*
Theremin, ix, 4–7, 8, 17, 17*f*, 22, 23*f*, 34, 35, 87, 244
Theremin, Leon (Lev Sergeyevich Termen), ix, 4–6
three-band EQ, 166
through-hole technology, 188–190, 189*f*, 287
　　vs. surface-mount technology, 189–190
timbral animation, 55
Tiptop Audio, 258, 258*f*, 260*f*,
　　Happy Ending Kit powered rackmount frame for Eurorack modules, 261*f*
　　Stackcables 3.5mm stacking plugs, 252, 253*f*
　　Station 252 Case, 259*f*, 260*f*
　　Z-DSP VC-Digital Signal Processor module, 200, 202*f*
　　Z8000 Matrix Sequencer module, 178, 180*f*
Tkacs, Ken, 266
Tomita, Isao, 50, 84, 311
Tom Oberheim.com. *See* Marion Systems
tonewheel organs, 3, 61, 78*f*, 125, 133, 184
TONTO (The Original New Timbral Orchestra) synth system, 26
Tonus, Inc., 93
touchplate/pad/ribbon controllers, ix, 6, 11, 13, 14*f*, 21, 22, 28, 87–88, 91, 94, 99*f*, 100, 170, 178–180, 179*f*, 205*f*, 207–209, 208*f*, 213*f*, 214*f*, 268*f*, 286–301, 287*f*, 288*f*, 289*f*, 290*f*, 291*f*, 292*f*, 293*f*, 294*f*, 295*f*, 296*f*, 297*f*, 298*f*, 299*f*, 300*f*, 301*f*, 307, 308*f*, 321, 348*f*
touch-sensitivity, 12, 18, 94
transistor-transistor-logic (TTL) circuitry, 99
Transoniq Hacker, 123*f*
Transsphere mode, 66
Traum, Matt, 285–286
Trautwein, Friedrich, ix, 8–9
Treanor, Vince, III, 26
tremolo, 42 (definition), 66, 124, 132, 154, 155, 171, 186*f*, 207
triangle waveform, 11 (definition), 41, 102, 105*f*, 137 (definition), 155
trigger, 21, 30, 31, 35, 43, 128, 130 (definition), 154, 155, 157, 161, 162, 163, 164, 172, 173, 174, 175, 176, 196, 197, 223, 252, 266, 267, 269–270 (S-trigger definition), 269*f*, 270*f*, 271, 272–273, 274, 275, 280, 282, 287, 293, 294*f*, 296*f*, 297, 298, 301–304, 316, 322

Tripp, Jeff, 279, 281*f*
trumpet sound, 12, 244, 285, 330
Tudor, David, 187
tuning-fork oscillators, 115, 117
Tuning In: Microtonality in Electronic Music, 44
Turnidge, Steve, 289*f*
turntable and scratch artists, 117, 126, 198
Tutti, 36
TV and film, orchestration for, 310–316, 322, 354–359
two-band shelving EQ, 124, 166
2Box Music Applications, 302

U&I Software MetaSynth graphic audio editing for the Macintosh, xv, 106–107, 107*f*
upper partials, 138
username and password to companion website, xv
Ussachevsky, Vladimir, ix, 20, 116, 152

vactrols, 265 (definition), 334
vacuum tube, 11, 25, 37, 102, 114, 115, 154, 239, 242*f*, 325, 362, 364
Vail, Mark, 83*f*
Vako Orchestron, 71–72, 71*f*
Van Koevering, David, 71, 71*f*
variable control voltage (VCV), 155
variable pulse-width wave, 137, 138 (definition)
VCA (voltage-controlled amplifier), 55, 56 (definition), 74, 143*f*, 150, 151 (definition), 154, 168, 172, 195, 250*f*, 251*f*, 266, 269–270, 327, 334
VCF (voltage-controlled filter). *See* filters
VCO (voltage-controlled oscillator). *See* oscillator
vector synthesis, 55–57, 61, 135, 136*f*
Vercoe, Barry, 102
vibration, ix, 36, 131, 184, 325
vibrato, 10, 11 (definition), 24, 25, 35, 41, 42, 87, 100, 125, 132 (definition), 138, 153, 154, 165, 188, 199, 204, 281, 285, 291*f*, 297
videos. *See* films
Vintage Computer Festival, 98*f*
vintage modular synth warning, 245–246
violin-like expression, 11, 12, 285, 324, 330, 331
virtual/modeled analog synths, 63–64, 64*f*, 65*f*, 79*f*, 108, 145 (definition), 216*f*, 234, 237, 239–240, 274
Virtuality, 244
Visser, Felix, 91
vocoder, 18 (definition), 33, 60, 88, 109*f*, 168, 170 (definition), 200–201, 202*f*, 203*f*, 204*f*, 207, 218*f*, 340*f*, 343*f*,
Voder (Voice Operation DEmonstratoR), 31–33
voice layering, 16, 38, 43 (definition), 52*f*, 63, 78, 82, 99, 311, 334–335, 337*f*
voltage control, 11, 13 (definition), 14*f*, 15, 20, 26, 38, 39, 41, 54, 55, 56, 63, 88, 102, 132, 137, 141*f*, 150, 151, 153, 156, 157, 160, 166, 167–168, 175, 193, 194*f*, 195, 200, 201, 201*f*, 204, 210, 265, 268*f*, 291*f*, 329, 348*f*
  digital voltage-control generators, 210
  nonprogrammable voltage-controlled hardware, 210, 223
  See also control voltage
voltage meter, 120
von Helmholtz, Hermann, 115, 152
VST (Virtual Studio Technology) plug-in software, 113 (definition)

wah effect, 161 (definition), 170
Waits, Tom, 71
Wakeman, Rick, 21
Waldorf Music GmbH, 64, 226, 326–327
  Blofeld wavetable synth module, 46, 67, 231*f*
  Micro Q modeled-analog synth module, 328*f*
  Microwave wavetable synth module, 46, 67, 229*f*, 326, 328*f*, 338*f*
  Microwave XT wavetable synth module, 326–327, 338*f*
  Microwave II wavetable synth module, 328*f*
  Microwave IIXT wavetable synth module, 328*f*
  Pulse Plus analog monosynth module, 324
  Q modeled-analog polysynth, 67, 158, 184, 225*f*, 226*f*, 229*f*, 338*f*
  Q rack modeled-analog synth module, 338*f*
  Wave wavetable synth, 46, 47*f*, 67, 229*f*, 231*f*, 338, 359
  Wave Shadow Edition wavetable synth, 328*f*
Walsh, Joe, 171, 173
Warnow, Harry, 118
wave sequencing, 54, 61 (definition), 135–136
Waveboy Industries Voder, 31–33
waveform, ix, 9, 137
waveguide equation, 30
waveguide filter, 136
waveshape, 46*f*, 137 (definition), 141*f*, 201*f*
waveshaper, 94 (definition), 101, 105, 106, 106*f*, 111*f*, 160, 164
wavetable, 45, 46 (definition), 47, 106, 106*f*, 108, 111, 123*f*, 134–135, 135*f*, 146, 147*f*, 148
websites
  companion website, explanation of, xv
  sites related to manufacturers, dealers, periodicals, etc., 253, 254, 373–382
Wedge, Scott, 73
Wenger, Eric, 106
"WhatThe," 322
whistle-like tones, 149, 158, 162*f*, 308*f*, 309
White, Thomas, 248*f*, 332*f*, 334
white noise, 21, 25, 106*f*, 117, 149, 173, 334
Who Framed Roger Rabbit?, 313
The Who, 91
Wiard Synthesizer Company, 160, 161*f*, 246, 247*f*, 251, 255*f*, 313*f*, 314, 314*f*, 339, 359, 359*f*
  Boogie Lowpass filter module, 160, 161*f*

Index

Wiard Synthesizer Company (*continued*)
    Model 331 Envelator envelope generator module, 255*f*
    Model 341 Classic VCO module, 247*f*
    300 modular synth system, 314, 314*f*, 359, 359*f*
The Wild Thornberrys, 224, 312
Wilkinson, Scott R., 44
Williams, Bob, 157, 262
Williams, Tony, 29
Wilson, George Balch, 24
WIMP (Wideband Interface for Music Performance), 17
wind controllers, 30, 31, 210, 284–286
Winde, Niklas, xv, 170
Windows platform, 41, 47, 61, 67, 79, 101, 102, 107, 110, 113, 210, 212*f*, 215*f*, 235*f*, 274, 276, 279, 285, 292, 295, 298, 305
Winterble, Charlie, 75
Wizdom Music SampleWiz, 213*f*
Wonder, Stevie, 26, 28, 72, 73, 76
Wonderland studio, 76
Wood, Chet, 267
Wood, Robin, 89
Wooster Audio Space Baby delay processor, 196, 197*f*, 307
world's most dangerous synth, 346, 347
"wow" tonal change, 161
Wright, Jim, 342
Wurlitzer electric piano, 53, 293
Wyman, Dan, 166

Xenakis, Iannis, 134
Xenon Groove Synthesizer, 216*f*

Yamaha, 13, 28, 41, 48–49, 53, 56, 64, 80, 81, 133, 135, 136*f*, 139, 142, 157, 235, 237, 240, 267, 270*f*, 272, 276, 302, 335, 342
    CS-80 analog polysynth, 28, 28*f*, 49, 227, 228, 235*f*, 236*f*, 237*f*, 240, 277
    DX7 linear FM synth, 48, 48*f*, 49, 53, 61, 108, 110, 133, 142, 232*f*, 243*f*, 344
    DX7II linear FM synth, 49, 53, 243*f*
    GS1 and GS2 linear FM synths, 49
    GX-1 analog polysynth, 346*f*
    MM series synth with Motif sounds, 49
    Motif ES7 music workstation, 344
    Motif music workstation, 49, 181, 344*f*
    Motif XF8 music workstation, 49
    Pro-Mix 01 digital mixer, 360–361
    RM1x Sequence Remixer module, 248*f*
    S series stage-piano, 49
    SY22 vector synth, 56, 135
    Tenori-On MIDI controller, tone generator, and sampler with matrix LED interface, 299–300
    TNR-i virtual Tenori-On for iOS devices, 300
    TF1 linear FM module, 240, 243*f*
    TG33 vector synth module, 56, 135
    TX216 rackmount modular linear FM synth module, 243*f*
    TX416 rackmount modular linear FM synth module, 243*f*
    TX816 rackmount modular linear FM synth module, 240, 243*f*, 337*f*
    TX802 rackmount linear synth module, 244, 328*f*
    Virtual Lead (VL) synthesis engine, 30, 31
    VL1 physical-modeling synth, 30, 30*f*, 33, 136, 225*f*, 226*f*, 237
    WX5 woodwind-style MIDI controller, 31, 285–286
    WX7 woodwind-style MIDI controller, 285–286
    WX11 woodwind-style MIDI controller, 285–286
    YAS-275 alto saxophone, 285
    03D digital mixer, 361
Yannes, Bob, 75, 104, 123
Yes, 91
Young, Alan, 37*f*
Young Chang, 78–79

Zappa, Frank, 121, 123
Zawinul, Joe, 93*f*
Zetterquist, Marcus, 108
Zicarelli, David, 104
Zinovieff, Peter, 89
Zoom R16 digital multitrack recorder, 354

Printed in Great Britain
by Amazon